GENERAL
NE WIN

A POLITICAL BIOGRAPHY

GENERAL NE WIN

A POLITICAL BIOGRAPHY

ROBERT TAYLOR

INSTITUTE OF SOUTHEAST ASIAN STUDIES
Singapore

First published in Singapore in 2015 by
ISEAS Publishing
Institute of Southeast Asian Studies
30 Heng Mui Keng Terrace, Pasir Panjang
Singapore 119614

E-mail: publish@iseas.edu.sg   • Website: bookshop.iseas.edu.sg

The responsibility for facts and opinions in this publication rests exclusively with the author and her interpretation do not necessarily reflect the views or the policy of the publisher or its supporters.

ISEAS Library Cataloguing-in-Publication Data

Taylor, Robert.
  General Ne Win : a political biography.
  1. Ne Vaṅ ʿʾ, Ū", 1911–2002.
  2. Prime ministers—Myanmar—Biography.
  3. Heads of state—Myanmar—Biography.
  4. Burma—Politics and government—1962-1988.
  I. Title
DS530.53 N54T24   2015

ISBN 978-981-4620-13-0 (soft cover)
ISBN 978-981-4620-14-7 (E-book PDF)

Cover photo: Ne Win in the 1950s. Reproduced with kind permission of the author.

Typeset by International Typesetters Pte Ltd
Printed in Singapore by Markono Print Media Pte Ltd

CONTENTS

LIST OF TABLES

Tables

Epilogue Tables

ACKNOWLEDGEMENTS

I have received much assistance from many people and institutions in the preparation of this volume. I am bound to forget some and overlook others, but I hope they will attribute this to a fallible memory rather than intentional neglect. Professor Ian Brown and Professor Sir Christopher Bayly started this project off when they kindly wrote letters of recommendation to the Leverhulme Trust in support of an application for an Emeritus Fellowship. Thanks to them, the Trust awarded me a grant which subsidized much of the initial archival research in the United States, China, Myanmar, and elsewhere. I am most grateful to the Trust and for their patience and faith that I would eventually return something for their funds. Professor Jane Ridley kindly introduced me to the literature on the art of biography which assisted me on my way.

Indirectly, the City University of Hong Kong subsidized some of the costs of the research work by providing me with a two-year visiting professorship at the Department of Asian and International Studies during 2010 and 2011. More recently, the drafting of the book was completed as a Visiting Professorial Fellow at the Institute of Southeast Asian Studies (ISEAS) in Singapore for one year in 2012–13. The Institute, its Directors and staff, over more than three decades, has provided me with research facilities and support for which I am extremely grateful. Back then, before 1988, when few were interested in research on Myanmar, ISEAS recognized that the country was part of Southeast Asia and therefore deserving of study. ISEAS library has been particularly helpful in the final stages of research. Its unparalleled collection of journals and periodicals relevant to modern Southeast Asian history is a memory bank for the region.

A number of individuals in, or connected with, Myanmar have come to my assistance in the writing of this volume. Included among them are the late Dr Myo Myint, Ma Thanegi, U Thuta Aung, U Sonny Nyunt Thein, U Sai Aung Tun, U Thein Nyunt, Dr Thant Thaw Kaung, Dr Nyi Nyi, Thakin Tin Mya, U Chit Hlaing, Dr Tin Maung Maung Than, U Nay Win, Professor Tin Aung, Professor Elizabeth Moore, Professor Dr Franz Gerstenbrandt, Dr Aung Myoe, Andrew Selth and Dr Ingrid Jordt. Deserving of particular thanks are Dr Kyaw Yin Hlaing, U Kyee Myint, and U Thaw Kaung. Dr Kyaw Yin Hlaing undertook to do many of the interviews with me with persons who worked with General Ne Win throughout his career. U Kyee Myint also assisted with interviewing and note-taking. While Dr Kyaw Yin Hlaing is an academic-turned-advisor, U Kyee Myint, a diplomat by profession, was lost to academia, which was perhaps his natural home. Finally, U Thaw Kaung, a retired librarian, historian, literary critic, and research bank extraordinaire, has assisted me in innumerable ways not only with this book but with almost everything else that I have written. Others who assisted me over the years are no longer available to read of my debt to them. U Lay Myint, U Tin Tun, Sagaing Han Tin, U Aye, U Maung Maung (retired Brigadier), Dr Maung Maung, and Dr Kyaw Win would have improved this book tremendously were they still around to help, as they often did in the past. They are greatly missed.

Outside of Myanmar, the archivists and librarians at the National Archives and Records Administration in Washington, D.C., the Lyndon Baines Johnson Library and Archives in Austin, Texas, and the Public Record Office in Kew, now for some unknown reason named the National Archives, provided a wealth of assistance. Cliff Callahan mainly helped me to search for details of a number of records in Washington. Dr Kenton Clymer pointed me to a number of useful sources and saved me from error. Dr Hans-Bernd Zoellner was very responsive to my requests for assistance, often beyond what could reasonably be expected. My former student, Dr Choi Dung Ju, extracted documents for me from the South Korean National Archives. In China, I am grateful for assistance from Professor Fan Hongwei and his former students, Li Tong and Qi Tianjiao. These young ladies spent a summer in Beijing visiting the archives and photographing documents for me which greatly enhance this volume. The late Jane Elliot translated the documents. Special thanks are also due to Tobias Esche who spent weeks going through the archives at the German foreign ministry and reading and translating relevant materials for me. His heroic and uncompensated work adds immensely to the Ne Win story.

Special thanks are due to U Pyo Win, General Ne Win's youngest son, and Daw Khin Sanda Win, his daughter with whom he lived in his final years. Pyo kindly came to London for me to interview and ceaselessly answered email queries when questions occurred to me in the course of writing. Daw Khin Sanda Win always received me graciously and was helpful in arranging several interviews and for sharing some of her views with me. Both placed no obstacles in my way, but their own resources were limited by the fact that many of Ne Win's effects were removed from his home in 2002. Aye Ne Win provided me with a number of family photographs, some of which are included in this volume.

In addition to four nearly anonymous readers selected by my publisher, a former student from my days at the School of Oriental and African Studies, Professor Ang Cheng Guan, kindly read and commented on the entire manuscript. He also introduced me to the new literature on the history of the Cold War and particularly the American wars in Indochina, on which he is a renowned authority. Professor Ian Brown saw this book project off from its beginning, and towards the end not only read and commented on the entire manuscript, but also guided me and steadied my hand when I was about to waver. To him, and everyone else mentioned, and should have been mentioned, *thadu, thadu, thadu.* Finally, thanks to my wife, Ingrid, for tolerating my frequent absences from my domestic responsibilities to pursue my reveries. Needless to say, all errors of fact, omission, and interpretation are mine and mine alone.

Robert H. Taylor
London
17 March 2014

1950s

4 AUNG ...
5 SAN HTWE
6 BA YIN GLAY
7 KYI MYINT
8 THEIN MG GYI
9 HTUN AUNG ...
10 TIN MG

Ne Win at the Rangoon Turf Club, 1950s, betting on the jockeys, not the horses.

Source: All photos are reproduced with kind permission of the author.

Ne Win and the Caretaker Cabinet, 1958.

(last row): Daw Khin May Than, Nikita Khrushchev, Ne Win, and Alexi Kosygin
(front rows): Daw Khin May Than's three daughters from a previous marriage, and her and
Ne Win's two daughters and son at the Chief of Staff's residence, 1960.

1960s Cold War Statesman

Ne Win meeting Mao Tse-tung.

Ne Win and Daw Khin May Than being received at Beijing airport by Chinese Premier Chou En-lai.

Map showing attempted incursions of Chinese KMT troops into Communist China in 1951 (UK National Archives FO371/92143).

Ne Win, Daw Khin May Than, and
UN Secretary General U Thant in
receiving line, July 1964.

Ne Win meeting UN Secretary
General U Thant in New York, 1966.

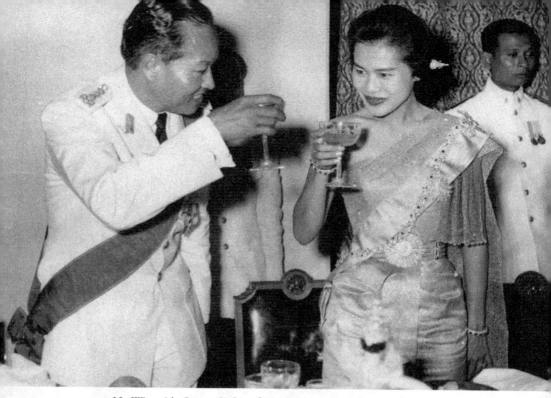

Ne Win with Queen Sirikit of Thailand, toasting at a state banquet.

Daw Khin May Than with King Bhomipol of Thailand at a state banquet.

Ne Win meeting Indian
Prime Minister Indira
Gandhi.

Ne Win and US President
Johnson shaking hands in the
Rose Garden of the White House
as their wives look on.

Ne Win meeting
the Emperor of Japan.

Ne Win and Daw Khin May Than in Japan.

1960s Internal

Ne Win addressing the Peasants Seminar at Ohndaw, December 1962.

Ne Win leads a peasant procession at Hkapaung Peasants Seminar.

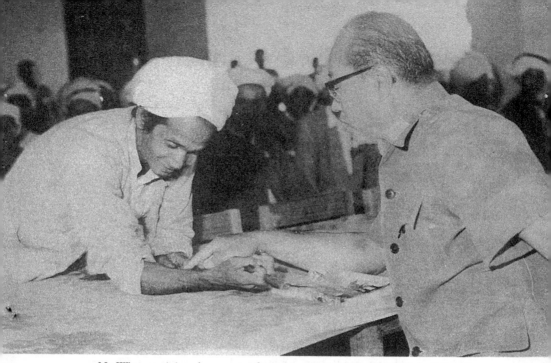

Ne Win examining the tattoos of veterans of the 1930s Hsaya San's Galon Tat.

Ne Win meeting the thirty-three member Internal Unity Advisory Board.

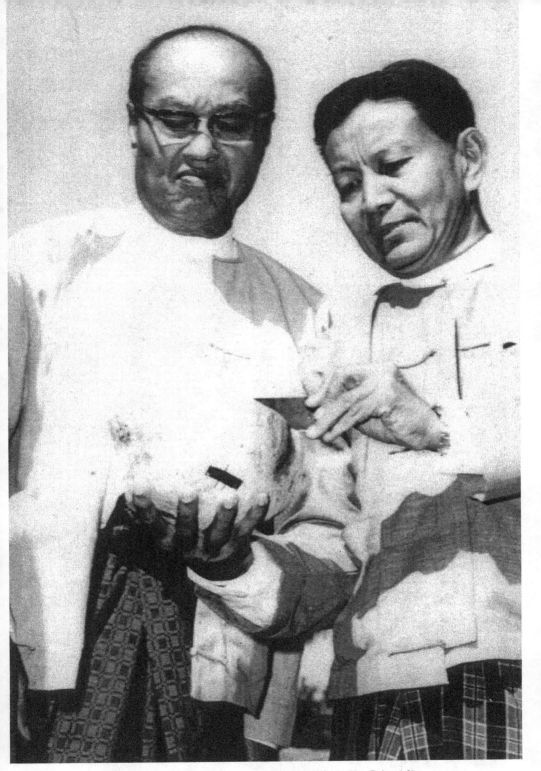

Ne Win examining gem stones with Colonel Ko Ko Gyi, 1960s.

mid-1970s

Ne Win in official photo at the time
of the First BSPP Congress, 1971.

Ne Win doing a Kachin dance.

Ne Win playing chess in Switzerland, with Daw Ni Ni Myint at his side, circa 1973.

Picture of Ne Win with Yadana Nat Mae on their wedding day as published in the Yangon newspapers, 24 December 1974.

Map showing major areas of insurgent activities in 1975 (UK National Archives FCO15/2045).

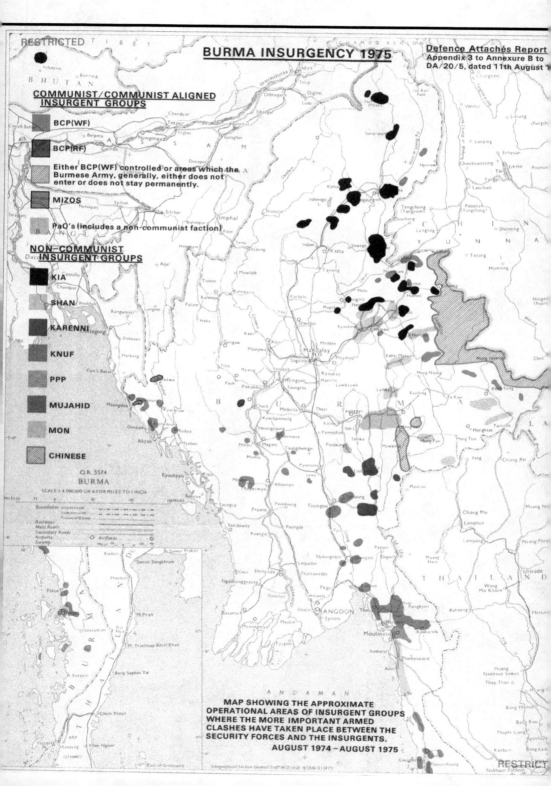

Map showing locations of army deployments, September 1975 (UK National Archives FCO15/2045).

1980s

Ne Win presenting the Aung San Tagun award to Lord Bottomley.

Ne Win with the King and Queen of Thailand and the Crown Prince.

Ne Win being
escorted by Colonel
Khin Nyunt to his
waiting plane.

Ne Win and President San Yu on an inspection tour.

Ne Win and senior BSPP leaders at a Party Congress, with Dr Maung Maung on the extreme left, circa 1981.

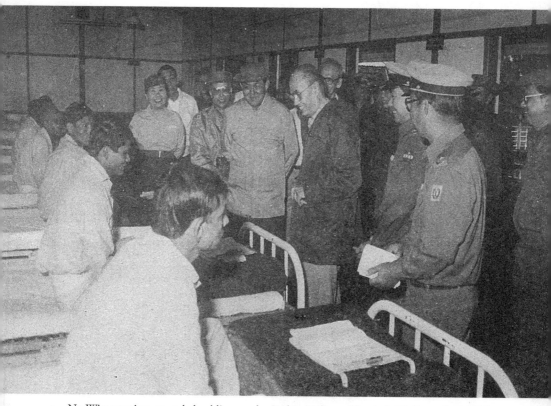

Ne Win meeting wounded soldiers at the Lashio Military Hospital, 25 December 1986.

Ne Win being briefed at the Metallurgical Research and Development Centre, 25 January 1988.

Ne Win bidding farewell to Malaysian Prime Minister Mahathir and his wife at the state guest house, Yangon, 27 February 1988.

1990s

Ne Win and Singapore Senior Minister Lee Kuan Yew, circa 1994.

Ne Win and his daughter Daw Khin Sanda Win and her husband and sons standing behind at a party, March 1998.

1

INTRODUCTION

It is both too soon and too late to write a political biography of General Ne Win. Too soon for several reasons: one is that his name still stirs political passions, though not as strongly as two or three decades ago. Another reason is that a number of diplomatic records necessary for a full account are not yet available. Under the thirty-year rule that applies in many archives, most of Ne Win's final decade in power is still under a blanket and this book is weaker for that. Moreover, the Myanmar archives and the archives of other countries crucial for a complete account are partially or totally unavailable. If I had more time, more money, and an even more tolerant publisher, the book would be substantially longer than it is now.

A political biography of General Ne Win is also too late in that many people who might have been interviewed and provided first-hand accounts of events and circumstances are no longer here. The Grim Reaper reached them before I did. Especially, the subject of the volume, General Ne Win, whom I never met, has been gone for more than a decade as I write. He does not have the chance to rebut and refute what I have written about him. However, given his lack of interest in what others said about him, and his unwillingness to encourage a cult of personality around himself, other than in the reflected glory of General Aung San, it is unlikely that he would do so even if he were alive.

A question that readers might ask is why have I bothered to write this book? I do not need to do so as I am under no obligation to a university to drive it up the league tables or a funding council to demonstrate that I deserve my noodles and potatoes.[1] There are, however, reasons which grew out of my academic career. I lived in Myanmar in 1978

1

and in 1982 for periods of six months each, and visited the country almost every year between 1975 and 1987, the year before Ne Win stepped down from formal office. Though I was unable to travel widely before 1989, and never reached the furthest regions of the country until this century, I did experience a little of what life in socialist Myanmar was like. In many ways, despite the lack of many of the creature comforts which I took for granted in my cosseted American/Australian/British existence when not in Myanmar, I found my life there constantly rewarding and interesting. The pace was slower, the people more friendly, the shortage of goods usually made up for by the black market or local substitutes, and generally I got my research done despite the claims that Myanmar was closed to the world. True, Military Intelligence followed me initially and later set silly traps to expose me as a combined CIA/ASIS/MI5 agent, but it was not hard to have a laugh at what was attempted.

Living in Ne Win's socialist Burma in the second decade of his rule provided me with experiences which I would not otherwise have had. This got me interested in the history of Myanmar nationalism and socialism as revealed in many memoirs and political texts published in the 1930s through the 1970s. It is no wonder that students in Yangon and elsewhere believed in their right and duty to rebel against the government in 1988. They had been provided with a steady diet of revolutionary nationalist literature readily available at any bookshop or private lending library, of which there were many in those days. Whereas today students seem merely to read "how-to-get-rich" manuals, then they and I were studying the efforts of student nationalists to oust the British, rid the country of foreign influence, and establish a socialist paradise.

A memorable experience concerning Ne Win occurred in 1977, on my first trip to Mandalay. In those more relaxed days, before mass tourism and heightened fears about security, one could wander almost anywhere in and around the city unhampered. One day I was strolling in the grounds of the old royal palace, not yet then rebuilt of cold cement rather than the timber which would have provided its warmth. Within the walls there was a small army base, within which one could equally stroll. As I did so, walking towards a dusty car shed containing three or four ancient Mercedes-Benz automobiles covered in bird droppings and dirt, I struck up a conversation with a middle-aged sergeant. I asked him whether General Ne Win ever used those cars. Indicating that he did, I asked whether he had ever met the General. He had and quickly explained that he would do anything for him to the point of death. He told me of the impact of Ne Win on him personally. Once, in the 1950s, as a young private, he had met Ne Win, who asked him about his domestic circumstances, including his marital status and about his children. Twenty years later, the sergeant had had the task of opening a car door for Ne Win on a visit to Mandalay. As he emerged from the backseat, Ne Win, addressing the sergeant by name, referring to him as *yebaw* (comrade), asked about his wife and children by name. He was flabbergasted at his feat of memory. Such a man had a hold over his army which deserves to be understood in terms other than the theories of despotism that I had been taught in school.

I subsequently heard others speak not only of Ne Win's prodigious memory, but also of his personal touch in human relations. Deferential and polite to the educated, he could be cruel and demanding towards those close to him, particularly in the army. As told later in this book, he physically beat his own men out of rage at their alleged ignorance or slavishness. His personal cook and valet for many years, Raju, told the story about how, when Ne Win got angry with him, he would strike him. Raju said he did not mind because after Ne Win's mood had been restored to equanimity, he often felt sorry for what he had done. Raju would then receive an increase in salary. For every account of Ne Win's brutality, there is a story about his devotion to duty and kindness towards others, often going out of his way to pay respects to his opponents in death or adversity, and revealing a humanity often denied by his critics. His emotions were always near the surface.

The persons with whom I talked most frequently about Ne Win in the 1970s and 1980s were his allies and confidents in the 1940s, 1950s, and 1960s, but then his opponents and political victims in the 1960s and 1970s. I expected these men and women to be angry at him and condemn him in no uncertain terms. A few did, particularly the wives of men whom Ne Win had imprisoned. However, many still retained a degree of respect for his integrity and patriotism, admitting that the economic policies over which he presided were a failure, as he did in the end, but he nonetheless had good intentions for the country. Of course, after 1988, when the anti-military exile community was in full voice, such views were drowned out by louder and more strident, younger voices.

Burmese voices of my age, living throughout Ne Win's socialist revolution, took a broader view of the man and his times, and were found to condemn less that those who fled abroad. One now-retired captain of a boat on the Ayeyawady River told me in the strongest terms how much he admired Ne Win. As this was more than a decade after his fall from power, when even the then military regime had nothing good to say about the socialist past, I pressed him to explain the grounds for his admiration. With a chuckle, he explained how he admired any man who could, for twenty-six years, alone and unaided, walk backward and never stumble. Whether Ne Win ever saw Clarke Gable, in the film *Honky Tonk*, remark as he backed out of a saloon covering his opponents with his pistol, "This reminds me of the days when we used to do all our walking backwards",[2] remains among the many questions I cannot answer about Ne Win and his times.

Ne Win was born into a Burma which was a colony that, politically, economically, and militarily, was intimately linked with the British Empire, especially British India. He spent his entire political life attempting to undo the consequences of binding and bending Myanmar to outside interests. His purpose was to restore Myanmar to self-mastery, only to realize that this was an impossible dream in modern conditions. More immediately, he had replaced a multiparty political system and a mixed economy with a single-party political system and a state-run economy, though with a large private sector, only to later admit that to go back after twenty-six years to what he had abolished, was the way forward.

This brings me to another reason for writing this book. Judged even on his own terms, Ne Win would have had to admit his revolution was a failure. Even so, it would be a mistake to argue from that perspective. To quote George MacDonald Fraser, who composed his memoirs, "to illustrate ... the difference between 'then' and 'now', and to assure a later generation that much modern wisdom, applied in retrospect ... is not to be trusted". He was writing about the Second World War as a man who had fought in it. If we look at the past through a lens distorted by "myth, revisionist history, fashionable ideas and reactions, social change, and the cinema and television", then much of the world Ne Win lived in and through seems apparent madness.[3] Our ideas of race, nation, economic justice, and political necessity are not those of our parents and grandparents, nor are they the same as Ne Win's and those with whom he lived and worked. Of course, basic beliefs in human dignity and the sanctity of life do not change, and Ne Win and his generation share these values with us, though they were displayed in different languages, often which the current generation would find politically incorrect.

Ne Win's life was lived as European imperialism was dying and new or restored states were emerging in the name of nationalism. War and conflict dominated the twentieth century in Europe and Asia. From the time Ne Win entered politics until he stepped down from formal office and beyond, he never knew peace. During the Cold War, which dominates this book, he attempted to keep Myanmar, despite its neighbours' machinations on various sides of the Cold War divide, out of their armed conflicts. Regrettable as the deaths of those who died in Myanmar's civil war over the years, perhaps as many as several thousand in the worst years, they were, in comparison to the many millions killed in Vietnam, Cambodia and Laos between 1960 and 1980, relatively few. Myanmar, despite its avowal of revolutionary socialism, also avoided the excesses of the Maoist revolution in China or the Stalinist era of the Soviet Union or the bloodbath in Indonesia of 1965. His revolution, in terms of its human toll, was not a bloody revolution. His political opponents died in their own beds or at the hands of other opponents.

That is not to say that the Ne Win era was cost free. Many lives were not only lost but stunted and opportunities for development and enrichment were destroyed. The cosmopolitan life of the privileged few that colonialism had created, and Ne Win had enjoyed himself, and continued to enjoy when abroad, was obliterated. Myanmar "fell behind" in the development race which has come to define political success in the late twentieth and early twenty-first centuries because of his single-minded pursuit of the Burmese Way to Socialism. However, seen from other perspectives, not shared by his most severe critics, he created a nation which had the resilience from its own resources to withstand more than twenty years of post–Cold War economic sanctions applied by his sometime collaborators at the height of the Cold War. I shall revert to this subject in the Epilogue. For now, to quote Fraser again,

> You cannot, you must not, judge the past by the present; you must try
> to see it in its own terms and values, if you are to have some inkling
> of it. You may not like what you see, but do not on that account fall
> into the error to trying to adjust it to suit your own vision of what
> it ought to have been.[4]

Finally, this is a very long book and it raises many questions and issues in the complex politics of twentieth-century Myanmar. The length and detail is justified by the need to detail for the record not only Ne Win's political thought as expressed in his speeches, but also his longstanding and close relations with many other leaders during the Cold War. For the uninitiated, this complexity may seem bewildering. For reference to the background and details to various sections, readers may wish to consult one or more of the standard histories of modern Myanmar. Unfortunately, there are few such available. I immodestly suggest, if they wish, they might consult the relevant sections of the author's *State in Myanmar* (2009). Throughout the book, I have used both the traditional transliteration of Burmese words and names as commonly found in books published prior to 1989, and the Myanmar Language Commission system published in 1980. By now, most readers will be familiar with both systems.

Notes

1. As H.L. Mencken wrote, in considering the biographies of President Theodore Roosevelt,

    > Nearly all our professional historians are poor men holding college posts, and they are ten times more cruelly beset by the ruling politico-plutocratic-social oligarchy than ever the Prussian professors under the Hohenzollerns. Let them diverge in the slightest from the current official doctrine, and they are turned out of their chairs with a ceremony suitable for the expulsion of a drunken valet.

    "Roosevelt: An Autopsy", in *Prejudices: A Selection* (New York: Vintage Books, 1955), p. 49.
2. Quoted in George MacDonald Fraser, *Quartered Safe Out Here: A Recollection of the War in Burma* (London: Harper Collins, 2000), p. 125.
3. Ibid., p. xix.
4. Ibid., p. xxi.

2

THE FORMATIVE YEARS
(July 1910 to December 1941)

The fault, dear Brutus, is not in our stars, but in ourselves, that we are underlings.

Julius Caesar (I, 1)

Despite his more than six decades in the public eye, relatively little is known about General Ne Win's youth and the formative years before he launched the military and political career whence his legend stems. There is much speculation about various aspects of his early days, as is to be expected of one who lived a long and controversial life. He provided little assistance to would-be biographers and kept the private information revealed about his life limited. Consequently, rumours and allegations abound but hard facts are rare. Even his date of birth remains wrapped in mystery, as there are several in circulation.[1]

According to Dr Maung Maung, his only official biographer and a close associate from the 1940s until his own death in 1994, General Ne Win, named Shu Maung at birth, was born on 24 May 1911, a Wednesday, at Paungdale in Paukkaung Township and Pyay District of what is now Bago Region (Maung Maung 1969, p. 26). *Who's Who in Burma 1961* places his birth date ten days earlier, on 14 May 1911, a Sunday, as does Ne Win's entry in the list of candidate members of the Central Committee of the Burma Socialist Programme Party at the 1971 Party Congress.[2] The former date was generally favoured in most English-language international media accounts of his life. However, his younger brother, U Thein Nyunt, himself born in 1927, states that his sibling was born on 6 July 1910, on the 15th day of the month of Waso, 1272, in the Burmese calendar, also a Wednesday, just after six o'clock in the evening.[3] His children concur with their uncle on the date, 6 July. U Thant also records that baby Shu Maung was born in 1910, not 1911.[4] It is universally agreed that he arrived in a little village then called Aung Thwe Ma Sha, now known as Kyaung Su, a short walk from Paungdale. Kyaung Su is a small settlement which has since moved further from Paungdale, but the original site still has a small Buddhist pagoda and a now dry well, as well as a new railway station for Paungdale.

The significance of the conflicting days of birth may not seem immediately obvious other than as an indication of mystery surrounding General Ne Win's origins. However, in Myanmar, the day of birth is thought to indicate qualities of the character of an individual and is a guide to his or her name. If his birth date had been Sunday, 14 May 1911, his birth name by which he was known until he took the *nom de guerre* of Ne Win in 1941, would probably not have been Ko[5] Shu Maung, but perhaps Ko Aung or Ko Aye. In Burmese culture, the significance of his brother's statement that he was born after six in the evening on a Wednesday is that his birth sign would be that of a tuskless elephant; earlier in the day it would have been a tusked elephant, Wednesday being divided in order to create eight birth signs in a week.

Persons born in the first half of Wednesday fall under Mercury and are said to be quick-tempered but as quick to forgive, although they do not forget. They are believed to be brave, optimistic, impulsive, and witty, as well as lucky. Many would say that these were the characteristics of General Ne Win. Those born in the second half of Wednesday are protected by the heavenly body of Rahu, which was believed by ancient astrologers to be the planet that causes the eclipse of the moon and the sun. Wednesday-afternoon born are described as cautious, highly attached to their families and tend to be moody. This too could have been a description of him, some might say. Certainly he displayed a strong sense of family loyalty and responsibility, though not indulgence.

Young Shu Maung's father, U Po Kha, had worked as a revenue surveyor, or *myei daing*, in the British–Indian government Land Records Department, one of the few parts of the colonial administration composed largely of persons indigenous to Myanmar, as opposed to the norm for the administration, which was largely staffed by British, Indian, and persons of mixed parentage (Donnison 1953, p. 66). Though poorly paid, revenue surveyors were "frequently very knowledgeable", and the basis upon which the maintenance of one of the primary sources of government finance, land taxes, depended.[6] Being poorly paid, they were also open to bribery.[7] U Po Kha was thus in a position in which he would have become well-informed about local land prices and income prospects. Upon retirement, he acquired sufficient land to live prosperously, growing and selling mixed crops, including groundnuts and corn as well as rice. He eventually became a broker and trader in many commodities, and could afford to build a substantial house, now gone, on the main road in the centre of Paungdale, a relatively prosperous town, unlike some parts of Pyay District.

Ne Win was definitely not born a worldly cosmopolitan, a trait that he eventually acquired. At the time of Shu Maung's birth, Paukkaung Township, where Paungdale is located, had a population of 28,600 residing in 77 village tracts. Both Paukkaung town and Paungdale had just over 2,000 residents, in over 400 households each. The total population of Pyay District of 379,000 persons in 1911 was overwhelmingly Bamar Buddhist, with Chin (11,600) being the second-largest ethnic group, with over 4,600 Karen (Kayin) and 1,000 Shan. There were more than 5,000 Hindu and 3,500 Muslim South Asians speaking Tamil, Telegu, Oriya, Bengali and Hindi. The Chinese population was fewer than 1,500 and there were 89 Europeans and 41 Anglo-Indians.[8] The ethnic mix of Pyay, like most of Myanmar at that time, created two interlocking discourses about ethnicity in subsequent Myanmar politics. These discourses dominated Myanmar politics in the twentieth century, though Ne Win's nationalization of much of the economy placed the discourse about foreign, primarily Indian and Chinese, ethnics in Myanmar life in the background until the twenty-first century. Claims about the putative rights of indigenous ethnic "groups", or minorities, starting with the Karen, were what helped catapult Ne Win to national prominence.

Though not cosmopolitan, Pyay was not cut off from the world. Some of the rice grown in the district, particularly Emata, was particularly sought after in Europe and Singapore because of its durable nature in transport after parboiling, and was sold at a premium in the markets, from whence it was shipped down to Yangon by rail from Pyay town, a journey of just 163 miles. However, some parts of Pyay District were noted for the small size of their land holdings, forcing many farming families into the poverty of subsistence agriculture. Much of the rice farming in the district was financed by Indian moneylenders known as Chettiars.[9] The Chettiars became the focus of much resentment in the 1920s and 1930s as Burmese nationalism mounted. Pyay sits on the nominal border between the dry zone of upper Myanmar and the wet zone of the delta in lower Myanmar, hence the mixed cropping pattern rarely found further north or south. Pyay town itself was sprawling and relatively affluent, being a major trading point for goods moving between upper and lower Myanmar as well as where logs floated down the Ayeyawady River from the northern forests were gathered into rafts or transferred to railway wagons for onward shipment to Yangon. Before the British occupied lower Myanmar in 1853, Pyay had been a major city of the old regime, given its strategic location and resources, crucial for "control of the middle reaches of the Ayeyawady as well as for relations with Rahkine" (Tun Aung Chain 2013, p. 28).

Industry, other than rice mills, was absent from Pyay District, as well as the rest of the country. Between 1903, when the first rice mill was erected, and the late 1930s, more than thirty rice mills were constructed in Pyay District, largely owned by British, Indian or Chinese individuals or firms. The labour force of the rice mills was typical of the employment competition which existed between the indigenous population and immigrant labourers from South Asia during the colonial period. The development of the mills attracted Indian workers north from Yangon into central Myanmar as well as the Delta. By 1939, while Burmese (i.e., the indigenous population) made up 39.6 per cent of the small skilled labour force in Pyay, Indians composed the majority at 60.4 per cent. With regards to unskilled labour, Indians made up 68 per cent while Burmese were just 32 per cent.[10] Burmese were relegated largely to farming and petty trade. Anyone growing up in Pyay after the First World War would have been reminded daily of immigration as a festering issue in Myanmar life. As many of the South Asian migrants were also followers of Islam, the perception that colonial rule was threatening the perpetuation of Theravada Buddhism, the religion of the indigenous majority, added to the so-called "race" question, which was the code for discussing immigration.

U Pho Kha was described by his family as friendly and outgoing, while Shu Maung's mother, Daw Mi Lay, was typically known for her good business sense. She was from Paukkaung, the township headquarters of Paungdale, twelve miles away. Paungdale was U Pho Kha's birthplace, and while in government service he would have visited Paukkaung frequently.[11] Ko Shu Maung's youngest brother remembers their father as being helpful, restrained and very sensitive to others, though others describe him as a jolly alcoholic. His mother, who passed away at the age of thirty-five, was a strict disciplinarian with intense spirit, one not to be caught out by others. Some even alleged that she was excessively outspoken in her views. Like many Southeast Asians several generations back, one or more of her ancestors had probably migrated from China to Myanmar, as she was said to have had a fair complexion.[12] Like many a son, General Ne Win, who was a finicky eater and an adept cook, said that no one's cooking was as good as his mother's.

After her passing, his father took up with a mistress from among the family's servants. Ko Shu Maung recounted in later years that he had a happy childhood, though he missed his mother a great deal after her death. Growing up in a very prosperous family in a small town, his early life might best be compared to that of the eldest son of the village squire, and perhaps assuming the privileges and licences which went with such putative rank. Unusually for a Myanmar boy growing up in the countryside, he apparently had no appreciable period of time as a novice monk, a normal rite of passage of Theravada Buddhist sons. He experienced a *shin byu*,[13] a nominal "baptism", but apparently received little else by way of religious education (Maung Maung 1969, p. 306). His parents were apparently not particularly religious.

There is much speculation that General Ne Win was of Chinese descent.[14] There is no evidence for this, although, as noted above, his mother probably did have a Chinese ancestor, perhaps Ne Win's grandfather. Certainly, the Chinese population in Pyay district was proportionately small. His father was said to have been tattooed from the waist down in a style typical of a Myanmar in the nineteenth century. A picture of him was apparently once published in a Yangon newspaper showing the tattoos. His cousin, a retired village schoolteacher, when interviewed in Paungdale in 2008, insisted that the family was thoroughly Myanmar and both he and U Thein Nyunt, the General's youngest brother, have the typical dark brown complexion and demeanour of a central Myanmar.

There is some belief that he was descended from a son of King Bodawpaya (1745–1819), the sixth king of the Konbaung dynasty, Myanmar's last. There is reportedly a Ne Win family tree recorded on a *parabeik*[15] in the possession of the late U Maung Maung Tin, an historian of old Myanmar and hoarder of documents, showing that General Ne Win was descended from Ein She Min, the Rakhine Naing Min Tha (Crown Prince Conqueror of Rakhine) in the eighteenth century, a son of Bodaw

U Waing, as he was known before he took the throne. The author of the *parabeik* was reportedly U Chan Thar, a member of the British Indian Civil Service (ICS). The famous Myanmar journalist and author, U Nyo Mya, apparently wrote a chapter on this subject to be included in a book he published soon after the formation of the Revolutionary Council government in 1962, but General Ne Win forbade its inclusion in the text as inappropriate for the new socialist era he was introducing.[16] As Bodawpaya fathered at least a hundred children, many Myanmar may be descended from him.

By all accounts, Shu Maung's parents made a happy couple until Daw Mi Lay's early death in 1931, despite the loss of four children. Two daughters and two sons died early in childhood but three sons survived, with Shu Maung being the eldest, followed by Hla Htun born in October 1917 and Thein Nyunt in April 1927.[17] In addition to assisting on his father's farm, as the eldest, Shu Maung also helped his mother with her first daughter and did a number of domestic chores before going off to school. After primary school in Paungdale, he went to Paukkaung to complete his middle school education, leaving at the end of the seventh standard.[18]

Subsequently in 1926 and at age sixteen, Shu Maung went to Pyay and initially enrolled in the National High School. National high schools were established throughout Myanmar following the 1920 students' strike at University College and Judson College, protesting government plans to create a new Rangoon University on the elitist model of a British university of the period. Suspecting an ulterior motive to retard Myanmar's political evolution to dominion status or even independence and to hold back the development of the people of Myanmar in favour of foreigners, the students demanded a more open, egalitarian institution. In this, they received wide support from the emerging political classes of the country. Following the strike, a Council of National Education was established to keep education as free and open as possible as a route to advancement for nationalistic youth, separate from government control. The movement soon became badly split, however, between those willing to accept a government offer of financial assistance, with, of course, mandatory regulations attached, and those who insisted on remaining independent. The split also affected the National School at Pyay, and it was closed after the founder and headmaster departed. Shu Maung then entered the Government Anglo-Vernacular High School, and though much of the teaching was in English, all of the teachers would have been Burmese or Indian.

During his school days, Ko Shu Maung was said to have disliked bullies and intervened when he saw younger children being coerced by older ones. Once, when he was at home in Paungdale during the school recess, he threw a shoe at some boys from a neighbouring village who were teasing some of his teammates on a local football team for not wearing shoes. In later years as adults, two of the younger fellows, U Than Daing and U Win Mya, were appointed to the state Trade Council in the 1960s, and another, U San Myint, became Burma Socialist Programme Party unit chairman in Pantaung Township.[19] Persons from his youth in and around Pyay often played major, as well as minor, roles in his subsequent career. A key associate in the army until 1963, Brigadier Aung Gyi, was from Paungde, just south of Pyay, and General San Yu, who succeeded Aung Gyi as General Ne Win's loyal, and long silent, deputy, eventually becoming President of the Socialist Republic of the Union of Burma, was eight years his junior at the Pyay Government High School. San Yu's elder brother was Ne Win's high school English teacher.

General Ne Win's famous irascibility was marked from a young age. Ko Shu Maung grew up quite close to his cousin, Ko Nyi, just four years older than himself. In Pyay, they were often together. On one occasion they went to a favourite stall run by Ma Khin Thaung, or Ni Ni, whom he was courting. Something, however, displeased Shu Maung, and he left the stall in a fit of pique, being generally rude to all about. When they returned to the market, Ko Nyi accused Shu Maung of embarrassing him by acting like a "prince sorcerer, like a little prince, like a lord who goes to school". Shu Maung just stomped off in high temper. Subsequently, according to his youngest brother, his mother consulted a fortune teller who predicted that her son was born to greatness, but would never have a satisfactory wife. She attributed his behaviour, including his short temper, to his stars. His mother was said to have made him promise to never "exceed the limit" (i.e., physically abuse) when dealing with women.[20]

General Ne Win's brothers had very different careers from his own. U Hla Htun, also known as U Nyi Hla, was a heavy drinker. He left Burma in 1946, and settled in Indonesia where he remained until 1948 or 1949. His journey to Indonesia was probably to help his uncle, U Ba Sein, a nationalist politician about which more below, who was in exile. Hla Htun married an Indonesian woman who, however, did not return to Burma with him. He made his living by operating a ferry boat, but was in trouble occasionally with the law and went to gaol a few times. He was known for his generosity and affability, the latter a strong family trait. The youngest brother, U Thein Nyunt, had been a businessman like his father, but when the government nationalized most concerns after 1962, he took up a post at the government trade corporation which dealt with cement, and later worked at the Myanmar Trade Commission in London.

Shu Maung was said to have done well at school, both in terms of his academic skills and at various sports. Some have claimed that he had a photographic memory and certainly learning seems to have come easily to him. He was articulate both in Burmese and English from a young age and even tried his hand as a youthful journalist, submitting articles from Pyay to the Yangon press, for which he was paid with postage stamps (Maung Maung 1999, p. 126). His athletic prowess is well-known, having been a devotee of tennis into his 50s, until he was forced for physical reasons, "tennis elbow", to abandon the game, and then a keen golfer, thus certifying a Myanmar national elite pastime. His parents provided generously for his needs while away from home, and he would have appeared to many to be the son of profligate and sympathetic, if not doting, parents. His success at high school was clearly good enough to provide him with the qualifications to enter the elite University College, which he did in June 1929, to read for a two-year intermediate degree in biology, preparatory to enrolling in the highly selective Rangoon University medical school. Then the only medical school in Myanmar, it admitted relatively few indigenes in favour of the sons and daughters of better off Indian and Chinese families resident in what was then a province of India.[21]

Students arriving in Yangon in the 1920s and 1930s would have found the capital of their country to be almost an alien city. Hindi was more frequently heard than Burmese in the market as the majority of the population were of South Asian descent. It was a cosmopolitan but highly class and race conscious city, with separate clubs, places of worship, and restaurants for the British, South Asian, Chinese and Myanmar populations. These communities were further divided into those who were Christian, Hindu, Muslim or Buddhist. In the words of the leading analyst of colonial Burma, writing on the cusp of independence but reflecting on pre–Second World War Myanmar, the population was then,

> ... in the strictest sense a medley, for they mix but do not combine. Each group holds to its own religion, its own culture and language, its own ideas and ways. As individuals, they meet, but only in the market-place, in buying and selling. There is a plural society, with different sections of the community living side by side, but separately, within the same political unit. Even in the economic sphere there is a division of labour along racial lines. (Furnivall 1956, pp. 304–5)

Other than enrolling initially in the National High School in Pyay, which may have been his parents' choice, there is no evidence that the young Shu Maung was particularly interested in nationalist politics or colonial Burma's myriad social, economic and ethnic problems. While leading politicians of the day from the *Myanma Athin Chokkyi* (General Council of Burmese Associations/GCBA), such as U Chit Hlaing, visited and stayed with Ne Win's parents in the 1920s, and debates about village nationalist organizations such as the *bu-athin* and *wunthanu athin*, which advocated boycotting elections and the non-payment of taxes and rents, and the fierce reprisal for their actions by the Indian mounted police, who sometimes razed entire villages, certainly would have taken place around Daw Mi Lay's and U Po Kha's table, Pyay and Paungdale were not centres of overt nationalist ferment in the 1920s. That would change in the subsequent decade.

Shu Maung took three years to complete the intermediate degree, having failed his examinations in the second year the first time round. This was attributed by his brother not to intellectual incompetence but to an excess of youthful enthusiasm for entertainment and an active night life. Attending the Rangoon Turf Club to gamble on the horses was a major occupation of his university days and subsequently. He did this in the company of two other young, prosperous, men from Pyay. One was the budding film star A-1 Tin Maung[22] who, as the youngest brother of the famous early Myanmar cinema actor Nyi Pu, appeared in his first film at the age of ten in 1923. The other was Ko Ba Win, son of a wealthy broker in Pyay who was attending Judson College. These three affluent blades whiled away the days in each other's company, leaving the library and laboratory far behind. Having completed the intermediate degree, Shu Maung left the university in 1932 at twenty-two years of age and sought to occupy himself with other activities, never returning to reside in Pyay again, but visiting frequently in later years.[23]

Despite his devoted attention to the Turf Club, a cosmopolitan gathering place for the well-to-do and powerful, and other pleasure spots in Yangon,[24] Shu Maung could not have been oblivious to the political issues that dominated the Rangoon press and tea shops. Whether any of the occasional articles he submitted to the English language weekly, *New Burma*, during his university days had any political content is unknown, but it would seem likely, unless, of course, they pertained to racing (Maung Maung 1999, p. 126). He was living in the capital of a prosperous colony in which wealth was a function of race and privileges were easier for foreigners to receive than for the indigenous population. It was also a colony in which nationalist ferment was growing and British–Indian constitutional policy struggled to keep up with the increasing political pressure for further reforms leading to self-government, if not independence. A system known as dyarchy, a form of mixed government between an elected legislative assembly and the British governor and his civil servants, had been established in 1923. Political parties had been formed and "race" reified into the language and institutions of Myanmar politics.[25] This prompted further discussion of additional steps to involve Myanmar politicians in the administration of the country, leading to eventual dominion status at the Burma Roundtable Conference in London in 1931. There the next stages of "constitutional advance" for Burma were explained and debated between British ministers and officials and Burmese cooperating nationalist politicians. The newspapers of the day were full of news of such events, as well as protests to the effect that they were not enough.

After the Round Table Conference, the main issue to be decided in the 1932 elections was whether Burma should remain a province of India or become a separate political entity under the authority of a Secretary of State for India and Burma.[26] One of Shu Maung's hostel mates at the university, and a distant uncle, was Ko Ba Sein. Ba Sein arrived in Yangon from Henzada in the Ayeyawady Delta three years before Shu Maung did. Though he admired his uncle, they were not particularly close, having grown up at some distance apart. Ko Ba Sein was soon to be one of the main leaders of a growing political movement which rejected all of what the British had to offer in terms of political and constitutional reforms, the *Dobama Asiayon* (We Burmans, or Our Burma Association).[27]

While some nationalist politicians cooperated in the institutions created by the colonial state and were grudgingly willing to accept the good intentions of their British masters, while urging them to hurry with reforms leading to eventual dominion status and perhaps complete independence, others, like Ko Ba Sein, were less considerate of constitutional niceties and the process of semi-polite debate and reform implicit in the evolution of political institutions. In addition to political domination concomitant with colonial rule, the consequences of the style of governance the British introduced, and the laissez-faire economic and social policies pursued, a number of grievances amongst the bulk of the Myanmar population had been generated. In many ways they had been made to feel foreigners in their own country, ruled by British–Indian personnel, both British and South Asian, British–Indian law, and exposed to cheap labour as a result of open immigration into Burma, which was relatively more affluent than India proper, for the poorest and richest populations of the subcontinent.

The Burmese population felt that they were doubly colonized, once by the British who imposed the modern state upon them through the institutions of British India, and secondly by India, through large-scale immigration and capital flows. The Burmese felt excluded from the modern institutions of the state and economy that imperialism imported and imposed. The resulting sense of frustration generated a number of complaints, centring on the future of the Buddhist faith, the role and nature of educational institutions and their personnel, the exclusion of Burmese from the civil service and modern sectors of the economy, and the near banishment of the majority linguistic group, the Bamar, from the army, in favour of so-called "martial races" from the non-Bamar border areas of the province. The latter was particularly galling to many young Burmese who were taught not only about Buddhism under the Burmese kings but also of the proud military history of the pre-modern monarchies which had lost power and ultimately the independence of the Myanmar state by the inability to modernize fast enough to ward off the colonial onslaught in the nineteenth century. The use of Indian, often Punjabi, troops, supplemented by members of the sometimes Christian-convert border minorities, what the British referred to as the "hill tribes", Karen, Kachin and Chin, caused deep anger in a population which had seen their own king denigrated and marched into ignoble exile in Ratnigiri, India, within their and their parents' lifetimes (Taylor 2006, pp. 195–210).

Not only were indigenous political institutions destroyed by the colonial rulers, but concomitant with that, the institutions and practices of the religion of the overwhelming majority of the population, Theravada Buddhism, were felt to be denigrated by rulers who had destroyed the central pillar of old Myanmar, the monarchy, and imported educational and missionary institutions to compete with the moral and ethical teachings of Buddhist monks. In seeking an explanation and solution to the totality of Myanmar's ills, Western ideologies, other than the ideology of the colonizer, liberalism, were increasingly studied and revered by Myanmar nationalists.[28] Marxism, in both its communist and socialist varieties, eventually became the dominant, if not the only, language of politics in the colony from the late 1930s onwards.[29]

The resentment generated by colonial rule erupted in violence in what became known as the Saya San rebellion that took place during the three years that Shu Maung was a student at Yangon University. The trigger for this peasant uprising was the great worldwide depression of the 1930s. Indian moneylenders, the Chettiars, became a focus of attack during the rising and the *bête noire* of Myanmar nationalists ever since. The Chettiars, being the most obvious local link in the great chain of imperial capitalism, connecting the great banks of New York and London via financial institutions in India to rural Burma, were the source of most of the rural credit in the major rice growing districts of Myanmar. After the depression, the Chettiars had unwillingly become the owners of half of the prime agricultural land in the Ayeyawady Delta, as they were forced to foreclose on loans granted in the days of high rice prices before the depression and the collapse of the world food prices.[30] This peasant uprising, with elements of a potential *pogrom*, which required the mobilization of an additional 3,640 troops from India, plus 8,100 Burma-domiciled troops, and much of the foreign personnel of British firms to suppress (Cady 1958, p. 316), affected almost all of lower Burma and parts of the Shan States and upper Burma as well.[31] Ne Win's father, U Po Kha, however, was largely unaffected by the depression or the rebellion, and his wealth was more than adequate to maintain his wayward pre-medical student son in his cavorting in Yangon.

Ko or Thakin Nyi, Ko Shu Maung's uncle, but more like a brother as they grew up together, could not resist the lure of the nationalist cause and became involved in politics at about this time. He would eventually lead his nephew/younger brother into politics via the nationalist organization, the *Dobama Asiayon*, which his distant relative, Thakin Ba Sein, led.[32] Founded in the early 1930s by Thakin Ba Thaung and Thakin Thein Maung, young men around the famous Burmese poet and writer Thakin Kodaw Hmaing, it was further evidence of the growing issues of race and immigration in colonial Myanmar politics. The deaths of both Indian and Myanmar workers in labour riots in Yangon in 1930, five months prior to the start of the Saya San rebellion, and anti-Chinese riots at its cusp (Pearn 1939, p. 291), forced a response from ardent nationalists to articulate public demands in political form. The *Dobama Asiayon* organized around the slogans of

Bama	Our country
Bama language	Our language
Bama literature	Our literature
Our country	Love it
Our literature	Cherish it
Our language	Revere our language (Ko Ko Maung Kyi, p. 29)

Ko Nyi joined the *Dobama Asiayon* in the formative period of the organization and was a devotee of his distant relative, Thakin Ba Sein. Thakin first entered into electoral politics in 1933 when a by-election for the legislative assembly was called for the seat of Shwebo, a town famous as the home of founder of Myanmar's last dynasty, Alaungpaya, and the site where would-be rulers of Myanmar sought to walk on the "victory soil" of the town. Three Thakin, having given, in support of their party, the *Komin Kochin*[33] and its candidate, forty rousing but seditious speeches in the eyes of local officials, were ordered to leave the town but refused to do so. They were consequently arrested and detained. These arrests attracted much attention and spurred the subsequent growth of interest and support for the *Dobama Asiayon*. The expansion of the organization, including encouragement from some in the Buddhist monkhood who saw its emergence as a force to protect indigenous society and its values, became a major preoccupation of the colonial police (Khin Yi 1988, pp. 21–22). Buddhist monks had become deeply involved in various political parties and newspapers during the 1920s and 1930s, contrary to their vows to abstain from political matters. They justified their violation of the *vinaya*, the disciplinary code of the monkhood, as essential to preserve the essence of Buddhism from the inevitable decay which would result from the absence of a Buddhist king or a Burmese government to protect the faith.[34]

In 1934, Ko Shu Maung's uncle/brother, together with Thakin Tun Ok and his younger brother, Thakin Hla Htun, formed a branch of the increasingly radical nationalist organization in Pyay (Sein Tin 2011, p. 106). Thakin Nyi and Thakin Tun Ok soon became prominent in the *Dobama Asiayon* and were elected to a temporary Executive Committee in September 1934, while their close colleague, Thakin Ba Sein, became General Secretary, eventually ousting two of the founders of the organization, Thakin Thein Maung and Thakin Lay Maung, from the leadership. They would seek their revenge later, for the rivalry persisted. Tun Ok became Joint Secretary and Nyi, one of two Propaganda Officers (Khin Yi, pp. 23–34). Next Thakin Nyi became in charge of Information in the *Dobama* Executive Committee, presided over by Thakin Ba Sein (Khin Yi, p. 32). At the Myingyan Conference in 1936, Thakin Nyi was elevated to Vice-President and Thakin Tun Ok to Secretary, while Thakin Ba Sein was reduced to an ordinary member of the Executive as Thakin Lay Maung returned to the Presidency (Khin Yi, p. 36). After the conference, Thakin Ba Sein, Thakin Aung Than, and Thakin Nyi, along with two others, were arrested for speeches they had made earlier in Mawlamyine (Maung Maung 1980, p. 126).

However, whilst political factionalism plagued the most radical element of the Burmese nationalist movement, Ko Shu Maung apparently took no active part in these machinations until at least 1937 or 1938. Initially on departing his student hostel and taking up residence on 101st Street in Yangon, he attempted to set up a business competing against the Indian charcoal suppliers in the city.[35] Pyay was a production centre for charcoal and Shu Maung adduced that he could bring it to Yangon and sell at a profit. His brother/uncle in Pyay, Thakin Nyi, became the supplier and he would develop the downmarket distribution and sales organization. The venture promptly failed, allegedly because of the unfair practices of the Indians already in the business who distorted the market to drive up the wholesale purchase price and undercut the actual cost at the retail end, making the business unprofitable for one with little capital to wait out the price distortions. He apparently learned a lesson that "puny measures could not dislodge the massive interests which were so deeply entrenched" (Maung Maung 1969, p. 41). This foray into capitalism may have contributed to many of his attitudes towards capitalists and the market in subsequent years.

Having failed at his first venture into capitalism, Shu Maung fell back on the state for employment. In subsequent years, he often spoke of the dilemma of nationalists, forced by circumstances, to work for the colonial state. First he served, in 1934, as a clerk in the Burma Railways office near Kyaiklat, west of Yangon in the Ayeyawady Delta, and then at the Rangoon post office, latterly at the Shwe Gon Daing branch.[36] In both those sections of the government administration, as well as the Customs Department, Anglo-Indians and Anglo-Burmese were employed in the higher technical sections of their operations grossly out of proportion to their total number in the overall population. The lower skilled were almost entirely persons from the Asian subcontinent (Donnison 1953, pp. 65–66). Working in such a non-Myanmar context may well have confirmed Ko Shu Maung's perceptions of what, as noted, was known at that time as the "race problem" in Burma, that lay behind the formation of the *Dobama Asiayon* and other nationalist groups.

While anti-Indian and anti-Chinese riots in 1930–31 and 1938 were the obvious markers of a deep-seated grievance felt by the majority of the population over competition for jobs, land, and spouses, in the departments of government in which Shu Maung worked, the disproportionate employment of what were to Myanmar people foreign labour would have been a daily reminder of the problem of unfettered immigration. The Myanmar economy before independence provided little employment for the indigenous population other than in agriculture and petty trade. What manufacturing did exist, in the making of cement (known as *Bilot myei*, i.e., British earth[37]), plimsolls and rubber shoes, matches, soap, beer, soda water (known as *Bilot yei*, i.e., British water), and leather goods, were almost entirely owned by British and Indian firms and employed overwhelmingly South Asian workers (Andrus 1948, pp. 140–62).

Taking up residence on 35th Street in central Yangon, an overwhelmingly Indian neighbourhood, Shu Maung followed his uncle's/brother's increasing involvement in the *Dobama Asiayon*. Thakin Nyi was devoting much of his money to the organization, but Shu Maung was initially sceptical and told him that he was just being exploited, and when his money was gone they would have no more use for him (Maung Maung 1969, pp. 47–48). However, before long Shu Maung also came under the spell of Thakin Ba Sein, one of the more controversial but ultimately unsuccessful nationalist politicians and, like his uncle, provided him with financial support from his own funds. In the mid-1930s, before Marxism and socialism came to be a dominant ideological motivation, second only to the goal of independence, Thakin Ba Sein, known for his forthright speaking and courageous behaviour in the face of the British–Indian police, was one of the most prominent staunch nationalists, advocating firm opposition to any sort of cooperation with the British colonial government. Thakin Ba Sein's nationalism was unclouded by other ideological issues, even if he did, almost certainly for tactical reasons, subsequently claim to be a Marxist, but not until 1940 and then but briefly.[38]

In the mid-1930s, many Thakins were arrested under the penal code for various acts of sedition, as noted above, with Thakin Nyi being one of them. Along with Thakin Ba Sein and others, he entered "into a fast", though unlikely for forty-six days as claimed, and was released from prison in an amnesty to mark the coronation of King George VI on 12 May 1937. His brother/nephew then nursed Thakin Nyi, who was never particularly strong, back to health and Shu Maung's faith in the Dobama cause was now confirmed, convinced by the determination of its supporters, including one who was very close to him. From then on, Shu Maung spent more of his free time at the *Asiayon* headquarters, eventually helping the printer and publisher, Thakinma[39] Khin Khin, the wife and primary financial backer of Thakin Ba Sein and his political career, find new quarters for the organization on Phayre Street (now Pansodan), moving from the corner of 39th Street and Montgomery (now Bogyoke Aung San Street). During one of Thakin Ba Sein's many periods of hiding to avoid arrest, Shu Maung and Thakin Chit Tin looked after him in a safe house on 126th Street North West (Sein Tin 2011, pp. 120–21). Amongst the editorial chores he undertook was proofreading Thakin Ba Sein's translation of Marx and Engel's *Communist Manifesto* into Burmese (Maung Maung 1969, pp. 48–49). There is a certain irony in this as Thakin Ba Sein became one of Myanmar's few anti-Marxist and anti-socialist politicians before 1988.

Following the elections of 1936 and the formation of a legislatively responsible government under a new constitutional order on 1 April 1937, politics, the British hoped, would be confined to the legislative arena and the press. Dyarchy gave way to what was referred to as the "91 Departments Government". The new dispensation gave the separated government of now British Burma, rather than British–Indian Burma, powers over all matters other than defence, foreign affairs, finance and the Shan States and frontier areas,[40] these remaining the preserve of the Governor and his appointed Counsellors. The cooperating nationalist politicians could now scheme and plot to achieve their goals via a tame parliamentary process, or so was the plan. Certainly, Dr Ba Maw's government was followed by that of U Pu, and before long U Saw had made himself the master of the lower house of the assembly and became the third elected Premier of Myanmar (Taylor 1976, pp. 161–64).

The British were soon disappointed, however, as the year 1300 (1938–39) in the Burmese era became a year of turmoil, including strikes and marches on Yangon by workers at the vital Burmah Oil Company in Yeinangyaung and Chauk, anti-Indian and anti-Muslim riots sparked by the republication of a pamphlet by an alleged Muslim attacking Buddhism, and students strikes leading to one death in a *lathi* charge by police outside the Secretariat, the seat of the administration, in Yangon.[41] The student strike, under the auspices of the All Burma Students Union, and spurred on by the *Dobama Asiayon*, spread nationwide, affecting even missionary schools as well as state-funded institutions (Leigh 2011, pp. 102–6). Monks also joined in the anti-government protests and soon the government of Dr Ba Maw fell from office as the politics of the street threatened to destabilize the processes of orderly government.

The expansion of the *Dobama Asiayon* and the introduction of Marxist thought into Burmese politics through organizations such as the

Nagani (Red Dragon) Book Club (Guyot 1970, pp. 13–16) and Dr Ba Maw's *Hsinyeitha* (Poor Man's) Party, led to increasing disputes among the radical nationalists, further threatening the unity of the *Dobama Asiayon*. Following the arrest of the then President of the *Asiayon*, Thakin Tun Ok, a conference of the organization was held at Pyay to choose his successor. This was expected to be Thakin Nyi, who was to run unopposed. However, he narrowly lost an eventual contested ballot to Thakin Thein Maung on the casting vote of the conference chairman, Thakin Lay Maung (Khin Yi 1988, p. 52). Thakin Ba Sein and Thakin Tun Ok were elected to much less elevated offices than they had previously occupied. Before long they would lose all control of the main organization to former student activists who sided with their rivals in the old leadership. Heady with their successes in the 1300 Revolution,[42] young men such as Thakin Aung San, Ko Hla Pe, Thakin Than Tun, and the slightly older Thakin Nu, thrust aside their ideologically uninformed elders.

The success of youthful nationalists, both students and recent graduates of Rangoon University, in leading and directing the 1300 Revolution gave them newfound confidence and ambition. With confidence and ambition came more factionalism and the eventual bifurcation of the *Dobama Asiayon*. Thakin Shu Maung was apparently so angry at the loss of his uncle in the leadership race that he had to be physically restrained by Thakin Nyi and others. The association became further divided over the issue of whether the three Thakins elected to the Legislative Assembly should, contrary to a pre-election commitment, accept their salaries as the government insisted. The Thakin Ba Sein faction held out against accepting.

The *Dobama Asiayon* finally split into the Thakin Kodaw Hmaing faction, nominally chaired by the doyen of Myanmar literature, and the Thakin Ba Sein–Thakin Tun Ok faction, over an attempt to expel Thakin Ba Sein for an allegedly intemperate attack on the now rather dotard-like figure of U Ottama, a veteran nationalist monk who had been appearing in rallies giving his support to cooperating nationalist politicians such as U Ba Pe. Other charges against Thakin Ba Sein were also made, including the usual one advanced within such organizations that he was a police spy. At the next *Dobama Asiayon* conference at Panswe, the new leaders failed to attend, and from then on Thakin Ba Sein, Thakin Tun Ok and their followers formed their own faction, which included Thakin Nyi and, following their family loyalties and old friends, Thakin Shu Maung and his younger brother, Thakin Hla Htun (Maung Maung 1969, p. 60; Sein Tin

2011, p. 106; Khin Yi 1988, p. 94). In the main organizations, Thakin Aung San succeeded Thakin Nyi as General Secretary, with Thakin Than Tun joining the Executive Committee for Peasant Affairs and Thakin Nu for Information (Ko Ko Maung Kyi 2012, p. 50).

The split in the *Dobama Asiayon* was not just over Thakin Ba Sein's allegedly intemperate remarks and other accusations, but was also created by personality clashes and the desire for power, as well as minor programmatic or ideological issues. All were driven by an intense spirit of nationalism, but when the younger members entered from their heady days of student politics and with their adoption of Marxist rhetoric, the older members, who had been involved with Thakin Ba Sein since the early 1930s, felt they were not given adequate respect and regard for their pioneering activities.[43] Such splits had occurred in earlier nationalist organizations such as the *Myanma Athin Chokkyi* and would continue to plague Myanmar politics throughout the 1940s, 1950s and early 1960s.

Whilst being drawn into the factional politics of the *Dobama Asiayon*, and working at the post office, Thakin Shu Maung was also busy having an affair with his landlady. Following his first marriage to Daw Than Nyunt,[44] the first of his children, Kyaw Thein, was born. He looked after his son, seeing to his educational and other needs, and never denied his paternity, keeping in touch with him all his life. In adulthood, U Kyaw Thein worked for the government oil and gas combine, Myanmar Oil Company, which monopolized the industry following the complete nationalization of the Burmah Oil Company in 1963.

After the 1300 Revolution, the major issue which dominated Myanmar nationalist politics was how the colony might best capitalize on the Second World War, which began in September 1939 in Europe, to achieve independence. U Pu and then U Saw, as Premiers in succession, pressed the British Governor, latterly Sir Reginald Dorman-Smith, and through him, the British government, to give a promise of dominion status in exchange for Burma's cooperation in the war effort. This they failed to do to everyone's satisfaction, with the British Cabinet, led by Prime Minister Winston Churchill, responding with the most calculated and ambiguous replies.

Seeing an opportunity to gain an advantage over those nationalists now in ministerial office and being blamed for not taking advantage of Great Britain's crisis, Dr Ba Maw entered into an alliance with his erstwhile student opponents, now dominating the major branch of the *Dobama Asiayon*. Thakin Nu and Thakin Aung San led their colleagues into a coalition with Dr Ba Maw's *Hsinyeitha* Party and the All Burma Students Union to form the *Bama Htwet Yat Gaing*, or Freedom Bloc. The Bloc, formed in October 1939, held that "Britain's difficulty is Burma's opportunity" and until a firm promise of post-war independence was received, as well as the formation of a constituent assembly to draft a new constitution and an interim responsible cabinet government, they would not cooperate in any way with the government in the anti-Axis or anti-fascist war (Guyot 1970, pp. 22 and 35). As a result of their firm political advocacy of this position, many members ran afoul of the wartime emergency Defence of Burma Rules and were arrested, including Thakin Nu, Thakin Than Tun, Thakin Soe, and Dr Ba Maw. In all more than a hundred were gaoled by the end of the following August (Guyot 1970, p. 40). Thakin Aung San, with an arrest warrant out for him from the end of June, had earlier gone underground, prompting his eventual departure in search of succour for the nationalist cause abroad (Naw 2011, p. 62).

While the politicians jockeyed for position in 1939–41, before the war came to Southeast Asia, other debates stormed among those who were concerned about the future of Burma and the world. Many saw the rising power of Japan as a possible saviour of Asia and considered turning to Japan for support. U Saw, who had visited Japan in 1936 and was known to have close contacts with the Japanese embassy, toyed with that idea both before and after he became Premier.[45] Others, particularly those of a left-wing or Marxist persuasion, took the view that Japan could not be trusted and indeed represented a greater threat to Myanmar than did even British imperialism.

The *Deedok* newspaper, edited by Thakin Nu's close friend Fabian U Ba Cho, published a series of anti-Japanese articles in 1939–40 (Thakin Nu 1975, p. 76, fn. 10). And U Tun Pe's translation of the Italian Amleto Vespa's *Secret Agent of the Japanese*, subtitled *A Handbook of Japanese Imperialism*, about the duplicitous behaviour of the Japanese in so-called independent Manchukuo, was a best-seller.[46] To those of this persuasion, especially after the German attack on Soviet Russia in June 1941, Burma had to join the anti-Axis war and reap the inevitable benefits of doing so after the greater evil of fascism was defeated. Others, led by Aung San, disagreed despite their leftist views. As the war came to its eventual end, Ne Win, in an address over Rangoon radio, conceded that he and others were aware of the "terror and ravage Japanese Fascists … wrought in China", but as seekers of independence, they had no choice but to collaborate with Japan.[47]

Advocates of Marxism such as Thakin Soe and Thein Pe Myint took the view that cooperation with the Japanese was unacceptable. This was the line at that time of the Indian Communist Party, which Burmese Communists such as Soe tended to follow slavishly, as well as the Indian National Congress. A delegation from the *Dobama Asiayon*, including Thakin Aung San, then the General Secretary of the Freedom Bloc, attended the organization's March 1940 Ramgarth conference. A small Communist party cell had been formed in August 1939, with Thakin Aung San as General Secretary, Thakin Soe in charge of organization, and Thakin Hla Pe as treasurer.[48]

Non- or anti-Communist Thakin and students formed their own organizations around the same time. One was the People's or Burma Revolutionary Party (PRP) formed as a counter to the Communists. Composed of young nationalists such as Kyaw Nyein, and led by Thakin Mya and Thakin Chit (Butwell 1963, pp. 29–30), Thakin Shu Maung was also a member.[49] Thakin Ba Sein dissented from this view and wrote that if the Freedom Bloc position was accepted by the British, or worse, the anti-fascist argument prevailed, "it would mean that the Burmese people would be involved in fighting a war for the British" (Sein Tin 2011, p. 115).

At a secret meeting of the Ba Sein–Tun Ok *Dobama Asiayon* at Pyapon on 10 April 1940, one of a series of conspiratorial gatherings over the previous months, a resolution was made to seek arms and military training abroad. A member of the Japanese Imperial Diet, Mr J. Ito, met Thakin Ba Sein while on a fact-finding mission to British Burma and introduced him to the Japanese consul. After their conversations, he resolved to go to Tokyo to seek arms and other assistance. He was also encouraged by Prince Damrong of Thailand, on a friendship delegation to Burma in September 1940, who suggested he walk across the border into the neighbouring country in order to make his way to the airport at Bangkok for a flight to Japan (Sein Tin 2011, pp. 117–18).

In the meantime, Thakin Ba Sein had met in June 1940 Shozo Kokubu,[50] the husband of a Japanese dentist in Yangon, then working as an unofficial agent of the Japanese navy, late one evening at the Jubilee Hall on Shwe Dagon Pagoda Road, then Yangon's premier venue for public events. He gave him a plan for his faction of the *Asiayon* to mount operations against the British in aid of the Japanese desire to close the Burma Road and speed independence. Burma at that time was the primary transhipment point for American and other foreign materiel to the beleaguered government of Chiang Kai-shek and the Kuomintang army, which had lost control of China's eastern seaboard to the Japanese military. The plan, which called for sending Myanmar youth to Japan for training and the provision of arms for an anti-British rising, was drafted by Thakin Ba Sein, Thakin Tun Ok and Thakin Nyi, among others. Subsequently, the police searched Kokubu's residence and found papers secreted away by Thakin Aung Than, another member of their faction, and was ordered out of Burma (Sein Tin 2011, p. 119–20; Guyot 1970, p. 50).

However, Thakin Ba Sein and Mr Kokubu played only minor roles in arranging for the departure of young Burmese for military training in Japan. Colonel Keiji Suzuki, Thakin Aung San and, after Dr Ba Maw's arrest, Dr Thein Maung, were much more crucial to an eventual operation organized not by the Japanese navy, but by the Japanese army, which belatedly recognized the navy's efforts (Guyot 1970, pp. 51, 62 and 65). Nonetheless, as will soon be obvious, had it not been for him, Thakin Shu Maung and other members of the Ba Sein–Tun Ok faction probably would not have been included amongst the Burmese chosen to lead the revolt against the British.

Activities of the *Dobama Asiayon* were largely funded by soliciting financial contributions from members and supporters on an ad hoc basis. In order to finance his walk to Thailand, Thakin Ba Sein received support from Daw May Sein and the Sayadaw of Thonze, as well as Thakin Shu Maung and others. Shu Maung was lauded subsequently by Thakin Ba Sein as a key fundraiser (Sein Tin 2011, p. 130). Having made his way south from Yangon as far as the Wywan railway station, from whence he set out on foot for the border, Thakin Ba Sein was soon arrested, along with a local guide, by a policeman, Ali Hussein, who took him to Moulmein police station. He was subsequently imprisoned at Monywa where he remained until the Japanese invasion in 1942 (Sein Tin 2011, pp. 131–32).

Whilst hundreds of Thakin and less-radical politicians such as U Ba Pe and U Ba U were being arrested under the Defence of Burma Rules for defying the colonial authorities during Britain's darkest days of the war in Europe, Thakin Shu Maung continued working at the post office. In addition, he was said to be honing the skills of an intelligence officer, checking on documents passing through his hands for information on the police to convey to his colleagues in the Ba Sein–Tun Ok faction. He also gathered politically relevant information at the Turf Club, which he continued to habituate, and from informants in government departments, as well as noting vehicle number plates and interrogating drivers of government cars, including that of the head of the police, Mr Prescott.

He also organized more safe houses in which he could hide colleagues from the police, including one at the stables of a horse owner, one U Po Pe, and a rented room on the fourth floor of a building on 29th Street, in the Bengali quarter of downtown Yangon. One of his charges in a safe house for a period prior to his abortive walk to Thailand was Thakin Ba Sein, to whom he supplied "Bisquit" brand brandy, one presumes to keep up his spirits between visits by his wife. Unlike many in the world of "revolutionary" politics, Shu Maung remained mum about his clandestine activities and "did not go round the town, carrying a Shan bag stuffed with papers, telling friends he was engaged in highly secret political work" (Maung Maung 1969, pp. 69–70). Such swollen and deceived heads were at that time, and later, plentiful in Myanmar political circles.

In the meantime, through the agency of Dr Ba Maw and others, the Japanese had already put into effect a plan to bring young Myanmar men out of the country and secretly train them on the then Japanese-occupied Chinese island of Hainan. Thakin Aung San was the first to be spirited out of the country, leaving on 8 August 1940, though in his case with no assistance from the Japanese but rather with the intent of reaching Communist-controlled areas of China in order to seek assistance from the Chinese Communist Party. He, however, was intercepted by the Japanese in Amoy (now Xiamen), thanks to information from Dr Ba Maw and Dr Thein Maung, and sent off to Japan.

After being convinced of the sincerity of the Japanese by a Colonel Suzuki, an officer of the Imperial Japanese Army, Thakin Aung San returned to Yangon to select and aid in the departure of a total of twenty-one young men from the main *Dobama Asiayon* faction via Japanese ships. Thanks to the earlier activities of Thakin Ba Sein, six young men from the Ba Sein–Tun Ok faction were also sent to Japan and then Hainan for military training. The twenty-seven of them were joined by three others, two, including Thakin Aung Than, of the Ba Sein–Tun Ok faction, who had gone on their own to Bangkok to contact the Japanese and one, a state scholar already in Japan (Naw 2001, pp. 57–73). These men together became the legendary Thirty Comrades, the origins of the first Myanmar army since the abolition of the Myanmar monarchy by the British in 1885.

With Thakin Ba Sein in jail, his wife, Daw Khin Khin, and other members of his faction, including Thakin Tun Ok, chose the members to be sent to Japan for training. Included were Thakin Tun Ok himself, Thakin Shu Maung, and younger men, Thakin Tun Khin, Thakin Ngwe, Thakin

Thit, Thakin Than Tin, and Thakin Kyaw Sein (Sein Tin 2011, p. 129). Finding men to join on what was an unknown adventure was not easy and they had to choose from those who were at hand, some of whom were very young and inexperienced. Men with little expectation of leadership or promising careers were chosen because they happened, by chance, to be available on the day. The Japanese organization which facilitated their departure and arranged their training was known as the *Minami Kikan*. It was led by a staff officer from the Imperial Headquarters of the Japanese Army known for his headstrong views, Colonel Keiji Suzuki. He became enamoured with the Burmese goal for independence and the men he trained and led (Yoon 1971, pp. 92–99).

Colonel Suzuki arrived in Yangon in May 1940, disguised as a correspondent for the *Yomiuri* newspaper with two colleagues, a businessman-cum-researcher and someone from the Manchukuo railways. As honorary secretary of the Japan–Burma Friendship Association, he met with U Saw and they discussed Japanese assistance for a Burma rising against the British. However, his main liaison was with Dr Ba Maw's associate, Dr Thein Maung, through whom he arranged to spirit away the twenty-one members of the Kodaw Hmaing faction after Thakin Aung San returned secretly from his initial foray the previous year (Maung Maung 1969, pp. 73–74). The inclusion of the Ba Sein–Tun Ok faction members only resulted after Suzuki had heard rumours in Tokyo of Mr Kokubu's assignations with Thakin Ba Sein and Thakin Aung Than. At first he was furious but was later convinced of the utility of involving the Ba Sein–Tun Ok Thakin after Naval officers, taking a larger strategic view than Colonel Suzuki, assuaged his ego by conceding his control of subversive operations in British Burma (Tatsuro 1981, pp. 45–46).

Three batches from the Kodaw Maing faction of the *Dobama Asiayon*, as arranged by Colonel Suzuki and Thakin Aung San, left prior to the Ba Sein–Tun Ok faction members. Thakin Shu Maung, one of the oldest of the Thirty Comrades, and ten others were in the last group to sail from Yangon, departing on the *Asahiyama-maur* of the Daitoa Shipping Company on 8 July 1941.[51] Five were from the Kodaw Hmaing faction, and six from the Ba Sein–Tun Ok faction, including Thakin Tun Ok himself, who had avoided an arrest warrant for some time. Neither group expected to find the other on board (Guyot 1970, p. 65). For his first of what would be many trips to foreign countries in the service of his country, Thakin Shu Maung bought a set of European-style clothes in order to disguise himself when boarding the ship, having previously always worn the Myanmar *longyi* (sarong) and *eingyi* (jacket) (Maung Maung 1969, p. 79). He, along with his new and old colleagues, was stowed in a steaming hold until the ship was outside of Burmese territorial waters.

As Dorothy Guyot points out, "the Thirty Comrades did not form a homogenous group". Thakin Tun Ok was sixteen years older than the youngest member, Min Gaung, who was just nineteen. Twenty-four years was the median age. In terms of educational attainment, four had only a middle school education, fifteen had some high school education, and eight had attended university, but only two of them had completed their course of study. The majority were from towns in lower Burma. While twenty-six were members of one or the other factions of the *Dobama Asiayon*, four had never been part of the organization (Guyot 1970, pp. 65–66). They were all willing to take a risk on an adventure with no certain outcome, but with the single-minded intent of speeding Myanmar's independence and wiping away the scar on Burmese nationalist sentiments caused by the humiliation of the Myanmar army in the loss of three wars to the forces of British India.

Most of the group arrived on Hainan via Tokyo by the middle of June, and were looked after by one of their training officers, Captain Kawashima (Tatsuro 1981, p. 52). Once on Hainan, they were divided into three groups for training purposes. Aung San, Let Ya, Setkya and Tun Ok were chosen to specialize in high command and administration, though Tun Ok, because of his age and condition, was spared military training; Ne Win, Yan Naing, Zeya, and Kyaw Zaw for field command, sabotage and guerrilla operations behind enemy lines; and the remainder for troop command and general warfare, with particular attention to guerrilla methods.[52]

Shu Maung was also given additional training, along with the group chosen for high command and administration because he "possessed outstanding leadership qualities".[53] To these five, Kawashima gave "lectures in political and military strategy", though this took up less than a tenth of their training time (Guyot 1970, p. 67). The divisions amongst the Thakin factions soon lessened under training, and though Thakin Tun Ok objected to the choice of Thakin Aung San as leader of the group, the other twenty-nine concurred, demonstrating that the rifts that had divided the *Dobama Asiayon* in Myanmar could be overcome for a larger cause and in a different context. Tun Ok became increasingly isolated and in the end took little part in the training, but rather spent his time drafting a constitution for the country after independence and recording radio broadcasts in Tokyo for later transmission (Guyot 1970, p. 68).

TABLE 2.1
The Thirty Comrades*

Civilian Name	Military Name	Year of Birth
1. Thakin **Aung San**	**Bo Teza**	1915
2. Thakin **Hle Pe**	**Bo Let Ya**	1911
3. Thakin **Shu Maung**	**Bo Ne Win**	1910
4. Thakin **Hla Maung**	**Bo Zeya**	1918
5. Ko **Tun Shein**	**Bo Yan Naing**	1918
6. Thakin **Hla Myaing**	**Bo Yan Aung**	1918
7. Ko **Shwe**	**Bo Kyaw Zaw**	1918
8. Thakin San Hlaing	Bo Aung	1910
9. Ko Saung	Bo Htein Win	1914
10. Thakin Tun Shwe	Bo Lin Yone	1917
11. Thakin **Aung Thein**	**Bo Ye Htut**	1922
12. Thakin Ba Gyan	Bo La Yaung	1911
13. Thakin Tin Aye	Bo Hpone Myint	1920
14. Thakin Tun Kin	Bo Myint Swe	1922
15. Thakin **Aung Than**	**Bo Set Kya**	1919
16. Thakin Soe	Bo Myint Aung	1917
17. Thakin San Mya	Bo Tauk Htein	1911
18. Ko Hla	Bo Min Yaung	1917
19. Thakin **Saw Lwin**	**Bo Min Gaung**	1920
20. Thakin Kyaw Sein	Bo Mo Nyo	1917
21. Thakin Thit	Bo Saw Naing	1920
22. Thakin Khin Maung	Bo Taya	1919
23. Thakin Tun Lwin	Bo Ba La	1917
24. Thakin Than Nyunt	Bo Zin Yaw	1919
25. Thakin Aye Maung	Bo Moe	1918
26. Thakin Maung Maung	Bo Nyana	1914
27. Thakin Ngwe	Bo Saw Aung	1914
28. Thakin Than Tin	Bo Mya Din	1920
29. Thakin Tun Ok		1907
30. Thakin Than Tin		1920

Note: *Names in bold are both used in this volume without necessarily reminding the reader of the pre-war and subsequent usage. Letya/Hla Pe (or Hla Hpei) and Set Kya/ Aung Than were known by either name after the war, whereas Aung San and Ne Win became identified with the old or new names respectively.

Source: Adapted from Tekkathi Sein Tin, *Yebaw Thon-gyaik Mawkun* (*Record of the Thirty Comrades*) (Yangon: Arman Thit Sapei, fifth edition, 2010, first published 1968), np.

Hainan was then under the authority of the Japanese navy. A camp was established at San-a, deep in some wooded jungle in the midst of a new naval base in the south of the island, disguised under the name of the San-a Agricultural Training Institute and under the command of Lieutenant Commander Fukuike, with Captain Kawashima and fifteen instructors from the army. All of the trainees were given Japanese names; Shu Maung, the tallest of the trainees, was called Takasugi Shin, Tall Cedar Tree (Nakanishi 2013, p. 55). The training camp opened on 11 April 1941 and terminated on 5 October of the same year, hence some of the trainees, including Shu Maung, missed the first several weeks of training (Yoon 1971, pp. 99–101).

The trainees were treated the same way as the peasant youths who were recruited into the Imperial Army in Japan, with the intention of making them hardened and fearless. Amongst the Burmese, Shu Maung was identified as seemingly "frail" and initially his personality did not stand out. However, that impression soon changed. He was said to be "unusually quick of understanding and both in practical skills and in theoretical subjects he would offer" to take the instructor's place "and explain things so that the others could understand more readily". When disagreements or misunderstandings occurred between the Japanese instructors and the Burmese trainees, often due to language barriers, "Thakin Shu Maung became a mediator and endeavoured to provide a solution" (Tatsuro 1981, pp. 53–54).

The training was accelerated and made more intensive in the expectation that the planned uprising in Myanmar might take place sooner than expected. They had night exercises on a regular basis, forced marches, and bayonet training. Some of the younger men appeared to crack under the strain and sought to steal a boat in order to escape from the island, but were persuaded to abandon their foolhardy plan. Some threatened to attack their instructors and had to be coaxed by Aung San into cooperation. Thakin Aung Than and several others became ill from the extreme conditions and had to be flown to Tokyo for hospitalization.

Distrust of Japanese intentions developed in the training camp as the planned date of the uprising in Myanmar was postponed in order to fit Japanese military plans (Yoon 1971, pp. 101–3). As Japanese preparations for war against the United States and European powers in Asia advanced, they were transferred to Taiwan to await developments. Though they had initially been led to believe that they would operate on their own in organizing a revolt in Burma, the longer the delay in invading their country, the deeper their suspicions grew that the Japanese were being duplicitous. However, they had no choice but to wait, and while doing so, one of them, Thakin Than Tin, died of acute appendicitis.

The training they received apparently had different impressions on the young Burmese nationalists. Kyaw Zaw was said to have "been deeply affected by the training in Hainan and the indoctrination in Tokyo". Three of them, including Ne Win, "returned with a distinct resentment of the imposition of Japanese ideals and culture on them". In conversations after the war, Ne Win indicated that Japanese expansionism and its accompanying militarist ideology had little impact on him (Fairbairn 1968, p. 69, fn. 2). "Militarism", however, was claimed to have become engrained in most, though some remained indifferent or uninterested. Yan Naing, Zeya, Ye Htut, and Myint Aung attempted to emulate the dress and behaviour of a Japanese officer in order to become as alike to them as possible.[54] Years later, General Ne Win recalled, "We learned our lesson, for the Japanese recruited from both our factions, knowing full well the two were far from friendly. So long as we were useful, they were willing to use us. Self-interest was all that mattered. That remains true today." (quoted in Maung Maung 1999, pp. 99–100). Thakin Shu Maung may have had a greater degree of detachment from his training than some of his fellow trainees, and became sceptical of Japanese motives earlier than most.

Interviewed forty-five years after the events on Hainan, Communist Thirty Comrade Kyaw Zaw, then a leading figure in the Burmese Communist resistance to the government of Burma, claimed that Ne Win and Aung San quarrelled frequently during their training. Noting Aung San's alleged puritanical streak, and Ne Win's notoriety for being a womanizer and a gambler, Kyaw Zaw went on to say that all of the Thirty Comrades agreed with Aung San and "despised" Ne Win. However, they kept together for the sake of the larger cause of independence (Lintner 1999, p. 42). He provided no evidence to support his claim, most of which does not accord with what happened subsequently, though no one could claim that Ne Win's relations with women were anything but frequent.

While Tokyo sought to find the most suitable date to commence the war in Southeast Asia, Colonel Suzuki began preparations for an eventual foray by the Thirty Comrades into Myanmar even before they commenced training. He opened a branch of the Minami Kikan in Bangkok under the name of the *Nampo Kygyo Chosa Kai* (Research Association for Southern Region Enterprise) in February 1941, and subsequently established four supply depots near the Myanmar border at Chiang Mai, Kaburi, Rahaeng (now Tak), and Ranaung. Imperial army headquarters initially authorized an incursion by four[55] of the Thirty Comrades on 10 October, but then cancelled that plan ten days after the new Japanese prime minister, the cautious Hedeki Tojo, feared if the British learned of the operations of the Thirty Comrades, it would upset his war plans. The four were ordered to return to Taiwan from Bangkok on 25 October (Yoon 1973, pp. 33–35). Two were subsequently ousted from the group for attempting to organize a revolt when they felt that the Japanese had betrayed their trust (Guyot 1970, pp. 69 and 73–74).

Colonel Suzuki, thinking the whole operation might be abandoned and refusing to give up his desire to help the Burmese liberate their country, telegraphed that the four Burmese had disappeared and could not be found. Learning in early November that the operation had not been cancelled by Tokyo, he ordered the four junior officers to infiltrate Myanmar to contact "underground" elements. Two did enter the country, possibly one being Ne Win, and evaded arrest by the British, but two were captured by Thai police before reaching the border. The entirety of the Minami Kikan organization in Thailand was finally ordered to close on 1 December and relocate to Saigon. This time Suzuki obeyed the orders. However, the Japanese bombing of Pearl Harbour on 8 December changed the entire situation, and those who had departed to French Cochin-China returned to Bangkok on 11 December along with all of their colleagues, under orders to organize a Burma Independence Army (BIA). A Japanese–Thai Military Agreement, concluded on 8 December, now made the operations of the Minami Kikan no longer technically illegal in Bangkok.[56]

Whether the Japanese army would actually invade Burma was still being debated almost to the day of the attack on Pearl Harbour and the American, British and Dutch colonies in Southeast Asia. However, the idea of assisting the BIA to initiate an anti-British uprising as a step towards independence was soon abandoned for a lesser role for the Thirty Comrades as adjuncts of a large-scale invasion of Burma by the Japanese army. Suzuki and his Myanmar confederates felt betrayed. Even before the beginning of operations, the Thirty Comrades felt they had been misled, but they were in no position to do anything about it. They had to go along with the Japanese plans, even with deep misgivings, as at that time there was no other alternative available (Yoon 1973, pp. 38–44). The BIA was officially established on 27 December 1941 in Bangkok. It included about 200 residents of Burmese descent in Thailand hurriedly recruited the day before and 73 Japanese, 29 commissioned and non-commissioned officers and 44 civilians (Yoon 1973, p. 44). They were equipped with three hundred tons of military materiel recently seized from the Kuomintang in China and shipped to Bangkok.[57]

Whilst waiting in Thailand for the war to commence, the BIA underwent additional training. Ne Win was in a small group which trained for parachute jumping. The plan that they would be parachuted behind British lines in order to inspire an uprising was put off repeatedly by inter-service rivalry within the Japanese forces and bureaucratic confusion. Plans for a parachute jump were further delayed by an absence of sufficient Japanese military aircraft and finally scuppered by the sinking of a Japanese supply ship, the *Mayu Maru*, loaded with arms and explosives for the planned operation.

The Thirty Comrades, with their Japanese trainers and officers, took the traditional Burmese (pre-HIV/Aids) blood-drinking oath, *thwe thauk*, on the day of the founding of the BIA. This entailed cutting their arms and draining blood into a silver bowl where it was mixed with that of the others and then drinking from the bowl after making a pledge of loyalty and comradeship. That evening the remaining twenty-seven Thirty Comrades, other than Thakin Tun Ok, also adopted *noms de guerre* at Bo[58] Aung San's suggestion. The idea of new names was either to protect their families should the British authorities discover their activities or to give them pride and a sense of mission.[59] Colonel Suzuki also adopted a Burmese *nom de guerre*, Bo Mogyo, or Thunderbolt. Shu Maung's choice of Ne Win was often translated as "Brilliant Like the Sun" (Yoon 1973, p. 46; Fredholm 1993, p. 32), or more accurately, "Bright Sun".[60]

The order of battle of the BIA at the time of its birth shows Japanese officers in leading positions, though Colonel Suzuki, having given himself the rank of General as the commander of an army, obviously consulted closely with Major General Aung San as the primary leader of the Burmese element. The Japanese would eventually be shed from the army, but initially they controlled the organization in its newly imposed role as support for the Japanese Southern Army.

At the age of thirty-one, Bo Ne Win was about to launch himself on his first military operation. As the leader of the only unit of the BIA without a Japanese commander, he was entrusted with the special task of infiltrating behind enemy lines and creating chaos amongst the British defences, as well as stimulating Burmese support for the incoming Japanese army. The other groups were expected to fall in behind the Japanese army as they approached the three main cities of Myeik, Dawei, and Mawlamyine

TABLE 2.2

Order of Battle of the Burma Independence Army (31 December 1941)

Unit	Name of Officer	Post	Rank
B. I. A. Main Force	Bo Mogyo (Keiji Suzuki)	Commander of the B. I. A.	Gen.
	Noda, Takeshi	Chief of Staff	Maj. Gen.
	Bo Aung San	Senior Staff Officer	Maj. Gen.
	Ba Yan Aung	Staff Officer	Lt. Col.
	Bo Set Kya	Staff Officer	Lt. Col.
	Kimata, Toyoji	Staff Officer	Lt. Col.
	Mizutani, Inao	Staff Officer	Lt. Col.
	Higuchi, Takeshi	Senior Adjutant	Col.
	Sugii, Mitsuru	Chief Accountant	Col.
	Suzuki, Taukasa	Chief of Medical Dept.	Maj. Gen.
Dawei Group	Kawashima, Takenori	Group Commander	Lt. Gen.
	Izumiya, Tatsuro	Chief of Staff	Col.
	Bo Let Ya	Staff Officer	Col.
	Bo La Yaung	Liaison Officer	Lt. Col.
	Doi, Yoshihara	Liaison Officer	Col.
	Tomoto, Shigeyuki	Chief of Sabotage	Lt. Col.
Hirayama Group	Hirayama, Suenobu	Group Commander	Col.
	Akikawa, Hiroshi	Staff Officer	Lt. Col.
	Sato, Taro	Staff Officer	Lt. Col.
	Bo Yan Naing	Staff Officer	Maj.
	Bo Min Gaung	Staff Officer	Capt.
Myeik Group	Tokunaga, Masao	Group Commander	Lt. Col.
Myanmar Interior Sabotage Group	Bo Ne Win	Group Commander	Lt. Col.

Source: Yoon, Won Z., *Japan's Scheme for the Liberation of Burma: The Role of the Minami Kikan and the "Thirty Comrades"* (Athens, Ohio: Ohio University Southeast Asia Program, 1973), p. 45.

in Tanintharyi, in preparation for making their way to Yangon before moving north to take all of Myanmar. Ne Win was in the vanguard with his "internal disturbance group" (Maung Maung 1969, p. 93), leading his men on his own, a position in which he would be in for the next five decades.

Venturing into territory occupied by the British, they did not know what to expect, other than that their allies might one day be their enemies, and their enemies one day their allies. That, of course, is a norm in politics. And war, as Clausewitz famously underscored, is politics by other means. Ne Win's career was to demonstrate the truth of the Prussian theorist's further linking of the psychological and political aspects of modern armed conflict.

Notes

1. See Larah Wessendorf, *The Era of General Ne Win: A Biographical Approach of His Military and Political Career Considering Burmese Traditions of Political Succession* (Berlin: regiospectra, 2012), p. 15. She provides three different days and three different years as permutations. However, several can be dismissed. She cites the unpublished doctoral dissertation of Hans-Bernd Zoellner for one, but he assures the author that he has no basis for raising 1909 as a possible year of Ne Win's birth. Personal communication to the author, 27 April 2013. Ms Wessendorf also cites Donald M. Seekins, *Historical Dictionary of Burma (Myanmar)* (Lanham, Maryland and Toronto: Scarecrow Press, 2006), p. 129, who gives 14 March 1911 as the date of Ne Win's birth. There is no authority cited and it can be dismissed without further consideration as no other authority supports this assertion. Curiously, on 11 June 1999, a *Straits Times* article quoted a diplomat in Yangon who claimed that his birthday was 12 June 1909, whereas other sources noted, in the same article, his birth as in 1919.

2. *Who's Who in Burma 1961* (Rangoon: People's Literature Committee and House, 1961 [compiled by U Tin Tut, information officer of the United States embassy in Yangon at that time]); *Baho Komiti Winlaung:mya: ei Koyei: Hmattan: Akyinchok* [Biodata of Candidate Members of the Central Committee] (Yangon: Myanmar Hsoshelit Lansin Pati, 1971), pp. 132–33. Also, *Thihmat Hpweya Koyei: AchetAlatmya* [Biographical Information for Recalling] (N.p.: N.p., N.d.) (available outside the Ministry of Information, News and Periodicals Department, Theinbyu Street, Yangon, for free in 2008), p. 119. This is the date used by Willard A. Hanna in his portrait of Ne Win in *Eight Nation Makers: Southeast Asia's Charismatic Statesmen* (New York: St. Martin's Press, 1964), p. 241.

3. Interview with U Thein Nyunt, Yangon, 10 July 2012; Thein Nyunt, "U Ne Win: Akyaung: Thi Kaung: Saya AkyetAlet Akyou" [Some Information about U Ne Win], photocopied typescript, unpublished paper (n.p., n.d.).

4. U Thant, then Secretary to the government in the Ministry of Information, provided a "Who's Who" appendix, pp. 127–30, to Thakin Nu, *Burma under the Japanese: Pictures and Portraits*, translated by J.S. Furnivall (London: Macmillan, 1954), p. 129. Furnivall explains this in his Introduction, p. xxvii.

5. Ko designates a young man; Maung, a younger male; U, an elder or respected male. Female titles are Ma for younger woman and Daw for older.

6.
> Surveyors were stationed throughout the district, each having a number of village tracts within his charge. They were responsible for keeping the field maps up to date, recording all physical changes in boundaries, noting every year what crops were planted on a holding, what plots were left fallow, and so forth. They also maintained registers showing changes of ownership, tenancies and mortgages.

> Robert Mole, *The Temple Bells Are Calling: Memories of Burma* (Bishop Auckland, County Durham: Pentland Books, 2001), p. 38.

7. U Kyan Aung, a corrupt revenue surveyor around the time that U Po Kha worked, is described in C.J. Richards, *Burma Retrospect and Others Essays* (Winchester, England: Herbert Curnow, The Cathedral Press, 1951), pp. 62–66.

8. "District Population Arranged by Race and Language", and "Table II, Distribution of Population", in *Burma Gazetteer, Prome District, Volume B* (Rangoon: Office of the Superintendent, Government Printing, Burma, 1913), pp. 7 and 10.

9. Burma Provincial Banking Enquiry, *Report of the Burma Provincial Banking Enquiry Committee, 1929–1930, Volume I: Banking and Credit in Burma* (Rangoon: Superintendent, Government Printing and Stationery, 1930), pp. 67–68. In Prome, the Chettiars provided one third of the direct finance to agriculturalists and another third indirectly.

10. The forgoing description of Pyay District is largely derived from Cheng Siok-Hwa, *The Rice Industry of Burma, 1852–1940* (Singapore: Institute of Southeast Asian Studies, 2012, reprint of Kuala Lumpur: University of Malaya Press, 1968), pp. 23, 32, 63, 64, 132, 215, Appendix V.6.: Percentage Distribution of Skilled and Unskilled Workers in Rice Mills in Selected Districts on 2 February 1939, and Appendix IV.B.: Distribution of Rice Mills in Burma by District and Division, 1892 to 1940.

11. *Thihmat Hpweya Koyei: AchetAlatmya*, p. 119.

12. Interview with U Thein Nyunt, 10 July 2012.

13. The *shin byu* ceremony re-enacts the last Buddha's passage from princely status to that of a monk and entails shaving the head and donning the robes of a monk. Most Burmese Buddhist boys undergo a *shin byu* and then remain

in the monkhood for varying lengths of time before returning to their families and secular life.

14. See, for example, Michael Fredholm, *Burma: Ethnicity and Insurgency* (Westport, Conn.: Praeger, 1993), p. 13; Martin Smith describes Ne Win's family as Sino-Burmese in his obituary in *The Guardian* (London), 6 December 2002. David I. Steinberg makes the same claim in *Burma: A Socialist Nation of Southeast Asia* (Boulder, Colorado: Westview Press, 1982), pp. 95 and 128; see also Martin Smith, *Burma: Insurgency and the Politics of Ethnicity*, 2nd ed. (London: Zed Books, 1999), pp. 37, 39; or Donald M. Seekins, *The Disorder in Order: The Army-State in Burma since 1962* (Bangkok: White Lotus Press, 2002), pp. 53–54. Speculation about Ne Win's alleged Chinese ancestry is rather like the earlier speculation that United States President Warren Harding had at least one ancestor of African descent, thus pipping Barack Obama as the first "black" president. See Francis Russell, *President Harding: His Life and Times, 1865–1923* (London: Eyre and Spottiswoode, 1969), *passim*.

15. A concertina-like lacquer book upon which was recorded birth, death, and other information including pagoda histories in pre-colonial Myanmar.

16. See note 4, *supra*. A copy of the Nyo Mya manuscript is in the Universities' Central Library, Yangon, but was missing at the time of writing.

17. See note 4, *supra*.

18. Interview with Dr Soe Lwin and U Ngwe Thein, 12 August 2012.

19. These were all institutions created after the 1962 coup when General Ne Win and his army and socialist colleagues recreated the state and will be discussed in Chapter 8.

20. See note 4, *supra*.

21. As late as 1940, only 16 of the 153 students at the Rangoon Medical School were indigenous. Two years before Shu Maung entered University, only 55 per cent of all students in Yangon University were from Myanmar. *Report on Public Instruction in Burma, 1927* and *1940* (Rangoon: Superintendent, Government Printing and Stationery, 1927 and 1940). The percentage of Burmese nationals enrolled in the medical faculty between 1929–30 and 1940–41 varied from as little as 13.6 per cent in 1940–41 to as large as 31.6 per cent in 1932–33. The remainder were all Indians, Anglo-Indians and others. Mya Oo, *History of Medical Education in Myanmar During Colonial Administration* (Yangon: Institute of Medicine 1, 9 May 1995), pp. 28–29.

22. A-1 refers to the film studio that he developed at Eight and a Half Mile, Pyay Road, just south of the major military base and international airport at Mingaladon, on the northern edges of Yangon. A-1 Tin Maung joined the Burma army during the Second World War, but returned to develop his studios, and direct and act in many films. He was chairman of the Film Council from 1964 to 1966 and died in 2000.

23. Whether he actually received the intermediate degree remains in dispute. Dr Maung Maung in *Burma and General Ne Win* (London: Asia Publishing House, 1969) writes that Professor Meggitt, whom Shu Maung apparently disliked because of how he bullied his students, together with biology, caused him to fail. His brother contends he did complete the course satisfactorily. *Thihmat Hpweya Koyei: AchetAlatmya* (p. 119) also indicates that he completed the course, but is ambivalent as to whether he received the intermediate diploma. As the records were destroyed in the Second World War, we shall perhaps never know. Whether he won any money at the races is also in dispute, but doubtful.

24. Hanna captures Ne Win at the races but is misleading on his educational experiences and otherwise in his "From *Thakin* to *Bo* to Chairman", *Eight Nation Makers*, pp. 239–65, esp. p. 242.

25. Between 1923 and 1947, legislative seats were created for "general" (i.e., largely Burman) constituencies plus special constituencies for rural and urban Indian labour (i.e., immigrants), Kayin (i.e., an indigenous minority living mixed with Burmans), Anglo-Burmans and Anglo-Indians (i.e., descendants of mixed race unions), and British business and the University of Yangon.

26. For details of these issues, see Robert H. Taylor, "British Policy Toward Burma in the 1920's and 1930's: Separation and Responsible Self-Government", in "The Relationship between Burmese Social Classes and British-Indian Policy on the Behavior of the Burmese Political Elite, 1937–1942" (unpublished PhD dissertation, Cornell University, 1974), pp. 89–149.

27. Burmese nationalists studied many Western and Eastern ideologies in search for a political explanation and solution to their colonial existence. The founders of the *Dobama Asiayon* studied Nietzsche, National Socialism, and Marxism as well as foreign nationalist movements such as that of the Irish Sein Fein (Ourselves or We Ourselves). The British, to disparage the Burmese nationalists, often called the Burmese the "Irish of the East".

28. As liberalism was advocated by the British, it was perceived as the ideology of imperialism and therefore rejected as part of the "slave education" offered in British schools and the university.

29. For a discussion of the introduction of Marxist and Socialist thought in Myanmar, see N. Nyun-Han, "Burma's Experiment in Socialism" (unpublished PhD dissertation, University of Colorado, 1970), pp. 25–32; or Robert H. Taylor, "Introduction: Marxism and Resistance in Wartime Burma", in *Marxism and Resistance in Burma, 1942–1945: Thein Pe Myint's 'Wartime Traveler'* (Athens, Ohio: Ohio University Press, 1984), pp. 2–7.

30. The most complete study of the economics of the rebellion, as opposed to its political issues, is Ian Brown, *A Colonial Economy in Crisis: Burma's Rice Cultivators and the World Depression of the 1930s* (London: Routledge/Curzon, 2005).

31. The most recent study is Maitrii Aung-Thwin, *The Galon King: History, Law and Rebellion in Colonial Burma* (Athens, Ohio: Ohio University Press, 2011).
32. Members of the *Dobama Asiayon* adopted the title of Thakin.

> Thakin means Lord or Master. Earliest mention of this word can be found in the Raza Kumar inscriptions of AD 1112. What prompted the young patriots to adopt the word was not love of the word itself but aversion when an Englishman or, worse still, an Indian used it in place of Mister, such as Brown Thakin or Banerjee Thakin. Usage of this appellation also earned the young Thakins much ridicule and contempt from the older generation of politicians and the general public alike. It was considered too presumptuous on the part of the young and seemingly unimportant men to use such a noble term of address.

Khin Yi, *The Dobama Movement in Burma (1930–1938)* (Ithaca: Southeast Asis Program Monograph, 1988), p. 3, fn. 2. British officials in the colonial period used the term rather like *sahib* in India. Myanmar nationalists who were members of the *Dobama Asiayon* (DBA, often mistakenly called the DAA) took the title unto themselves in the 1930s, implying that they were both equal to the British and themselves the proper masters of the country.

33. One's own king, one's own kind or self-government.
34. Maung Maung, *From Sangha to Laity: Nationalist Movements in Burma, 1920–1940* (New Delhi: Manohar, 1980), is the most detailed source on this subject.
35. Charcoal was the main and cheapest form of cooking fire for the majority of residents.
36. *Thihmat Hpweya Koyei: AchetAlatmya*, p. 119. This source spells the town as Kyauklat, but no such town appears on any available map.
37. Further demonstrating the foreign nature of the miniscule manufacturing sector, *Bilot* is the Hindi word for Britain, the origins of the British Indian army reference to home, Blighty. I am indebted to U Tun Aung Chain for this information.
38. Maung Maung, *From Sangha to Laity*, p. 147, claims that Thakin Ba Sein "was increasingly drawn towards national socialism and the totalitarian system of Germany and Italy".
39. Female Thakin.
40. The Shan States and the frontier areas, basically the border areas of northern Myanmar where the majority of the indigenous ethnic minorities resided, were not to come under the control of an elected government until after independence in 1948.
41. While the turmoil commenced in 1938, it extended into 1939 when Dr Ba Maw's government fell to U Pu following a no confidence motion moved by U Saw.

A full account of the 1300 Revolution can be found in Lei: Maung, "1300 Pyi Ayeidawpun" [1300 Revolution], *Myanmar Nainganyei: Thamaing* [History of Myanmar Politics] (Yangon: Sapei Beikman Press, 1974), pp. 467–73.

42. For a discussion of Burmese concepts of revolution, see Robert H. Taylor, "The Burmese Concept of Revolution", in *Context, Meaning and Power in Southeast Asia*, edited by Mark Hobart and Robert H. Taylor (Ithaca: Cornell University Southeast Asia Program, 1986), pp. 79–92.

43. For a discussion of the allegations made by each side against the other, see Khin Yi, *Dobama Movement in Burma*, pp. 133–36. For another version of these events, see Maung Maung, *From Sangha to Laity*, pp. 146–51.

44. Interview with U Thein Nyunt, 28 November 2014.

45. His account of his Japanese visit, which clearly impressed him, is found in Saw, *Gyapan Lan Nyunt* [Japan Points the Way] (Yangon: Thuriya, 1936). His argument would have been widely read as it was also serialized in the *Thuriya* (*Sun*) newspaper, the oldest nationalist paper, which he purchased from U Ba Pe, the veteran politician, after he returned from Japan.

46. The book was originally published in English in London by Victor Gollanca in October 1938. See Tun Pe, *Sun Over Burma* (Rangoon: Rasika Ranjani Press, 1949), p. 3. Contrary to On Kin, *Burma Under the Japanese* (Lucknow: Lucknow Publishing House, 1947), p. 22, U Tun Pe was not "tortured to death" by the Japanese secret police, the *Kempetai*, during the Second World War.

47. "Radio Address by Colonel Naywin (7–5–45) to the people of Burma", in *From Fascist Bondage to New Democracy: The New Burma in the New World* (Rangoon: Anti-Fascist People's Freedom League, 1945), p. 31.

48. Taylor, "Introduction", in Thein Pe Myint's '*Wartime Traveler*', pp. 5–8.

49. Khin Let Ya, *Hpei Hpei Bo Let Ya* [Daddy Bo Let Ya] (Yangon: Zwun Pwint Sa Ok, 2012), p. 149.

50. Kokubu had been dismissed from the Japanese Navy after a court martial during the First World War and later tried to farm in the Shan States of northeast Myanmar. After failing at farming, he moved to Yangon and, on his own initiative, regularly sent reports to the Japanese navy on conditions in the country. The Japanese consulate avoided him because of his indiscrete behaviour, for which he was once arrested. When the Navy and the Army eventually brought Suzuki, about whom more below, and Kokubu together, they clashed repeatedly and finally, when the Army assumed sole responsibility for the mainland Southeast Asian operations, they separated. Later, he wandered in Manchukuo and China, seeking funds to aid the Burmese independence movement. Dorothy Guyot, "The Political Impact of the Japanese Occupation of Burma" (unpublished PhD dissertation, Yale University, 1970), pp. 50–51 and 61–62. Sein Tin, and possibly Thakin Ba Sein himself, seem to have believed that he was an official agent of the Japanese government, which he

briefly became again before being dismissed when the Army took control of the operation.

51. Angelene Naw, *Aung San and the Burmese Struggle for Independence* (Copenhagen: Nordic Institute of Asian Studies, 2001), p. 72; Maung Maung, *Burma and General Ne Win*, pp. 79 and 84. Maung Maung gives the name of the ship as the *Kouryo Maru*.

52. Naw, *Aung San and the Burmese Struggle for Independence*, pp. 72–73; Keiji Suzuki (Bo Mogyoe), "Aung San and the Burma Independence Army", in *Aung San of Burma*, edited by Maung Maung (The Hague: Martinus Nijhoff, 1962), p. 57.

53. Maruyama Shizno, *The NAKANO School: Memoirs of a Member of the Takuma Kikan* (Tokyo: Heiwa Shoba, 3 April 1948), mimeographed translation by American intelligence, held in the Public Record Office as KV3/297, Japanese Security Service Home Organisation.

54. Maung Maung, *Burmese Nationalist Movements, 1940–1948* (Edinburgh: Kiscadale, 1989), p. 42. One might view these remarks from former Brigadier Maung Maung somewhat skeptically, in as much as two of the trainees referred to, Zeya and Ye Htut, eventually joined the Communist Party in the late 1940s. Brigadier Maung Maung was known for his strong hostility to anyone who smacked of Communism. Yan Naing, however, was known as a bit of a dandy, and married the daughter of the wartime head of state, Dr Ba Maw, who also was known for his love of finery.

55. The sources are not totally clear on this point. It would seem that actually six were taken for the operation but two subsequently were removed for insubordination subsequent to operations and they were then removed from the record, or at least memory.

56. Won Z. Yoon, *Japan's Scheme for the Liberation of Burma: The Role of the Minami Kikan and the "Thirty Comrades"* (Athens, Ohio: Ohio University Southeast Asia Program, 1973), pp. 36–37. Research by Won Z. Yoon, based on Japanese publications, indicates that those who attempted to enter British territory were Bo Let Ya, Bo La Yaung, Bo Zeya and Bo Myint Swe. Won Z. Yoon, "Japan's Occupation of Burma, 1941–1945" (unpublished PhD dissertation, New York University, 1971), p. 108; see also Guyot, "Political Impact of the Japanese Occupation", p. 74. However, in Colonel Suzuki's account of the formation of the BIA, he writes that Bo Ne Win was also part of the pre-war parties into Myanmar while Suzuki and Aung San remained in Bangkok. "I went ahead to Bangkok with Aung San and Ne Win, and we sent Ne Win, Let Ya, and a small group into Burma to scout and prepare." Suzuki, "Aung San and the Burma Independence Army", in Maung Maung, ed., *Aung San of Burma*, p. 58. They had to do this in great secrecy as the Imperial General Staff were opposed to such risky operations so near to the intended date of attack in Southeast Asia and the

Pacific. Yoon cites the Suzuki memoir but provides no explanation as to why he disbelieves Suzuki.

57. Guyot, "Political Impact of the Japanese Occupation", p. 75; she gives the figure of 150 Thais of Burmese descent and indicates that Japanese businessmen joined the Minami Kikan, not the BIA. Later, Guyot (p. 112) suggests that "perhaps three hundred Thais of Burmese origin" joined the BIA.

58. *Bo* loosely means an officer, leader, boss, or, in colonial times and until relatively recently, a European male. In terms of formal rank, a *Bo* is a Lieutenant; *Bokyi* is a Major; *Bohmu* is a Captain; *Bohmukyi* is a Colonel; *Bohmukyichok* is a Brigadier General; and *Bochok* or Bogyoke is a General.

59. Guyot, "Political Impact of the Japanese Occupation", p. 46; Naw, *Aung San and the Burmese Struggle for Independence*, p. 77, citing Bo Let Ya's and Bo Min Gaung's accounts in Maung Maung, ed., *Aung San of Burma*, pp. 190–91 and 47.

60. Maung Maung, *Burma and General Ne Win*, translates Ne Win as "brilliant as the sun", p. 95; Martin Smith gives "Brilliant Like the Sun", *Burma: Insurgency and the Politics of Ethnicity*, p. 55. Hugh Tinker, The *Union of Burma: A Study of the First Years of Independence*, 4th ed. (London: Oxford University Press, 1967), p. 8, trumps these with "Sun of Glory General", which Bertil Lintner follows, *Burma in Revolt: Opium and Insurgency since 1948*, 2nd ed. (Chiang Mai: Silkworm Books, 1999), p. 44. Another common mistake, based on having only a speaking knowledge of Burmese is that Ne Win means "Setting Sun". "Is There Anything to Be Said for Ne Win's Rule?", Confidential Diplomatic Report No. 188/78 by C.L. Booth, 13 July 1978, FCO15/2318.

3

THE BIA AND THE RESISTANCE
(January 1942 to August 1945)

The enemy of my enemy is my friend.

Arabic and Chinese proverb

Bo Ne Win was in the forefront of the Burma Independence Army (BIA) when it crossed the border from Thailand back into his homeland in January 1942. He had left a scant half year before.[1] Ne Win's party, including two Japanese majors and three other members of the Thirty Comrades, were the first to cross the Thaungyin River (Sop Moei in Thai) which forms the Thai–Burma border at that point. They did this by raft, with Ne Win being ceremoniously lifted on to Burmese soil by the Japanese officers. The two Japanese then returned to Bangkok, leaving the Burmese to proceed on their own, after changing from Thai to Burmese clothing. Across the river, they passed through Kayin and Thai villages. Their presence evoked some suspicion and curiosity about who this motley group was and what they were doing.

Eventually, they took a boat down the Thanlwin (Salween) River, but this was not until after Ne Win's attempted disguise as a forest officer searching for an elephant was doubted by a village headman who threatened to disarm the group until he was told the truth about their mission. One night they stayed at the monastery of a pro-Thakin monk, U Zawkita, but were rejected by another monk when seeking refuge at his monastery in order to avoid a police patrol. The party then divided, with his three

45

colleagues leaving for Pyinmana, Pyay and Bago, while Ne Win headed to Yangon. Each was to find and encourage members of the resistance to the British they hoped to raise from among their nationalist associates from the *Dobama Asiayon* and the Students Unions (Maung Maung 1969, pp. 101–3). They moved stealthily into yet British held territory and, evading arrest, and made their way towards the Ayeyawady Delta, east of Yangon. The Japanese army was then approaching the Sittaung River where the defending British would suffer a major disaster in February when the only bridge across was blown before many of the retreating Indian and British troops had crossed, thus further weakening their defence of Yangon.

Ne Win entered Yangon on 2 February, more than a month before the Japanese army. There was no evidence that his mission disrupted the British defence of the capital in any way. Indeed, though the British were aware that some Thakins were accompanying the invading Japanese, they apparently did not know that any group had infiltrated the city as early as 2 February. Yangon, in any event, was becoming increasingly chaotic, following the beginning of a Japanese bombing offensive on 23 December and the British-organized destruction of important assets such as the oil refinery at Thanlwin and materiel stored in the docks in February. As law and order broke down, looting and arson became widespread and municipal services collapsed.

Bo Ne Win, with a guide, travelled to Yangon by train from Hninpale Station. By chance, he encountered a former flatmate who secreted him the key to a residence in Shwe Gon Daing where they subsequently met and exchanged confidences. Many of his former associates, such as Thakin Nyi, were in prison, but eventually Ne Win was able to meet up with a group, calling themselves the Burma Revolutionary Party (BRP), consisting of future Communist and Socialist political leaders who were working in government offices or students lying low and reading military manuals. While discussing the future of the resistance with his colleagues, Ne Win also attempted to rescue a number of Thakin in prison who were being transferred by train from Tharrawaddy to Mandalay via Yangon. He succeeded in leading ten of them away from the tail end of a column waiting at the main station, but none were the senior figures such as Thakin Nu or Thakin Than Tun whom he was hoping to find. Ko Kyaw Nyein, with whom Ne Win was then conspiring, managed to convince a few members of the Burma Rifles to join the incipient resistance, bringing with them their weapons. In a stolen government truck, they headed north towards Pyay with Bo Ne Win, only to have the truck confiscated in Tharrawaddy by a sharp-eyed British officer. The group had dispersed by then and

Ne Win and Kyaw Nyein resolved to walk seventy-five miles back to Yangon (Maung Maung 1969, pp. 104–5).

Walking through the night, they managed to convince a suspicious police post at Okkan that they were government officials returning from making arrangements for their department to evacuate Yangon, and spent the remainder of the night there. Given the decisions being made by the British government as it was increasingly obvious that a defence of Rangoon was impossible, this was a very plausible explanation. The next morning they walked to Taikkyi only to learn that martial law had been declared by the British Governor, Sir Reginald Dorman-Smith. At that point, Ne Win and Kyaw Nyein separated and made their individual ways back to Yangon. Bo Ne Win and his aid, *Yebaw*[2] Toke Shwe, walked on and rested at Hmawbi before reaching Hlegu. They tried to board a train there but *Yebaw* Toke Shwe was hobbling and they could not catch it before it left. Entering Yangon at Kamayut, they found the university campus occupied by Indian troops and made their way to Bauktaw, east of the Rangoon Turf Club, where a BRP cell was located (Maung Maung 1969, pp. 106–7).

Ne Win's orders were to raise a rebellion by 27 February but he hardly had time to train the local area commanders before operations were to commence. Bringing with him "fewer than a dozen .22-caliber pistols", there was little evidence to show that the resistance he was to raise had any noticeable military effect (Callahan 2004, p. 49). However, his group was able to organize a military training centre at Bago in order to turn members of the inchoate underground resistance into viable military units (Yoon 1971, pp. 172–73). The British, who had only lightly defended the Delta in any event, had already withdrawn into Yangon in preparation for evacuating to the north. However, the presence of Burmese soldiers leading a revolt against the colonial rulers created a minor sensation among residents of the area. Now outside the range of command of the Minami Kikan and the Japanese army, bands such as that led by Ne Win were operating on their own initiative, acting with impunity wherever they went. Cloaking themselves with the mantle of nationalism and the reputation of the *Dobama Asiayon*, they assumed authority where none existed. As the BIA grew with the addition of more and more untrained but enthusiastic youths, the Japanese army occasionally clashed with the force they had created but no longer controlled.

Using their local knowledge and contacts, the BIA easily recruited members of the *Dobama Asiayon* and other nationalist and student organizations, as well as local toughs and other adventurous spirits.

Previously, the only military experience they had were in the so-called *tat*, or unarmed volunteer corps, that many political parties, both cooperating and nationalist, organized in the 1930s as auxiliary forces (Taylor 2006, pp. 201–5). Very few had been members of the University Training Corps, which the British army expanded only on the cusp of war. The *tat* of the *Dobama Asiayon*, the *Bama Let Yon Tat*, would have been a prime source. Quickly, young men who had been looked upon as untrained and perhaps untrustworthy, at least by established political opinion, were thrust into temporary positions of leadership within their communities as the BIA set about organizing local administrations following the rapid collapse of the colonial administration as the British withdrew.[3] Many BIA units, until they were brought under military discipline, behaved as bullies, arbitrarily demanding "taxes", food and weapons from the villagers (for example, see Zan 2007, pp. 65–66).

The Japanese army entered Yangon on 8 March, having reached Taukkyan and Mingaladon on the 7th together with contingents of the BIA. Bo Ne Win went out to Mingaladon to welcome Captain Kawashima, his training officer in Hainan, and about 2,000 hastily raised BIA troops. They entered the city on 9 March. Kawashima then commandeered the residences of the senior managers of the Irrawaddy Flotilla Company on Signal Pagoda Road, opposite the British army cantonment, and he and Ne Win took up residence in a compound of prepossessing, quintessential colonial residences.[4] Earlier, Ne Win had requisitioned other structures, including the deserted Methodist High School, also on Signal Pagoda Road, the Park Hotel and Devon Court as accommodation for the BIA. Unlike many other BIA units, Ne Win was said to have imposed strict discipline on the troops he raised and commanded (Maung Maung 1969, pp. 106–7). Ne Win, with his local knowledge, having lived in Yangon the previous decade, proved invaluable to Kawashima. He quickly made himself indispensable to the Japanese officer on his first visit to the city (Tatsuro 1981, p. 168). The Japanese army commander, General Shojiro Iida, occupied the Government House, residence of the British governor, on 15 March, and soon after the BIA held a parade to mark their arrival in the city at the Burma Athletic Association football grounds.

The Japanese army, rather like Goethe's sorcerer's apprentice, now sought to rein in the BIA and its youthful, if not criminal, excesses. They were about as successful as the apprentice as well. While the Japanese tamed the BIA, they ultimately could not control it.[5] In late March, they undertook to organize the hastily raised army into two units in preparation for a march north with the Japanese army in pursuit of the British. This consolidation worked to the BIA's advantage as it gave the senior officer corps time to shape the core as a national army. Following a démarche to Colonel Suzuki, who felt that his fellow Japanese had failed to fulfil their initial guarantees to declare Myanmar's independence, Bo Aung San was made commander of the BIA with Bo Let Ya, his deputy, as the chief-of-staff, with one new unit, the first division, commanded by Bo Zeya, and the second by Bo Ne Win (Naw 2001, p. 87). Eight Japanese officers were assigned to supervise the Rangoon headquarters and three to five to each of the divisions to work with the divisional commanders. In all, approximately 7,000 men were brought under military discipline and arrayed in Japanese uniforms. As the officers were now responsible for their discipline, a command structure quickly emerged and what had been a rabble began to cohere as a more coordinated force. Unknown in March, however, this organization was the prelude to the disbandment of the BIA just three months later (Callahan 2004, p. 54).

The two divisions of the BIA were ordered to march north on either side of the Ayeyawady River. Ne Win's column took the west bank, going via Henzada. There he called on Kayin leaders as well as members of U Saw's *Myochit* (Patriots) Party, the wealthy landowner Henzada U Mya and U Aung Tha. Though U Saw's followers had been, once he became Prime Minister, political opponents of the Thakin, Ne Win now urged unity among all parties as well as ethnic and social strata, indicating that the Japanese would only respect the Burmese if they stood up to them in a united manner. While Ne Win's men wearily trod up to Sagaing and then Mandalay in the heat of April and May, unopposed by the British, the other column clashed with the rear of a British unit at Shwedaung. The ensuing skirmish, in which the BIA led by Bo Yan Naing, became the stuff of songs and legends, was of little military significance. One of the BIA's opponents in the Battle of Shwedaung was a Myanmar from the Kayin minority, one Smith Dun. He would be the first commander of independent Burma's army in less than six years. After reaching Mandalay, it took the BIA a further period to reach Myitkyina and Bhamo in the far north (Maung Maung 1969, pp. 112–13).

The early installation of discipline into the BIA began to wane as the army outgrew its only disciplined officer corps and the behaviour of undisciplined soldiers became a source of one of Myanmar's most enduring post-colonial ethnic conflicts. The young men who rallied to the BIA had been told by nationalist politicians and politicized Buddhist monks of the nefarious actions of the British and their alleged collaborators, the Indians and indigenous ethnic minorities, especially the Kayin community, in denigrating Buddhism and suppressing the rights of the majority of the population. The fact that the British had given special privileges to the Kayin in terms of recruitment into the colonial army and Kayin-designated legislative council constituencies, and a minority of the Sgaw-dialect Kayin had converted to Christianity and were highly articulate in English, allowed the entire Kayin community to be demonized by those whipped into a fury, feeling that they were now in charge. With the British gone, the Kayin were defenceless, so the raging mob believed, and they turned their attention to reversing the distorted picture that extreme nationalist demagogues had taught them. In the middle of the Ayeyawady Delta, though the overwhelming majority of the population were Bamar, there were both predominantly Indian and Kayin villages and, particularly in and around the town of Myaungmya, a rough equivalency in the population of Bamar and Kayin. Revenge for alleged anti-nationalist sentiments was sought there. The area was ripe for conflict.

It was upon these Kayin that the rogue BIA youths wrought their most vengeful fury. Though the myth of Bamar-Kayin enmity had developed during the colonial period, there was no evidence of any actual serious conflict between the two communities either before or after the advent of colonialism until April–May 1942. The events of those months created a fissure in the Myanmar polity which has yet to heal completely. Over a period of weeks, fifty-eight Karen villages were destroyed by fires set by the BIA and their Bamar collaborators while probably a larger number of Bamar villages were destroyed by Kayin, many led by a Buddhist Pwo-dialect Kayin village headman named Mahn Shwe Tun Kya.[6] Bamar tended to flee for refuge into the towns, particularly Myaungmya, while Kayin retreated into fortified villages to defend themselves. The Japanese military police, the *Kempeitai*, became involved in the multi-sided conflict, as did the local Indian villages. In the midst of the conflict, the Ba Maw government, and its Central Karen Committee, protested to the Japanese over the organization of several Kayin self-defence organizations in the Delta in opposition to the efforts of the government to restore order. Only after the Japanese army imposed control was the bloodshed brought to a halt.

Realizing that their goal of immediate independence on the defeat of the British was thwarted, the BIA officer corps got down to the process of army and state building. While in private, Bo Ne Win, "as was his habit", referred to the Japanese as "mother-fuckers", in public he and others were forced to defer to the Japanese (Taylor 1984, p. 133). As the Japanese began to replace the hastily organized and amateur local administrations of the *Dobama Asiayon* with civil servants who had served under the British, and called the older generation of politicians out of hiding to join in providing a facade for continued Japanese military rule, the BIA officer corps were forced to go along. In mid-May, after the British lost control of Bhamo in the north of the country, the Japanese commander called a meeting in Pwin-Oo-Lwin (then known as Maymyo) of senior Burmese military and political figures. From the army came Aung San, Let Ya and Ne Win; from former students and *Dobama Asiayon* nationalists were Thakin Kodaw Hmaing, Thakin Mya, Thakin Than Tun, Thakin Ba Sein, Thakin Tun Ok, and Thakin Nu; from the established politicians came Dr Ba Maw, Bandoola U Sein, Dama Ba Thein, U Tun Aung, the Buddhist Kayin U Hla Pe, and U Ba Pe. The Burmese leaders agreed with the Japanese to nominate Dr Ba Maw, who like many others had been recently released from prison, as the head of government and eventually of state.[7]

Only Thakin Ba Sein and Thakin Tun Ok objected to the choice of Dr Ba Maw (Tatsuro 1981, pp. 193–94). Tun Ok, who had been appointed while still in Hainan to organize a central, or *Baho*, administration, was quickly shunted aside, presaging both his and Thakin Ba Sein's exile the next year to Singapore and then the Japanese-occupied Dutch East Indies. In Hainan, Bo Ne Win, like his fellow officer and former member of the Ba Sein–Tun Ok faction, Thakin Aung Than (Bo Set Kya) (Guyot 1970, pp. 140–41), remained loyal to the chain of command and the leadership of Bo Aung San, never returning to their former mentors in the waning faction of the *Dobama Asiayon*. At the time of the meeting at Pwin-Oo-Lwin, "Bo Aung San, Bo Ne Win and the other leaders of the army had left a note for Dr Ba Maw in Maymyo to the effect that they know the Japanese had cheated us, and the only hope for Burmans was to remain united." They also suggested to him to find a way to keep the army posted at one place in order for it to remain intact and not be emasculated by the Japanese.[8] Following the Pwin-Oo-Lwin meeting, the Japanese commander, General Iida, installed a Central Executive Administration, chaired by Dr Ba Maw, and consisting of all the persons who attended the Pwin-Oo-Lwin meeting, except the military commanders and U Ba Pe (Maung Maung 1989, p. 45).

After the formation of the Ba Maw administrative committee, the BIA was centred on Mandalay, with Amarapura as the headquarters, under the command of Bo Let Ya, with the rank of Lieutenant Colonel. Aung San, as the overall commander of the army, was given the rank of Colonel by Colonels Suzuki and Nasu. Aung San, together with Ne Win, met Thakin Than Tun, himself not yet a Communist, in Mandalay and dropped hints about resisting the Japanese eventually. Moving on to Shwebo, they ran into Thein Pe Myint and took him south of Sagaing.[9] When it was decided that Bogyoke Aung San should make a ceremonial re-entrance into Mandalay, the city in which the last Myanmar army surrendered, Ne Win was sent ahead to make the necessary arrangements for his commander to be received in style with an appropriate parade organized with the town dignitaries and elders.

As the Ava (Innwa) Bridge was closed at that time, it was necessary to cross by ferry and Ne Win did so together with the then fugitive Communist and nationalist writer Thein Pe Myint, a member of a secret underground movement, seeking to walk out to India in order to convince the British of the seriousness of the indigenous resistance to the Japanese. If successful, he intended to encourage the Allies to assist the resistance when circumstances permitted. Ne Win rushed to the ferry despite the May heat, and Thein Pe Myint had to hurry to keep up with him. Not knowing that the Japanese were searching for Thein Pe Myint, Ne Win provided him with the password with which to ride the ferry. When they boarded the boat, Japanese officers seemed to despise the insignia of Ne Win's Japanese-style uniform, distaining the Burmese army that he represented. Hence, his oath that the Japanese were "mother-fuckers", against whom the Burmese must eventually revolt, but only when conditions were propitious (Taylor 1984, p. 188; Maung Maung 1969, p. 119).

The further consolidation of the grip of the officer corps, under Bo Aung San and his senior colleagues, came about as a result of the decision of the Japanese to dissolve the BIA on 27 July 1942 and to recruit a smaller number of men into a new Burma Defence Army (BDA).[10] Initially planned to involve up to 5,000 men, it became an initial force of only 2,000 in the end. The smaller size made it possible for the unit commanders to get to know their troops much better than if the organization had remained unwieldy. Ne Win was made commander of one of the two core units and promoted to full Colonel at the same time. This lean and tightly controlled organization recruited only the most reliable and capable men and, in the words of a directive written by Bohmu Ne Win to those involved in choosing the rank and file of the BDA, excluded "persons of dubious character". Thousands of villagers mobilized into the BIA were dismissed and returned to their homes, many disgruntled and open to appeals from the Communists and other leftists in the initially thwarted civilian underground resistance.

The two units were grouped in Rangoon and Mandalay, before being unified in a training camp at Pyinmana for several months. The Japanese officers who supervised this operation gave Bo Ne Win and Bo Yan Naing, the officers in charge, a degree of latitude in mounting the reorganization (Callahan 2004, p. 58). Army building and the imposition of discipline and order became a hallmark of the BDA, in emulation of the Japanese army, particularly in contrast to the indiscipline of the BIA. Many of the new army's manuals, however, were translations of British Indian army materials.[11]

Reduced to the hard core of 2,000, the Burma army then began to expand. Over the next three years, it grew to a force of approximately 15,000 men, with the formation of additional battalions and the development of specialist corps such as anti-aircraft, supplies and transport, engineers and, after many months had passed, a special unit recruited from the Kayin community, the Karen Rifles. As the BIA had provoked significant conflict with the Kayin community, especially in the Ayeyawady Delta, the latter development was designed to establish good relations with the Kayin and their leaders. The Japanese also opened an officer's training school at Mingaladon, from whence most officers were chosen until the end of the Japanese occupation. Ne Win and Yan Naing, with Captain La Yaung, were sent to choose men from the camps at Pyinmana, Mandalay, and Rangoon for the first class. They chose those with firm mental toughness, putting them through a rigorous pre-selection process on the assumption that the training they received would be as intimidating as that in Hainan (Callahan 2004, pp. 61–62).

The formation of the BDA led to the eclipse of the majority of the Thirty Comrades within the army leadership. Except for a distinctive minority which obviously included Aung San, along with Let Ya, Set Kya, Yan Naing, Zeya, Kyaw Zaw, Ye Htut and Ne Win, the fame of the Thirty Comrades was derived from venturing abroad, not what they were capable of doing at home. Aung San called for a meeting of the Hainan returnees after receiving a number of complaints from many of the Thirty Comrades that they had not been promoted. Most were still captains, while only Let Ya, Ne Win and a handful of others had been promoted to major or colonel. Ne Win, however, argued that they needed to be retrained as their education were insufficient for higher command posts. The training they had received in Hainan had been truncated in terms of military tactics and their education needed to be enhanced. Consequently, they were removed from their commands and their places given to men from the resistance who had joined the BIA on the march north. There was further jockeying for power and influence in the army and Aung San undertook a complete reorganization, ensuring the army's loyalty to him. Whether he trusted Ne Win or not is unclear. Ne Win, however, never displayed any sign of disloyalty, in words or deeds, to his commander at that point or later (Maung Maung 1989, pp. 83–85).

After the BDA had begun to expand, it was divided into three battalions. The Third Battalion remained at Pyinmana and became the training and recruitment centre of the army, while the second was posted to Yangon. The First Battalion, under Bo Ne Win, was sent west over the Rakhine Yoma, via the Taungup Pass, to perform mainly garrison duties and keep the lines of communication with the Japanese open. Initially at Pyinmana and then in Rakhine at a camp established at Lamu, 100 miles north of Thandwe (Sandoway), Ne Win put his troops through a tight training schedule. Japanese army manuals were translated into English by Japanese officers, and then into Burmese by Ne Win. Bo Aung Gyi served as his supply officer and several of the Thirty Comrades were in his command along with Bo Tin Pe (Maung Maung 1969, pp. 130–31). Controlling the islands of the Rakhine coast was seen as important as the British might try to land infiltrators into the area or use it for potential resistance forces to exit Burma to link up with the British in India (Maung Maung 1989, p. 74). It was through this area that Thein Pe Myint and his colleague, Tin Shwe, passed on their way to India, eventually meeting with the British forces in Chittagong (Taylor 1984, pp. 146–56).

The Japanese, in order to provide and supply the BDA, also organized Burma's first War Office in 1942–43. Initially under a Japanese officer and a mixed Japanese-Burmese staff, the Japanese element was greatly reduced, allowing General Aung San, and later Colonel Ne Win, to run the army on a day-to-day basis. The War Office attracted students from Rangoon University who jealously protected its increasing independence from the nominal Burmese administration as well as the Japanese (Guyot 1970, p. 149). Key officers in the early War Office were Bo Aung Gyi and Bo Maung Maung. It was at this time that Ne Win came to work with and rely heavily upon these two stalwart staff officers. Both were strongly nationalistic; they became masters of the organizational logic of military affairs. Maung Maung, who in 1943 served as General Aung San's staff officer, witnessed meetings between the Minister of Defence and his two major divisional commanders, then Ne Win and Zeya.[12] By 1944–45, the War Office was functioning with almost no Japanese involvement, establishing a command-and-control function separate from the Japanese army, thus allowing the Burmese army to organize the eventual resistance unbeknownst to their nominal allies (Callahan 2004, p. 64). The officers in the War Office, and those who attended the officer's training courses at Mingaladon, were a small and select group who, though from various backgrounds and different parts of the country, developed a strong sense of camaraderie, which maintained the army's essential unity until 1948 and independence from the British.

The BDA was never used by the Japanese in any major military campaign. While small units were attached to some forward units, others were used for road construction in Rakhine, air raid precautions in Yangon, manufacturing munitions, and general garrisoning and security details. Just before the end of the war, the Japanese did order the army to assemble at Yangon and prepare to march north to defend the capital, but this merely strengthened its ability eventually to revolt against the military occupation forces (Callahan 2004, p. 314). Before then, some BDA troops did penetrate as far north as what is today the Kachin State where they clashed, along with larger Japanese units, with some units of the Chindits in 1943 (Callahan 2004, pp. 312–13). The Chindits were British units flown into northern Burma as long range penetration units to test Japan defences and assist the American army in attempting to open the Ledo Road between Assam in India and Yunnan in China in order to supply Chiang Kai-shek's armies. While militarily insignificant, the use of locally recruited Kachin men, often raised and armed by the American Office of Strategic Services (OSS), the forerunner to the Central Intelligence Agency,[13] into irregular forces continued the British tradition of seeing the Kachin and other residents of the northern hills as plucky fighters loyal to the Empire and its perpetuation. Amongst the residents of the northern hills, it created a sense of ethnic exclusivity and added to a belief in military prowess, conceived out of the British Indian army's notion of "martial races", that contributed to subsequent conflicts in Myanmar's post-independence politics.[14]

The most careful study of the characteristics of the BDA and its successors is that by Dorothy Guyot. She concludes that there were four aspects of its structure which shaped its character and, by implication, its form after independence, even after being reorganized by the British. One was that it was small, never exceeding 15,000 troops and the officer corps was "able to maintain great intimacy, and the men shared a strong sense of brotherhood". Secondly, the army grew at a reasonable rate, allowing for a "satisfying rate of promotion". It also remained entirely an infantry force with little technical training other than in transportation and weaponry and, lastly, it was tightly controlled by the Japanese, in the sense of not being militarily utilized, thus increasing the sense of resentment against the occupiers by the Burmese officer corps (Guyot 1970, p. 314–26, quotation from p. 315).

The success of Dr Ba Maw's Central Executive Administration at resurrecting the core of the former British administrative system, and the pressure for a grant of independence to Japan's new colonies in order to make good the promise of a "Co-Prosperity Sphere" rather than another colonial empire, led the Japanese to form a Central Administration Programme Committee in early June 1943. Eventually, Dr Ba Maw, General Aung San and others were invited to Tokyo to meet the Japanese government, and on 1 August 1943, Burma was declared officially independent. At that time, Dr Ba Maw became *Naingngantaw Adipati* (head of state) and premier with the strong backing of the Japanese Prime Minister. The Japanese army would have preferred a more compliant candidate such as Thakin Nu (Nemoto 2007, p. 7). However, a secret treaty was entered at the time by Dr Ba Maw and the Japanese government, thus rendering the independence more nominal than real.

After the formal declaration of Burma's independence and the subsequent formation of the Burma National Army (BNA) on 6 August 1943, the new name for the BDA, supposedly hallmarking its role in an independent state, Ne Win was appointed as Aung San's successor as Commander-in-Chief of the armed forces, reporting directly to him as Minister of Defence (Naw 2001, p. 98). Ne Win announced the name change for the army at a press conference on the same day at the War Office and the decision was ratified by the Defence Council on 15 September (Defence Services Museum and Army Archives Office 1994, p. 293; Min Maung Maung 1995, p. 22). The headquarters of the army was at that time moved from Pyinmana to Bago in order to be nearer to the War Office in Yangon. Bo Yan Aung was ordered to serve as Ne Win's chief of staff, replacing Aung Gyi, who was moved to the War Office, along with Maung Maung. He was highly trusted by Aung San, having accompanied him to China in 1940 (Maung Maung 1989, p. 85). One may suspect that Aung San put Yan Aung in a position to report on the actions of his nominal superior. However, Aung San apparently had no reason to be suspicious of Ne Win as he had proven to be loyal to Aung San in Hainan and at the Pwin-Oo-Lwin meeting in May 1942. Nonetheless, it was felt that Aung San did not trust Ne Win.

Dr Ba Maw had his own doubts about the loyalty of his subordinates. He attempted to control the BDA and his nominal Minister for Defence, Aung San, through a seven-member Supreme Defence Council composed of himself as chairman; the vice-chairman of the Privy Council, U Ba Hlaing; Aung San; the Vice Minister of War, Bo Set Kya; the Commander in Chief, Colonel Ne Win; the Principal of the Military Academy, Bo Zeya; and his aide-de-camp and eventual son-in-law, Bo Yan Naing. This hollow institution had no control over the armed forces and Aung San did not even bother to attend the cabinet meetings where the budget was discussed. Instead, he sent one of his Japanese advisors. In any case, the army budget was provided by the Japanese army, so any control by Ba Maw's government was purely perfunctory (Guyot 1970, pp. 323–24. fn. 4).

Relations between the Japanese military headquarters and the BNA were largely handled by Aung San and Ne Win. A series of Japanese officers were appointed to liaise with the headquarters of the Burma army. One of them was Lieutenant Colonel Kutsuda, with whom both Aung San and Ne Win negotiated amiably (Maung Maung 1989, p. 83). Though a Major General in the Japanese army, Sawamoto Rikichiro, was the Chief Military Advisor during most of the post-independence period, the main work was done by Captain Takahashi Hachiro, the only remaining member of the original Minami Kikan, and therefore well known to Aung San and Ne Win. Captain Takahashi "managed to win the respect and close friendship of every Burmese Army officer he met". Physically, the War Office was removed from the proximity of the Japanese headquarters and placed in a Burmese quarter. In June 1944, Ne Win organized a tour of BNA camps for Aung San and Sawamoto. They visited Mandalay, Pwin-Oo-Lwin, Shwebo, Namkhan, Indaw, Yeinangyaung, Allanmyo, Pyay and Paungde. The travels also involved meetings with the local dignitaries (Maung Maung 1969, p. 141). Sawamoto was eventually replaced by an officer who attempted to ingratiate himself with the headquarters staff, who, however, completely bamboozled him, believing until the day the BNA began shooting at the Japanese that they were completely loyal and ready to fight the British (Maung Maung 1989, pp. 82–83).

The structure of the Burma National Army at the top was similar to that of the Japanese Army, at least initially. Aung San became Minister of Defence with Bo Set Kya as his deputy. Bo Let Ya was appointed Chief of the Military Affairs Bureau and, like the Deputy Defence Minister, given the rank of Colonel. Set Kya was soon removed at the insistence of the Japanese police who suspected him of being in contact with a British agent in the Karen hills in the east of the country, the famous Major Hugh Seagrim.[15] Indeed, Set Kya was in touch not only with Seagrim but also with Karen officers from the British army who had remained behind after the Japanese fled, including Saw Kya Doe, and anti-Japanese Karen leaders such as Saw San Po Thin.[16] Set Kya was sent to Japan as military attaché and the deputy's post was left vacant. Dr Ba Maw requested Bo Yan Naing, who accompanied Aung San to Japan in 1943, as his aide-de-camp, with the rank of Major. Bo Zeya, now a Lieutenant, became the first Burmese commandant of the officer training school at Mingaladon (Maung Maung 1989, p. 85). Reorganization became a substitute for military action.

Ne Win's office was at Bago, also the site of the Model Battalion under the command of Bo Kyaw Zaw. Supposedly an exemplar of a modern army, the Model Battalion was where the remaining Hainan-trained officers, other than Bo Ye Htut, were located for further training, along with a number of new officer recruits to the BNA from the anti-British resistance. The camp was highly politicized and in time became a major centre for Communist training within the armed forces. Kyaw Zaw himself became a Communist. Anti-Communist junior cadet officers, fearful of losing future influence to the leftists, initially refused to study Japanese in order to prepare themselves to be sent to Japan to attend the Imperial Military Academy. Ne Win ordered them to do so, saying that others would manage the resistance (Maung Maung 1989, p. 117).

In his capacity as Commander-in-Chief, Colonel Ne Win was not only in charge of the army headquarters, but also supervised the work of the Model Battalion. However, the Hainan-trained officers at Bago, many of whom were Communists, whom Ne Win had previously insisted required additional training, went to Aung San's confidant, Bo Let Ya, and through him convinced Aung San that he should not leave operational control of the army in the hands of one man, Ne Win. Consequently, in March 1944, Ne Win was moved to Yangon and made Chief-of-Staff of the General Staff Department, with Aung San himself remaining as Commander-in-Chief (Maung Maung 1989, pp. 86–87 and 119). Aung San's apparent acceptance of leftist dislike of Ne Win, however, never affected their relationship and they often appeared at events together, solidifying their relationship with their troops, such as the graduates of the Mingaladon Military Academy (Maung Maung 1974, pp. iv, 45 and 53–54).

The month following the renaming of the army, Aung San called for a meeting of his five senior officers, Let Ya, Ne Win, Zeya, Kyaw Zaw, and

Ye Htut. They discussed whether and how they should organize a resistance movement against the Japanese, but the meeting proved to be inconclusive. The polished, Calcutta-educated Bo Let Ya, whom Aung San relied upon for his administrative abilities and political support since their days together in the Rangoon University Students Union and the *Dobama Asiayon*, argued that the timing was premature and the resistance forces were not prepared for such an action. Aung San, inherently cautious and unconvinced of the military strength of the army, only came round to seeing the possibility for a successful resistance movement in the future after discussions with Thakin Than Tun.[17] Than Tun was in touch with Thakin Soe, the leader of the putative Communist resistance organization in the Ayeyawady Delta, who in turn had contacts with the plans being developed in India by Thein Pe Myint and the British Special Operations Executive (SOE), Force 136. Aung San and Than Tun were also brothers-in-law: Aung San married his nurse in hospital, Daw Khin Kyi, and Than Tun, married her sister, Daw Khin Gyi, so the bonds between them in the war years were very close.

Aung San and Than Tun were not the only leaders who married either during or immediately after the war. Bachelor officers of the BNA and government ministers were obviously prime candidates for marriage and the wives of Aung San and Than Tun came from a wealthy and established Myaungmya Delta Christian-Buddhist family, capable of affording to have their daughters study at the Kyemyindine American Baptist Mission School in Yangon, the Teachers Training College in Mawlamyine, and eventually nursing training.[18] Bo Yan Naing, the hero of the battle of Shwedaung, parlayed his post as aide-de-camp to the Adipati to become the son-in-law of the head of state, Dr Ba Maw.

Bo Ne Win also married either during or immediately after the war to a young lady named Daw Tin Tin. Daw Tin Tin was a telephone operator,[19] with no illustrious connections, and Bo Ne Win's father was not reconciled with the marriage. The union resulted in two sons, Aye Aung, who passed away in the mid-1990s, and Ngwe Soe. Daw Tin Tin, with whom Ne Win remained in contact, died in 1979.[20]

The senior officer corps remained behind the leadership of Aung San, but his cautious nature frustrated some of the junior officers, particularly in the War Office, which was a centre of gossip and intrigue. The question of resistance against the Japanese potentially could have led to a disastrous split had not cooler heads prevailed. Junior officers around Maung Maung and Aung Gyi considered revolting as early as February 1944, and initially Ne Win apparently indicated he would go along with them even if Aung

San refused. However, when Kyaw Nyein indicated that no one on the civilian side of the government had even considered revolting, they decided to postpone the plan (Maung Maung 1989, p. 118).

Bo Ne Win learned of a later plot by the so-called Young Officers Group to organize what Aung San saw as a premature move against the Japanese. They had decided to commence an uprising on 22 July 1944, but Colonel Ne Win, then at Allanmyo, when informed of the plot, almost certainly from his former staff officer, Maung Maung,[21] returned to Yangon to relay the information to General Aung San (Ba Than 1962, p. 47). The Minister of Defence sent Ne Win back to talk them out of the plan (Callahan 2004, p. 65). Unlike Bo Let Ya, whom Aung San relied upon for his administrative skills and political contacts, Ne Win's close rapport with the troops gave him access to information and influence within the inward-looking army which provided him with a kind of power over his men that only the Communists Kyaw Zaw, Zeya and Ye Htut might match. Given his superior rank and reputation for being close to the troops, he was able to effectively control the rebellious junior officers.

The deep distrust created in 1942 between the Kayin ethnic minority and the army began to be healed late in the war with the recruitment of Saw Kya Doe, a Karen officer from the old British army in Burma. Getting Saw Kya Doe into the army and raising the Karen Rifles as an all Kayin unit was important not only because of his training and experience as a British army officer, something which the Thirty Comrades and the Thakins would have despised before 1942, but for the symbolism of unity as the army leadership attempted to heal the deep rift which had developed between the BIA and the Karen community in the Delta at the start of the war.

Finally, a month after the major defeat of the Japanese army by the British at Imphal in July 1944, a battle which marked the beginning of the British re-conquest of Burma, Aung San decided that it was time to begin organizing a resistance movement against the Japanese in central and southern Burma. Initially doubting the news of the Japanese loss at Imphal, Aung San had hesitated to act, but when pressed by Bo Tin Pe, and subsequently Ne Win who was convinced of the defeat, Aung San authorized preparations for a resistance campaign. Bringing together three organizations which had their roots in the student and *Dobama Asiayon* politics of the 1930s, and initially excluding older politicians who had cooperated with Dr Ba Maw's government, the resistance marked the high point of political unity amongst the younger generation of Burmese nationalists. The three groups, though they had their origins in the 1930s, were in fact products of the 1940s. One was the BNA led by Bogyoke Aung San, Bo Let Ya, Bo Ne Win and others; the second was the Burma Communist Party (BCP), led by Thakin Soe and Thakin Than Tun; and the third was the newly formed People's Revolution Party (PRP), which had its roots, along with the Communists, in the resistance cells established at the time of the Japanese invasion in 1942. Key figures in the PRP were Kyaw Nyein, Ba Swe, Hla Maung and Chit. The three groups formed the Anti-Fascist Organisation (AFO) and initially agreed that Thakin Soe was the primary leader but with Bogyoke Aung San in charge of the army.

Earlier, whilst the BNA officers considered when and how to rebel against the Japanese, their civilian nationalist colleagues had not been idle, particularly the Communists. Members of the newly formed BCP, led underground in the Delta by Thakin Soe, and above ground in the government by Thakin Than Tun, were the first to do so. Within Japanese-sponsored groups such as the East Asia Youth League, and outside, the Communists had been organizing cells and clandestinely teaching Marxist doctrine in the towns and villages of the country. While Thakin Than Tun could travel freely in his capacity as Minister of Agriculture and Transportation without drawing Japanese suspicion, Thakin Soe operated underground, organizing secret cells in towns and villages, particularly in the Delta region.

Anti-Communist but still Marxist and socialistically inclined young nationalists such as Kyaw Nyein and Ba Swe, realizing that the BCP was gaining strong support from the workers and especially the peasants, began organizing their own party, the PRP. The PRP also had a number of followers among the junior officers of the BNA, especially in the War Office, as did the BCP. The basis for future conflict in Myanmar politics was unfolding within the nationalist movement before the prospect of independence from the British could even be contemplated as a realistic demand. However, this incipient conflict lay hidden under the surface of the immediate issue of turning against the Japanese and, in the process, the AFO was seen as a potential ally of the British.

The core of the civilian resistance, both Communist and anti-Communist, was developed out of the Rangoon University Students Union and *Dobama Asiayon* faction which opposed any collaboration with the Japanese. While the BIA was marching north with the Japanese, the civilian core of resistance were actively laying plans for an eventual revolt against what were described as the Fascist aggressors. Led by Thakin Soe, the eventual head of the Communist Party (Burma), the civilian resistance began training cadres and building the resistance organization. The youthful resistance leaders divided tasks amongst themselves. It was agreed that Thakin Nu and Ko Kyaw Nyein should remain in Burma while Thein Pe Myint, whose name was prominent because of his anti-Japanese writings, should go to India with Thakin Tin Shwe and seek assistance from the British.

Initially the British largely ignored Thein Pe Myint's entreaties, but in 1943 Force 136, the India element of the wartime SOE, which existed to gather intelligence, and only secondarily organize resistance movements in Axis-occupied territories, decided to work with the resistance within Burma. By October 1943, Force 136 was pressing Governor Dorman-Smith to cooperate with the resistance and the BNA, whereas his staff were still referring to them as the "Burma Puppet Troops" of the Japanese (Maung Maung 1989, p. 93). The internal resistance had its numbers bolstered by disgruntled ex-BIA volunteers who were demobilized from the army in mid-1942 but were still filled with zeal for gaining genuine independence, amongst other less honourable motivations. Force 136 also worked with members of various ethnic minorities, particularly the Kayin. It launched its initial operations in Rakhine in 1944, in conjunction with British army operations, with the cooperation of Burmese from the resistance who had come out to join Thein Pe Myint in India (Taylor 1984, pp. 255–57).

As noted above, in the first week of August 1944, Aung San, representing both the Burma Army and the PRP, met with Communist party leaders Thakin Soe, Thakin Than Tun, and Ko Ba Hein, at the Bago Model Battalion camp and agreed to form the Anti-Fascist Organisation (AFO). This followed from an approach made by Thakin Soe through Second Lieutenant Thein Dan and the Bogale/Dedaye commander, Bo Ba Swe Lay, to Aung San. Aung San was named Chairman and Than Tun, Secretary. However, in meetings at Kyaw Nyein's and Ne Win's homes, Aung San's action led to opposition within the army and the PRP, and Aung San then directed Colonel Ne Win and Lieutenant Ye Htut, along with PRP leaders Ba Swe and Kyaw Nyein, to meet with Thakin Soe at Dedaye to discuss how the resistance should be organized. Further prolonged discussions between Thakin Soe and the junior officers, including Captain Maung Maung, Lieutenant Aung Gyi, Captain Khin Maung Gale and Bo Ba Swe Lay were necessary to reach accord, but that did not happen until the first week of October. Part of these meetings, which seriously tested the patience of the army officers, were lengthy readings by

Thakin Soe of works on Leninism published by the Left Book Club in London (Maung Maung 1969, pp. 121–22). Subsequently, classes in Marxist ideology and revolutionary theory began to be taught openly in the army as the Communists and Socialists were preparing to work together to resist the Japanese and declare Myanmar's independence.

Thakin Soe convinced Aung San that he should be leader and Aung San the military chief and, arguing the Browderist line then in vogue with the international Communist movement, they should postpone indefinitely any revolt against the British.[22] Consequent to the formation of the AFO, Maung Maung and Aung Gyi came to believe that Aung San, Kyaw Nyein and even Ne Win had came under the influence of the Communists Soe and Than Tun. Ne Win and Kyaw Nyein, however, were convinced that they could manage Thakin Soe and expressed their dissatisfaction with how the junior officers had handled the negotiations with Soe in October (Maung Maung 1969, pp. 123–24). Amongst the decisions made at that meeting was that the resistance would be divided into seven zones, each with a military commander and a political party representative from either the Communist or People's Revolution Party, presumably an idea derived from Soe's reading of Lenin. The zone to which Ne Win was assigned command had as its political advisor Thakin Soe himself.[23]

Later in 1944, after being convinced by Aung San, Ne Win and Thakin Than Tun that the BNA and the civilian resistance would eventually rise against the Japanese, Saw Kya Doe joined the army and formed the 170-member Kayin battalion. Hanson Kya Doe, wishing to avoid detection by the Japanese secret police, the *Kempeitai*, had lived in obscurity, but eventually Saw San Po Thin, a Karen community leader and politician who had once performed in the Barnum and Bailey-Ringling Brothers Circus in the United States, made contact with him. Saw San Po Thin, a minister in Dr Ba Maw's government,[24] took Saw Kya Doe to meet with General Aung San. Convinced of Aung San's sincerity, he accepted a commission in the BNA at the rank of Lieutenant Colonel. At that time, only Let Ya, Setkya, Ne Win and Zeya, all members of the Thirty Comrades, had attained the higher rank of Colonel, with Aung San the only General in the army (Callahan 2004, p. 76; Maung Maung 1999, pp. 145–46).

As the war progressed, the name Bo Ne Win became more widely known, whereas the name Thakin Shu Maung would be unknown to most people in 1942. The obscure postal clerk and follower of now exiled Thakin Ba Sein and Thakin Tun Oke had by 1944 become a name to conjure with in Yangon, if not beyond. Known to his troops for his earthy language and concern for their welfare, he was much closer to the troops in the field than Aung San and Let Ya, who were tied down to desk jobs and political routines. At the same time, he moved amongst the upper circles of the Ba Maw government which included almost all of the pre-war political elite except for a handful who had fled to India with the British government (Nemoto 2007, p. 7). Ne Win did not hide his views, and particularly his anti-Japanese sentiments, from his fellow Burmese. Late in the war, the journalist and later minister, U Tun Pe, "met a well dressed young Burman at the home of a friend in Golden Valley", where the residences of the Burmese elite were to be found. As U Tun Pe did not recognize his interlocutor, he said that he was Bo Ne Win. "In the course of conversation, he showed himself to be definitely anti-Japanese." (Tun Pe 1949, p. 105).

The fame of Bo Ne Win at organizing military affairs in the resistance, and earlier as one of the famed Thirty Comrades, spread far and wide, even into the pages of post-war British fiction. *The Chequer Board*, published in 1947 and written by Neville Shute, is essentially a fanciful story of romance between a British pilot who arrived after his plane was shot down into the western Ayeyawady Delta near Pathein, and a local Myanmar woman. Initially, however, the pilot was captured by the local anti-Japanese resistance who has learned of a V Force[25] intelligence officer in the still Japanese-occupied region. Led by one strangely named Utt Nee, the resistance members, none of whom spoke much English, enlisted Utt Nee's presumably missionary-educated English-speaking sister, to take the pilot, Captain Morgan, to see the V Force agent. Utt Nee told his faithful subordinate, one Thet Shay, that if Captain Morgan "... says he will give us arms, then I will come to see him with Colonel Ne Win and we will arrange the details." (Shute 1962, p. 117).

By March 1945, conditions had become sufficiently propitious for Aung San and his colleagues to act against their Japanese mentors and formal allies. By then the British had fought their way down from Imphal and Kohima, retaking Myanmar as far south as Meiktila, bypassing Mandalay, and contacts had been firmly established via the BCP between Thein Pe Myint and his colleagues in Force 136 in India and the resistance forces within the country. Over 3 and 4 March, Aung San conducted a clandestine planning conference at his home with senior military figures, including Ne Win, Saw Kya Doe and about thirty other officers as well as the Communist leaders Thakin Soe and Thakin Than Tun and representatives of the PRP, Kyaw Nyein, Ba Swe, Hla Maung, and Chit (Naw 2001, p. 108; Maung Maung 1969, p. 140). On 27 March, Aung San declared that the Burma National Army would "fight the enemy", ambiguously not specifying the enemy's name. The date, 27 March became known for many years as *Towhlanyei* (Resistance or Revolution) Day, until subsequently renamed Army Day.[26] Once the resistance commenced, the British sent an Anglo-Burmese officer, Raymond Campagnac, son of a former mayor of Yangon, to serve as the liaison officer with Ne Win and also Bo Let Ya (Campagnac 2010).

The military value of the assistance that the BNA provided the Allies after their rising against the Japanese has long been in dispute. For political reasons, even British officers inclined to look positively on Aung San and his colleagues, tended to deny that it was of any real military assistance.[27] Once a clear message was received that the BNA of 8,000 men was available to assist the allies as early as 1 January 1945, Force 136 began to send in wireless teams to rendezvous with the resistance, mainly to gather intelligence, but also to raise guerrilla forces behind Japanese lines (Kirby et al. 1965, pp. 33 and 225). By early March, they had established an intelligence network as far north as Pyinmana from an initial drop at Toungoo. British officers reported the resistance was ready to rise. Other reports from Force 136 provided similar news from Pyu and other areas (Kirby et al. 1965, pp. 332–34). Intelligence provided enabled "useful airstrikes to be carried out, at times in co-operation with attacks by guerrillas". However, the BNA would only operate under orders from Aung San, hence the British were desirous of contacting him as soon as possible (Kirby et al. 1965, p. 337). Records produced after the 27 March resistance declaration provide a different version. The Fourth Corps commander reported on 11 April that 360 members of the Fifth Battalion of the BNA were "being employed. They were a 'well drilled', disciplined armed and organised body'."[28] Eight days later, General Slim was reported as saying "that the help already provided by the BNA ha[d] gone a long way toward expiation of political crimes. He pointed out that BNA ha[d] already given valuable help to own troops and that this help [wa]s increasing."[29] The official British army history of the re-conquest of Burma complains that the BNA troops merely delayed the progress of the Fourteenth Army (Kirby et al. 1965, p. 387). On 10 May, Slim reported that the BNA units had refused to cooperate with his forces and were practising *dacoity*[30] (Kirby et al. 1969, p. 50). By early June, British Intelligence was receiving every assistance from the local inhabitants in central Burma, south of Meiktila and north of Yangon, no doubt thanks to encouragement by the resistance (Kirby et al. 1969, p. 38). At a post-war conference, in words designed to deflate the sense of importance in the war effort on the part of Aung San and his colleagues, and paraphrased by the British army's official historians, the BNA

> so far as he knew … had co-operated with the British forces loyally since the end of March and had killed many Japanese, but the B.N.A. had not been taken into account in any of the British operations, although the British had been glad to have had its co-operation (Kirby et al. 1969, p. 255).

The Burma National Army entered Rangoon on 1 May 1945, the Japanese having already withdrawn to the south and east, attempting a breakout to Thailand or Malaya. The allied commander, Lord Mountbatten, was informed by Force 136 that the Japanese would abandon the city on that same day. British forces entered Rangoon two days later on 3 May. Colonel Ne Win, commanding troops in the Pyapon region of the delta, moved up to Yangon before the British. He took control of the BNA headquarters, sharing rooms at 77 Sanchaung Street, with Bo Khin Maung Gale. Ne Win established an army hospital, under his future father-in-law, Dr Ba Than, and managed to get a radio transmitter repaired and began broadcasting from 2 Park Road (Maung Maung 1969, p. 152). As the senior BNA officer in the capital, he addressed the nation over the radio on 7 May, explaining the reasons why the BIA had accepted Japan's false promise of independence in 1942.[31] He gave a press conference three days later (Taylor 1984, p. 287). The speech was written by Ne Win in English with assistance from *Journal Gyaw* U Chit Maung[32] and Bo Aung Gyi. U Htin Fatt translated it into Burmese. Both the Burmese and English versions were read out by others, U Tun Sein, his wife and U Htin Fatt, as Ne Win was meeting Colonel Holden of the British army and V Force at the time of the broadcast (Maung Maung 1969, p. 158).

Colonel Ne Win was not shy about making his mark in Burmese history and seizing an opportunity to publicize the role of the BIA and its successors, and the AFO, in the nationalist cause. Despite instructions from London that no undue publicity should be given to the resistance movement, Ne Win's speech was not only broadcast as an address to the nation but was subsequently included in the first major English-language publication of the political position of the Anti-Fascist People's Freedom

TABLE 3.1

Zones of the Resistance and Initial Leaders

Zone Number	Military Commander	Political Leader	Party Affiliation
1	Bogyoke Aung San	Thakin Ba Hein	Communist
2	Bohmukyi Ne Win	Thakin Soe	Communist
3	Bohmukyi Kya Doe		
4	Bohmu Kyaw Zaw	Thakin Chit	People's Revolution
5	Bokyi Htin Htun	Thakin Thein Tin	Communist
6	Bohmu Ye Htut	Ko Kyaw Nyein	People's Revolution
7	Bohmu Aung	Thakin Tin Mya	Communist

Source: Tin Mya, *Hpakhsit Towhlanyei Danachok hnin Tain Hse Tainmya*. Yangon: Maha Dana Sapei, 1968, third printing, 1976, p. 72.

The official version of the resistance published by the AFPFL a year after the event gives a different picture. It suggests that the following leadership responsibilities were assigned in 1945:

1. Aung San and Thakin Tin Mya in Theyet, Pyi, Allan and the Rakhine Yoma.
2. Thakin Than Tun in Toungoo and relations with the allies.
3. Thakin Soe and Bo Ne Win in the western delta
4. Bo Let Ya and Karen troops in the eastern delta
5. Thakin Chi and Bo Kyaw Zaw at Bago, Thaton, Hpa-an and Mawlamyaing
6. Socialist Ko Kyaw Nyein and Bo Ye Htut at Pyinmana
7. Ko Ba Swe and Workers Union Ko Kyaw Nyein at Yangon

Also, Thakin Ba Hein was at Toungoo and Bo Ba Htu lead the rebellion in upper Burma prior to 27 March. Hpa Hsa Pa La Apweikyok, *Tawhlanyei Sahkaing* (AFPFL, *Resistance Memorial*), nd [1946], p. 8.

League (AFPFL), as the AFO was soon renamed. In his remarks, he, in Dr Guyot's view, exaggerated the role of the nationalist youth movement, including the BIA and the AFO, in both inviting the Japanese invasion and ensuring the eviction of the Japanese fascist foe (Guyot 1970, p. 382, fn. 3). Others might view his remarks as a carefully phrased apology and an explanation of the behaviour of the youthful nationalist forces, particularly the army, over the preceding four years in order to rally support for the national cause in the forthcoming political conflict with the British until independence was achieved.[33] He also held a press conference on 10 May to explain what was happening within the country. He reported all these activities to General Aung San on 19 May (Maung Maung 1969, pp. 155–57). Ne Win had operated very much on his own in Yangon for nearly a month.

His press conference, on 10 May, one of the few Ne Win ever gave in his long career, was memorable for one of the journalists who attended. Harry Hopkins subsequently wrote, "Some of the journalists were inclined to be hostile, but Ne Win sat there at the head of the long table, cool, imperturbable, charming, and looked fantastically young." Hopkins concluded that, "for all his nonchalance", he was courting the goodwill of the British and perhaps the larger world (Hopkins 1952, pp. 211–12).

At that time, the AFO leadership was still uncertain how the British might deal with the resistance. Some on the British side referred to the BNA as the BTA, the Burmese Traitor Army. Rumours had it that Aung San and others would be placed on trial. The BNA, under Ne Win, cooperated with the First Corps paratroopers of the British forces in the reoccupation of Yangon, but when the first officer of the military administration arrived, Civil Affairs Service (Burma), in the form of former ICS officer C.J. Richards, Thakin Soe accused Ne Win and his troops of preparing to attack the British (Maung Maung 1969, p. 152). Nothing came of the allegation, however, and with the BNA and the British army cooperating in the reoccupation of the city, work went on relatively smoothly at restoring basic services. As early as 8 May, the harbour had been cleared of all mines and the port was once more operating, though on a reduced level. However, the water supply was not restored until 24 June, the Japanese having attempted to destroy the major pipelines from the reservoirs north of the city (McEnery 2000, p. 26).

The activities of Ne Win's troops in Zone 2 of the resistance irritated Thakin Soe and he persuaded Thakin Than Tun to pressure Aung San into disarming and disbanding the group, the order being conveyed via Bo Let Ya to Aung Gyi and Tin Pe. Some of the troops consequently escaped to join Zone 1 at Minhla, Tharrawady District, but the Communists managed to have them disbanded. These troops later emerged as part of the Socialist Party with which Maung Maung and Aung Gyi were closely associated. According to Maung Maung,

> The Zone Commanders and other BNA leaders and the troops were shocked when they heard what had happened to Ne Win's forces, and relations with the British forces, which had often been personally close

between commanders, BNA zones and the Indian Divisions, extending
to unreserved cooperation through the Force 136 liaison officers, became
more cautious and formal (Maung Maung 1969, p. 153).

At this time, Aung San was apparently very much under the influence of
Communist ideologue Thakin Soe.

Though the BNA continued to pursue the retreating Japanese army
eastward towards the Thai border, gaining leverage with the returning
British was the greatest challenge. As the Communists and non-Communists
were together with the army at that time, they presented a united front,
but first contact had to be made at the highest level. While Ne Win was
operating alone in Yangon and reaching local agreements with the British,
the centre of the British army was still at Meiktila in the central zone. The
task of dealing on a policy level with the British fell to General Aung San
as commander-in-chief of the Burma Army and representative of the
AFO. He made contact with the British forces on 15 May, eight days after
Ne Win's broadcast, and was flown to Meiktila the next day where he met
for the first time with a senior British officer, Field Marshall Sir William
Slim. At that time, Aung San told Slim that he represented a provisional
government of Burma, formed by the Supreme Council of the Anti-Fascist
Organisation. His government was headed by Thakin Soe and included
Thakin Than Tun, U Ba Swe, Ko Ba Hein, Colonel Ne Win, Thakin
Nu, and Thakin Aut (sic), in addition to himself.[34] This "government"
was, in effect, dismissed by Slim, on instructions from the Supreme Allied
Commander of Southeast Asia, Lord Mountbatten, and Aung San set out
on 18 May from Meiktila to Yangon to consult with his colleagues on the
Supreme Council. Though his political pretence was dismissed, Aung San
made clear to Slim that he would be willing to place his army under the
command of an allied force.[35]

Aung San indicated to Field Marshall Slim that he was in command
of approximately 7,000 men divided into seven resistance zones. Under
Major Maung Maung, there were two battalions plus cadets from the
Mingaladon military academy, now in the Paungde region. Other units
were Major Kyaw Zaw with 2,000 at Pegu; Major Ye Htut with 1,200 at
Pyinmana; Captain Tin Tun with 300 at Dawei; Major Aung with 1,000
at Thayetmyo. Colonel Hanson Kya Doe was in command of 600 to 700
Karens in the Pathein region. Zone 2, centred at Pyapon, under the command
of Colonel Ne Win originally had 400 troops, including some Karens, but
that number had probably grown since then. Liaison between Ne Win and
Saw Kya Doe's Kayin Rifles was managed by Bo Let Ya.[36] However, as the

resistance continued, Ne Win took command of the troops in Zone 4 in the Bago and Toungoo districts as Eastern Commander in conjunction with the British forces. Aung Gyi, his former staff officer, then took control of Zone 2.[37]

In the interim, the British government in London issued a "White Paper on Burma Policy" on the future government of the colony on 17 May, promising eventual self-government as a Dominion within the British Commonwealth, but only after an indefinite period of reconstruction under a non-elected government controlled only by the Governor at least until 1948. Furthermore, the policy contained within it the likelihood that "Burma proper" and the Shan States and Frontier Areas would remain under separate administrative and political arrangements, as set out in the 1935 Government of Burma Act, or indeed the 1923 arrangements (Secretary of State for Burma 1945). This was clearly unacceptable to the Burmese nationalists as it promised even less autonomy than experienced either under the 1935 dispensation or under the Japanese (Tinker 1967, p. 18). Moreover, it once more implied to sensitive Burmese nationalists that Burma would again be treated separately and less liberally than India.

While the AFO decided what to do next, the British war against the Japanese progressed, with the Fourteenth Army ordered to leave Burma to retake Malaya and the Twelfth Army constituted in Burma under the command of Lieutenant General Sir Montagu Stopford on 28 May (McEnery 2000, p. 27). The nationalist movement in Burma, separate from the machinations of the British, now focused its energy and enthusiasm on the AFO or AFPFL. Its Central Committee had expanded to sixteen members and the original three organizations which composed the body, the Burma army, the BCP and the PRP, were joined by the Fabian Party, the *Myochit* Party, the Arakanese Parliamentary Party, the Central Karen Organisation, journalists, and a youth organization. Aung San had also replaced Thakin Soe as the primary leader, and the beginnings of the conflicts between the army and PRP with the Communists were being generated.[38]

The British plans were predicated on the necessity of rebuilding the economy and finances of Burma from the destruction it had faced as a consequence of first the Japanese invasion and the British scorched-earth withdrawal, and subsequently the conflict between the Japanese and the British as the latter returned three years later. The country was in an economic shambles. As late as 1959, real per capita gross domestic product (GDP) had yet to return to pre-1938 levels of production (Steinberg, p. 78, Table 5.1). GDP declined by at least 20 per cent during the war

(Mya Maung 1964, p. 1189). The oil wells at Chauk and Yeinangyaung and the refinery at Thanlyin were made inoperative in 1942 and regained pre-war levels only years after the war ended.[39] More than 600 ships of the Irrawaddy Flotilla Company were scuppered off Katha as the British fled.

The ability of the government to tax and spend also declined precipitously during the war. The average level of government expenditure between 1937 and 1941 was 158 million rupees. Despite massive inflation, actual government expenditure in 1943–44 was only 30 million rupees. Calculated in rupees at the 1937–41 value, actual expenditure in 1943–44 was only 5 per cent of the pre-war level. Budget estimates for 1944–45 were 3 per cent of the pre-war level (Guyot 1970, p. 208, Table 8). The taxation system also collapsed, especially the land tax system, and was never re-established after the war. Paddy production also declined and rice exports, with shipping disrupted, and historic markets unavailable, fell to next to nothing. Disease killed off nearly half of all draught cattle as the veterinary service collapsed (Saito and Lee 1999, p. 83, Table II–8). What little manufacturing industry Myanmar had before the war ceased to function and there was virtually none after.

Despite the posturing of the British government and the AFPFL, in terms of military developments, the British Twelfth Army was in charge of both the administration of Burma under the Civil Affairs Service (Burma) and the military operations to defeat the fleeing Japanese troops. Particularly in the latter regard, the cooperation of the Burma army was much sought after. On 30 May, Brigadier K.J.H. Lindop, the Deputy Chief Civil Affairs Officer of the Twelfth Army, met with General Aung San, Colonel Ne Win, and Thakin Than Tun in Yangon. Complying with a policy laid down by the British government designed to limit the availability of weapons to unauthorized forces, they reported that all the weapons which had been supplied in the Yangon area by V Force in the early days of the resistance had been returned and if people claimed they had such weapons, they were imposters and should be dealt with as such.[40]

Lindop then "told Aung San that we should welcome his troops taking part in an operation in the [Bago] Yomas" in pursuit of the Japanese. According to Lindop, Aung San and Ne Win, as battalion commanders, "were enthusiastic to take part". Ne Win offered to provide "a statement of the force he can put in the field within three days" and, he hoped, "earlier". Next, Lindop told Aung San to see the local area commander and they set off to do so. Lindop concluded that "they were very ready to receive friendly advice or instruction", but he was "not so sure that they will find the smaller fry amenable to discipline".[41]

From then onwards, whatever political differences between the AFPFL and the British, militarily the Burma Army accepted the Browderist line advanced by Thakin Soe and the Communists that collaboration with the Allies for the final defeat of fascism meant that there should be no significant conflicts between the British military and their former opponents. To many, the war in Burma appeared to be over when a Victory Parade was held in Yangon on 15 June in which Lord Louis Mountbatten, visiting Rangoon from his headquarters in Ceylon, took the salute. Troops of the Burma army participated as an allied force in that parade and the red flag with a white star of the AFO was flown next to the Union Jack (Tinker 1967, p. 16). The next day, Mountbatten hosted a meeting with Burmese political leaders, at the end of which he remained behind with Thakin Than Tun and General Aung San, rather than granting them a separate meeting. Colonel Ne Win and Thakin Ba Hein[42] joined them in the private session of about fifteen to twenty minutes, along with the commander of the Twelfth Army, Lieutenant General Sir Montagu Stopford, the head of CAS(B), Major General H.E. Rance, and the representative of the Governor of Burma, Mr T.L. Hughes.[43]

Explaining that he had no responsibility for political matters, but only for military administration, the Supreme Allied Commander noted that it was the policy of the British government to grant dominion status and that he was anxious to avoid conflict with the organizations they represented. Both Than Tun and Aung San expressed the view that they and their organizations also wished to avoid conflict and to cooperate with the British army. Mountbatten also stated that charges of unlawful behaviour might be brought against some members of the resistance, to which Aung San requested advanced notice as some of his best men might be detained, and he would need time to find replacements in order not to disrupt operations. They then discussed the possibility, originally raised in the meeting between Slim and Aung San in May, of enrolling members of the Burma army into the regular British army. No firm decision had yet been made, but informally Mountbatten was willing to proceed with the idea. Having abandoned the claim to be the military commander of an independent government, Aung San requested medical treatment for his soldiers from the British as well as consideration of awarding British gallantry medals to Burma army troops. The meeting concluded with an inconclusive discussion of finding a new name for the Japanese-era Burma National Army, the Burmese resisting Mountbatten's preferred Local Burmese Forces.[44]

During the next month, a series of meetings took place between senior Burmese figures and the British military and civilian representatives. On 28 June, Governor Dorman-Smith met with a limited number of representatives on H.M.S. *Cumberland* in Yangon harbour. Some of the meetings concerned what to name the Burma army as well as processes of incorporating its members into the British forces. Ne Win was not involved in these matters, however, as Aung San now relied on his deputy, Bo Let Ya, who reverted to his pre–Thirty Comrades title, to be called Lieutenant Colonel Hla Pe. At such meetings, issues which irked the British were often raised. Hla Pe was forced to concede that some of the arms surrendered by the Burma army were not those supplied by Force 136 as agreed, and Aung San had to feign ignorance of the incident at Myaungmya in 1942 when the BIA clashed with Karen villagers, leading to widespread communal unrest.[45] On 23 July, the Burma National Army was renamed the Patriotic Burmese Forces (PBF).

Ne Win was back with the troops, solidifying his identity with their interests and welfare, as he had done at the time of the dissolution of the BIA in June/July 1942. From events at that time, such as that described in a short story by the famous writer Min Shin, Ne Win's fame as a friend of the *yebaw* spread and was nurtured. In "Sit Pyan" [War Returnee or Veteran], Min Shin tells the story of how he, as a private in the BNA, was sent to deliver a message at the Lowis Road headquarters of the army. There he met Colonel Ne Win who asked him if he had eaten. Conceding he had not, Ne Win insisted that he do so, and personally filled his plate, not once but twice. The *yebaw* thus was unable to eat his favourite food, lovingly prepared by his mother, when he returned home from serving in the army at the end of the resistance.[46] Ne Win was also involved in political matters, attending a series of seminars or meetings on Marxism led by U Ko Ko Gyi of the Burma Socialist Party, along with Bo Tin Pe in a house in Sanchaung quarter of Yangon not far from the war office (Kyaw Zaw Win 2008, pp. 63–66, fn. 122). He also attended an early meeting of the Socialist Party at the residence of U Kyaw Nyein with a number of senior Socialist leaders, including Thakin Mya (Kyaw Zaw Win 2008, p. 64).

If the anti-fascist resistance of the nationalist struggle for independence was effectively harnessed by a combination of the current Communist position on cooperating with the Allies and Lord Mountbatten's bromides, its rationale was ended with the atomic bombing of Hiroshima and Nagasaki on 6 and 9 August and Japan's surrender on 14 August. The next phase of the struggle was about to commence, this time to force the British to grant Myanmar's independence as quickly as possible. The future of the army that Aung San and the Thirty Comrades had founded in December 1941 was at that time a key aspect of the struggle in the recast circumstances. A meeting of the top forty commanders of the Patriotic Burmese Forces was held with British officers at the Bago Model Battalion to discuss the future on 10 August. Colonel Ne Win attended as third in command of the PBF (Tin Mya 1968, p. 114).

Political relations, however, were soon to become tense. Decisions were to be made which would change the political climate. The Supreme Council of the AFPFL met at the Churchill Road headquarters of the League from 16 to 18 August. There it was decided to hold a mass meeting, known in history as the Naythuyein meeting, named after the cinema hall where it was held on 19 August. At that meeting, the public demand of the AFPFL became not dominion status, but full and immediate independence outside of the British Commonwealth and that the PBF remain a coherent military force. The meeting had grown out of British pressure to disband the PBF, which was resisted at the meeting of army commanders earlier in the month. The Naythuyein meeting also confirmed that Ne Win, along with Bogyoke Aung San and Bo Let Ya, were the army members of the AFPFL Supreme Council (Maung Maung 1969, p. 181). Thus, the army was formally identified as a political actor, along with the PRP, the BCP, and various minority interests. Furthermore, after 26 July, the stage was now set for confrontation between the British government, the Labour Party led by Clement Attlee, governing in their own right, and the AFPFL.

Notes

1. As with Ne Win's date of birth, establishing with certainty when he returned to Myanmar is fraught with difficulties. Tatsuro, a former member of the *Minami Kikan*, who tends to bolster Ne Win's prominence and abilities, states that he entered ahead of the Japanese on 14 January 1942, five days before the Japanese Fifteenth Army took Dawei from the British. See Izumiya Tatsuro, *The Minami Organ*, translated from Japanese by Tun Aung Chain (Rangoon: Translation and Publications Department, Department of Higher Education, March 1981), pp. 81, 109 and 120. Actually, the first

Japanese troops entered in December and took Victoria Point (Kawthaung) in the extreme south of the country but the main Japanese army did not cross the border until 22 January. According to Tatsuro, the mission followed on from an earlier failed attempt led by Bo Hla Pe (Bo Let Ya) and Bo Gyan. Colonel Ba Than writes that Ne Win and his party crossed from Rahaeng on 25 January, having left Bangkok for the border area on 12 January, and immediately went off in the direction of Rangoon. See Ba Than, *The Roots of the Revolution: A Brief History of the Defence Services of the Union of Burma and the Ideals for which They Stand* (Rangoon: Director of Information, 1962), p. 25. Yoon contends that Ne Win and his group, the last to leave Bangkok and the first to enter Myanmar, travelling via Rahaeng, Chiang Mai, and Tha Song Yang. See Won Z. Yoon, "Japan's Occupation of Burma, 1941–1945" (unpublished PhD dissertation, New York University, 1971), pp. 172–73.

2. *Yebaw* means comrade, colleague, or soldier, and is used to refer to privates and non-commissioned officers in the Myanmar army and police.

3. There are a number of accounts of the collapse of the British and the swift advance of the Japanese. A recent example of the genre is Alan Warren, *Burma 1942: The Road from Rangoon to Mandalay* (London and New York: Continuum Books, 2011).

4. Tatsuro, *Minami Organ*, p. 81; Ba Than, *Roots of the Revolution*, p. 31. Their quarters is now the residence of the British ambassador.

5. By June, as many as 23,000 young men, mainly peasants, had rallied to the call of the BIA, though it was doubtful if that number was actually enrolled in the army in any formal sense. See Dorothy Guyot, "The Political Impact of the Japanese Occupation of Burma" (unpublished PhD dissertation, Yale University, 1970), p. 112. In her thesis, much shaped by social science theories of its time, Guyot argued that there were four characteristics of the membership of the BIA: (a) and (b) that they were recruited from lower Burma and were entirely made up of Bamar and, presumably, highly assimilated Mon; Kayin were, she contends, already politically mobilized and anti-Bamar; (c) "it was led and composed of youths", and (d) it mingled for the first time villagers with townspersons. While (a) and (c) are incontestable, there is little reason to assume that (b) and (d) are as obvious as she argues.

6. Kazuto Ikeda, "The *Myaungmya* Incident during the Japanese Occupation of Burma: Karens and Shwe Tun Kya", in *Reconsidering the Japanese Military Occupation of Burma (1942–45)*, edited by Kei Nemoto (Tokyo: Research Institute for Languages and Cultures of Asia and Africa, Tokyo University of Foreign Studies, 2007), p. 65. This article and Dorothy H. Guyot, "Communal Conflict in the Burma Delta", in *Southeast Asian Transitions: Approaches through Social History*, edited by Ruth T. McVey (New Haven and London: Yale University Press, 1978), pp. 191–234 are the two major studies of this seminal incident in modern Myanmar history. Ikeda's analysis

is more sophisticated, noting the ethnic complexity and ambiguous nature of many of the underlying causes of the outbreak of violence in 1942. See also John F. Cady, *A History of Modern Burma* (Ithaca: Cornell University Press, 1958), pp. 443–44; and Maung Maung, *Burma and General Ne Win* (London: Asia Publishing House, 1969), pp. 121–22.

7. Maung Maung, *Burmese Nationalist Movements, 1940–1948* (Edinburgh: Kiscadale, 1989), pp. 44–45. U Ba Pe, the grand old man of Burmese politics and a founder of the YMBA, refused to deal further with the Japanese after this meeting and retired from public life until after the war. See Guyot, "Political Impact of the Japanese Occupation", p. 24; and Maung Maung, *Burma and General Ne Win*, pp. 118–19. Tekkatho Sein Tin (co-translator Kan Nyunt Sein), *Thakin Ba Sein and Burma's Struggle for Independence* (Saarbrucken: VDN Verlag Dr Muller GumbH and Co., 2011), p. 141, includes Bo Let Ya whom Tatsuro omits. Maung Maung, *Burmese Nationalist Movements*, p. 44, also includes Bo Let Ya.

8. Thakin Nu, *Burma under the Japanese: Pictures and Portraits*, translated by J.S. Furnivall (London: Macmillan, 1954), p. 42. The volume was originally published in 1945 as Nu, *Nga Hnit Yathi — Bama Pyi 1941–1945* [Five Seasons in Burma, 1941–1945] (Yangon: Myanma Pyi Saok Taik, 1946, 2nd printing, 1961).

9. Aung San, "A First Hand Report", in *Aung San of Burma*, edited by Maung Maung (The Hague: Martinus Nijhoff, 1962), pp. 36–37. Aung San, "The Resistance Movement", in *Burma's Challenge (1945)* (Rangoon: Tathetta Sapei, March 1974), p. 39.

10. Tatsuro, *Minami Organ*, p. 197. Yoon, citing Japanese sources, states that the BIA was dissolved on 10 June 1942. This may be the date on which the Japanese decided to dissolve the BIA. See Yoon, "Japan's Occupation of Burma", p. 150. Guyot gives the date as 24 July 1942, as does Tinker. Guyot, "Political Impact of the Japanese Occupation", pp. 111 and 127; Hugh Tinker, *The Union of Burma: A Study of the First Years of Independence*, 4th ed. (London: Oxford University Press, 1967), p. 10. Guyot states that the BDA was formed on 2 August 1942 whilst others state 1 August or 27 July. "Political Impact of the Japanese Occupation", p. 312.

11. Dr Maung Maung, the nearest to being Ne Win's official biographer, spent some time during the war translating British manuals in a house on U Wisara Road near the Dhamazedi (former Boundary) Road crossing. Now a restaurant, known as the House of Memory, it is the former residence of a wealthy Indian landowner named Nath. It became the first War Office of the Myanmar government.

12. Maung Maung, "On the March with Aung San", in Maung Maung, ed., *Aung San of Burma*, p. 61; never shy about his considerable abilities and achievements, former Brigadier Maung Maung described himself as Aung San's intelligence officer. Guyot, "Political Impact of the Japanese Occupation", p. 61.

13. Roger Hilsman, *To Move a Nation: The Politics of Foreign Policy in the Administration of John F. Kennedy* (New York: Delta, 1964, 1967), p. 115; Roger Hilsman, *American Guerrilla: My War Behind Japanese Lines* (Washington, D.C.: Brassey's, 1990). Though Hilsman mentions the Kachins as the backbone of Force 101 (pp. 122 and 150), he describes the battalion with which he was an officer as gradually composed of "one Englishman, three Americans, about one hundred and fifty Chinese [recruited in Myanmar], another one hundred and fifty Karens [living in the Shan State], a couple of dozen Kachins and Shans, one Bengali, two Sikhs, and ... about one hundred ethic Burmese in Japanese uniforms" (p. 213).

14. Richard B. Laidlaw, "The OSS and the Burma Road, 1942–1945", in *North American Spies*, edited by Rhodri Jeffrey-Jones and Andrew Lownie (Lawrence: University of Kansas Press, 1992), pp. 102–22. The fighting in northern Burma during the war also helped shape United States policy towards anti-Communist guerrilla warfare in Laos and elsewhere during the Kennedy and Johnson presidencies. See Stephen E. Pelz, "Documents: 'When Do I Have Time to Think?' John F. Kennedy, Roger Hilsman, and the Laotian Crisis of 1962", *Diplomatic History*, vol. 3, no. 2 (Spring 1979): 215–29. See also Lawrence Freedman, *Kennedy's Wars: Berlin, Cuba, Laos and Vietnam* (New York and Oxford: Oxford University Press, 2000), p. 335.

15. Major Hugh Seagrim remained behind after the British retreated to India and worked within the Kayin communities in the eastern hills of Myanmar gathering intelligence. He voluntarily gave himself up to the Japanese in order to obviate more violence by the Japanese on the Kayin with whom he was working. See Louis Allen, *Burma: The Longest War 1941–45* (London and Melbourne: J.M. Dent, 1984), pp. 575–78. Also, Ian Morrison, *Grandfather Longlegs: The Life and Gallant Death of Major H.P. Seagrim, GC* (London: Faber and Faber, 1947).

16. Kya Doe, "The Bogyoke", in Maung Maung, ed., *Aung San of Burma*, p. 71. Maung Maung, *Burmese Nationalist Movements*, p. 88.

17. Let Ya, "The March to National Leadership", in Maung Maung, ed., *Aung San of Burma*, p. 50.

18. Kya Doe, "The Bogyoke", in Maung Maung, ed., *Aung San of Burma*, p. 72.

19. Prior to the war, if you could not speak Hindi or English, according to Furnivall, you could not use the telephone. The telephone department was an Indian preserve. See J.S. Furnivall, *Colonial Policy and Practice: A Comparative Study of Burma and Netherlands India* (New York: New York University Press, 1956, reprint of Cambridge University Press edition, 1948), p. 121.

20. Aye Aung was a merchant seaman, eventually becoming a First Officer. He passed away in 1993. Ngwe Soe passed away in Milton Keynes in September 2012, having lived for many years in Perth, Scotland. General Ne Win remained in contact with him throughout his life. He was trained as a pilot at Darjeeling

and after serving in the Burma Air Force, flew for Union of Burma Airlines. Arrested for drug smuggling and use, he was imprisoned for five years. He married seven times. General Ne Win may have taken another woman as a wife during the war, but this is uncertain. I met Ngwe Soe in 1982 when attending a *soon swe* (offering to monks on auspicious occasions) in Yangon. He was much more shabbily dressed than the other attendees and was on weekend release from prison. His hardened appearance suggested a man who was working outdoors doing manual labour. For his assistance in helping Ngwe Soe end his drug taking, General Ne Win allowed a British man, who had worked in Yangon for Imperial Chemical Industries, to own and rent to the Australian embassy a residence, off Kaba Aye Pagoda Road. The house became La Planteur Franco-Swiss restaurant sometime after 1995.

21. This is determined by implication as Maung Maung tends to code some of his activities including the plotting he and Aung Gyi had undertaken. Maung Maung, *Burmese Nationalist Movements*, pp. 118–19.

22. This discussion is based upon Robert H. Taylor, "Burma in the Anti-Fascist War", in *Southeast Asia under Japanese Occupation*, edited by Alfred W. McCoy (New Haven: Yale University Southeast Asia Studies No. 22, 1980), pp. 169–74. See also Jan Becka, *The National Liberation Movement in Burma during the Japanese Occupation Period (1941–1945)* (Prague: Oriental Institute in Academia, Czechoslovak Academy of Sciences, 1983), pp. 166–73. Earl Browder was the chairman of the American Communist Party. He argued that the Second World War and its aftermath would ensure the success of Communism via peaceful means because progressive elements would drive the United States and other capitalist countries to cooperate with the Communists.

23. Maung Maung goes on at some length arguing that it was the young officers including himself and Aung Gyi who put pressure on Aung San and the senior officers, and also on Thakin Soe, to eventually revolt against the Japanese on 27 March. This fits only to a certain degree with other accounts, but does underscore the confusion and uncertainty of lines of command and decision within the army and the resistance at that time. Maung Maung, *Burmese Nationalist Movements*, pp. 123–29.

24. Mary P. Callahan, *Making Enemies: War and State Building in Burma* (Ithaca: Cornell University Press; Singapore University Press, 2004), p. 75. Tinker, *Union of Burma*, pp. 9–11 suggests that San Po Thin helped precipitate the Myaungmya incident, was arrested by the Japanese, ingratiated himself with Aung San, and generally displayed a duplicity that undermined the "Karen cause".

25. V Force was an intelligence and reconnaissance unit established in Burma after 1942 to assist the allies eventual return. It became the key link between the indigenous anti-Fascist resistance and the British army during 1944–45.

26. After the army turned against the Japanese, according to Tatsuro, Ne Win spared the life of the last Minami Kikan officer in Burma. However, he provides no details or explanation. Tatsuro, *Minami Organ*, p. 205.

27. This was a theme at the post-war Kandy Conference. See the discussion of the Kandy Conference in the following chapter, pp. 87–90.

28. Hugh Tinker, ed., *Burma: The Struggle for Independence, Documents from Official and Private Sources, Volume I: From Military Occupation to Civil Government, 1 January 1944 to 31 August 1946* (London: Her Majesty's Stationery Office, 1983), Doc 121, Telegram, Headquarters Fourteenth Army to Advanced Headquarters AFFSEA, 11 April 1945, PRO: WO 203/38, p. 221.

29. Ibid., Do. 124, Telegram, Major General G.P. Walsh (Advanced Headquarters ALFSEA) to Lieutenant General F.A.M. Browning (Chief of Staff, Headquarters SACSEA), 19 April 1945, PRO: WO 203/58.

30. Dacoity is defined by the *Oxford Dictionary of English* as "an act of violent robbery committed by an armed gang".

31. "Appendix 2B. Radio Address by Colonel Naywin (7–5–45). To the people of Burma", in [Anti-Fascist People's Freedom League], *From Fascist Bondage to New Democracy: The New Burma in the New World* (Rangoon, 1945), pp. 30–35.

32. Htin Fatt, "As I Remember", *The Guardian*, vol. XV, no. 5 (May 1969), p. 21. For an affectionate portrait of U Chit Maung by his wife, see Ma Ma Lay, *A Man Like Him: Portrait of a Burmese Journalist, Journal Kyaw U Chit Maung*, translated by Ma Thanegi (Ithaca, New York: Cornell University Southeast Asia Program, 2008).

33. The speech is reprinted as an appendix at the end of this book.

34. The choice of Thakin Soe as head of the provisional government was apparently made by Aung San without consulting anyone else in the resistance movement. This decision was soon dropped. Let Ya, "The March to National Leadership", in Maung Maung, ed., *Aung San of Burma*, p. 51.

35. Robert H. Taylor, "Introduction", in *Marxism and Resistance in Burma, 1942–1945: Thein Pe Myint's 'Wartime Traveler'*, (Athens, Ohio: Ohio University Press, 1984), pp. 37–38. See also Document 156, Supreme Allied Commander, South East Asia to Chiefs of Staff, 19 May 1945, IOR R/8/20, in Tinkers, ed., *Burma: The Struggle, Volume I*, p. 266. Slim's subsequent account of his first meeting with Aung San puts a more positive gloss on the event than is justified by contemporaneous documents. See William Slim, *Defeat into Victory* (London: Cassell, 1956), p. 515ff.

36. Document 169. Supreme Allied Commander, South East Asia to Chiefs of Staff, 23 May 1945, IOR M/4/1320, in Tinker, ed., *Burma: The Struggle, Volume I*, p. 169. This is in accord with the orders given by General Aung San at the start of the resistance. Zone 1, under Bohmu Maung Maung was centred on Tharrawaddy; Zone 2, the Delta, was under Bohmukyi Ne Win; Zone 3, in Maubin, under Saw Kya Doe; Zone 4, Bago, the new model

army, under Bohmu Kyaw Zaw; Zone 5, Dawei under Bokyi Tin Htun; Zone 6, the Meiktila and Pyinmana railway line under Bohmu Ye Htut; and Zone 7, Thayet to Minbu, under Bohmu Aung. See Tin Mya, *Fascist Tawlonyei Danakyuk hnit Tain (10) Tain* [The Fascist Resistance Headquarters and the Ten Divisions] (Yangon: Pyi Loung Kywat Hpyan Hkyi Yei Hla Maw Sapei Taik, 1968), p. 74.

37. Ibid., p. 74 and p. 106.
38. Prominent newcomers to the AFPFL Central Committee were Thein Pe Myint, though still in India; Fabian U Ba Choe; wealthy landowner Henzada U Mya; Rakhine U Aung Zan Wei; Saw Ba Aye from the Karen Central Organisation; and *Journalkyaw* U Chit Maung.
39. Teroko Saito and Lee Kin Kiong, *Statistics on the Burmese Economy: The 19th and 20th Centuries* (Singapore: Institute of Southeast Asian Studies, 1999), Table V-2 (ii) Production of Minerals (1897/98–1993), five-year averages, p. 150.
40. Document 184. Brigadier K.J.H. Lindop, Deputy CCAO Twelfth Army to Brigadier, General Staff, Twelfth Army, 30 May 1945, PRO: WO203/59, in Tinker, ed., *Burma: The Struggle, Volume I*, pp. 184–85.
41. Ibid.
42. One of the senior Communists in the AFPFL with Thakin Than Tun, he was organizing Yangon labour into a Communist trade union at the time.
43. Tinker, ed., *Burma: The Struggle, Volume I*, Document 202. Headquarters Camp, Supreme Allied Commander, South East Asia SAC (Misc.) Twelfth Meeting, 16 June 1945, IOR R/8/30, pp. 331–34.
44. Ibid.
45. See, for example, Document 217, Conference to discuss the disposal of the LBF/PBF, 9 July 1945, IOR R/8/30, in Tinker, ed., *Burma: The Struggle*, Vol. I, pp. 216–17. See also Document 219. Conference to discuss certain points regarding the enrolment of PBF into the Burma Army, and the handling of arms by those not immediately required for operations, 11 July 1945, in ibid., pp. 362–65.
46. The story is translated as "Back from the Wars", *Forward*, vol. 1, no. 11 (7 January 1963): 25–27, and reprinted in Min Shin, *Ta-hka-don-ga Do Yebaw* (Yangon: Mya Sarpay Taik, 1963). See Thaw Kaung, "Mirrored in Short Stories: Some Glimpses of Myanmar Life and Society in the 20th Century", in *From the Librarian's Window*, by Thaw Kaung (Yangon: Myanmar Book Centre, 2008), p. 115. Others also remarked about how Ne Win, often travelling to or from work on foot or in a sidecar (three-wheel bicycle) would hail a yebaw and take him for a meal. Maung Maung, *To a Soldier Son* (Rangoon: Sarpay Beikman, 1974), p. 70.

4

SHOWING THE BRITISH OUT
(September 1945 to December 1947)

Keep your friends close and your enemies closer.

Attributed to Sun Tzu

Not surprisingly, war and the threat of war, in all their varieties, punctuated the life of General Ne Win. After all, warfare is the trade of the military. War also creates strange alliances. Alliances of partners who have fundamentally conflicting goals place great strains on the relationships formed. These strains grow out of not only conflicting goals, but contradictory understandings of the history and nature of the societies from which and over which they are contesting, even if they are nominal allies. If the relationship between the Burmese Independence Army and their Japanese mentors deteriorated to disgust and then hatred in less than a year, the British and the Burmese had had thirteen decades to grow to dislike each other by the end of the Second World War. Ne Win, who had started his political career as an acolyte of one of the most radical nationalist leaders of the *Dobama Asiayon*, had now to serve under, take orders from, and accept the terms of service of the organization he had sworn to remove from his country, the British colonial state and its armed forces. However, conditions change as politics evolve, and while at the beginning of the next phase of Ne Win's career he may have felt he was working with his enemy, by the end he had learned to work with the British and even adopt some of their ways, if unwittingly.

In September 1945, Colonel Ne Win and other officers of the Patriotic Burmese Forces (PBF) were once more rebranded. From being officers of the *Minami Kikan* of the Japanese Imperial Army, to being officers of the Burma Independence Army (BIA), the Burma Defence Army (BDA), the Burma National Army (BNA), followed by the Patriotic Burmese Forces (PBF), they were sworn in as loyal officers of His Britannic Majesty's Army in Burma. Ne Win was Burma Commission Number Two, with Number One being Bo Let Ya. This was the result of decisions finalized at a conference held at the headquarters of the Supreme Allied Commander, South East Asia, Lord Louis Mountbatten, in Kandy, Ceylon (Sri Lanka), which was, in turn, required as a result of the earlier Anti-Fascist People's Freedom League (AFPFL) resolution at the Naythuyein meeting that Aung San had convened in August. On 6 and 7 September, nine weeks after Bogyoke Aung San and his party had met the cousin of the British King following the Victory Parade in Yangon, they met again. In the interim, members of the BNA had begun to be inducted into the British army as the resistance continued to assist the British in pursuit of the rapidly retreating Japanese. In what became known as "the battle of the breakout", five PBF battalions of approximately 400 men each, "gave a good account of themselves", in providing reconnaissance to the 17th Indian Division and mopping up small pockets of Japanese troops (McEnery 2000, p. 27). Ne Win commanded the troops on the "Sittang front" at that time (Aung San 1974, p. 39).

The twenty-eight months between the defeat of the Japanese and the achievement of the independence of Myanmar on 4 January 1948 were perhaps the most politically fraught of the country's twentieth-century history. They were not the bloodiest, for more died both before and after this period in the Second World War and Myanmar's post-independence civil war. They were politically fraught because they were the years of maximum political uncertainty. Individuals knew that the distribution of political power and rewards that had existed either before or during the Second World War was not going to be re-established. What would be established was still unknown. The prize of independence, which almost all of the country sought, to a greater or lesser degree, contained within it the gift of power, power for personal glory, "group rights", ideological certainties, or the re-establishment of a lost but dreamed of past, of Buddhist kings and Myanmar military prowess. Whoever achieved the prize would inherit the state the British built and which the war had severely battered. Many other colonial societies faced the same fraught period on the cusp of their independence, but few in such a shattered condition as Myanmar. Ideals of national unity and a shared fate were abandoned, if they ever existed, as the reality of real, and seemingly complete and final, power became nearer and nearer. While it is easy to conceptualize such a process, the reality was very muddled and many seemingly unrelated events came together to create these fraught months and their terrible legacy for the people of Myanmar.

The seeds of the civil war that engulfed Myanmar within two months of the country regaining independence in January 1948 were sown in the previous chapter. The two-and-a-half years which followed, the subject of this chapter, are very complex. There are many actors and many seemingly unrelated events. They all, in one way or another, contributed to the strife that grew after March 1948 until it was contained in 1950. Ne Win was not initially a central figure in immediate post-war political developments. Rather, his career seemed to be set then as that of a conventional army officer, relearning from the British the lessons he had first learned from the Japanese, as ordered to do by his leader, Aung San.[1]

The first of those manifold events leading up to independence and civil war was the Kandy Conference. That meeting marked a high point of British cooperation with the Anti-Fascist People's Freedom League until General Aung San was invited to London sixteen months later to negotiate Burma's independence. It also marked Ne Win's return to second rank politics to concentrate on managing the Burma army within, potentially against, but later in cooperation with, the British army. Initially, his role was to prepare for a possible attack on the British if the AFPFL's bid for early and complete independence was thwarted. When independence was assured, it was to build a force to defend the sovereignty and integrity of the new Burma in the new post-war international order, as well as shore up the crumbling foundations of the state. But before all those things could happen, trust had to be established between the British and the PBF. Aung San indicated that this did not yet exist when he halted recruitment of former members of the PBF into the British army on 24 August. The PBF officer corps saw the recruitment of the PBF on an individual basis as an attempt to break up the unity of the army by assigning the men to different units (Maung Maung 1989, pp. 155–56; McEnery 2000, p. 32. For the official British army version, see Kirby et al. 1969, pp. 50–56 and 254–56). Thus was necessitated the Kandy Conference.

While Colonel Ne Win was in the midst of the politicking involved in ensuring that the force which had been created by the Thirty Comrades in 1941 survived in order to be of use in the ensuing struggle for independence and after, he had his personal and private commitments, some of which involved politics and family. Of course, there were his wife and sons. Also, at the end of the war, his cousin and near brother, Thakin Nyi, whose political career has lapsed when his patron Thakin Ba Sein was sent into exile by the Japanese in 1943, was in ill health and Ne Win brought him down to Yangon from Pyay to ensure he got adequate medical attention. When his health had been sufficiently restored to go back to politics, Thakin Nyi joined the AFPFL executive, thus ensuring a role for the old Ba Sein–Tun Ok faction of the *Dobama Asiayon* in the larger nationalist front. Thakin Nyi was then in a position to assist, together with the wealthy landowner and supporter of Galon U Saw, Henzada U Mya, whom Ne Win had visited in 1942 on his first march with the BIA, with the arrangements for him and Bo Maung Maung to travel to Kandy (Sein Tin 2011, p. 107). The AFPFL was strapped for cash at that time and the assistance of wealthy private donors was essential, though compromising, for the front's avowed leftist leadership.

On the Burmese side, the Kandy Conference was attended by Major General Aung San, his chief civilian adviser, U Tin Tut;[2] Bo Let Ya, Bo Ne Win, Bo Zeya, Bo Zaw Min, Bo Kyaw Zaw, and Bo Maung Maung, from the PBF; Communist leader Thakin Than Tun; veteran nationalist politician U Ba Pe; Kayin leader Saw Ba U Gyi; and journalist and former resistance member Ko Nyo Tun. Lord Mountbatten chaired the meeting, leading twenty-three British attendees, mainly military but including representatives of the Governor, the head of the Special Operations Executive (SOE) in India, and the radical camp left-wing Labour Member of Parliament and correspondent for *Reynolds News*, Tom Driberg.[3] At the Kandy Conference it was confirmed, as agreed in July (Callahan 2003, p. 95), that a Burma army would be created from the forces which had composed the PBF and the British Burma Army which the British had raised after 1937, mainly from the ethnic minorities who had been recruited during the Second World War. However, rather than being inducted into the British army on the basis of existing military units, as Aung San and the others wanted, the British insisted on recruitment on an individual basis, thus potentially breaking up the solidarity of the old forces (Maung Maung 1989, pp. 156–57).

From the perspective of the British, the purpose of the Kandy meeting, as stated in the minutes of the meeting on 5 September amongst only the British delegates, was to disarm the PBF and render it harmless.

Mountbatten was of the view that without the PBF as its core, the AFPFL would disintegrate and the political situation would return to something more like before the war. It was the consensus of the British, including the Supreme Commander and the Governor, that Aung San had defaulted on his agreement in July and was merely "playing for time". From Mountbatten's perspective, reining in the PBF would set a precedent for other Southeast Asian colonies as they were retaken and their resistance movements brought under control. If Aung San and the Burmese delegation proved unwilling to bring their troops under British control, the Governor's idea of inducting them into a Burma National Militia would be offered, but only as a second best option to direct British military control.[4] Aung San accepted Mountbatten's plan and for the next twenty months, until six months after independence had been agreed, all military units in Burma were under the command of British officers applying British rules and regulations.

At Aung San's request, the new army units would be organized on what the British referred to as "class battalions", class in this case referring to ethnicity or identity. Unlike the British Indian army, which was organized on the basis of "class companies", which would then be combined in mixed battalions, the new Burma army would be organized on the basis of larger, mainly single identity units. The issue of "race", which the British had introduced into Burmese political institutions in 1923, was now firmly insinuated into the army, with major consequences for the future. The idea of single identity units was to ensure that both the former PBF and the Karen, Kachin, Chin and Gurkha units of the British army remained distinct units.[5] As almost all the members of the BIA had been recruited from predominantly Bamar areas, they were *ipso facto* Bamar units. It was agreed that there were to be four Bamar battalions,[6] two Chin battalions, two Karen battalions, and two Kachin battalions, all of which were infantry. This became, as Mountbatten envisaged, a "two wing" army, rather than a unified national defence force.

A majority of the 12,000 men envisaged for the force were to come from former British units with 5,000 men, plus an additional 300 reserves, from the PBF. Two hundred PBF officers were to be selected along with another 200 reserve officers. In addition to the infantry battalions, there would be one field artillery regiment, an armoured car regiment, and various reserve and ancillary units, including engineers. The service units of the army, as well as the artillery and armoured car units, would also be organized on the basis of ethnic or previous military identity.[7] The commander-in-chief would be British, but one of his deputies, known as Deputy Inspector General, would be from the PBF, and one from the old British Burma army.[8] Mountbatten, with the approval of the British government, offered the post of junior Deputy Inspector General to Aung San who refused it and recommended that Bo Let Ya be appointed instead. He also suggested that Sandhurst-trained Colonel Kya Doe, who had served with the BNA and PBF as commander of a Kayin battalion, be appointed the Deputy Inspector General from the Burma army side.[9]

While Mountbatten accepted Aung San's recommendation of Bo Let Ya as junior Deputy Inspector General, he chose Colonel Smith Dun, a rapidly promoted officer of Karen ethnicity, as the other and slightly more senior Deputy Inspector General from the old Burma army. Smith Dun, one of the two Karen officers in the British Burma Army, the other being Saw Kya Doe, had served six years in the ranks before becoming a Viceroy's Commissioned Officer in the Indian Army in 1931 and a King's Commissoned Officer in 1934.[10] Both served under the overall command of Major General Lechmere Cay Thomas, CBE, DSO.[11] A Sandhurst graduate, Thomas had been wounded in the First World War and had led several Indian army units before being assigned to Burma.[12] At the time of the formation of the new force, Ne Win, along with the other officers of the PBF, was reduced in rank, in his case from Colonel to Major, in keeping with British practice.

On the way to the Kandy Conference, the delegates flew via Calcutta in order to call upon their colleague, Thein Pe Myint, then recuperating from spinal tuberculosis at "Sandy Villa" in Behala. A Burmese Indian Communist, later to become prominent in the Burma Communist Party (BCP), one H.N. Ghoshal, who had spent the war years in Bengal and was closely connected with the Indian Communist Party, together with Thakin Than Tun, urged Aung San to remain in the army and accept the King's Commission, rather than resigning to lead the AFPFL. Thein Pe Myint and Bo Let Ya objected, arguing that Aung San's position was now that of national leader and it would be peculiar for him to withdraw to behind-the-scenes politics. Ghoshal tried to convince Aung San to return from Kandy via Calcutta in order to have further talks with the Indian Communist Party but was unsuccessful. Thakin Than Tun was convinced that Aung San would grab the leadership by playing the Communists against the others, presumably the People's Revolution Party (PRP), increasingly identified as the Socialists.[13] The personal and ideological rivalries which formed the basis of one of Myanmar's civil wars between the non-Communist army and Socialist-dominated government against the BCP, were being realized two-and-a-half years before independence.

The final Japanese surrender in Burma took place on 13 September and the Civil Affairs Service (Burma) (CAS[B]) handed the administration over to Governor Dorman-Smith on 16 October, though the full handover took several more months (McEnery 2000, pp. 30 and 33). While politically the handover was significant, for now Aung San and the AFPFL had a political government with which to negotiate, administratively it made little difference as many of the key CAS(B) officers were former members of the Burma Civil Service (BCS, Class I) who now doffed their uniforms for mufti. Military organization proceeded parallel with political developments. The Socialist Party had finally emerged on 1 September after Thakin Mya returned to Yangon and was appointed its first chairman (Tinker 1967, p. 19).

When the Governor would not accept Aung San's demand for an essentially AFPFL cabinet with executive power, and instead appointed his own nominees, including four members of the League executive from pre-war legislative parties, on 3 November, the nationalist movement began to take action to halt the re-establishment of the old political order and force the pace of independence. Soon after, on 7 November, Dorman-Smith learned of a possible charge of murder to be laid against Aung San, an action which would certainly have had significant consequences had the British government chosen to prosecute him. The AFPFL also began forming an auxiliary military force of former members of the resistance and PBF men not drawn into the new Burma Army, possibly as many as 15,000 men. Formally organized on 1 December 1945, the *Pyithu Yebaw Tat*, or People's Volunteer Organisation (PVO), emerged in time to become another product of the sorcerer's apprentice, one which Ne Win would have to deal with in the years to come as the political-cum-military officer who had the closest contacts with the rank and file of the dismissed veterans.

Originally described as a welfare organization for ex-members of the PBF, the PVO became Aung San's personal army, consisting of former members of the Japanese-era forces and organized into thirty-two districts. Its members became involved in politics, black market activities and crime, and as political warlords. Affiliated with various political groups, their loyalties, other than to Aung San and the idea of independence, were as fluid as their organization. The British initially ignored the growth of the

PVO, but by April 1946, Governor Dorman-Smith issued orders to bring a halt to its military training. This led to the so-called Tantabin incident, where police opened fire on unarmed demonstrators protesting at the arrest of eleven PVO members. Three were killed and six injured. One of many clashes between the authorities and the AFPFL, it managed to pressure the government to find a political solution to Myanmar's increasingly chaotic politics.[14]

However, Bo Ne Win's first task in the British army was to help form and train the Fourth Burma Rifles.[15] He had already re-established an army headquarter at Bago in conjunction with the British IV Corps and was involved in the selection of men to be inducted into the new force. Almost all, like Ne Win, were at lower ranks than they had in the PBF. When assigned to form the Fourth Burma Rifles, Ne Win moved to a camp at Legyun-Simee near Pyay. There, sharing command with British Lieutenant Colonels,[16] he was soon promoted to the same rank (Maung Maung 1969, pp. 164–65). At the Legyun-Simee camp, he was surrounded by a number of former BIA/BNA officers and men with whom he had worked before and with whom he would work for many years to come. Many, such as Tin Pe, Maung Maung and Aung Gyi, like Ne Win, were close to the Socialist Party leaders in the AFPFL, and political issues dominated conversation in the mess tents before and after military training each day and on frequent trips to Yangon. As the officer corps of the Fourth Burma Rifles trained together and spent their weekends having rum and beer drinking sessions and retelling stories of the war, they got to know one another very well and in the process became a tightly knit unit. Ne Win's leadership was never in doubt (Maung Maung 1969, pp. 168–69).

Building the army, rather than politics, dominated the working days. Creating a cadre of Burmese officers was a priority, especially if the desired goal of an early independence was not to create a state bereft of defence capability and beholden to other powers. The army set up a training school at Maymyo and by March 1946, 156 former members of the PBF were recruited as officers.[17] Many of these Ne Win knew and perhaps selected for their preferment to the officer ranks. During the uncertain politics of 1946, during which Aung San and other political actors sought both to gain preferment in the political order and to pressure the British for a promise of prompt independence, the army remained under the control of the British. Nevertheless, Ne Win and his colleagues discussed how they could overthrow their commanders, just as they had done against the Japanese the previous year. Their consideration of the future and their roles in it were conditioned not only by the politics of Myanmar, but also by the process of India's independence, including the breaking up of the Indian state with the creation of Pakistan and the threat of communal violence. Also looming in the background was the outcome of the Chinese civil war and the implications of a Communist victory as well as Chinese claims to large parts of northern Myanmar. The implications of independence for other European and American colonies in Southeast Asia were less pressing, but certainly news of developments in French Indochina and the Dutch East Indies would have been noted, as well as the grant of independence to the Philippines in 1946.

Myanmar's fissiparous politics also saw the beginnings of new conflicts out of grievances in the administratively and militarily disturbed condition of the country separate from the high politics over the independence issue in Yangon and London. West Myanmar, only reincorporated into Konbaung Myanmar in 1784, and the site of the first resistance against the Japanese in January 1944, became particularly unruly and partially outside of the control not only of the British but also of the AFPFL. U Sein Da, a radical Buddhist monk with Communist affiliations, almost immediately at the end of the resistance, set up his own Arakan People's Liberation Party (ALPA) in the Rakhine region and began to collect arms and organize his own revolutionary force in a bid for autonomy (Smith 1999, p. 64). Revolution was in the air and the inability of Governor Dorman-Smith to find a modus vivendi within the remit he was given by the British government with Aung San and the AFPFL leadership, encouraged the League to increase its pressure on the British Labour government to change its stance towards Myanmar's future.

Events unfolded in early 1946 with dramatic implications for the future. On 17–19 January 1946, mass meetings were held at the Shwedagon by the AFPFL to demonstrate the popular demand for independence. On 3 February, Karen politicians and community leaders met again in Yangon to plan for a British withdrawal. Thakin Soe split from the Burma Communist Party (BCP) on 22 February and set up his own Red Flag Communist Party (Burma) (CP[B]) in March with seven of the thirty-one members of the BCP's executive committee. In March, Shan Sawbwa, the hereditary heads of the governments in the Shan State which the British had confirmed in power after the occupation of all of Burma in 1886, met at Panglong for the first time to discuss with Burmese politicians the future of the frontier areas. Chin, Kachin and Karen observers were also invited to attend. The great political and administrative divide the British had imposed in 1886, and imbedded in the country's political institutions in the 1920s, was beginning to crumble. While the AFPFL was championing the cause of independence, its constituent elements, not only Socialist and Communist, but also intra-Communist, were planning for an eventual confrontation over who carried the correct ideological banner for the future of the state. In the meantime, those groups which had mostly benefitted from British rule, or had been excluded from the tumultuous changes of central and southern Myanmar during the previous century, were beginning to seek ways to protect their interests if or when majority rule was created in the emerging re-unified state.

By the time of the first anniversary of the resistance on 27 March 1946, the Central War Council of the AFPFL was composed of Bogyoke Aung San, Thakin Soe, Thakin Than Tun, Ko Kyaw Nyein, Thakin Chit, Bo Let Ya and Bo Ne Win.[18] Although united on the goal of independence, these seven men were divided on the future beyond independence. Thakin Soe's Communists had split from Thakin Than Tun's, both Communist parties saw the socialists Kyaw Nyein and Chit as their political opponents; and Let Ya and Ne Win, though both from the army, were known to have socialist proclivities. Aung San's position was more ambivalent, and while many nationalist Myanmar writers subsequently claimed that he was above politics and represented, like the army, the elusive "national interest", it is unlikely that anyone on the Central War Council thought so in 1946. To his Communist brother-in-law Than Tun and his former Communist guru Soe, he represented a rival, the army, increasingly aligned with the socialists, and therefore a threat to their desire for power in the name of their ideology.

In April, Bo Ne Win's former political leader, Thakin Ba Sein, returned to Yangon from exile in Singapore and the Dutch East Indies with Thakin Tun Ok. He met with Thakin Nyi and Thakin Kyaw Sein from the former Ba Sein–Tun Ok faction of the *Dobama Asiayon* and planned for his new role in politics. Obviously taken by the left-wing bias of the major political actors in the AFPFL and the difficulties the British were facing in terms of trying to implement an anti-AFPFL policy, the American Consulate, in an early Cold War comment, thought that perhaps Thakin Ba Sein might take an anti-Communist leadership role in Myanmar politics.[19] He and Thakin Tun Ok eventually joined the governor's council under Sir Paw Tun with three members of Galon U Saw's *Myochit* Party. They also re-founded the *Dobama Asiayon* during the year (Tinker 1967, p. 19), but it never regained the prominence it held before the war. Ne Win considered becoming involved in the re-established *Asiayon* but, at Aung San's urging, decided to avoid any overt political party role and remain solely loyal to the army (Maung Maung 1969, p. 165).

The American Consul in Rangoon in 1946 was not at all sanguine about the ability of the country to survive as an independent nation state, given the prostrate condition of the economy. He attributed this to three factors: "(a) the complete lack of public financial assets; (b) the peculiar Burmese lack of acumen with respect to business; and (3) their lack of political and administrative experience." (sic)[20] The consul took the reorganization of the Burma Army then taking place as evidence of the British desire to grant dominion status to Myanmar as soon as possible, but was clearly drawing attention to the third point — the absence of a large administrative and technical class of indigenous personnel experienced in managing a modern state. Other than the three years of Japanese occupation and the limited rule of the Ba Maw government, the Burmese had been largely excluded from such roles and it was primarily in the army where the British were starting to make up for that deficiency. Otherwise, the senior administrative group, the ICS or BCS officers, British, Indian or the few Burmese, were not keen on early dominion status.[21]

As a resolution of Burma's political future seemed as remote as ever, violence was increasingly resorted to as a substitute for politics. Following a number of militant actions by Thakin Soe's Red Flag Communists, the party was declared illegal on 10 July. Thakin Than Tun's Communists however could not stand aside and let Soe steal the banner of revolution. The Burma Communist Party organized peasant uprisings in the Yamethin and Toungoo districts at the end of August. Governor Dorman-Smith, whose health deteriorated during the rainy season and the toll of political conflict increasingly weighed upon him, had been recalled to London and unceremoniously sacked in June. After a brief interregnum under an acting civil servant governor, Sir Hubert Rance, on the recommendation of Lord Mountbatten, arrived to assume the Governorship on 31 August 1946.

Many Burmese thought the appointment of Rance, a former Major General and head of the military administration of Burma after the war, was a precursor to the imposition of military rule. However, he soon managed to open negotiations with Aung San and the AFPFL following new and far more liberal policy guidance from Prime Minister Clement Attlee. With a freer hand than had been imposed upon Dorman-Smith, Rance immediately sought to reach an understanding with Aung San and the AFPFL leadership in order to thwart a further drift to the left to the advantage of the Communists. Prime Minister Attlee was clearly worried that if a deal was not made with Aung San, the only beneficiary would be the Communists.[22] Myanmar nationalists, aware that India had already achieved an interim government, were particularly incensed that they had once more been "left behind". Rance also knew that he could rely neither on the "two-wing" Burma army nor the remaining Indian troops in Burma to suppress a rebellion should the AFPFL feel forced in that direction. While he did not like what he saw as the AFPFL's authoritarian methods, and feared its leftist orientation, he had few options other than to try to do a deal with Aung San.[23]

The leaders of the Karen Christian minority, anticipating that Myanmar's ties with Britain were fast weakening, sent a goodwill mission to London from August to December 1946 in the hopes of getting their case for a separate Karen state heard (Keenan 2008, p. 5). They had little luck. The British government faced more pressing problems than the possible future of the Karen community and its political leaders. Myanmar was just a minor issue on the Labour Cabinet table and resolving it was fast becoming a priority. Control of Burma was slipping away, as indicated by a strike of the predominantly indigenous police in Rangoon and elsewhere in the country on 5 September (Maung Maung 1989, pp. 231–37). The AFPFL then called for a general strike on 23 September and soon the Governor was forced to bow to what now, in retrospect, seems to have been inevitable. Governor Rance issued an invitation to Aung San and the AFPFL to join his Executive Council government. On 27 September, six representatives from the AFPFL joined the Council, including its leader and the idiosyncratic Communist Thein Pe Myint.[24] The League now had a majority of the eleven-member Council. The Karen leader, Saw Ba U Gyi, was also included as Information Minister.

As the AFPFL was calling for a general strike in Yangon and other cities across Myanmar, Ne Win was not idle. He was involved in assisting the British in carrying out the Governor's plans. Ne Win was second in command of the Fourth Burma Rifles, still stationed near Pyay. As there was a problem with dacoits in the Thayetmyo area, Ne Win was ordered to command his troops to deal with the issue. In what was "an extended operation lasting over a month", Ne Win introduced his own ideas of how to resolve with the trouble.

> Police patrols were withdrawn to enable it [i.e., the Fourth Burma Rifles] to communicate with the dacoits. The company did not have to fire a shot in anger but did well, receiving the surrender of eight dacoits on 20 September and an undertaking to surrender from the dacoit leader on 24 September. Lt. Colonel Ne Win had ideas for improving military co-operation with the armed police and put these to the [British] Brigadier [commander], who thought them good. He looked like a Burma officer who would go far (McEnery 2000, pp. 67–68).

Ne Win had other ideas, including that the British instructors they received to train the troops were not up to the task for linguistic reasons and that there were inadequate handbooks and manuals in Burmese for his troops (McEnery 2000, p. 71, fn. 1). Despite displays of cooperation between Ne Win and his colleagues, including Tin Pe and Aung Gyi, with their British superiors, relations were often strained. They resented being referred to as "ex-PBF" and their facilities and rations, supplied by Indian contractors, were inferior in comparison to those of the British (McEnery 2000, p. 106). Racial distinctions had obviously yet to disappear. On 16 November, Ne Win was confirmed as Lt. Colonel and deputy commander of the Fourth Burma Rifles.[25]

Thein Pe Myint was not to serve long in the final colonial equivalent to a cabinet. Thakin Than Tun and the Communist Party expressed extreme displeasure with his decision to join the Govenor's Council, and Thein Pe Myint resigned on 22 October. Soon the BCP was expelled from the Supreme Council of the AFPFL for its criticism of the League's drift to the political right and Aung San's willingness to eschew revolution and chose negotiation and compromise as the route to independence. The Communists, now excluded from the prospect of power, and already divided between the Red Flags and Than Tun's majority party, now known as the White Flags, were able to entice some members of the PVO which Aung San had formed the year before to follow them in the direction of revolution (Maung Maung 1969, pp. 185–86).

During the next two months there were many exchanges of views between Governor Rance, Aung San and the Burma Office in London. Both independence and the unification of the Shan States and the frontier areas with "Burma proper" were still outstanding issues. Finally, on 20 December 1946, Prime Minister Attlee announced in the British Parliament a new policy towards Burma and invited Aung San to London to negotiate Myanmar's future inside or outside the British Commonwealth. He soon departed, accompanied by Socialist Party Chairman Thakin Mya, ICS U Tin Tut as his chief advisor, U Kyaw Nyein, Galon U Saw and Thakin Ba Sein. No Communists or members of the former BIA other than Aung San were included. Just over a month after Attlee's announcement, the Aung San–Attlee Agreement was signed in London, establishing an interim government and the promise of independence either inside or outside the British Commonwealth. The unification of the country was foretold in the agreement, following some procedures to ensure that consultation with the local leaders would take place. Thakin Ba Sein, Ne Win's old mentor, together with U Saw, refused to sign the agreement, knowing full well that Aung San's victory possibly meant the end of their political careers. While talks were under way in London, the AFPFL back in Myanmar was trying to maintain peace and Thakin Soe's Red Flag Communists were attempting to create as much disturbance as possible. Lieutenant Colonel Ne Win was called upon to disarm one such group marching from Seikpyu to Minbu.[26]

As noted, the Aung San-Attlee Agreement also called for a resolution of the issue of the future of the frontier areas and the Shan States. Long suspicious of the British intention to break up Burma into an independent central and lower Burma and a separate remaining British colony in the north, Burmese politicians were desirous of finding a prompt solution to the issue. Similarly, the British government, feeling some sense of obligation towards the rulers and their peoples in the Shan States and the frontier areas, sought a solution which would protect the rights and privileges they had established for those who had been the bulwarks of colonial authority, particularly the Shan Sawbwa, Kachin Duwa, and other recognized political leaders. Radical nationalists, both among the majority Bamar population and the minorities, sought to end what they saw as the "feudalism" that the British had preserved in the northern reaches, and demanded equality as a principle of future governance. Meanwhile, Kachin, Chin and other groups, having been armed and trained as guerrilla fighters by the American OSS and the British V Force during the war, and with vague talk of post-war autonomy as their future, were gearing to defend their newly discovered "group rights". It was a volatile mix, not assisted by at least one senior Frontier Service Officer, Noel Stevenson, whipping up support for a separate nation in the Commonwealth from the Frontier areas and autonomy for the Karens (Bayly and Harper 2007, p. 306).

Both Aung San and Rance had to tread warily. The solution they sought came through two mechanisms. One was the second Panglong Conference at which Aung San and other AFPFL leaders met with Shan Sawbwa, Kachin Duwa, and Chin chiefs and reached a vague agreement. That agreement, the meaning of which has long been in dispute and has caused much wrangling in Myanmar's modern politics, was then followed by the Frontier Areas Commission. Chaired by a member of the British parliament, the Commission met in March and issued its report on 23 May, basically concluding that things were set fair for a unified Myanmar. The Karen communities of the delta and eastern border reaches were not included in these agreements, though they sent observers to keep a close watch on the kinds of "autonomy" that would be provided to the minority territories in the future independent Myanmar. Karen politicians, in the midst of the constitutional uncertainties unfolding, changed positions and sought support where they could find it. Saw Ba U Gyi, the senior Karen leader to join Aung San in the League Supreme Council, resigned on 4 March, while Saw San Po Thin, Saw Kya Doe's former patron, broke away from the newly formed Karen National Union (KNU), and brought his Karen Youth Organization into the League. He replaced Saw Ba U Gyi on the Governor's Council on 10 March. Lines were being drawn laying out the patterns of future armed conflict.

In April 1947, elections for a constituent assembly to approve a constitution for independent Burma were held. Before the elections could be held, however, the new Burma army, in the form of the Fourth Burma Rifles, together with British and Indian forces, was called upon to restore order in the oilfields of central Burma and around the Yamethin and Toungoo areas, reaching down to Nyaunglebin in Bago division. Known as "Operation Flush", as a British officer in Burma at the time noted, "despite, or perhaps because of" Ne Win's involvement in the operation, it has been largely ignored by historians of Myanmar. The area of conflict, a centre of nationalist and radical peasant politics preceding the Second World War, had subsequently become, with the collapse of civil administration, an organizational area for the Red Flag Communists and renegade Japanese soldiers. Both were suspected to be training dacoit gangs to attack trains and villages, creating a "dacoit dictatorship", a "synonym for the Communist underground" (Tinker 1984, p. xxvii).

There were daily attacks on buses and villages, copper cables were continually removed, and forest work disrupted. Gangs armed with automatic weapons and *dahs*,[27] one near Pyinmana led by a woman, were said to have been marauding the area for the previous six months.[28] Ne Win was in command not only of the Fourth Burma Rifles but of all the police and People's Volunteers (*Pyithu Yebaw Tat*) in his operational area.[29] In total, there were believed to be at least a thousand dacoits, in at least four gangs, who had taken possession of the territory between Tatkon in the north to near Bago. The government of Burma, now firmly in the hands of Aung San and the AFPFL, requested the army to clear the area before the elections (McEnery 2000, pp. 98–99). During March and April, in a combined operation, including the British Indian "Black Cats", as the Indian Seventeenth Infantry Division were known, three companies of the Fourth Burma Rifles, and the Fifth Burma Rifles, under a British officer, all under the joint command of Brigadier Charles Jarrard and Colonel Ne Win, were ordered to restore order in the area (Bayly and Harper 2007, pp. 311–12; Maung Maung 1969, p. 181). Though in an earlier experience at trying to control a politically motivated display of public discontent, the Fourth Burma Rifles had demonstrated that they were on the side of the government, the British remained in doubt of their loyalty until after the campaign commenced (McEnery 2000, p. 99). Ne Win met demonstrators at Sinbyugyun, disarmed them, and convinced their leaders to avoid further conflict with the "Black Cats". When they insisted on marching on, he provided an escort for them until they dispersed of their own volition.[30] At the conclusion of "Operation Flush", the Fourth Burma Rifles were handed over solely to the command of Ne Win, though this was not confirmed until August,[31] the first unit of the new Burma army to come under indigenous control.

Assessing "Operation Flush" at the end of April, Governor Rance wrote to the Secretary of State:

> At first it was found that little help was given by the local inhabitants who were suspicious of the motive of the troops. As time went on and an ascendancy was gained over the dacoits this attitude changed. The operations were conducted vigorously and with a strict regard to entailing the minimum of hardship to loyal element of the population. All the troops, British, Indian and Burmese, displayed skill and firmness tempered by due moderation, and the local inhabitants have now

appreciated their efforts and are cooperating to a greater extent than ever before in the maintenance of law and order. The Burma Army troops who are still comparatively less well trained were largely those recruited from the PBF and have shown great promise and should soon be fully capable of standing on their own.[32]

While there were still small bands of dacoits hiding in the area, normal agricultural and forestry work had resumed and police morale restored. The area would soon be garrisoned by only Burmese troops in the form of two battalions which, Rance optimistically wrote, would be sufficient to maintain order in the future. Among the casualties of the two-month campaign were 58 dacoits killed and 38 wounded, with 219 arrested. Against that, the army lost 2 men and 5 were wounded; the police and PVOs 2 dead and 5 wounded; and 15 civilians were killed and 6 wounded.[33] While Communist influence was not eradicated from the operational area, it was sufficiently kept in check that polling could take place on the designated day in April (Smith 1999, p. 70).

Writing more than thirty years after the successful culmination of "Operation Flush", the District Commissioner of Bago, during the early months of 1947, recalled a trip he made to Toungoo, then in the northern part of his area of concern. There, "it was a pleasure to meet Lt. Col. Ne Win again, now as the leading Burmese regular officer in this operation. His participation obviously was of the greatest political importance, and what was additionally valuable — and hopeful for the future — was that he was there on merit as a professional soldier."[34] As one British soldier who had served in Burma after the war also subsequently wrote, "... 'Operation Flush' contributed in no small measure to the establishment of an independent Burma." He also noted that the army and the police worked closely together to gain the support and cooperation of the local populace (McEnery 2000, p. 100), concluding,

> And what was most reassuring, the men of the 4th and 5th Burma Rifles had given a very good account of themselves in the anti-dacoit operations. The hand-over to the Burma Army of responsibility for Internal Security in all Burma, now scheduled for 15 June, looked a lot less risky.[35]

The general election was held on 9 April, under the rules of the Government of Burma Act (1935), and as expected, given that both the KNU and the Communists boycotted the vote, the AFPFL won an overwhelming majority of the seats, with approximately 60 per cent of the vote. The AFPFL gained 171 out of 255 seats in the *Pyithu Hluttaw* (People's Assembly). A majority, 182, of seats were not reserved for persons of recognized ethnicities, but 24 were only for Karen, 4 for Anglo-Burmese, and 45 were elected from the Frontier Areas. This was the first time that elections had been held in the northern regions. Though the Communists did not run in the election, 28 members of the BCP did so as independents, of which 7 were elected.[36] The Constituent Assembly convened in Rangoon on 8 June and began deliberations on a constitution for the new state, with legal advisers from India and the United Kingdom. Thakin Nu was elected speaker of the body.

With less than six months before independence would be declared, the pace of developments in Myanmar became frenetic. On 17 July, the KNU established an armed wing, the Karen National Defense Organisation (KNDO). Two days later, gunmen posing as members of the Fourth Burma Rifles, riding in a jeep with British Twelfth Army markings, stormed into the Secretariat and assassinated Aung San and six other cabinet members.[37] This was a mortal blow to the government in all senses. Despite the rivalries between Than Tun, Soe and Aung San, to many in the general public, the Bogyoke had been the primary national leader since he entered Burma with the BIA in January 1942. In that sense, he was irreplaceable and any chance of creating a reconciliation between the Socialist and Communist movements, despite Nu's later attempts, slipped away with his life.

Similarly, as the architect of the Panglong Agreement, Bogyoke had established a rapport with the leaders of the various political movements in the Frontier Areas and the Shan States, though whether his death had any impact on the possibility of peace with the KNU is a moot point. It is extremely doubtful that Aung San would have had any ability to deflect the growing hostility towards the emerging state from the Muslim population in northern Rakhine which sought to merge with Pakistan. The *Mujahid*, as they were known, formed a resistance army in Buthidaung, Maungdaw and Rathedaung townships led by one Jafar Hussain, or Jafar Kawwal, a popular singer, in August (Smith 1999, pp. 64 and 87).

Ne Win was at Pyinmana at the time of the assassination. On learning of the deed, he, together with Bo Maung Maung and Bo Ye Htut, drove to Yangon,[38] arriving the next day, to meet with other members of the

Supreme Council of the AFPFL in order to consider the new situation. However, the British had surrounded the city with road blocks and Ne Win and his party were stopped at a checkpoint at Toungoo and finally detained at an additional checkpoint near the Kyaikkalo Pagoda on the approach to Mingaldon, the army camp north of Yangon. No one was allowed to enter the city and the party was told to disarm and remain at the nearby camp of the Third Burma Rifles. After a lengthy outburst of unprintable language on the part of all three men, lead by Ne Win, General Stopford was finally reached and permission was given for them to continue into Yangon (Maung Maung 1969, pp. 291–92; 1989, p. 319).

Thakin Nu was chosen by Governor Rance as Aung San's successor as putative Prime Minister and Bo Let Ya became the Defence Councillor in the Governor's Executive Committee, effectively Deputy Prime Minister and Defence Minister, in an interim government. Though both men were closely identified with Aung San from Student Union politics, the *Dobama Asiayon* and the politics of the war period, neither had his charismatic ability to inspire confidence in the future. Galon U Saw was soon arrested for organizing the conspiracy which led to the assassination, as the British sought to limit speculation about the involvement of members of the British army, several known to be drinking companions of the convivial Saw.[39] The Governor and Thakin Nu and their colleagues, however, managed to maintain a semblance of order and the constitutional processes continued despite the loss of Aung San and the other *Arzani* (martyrs), as they became known.

Now Prime Minister Nu and Defence Minister Let Ya met with leaders of the PVO at its headquarters on Lowis Road. Aung San's private army was now left without a leader and presumably Nu and Let Ya were concerned at what his former subordinates, Bo Aung, Bo Sein Hman, and Bo Htein Lin, might do. Ne Win, Maung Maung and Ye Htut also attended the meeting. Rumours were rife and it was believed that a foreign invasion was imminent. And as often the case, there was a modicum of truth in the rumour, as Bo Let Ya reported to his colleagues that the British Headquarters, Burma Command, and South East Asia Land Forces Headquarters, were both advising the Governor to fly in an entire Brigade Group from Singapore to Mingaladon. The Governor turned down the offer (Maung Maung 1989, pp. 317–18). Maintaining calm and restoring order were clearly in the interests of the government and the army (Maung Maung 1969, p. 193). Ne Win promised Nu that he would keep the army, or at least the three ex-BIA units of the Burma Rifles, united behind his government and the AFPFL. In addition to his own Fourth Burma Rifles, he visited the camps of the Third and Fifth in order to rally the troops and steady them for what remained unknown. Overtures to Thakin Than Tun and the majority Communists by Prime Minister Nu remained unheeded, maintaining the tensions within the nationalist movement despite the crisis of Aung San's death.[40]

The Constituent Assembly concluded on 24 September, producing a new constitution which provided for three territories with ethnic designations, Shan, Karenni and Kachin; one special division, named after the various linguistic groups lumped together as Chin; the possibility of a territory named Karen in the future; and the remainder of Myanmar. It established the right, under conditions very difficult to fulfil, for the Shan and Karenni areas to secede from the Union of Burma after ten years (Silverstein 1958, pp. 43–57). Like the Panglong Agreement, the 1947 Constitution of Myanmar provided many things over which political leaders, purporting to represent different factions of the population, would argue and fight over in the years to come.

Almost everything that was done during this time held within it the seeds of future conflict and misunderstanding. In terms of the future defence of the new state, the British and the interim government reached a separate agreement to the Aung San–Attlee Agreement and subsequent Nu–Attlee Agreement that sealed Burma's independence.[41] Bo Let Ya, a month after assuming office as Defence Minister, signed the Let Ya–Freeman Agreement with the British Labour Defence Minister, John Freeman, MP, and later incorporated into the treaty with the United Kingdom which established the independence of Myanmar (Darby 1973, pp. 12–13). This agreement, a precedent-setting "run down agreement" for when Britain granted independence to former colonies, established a British Services Mission which would remain in Myanmar after independence, paid for by the Burmese government to provide advisers and training for the post-independence army, as well as serving as a purchasing agency for British military equipment and ammunition. The agreement also committed the government of Burma not to enter into any military commitments with non-Commonwealth countries, and to provide harbour and airport facilities to the Royal Navy and Royal Air Force. The agreement was condemned by the Communists and others as further proof of the willingness of the AFPFL government to subordinate Burma to its imperialist rulers. Within the army and the PVO, both the agreement and Let Ya were condemned, the latter for selling out to the very people implicated in the assassination of General Aung San (Callahan 2003, p. 104). The necessity for a defence agreement was denied by the entire officer corps of the army, according to Brigadier Maung Maung, led by Bo Ne Win (Maung Maung 1989, p. 355).

Bo Let Ya, who had a free hand in defence policy as Prime Minister Nu and other ministers left such matters entirely to him, was also accused by the former PBF officers of handing control of the army over to the British and the Karen officers who collaborated with the British. The unpopular choice of the Karen Colonel Smith Dun to command the Burma Army at the time of independence was attributed to Bo Let Ya, in collusion with the outgoing British officers (Maung Maung 1989, pp. 351–52). It would take a man with a commanding presence to control the Burma army after independence. Smith Dun, who had fought against the BIA in the skirmish at Shwedaung (Smith 1980, p. 26), faced a daunting task. Dissent was rife and insubordination was in the air. Nevertheless, Bo Let Ya confirmed in place as the head of the Burma Air Force a Karen, Wing Commander Saw Shi Sho, and the head of the Burma Navy the British-appointed Commander Khin Maung Bo (Khin Maung Saw 2008, p. 21, fn. 1).

Delegations representing the various Karen communities gathered together in Mawlamyine, under the KNU/KNDO banner, in early October to demand once more an independent Karen State, including, some claimed, parts of Thailand.[42] The British ignored KNU's demands for what are now (2014) Tanintharyi region, Mon state, Kayin state, Ayeyawady region, all of Yangon region other than central Yangon and its immediate suburbs, and parts of the Bago region.[43] For the KNU to demand this arc of land surrounding Yangon, separating the then capital from the remainder of the country, was so impractical as to evoke no rational response from any British political leader. However, it demonstrated the irrationality that gripped the country on the eve of independence. The political demonstrations and violence that the Communists had mounted earlier in the year and was suppressed in "Operation Flush", lay just beneath the political surface and new sources of violence emerged above. In November, U Sein Da's Arakan People's Liberation Party began small-scale guerrilla warfare against the remaining largely Indian British troops and the Burma Army around Sittwe, and Chin troops in March near Thandwe, further south.[44] In the following month, fighting commenced in northern Rakhine's Buthidaung, Rathedaung and Maungdaw townships, led by Jafar Kawwal and his *Mujahid* (or *Mujahedin*), demanding to be merged into East Pakistan (Tinker 1967, p. 34).

The old and new were coming together and the new Burma in the new world, as the AFPFL described the country optimistically in 1945, looked on the cusp of independence to be a fragile and uncertain union blighted with many old wounds. The structures of the British state were in place, though few of the personnel who had manned it until 1942 remained. British and Indian firms were struggling to survive, but with the expectation of nationalization by the new socialist government imminent, new investments were few. Many had already bowed to the inevitable and had replaced many of their Indian and British employees with Burmese. For those who had skills and opportunities, independence meant social mobility and an ability to finally reach the riches which others had held. For the politicians of the Anti-Fascist People's Freedom League, power was now theirs, along with the trappings of state authority. However, that power was very weak and those trappings were already tattered and worn. Three weeks before independence, on 12 December, at the age of thirty-nine, Colonel Ne Win was promoted to the rank of Brigadier General and was placed in charge of the Northern Command, basically half of the country, including the frontier areas and the Shan States.[45] Brigadier Saw Kya Doe was appointed to the Southern Command. Neither would be in the same place a year later.

Notes

1. A helpful chronology of these years is provided by Bertil Lintner as Appendix 2, "Burma's Civil Strife — A Chronology", in *Burma in Revolt: Opium and Insurgency since 1948,* 2nd ed. (Chiang Mai: Silkworm Books, 1999), pp. 430–33. The text of the volume, however, largely covers events after 1948. I have relied on the chronology in this and later chapters to provide background and context for Ne Win's military and political career.

2. U Tin Tut, a graduate of Dulwich College and Cambridge University, was the first Myanmar member of the Indian Civil Service. He was the son of a wealthy Rakhine landowner, the eldest of a distinguished family which included an eventual Chief Justice and a Professor of History at Rangoon University. In 1947, his daughter was the correspondent for *The Times* of London in Yangon. U Tin Tut had travelled with U Saw to London and Washington, D.C., as his adviser. As he was not implicated in Saw's contacts with the Japanese embassy in Lisbon in 1942, he returned to serve as an adviser to the Governor of Burma-in-exile at Simla during the Japanese Occupation. At the Kandy Conference, he was once more transmogrified, this time as Aung San's chief adviser in negotiations with the British. He was Burma's first Foreign Minister and was assassinated in 1948.

3. Christopher Bayly and Tim Harper, *Forgotten Wars: Freedom and Revolution in Southeast Asia* (Cambridge, Mass.: The Belknap Press of Harvard University Press, 2007), pp. 27–28. Driberg returned with the Burmese delegation to Rangoon and offered his advice to his new leftist friends. Ibid., pp. 70–71.

4. See Supreme Allied Commander's Meetings, 21st Miscellaneous Meeting, Minutes, 5 September 1945. BOF P&G 623/46. Also, Robert H. Taylor, "Introduction: Marxism and Resistance in Wartime Burma", in *Marxism and Resistance in Burma, 1942–1945, Thein Pe Myint's 'Wartime Traveler'* (Athens, Ohio: Ohio University Press, 1984), pp. 54–55.

5. At that time, the British army was composed of the First and Second Burma Rifles, of mixed ethnicity, largely Gurkhas and Bamar; the First and Second Kachins; the First and Second Karens; and the First and Second Chins. The Third Battalion, Burma Rifles, had begun to be organized in July, prior to the Kandy Conference, under the command of Bo Zeya. The Fourth and Fifth Burma Rifles were organized subsequently. Hugh Tinker, "Note on the Development of the Armed Forces in Burma", in *Burma: The Struggle for Independence, Documents from Official and Private Sources, Volume I: The Military Occupation to Civil Government, 1 January 1944 to 31 August 1946*, edited by Hugh Tinker (London: Her Majesty's Stationary Office, 1983), p. 1061.

6. One of which was composed not of members of the PBF but of Bamar who had served in the British Army.

7. Tinker, "Note on the Development of the Armed Forces in Burma", in Tinker, ed., *Burma: The Struggle, Volume I*, p. 1062.

8. Abridged documents relevant to the Kandy meeting are found in Tinker, ed., *Burma: The Struggle, Volume I*, pp. 436–65.

9. Letter, Aung San to Mountbatten, 25 September 1945, in Maung Maung, ed., *Aung San of Burma* (The Hague: Martinus Nijhoff, 1962), pp. 90–91.

10. Tinker, "Note on the Development of the Armed Forces in Burma", in Tinker, ed., *Burma: The Struggle, Volume I*, p. 1059.

11. Commander of the Most Excellent Order of the British Empire, Distinguished Service Officer.

12. British Army Officers 1939–45, available at <www.unithistories.com/army_officers> (accessed 5 December 2012).

13. Let Ya, "The March to National Leadership", in Maung Maung, ed., *Aung San of Burma*, p. 42; and Thein Pe Myint, "A Note from My Diary", in ibid., p. 86.

14. The most complete account of the PVO is that provided by Mary P. Callahan, *Making Enemies: War and State Building in Burma* (Ithaca: Cornell University Press; Singapore University Press, 2004), pp. 109–12.

15. Tinker, "Note on the Development of the Armed Forces in Burma", in Tinker, ed., *Burma: The Struggle, Volume I*, p. 1061.

16. First, Lt. Col. Burlance, then Lt. Col. Mitchell, and finally Lt. Col Scott. See Min Maung Maung, *Tatmadaw hnin Amyotha Naingngan Uhsaunghmu Ahknankagna* [Collected Articles on the Army and National Politics] (Yangon: News and Periodicals Corporation, July 1995), p. 43.

17. Tinker, "Note on the Development of the Armed Forces in Burma", in Tinker, ed., *Burma: The Struggle, Volume I*, p. 1061.

18. Hpa Has Pa La Ahpweikyok, *Tawhlanyei Sakhaung* [Revolution Memorial] (N.p.: N.p., N.d.), p. 8. Pamphlet published to mark first anniversary of Resistance Day, 27 March 1946.

19. Telegram, Rangoon (Abbey) to Secretary of State, 26 April 1946, 845C.00/4-846, No. A-36.

20. Telegram, Abbey to Secretary of State, 22 April 1946, in *Foreign Relations of the United States 1946, Volume VIII: The Far East* (Washington, D.C.: United States Government Printing Office, 1971), p. 1.

21. Ibid.

22. Clement Attlee, *As It Happened* (London: Heinemann, 1954), p. 188; Francis Williams, *Twilight of Empire: Memoirs of Prime Minister Clement Attlee* (New York: A.S. Barnes, 1962), pp. 213–15. Though Attlee mentions in both volumes of the memoirs his concern that the Communists might take over power in Burma, he is silent on the question of the Karens whom he championed during the post-independence civil war.

23. Bayly and Harper, *Forgotten Wars*, pp. 253–65 provide a very readable summary of the period.

24. The other members included none from the left but comprised of U Tin Tut, U Ba Pe and Sir Maung Gyee as AFPFL Councillors.

25. *Thihmat Hpweya Koyei: AchetAlatmya* [Biographical Information for Recalling] (N.p.: N.p., N.d.).

26. Hugh Tinker, ed., *Burma: The Struggle for Independence, Documents from Official and Private Sources, Volume II: From General Strike to Independence, 31 August 1946 to 4 January 1948* (London: Her Majesty's Stationery Office, 1984), Doc. 240, Telegram, South East Asia Land Forces to War Office, 24 January 1947, IOR: L/WS/1/1053, p. 356.

27. Burmese farmers' commonly used knives.

28. Tinker, ed., *Burma: The Struggle, Volume II*, Doc. 314, Cutting from the *New Times of Burma*, 10 March 1947, IOR/M/4/2501, pp. 454–555.

29. Ibid., Doc 321, Telegram, Chief Secretary, Government of Burma to Secretary of State for Burma, IOR: M/4/2501, p. 464.

30. Maung Maung, *Burma and General Ne Win* (London: Asia Publishing House, 1969), p. 181. Maung Maung's account is rather confusing and he states that "Operation Flush" was a purely Burmese affair, but that overstates the situation.

31. *Thihmat Hpweya Koyei: AchetAlatmya* [Biographical Information for Recalling].

32. Tinker, ed., *Burma: The Struggle, Volume II*, Doc 341, Telegram, Governor of Burma to Secretary of State for Burma, 30 April 1947, IOR: M/4/2501, p. 497.

33. Ibid., p. 498.

34. Tinker, ed., *Burma: The Struggle, Volume II*, Walter Ian James Wallace, OBE, ICS, "Narratives of Events", IOR: MSS EUR E 362/17, pp. 886–98 and 897.

35. John H. McEnery, *Epilogue in Burma 1945–1948: The Military Dimensions of the British Withdrawal* (Bangkok: White Lotus, 2000; orginally published Tunbridge Wells: Spellmount, 1990), p. 101. He provides slightly different casualty figures than those provided by the Governor. He reported 54 dacoits killed, another 20 believed killed, 34 wounded, 255 captured and 871 detained under suspicion. Also, four Japanese deserters were captured. McEnery, *Epilogue in Burma*, p. 100 and p. 101, fn. 3. Bertil Lintner, who generally can find nothing positive to write about Ne Win, alleges that the Fourth Burma Rifles were "heavy handed" during "Operation Flush", contributing to disaffection toward the government. He also contends, on the basis of an interview in New York City in 1992 that officers of the Fourth Burma Rifles stole jewellery and sold it to Muslim female jeweller and moneylender in Pyinmana, getting rich as a consequence. Lintner, *Burma in Revolt*, pp. 5–6.

36. Tinker, ed., *Burma: The Struggle, Volume II*, Doc No. 342, Telegram, P.G.E. Nash to Sir Gilbert Laithwaite, 30 April 1947 (IOR: M/4/2677), pp. 498–500.

37. Thakin Mya, Deedok U Ba Choe, Mahn Ba Khine, Mr A. Razak, U Ba Win, and the Sawbwa of Mongpawn. U Ohn Maung, a secretary, and Bo Htwe, a bodyguard, were also killed.

38. Either in an old convertible or a truck, depending on which Maung Maung you believe.

39. Bayly and Harper, *Forgotten Wars*, pp. 313–20; subsequently, a number of implausible theories were advanced that somehow General Ne Win had plotted the assassination of his leader. See, for example, Shelby Tucker, *Burma: The Curse of Independence* (London: Pluto Press, 2001), pp. 155–59, or Kin Oung, *Who Killed Aung San?*, 2nd ed. (Bangkok: White Lotus, 1996). Ne Win's old mentor, Thakin Ba Sein, along with the other politicians, were taken into protective custody after the assassination but were soon released uncharged. Tinker, ed., *Burma: The Struggle, Volume II*, fn. 3, p. 675.

40. Then, and later, there was much speculation, particularly among the leftists, that the reason for Aung San's assassination was that he and Than Tun had agreed that after independence the Communists would be invited to join the government.

41. Signed on 17 October, this confirmed that Myanmar would be independent outside of the British Commonwealth.

42. The initial demands, made by the Karen Central Organisation (KCO) in September 1945, were for a "United Frontier Karen State — which they stated should include all of Tenasserim, Nyaunglebin, a sub-division of Pegu, and parts of Thailand as far as Chiang Mai". Paul Keenan, *Saw Ba U Gyi* (N.p.: Karen History and Culture Preservation Society, March 2008), p. 4.

43. Ibid., p. 8.

44. Tinker, ed., *Burma: The Struggle, Volume II*, Doc 323, Telegram, Chief Secretary, Government of Burma to Secretary of State for Burma, 22 March 1947, IOR: M/4/2502, pp. 466–67.

45. *Thihmat Hpweya Koyei: AchetAlatmya* [Biographical Information for Recalling].

5

INDEPENDENCE AND CIVIL WAR
(January 1948 to September 1950)

He should be appointed Commander-in-Chief who is experienced in
the subjugation of others, who knows how to choose a victory-giving
battlefield, who does not abandon his forces in misfortune, who remains
the same in adversity or prosperity, who is strong, of irreproachable
character, well versed in military treatises, who can bear fatigues riding
and is replete with diligence and bravery.

Myanma Min Okchokpon Sadan

When Myanmar received its independence from Great Britain at 4:20 in
the morning of 4 January 1948, Ne Win, as commander of the Northern
region, was responsible for defending the country's borders with India,
China, French Indochina, and Thailand. India was convulsed with the
consequences of the partition from Pakistan and China was in the final
throes of the civil war between Mao Tse-tung's Red Army and Chiang
Kai-shek's Kuomintang (KMT). Laos, as a French colony was relatively
peaceful and Thailand was just two months back under the military rule
of Marshall Pibul Songram. None of these at that time appeared to pose
a threat to the territorial integrity or the sovereignty of Myanmar but
with Chinese Communist victory apparently imminent, and Thailand
having only recently given up administrative control of the cis-Salween
(Thanlwin) Shan State of Kengtung which had been given by Japan, the
future appeared ominous.

Moreover, both putative Chinese governments maintained claims to territory bequeathed by Britain to Burma to a line deep into Ne Win's command, roughly from Myitkyina west to the Indian border.[1] In January 1948, it was fortunate that no neighbouring government either wished, or was in a position, to challenge Burma's borders. The northern command had neither the troops nor the equipment to move up to the borders and defend them. During the sixty-two years that Britain had controlled this vast territory, little had been done to develop the roads and railways of the region. Being a rough mountainous country with few obvious economic assets, most of the border areas remained largely undisturbed except for the many Western and Karen missionaries who were converting the peoples of the area who were non-Buddhists, particularly the Kachin, to one or another variety of Christianity. Like the Bamar, however, the Shan remained overwhelming followers of Theravada Buddhism.

Despite the placid surface of the northern reaches of Myanmar in 1948, processes were at work which would pose great challenges to the government in the years to come. The area had been a recruiting ground for the British Indian army in Burma and army recruiting officers often worked closely with village headmen and Christian pastors to encourage men to join the colonial army and see the world beyond their own mountains and valleys.[2] During the Second World War, more men from the Kachin hills were brought under arms in guerrilla bands and loose talk of independence for the "Kachin nation" began to be encouraged by fast talking, loose thinking American and British soldiers and "spies" who used the local men to pursue the Japanese (Laidlaw 1991, pp. 102–22). Guns were now widespread in the hills.

Moreover, the process of social change which turns tribesmen into citizens, and tribal communities into larger amalgams, sometimes with claims to be made through a process of ethnic reification was under way. This was largely unnoticed except to a perceptive anthropologist-turned-army recruiting officer, Edmund Leach, who observed and documented the end of an old order, where ethnicity was a negotiated phenomenon, to one in which ethnicity was seen as being somehow primordial and bearing with it terms such as "rights" and "cultures". The daily struggle to survive was now becoming part of global political and economic processes. The ease with which an individual could be born a Kachin and die a Shan had not disappeared (Leach 1965), but was being challenged by imported ideas of ethnicity and nationality. People were being defined by censuses and nationality certificates.

The plasticity of the hillman's world was being replaced by the certainties of categorization. Thanks to the 1931 British Indian census of Burma, the country now had 135 ethnic groups, or "national races", as they became known. The ethnic conflicts which had been created during the previous hundred years between the "Kayin" and the "Bamar" were then being created among the "Kachin", "Shan", "Chin", "Naga", "Pa-O", "Pa-Laung", and the "Bamar". The consequences of this were for the future and nothing was being done to think about the problems that were to come in 1948, other than the vague and untested words of the Panglong Agreement and the 1947 Constitution which apparently promised to leave things as they were.

If the task of defending northern Burma, with its vast, largely undeveloped spaces and its few cities and towns, such as Taunggyi, Lashio, Myitkyina, Bhamo, Katha, and Kalemyo, as well as the central plains around Mandalay, appeared daunting to a new, small and untried army, the problems faced in the south were much more threatening on 4 January 1948. In Yangon, the euphoria of independence lasted but days before the reality of the continuity of life, political and as lived, sank in. For most people, nothing had changed in their way of living, which had been hard under the British, and was also hard under the government of Prime Minister Nu and his Socialist and aristocratic, wealthy colleagues, including the country's first President, Sao Shwe Thaik, the Sawbwa of Yawnghwe.[3]

The aristocratic Sawbwa, and the left-leaning but deeply religious Prime Minister, symbolized one of the many compromises and unresolved issues which the country faced. In November 1946, Sao Shwe Thaik, the first president of the Supreme Council of the United Hills Peoples, had made it clear that he, speaking for the Shan and other people's of northern Myanmar, considered the future to be in doubt, having insisted that the constitution provide the Shan State and Kayinni State a ten-year opt out clause if he and others found the new order not to their satisfaction. What they would opt out to, of course, remained unstated and perhaps not even considered.

While the Shan Sawbwa kept their options open for the future, other political leaders in Myanmar saw their options rapidly being foreclosed and they decided to act soon in order to gain the power that they thought was theirs by the laws of "scientific socialism" or primordial "racial" lineage. Thakin Than Tun, Thakin Soe and the other leaders of the several Communist parties of Burma each felt they had been betrayed by Aung San and his successors, led by Nu and the Socialists, from their right to power.[4] As the largest and first members of the resistance, in some ways a more useful asset to the British in 1945 than the Burma National Army (BNA) had been, the existence of the Communists and the likelihood of them seizing power if a negotiated settlement was not reached with Aung San, prompted the British to grant independence. Power should have been theirs and revolution the result, except for the collusion of the new government of Burma and the now largely departed imperialists. Similarly, the leaders of the Karen National Union (KNU) felt their chance of seizing the independent state that they thought the British had promised them, and then reneged on, would soon disappear if the new political order became imbedded.

Both of these groups had their supporters and allies, particularly in the new army of Burma. Mountbatten's two-wing army and Aung San's resistance forces were both divided within themselves. If the unity of the country would not hold, would the unity of the army survive? This must have been a question on every officer's mind at dawn on 4 January 1948. Did their loyalty lie with the state, their ideology, their leader, or their ethnicity? Did they take orders solely from their military superiors or follow the leads of their political colleagues or putative kin? The first year of independence would find the answer to those questions. Politics ruled and the politicians, no sooner than the Union Jack was lowered, were making decisions, concocting plots, and seeking to redistribute power in a manner which shaped the next half century and more.

In addition to the existing issues of ideology and ethnicity, a new element entered into Myanmar politics on Independence Day. Myanmar was now a nation-state, its foreign relations no longer determined in London. The new state joined the United Nations on 19 April 1948 under the sponsorship of Nationalist China. Diplomatic relations were established in the first year of independence with the United Kingdom, the United States, Chiang Kai-Shek's China, India, France, the Netherlands, Pakistan and Thailand, but an agreement to establish diplomatic relations with the Soviet Union was made only in 1950 and formal relations not established until the following year (Trager 1966, p. 216). In the global Cold War which was emerging at the time of Myanmar's independence, Myanmar foreign policy talked of neutrality and independence, but in reality leaned towards the West.

This was underlined by the close contacts maintained with the British Commonwealth nations, particularly India and Pakistan, and made emphatic by the Let Ya–Freeman Defence Agreement establishing the British Services Mission (BSM).[5] With the army under the leadership of Bo Let Ya as the country's first Minister of Defence and General Smith Dun, the British Ambassador, was pleased with the "excellent relations" that existed between the BSM and Burmese officers during the first months of independence.[6] This view, however, was not shared by others. Lieutenant Colonel Maung Maung, for example, declared, "I don't want any British advisers." Brigadier Ne Win echoed these sentiments, claiming that "Too many British officers here do not realise what happened on 4th January and carry on much as before."[7] He did not like to see British advisers attached to various units of the army and was galled, as were other Burmese officers, by the fact that the British were living in 90 per cent of the best officers' accommodation while the Burmese lived in bamboo huts.[8] These sentiments were to grow and become a source of contention.

However, more pressing matters were at the centre of attention. Communist and Karen National Union leaders were busy plotting against the government[9] and even members of the government were creating chaos and mayhem. On 12 March, for example, U Kyaw Nyein, the Home Minister, organized a party which wrecked three newspaper offices, after articles critical of the government were published (Nu 1975, pp. 143–45; Tun Pe 1949). Both the Burma Communist Party (BCP) and the KNU leaders were in talks with the government after independence but a compromise to share power or abandon any of the territory of the new state was impossible, and tensions grew until, on 25 March, Prime Minister Nu, at Kyaw Nyein's urging, ordered the arrest of BCP leader Thakin Than Tun. Three days later the party went underground, abandoned politics, and took up arms against the government. Burma's civil war had commenced. Even then, more groups were formed to advance unacceptable claims and during the same month, around Mawlamyine, Mon nationalists formed the Mon National Defence Organisation (MNDO), in alliance with the KNU's armed Karen National Defence Organisation (KNDO) established the previous year.

By early April, Communist guerrillas had seized many towns in central Burma and the delta, often raiding government offices and making off with arms and money. One of the areas particularly prone to conflict was the territory where "Operation Flush" had imposed order just two years before. As the power of the Communists grew, and the government's control of the territory declined, U Nu's government sought political means to bring the Communists back into the realm of peaceful politics. The day after the burial of General Aung San,[10] 12 April, on the cusp of Buddhist New Year celebrations, the Prime Minister called a meeting at his residence to discuss a plan for "leftist unity" to entice the Communists to lay down their arms. Those present, in addition to the Prime Minster, were Bo Let Ya, Bohmu Aung, Ko Sein Hman, U Kyaw Nyein, U Ba Swe, U Ohn and Thakin Thein Pe Myint (San San Myint 1979, p. 207). Meanwhile, government forces had regained some areas lost earlier in the month but lost other areas to the marauding Communist bands.

On 25 May, U Nu announced his fifteen-point "Leftist Unity Plan" designed to bring the Communists back into a broad united front, with the Anti-Fascist People's Freedom League (AFPFL), the nominal ruling party. The plan, which was modelled on a story related to one of the lives of the Buddha, did little to attract the Communists, but badly frightened the Western governments who thought that the country was "going Communist" (Nu 1975, pp. 147–50; Trager 1966, p. 109). While the first fourteen points echoed a socialist plan outlined by Aung San the previous year, the 15th point was "to form a League for the propagation of Marxist doctrine, composed of Socialists, Communists, *Pyithu Yebaw* (PVO) and other who lean towards Marxism", after which the pre-existing parties would be dissolved into the new League (Tinker 1967, pp. 30, 101–2).

The Communists rejected the plan and it was withdrawn as fast as it had been offered. The failure of the Leftist Unity Plan also exposed growing rifts between supporters of the Socialists and the Communists in the *Pyithu Yebaw*, known as the Yellow Flags and the White Flags respectively. As noted above, the PVO was a militia force of volunteers organized by Aung San to hold in reserve to attack the British if independence had not been granted. After Aung San's death, it became factionalized behind leaders of different Communist and Socialist organizations, becoming both a threat to and an occasional ally of the government. Ne Win and his army colleagues had to learn how to manage the PVO and eventually many were absorbed into the army.

The Leftist Unity Plan became embroiled in growing frustrations in the army over leadership and tactics. The ex-PBF officers, including key persons such as Bo Chit Myaing, complained to the Defence Minister about the dominance of Karen officers and the tactics they employed to raze Communist-controlled villages, thus further alienating the population from the government. Let Ya replied that he preferred the Karen officers as they were apolitical and professional, unlike the Japanese-trained former BNA officers. The matter was discussed at the First Commanding Officers Conference held on 1 June 1948. In the afternoon of the conference, the discussion became heated and Ne Win joined the junior officers in criticizing the failure of the government to come to terms with the Communists, thus creating widespread chaos across the country (Aung Myoe 1998, pp. 2–3).

The army stayed united until mid-June when some members of the First Burma Rifles mutinied and, together with their arms, joined the Communist insurgency. Soon two others followed, the Fourth Burma Rifles, in the view of Hugh Tinker, remained loyal to the government solely because of its connections with Ne Win (Tinker 1967, p. 323). As relations between different political factions in the army became strained, so did relations with the BSM. Following the opening of a new War Office by Prime Minister Nu and Defence Minister Let Ya on 26 May, it was made clear that the War Office, manned by men close to Ne Win, including Maung Maung and Aung Gyi, would no longer have British advisers.[11] The British government, fearful that Burma was too willing to compromise with the Communists following Nu's leftist unity scheme, had adopted a "go slow" policy on supplying arms to the army, thus inhibiting its ability to fight the Communists and regain the towns and cities lost in the ongoing civil war.[12] It estimated that the BCP had as many as 15,000 to 20,000 troops attacking the government in 1949.

Many members of the PVO became increasingly disgruntled with Nu's failure to bring Than Tun and other Communists into the government. The PVO split in July with the majority White Flag PVO joining the revolt of the BCP, while the minority Yellow Flags remained loyal to the government and Ne Win. At about this time, some officers in the Burma Rifles, and politicians such as Thein Pe Myint, considered how they might be able to organize a coup in which Ne Win would be involved, perhaps taking over the government in his own name. Ne Win resisted the efforts of the officers and resolved to stay away from Thein Pe Myint and his mad cap schemes. When Ne Win refused to cooperate with the coup plans and reported them to Prime Minister Nu, some officers of a Communist persuasion switched their allegiances to Lieutenant Colonel Ye Htut instead (Maung Maung 1969, pp. 204–5).

As the law and order situation continued to deteriorate, the government took steps to increase the power of the army. The chiefs of the north and south army commands, Ne Win and Kya Doe respectively, were made Special Commissioners and given powers tantamount to martial law.[13] Dissatisfaction within the senior ranks of the army with Bo Let Ya's performance as Defence Minister became increasingly apparent.[14] A "Group of Nine", including Chit Myaing and Ye Htut came together and, with the approval of Bo Let Ya, attempted to persuade the White Flag Communists and the White Flag PVOs to cooperate with the AFPFL government. When the National Security Council, composed largely of Karen officers, and including former ICS member U Tin Tut, learned of the efforts of the "Group of Nine" to do a deal with the Communists, it decided to disarm the ex-PBF forces. Words leaked to Bo Zeya and Bo Ye Htut, and they plotted a coup against the government, but Ne Win refused to join them, believing that the government's response would be to invite the British and other foreign forces to intervene and disband the ex-Japanese allies. In the meantime anger at Bo Let Ya continued to grow, some arguing that "his actions had caused a lot of misunderstanding in the army". They encouraged Prime Minister Nu to dismiss Let Ya and he agreed, but the Group of Nine nominated no one in particular to succeed. Either Ne Win or Lieutenant Colonel Zeya would have been satisfactory (Chit Myaing 1997, p. 13).

Prime Minister Nu describes how he came to favour Ne Win over rival officers in mid-1948. In July, Kyaw Nyein came to see Nu and demanded that he appoint either Ne Win or Bo Zeya as Defence Minister in lieu of Bo Let Ya. Nu felt that he was being coerced into making a decision. After being persuaded by Kyaw Nyein, Nu agreed to see both Ne Win and Zeya and they arrived with several other officers, and also Thein Pe Myint. Thein Pe Myint insisted that Nu appoint either Ne Win or Zeya within three days. Though Nu had already decided to appoint Ne Win, as he believed that only his Fourth Burma Rifles and the Chin and Kachin troops were loyal to the government, this ultimatum put his back up. He once more refused. After the meeting ended, Bo Let Ya asked Nu to give Bo Zeya a private hearing. Bo Zeya then came back but Nu reiterated his refusal. Kyaw Nyein, when he learned of this, told Ne Win who felt that Zeya had double-crossed him and from then on they became sworn enemies (Nu 1975, pp. 151–60; Callahan 2004, pp. 124–25). Soon after, most of the PVO went underground.

On 1 August, Prime Minister Nu appointed himself as the Minister of Defence. Initially, Ne Win was ordered to return to his duties at Mandalay but the Group of Nine insisted that he ignore the order. Chit Myaing recalls the Group of Nine saying to Ne Win, "The government would not dare to touch you as long as we are behind you. We are with you 100 per cent, don't leave Rangoon" (Chit Myaing 1997, p. 14). Ne Win was then appointed as the Deputy Defence Minister.[15] Under the new dispensation, Smith Dun, as Chief of the General Staff, was to have direct access to the Prime Minister in case of disagreements with Ne Win, an arrangement which the BSM chief, General Bourne, founded highly unsatisfactory.[16] Rumours of these moves, including Bo Let Ya's resignation and Thakin Than Tun's refusal to join the cabinet under Nu, were circulating in Yangon days before they were brought into effect.[17]

Following Nu's refusal to appoint Bo Zeya or Bo Ne Win as the Defence Minister, the largest mutiny of Burma Army troops ever to occur took place on 10 August. On the night of the refusal, the officers of the Third Burma Rifles met and determined that those who supported Bo Zeya and the Communists would mutiny (Nu 1975, p. 157). Prior to then, Ye Htut and Chit Myaing had argued over whether they should allow Thein Pe Myint to address the troops in order to convince them to join the Communists underground. Chit Myaing insisted that if Thein Pe Myint were invited to put the case for the Communists, Ne Win should be invited to make the case for remaining loyal to the government. Subsequently Ye Htut, in collaboration with Thein Pe Myint and others, caused the Third Burma Rifles to split. Bo Ye Htut, with 350 officers and men from the Third Burma Rifles and the Number Three General Transport Company, with 32 trucks, deserted.[18] When Major Chit Myaing reported to Ne Win about the defection of Zeya and his followers, he replied, "Good. Now we know who is black and who is white."[19]

Three days later, Smith Dun was promoted to Lieutenant General, Ne Win to Major General as Deputy Commander of the Army, and U Tun Hla Aung, a British trained officer, to Major General in charge of the police.[20] Nominally, at least, Smith Dun was now in charge of both the police and the army. Thein Pe Myint and Bo Thein Swe, founders of the radical leftist Aung San League, were arrested, Thein Pe Myint for his role in the defection of the Third Burma Rifles to the Communists. Rumours abounded, including that General Aung San's widow, Daw Khin Kyi, had disappeared to join the insurgents led by her brother-in-law.[21]

At about the same time, members of the Military Police of Karen descent began to desert their posts and the KNDO and MNDO began attacking towns in the delta and around Thaton, near Mawlamyine. The fighting was spreading and the government was facing not one enemy, but several. Moreover, the question of whether the troops were loyal to the government, or to their ideological or ethnically designated leaders, was being answered. It was a perilous time for the government. U Nu sought to shore up his regime as best as he could and came up with a scheme to arm four-and-a-half battalions of auxiliary forces, mainly from the ethnic minorities. This plan did not find favour with the BSM, which was asked to find the weapons the new battalions would require. However, the British Ambassador, James Bowker, warned the Foreign Office that if the arms were not provided, the Burmese would turn to the United States instead.[22] On the same day as the Ambassador issued his warning, combined KNDO/ MNDO forces occupied the city of Mawlamyine only to be evicted from it shortly after by government forces.

Ne Win, now back in Yangon permanently from his brief posting in the north, was distrusted by General Geoffrey Bourne, the head of the BSM.[23] Believed to be in touch with Bo Ye Htut, the leader of the mutiny who was reported to have been seen in Yangon,[24] Ne Win's popularity with the troops was widely known. Whether he was in touch with Ye Htut, or with the other mutineers, is unknown, but a "considerable number" of them surrendered within two weeks of their desertion.[25] Ne Win had convinced at least the sceptical Bourne that he was "fairly deeply committed as an anti-Communist". He reached this conclusion on the basis of his performance in "Operation Flush" and his subsequent dismissal of civilians with Communist leanings. He was, however, working with Bo Ye Htut and leftist Bo Zeya to try to pull the old BNA troops together behind the government.[26]

Bo Let Ya told Bourne that many men in the army were loyal to Ne Win and if a crisis were to occur, they would follow him. Included amongst the Ne Win loyalists were the entire Fourth and Fifth Burma Rifles, the Fourth Union Military Police Battalion and probably the Sixth Burma Rifles, then under the command of Colonel Tin U. Tin U had been approached by Bo Zeya to bring his troops over to the Communist side but Tin U just passed the message to Ne Win. Smith Dun took no action to counter the contact with the mutinous troops on the part of Ne Win and his subordinates.[27] Bourne was convinced that Ne Win was very close to the Socialists in the Cabinet but the British Ambassador, James Bowker, did not believe so.[28] Bourne also believed that despite being a Socialist-inclined anti-Communist, Ne Win was also "awkwardly anti-British" while Prime Minister Nu was a "hapless" Defence Minister.[29]

Tun Hla Aung was soon after relieved of his command probably for opposing the arming of what he saw as political levies or *sitwundan*, irregular forces under the control of the Socialists,[30] and sent to London as military attaché.[31] At Insein, and at another undisclosed location, Ne Win was using officers from the Fifth Burma Rifles to train police levies to attack the Communists and the KNDO/MNDO. He was said to have bypassed his nominal commanding officer, Smith Dun, and was opposed by non-Socialists in and near the government, including Tin Tut, Let Ya and Brigadier Aung Thin, the latter a Bamar who had served in the British army.[32] Ne Win's reliance on the police and irregulars, such as the *sitwundan*, in controlling public disorder went back to "Operation Flush" and he used similar tactics to deal with the civil war situation.

Connections between the British and the Karen rebels were documented on 11 September when Burma Military Intelligence revealed that a British journalist for the *Daily Mail* in Yangon, Alexander Campbell, and a Colonel John McCromarty-Tulloch, were in league with the KNU and assisting their rebellion. Campbell was subsequently expelled from Myanmar. The *Daily Mail* at that time was edited by Frank Owen, who had been the editor of the newspaper of the South East Asian Command during the Second World War. According to the diaries of Malcolm Muggeridge reporting on a conversation with a friend from the Foreign Office, Campbell and McCromarty-Tulloch were part of a plan whereby Owen and his foreign editor had "engineered a revolt in Burma", the end of which was to see "Owen marching on Rangoon with the victorious Karen army." However, "after a little while, Owen characteristically lost interest in the project, and went off to Africa".[33] Diverting as this tale was, the KNU were a serious threat to the government and even more so when Karen troops in the Burma army began to revolt in late September. Owen was not the only one involved in an effort to "revive SOE assistance" to the KNDO. Winston Churchill, former Governor Dorman-Smith and others were also involved, including the then commander of the Burma Army, General Smith Dun (Aldrich 1999, pp. 136–42).

In late September, Karen military police were reported to have mutinied at Kengtung in the eastern Shan hills, looted the Loilem government offices, and captured Loikaw in the Kayinni State. Kayinni, Myanmar's smallest and poorest state, its existence an accident of history, was said to be almost completely under the control of Karen rebels. Karen insurgents were facing Karen government troops near Nyaunglebin and the loyalty of the troops was doubtful. While Smith Dun contends he ordered Saw Kya Doe to use Karen troops to fight the Karen rebels, the British embassy did not believe they would do so. The KNU and other Karen groups were saying their real enemy was the Communists and were requesting for government support to oppose them. While the Karen troops were rebelling on the eastern borders of Burma, in Rakhine State, north of Sittwe, part of the Fifth Burma Rifles were surrounded, probably by *Mujahid* rebels, and reinforcements had to be rushed to their defence from Yangon.[34] While the Burma army was fighting the *Mujahid* in Rakhine, the government of neighbouring East Pakistan was shoring up its defences against a perceived Communist threat from Burma.[35] Conflict on the Pakistani border continued into 1950, with clashes between Arakanese Buddhists and Chittagonian Muslims, as the government tried to halt the smuggling of rice into East Pakistan.[36] The chaos of September was punctuated on the 18th with the assassination of U Tin Tut, who had resigned as Foreign Minister to join the army on a special commission. Yellow Flag PVOs or perhaps Socialists under Bo Min Gaung were suspected of carrying out the deed.[37]

Fighting was raging across the country and Nu's beleaguered government was referred to merely as the "Rangoon government" by foreign media. It seemed as if it controlled little else and Yangon and other cities were rapidly filled with refugees fleeing the conflicts. Ne Win was obviously in the thick of all these activities. For example, he and a senior Karen leader, Mahn James, travelled from Yangon to Maubin in the delta on 21 October on a mission to defuse a possible communal clash between the Karen and Burman residents of the area. They were successful, but there were doubts whether the peace would be perpetual.[38]

Command of the armed forces was slowly slipping away from Smith Dun as the loyalty of the Karen troops came into doubt and Ne Win increasingly operated on his own with the loyal troops of the Burma Rifles and other units. The levies which had been raised were completely under Ne Win's control and were "playing a useful part in operations". His behaviour, however, was found wanting by General Bourne. He had "done no desk work except to transfer the levies from the Home Office to War Office control". While outwardly loyal to Smith Dun, the cooperation was only superficial. Ne Win was moving officers from the Fourth, Fifth and Sixth Burma Rifles at will and was not cooperating with the BSM. At least half the War Office was under his complete control and if he was away things were "held up for days". Ne Win was gradually gaining more and more power. Smith Dun, who did consult with British officers, unlike Ne Win, told Bourne that even the Prime Minister was afraid of Ne Win because of his close affiliation with the Socialists in the government, as well as his alleged contacts with the Communist and PVO White Flags in revolt. On the other hand, perhaps Ne Win had to act as he did because, in Bourne's view, Smith Dun was "a great disappointment as the Supreme Commander".[39]

The situation was getting desperate for the government. A senior Kachin political figure, the Sima Duwa Singwa Nawng, reported to Prime Minister Nu on 24 November that the KNDO were attempting to rally the Kachin population to support them in seizing power. He recommended, and Nu agreed, to organize frontier area forces, or Burma Territorial Force battalions before the end of January.[40] This became known as the Ten Battalions Scheme. Nu called Ne Win and his deputy, Aung Gyi, to implement the plan and himself went off to the north to rally the population there to support the government (Maung Maung 1969, p. 207).

At the end of Myanmar's first year of independence, the country was in turmoil. Luckily for U Nu's government, some Karen and most Kachin and Chin troops remained loyal to it, as were the forces led by Ne Win. While the First Karen and First Kachin were attacking the Communist forces in the Pyinmana area, Nu was still hoping to end the civil war by doing a political deal with the Communist leaders. He invited four Communist military leaders, including former Thirty Comrades Bo Zeya and Bo Ye Htut, to Yangon for peace talks but they indicated that they would not reply to the offer until at least 15 March. Clearly, the Communist and other rebel forces suspected that they had time on their side and victory was in sight. Perhaps they had an inkling of what the forces they were fighting were thinking of doing, for around 26 January, the First Karen Rifles mutinied at Toungoo, south of Pyinmana, seized Pyu and Htantabin and began to march towards Yangon. Karen units at Pyay also revolted and when words of these mutinies reached Pathein, Karen Union Military Police revolted there, too (Smith 1980, p. 62). Yangon was rapidly being surrounded by Karen forces, especially after the KNDO seized Twante, across the river from Yangon on New Year's Day 1949. At the end of the month, the KNU's armed wing was declared an illegal organization.

On the last day of January, with the Karen mutineers marching towards Insein in two columns from Pyay and Toungoo, Smith Dun was in his residence, Flagstaff House, in the military compound south of what is now Inya Lake Hotel Street in Yangon, discussing affairs with Brigadiers Let Ya[41] and Kya Doe. According to Smith Dun, Ne Win entered the room and the Commander-in-Chief,

doubting [Ne Win's] capacity to read orders, briefed him about [a] conference that was to take place. He listened quite attentively, but at the end he got up and said, "If only the Karens had started two months ago it would be alright for them, not now," and left. The two Brigadiers were just left there, stunned at such an attitude and behaviour. No doubt it would seem strange and funny in some countries for a deputy to be so brazen as to make such remarks in the face of his Commander, but nothing was strange in Burma then (Smith 1980, p. 53).

That night, Karen quarters in Yangon, Ahlone and Thamaing were searched for arms, and shots were exchanged. When Smith Dun learned of this via a phone call from a Karen elder in Thamaing, he phoned Prime and Defence Minister Nu who in turn said he would contact Ne Win to find out what was going on. Karen troops at the military base at Mingaladon, on learning what had happened, marched off to nearby Insein and the battle for Yangon commenced. It looked not completely impossible that Frank Owen's alleged plan to march on to Yangon with victorious Karen troops might be fulfilled, even if he was away in Africa then. Smith Dun's position was not tenable and he resigned on 1 February and went into internal exile in Myitkyina (Smith 1980).

The mutiny of the Karen troops at Mingladon was done in coordination with a KNDO attack on Insein, then a separate town from Yangon (Smith 1980, p. 62). A major facility of the Burma Railways and possessing one of the country's main prisons, Insein was also a place of residence for many Kayin and the location of the Baptist Theological College. Just seven-and-a-half miles from Yangon, and much nearer to the international airport and military base at Mingaladon, Insein was an important location for the KNDO. The army had to move quickly to shore up the government or it might soon fall. By 2 February, Insein was completely under the control of the KNDO. Immediately after Smith Dun's resignation, Ne Win was appointed the Commander-in-Chief in his place and gave orders to defend Yangon. As a consequence of the prior mutinies of troops sympathetic to one insurgent group or another, the army he commanded probably had fewer than 2,000 troops, some of doubtful loyalty, at least when facing their compatriots (Callahan 2004, p. 114). The upper reaches of the Burma Army was dominated by officers, mainly Karen, who had served with the British before or during the Second World War. "Of the thirty-three senior officers who attended a commanding officers' (COs') conference on 31 January 1949, only four had experience in the PBF." The others included nine Kayin, four Bamar of doubtful loyalty to Ne Win, and the rest were Chin, Kachin and other minority officers (Callahan 2004, p. 119). The new Commander-in-Chief may have found his position very lonely, but as the Kayin officers were soon placed on leave and temporarily confined as their troops mutinied, the situation was clarified. Karen troops who had not yet revolted were also disarmed and placed in camps for several years until their political loyalty could be determined. During that time, racist rumours and crude documents threatening the extermination of both Kayin and Bamar were in circulation.[42]

The 2,000 men whom Ne Win could possibly command were "scattered", as Bertil Lintner writes, "in decimated, weak battalions and companies" (Lintner 1999, p. 96). Losses of weapons to the insurgent forces amounted to nearly half of the army's stocks (Tinker 1967, p. 323). During its first year of existence, the government lost control of 75 per cent of the towns and cities across the country. Only Yangon was in its grip and that was tenuous. Soon after Ne Win took control, part of the Third Burma Rifles, then stationed in the Delta at Pyapon, Maubin and Dedaye, were ordered with their families to Yangon. The Burma Navy was ordered to provide escort as the waterways were filled with KNDO forces. As the Twante canal was closed by the KNDO, an indirect route had to be sought (Myoma-Lwin 2011, pp. 66–72). At that time, the Southern Command was under British-trained Brigadier General Aung Thin and the Northern under Brigadier General Lazum Tang, a British-trained Kachin.[43] The following November (Lintner 1999, p. 98), Lazum Tang was replaced by Brigadier General Kyaw Zaw, the Communist Thirty Comrade, who was replaced later by the Anglo-Burmese, Douglas Blake.

Improvization was clearly required and soon a Navy Bofor gun, put on wheels, was rolled into position to assist the Third Burma Rifles, under the command of Bo Chit Myaing, to halt the KNDO and prevent the Karen Rifle mutiners passing down the road from Pyay to reach Insein and join their comrades there.[44] Though the KNDO were forced back at the battle of Wetkaw on 11 February, their forces were soon to be augmented by additional deserters from the Burma army. Ordered to retake Toungoo from the KNDO, the First Kachin Rifles under Colonel Naw Seng (Fellowes-Gordon 1971), now in league with the rebel forces, occupied Meiktila on 20 February, seized two Dakotas on the ground at the Meiktila airfield, and forced the British and American pilots to fly them to an army camp near Maymyo,[45] the hill station outside Mandalay to which the British moved the government of Myanmar during the hot season every year until 1940. Government forces retook the city two days later.

In the midst of this conflagration, Ne Win met with General Temple, the successor to General Bourne, as head of the Burma Services Mission, to discuss strategy. A sanguine Ne Win believed the only real threat to Burma arose from the impending success of the Chinese People's Liberation Army in China. In the case of aggression by the Chinese Communists, his view was that only external assistance could save Burma from Chinese occupation. Indian or Pakistani troops would have to be brought in to support the Burma army with field batteries and armoured cars.[46]

Facing more than 15,000 armed insurgents,[47] the weakest period for the Burma army was in February 1949. However, from then on, Ne Win and his colleagues worked to expand the force to cope with the situation. While they could rely on the British legacy air force, and navy to provide support, the infantry bore the main burden of fighting and its expansion was essential for regaining control of the country. New battalions were formed, including three new Kachin battalions and three Shan battalions. Later, a Kayah battalion was formed, comprising of Shan, Kayinni, and other hill people, as well as a fourth Burma Regiment. By early 1953, a total of 41 battalions existed, up from a mere six four years earlier. The rapid expansion came from taking in the irregular forces, *sitwundan*, raised during the height of the insurgency. This rapid expansion provided many opportunities for rapid promotions and the army was often unable to provide trained leadership as quickly as required. *Sitwundan* and other irregular home guards continued to exist, in part as a way of controlling former insurgents who surrendered with their arms and had to found useful employment. While few officers were promoted to the higher ranks, all were well paid in comparison with the civilian civil service (Tinker 1967, pp. 325–29).

As the civil war raged across the country, with more than an estimated 30,000 casualties in the first year of independence,[48] the siege of Insein entered its second month. With towns being lost and retaken by government forces on a daily basis, the army having to improvise, and the generals speculating on a Chinese invasion, politics continued in Rangoon. On 7 February, civil servants in Yangon had gone on a strike for improved wages and conditions, to be joined the following week by railway workers. Conditions in the cities were hard and travel was unsafe, forcing up prices and rendering normal life impossible. Deputy Prime Minister Kyaw Nyein, Ne Win's associate from time to time since the Japanese invasion in 1942, with a reputation for demanding robust action against those who opposed him, apparently insisted that the armed forces be brought in to break up the strikes which he saw as irresponsible. Ne Win refused and the resulting argument allegedly resulted in fisticuffs.[49] Several weeks later, Ne Win was promoted to Lieutenant General.[50] Others, such as veteran nationalist leader U Ba Pe, allegedly backed by Indian and Burmese landlords and British businesses, advocated Ne Win to take over the government, suspend parliament and eventually hold new elections.[51]

According to Dr Maung Maung, during the height of the civil war, Ne Win often worked at the War Office, or the Police Barracks on Pyay Road, "in his vest, sweating in the heat", moving his sparse forces to where they could be most effective (Maung Maung 1969, p. 210). He still had time, however, for enjoyment with his colleagues, drinking champagne with Bo Set Kya one night.[52] Rumours were in abundance in Yangon. One was that Ne Win was negotiating with the PVO for a "drastic cabinet shake-up, presumably involving ousting the Socialists". Socialists reported that they would go underground if Ne Win, with the PVO, took over the government.[53]

They were apparently responding to a Ne Win plan for the entire cabinet to resign except Nu and the BCP to be invited to form a government in order to end the civil war. According to Trager, Nu and Ne Win went north together on 16 March to plan the recapture of Mandalay which was being held by a combined force of Communists, KNDO, and PVO. Nu was called back to Yangon but the Communists made contact with Ne Win and he began negotiating their entrée into the cabinet under Nu. If successful, peace would be restored and new elections held within the next year (Trager 1966, pp. 112–13). Ne Win would have ensured that the Communists did not control the army, but as "the insurrection weakened the country and compromise would have been preferable" (Trager 1966, p. 54). Whatever the truth of the rumours, the Socialists soon resigned and Ne Win was appointed by Prime Minister Nu as the Deputy Prime Minister as well as Home and Defence Ministers on 1 April (Nu 1975, pp. 181–83). Nu's account of what took place implies the veracity of this version of events and downplays the claim that Ne Win was about to grab power for himself or join with the Communists. In Nu's memoirs, he returned from the trip to find that all the Socialist Ministers had resigned. When he asked one of the resigning ministers why they had done so, he replied:

Bo Ne Win was constantly at us, saying that the army were not watchdogs for ministers, and that they could not go on protecting us. Because he was forever egging us on to invite the rebels into a new government, we thought we should resign (Nu 1975, p. 182).

The following morning, Kyaw Nyein arrived with Ne Win. The latter did not say anything and Kyaw Nyein repeated the explanation of the previous day. Having been deserted by his Socialist colleagues, Nu, nonetheless, refused to appoint ministers from among the rebels. Without explanation, he merely appointed Ne Win to his three portfolios and Dr E Maung as Foreign Minister.

Ne Win also retained his post as Supreme Commander of the Armed Forces. He was clearly, if not the most powerful, the second most powerful person in the government. The American ambassador disparaging Ne Win's military abilities, described "Operation Flush" as a failure. Without doubt, the ambassador had not read Communist leader Thakin Than Tun's speech at the second congress of the Indian Communist Party, a month before going underground. In it, Than Tun drew particular attention to "Operation Flush" as an example of the "'anti-Communist Annihilation Drive' of the 'imperialists-bourgeoisie Government' which was 'following the dictates of Anglo-American imperialism'".[55] The ambassador described Ne Win as having "a good appearance, a pleasant personality, and is reasonably intelligent".[56] The Americans were to keep an eye on Ne Win from then on.

The British government was clearly concerned about developments in Burma and Labour MP Woodrow Wyatt, on a fact-finding visit to the former colony, felt that the British had to do more to force the KNU to agree with the government and end their relations with the Communists. The British Services Mission had set itself up to be opposed by the army as it kept recommending Karen officers for promotion in the midst of the civil war and Ne Win took no notice of it. Wyatt recommended that an English person be appointed to negotiate between the KNU and the government, something unacceptable to U Nu and Ne Win, and that the BSM be halved in size, if not withdrawn completely.[57] Wyatt's concerns about the position of the Karen rebels was shared by many in London, with obvious implications for relations between the BSM and Ne Win and the Burmese government. U Nu and Ne Win did enter into peace talks with the KNU leader, Saw Ba U Gyi, in Yangon soon after but to no conclusion.

While Wyatt was advising from Yangon, the Myanmar minister for the Shan States, Sao Hkun Hkio, the Sawbaw of Mongmit,[58] and the Myanmar ambassador to London, U Nu's close adviser, U Ohn, were consulting with the British Chancellor of the Exchequer, Sir Stafford Cripps, in a vain attempt to raise British weapons and arm ten battalions of Kachin and other loyal "hill tribe" troops to take on the BCP, the White Flag PVO, and the KNU. The British position was that they could not defeat all three and should do a deal with the KNU in order to take on the Communists effectively.[59] Ne Win was of the view that the existing Burmese and Kachin officers were sufficiently qualified to raise and train such battalions without BSM assistance.[60] The plan to raise the ten battalions in the north of the country had been developed by Nu and Ne Win without consulting the BSM, which was why the mission of Sao Hkun Hkio to London came as a surprise to the British.[61] The next day Sao Khun Khio requested free British air transport for the shipment of Indian small arms to Burma to fight the KNU and perhaps Chinese Communists infiltrating from Yunnan province.[62] This was the first hint of what became not Chinese Communist infiltration into the eastern Shan States but defeated troops of the Kuomintang seeking refuge in Burma, the origins of the KMT issue, about which more below.

On 20 April, the same day Cripps met with Hkun Hkio, Ne Win, at his request, had a "very friendly" interview with the head of the BSM, General Temple. At this meeting, Ne Win explained the basis of his distrust of the BSM. First, the quality of the officers assigned to the Mission had been below the expected standard. Second, he was convinced that BSM officers at Myamyo were complicit in the KNU seizure of the town and its resources the previous month. Third, as the British were unwilling to supply the arms that the army required, he would turn to India for support. Therefore, he requested the size of the Mission be reduced as the British tactical training was inappropriate and he would write a new manual for Myanmar's conditions, and British officers were no longer needed for routine work in the War Office.[63] The British ambassador doubted that Ne Win was in favour of raising the ten Kachin and other "tribal" troops because of his alleged preference for Burman predominance in the army. In any event, he advised against flying any weapons directly to the frontier territories outside of army control.[64]

Clearly, relations between the British government and General Ne Win, if not the entire government of Burma a year and four months after independence, were severely strained. Arms shipments from India began to arrive in Yangon in June as the fighting began to turn in the government's flavour. Both KNU and BCP rebels withdrew from a number of towns and cities during May. The 112-days seige of Insein ended on 22 May and the threat to Rangoon was finally terminated.[65] As the civil war seemed to be turning in the direction of the government, Ne Win decided to take a holiday, flying off to Bangkok, where he and the other Thirty Comrades had drunk the blood oath in 1941. While in Bangkok, he called on the Thai Prime Minister, Marshall Pibul Songram, who in February of that year had survived a plot by part of the armed forces to oust him from office. Ne Win apparently had a general conversation with Pibul, and while hoping for cooperation on their joint border, made no request for assistance.[66] His first of many quasi-political trips abroad was back to the scene of one of his earlier triumphs.

Ne Win's rise to power as Deputy Prime Minister, Minister of Defence, Minister of Home Affairs, and Supreme Commander of the Armed Forces not only caused the Americans, but also the British, to take note of his skills and abilities. General Temple, head of the BSM, penned an Orientalist note on his character, stating that

> Bo Ne Win's success is due mainly to a certain personal magnetism and charm combined with ruthlessness and a fair measure of energy and determination (qualities never very marked among the Burmese). He is undoubtedly quick and intelligent though lacking a real intellect.

He went on to write that he had "no aptitude for detailed work such as planning and administration!" but had created a "loyal officers net" around himself.[67] In a separate assessment, Temple indicated he thought that political loyalty to Ne Win was more important than other considerations such as technical competence or intelligence.

Noting a Burmese "intense feeling of national pride and a desire to show that they are independent and capable of standing on their own feet", in a report on the future of the BSM, General Temple advised setting up a staff college with British instructors to shape future developments. Prime Minister Nu indicated support for the idea but Ne Win "always asserts that he had no officer personnel available to undergo training". Ne Win apparently found the technical provision in the air force and navy contingents of the BSM to be worthwhile but the army element was seriously undervalued.

Temple believed "that so long as Ne Win is Supreme Commander and virtual dictator of Burma", the army element of the mission would be unable to function as he intended. Temple clearly found Ne Win exasperating to work with. He wrote,

> I find it increasingly difficult to make any specific recommendation to General Ne Win as he is not clear in his own mind what he really wants. His superficial ideas change every time I see him. He has never given me the opportunity to discuss basic matters with him and thus to help him form a sound plan.
>
> Sometimes he appears to be opposed to the Mission, on other occasions he gives a half-hearted impression of wishing to keep part of the Mission, especially the more senior officers. But the point on which I think he is clear is a dislike of the Army element as a whole except perhaps the technical arms which he realises are almost essential to him and he thus appears prepared to put up with them.[68]

Temple wrote in apparent despair at the end of the June that "the whole Burma problem tends to revolve around the personality of Lieutenant General Ne Win."[69]

Ne Win, as soon as he had taken charge as Chief-of-Staff, began to plan to reorganize the War Office to ensure that the ex-PBF officers were in control. With both Let Ya and Smith Dun removed from power, Ne Win had a free hand in making the War Office loyal to him, so that he could be away from his office for long periods with no fear of anyone threatening to supplant his authority. At the Second Commanding Officers Conference held in January 1950, Ne Win discussed with his subordinates how to distribute promotions equitably among the ex-PBF, British army veterans, and ethnic minority officers in order to avoid civilian interference in army internal affairs. The divisions which the British proposed between the army, navy and air force were ignored in order to form a more unified defence services organization which allegedly operated more efficiently, undermining inter-service rivalries (Aung Myoe 1998, pp. 5–6).

The British were frustrated with Ne Win, but Prime Minister U Nu faced even more serious problems. His deputy was clearly in a much more powerful position than himself. Ne Win had moved into the Cabinet and the army, or at least the former BNA elements of the army, and the Yellow Flag PVOs were his power base, something far stronger than the political support provided by the fractured AFPFL. What to do with

Ne Win, in the context of what to do about the British Services Mission, and British concerns about Burma not playing fair with the KNU or going Communist, must have lain at the back of people's minds when Prime Minister Nu and General Ne Win met with the British ambassador on 15 June. At that time, Ne Win proposed to visit London, together with General Temple, to discuss the way forward.[70] Ne Win had told Temple that he would remain in England for a week to a maximum of a fortnight. His plans, according to Temple, were very vague and subject to change. He also wanted to visit other European countries on what would be his first of many visits to Britain, Europe and the United States.[71] Subsequently, Ne Win hinted to Temple that he would like to be received by His Majesty King George VI, whose ancestors had been so despised by Burmese nationalists before independence.[72] He apparently met both the king and also Princess Elizabeth, the first of several meetings with the future queen (Tarling 2005, p. 22).

The American embassy in Rangoon was obviously interested in Ne Win's visit. He was seen as operating largely independent of Nu and the rest of the cabinet,[73] but it was hoped that the visit would clarify the work of the BSM, improve British-Burmese relations, and ultimately stabilize the situation. The ever active Yangon rumour mill had it also that Ne Win might visit Prague in Communist Czechoslovakia, or possibly even the centre of World Communism, Moscow. To give credence to the rumour was another rumour that he had met for four hours with a Soviet Minister in Bangkok during his visit earlier in the month. However, Myanmar Foreign Minister U E Maung informed the Americans that Ne Win had no intention of visiting the United States or either Prague or Moscow.[74]

The American embassy in London also took an interest in Ne Win's travel plans and intentions. Noting from their conversations with British officials in the capital that the Burmese government favoured the naval and air force contingent of the British Services Mission, but considered the army element too pro-Karen, the British believe that Ne Win was "without doubt the strongest man on the Burmese horizon", but was "unfortunately ... intolerant, suspicious and violently anti-Karen". The British felt that a settlement with the Karen was the "ultimate solution" to Burma's problems. As to Ne Win's rumoured interest in going to Prague to buy an ammunition or an arms factory, the British intended to put him off by pointing out the negative effect of such a move on British public opinion.[75] Soon after this, however, the Americans in Yangon got wind of a possible plan for Ne Win to visit the United States instead of eastern Europe, following an invitation from an unnamed American company interested in selling an "industrialization scheme".[76] Ne Win's earlier vague plans were taking shape as he flew to the West for the first time. The invitation had apparently come from a Mr A.L. Resnick, representing the Ameritex Industrial Export Corporation, a firm with mining interests and a penicillin factory in the Philippines. Ne Win had apparently met with Mr Resnick on 2 July, the day before his departure.[77]

As was to become a pattern in future years, Ne Win left Rangoon confident of his position and that his subordinates would carry on collectively in his absence. Day-to-day matters were being handled by a War Office Committee of four senior officers.[78] The British organized a tour for Ne Win, who was accompanied by Bo Chit Ko Ko, described as violently anti-British, and Wing Commander S. Khin.[79] The tour designed to impress him with what the old imperial armed forces could offer, included RAF bases, major naval bases, Sandhurst and other military training centres, and infantry and small arms training centres.[80] The heart of the visit, however, was meetings with British ministers, the first of which was with A.V. Alexander, the Secretary of State for Defence, held at the House of Commons. Ne Win was accompanied by U Hla Maung, U Aung Than,[81] and Ambassador U Ohn.[82] The lengthy British record of the meeting makes clear Ne Win's grounds for mistrusting the BSM because of its apparent support for the Karen insurgents and defectors from the Burma Army.[83]

First Ne Win explained that, in his view and that of his colleagues, certain officers in the BSM had instigated to make Karen officers hostile to the Union and had conspired and intrigued to foment a long-planned rebellion. He cited the case of one Major Parsonage who was the subject of a court of inquiry. He also noted that when it became necessary in March to evacuate British personnel from Maymyo, then occupied by the KNDO, information on the disposition of Burma army troops protecting the landing grounds "reached the Karen rebels, with the result that the Burmese forces were attacked and lives lost". This kind of situation had happened more than once and General Temple had admitted the complicity of "foolish" British officers. He also felt that the Karen at the Staff College received preferential treatment over the Kachin. Even if this and other points were difficult to prove, they led to suspicion and ill will. While he liked General Temple, he did not like complaining to him about the behaviour of individual officers.

However, General Temple "seemed to go out of his way to ask difficult and often unfriendly questions". Temple made it clear that he personally approved all requests for weapons purchases and tied this to concern about base security. Ne Win had assured him that the army was doing all it could to ensure that arms did not reach the wrong hands, and they requested only what was needed for the troops. Temple, and General Thomas before him, had both sought to reverse the proportion of Burmese to Karen troops in the army, two-thirds to one-third, which Admiral Mountbatten had agreed.

Ne Win said that he understood the position of the Labour government but the personnel in Burma were working in a different direction. He had not yet made up his mind on the future of the BSM but was convinced that "a united Burma would be a better friend of Great Britain than a disunited one and he hoped it would be possible to develop good feelings between the two countries." However, personnel of the BSM should not meddle in the internal affairs of Burma and instead confine themselves to military matters. Alexander attempted to calm the situation and explain that Britain was doing its best to supply what was requested, though supplies were not unlimited, and that Britain's military training in the Far East was of a high quality. In reply, Ne Win expressed confidence in British methods but doubted the best trainers were being sent. For example, sentries on duty were told they were allowed to sit, which struck him as distinctly odd. Alexander promised to look into the matter. Military disagreement between Ne Win and Temple was revealed in a press interview. Ne Win there explained, Burma "did not want highly mechanised equipment" as it could neither be afforded nor was it suitable to the reorientation of the Burma army to guerrilla warfare (quoted in Maung Maung 1969, p. 215). Moreover, the army was moving away from the British designed "strategy of the razing of villages suspected of harbouring or sympathizing with communists and executing their villagers" which, as Colonel Chit Myaing explained, was counterproductive and not the way to get the people to support the government (Callahan 2004, p. 112).

The same group met again on 13 July, joined by the British Ambassador to Rangoon, James Bowker. Alexander started the meeting by stating that the position of the British was one which Ne Win and the Burmese government should find satisfactory and even-handed. Ne Win responded by saying that he was now satisfied that partiality towards the Karen rebels was not the policy of the British government and he would return home and make decisions on that basis. His prior suspicions of British intentions towards the Karens had stemmed from the conditions the British ambassador had put on an offer of short-term financial assistance in a meeting with Prime

Minister Nu which Ne Win had not attended. In his understanding, the British were insisting on a Commonwealth-sponsored round-table conference between the government and the Karen rebels.[84] This was indeed a Karen proposal a few days prior to the meeting and smacked of an attempt to interfere in Myanmar's internal affairs to the advantage of the KNDO. To make settlement with the Karen a condition for assistance was unacceptable.[85] Also discussed was a confusion which had arisen following a conversation between the American journalist Edgar Snow and Kyaw Nyein which had led to a message from the Ambassador to London about the possibility of Burma withdrawing from the sterling bloc, a sensitive point for the British at that time. Ne Win concluded the meeting by saying, according to the British record,

> If he had not had faith in Britain he would not have made his visit. All that he had seen over here had impressed him with the value to Burma of Britain's friendship and in the technical field of the help that could be given to the Burmese Armed Forces. He must repeat however that though Burma asked for help from Britain, both material and moral, they could not accept conditions which implied any inferiority on the part of the Union of Burma.[86]

Ne Win and his party remained in Britain until 19 July, when he departed for New York. During that time he had lunch with U Aung Than and Arthur Bottomley, the Labour MP who had participated in the negotiations over the unity of Burma prior to independence.[87]

Before his departure, Ne Win was certainly informed of a welcoming message from the United States Secretary of State, Dean Acheson, to the American embassy in London, that they offer to facilitate him on his journey.[88] He arrived in New York with U Hla Maung and U Than Aung and was met by Mr Daniel Rose and Mr Paul Yee, who were described by an observer as "personal friends".[89] Five days later, Ne Win was in Washington where he called on Secretary of State Acheson at the old State Department Building next to the White House. In the interim, Ne Win and his party apparently visited the Ford Plant at Detroit, facilitated by Ameritex, which sold a DC-3 (Dakota) to Myanmar, probably to Bo Set Kya's private airline, the Burma Civil Aviation Company, during the visit.[90] In making preparations for the meeting, it was suggested to the Secretary of State that he avoid any opportunity for Ne Win to ask for American assistance, as he had apparently hinted in the past.[91]

Acheson did avoid that subject but Assistant Secretary of State George McGhee raised another topic which certainly raised Ne Win's suspicions — whether Burma would join the Commonwealth — a frequent topic in Western governments at that time. Ne Win said it would not happen. The rest of the discussion was very general, though the Point Four legislation, establishing the American foreign assistance programme then progressing through Congress, was mentioned. Ne Win was non-committal on that and indicated that there would be no military alliance with Britain. Ne Win indicated that he had few contacts with the American embassy as he was "not socially inclined" and, furthermore, was very busy with onerous responsibilities.[92] In Washington, Ne Win also met the U.S. Army Chief-of-Staff, General Omar Bradley.[93]

The party left the United States on 28 July. During their time in America, according to the State Department, they apparently did not engage in talks with armament firms.[94] They flew via Paris to Rome,[95] and then occurred one of the hiatuses in the Ne Win record. Hla Maung, Aung Than and Ne Win remained in Italy for nearly a month, with the General not going back till 27 August.[96] Rumours of an Italian connection continued for years after.[97] From March 1949, there were rumours abounding of mysterious Italian weapons arriving in Yangon harbour, though none had been seen at military supply depots. Two curious Italians were said to have arrived in a city which was not then a tourist spot.[98] Whether the Italian arms ever arrived is uncertain, but there were and have been rumours about them ever since.[99] The truth of the matter is, according to Andrew Selth, that U Nu's government purchased machinery from Italy for the manufacture of a submachine gun and Italian engineers came to Yangon to supervise the installation and initial operation of the equipment. By 1953, a slightly modified version of a Second World War Italian gun was the standard submachine gun of the Burma army (Selth 2002, p. 140).

The Burma army was seriously strapped for weapons and was seeking them wherever it could. The American ambassador was then particularly concerned that the bad relations which existed between the BSM and Ne Win might result in the British not supplying the required war materiel. During his trip to London in July, Ne Win allegedly met with Italian arms merchants,[100] and U E Maung, the Burmese foreign minister who followed Ne Win to London for further talks on supplying arms to the additional battalions of Kachin and other frontier area troops previously noted, indicated that Ne Win was in Italy seeking advice on building a munitions factory in Myanmar.[101] The two curious Italians rumoured in March might have been Messrs. Gigante and Spero, who were apparently supplying the Burma navy with river boats from a Long Beach, California company called Korady Marine.[102] The navy was badly in need of small river craft in order to try to retake control of the waterways of the Delta, then largely in the hands of the various insurgent groups.

Though the Burma Navy and Burma Air Force were both under Ne Win's command, he paid little attention to them at the start of the civil war. However, by the end of 1949, he began to take an interest in the Navy and relieved the captaincy of the *Mayu*, a Royal Navy ship given to Burma at independence, from the British-trained Lieutenant Commander Khin Pe Gyi, after an audit of ships records following a refit in Singapore revealed a shortfall in funds matching those found in Khin Pe Gyi's accounts. Members of the pre-war British Indian navy who had stayed in Burma following the Japanese occupation, including Lieutenant Commanders Chit Ko Ko and B.O. Barber, were restored in rank by order of Ne Win, leading to disgruntlement by those officers favoured by the British.[103]

Ne Win's first trip to the West, at least in the eyes of the BSM, changed little in terms of his attitude towards them or theirs towards him. In one review, probably written by General Temple, in mid-August, he was seen as "probably stronger and more ruthless than any potential rival", but the author did "not think he ha[d] the energy or ability to run a successful dictatorship; his regime would probably be corrupt, inefficient and short-lived".[104] More than a week after Ne Win had returned to Yangon, he had not seen Temple[105] and had not produced, together with the War Office, a promised Order of Battle of the Burma Army or a list of required supplies and equipment. Temple was increasingly suspicious that arms were being either sold or leaked to French Indochina where the Vietnamese Communist Party was fighting against the colonial regime.[106] Finally, on 10 September, Temple met Ne Win "for a few minutes only" but would not see him again for a while because of the sitting of the *Hluttaw* (legislature) on the Twelfth[107] as he was preoccupied with political matters. In any event, he had not made up his mind about future policy and remained evasive.[108] Little changed in Ne Win's relationship with Temple in subsequent months, at best described as "cordial but entirely superficial". It normally took Temple ten days to make an appointment with Ne Win.[109]

During the three months of Ne Win's absence abroad and his subsequent preoccupation with Yangon politics, the civil war continued to rage. U Nu's government and Ne Win's army subordinates coped with the situation. However, by March, in the assessment of Prime Minister Nu, the tide had turned in the government's favour and by the end of the year, he could abandon his post to retreat to a meditation centre. Amongst the factors he attributes to the government's success was the loyalty of the remaining armed forces, including the army, police, Union Military Police, and *sitwundan* forces,[110] all of which had been brought under Ne Win's control after he assumed the role of Supreme Commander in February and reinforced by his ministerial roles from April. However, he mentioned no particular individual amongst the armed forces he praised (Nu 1975, pp. 193–95). The achievement by the government to control at least the major towns, and, during the day, the roads between them, was down in part to the growth of the armed forces, believed to have more than doubled in the previous year to about 20,000 men.[111]

By November, relations between Ne Win and the BSM had improved, at least in part because the weapons the Burmese requested more than a year previously had begun to arrive.[112] One might speculate that the coming to power of the Chinese Communists across the border might also have affected Ne Win's views, given his ideas earlier on possible Communist aggression towards a militarily weak Burma. In early November, Ne Win hosted a dinner for all senior British Mission officers and was most cordial towards them. The British speculated that this was because of his trips to the UK and the United States, as well as to Pakistan, which had a large contingent of British trainers as well as officers in command of troops.[113] Ne Win had apparently also requested to visit Hong Kong to study British defences there.[114]

The threat of China was beginning to loom as a reality. The Chinese threat, however, was not so much from Communist Chinese aggression, but possible People's Liberation Army (PLA) attacks on defeated Chinese nationalist troops (KMT) crossing over the border and occupying the area around Kengtung. Pro-Communist militia men chased 100 KMT and the War Office responded by flying by chartered civilian DC-3s Kachin troops to take the surrender of the KMT troops. Prime Minister Nu and General Ne Win then flew to Kengtung together to reassure the local authorities. Ne Win returned to Kengtung again in March and at a press conference reassured the local people, the Burmese nation, and the new Chinese government in Beijing, that the army would ensure that all KMT would be disarmed once they were on Burmese territory (Gibson with Chen 2011, p. 18). Previously, on 17 December, Burma became the first non-Communist government to recognize the People's Republic, but formal diplomatic relations were not established until June the following year and relations were distant until 1954.

In 1948, and especially 1949, the lives of the majority valley- and delta-dwelling population of the country were disrupted in a manner not to be seen again. Villages were razed, towns occupied, trains and buses attacked, bridges blown, schools and hospitals raided, but for all of the chaos, actual casualties were apparently relatively few given the scale of the conflict. No reliable estimates have been made. As Thein Pe Myint described the period, through the eyes of two members of a dacoity gang, as they were making their way home to the Delta from prison in Yangon, and seeing burnt villages all around them,

> During their journey they came across several villages which had been burnt down, and they asked what had happened. Some explained that the Government had set fire to them, and others contradicted them, blaming it on the Communists. Some said it was the White Flag Communists, and others said it was the Red Flags. Some blamed the Karens, and some said "No, it was the Burman." Still others said the White P.V.O. were responsible, others the Government, and so on. But most of the people just said that the villages had been burnt down when they were fighting each other, and Maung Thit felt that this was probably correct.[115]

At the end of the year, General Temple reported that he and Ne Win had a "most cordial interview" and that his attitude was "more realistic and sensible". This was echoed by the British ambassador, noting that two battalions, to Ne Win's pleasure, were now equipped with new British arms.[116] Temple thought that the proposals finally made by the War Office for reorganization of the BSM were sensible. They included reduction of the number of British officers in the War Office; abolition of the adviser to the Southern Command, as already done in the north; the re-establishment of staff at training depots; and the placing of advisors in proposed artillery and armoured regiments.[117] Ne Win's attitude towards the United States and other foreign government's military attachés, all then either neutral or anti-Communist in the growing Cold War, were also more cordial than at any time in the past. He held a stag dinner for them to mark the annual Independence Day and "was especially friendly and cordial" towards the American military attaché.[118] For whatever reason, Ne Win's attitude towards the British and Americans seemed to be open to re-evaluation in changing circumstances.

However, old attitudes change slowly and new problems arise. A review of British military aid to Southeast Asia following Mao's victory in China concluded that Burma was largely a lost cause. Its government was unstable and could fall to the Communists at anytime. Moreover, it was attacking the pro-British Karens, and potentially, if the Arakanese Muslim separatist threat developed further, would destabilize Pakistan. This report inaccurately described the Karen as "a largely Christian, pro-British race of hardy fighting men" who could have been an asset in the defence of Southeast Asia. The crusty thinkers who drafted these words must have come from the pre-independence British Indian Army. They were scandalized when the British ambassador to Burma reported that "the Burmese, from General Ne Win downwards, believe that the British forces will come to their assistance without the formality of prior staff talks or planning, should it become necessary to deal with any external threat to Burma."[119] While old British soldiers would eventually fade away, Chinese Nationalist troops, who began entering the Burmese Shan States in February, about 2,000 of them in the first months of the year, would remain a thorn in Burmese relations with the United States for years to come.

Other Britons were equally dismayed at what they found in the former colony. A delegation of Members of Parliament visited Yangon in January 1950 and met with, amongst others, General Ne Win, over dinner. They found him to be uncommunicative as did the members of the BSM. The delegation could not help but conclude, rather callously, that he would "not or could not put much drive into the war effort, and was especially afraid of casualties. He mentioned, as if it were important, 5 or 6 casualties before [a recent battle to retake] Prome." The subject of recent rumours of a military coup against U Nu's government was also mentioned towards the end of the dinner, and Ne Win did advance the view that the big British firms of Steel Brothers and the Burmah Oil Company were probably financing the effort. There was apparently more truth to the rumours than some believed. In October 1954, Prime Minister Nu told a press conference of a plot involving British business figures which Ne Win reported to him. Apparently the heads of Burmah Oil and other companies were approached, almost certainly by veteran nationalist politician U Ba Pe, for funding to mount a coup.[120] The parliamentarians got more information from their conversations with the BSM, but conceded that its members like to "throw dirt" on Ne Win, such that he had a half share in Burma Civil Aviation Company with Bo Set Kya, perhaps because they did not trust him.[121]

As the insurgency within Myanmar became at least manageable, if not satisfactorily resolved, concern about the larger international situation, following the Communist victory in China began to concern not only the British and the Americans, but also the Burmese government. It shared the same assumptions about the potential threat of Communist aggression and, facing its own internal threat from the two Burmese Communist parties, the possibility of its internal problems becoming connected with international developments seemed very real. However, unlike the British and the Americans, Burma was a neighbour of China, and while the West discussed fighting wars in other people's countries, the Burmese were worried about wars being fought in theirs. Burma in 1950 had suffered nearly a decade of armed conflict, two major campaigns by world powers on its territory, and persistent low-level insurgency. The economy remained in tatters and much of the population dislocated, at least temporarily. In such circumstances, it is not surprising that personnel responsible for the defence of the internationally recognized government of Burma began to reconsider their options. U Nu had declared that Burma would be neutral in the Cold War, describing Burma as a "tender gourd amongst the thorns". However, neutrality might not always be sufficient against a determined opponent.

On 14 February 1950, U Aung Than (Bo Set Kya) discussed with an official of the United States embassy the possibility, advanced by Aung Than on behalf of Deputy Prime Minister General Ne Win, of entering into an alignment between Burma and the United States, and the West more generally, including the British. Concern was raised about the depth and ability of the British commitment to Burma. In exchange for the alignment, Burma would expect "long-range assistance including loans, military supplies and technicians, and Point Four type [technical development] assistance".[122] According to U Aung Than, "concrete proposals" were being "worked out by Ne Win group" who were confident that the government and the AFPFL leadership would accept the proposals if the Americans were interested. In the view of the embassy, this proposal chimed with earlier intimations of Ne Win's pro-West orientation.[123]

This tentative and semi-formal approach to the Americans by a trusted confidant of Ne Win, however, threatened to become enmeshed in a new intrigue in which domestic ethnic politics once more became entangled in international relations, raising the suspicions of Ne Win and others about the reliability and interests of foreign governments. The case of Dr Gordon Seagrave had come to Ne Win's attention. Seagrave, an American medical missionary from a family with deep missionary connections in Myanmar going back generations, was an egotistical self-publicist who had a sizeable following in the United States.[124] During the fighting in 1948–49, his hospital in Namkhan near the Chinese border was occupied by Kachin mutineers led by Captain Naw Seng.

The government was convinced that Seagrave was giving aid and succour to the rebels. The American embassy reported two days after a military confrontation between the government and rebel troops at Seagrave's hospital that Ne Win would approach them with evidence to that effect upon his return from touring northern Myanmar on 17 February. Deportation of the long-time missionary was the desired outcome from the Burmese perspective but the government did not want a scandal and Seagrave was persuaded to come to Yangon for discussions.[125] It was not Ne Win however, but the Permanent Secretary of the Foreign Office who produced the government's evidence.[126] Seagrave was eventually arrested by one Ali Hussein,[127] tried, convicted, released, and remained in Burma until his death in 1965 (the only full account is Clymer 2012, pp. 245–91).

Despite the opening of the Seagrave fracas by Nu and Ne Win, the latter remained publicly open to assistance and cooperation with the United States. The message that U Aung Than conveyed to the American embassy was reiterated, without the offer of an alliance or even an outline of details, by Ne Win in an interview with *New York Times* journalist Robert Trumbull on 6 March.[128] Despairing of the BSM, Ne Win indicated to Trumbull that he would like the Americans to take over the training tasks of the Burma army, though it was believed that he would give the Americans no more than the limited supervisory roles that he had given to the British. He believed that the Burma army was doing a better job of fighting the insurgents than what the British army, with their advanced equipment, was doing in Malaya.

When Trumbull mentioned the Anglo-Burmese officers in the army, Ne Win replied, "People with mixed blood may have mixed loyalties." Ne Win also criticized American press coverage of the KNDO and the Karen cause. U Nu refused to grant Trumbull an interview, despite his central position in reporting Burma to an important American audience. But Ne Win went to great length to make himself available, taking the *New York Times* reporter on a three-day tour of upper Burma, even sharing a room with him at various army camps.[129]

Ne Win's courting of the United States government, or their courting of him, was raised to another level when he met with a mission led by R. Allen Griffin that was touring Southeast Asia to assess the level of American military and economic assistance that was required "to shore up" the region. As U Nu was unavailable to receive Griffin, and the recently arrived United States ambassador, David McK. Key, it fell to Ne Win to do so. McKey was "impressed" by the General's "statesman-like attitude" and "apparently sincere desire [to] unify and strengthen Burma". They discussed current efforts to reach a settlement with the KNDO. Recognizing the threat posed to Burma by Communist China, Ne Win "stated he realized [the] danger to [the] country from any group embittered against [the] government" and his government sought to "restore unity within [the] country against [the] growing threat from Chinese Communists".[130]

Ne Win's role in U Nu's cabinet continued to grow and his involvement in foreign policy was becoming more apparent daily, but his ambitions were thought to be limited. In an assessment by the British ambassador, he was said to lack the "drive" of General Aung San and had "too much common sense and perhaps too little determination to make a dictator".[131] An American embassy assessment suggested, however, that "More recent evidence suggests that the General's capacity for self-abnegation may have been over-estimated." Rumours abounded that he was about to oust Nu from the Prime Ministership with Socialist backing,[132] and a press account to that effect led to the arrest of the publisher and editor of *Bama Hkit*,[133] presumably on the orders of the Home Minister, General Ne Win.[134] Whether it was Ne Win's order, as speculated, or not, the government order issued by the Foreign Ministry on 31 March that all diplomats provide full details "well in advance" of all journeys outside Yangon irked the embassies. The rationale, of course, was to ensure that the security situation in the area made it safe for them to travel.[135] With regard to policymaking in the government and cabinet, the American embassy was convinced that while the Socialists, particularly Kyaw Nyein, were key players, they could only do so "with the cooperation and consent of General Ne Win".[136]

Soon after the issuance of the order regarding diplomatic travel, Ne Win led a delegation of military attachés on a five-day visit to the Mandalay-Maymyo-Meiktila triangle. He assured them that the KNDO rebellion was now under control, though there would be resistance by "die-hard elements" for a long time to come.[137] On the trip and after, he talked affably with the American military attaché and explained the army's plans to retake Pyay from the BCP and White Flag PVOs. Intelligence indicated that the two groups were quarrelling with each other and their defence of the city would be slight. Though Ne Win made no request for American military assistance, he indicated repeatedly the shortage of equipment from which his troops suffered noting the need for vehicles, wireless equipment, Bailey bridges, and personal kit.[138] Indeed, the Americans were about to offer assistance, but in the form of coastal defence vessels. Nu's plan, mooted nearly a year before to arm ten battalions from the frontier areas, had yet to find a sponsor, as far as the British knew.[139]

In the midst of all the high and low politics that Ne Win was involved in during the civil war, he still found time for his family and associates from earlier times. His former leader in the *Dobama Asiayon*, the inveterate dabbler in right-wing politics, Thakin Ba Sein, was arrested for illegal contacts with the KNDO and detained in Insein Prison in 1950. Ne Win took time to visit him in prison when he went there for business (Sein Tin 2011, pp. 130–31).

Ne Win's cool relations with the British and apparent warm relations towards the Americans was underscored in a meeting he had with George Herman, a senior reporter from CBS news. Herman reported that Ne Win was "extremely hostile to Great Britain" and claimed to have proof that the British were supplying arms to the KNDO, even by submarine off the Tanintharyi coast.[140] When Malcolm MacDonald, the recently appointed British Commissioner-General for Southeast Asia, came to Yangon, Ne Win apparently made sure he was out of town. However, Nu wanted Ne Win to meet MacDonald, who subsequently stayed another day in order to join Nu and Ne Win on a river cruise.[141] MacDonald, with Bowker's apparent agreement, conceded to Ne Win that disloyal British officers in the BSM should be transferred to other posts but without being considered guilty of any offence or demoted in rank.[142] This was the first evidence of an attempt by a British official to deal with the doubtful loyalties of British officers. It was the beginning of a fairly friendly relationship between the General and the loquacious, fun loving, son of Britain's first Labour Prime Minister.

Ne Win indicated that he did not object to taking advice from the BSM but did not trust them when fighting against the KNDO. His confidence in the BSM was sapped by disloyal talk from Mission members, but he was still willing to discuss with the Ambassador the ten battalions scheme that he and Nu had advanced nearly a year before but upon which the British had taken no decision.[143] By then, the BSM had nearly half as many officers as at its peak.[144] In a lengthy discussion with Ambassador Bowker,

Ne Win explained that five of the ten battalions proposed had been raised and armed with weapons from India and Pakistan. They were initially under the control of a committee of frontier area leaders but they had proven unable to provide sufficient officers. They, and five more battalions yet to be raised, would be brought under the Burma Army Order of Battle and officered by regular army men. Lists of the required equipment had been provided to Prime Minister Nu, who was about to depart on a visit to London.[145] While in London, Nu too raised his own misgivings about the loyalty of BSM members and disappointed Prime Minister Atlee by insisting that rebel Karen troops should not be re-enlisted into the Burma army.[146] Though they may have expressed themselves differently, Nu and Ne Win were in agreement on the fundamentals of the civil war and relations with the British. After Nu's departure, Ne Win went off on holiday with General Temple and all the foreign military attachés at the old British hill station at Kalaw.[147]

Relations between the Western powers and Burma, especially Ne Win, were soon to be tested. On 8 June, Burma established diplomatic relations with Communist China, the sixteenth country to do so. On 14 June, Ne Win met with the United States military attaché at Kengtung in the Eastern Shan State to discuss the problem of marauding Chinese Nationalist (KMT) still entering Myanmar territory from Yunnan. At that time, the Burma Army was fighting KMT troops which had occupied Tachilek on the Myanmar–Thai border, retaking the town only on 21 July (Gibson with Chen 2011, p. 19 *et passim*). Ne Win reported at that time that the KMT were scattered and trying to enter Thailand and Laos, though a few had surrendered and been disarmed.[148] On 25 June, the Korean War began. These events were not unrelated and were to vex relations until the end of the Cold War.

The first reaction was from the Americans. The Griffin Mission had concluded in May that the entire Southeast Asia required little in terms of American assistance and recommended a mere US$60 million in military and economic assistance.[149] Another mission, the Melby Mission, a cover for a military mission led by Major General Graves B. Erskine and six, later sixteen, other officers from the army, navy and air force, was launched as the United States went on high alert about possible "Communist aggression" in Asia immediately after the start of the Korean War.[150] The Mission intended to visit Southeast Asia in order to assess how the United States could bolster the region's anti-Communist military forces. Ne Win also became more positive about the BSM following the start of the war, indicating not only that he did not wish the Mission to end, but that he would be using it more in future.[151]

The Korean War had other repercussions within Myanmar. When U Nu's government voted to support United Nations' action against North Korea, the left wing of the Socialists resigned and formed the Burma Workers' and Peasants' Party (BWPP), from then on known as the above-ground Communists, eventually transmogrifying into the National United Front (NUF). According to U Win, Ne Win's successor as Ministers of Home Affairs and Defence, the BWPP leadership approached Ne Win to join them, and when it was rumoured that Win had ordered their arrest, Ne Win "rushed round to see him and inquire if this was true". Ne Win then said cryptically "that the party had 'double crossed' him, and he would have nothing more to do with them".[152]

As the Cold War heated up and the military position of the government of Burma continued to improve, Ne Win went on a brief excursion to Singapore and Indonesia. With a party of ten, including U Hla Maung, who was presenting his credentials as ambassador to Indonesia, Ne Win first called at Singapore where he stayed at the Raffles Hotel. He declined to stay with MacDonald at his residence because of the size of his party but promised to call on him on his return. After dining with two Chinese bank managers and visiting the Great World Amusement Park, they went on to Bandung and Bali.[153] Ne Win met with the new Indonesian President and national hero, Sukarno, but mainly holidayed at Bali.[154]

After his visit to Indonesia, Ne Win was soon back at work in Yangon, agreeing with Temple on a plan to reorganize the BSM.[155] However, his meetings with the Americans were less cordial. On 10 August, he met with Colonel Thomas M. Davies, the American military attaché, and protested "against American meddling in Kengtung area". He noted that an official from the American embassy in Bangkok had visited the area for several days without permission from the government of Burma; another officer from the American military attaché's office in Bangkok visited the area; and the Bangkok air force attaché's aeroplane was spotted flying over Kengteng, far off its usual route from Bangkok to Yangon. The American ambassador was seeking information on what was going on in Bangkok and the Shan States from Washington.[156] In the same interview, Ne Win said that the Melby Mission would not be welcomed in Myanmar.[157]

In Ne Win's mind, the Melby Mission, and the prospect of American assistance, was now tied to his domestic military problems, just as the BSM had been linked to the KNDO insurrection and Karen Rifles mutinies.

While Ne Win claimed that the KMT had been reduced to fewer than a hundred men, they were tying up troops needed elsewhere. He apparently advocated, along with a majority in the cabinet, taking the KMT issue to the United Nations for an early resolution,[158] against the wishes of Nu and the Foreign Minister, who were being pressed by the British and Americans not to do so. The Melby Mission, Ne Win evidenced, was an example of American high-handedness, sending a mission without prior consultation and allowing it to be used in KNDO propaganda as evidence of Western support for their cause.[159] The arrest of Dr Gordon Seagrave came in the midst of the fracas over the KMT and the Melby Mission.[160] The Mission intended to arrive in Yangon on 21 August. Instead, it was cancelled on the same day. At the time, Prime Minister U Nu was out of Yangon on a meditation retreat, and Ne Win was the Acting Prime Minister and Minister of Defence. He made it clear to the American embassy that neither he nor any other Burmese officer would attend a reception the Mission planned to host and only members of the British Service Mission would be present. Therefore, the embassy recommended that the mission be cancelled.[161] Malcolm MacDonald noted that indeed there was talk in Yangon that the Melby Mission was coming to assist the KNDO and that a defence pact with Thailand had already been agreed.[162] The American embassy was in no doubt that the cancellation of the Mission was due to the KMT issue, Seagrave's arrest, the manner in which the Melby Mission was proposed, and the behaviour of American personnel from Bangkok in Kengtung State.[163] To some extent, however, the Americans remained convinced that Ne Win was fundamentally pro-American. However, for both domestic and international political reasons, neither he, nor the government of U Nu, could be seen as entering into an alliance with the United States.[164] In September, the United States government provided US$8 to US$10 million of military assistance to Burma, primarily in the form of ten river patrol boats.[165]

On 11 September, after U Nu returned from his meditation retreat, it was announced that Ne Win, unexpectedly to some, had resigned from the cabinet, retaining only his military post as Commander-in-Chief.[166] It was said that there were strong areas of disagreement over policy between Ne Win and Prime Minister Nu which contributed to Ne Win's frustration in office. Bo Set Kya, who described Ne Win as having an "unsteady head and heart", claimed that he advised Ne Win to resign and devote himself solely to military matters.[167] Bo Set Kya, however, also confided that the "motive underlying" his resignation was his "infatuation [with a] married

woman with whom he had been involved for many months and whom he
now desires [to] marry".[168] Ne Win's departure from the cabinet was said
to have resulted in much less emotion in policymaking and a more stable
government, at least from the perspectives of the British and the Americans.[169]
Two days later, the government of Burma signed a friendship treaty with
the United States and four days later, Ne Win issued the following Order
of the Day to the armed forces:

> You will remember that I took Office in the Ministry in April last
> year with no other aim than the restoration of peace in the country.
> As a result of this I have been shouldering the heavy responsibilities
> of a Minister besides those of the Supreme Commander and the
> Chief of General Staff. In consequence, I could not devote as much
> time and attention to the Union Armed Forces as I feel I should.
>
> Now that conditions have improved a great deal I consider the
> time has come for me to be relieved of the extra heavy responsibilities
> in order that I may devote my whole time to the Armed Forces.
> I have accordingly tendered my resignation from the Ministry and the
> resignation has been accepted.
>
> I ought to mention that usually on such occasions, mischievous
> rumours are spread either unwittingly or on purpose. I wish all
> Officers and men of the Union Armed Forces to pay no heed to such
> rumours, bearing in mind that the sole reason for my resignation is
> as stated above.
>
> I wish to stress above all the point that the devotion of my whole
> time as Supreme Commander of the Armed Forces will enable me and
> all Officers and men of the Forces to contribute all the more toward
> the country's stability.
>
> I greatly appreciate your trust and confidence in me and I am
> fully confident that with your cooperation and devotion to duty
> and unswerving loyalty to the Union, I will be able to achieve the
> following three objects which I laid down before assuming Office
> last year:
>
> (1) To help hold free elections as soon as possible.
> (2) To restore peace by any means, and
> (3) To resist and suppress any attempt to seize power by violence.[170]

Following Ne Win's resignation, the British and American embassies speculated
at length on Ne Win's alleged aversion to politics and administrative duties.
There was agreement that he and U Nu had differed over the acceptance

of the Melby Mission and whether the KMT issue should be taken to the United Nations. Soon, speculation that Ne Win might be planning a coup against Nu once more appeared, with an implausible story that Ne Win had asked a former Prime Minister, possibly Sir Paw Tun or maybe U Ba Pe, what the American and British reactions to a coup would be.[171] Ne Win was at that time busy consolidating the armed forces for planned operations against the various insurgent groups in both the northern and southern commands in the following January.[172] Washington was keen, as a consequence, for the American embassy's views on the nature of any possible Ne Win dominated government.[173] Speculation continued, but the only hard evidence of Ne Win's views came in a "lengthy and frank conversation" with the U.S. military attaché in late November. At that time, Ne Win drew a parallel between the levels of graft and corruption in the police and government of Burma and that of the former Kuomintang government of China. Only the Communists would benefit from Burma's problems, as happened in China, suggesting implicitly that one of the reasons he had resigned from the cabinet was from a distaste at the corruption he had observed there.[174]

Woodrow Wyatt, the visiting Labour member of parliament and prolific journalist, who had visited Myanmar during the height of the civil war, subsequently wrote a volume on conditions he found there. His observation that "the Burmans were unconscious that they were fighting one of the decisive battles of the post-war world" deserves more consideration than it has received. If Ne Win had failed to keep the Burma army loyal to the government of U Nu, Nu would have had to turn to the British for assistance which was unlikely to be given. The United States, however, would, as it did in Korea and French Indochina, most likely have stepped in to support Nu. Had this happened, the history of Cold War in Southeast Asia would have been completely changed. Wyatt's further comment that "certainly most of the West was oblivious of the fact" also rings true (Wyatt 1952, p. 106). Ne Win was in the middle of that decisive battle of the early Cold War. Though fought only in Myanmar, and with scant support and much opposition from Western sources, the Burma Army was able to keep U Nu's government in place not only against the Communists, but also the KNDO. Wyatt reminded his readers that the Communists might have ridden on the back of the KNDO to seize power. Those who accused Ne Win of being disloyal to Prime Minister Nu and a crypto Communist, would have to revise their views.

Notes

1. The Geographer, Office of the Geographer, Bureau of Intelligence and Research, United States Department of State, *International Boundary Study No. 42, Burma-China Boundary* (Washington, D.C.: 30 November 1964), p. 6.

2. See Colin Metcalf Dallas Enriquez, *The Races of Burma, Compiled under the Orders of the Government of India* (New York: AMS Press, 1981, reprint of 2nd ed., published Delhi: Manager of Publications, 1933). This recruiting manual for the Indian Army is available today in tourist shops across Myanmar. The implications for notions of primordialism of a British Indian army officer, a Major, with the name Enriquez, apparently never troubled him.

3. The Sawbwa of Yaunghwe, following Thakin Nu's joining the Governor's Executive Committee after General Aung San' assassination, was elected President of the Constituent Assembly. This decision was not welcomed by Governor Rance, who believed that "one of his major failings is that he is unable to express himself in Shan, Burmese or English." Hugh Tinker, ed., *Burma: The Struggle for Independence, Documents from Official and Private Sources, Volume II: From General Strike to Independence, 31 August 1946 to 4 January 1948* (London: Her Majesty's Stationery Office, 1984), Document 478, Telegram, Sir Hubert Rance to the Earl of Listowel, 31 July 1947, IOR: M/4/2719, pp. 705–6.

4. In ideological terms, the difference between the Communists and the Socialists hinged on an argument as to whether Myanmar was genuinely independent after 1948. While some would see the presence of the British Services Mission as evidence of a constraint on independence, after 1954, that was no longer an issue. However, the Communists continued to see U Nu's, and subsequently Ne Win's, governments in class terms as the tools of the "big bourgeoisie and landlord classes". See Thein Pe Myint, *Critique of the Communist Movement in Burma* (Yangon: mimeographed, circa 1967), pp. 27–29.

5. Many authors have overstated the degree to which Myanmar adopted military autarky after independence. See, for example, Odd Arne Westad, *The Global Cold War* (Cambridge: Cambridge University Press, 2007), p. 98.

6. Telegram, Bowker to Bevin, 26 February 1948, FO371/69482. Burma, unlike India and Pakistan where large numbers remained in command for up to a decade after independence, dispensed with all British officers at independence. Hugh Tinker, *The Union of Burma: A Study of the First Years of Independence,* 4th ed. (London: Oxford University Press, 1967), p. 322.

7. Old attitudes and prejudices amongst the small British community in Myanmar persisted into independence, as in the choice of Indians and Anglo-Indians

to staff the British Council in preference to Burmese. Report on a Visit to Burma by Mr J.A. Pilcher during a Tour of Information Posts in the Far East, January 1948, FO953/280.

8. Note on the Future of the British Services Mission to Burma, 15 May 1948, FO371/69482.

9. Bertil Linter provides a very helpful summary of the political and military developments during the early years of independence in "Appendix 2, Burma's Civil Strife — A Chronology", in *Burma in Revolt: Opium and Insurgency since 1948*, 2nd ed., edited by Bertil Lintner (Chiang Mai: Silkworm Books, 1999), pp. 431–41. A useful chart of the first years of the insurgency is found in *Burma and the Insurrections* (Rangoon: Government of Burma, 1949), pp. 59–63. Tinker, *Union of Burma*, provides maps and lists of dates that cities were taken by various insurgent groups, pp. 44–45 and *passim*.

10. The event had been postponed until after independence.

11. Telegram, Rangoon to Foreign Office, 29 May 1948, and Telegram, Bowker to Foreign Office, 12 June 1948, both in FO371/69482. The BSM at its peak membership in June 1948 had 117 officers, 67 non-commissioned officers, and 14 other ranks. Information in FO371/83175.

12. Letter, A.V. Alexander (Freeman's successor as Defense Minister) to Bevin, 24 June 1948, DEFE 7/159. See also papers in FO371/69483 on the "go slow" policy.

13. Telegram, British Services Mission to War Office, 5 July 1948, FO271/69483.

14. Telegram, Acly to Secretary of State (SOS), 30 July 1948, 845C.00/7-3048, Control 10643, No. 324.

15. *Thihmat Hpweiya Koyei: AchetAlatmya* [Biographical Information for Recalling] (N.p.: N.p., N.d.).

16. Telegram, BSM to War Office, 6 August 1948, FO371/69484.

17. Telegram, Acly to SOS, 30 July 1948, 845C.00/7-3048, Control 10643, No. 324.

18. Telegram, BSM to War Office, 10 August 1948, FO372/69484; Chit Myaing, "In His Own Words", *Burma Debate*, vol. IV, no. 3 (July/August 1997): 14.

19. DR 9453, Interview with Col. Chit Myaing for the History of the Tatmadaw, p. 50, quoted in Aung Myoe, *Building the Tatmadaw: Myanmar Armed Forces Since 1948* (Singapore: Institute of Southeast Asian Studies, 2009), p. 4.

20. Tun Hla Aung was the most senior officer who possessed a King's Commission in the British Army and a son of U May Oung, the first Minister under the diarchy constitution introduced in 1923.

21. *Thihmat Hpweiya Koyei: AchetAlatmya* [Biographical Information for Recalling]; Telegram, Acly to SOS, 14 August 1948, 845C.00/8-1448, No. 359; Telegram, BSM to War Office, 14 August 1948, FO/371/69484.

Writing more than fifty years after these events, former Brigadier Maung Maung claimed that Ne Win's promotion at this time was designed to keep him from joining the Communists and subverting the government of Prime Minister Nu. In his account, Ne Win was negotiating with the Communist just before the PVO split and the White Flags went underground to form a new National Government with Thakin Than Tun as Prime Minister, after a possible period of having a non-Communist figure head front man, and Ne Win as Defence Minister. As Ne Win was indiscreetly discussing this possibility with his subordinates, words leaked to U Nu who reacted by flattering Ne Win and offering the promotion and the Thadomaha Thiri Thudhamma title on the anniversary of the first independence day. Maung Maung, "Some Aspects of the 'Caretaker Government' 1958–1960: An Experiment in Democratic Process", unpublished manuscript, pp. 23–24. Maung Maung's account is skewed and does not fit with the accounts of Colonel Chit Myaing or the details in the study by Dr Aung Myoe.

22. Telegram, BSM to War Office, 21 August 1948, FO371/69484; Telegram, Bowker to FO, 31 August 1948, FO371/69484.

23. General Bourne (1902–82), prior to his year in Myanmar, had served in Hong Kong, the War Office in London, and the Joint Planning Staff in Washington, D.C., at the beginning of the Second World War. During the war, he fought in Italy and Belgium, before being posted as commander of the Fifth Indian Division in Java. After Myanmar, he was Commandant of the British sector of Berlin and commander British Forces Eastern Section, Malaya and the Middle East before retiring. After servicing as Aide-de-Camp General to Her Majesty the Queen, he was made a life peer as Baron Bourne of Atherstone.

24. Telegram, BSM to War Office, 25 August 1948, FO371/69484.

25. Telegram, Bowker to Bevin, 31 August 1948, FO371/69484 or DEFE7/159.

26. Review of the Situation in Burma on 14 September 1948, FO371/69485 or DEFE7/863.

27. Telegram, Bourne to Packard, War Office, 18 September 1948, FO371/69485. One commentator wrote of Smith Dun, he "was a man of little ability, and proved unable to enforce command over forces riddled with political intrigue, or to restore discipline". Letter, Edwin Haward, Secretary, India, Pakistan and Burma Association, 8 May 1950, to J.D. Murray, enclosing Who's Who in Burma, FO 371/83117. In contrast, Mr Haward wrote that Ne Win "has been for the past year the virtual dictator of the part of Burma which acknowledges the authority of the central government".

28. Letter, Bowker to Bevin, 18 September 1948, FO371/69485.

29. Third Quarterly Report of the British Services Mission, 30 September 1948 by G.K. Bourne, DEFE7/863.

30. Telegram, Foreign Office to Rangoon, 25 September 1948, DEFE 7/159.

31. Letter, Bowker to Foreign Office, 15 September 1948, FO371/69485.

32. Telegram, Acly to SOS, 10 September 1948, 845C.00/9-1048, Control 3125, No. 408.

33. Malcolm Muggeridge, *Like It Was* (London: Collins, 1981), pp. 310–11. The diary entry is for 30 November 1948.

34. Raymond Campagnac, the Anglo-Burmese led troops of the Fifth Burma Rifles against both the *Mujahid* and Communists in Rakhine for which he was decorated. Charles Haswell Campagnac, *The Autobiography of a Wanderer in England and Burma* (Raleigh, North Carolina: Sandra L. Carney, 2010), pp. 309–10.

35. Report on conversation with Pakistan Defence Secretary, 24 October 1948, WO208/3824.

36. Telegram, Key to SOS, 16 June 1950, 7908.00(W)/6-1650, Control 5728, No. 202.

37. Telegram, Rangoon to SOS, 1 October 1948, DEFE7/159.

38. Telegram, Bourne to Packard, War Office, 25 October 1948, FO371/69686.

39. Telegram, Bourne to Packard, War Office, 9 November 1948, FO371/69486.

40. Aung Myoe, *Building the Tatmadaw*, p. 4. An alternative version of this decision was provided by his son, Dr Seng Li. According to page 117 of an unknown publication shown to the author, the Sama Duwa Sinwa Nawng was the "Defence Minister for emergency measure". According to his son, this was done on or about 31 January 1949.

41. When Nu dismissed Let Ya, he briefly joined the army at the rank of brigadier but was soon placed on indefinite leave.

42. For example, a so-called "Operation Aung San" was alleged to have been ordered by the army high command with the intent of killing all Kayin soldiers. Spencer Zan, *Life's Journey in Faith: Burma, from Riches to Rags* (Bloomington, Indiana: Author House, 2007), pp. 126, 144–45.

43. Lazum Tang had fought with the American Office of Strategic Services Detachment 101 against the Japanese during the Second World War and raised several battalions of the Kachin Rifles during 1949 and 1950.

44. The full story is told in Lintner, *Burma in Revolt*.

45. Acly to SOS, 23 February 1949, 845C.00(W)/2-2349, Control 9550, No. 63.

46. Telegram, Temple to Foreign Office for Ministry of Defence, 22 Feburary 1949, DEFE7/160.

47. Composed of less than 5,000 armed Communists; more than 4,800 Karen and other ethnic minority army mutineers; 2,000 Union Military Police; over 1,700 other police and police reserves; and over 1,500 locally organized protection forces. Thakin Nu, *From Peace to Stability* (Rangoon: Ministry of Information, 1951), p. 202.

48. Speech by U Nu on 27 February 1949, in *Toward Peace and Democracy* (Rangoon: Ministry of Information, 1949), p. 182.

49. During the height of the Civil War, Ne Win maintained an air of confidence and went about his life as much as possible as if there was no crisis. He kept his box at the Rangoon Turf Club and attended the races as usual on Sundays. However, during the day officers such as Colonel Kyi Law would arrive at the races and Ne Win and he would withdraw to the men's room where they studied maps of the battle zone and Ne Win would issue instructions. Telegram, Rangoon to SOS, 23 February 1949, 845C.00(W)/2-2349, Control 9550, No. 63.

50. *Thihmat Hpweya Koyei: AchetAlatmya* [Biographical Information for Recalling].

51. Interview in Thuriya, 26 February 1949, cited in Maung Maung, *Burma and General Ne Win* (London: Asia Publishing House, 1969), p. 210. Ne Win discussed the approach of U Ba Pe to him in 1949 in an address in 1969. *Address Delivered by General Ne Win, Chairman of the Burma Socialist Programme Party, at the Opening Session of the Fourth Party Seminar on 6th November 1969* (Yangon: Burma Socialist Programme Party, November 1969), p. 17.

52. Former Foreign Minister Admiral (retired) Chit Hlaing was personal assistant to Set Kya in 1949. One evening he suggested they drink champagne. The proposal was accepted and he was sent out to a shop to buy the champagne for them. He convinced the shopkeeper that the champagne was for the president, subsequently joking with Ne Win that he appointed him president before anyone else. Interview, Admiral (retired) Chit Hlaing, 12 March 2006.

53. Telegram, Rangoon to SOS, 21 March 1949, 845C.00/3-2149, Control 8370, No. 106.

54. Letter, Colonel Berger to Director of Military Intelligence, 7 December 1955, FO371/123315.

55. "Thakin Than Tun's Speech of Greetings to the 2nd Congress of the Communist Party of India", Asia Research Institute, National University of Singapore, Documentary Database, The Cold War in Asia (1945–1980), available at <http://www.ari.nus.edu.sg/docs/SEA-China-interactions-Cluster/TheColdWarInAsia/1948%20Thakin%20Than%20Tuns%20Speech%20of%20Greetings%20to%20the%202nd%20Congress%20of%20the%20Communist%20Party%20of%20India.pdf>.

56. Airgram, Huddle to SOS, 11 April 1949, 845C.002/4949/3473, Airgram 135.

57. Brief Summary of Report on Southeast Asia by Woodrow Wyatt, MP, reached the Foreign Office on 1 April 1949, CO 825/75/4.

58. A Cambridge University graduate, and an old boy of Framlingham College, he succeeded his father in 1937 as Sawbwa of Mongmit. His wife, Mabel, was the daughter of an East London green grocer whom he allegedly met on one of his visits to the New Market racetrack. He, Mabel, and several

large dogs were the point of much unofficial memo writing in the Burma Office after his father insisted he return home without Mabel. He refused and eventually his father relented. Mabel will appear again below.

59. Note, Cripps to Prime Minister, 20 April 1949, FO 371/75682.
60. Telegram, Huddle to SOS, 20 April 1949, 845C.00/4-2049, Control 7513, No. 142.
61. Telegram, Bowker to FO, 20 April 1949, DEFE 7/160.
62. Telegram, Bevin to Bowker, 21 April 1949, FO 371/75682.
63. Telegram, BSM head to Minister of Defense, 20 April 1949, DEFE 7/160.
64. Telegram, Bowker to FO, 29 April 1949, DEFE 7/160.
65. For an account of the final battle, see Maung Maung, "The Mighty Drama", in *Dr. Maung Maung: Gentleman, Scholar, Patriot*, edited by Robert H. Taylor (Singapore: Institute of Southeast Asian Studies, 2008), pp. 395–98.
66. Airgram, Stanton, Bangkok, to SOS, 8 June 1949, 845C.00/6-649, Airgram 2902, A-221.
67. Letter, Temple to Permanent Secretary, Ministry of Defence, 6 June 1949, Appendix B: Note on the Character of General Ne Win, DEFE 7/865.
68. The Future Functions and Organisation of the British Services Mission to Burma by Major General Temple, 7 June 1949, DEFE 7/161.
69. Second Quarterly Report of BSM, 30 June 1949, by Temple, DEFE 7/865.
70. Telegram, Bowker to FO, 15 June 1949, FO371/75682.
71. Telegram, Bowker to FO, 16 June 1949, FO371/75682.
72. Telegram, Crombie to FO, 27 June 1949, FO371/75682.
73. Telegram, Huddle to SOS, 17 June 1949, 845C.00(W)/6-1749, Control 7599, No. 246.
74. Telegram, Huddle to SOS, 27 June 1949, 845C.002/6-2749, Control 11310, No. 256.
75. Telegram, Douglas (London) to SOS, 1 July 1949, 845C.002/7-149, Control 589, No. 2562.
76. Telegram, Huddle to SOS, 5 July 1949, 845C.002/7-549, Control 1289, No. 273.
77. Telegram, Huddle to SOS, 13 July 1949, 845C.002/7-1349, Control 4548, No. 279.
78. Telegram, Huddle to SOS, 8 July 1949, 845C.002(W)/7-849, Control 2819, No. 277.
79. Not included in the British notes on the visit but mentioned in Maung Maung, *Burma and General Ne Win*, p. 216.
80. Note in FO 371/75682.
81. Bo Set Kya; for reasons that will become clear later in this volume, Dr Maung Maung makes no mention of U Aung Than in the party. Maung Maung, *Burma and General Ne Win*, p. 245.
82. Ne Win also met with Ernest Bevin, Foreign Secretary, A.V. Alexander, Defence Minister, Emanuel Shinwell, War Minister, Arthur Henderson,

Air Minister, and Sir William Slim, Chief of the Imperial General Staff, but not with the Chancellor of the Exchequer, Sir Stafford Cripps. Letter, Atlee to Nu, 4 August 1949, CAB 127/151.

83. The following discussion is based on Annex to Notes on Meeting held in the Minister of Defence Rooms, House of Commons, 5:30 p.m., 12 July 1949, DEFE 7/161.

84. This was indeed what the Ambassador told U Nu. Thakin Nu, *U Nu — Saturday's Son*, translated by Law Yone and edited by Kyaw Win (New Haven and London: Yale University Press, 1975), pp. 183–84. The proposal originated in a meeting in Delhi between the Indian Prime Minister, the Australian External Affairs Minister, the British Secretary for Overseas Trade (Bottomley), the Ceylonese High Commissioner to India, and the British Commissioner General in Southeast Asia (MacDonald). Uma Shankar Singh, *Burma and India, 1948–1962* (New Delhi: Oxford and IBH Publishing, 1979), p. 54. This meeting was the first of a series which eventually ended in the formation of the Colombo Plan to provide economic assistance to Burma, and developing Commonwealth countries, from developed Commonwealth countries and the United States. See Ademola Adeke, "The Strings of Neutralism: Burma and the Colombo Plan", *Pacific Affairs*, vol. 76, no. 4 (Winter 2003–04): 593–610. See also Nicholas Tarling, *Britain, Southeast Asia and the Onset of the Cold War 1945–1950* (Cambridge: Cambridge University Press, 1998), pp. 348–51.

85. Nu's account of this episode does not contradict Ne Win's version, though he, customarily, puts the blame on himself for being rude. Nu, *U Nu — Saturday's Son*, pp. 183–84.

86. Notes on meeting held in the Minister of Defence Rooms, House of Commons, 5:30 p.m., 12 July 1949, 13 July 1949, DEFE 7/161.

87. At the lunch, U Aung Than pointed out that the locally employed staff of the British embassy were all former civil servants and this did not inspire trust between the embassy and Burmese government ministers. Note from Authur Bottomley to Secretary of State Bevin, 18 July 1949, FO 371/75684.

88. Telegram, SOS to London, 12 July 1949, 845C.002/7-1245, Control 4168, No. 2713.

89. Memo, James P. Cavanagh, Special Agent, Division of Security and Investigations, State Department, New York City, 25 July 1949, 845C.002/7-2549 CS/H, 188946. Mr Rose was in fact an arms dealer who after the Second World War supplied used and surplus equipment to many governments. I met him once over tea at the Ritz Hotel in London in about 1987 and he expressed dismay at Ne Win's socialist government. However, he also expressed great admiration for the independence movement in Burma and the role of the army in maintaining Burma's independence. He described himself in the late 1940s as being a great supporter of liberation movements and had special attachments to Israel.

90. Notes in FO371/75684; Telegram, SOS to Rangoon, 2 August 1949, 845C.002/8-249 CS/J, Control 398. The DC-3 was apparently subsequently sold to the government.

91. Memo from Mr McGhee to SOS, meeting with Ne Win at 2:15 p.m., 25 July 1949, 845C.002/7-2549 CS/A, 003277.

92. Memo by Acheson on Ne Win visit, 25 July 1949, 845C.002/7-2549 CS/N, 0043347; Telegram, SOS to Rangoon, 2 August 1949, 845C.002/7-8249 CS/J, Control 398.

93. Telegram, Acheson to American embassy in Rangoon, 2 August 1949, 845C.002/8-249 CS/J, Control 398.

94. Telegram, London to Rangoon, 15 September 1949, FO 25/9/49 and FO 371/75684.

95. Notes in FO 371/75684.

96. Burma: Monthly Summary Telegram, 3 September 1949, DO 142/553; Telegram, Rangoon to FO, 7 September 1949, DEFE 7/162.

97. The author heard in Yangon in the 1970s and 1980s that he returned with an Italian mistress in tow. She was apparently named Corice de Sevigny, although sometimes called Maria Minnelli. Wendy Law-Yone, *Golden Parasol: A Daughter's Memoir of Burma* (London: Chatto and Windus, 2013), pp. 127–28. This is rather similar to the story that U Saw returned from his prison stint in Uganda during the Second World War with a vivacious blond German mistress.

98. Telegram, Bowker to FO, 23 March 1949, DEFE 7/160; 1st quarterly report, British Services Mission, 31 March 1949 by Temple, DEFE 7/864.

99. It was alleged that the Italians might have built a small arms factory on an island in Inya Lake. Report of an interview between Major-General Temple, Head of the British Services Mission, and U Win, Minister for Defence, on 13 December 1950, enclosed with letter, Speaight to Secretary of State, 19 December 1950, FO371/83108. Edward Law-Yone recalled in 1971 that the Italian arms venture was the result of a trip by Kyaw Nyein to Europe in late 1948 to purchase arms. He met with arms dealers in Italy who had surplus U.S. equipment for sale. He asked Ne Win and Set Kya to go to Italy where they were placed on a yacht with a woman who claimed to be of "French noble stock". They remained on the boat for a month and she returned to Myanmar with them. When U Nu eventually got wind of the French woman's presence in Yangon, she was sent back. Author's interview with Edward Law-Yone, 13 August 1971. Edward Law-Yone's daughter states in her memoir of her father that the name of the company was SANE. The lady of "French noble stock" is presumably the person referred to in note 97 *supra*.

100. Notes in FO371/75684.

101. Note on Meeting between Minister of Defence and the Burma Foreign Minister U E Maung, 24 August 1949, DEFE 7/161. The British were thwarted in asking the Italian government about the possible arms link with Burma, despite the peace treaty ban on Italian arms exports, because of the lack of firm evidence. Letter, R.H. Scott to Bowker, 7 December 1949, DEFE 7/163.

102. Note, Naval Craft for Burma, 8 February 1950, by P V Jones, FO371/83168. An anonymous letter concerning the mysterious Italians, including Mr Giusippe Giganta and Mr Tento Spera, arrived at the British embassy in Yangon in April 1950. Posted from Milan, and written by "A Friend of the Truth", the letter was copied to various government officials and newspapers. The embassy believed it was written by another arms dealer who was aggrieved to have lost out on a deal with U Aung Than on behalf of the Burma navy. Letter, Chancery, Rangoon, to South East Asia Department, Foreign Office, 5 May 1950, DEFE 7/164.

103. Letter, Lieutenant Commander J.C. Brookes, RN (Naval Mission) to Secretary of the Admiralty, forwarding report on Ne Win influence in Burma Navy, 24 March 1950, PRO FO 371/83179.

104. Review of the situation in Burma as at 15 August 1949, DEFE 7/865.

105. Telegram, Rangoon to FO, 7 September 1949, DEFE 7/162.

106. Telegram, Rangoon to FO, 29 August 1949, DEFE 7/162.

107. Telegram, Rangoon to FO, 13 September 1949, DEFE 7/162.

108. BSM 3rd Quarterly Report, 30 September 1949, Temple, DEFE 7/866.

109. 1st Quarterly Report BSM, 31 March 1950 by Temple, DEFE 7/866.

110. Described by a senior police officer to an American embassy official as "Ne Win's private army". Telegram, Huddle to Secretary of State, 11 October 1949, 845C.008/10-1149, and Air Letter, Huddle to Secretary of State, 18 November 1949, 845C.008/11-1849.

111. Telegram, Huddle to SOS, 21 October 1949, 845C(W)/1[0]-2149, Control 8366, No. 460.

112. Telegram, Bowker to FO, 28 October 1949, DEFE 7/162.

113. Telegram, Rangoon to SOS, 7 November 1949, 845C.00/11-749, Control 2732, No. 489.

114. Telegram, Huddle to SOS, 10 November 1949, 846C.00(W)11-1059, Control 4309, No. 492.

115. Thein Pe Myint, *Selected Short Stories of Thein Pe Myint*, translated by Patricia M. Milne, Southeast Asia Program Data Paper No. 91 (Ithaca, New York: Cornell University, June 1973), "All is Well, Sir", p. 172. The translation of the same story, including this paragraph in Thein Pe Myint, *Sweet and Sour: Burmese Short Stories*, translated by Usha Narayanan (New Delhi: Sterling, 1999), p. 172 is less complete.

116. Letter, Bowker to H. McNeil, MP, 28 December 1949, FO 371/83163.

117. Fourth BSM Quarterly Report, 31 March 1949 by Temple, DEFE 7/866. These views were echoed in Despatch, Bowker to Bevin, Burma Annual Review for 1949, 11 February 1950, FO371/83013.

118. Telegram, Key to SOS, 5 January 1950, 1908.00/1450, Control 1450, No. 79.

119. Political implications of the provision of military aid by the United Kingdom, by Members of the Commonwealth, or by the United States to French Indo-China, Siam or Burma (reviewed as of 31 December 1949), 23 January 1950, by Commissioner General SEA Singapore for Joint Intelligence Committee, Far East, FO 371/84604. Such views were repeated to the visiting American Melby Mission on 8 August 1950. General Sir John Harding expressed the view that "The Karens are the fighting race." Record of Conversations of Melby Mission with MacDonald et al., 8 August 1950, FO371/84609. On the Melby Mission, see below.

120. Telegram, Gore-Booth to FO, 16 October 1954, FO371/111960; Monthly Summary for October 1954, FO 371/111595; Letter, R.S. Carey to U Nu, 15 October 1954, FO371/111960; Monthly Summary for November 1954, 9 November 1954, FO371/111959. For Ba Pe's "final intrigue", see John F. Cady, *A History of Modern Burma* (Ithaca: Cornell University Press, 1958), p. 628; he refers the reader on to *Hindu*, 3 January 1955 for the full details. Ba Pe was detained in prison between 1954 and 1958, but treason charges against him were then dropped and he was released. Tinker, *Union of Burma*, p. 384 and p. 384, fn. 2.

121. Note received from Col. Ponsonby, MP, to Minister of State on 1 February 1950, FO371/83109.

122. Point Four originated, almost as an afterthought, in President Harry Truman's inaugural address of January 1949. See Louis Joseph Halle, *The Cold War as History* (London: Chatto and Windus, 1967).

123. Telegram, Martin to SOS, 14 February 1950, 7908.00/2-1450, Control 6530, No. 85.

124. His numerous books before, during and after the Second World War, created an image of a one-man engine for good in a world which was stacked against the forthright man of God who fought valiantly against the odds. See, for example, *Burma Surgeon* (New York: Norton, 1943); *Burma Surgeon Returns* (New York: Norton, 1946); and *My Hospital in the Hills* (New York: W.W. Norton, 1955; London: R. Hale, 1957). The highly readable volume by Sue Mayes Newhall, *The Devil in God's Old Man: Life and Work of the Burma Surgeon* (New York: W.W. Norton, 1969), offers insights into Seagrave and his final three years of life.

125. Telegram, Rangoon to SOS, 14 February 1950, 7908.00/2-2750, Rangoon No. 75.

126. Air Letter, Day to SOS, 27 February 1950, 790B.00/3-650, Rangoon No. 75.

127. Presumably, the same policeman who arrested Thakin Ba Sein for attempting to reach Bangkok across the border in 1941.

128. When Trumbull phoned Ne Win's office, having been assured by an American military attaché that such appointments were rare, the General himself answered the phone and made an appointment for 10:30 a.m. the next day. Robert Trumbull, *The Scrutable East: A Correspondent's Report on Southeast Asia* (New York: David McKay, 1964), pp. 127–28.

129. Air Letter, Henry Day, CAD Rangoon to Department of State, 6 March 1950, 7908.00/3-650, Rangoon No. 99. Also, Trumbull, *Scrutable East*, p. 128.

130. Telegram, Key to Secretary of State, 25 March 1950, 790B.00/3-550, Control 11879, No. 160.

131. Bowker to Bevin, 3 March 1950, leading personalities in Burma, FO371/83168.

132. Political analysis by Herbert Spivack, 2nd Secretary, 7 April 1950, Embassy Despatch No. 238 790b.003-750.

133. Telegram, Rangoon to Foreign Office, Monthly Summary, 7 April 1950, FO371/83210.

134. Ambassador Bowker doubted repeated rumours that U Ba Swe of the Socialists and Ne Win were plotting to remove Nu. Ne Win did not like the limelight and enjoyed the success of recent military victories. The coup rumour may actually have been put up to On Khin, the *Bama Hkit* editor, by U Nu to test Ne Win. Telegram, Bowker to Foreign Office, 3 May 1950, FO 371/83106.

135. Letter, Bowker to Bevin, 8 April 1950, FO371/83210.

136. Telegram, Embassy to Secretary of State, 14 April 1950, 7908.00(W)/ 4-1450, Control 5728, No. 202.

137. Telegram, Key to SOS, 11 April 1950, 7908.00/4-1150, Control 6530, No. 85.

138. Telegram, Key to SOS, 14 April 1950, 7908.00(W)/4-1450, Control 5728, No. 202.

139. Letter, Bowker to Bevin, 14 April 1950, FO371/83170.

140. Letter, Foreign Office to Rangoon, 5 May 1950, FO371/83106.

141. Telegram, Bowker to Foreign Office, 27 April 1950, FO371/83174.

142. Telegram, MacDonald to Foreign Office, 11 May 1950, FO371/83174.

143. Telegram, Bowker to Foreign Office, 29 April 1950, FO371/83174.

144. In May 1950, there were 49 officers, 46 non-commissioned officers and 16 other ranks. Information in FO371/83175.

145. Telegram, Bowker to Foreign Office, 3 May 1950, DEFE 7/164, FO371/ 83166.

146. Memo, C.R. Atlee to Ernest Bevin, 13 May 1950, DO196/441; Letter, Thakin Nu to Mr E. Shinwell, 21 May 1950, FO 371/83174.

147. Telegram, Bowker to Foreign Office, 3 May 1950, FO371/83106.

148. Telegram, Key to SOS, 16 June 1950, 1923.01/1550, Control 6530, No. 99.

149. Press Release, Department of State, No. 485, 11 May 1950.
150. Letter, Sir O. Franks to Foreign Office, 3 July 1950, FO371/84610; Telegram, Washington to Foreign Office, 8 July 1950, FO371/87135.
151. Telegram, Bowker to Foreign Office, 10 July 1950, FO371/12280; Telegram, Bowker to Foreign Office, 10 July 1950, FO371/83175.
152. Report of an interview between Major-General Temple, Head of the British Services Mission, and U Win, Minister for Defence, on 13 December 1950, enclosed with Letter, Speaight to Secretary of State, 19 December 1950, FO371/83108.
153. Notes in FO371/83123; Telegram, Rangoon to Foreign Office, Monthly Summary, 4 August 1950, FO371/83105.
154. Letter, MacDonald to Bevin, 29 July 1950, FO371/93129.
155. Telegram, Temple to Minister of Defence, 3 August 1950, FO371/83175.
156. Telegram, Key to SOS, 10 August 1950, 7908.00/8-1050, Control 4560, No. 76.
157. Telegram, Henry Day to SOS, 10 August 1950, 7908.00/1052, Control 4560, No. 78.
158. Letter, H.W.A. Freese-Pennefather to R.H. Scott, 18 August 1950, FO371/83113; Telegram, Key to SOS, 12 August 1950, 708B.00/8-1250, Control 5530, No 85.
159. Telegram, Key to SOS, 12 August 1950, 708B.00/8-1250, Control 55530, No. 85. Subsequently, Ne Win confirmed this point with visiting American journalist Tilman Durdin. Telegram, Key to SOS, 22 September 1950, 7908.00/8-1250, Control 5492, No. 122.
160. Telegram, Rangoon to Foreign Office, Monthly Summary, 1 September 1950, FO371/83105.
161. Telegram, Langdon to SOS, 19 August 1950, 790B.5 MAP/8-1950, Control 8742, No. 113.
162. Talk notes of Final Meeting Melby Mission with MacDonald et al., 19 August 1950, FO371/84609.
163. Telegram, Rangoon to SOS, 23 August 1950, 7908.00/8-2350, Control 10418, No. 22.
164. Memo, "Political Background — Military Assistance to Burma" for meeting on 11 September 1950 by Martin G. Cramer, 8 September 1950, SEAC D-12.
165. "Military Assistance to Burma", *Department of State Bulletin* 23, no. 596 (27 November 1950), p. 856.
166. His influence on government policy remained, of course. A month after he resigned, he recommended and the government accepted that it acquire 11 Dakotas from Air Burma which went into liquidation on 10 October. Ne Win was thought to have an interest in Air Burma. Telegram, Temple to Ministry of Defence, 10 October 1950, DEFE 7/165.
167. Air Letter, Day, Counsellor, Rangoon, to State Department, 14 September 1950, 790B.00/9-1450, No. 184. This information was based on a

conversation with U Aung Than (Bo Set Kya) and Assistant Attaché L.M.
Purcell. Aung Than claimed to have his own men placed in the War Office
supervising all of Ne Win's activities.

168. Telegram, Key to Secretary of State, 17 July 1951, 7908.00/7/7-1571, Control
6244, No. 186.

169. Telegram, Rangoon to Foreign Office, Monthly Summary, 4 October 1950,
FO371/83105; Telegram, Key to SOS, 12 September 1950, 790B.00/9-250
Control 787, No. 156; Air Letter, Day to Department of State, 24 September
1950; Letter, Freese-Pennefather to Foreign Office, 14 September 1950,
FO371/83111.

170. Air Letter, Henry Day to SOS, 15 September 1950, 790B.13/9-1850 XR
790b.55.

171. The coup plot was apparently launched by U Ba Pe who wanted Ne Win
to take over the government and approached prominent British and Indian
business interests to back the plan. When Ne Win was approached, he
informed both U Nu and Kyaw Nyein. Kyaw Nyein encouraged Ne Win to
go along with the plot in order to learn more of the plans. Nu, Ne Win and
Kyaw Nyein testified in a trial of Ba Pe and Tharrawaddy Maung Maung.
Eventually, the trial was abandoned and the charges dropped against the aged
and increasingly frail veteran nationalist figures. Letter, Chancery to South
East Asia Department, 24 December 1956, FO371/129440; *New Times of
Burma*, extracts, 23 January and 25 July 1957, both in FO371/129440. See
also fn. 120 *supra*.

172. Telegram, Key to SOS, 16 November 1950, 790B.00/11-1650, Control 7705,
No. 320.

173. Telegram, SOS to Rangoon, 16 November 1950, 790.00/11-1650, Control
6083, No. 276.

174. Telegram, Key to SOS, 28 November 1950, 790B.00/11-2850, Control
12851, No. 345.

6

RELAXING AND REBUILDING
(October 1950 to March 1958)

When the enemy is close to your troops and each side does not
know the combat efficiency of the other, you must guard against the
inclination to fight the enemy who may lure your troops from the
jungle before you are prepared.

Letwetthondra, *Vyuuacakki*

As Ne Win entered his 41st year, he might well have felt that he had done
his share of creating and defending Myanmar as an independent state.
During the previous decade, he had been part of six organizations and
re-organizations of Myanmar's first army since 1885. He had climbed up
and been lowered down the chain of command of armies led by Japanese,
Burmese, British, and again Burmese officers. Always playing a leading
role, whatever his rank, he rose to the pinnacle of military power and had
political power within his grasp, but had refused to keep it. Seen by many
as the "virtual dictator" of those parts of the country where the government's
writ ran,[1] rather than grab for power, he eased back and for the next eight
years reverted to a man many people remember from his life in Yangon
during and after his stint at Yangon University, a rather shiftless, easygoing
playboy, intent on rather selfish and hedonistic pursuits, with little ambition
and less energy for the details of government.

During the next eight years, he married, for the third time, the woman
with whom he is most remembered in Myanmar and who bore him three

children who were closest to him. To the extent that Ne Win had a normal
domestic life, it was during this period. He travelled the world for business
and pleasure, playing golf in Scotland, lunching with prime ministers and
heads of state, taking what were in effect extensive holidays abroad, as well
as visiting foreign military bases and holding high-level strategic and political
discussions with governments of every political stripe, capitalist republics,
Communist one-party regimes, and the mixed bag that came to be known
as the Third World, of which Myanmar was a part. He clearly mellowed
during these years and the intensity which had driven him in the 1940s,
and especially during the height of the civil war, was gone, for a man
taking a more measured view of matters, even a degree of detachment. He
allowed his subordinates fairly free range to get on with matters, and even
when he disagreed with them over, for example, whether Myanmar's army
should be primarily designed to fight domestic insurgency, or equipped
with heavy and expensive weaponry to defend itself from foreign invasion,
he did not press his preference for the former.

Many people tried to read Ne Win during this period. Part of
his contradictory reputation was made between 1951 and 1958, and
commentators on his behaviour during these years often misjudged him
as they did during his earlier career. For example, one visiting journalist
wrote:

> How different in 1951 when the man who controlled the army could,
> if he chose, control Burma! Sometimes there were rumours about
> Ne Win: he had many friends on 'the other side'; he was playing a
> double game; he had dictatorial ambitions. But probably this young
> man from the post office is not clever enough, is too much a playboy,
> to undertake a Napoleonic role in Burma's post-war revolution
> (Hopkins 1952, p. 211).

Ne Win was a complex man and perhaps part of his complexity grew from
the fact that he knew people were perplexed by him, particularly foreigners.
Within Myanmar, he was a hero to his *yebaw* and subordinate officers, and
even when they disagreed with him, they still remained loyal to him. To
the politicians who made and shaped the governments of the day, he was
both a threat and a friend. His power was obvious but apparently he was
unwilling to make use of it. Prime Minister Nu went from seeing Ne Win
as someone whom he wanted to control to someone whom he wanted to
befriend. The years between 1951 and 1958 were amongst the least eventful
of Ne Win's life; they were, however, not necessarily, the least important.

Following General Ne Win's resignation from the cabinet, the new Defence Minister, U Win, attempted to gain greater control over him and the army. However, bureaucratic and political control was inadequately matched against the Commander-in-Chief's personal contact with his men and the control the War Office had over information and resources. As the army had shed its Communist and Karen elements, those who remained as the core of the ever-expanding army knew their leader and turned to him for guidance and advice. Politicians were seen as placemen in comparison to themselves and their leader. Relations between the cabinet and the army, from the Prime Minister and below, were strained, and U Nu found Ne Win just as difficult to control outside the cabinet as inside.[2] U Win, while outlining a request that the British provide weapons for the police as a counterforce to the army, in apparent exasperation, stated to General Temple, "'You must remember', he went on to say, 'that General Ne Win hates you, he hates me, the Prime Minister, Chins, Kachins, Karens, the Americans and the British, in fact everyone but himself.'" However, Temple went on to write, "But despite this he was of the opinion that General Ne Win was very loyal to the Union, and had not had any conversations with the Chinese."[3] He might well have mentioned politicians in his list, for Ne Win left the cabinet with a very low opinion of Burmese party politics and politicians. In the end, however, Nu was forced to conclude, despite his best efforts, that "the army means Ne Win".[4]

The Prime Minister openly told the British ambassador that he "could not trust Ne Win" and that he was a "complete opportunist" who would join the Communists if he thought they would win, an allegation made by the British themselves two years previously, but of course, Ne Win did not do so. Nu apparently attempted to use the prognostication of astrologers to convince Ne Win that the Communists would not win. As astrology and religion then had little hold on Ne Win's imagination, it was doubtful that this had much effect. Though he did not trust Ne Win, Nu however knew that if he attempted to remove him or move against him in any way, the resulting crisis would be out of his control.[5] The ten battalions scheme of 1949, Nu now argued, was designed to place units outside of Ne Win's control and in January 1951, the cabinet, in particular Defence Minister U Win, wanted to better arm the police in order to be able to take on the army under Ne Win. Just as the British failed to supply the arms for the ten battalions, so the Ambassador convinced the Defence Minister that such a scheme would not succeed. Besides, Britain could not supply the arms and Ne Win already had control of all the arms depots.[6]

The curious friendship between Ne Win and the British Special Commissioner for Southeast Asia, Malcolm MacDonald, burgeoned as Ne Win entered into a less fraught period of his career. MacDonald, who was visiting Myanmar for ten days in January 1951, spent three days with Ne Win, touring the central and eastern regions and staying in Kalaw and Maymyo. Apparently, no serious discussions took place but there was much entertaining,[7] a pattern that Ne Win followed in later years. At the time, the army launched its first major campaign against the KMT in the Shan States. Following this visit, U Nu latched on to the idea of using MacDonald to try to tame Ne Win and MacDonald willingly accepted the role. U Nu asked Macdonald, via the British Ambassador, now Richard Speaight, to invite Ne Win to Singapore. Both Nu and Win felt their combined efforts to reduce Ne Win's prominence was beginning to succeed.[8] Ne Win, together with Bo Min Gaung, did visit Singapore from 5 to 12 April, bringing with him two peacocks as gifts to "strut in the grounds of Buket Serene, Malcolm MacDonald's fantastic residence in Johor" (Hopkins 1952, p. 212). He and "a group of pleasant travelling companions" stayed as MacDonald's guests at Bukit Serene and the Raffles Hotel. Amongst others, he met with Field Marshall Slim and the British Minister of War, the socialist writer and politician, John Strachey. Eventually, MacDonald believed that Nu's campaign to control Ne Win was beginning to show success and the Socialists in the government, with whom Ne Win had split, were building up the Union Military Police under the Home Minister, now U Kyaw Nyein, to counter the army.[9] The possibility of an armed clash between the army and the Union Military Police, then just a notion, came near to reality seven years later.

In a lengthy despatch to London on his week with Ne Win, MacDonald, after repeating the view of Nu that Ne Win's character was one for which he had "complete contempt" and how he tried to use Bo Set Kya and U Hla Maung to control the Commander-in-Chief, he summarized Ne Win's views on various topics of the day. Ne Win was of the opinion that the Chinese People's Liberation Army (PLA) was not particularly strong, as witnessed by its performance in Korea. He opined, rather perspicaciously, that Russia did not want a strong China, and that even the Chinese people might withdraw their support for the Chinese Communist government. As for Myanmar's insurgencies, they were not that strong. The Communists were a mere 500 badly factionalized fanatics, though Thakin Than Tun, their leader, was an able man who would have made a good lawyer. Ne Win claimed that he had many spies within the Communist Party of

Burma. The Karens were equally divided amongst themselves and while various insurgent groups could and did collaborate with each other against the government, "they were too quarrelsome and would always fall out amongst themselves".[10]

Once more reminding his intended reader, Britain's Foreign Minister, MacDonald wrote that Nu felt Ne Win was someone with "no political convictions, ... an opportunist, an utterly selfish, unreliable man with personal ambitions". MacDonald went on,

> I must say ... that I like General Ne Win. There can ... be no serious doubt that Thakin Nu's estimate of his character comes fairly near the truth, and I would not necessarily trust him very far. Nevertheless, he is youthful, charming and gay, as well as clever and dynamic. Though unsociable on official occasions, he is excellent company amongst his private friends. He dislikes pomp, ceremony and stuffed shirts, but likes soldiering and various other manly sports and pastimes. He is perhaps superficial and vain, but he apparently has the quality which commands the confidence, loyalty and even affection of troops under his authority. He is a Burmese Nationalist with all the customary prejudices, as well as principles, of his kind; but his suspicion of Britain is lessening and does not prevent him from working with the United Kingdom representatives whom he feels to be sincere friends of Burma.[11]

MacDonald's assessment of Ne Win, and the Burmese more generally, was refreshingly free from the snide Orientalism of many British commentators at that time. For example, Major General Temple referred to Burmese as "unenterprising" and with no regard for "what the Western World calls efficiency".[12] Accusing Ne Win of taking money from Italian arms deals, but providing no evidence thereof, the British ambassador opined that

> It must be remembered that, if he possesses the usual charm and gaiety, Ne Win equally shows their vanity, their ignorance of the complexities of modern life, and their dislike of sustained application. ...

To his credit, however, Speaight was the first person to observe that Ne Win, "unlike most Burmese, had no use for religion".[13] General Temple remained convinced to the end of his time as head of the BSM that the Burman was not a member of a "martial race", as were allegedly the Karen.[14] He also despaired at the alleged unwillingness of the Burmese to concede "that a man does not automatically become a soldier when you give him a uniform, a rifle and thirty rounds of ammunition" (Hopkins 1952, p. 212).

One can see that Ne Win's views of an army and a soldier differed from those of his British interlocutors when he expounded at some length at a dinner hosted by General Temple on the subject of "good generalship". "His theme was that the winning of battles was only half the battle and that a good general must concern himself with the political follow-up." He also noted the importance of infiltrating one's opponent and seeking out intelligence as military movement is only part of a campaign.[15]

Ne Win discussed with MacDonald the issue of the KMT troops then being pursued by the Burma army in and around Kengtung. He felt "very bitter about American and Siamese aid to the K.M.T. troops in Burma" and the unwillingness of U Nu's government to take the issue to the United Nations. He instanced various incidents, including an attempt by the United States ambassador in Bangkok, Edwin Stanton, to visit Kengtung. Nu and his colleagues kept news of the impending visit from Ne Win, but U Hla Maung, then Myanmar ambassador to Thailand, and one of Nu's "handlers" of Ne Win, sent him a note about the impeding visit. Ne Win ordered a platoon to the Kengtung airport to arrest the American ambassador on arrival, and the trip was then cancelled.[16]

After departing Singapore, Ne Win and his party called at Bangkok for a five-day visit, Ne Win's second since independence. The visit was largely recreational, including some night clubbing, but he did call on the Thai Prime Minister Pibul Songram. While in Bangkok, Ne Win appeared to be unconcerned about the KMT issue, assuring the Thai government that there were only a few hundred of them and they were of no threat.[17] The next month, the KMT launched the first of several failed attempts to cross the border back into Communist China. Ne Win's unwillingness to confront the Thai government with his evidence for their collusion with the KMT was typical of his handling of international conflicts, trying not to exacerbate, but rather underplay, a problem.

In mid-July, Ne Win suddenly announced he was taking a month's leave of absence from the army. Complaining of being tired and dizzy, he felt he needed "liver shots". In early 1951, he was in Rangoon General Hospital for some time. In a meeting with the American military attaché, he admitted that the Socialists in the government were critical of his campaign against the insurgents, so why not "let government try for awhile?" To the rumours that his opponents were out to remove him, he indicated that "two or three months will tell the tale". Bo Setkya, now a wealthy man,[18] and at one time Ne Win's "partner and intimate", "but now his bitter enemy", said that he was going on leave to remarry.[19]

Rumours of his impending marriage had been heard for some time and had led to criticism of Ne Win for breaking up a marriage — his fiancé was then married to a Burmese doctor in training in Liverpool, England, and she was pregnant with twin daughters. He was also accused of allowing his personal affairs to interfere with his official duties.[20] Certainly, his love of horse racing had not diminished and he was frequently seen at the Sunday race meets in his private box. It was no secret that he could be found on many evenings, after playing tennis in the late afternoon, drinking at the Union or Lake Clubs. The general consensus around Yangon amongst those allegedly in the know was that Ne Win in mid-1951 was politically defeated and his withdrawal from power was inevitable.[21]

A month later, General Ne Win was back at his desk in the War Office after a honeymoon in Taunggyi with his new bride, Daw Khin May Than. She, the daughter of Dr Ba Than, the top surgeon in Rangoon and a *bon vivant* known to also enjoy the Turf Club and sports, as well as the ladies, had been trained as a nurse in Washington, D.C., and had lived with her doctor husband in England for the previous three years. Very Westernized and sophisticated in outlook, Daw Khin May Than, or Katy, often pronounced Kitty, as she was known by Western diplomats, seemed to be the antithesis to the General with his bluff manners and strongly nationalist views.[22]

Criticism within and without the army of Ne Win's behaviour was obviously rife but efforts to remove or control him were stymied. He seemed to rise above problems or resolve them, often pointing out unwelcome truths to those around him. After surviving the infighting within the army leadership among the Karens and the Communists, and those who remained loyal to the government throughout 1948 and 1949, by 1950 he had managed to create and maintain the unity of the army. Still an ad hoc, "learn-on-the-job" force, the young officers freely criticized each other at the Annual Commanders' Conference in 1951. There Ne Win had to intervene in disputes between staff and unit or field commands. The inability of the War Office to supply and equip the troops, a casualty of the British rationing of weapons and the rapid expansion of the army, and rotating officers from staff to units and vice versa, would do nothing to improve efficiency (Callahan 2004, pp. 152–53).

In August 1951, having returned from his honeymoon, Ne Win drafted a memo authorizing the establishment of what became the military planning committee under Colonel Aung Gyi. Analysing the problems of the army as it faced not only internal insurgency but also the KMT threat in terms of its inability to plan effectively, he laid the basis of the problem as the hybrid nature of the War Office — half Ministry of State and half military headquarters. Overwhelmed with detail, the bigger picture was often lost sight of. That had to change. As Dr Callahan writes, "the message of Ne Win's memo was that the time had come to turn the tatmadaw into a first-class fighting force, capable of repelling external aggression" (Callahan 2004, p. 161). Personnel changes in the War Office were also required, but whereas Ne Win just ignored such problem, such as his dislike of the permanent secretary, U Ba Tint, and his senior staff officer, Lieutenant Colonel Hla Aung, Maung Maung transferred Hla Aung out of the War Office (Callahan 2004, pp. 162, 164). At the 1952 conference, improving efficiency, as well as training, was the focus of the discussions (Callahan 2004, pp. 152–53).

At about this time, General Ne Win said that his top priority was to deal with the issue of the KMT troops in the Shan State.[23] It had become increasingly obvious to all that the American government was deeply implicated in the KMT affair even if the State Department was not officially informed. President Truman, early in 1951, after being briefed on what the Central Intelligence Agency (CIA) had been doing unofficially with the Chinese Nationalist and Thai governments, in support of the KMT troops in Myanmar, authorized forays into China (Beisner 2006, p. 496). Without knowing the details, almost everyone in Yangon remotely interested in the matter would have known about the CIA's support for the KMT, except the United States Ambassador.[24] It soon entered into popular fiction, disguised as operations further east.[25]

Though Burma was not part of Malcolm MacDonald's official brief, he was obviously becoming increasingly intrigued with the country and its leaders. He returned for another ten-day visit in November with Ne Win as his host. Ne Win planned to take him to the Chinese border to show him, presumably, evidence of the KMT's activities. However, word of the trip leaked to the press and it had to be cancelled because of objections by the American embassy at having been excluded from the tour party. At that time, Ne Win "showed not only intense dislike for the Americans, but intense suspicion of them too". He apparently believed, or at least speculated, that the United States was considering starting a Third World War by arming Yugoslavia and then Japan and Germany.[26] The American ambassador in Thailand, Stanton, and his colleagues in Rangoon suspected the same, though they believed that KMT *agent provocateurs*, not their own government, were doing the plotting.[27]

Ne Win was not out of politics just because he was out of the cabinet. His relationship with the Socialists in the government remained one of continual tension, though they often worked closely together. He and Kyaw Nyein were said early in the year to have made up and were once more cooperating,[28] but following the completion of the 1951–52 general elections, which were held seriatim in different parts of the country as the army was able to establish order, Ne Win apparently attempted to block the appointment of the Socialist U Ba Swe as Defence Minister.[29] The British ambassador was of the opinion that Lieutenant Colonel Maung Maung was appointed early in 1952 as Chief-of-Staff under Ne Win by the Socialists in order to control him.[30] Whether these or any other rumours and reports were true, such as the report by American intelligence that Ne Win was going to mount a coup at about the same time, is impossible to determine.[31] What remains undisputable was that Ne Win insisted that the War Office occupy the old Steel Brothers Chummery and the former Masonic Lodge on Signal Pagoda Road.[32] Kyaw Nyein apparently remained convinced that Ne Win would "toe the [Socialist] party line" as they had worked together since the 1930s.[33]

Ne Win's vow to have the KMT problem dealt with progressed in a meeting that he held with the United States Assistant Military Attaché in late January 1952. His solution to the problem was threefold:

1. That the United States government "instruct" the Chinese Nationalist Government to order the surrender of the KMT in Burma or their immediate withdrawal to Formosa via Thailand.
2. That the United States arrange the withdrawal with the Thai government.
3. That the government of Burma facilitate the withdrawal by allowing six senior KMT officials access to Burma.[34]

Since the United States admitted no responsibility for the KMT problem, despite the obvious evidence of their complicity, such a direct solution would find no favour in Washington. The unwillingness of the Americans to admit the CIA's involvement in the affair also resulted in the resignation of the United States ambassador upon his realization that he had been lied to and had told lies in his official capacity. As to a counter proposal to appoint a United Nations Commission to supervise the withdrawal, Ne Win was "definitely unfavourable and said it would be impossible to find members who would not be prejudiced in advance".[35] By March and with no solution yet in sight, 2,000 KMT troops were reported moving south and linking up with Karen rebels in the Kayah state and northern Karen hills (for the KMT-KNDO alliance, see Gibson with Chen 2011, pp. 121–30).

Fighting the KMT in the eastern Shan State was made especially difficult not only by the rugged terrain and lack of infrastructure, but also by the hostile local population. According to a journalist who was "embedded" in the army during the fighting, the KMT troops "were very cruel. Before they left the eastern side of the Thanlwin River, they wrote down in Chinese on trees that Burmese Communist bandits were coming." Not knowing that Myanmar was an independent country, the local people did not realize that the army was the Myanmar army. The problem was compounded by the fact that some of the government troops misbehaved when the locals were hostile towards them.[36]

It is unknown whether Ne Win knew that his old political mentor from the *Dobama Asiayon*, Thakin Ba Sein, was plotting with the KNDO and the KMT to bring U Nu's government down and install the right-wing politician as the head. If Ne Win did, he would not have been amused (Gibson with Chen 2011, pp. 103, 104, 111–12). The British Services Mission by early 1952 had been barred from offering any advice on policy and training and even the head of mission, General Temple, had to give forty-eight hours of notice before he could visit any base, even if British personnel were stationed there.[37]

The General's relations with the head of the BSM improved dramatically with the departure in mid-April of General Temple, and his replacement by Air Commodore E.L.S. Ward (1905–91). Ward, who had served briefly in Burma in 1946, and in India since 1926, as well as in China, was from a much more technologically advanced element of the British armed forces than his predecessor who brought all the prejudices of the British Indian army to his work in Burma. Ne Win met with Ward most cordially, but soon made it clear that if the British Mission could not supply the number of arms requested by the deadlines agreed, the Mission would have to depart.[38] Ne Win apparently conceded that the air element of the Mission was useful from the point of view of training, but the Burma Air Force was still incapable of putting many planes into the air.[39] Ward, who soon departed to London on a weapon purchasing mission in an attempt to demonstrate the utility of the BSM, was fully aware that Ne Win's strategy for the development of the army was to create a force of mobile brigades with a minimum of heavy equipment rather than the conventional European style army that Smith Dun, Let Ya, and the former heads of the

BSM had advocated. Nonetheless, Ne Win still wanted training in Great Britain for his officers.[40]

Despite his various personal and private commitments, Ne Win never lost sight of the problems of others, even those with no connection with the military and his official or familial responsibilities. When a senior civil servant from the Ministry of Education was killed in an automobile accident while on an official trip to Calcutta, Ne Win was the first person from the government to visit the family home in Yangon and give condolences to the family. He also ensured that a government plane was despatched to bring the body back and assured the family that they would be properly cared for in future. He never let them down in that regard.

With the growing relative peace in the countryside, and Ne Win's settling down to a new routine after his marriage to Katy Ba Than, he began to explain more clearly to Ward and other British officers his vision for the Burma army. In turn, the British began to see Ne Win in a more positive and sympathetic manner, although still not giving him high marks for fair dealing, noting, for example, that the Minister of Defence, Socialist U Ba Swe, was "just as unscrupulous as the General, and a good deal cleverer".[41] The British concluded, however, that there was no evidence that Ne Win or anyone else in the army was involved in any "arms racket" or leakage of weapons to the insurgents. Even if there was evidence of alleged shady dealing between Ne Win, and possibly Bo Set Kya, with purveyors of shoddy Italian arms at the height of the civil war, such activities had completely ceased.[42] In discussion with Air Commodore Ward, Ne Win explained that while he wanted to develop an army to fight primarily as a lightly armed force in order to combat its opponents who practised guerrilla warfare, it was still to be an army built on Western military lines. He was developing the necessary plans but had to concede to his colleagues in the War Office who wanted to purchase heavy weapons, including tanks. As far as he was concerned, gaining familiarity with tanks was merely to acclimatize his troops for fighting alongside an allied army if required.[43]

While Ne Win and the War Office were developing their plans for the future of the army, they continued to face a number of ongoing security problems. The KMT had sent units as far south as Hlaingbwe in KNU-dominated territory and then further south to Mottama (Amherst) where the army fought hard battles to drive them back from the coast. In addition, the Shan States were placed under martial law following fighting between the army and the KMT along with Pa-O rebels. The powers of the Shan State government were increasingly being supplanted by the army, leading to growing resistance by the Shan Sawbwa at the undermining of their powers, territory and revenue streams.

Against a backdrop of improved relations with the BSM under Ward's leadership, and the ongoing problem of driving the American-backed KMT out of the country, Ne Win set out on his second trip to Great Britain and the United States in mid-October 1952. The request to visit the United States to explore the possibility of purchasing arms was made at short notice, to the discomfort of the Americans who asked for the trip to be postponed by three weeks.[44] Ne Win was accompanied by senior military colleagues, including Colonel Kyaw Win, Colonel Maung Maung, Lieutenant Colonel San Yu, Major Yai Ye, Lieutenant Commander Khin Maung Maung, Squadron Leader Tun Tha, Flight Lieutenant Thaung Dan, and one civilian, U Thi Han, but only on the American leg of the trip.[45] In the UK, he was accompanied only by two members of staff.[46]

Initially, Ne Win and his party were in the United Kingdom for only two days, meeting with Lord Reading, the Parliamentary Undersecretary for Foreign Affairs in the Churchill government on the first day, and also lunching with the Minister for Defence, Lord (former Field Mashall) Alexander, the same day. In the course of his conversation with Reading, Ne Win expressed the view that the KMT never amounted to more than 7,000 men who, when under the control of General Li Mi, were well-disciplined. However, many have broken into groups of about fifty and were marauding the countryside in search of food and booty. The KNU were trying to use the KMT to their advantage.[47] Alexander assured Ne Win that the British would provide the weapons he had requested over the next two years, and Ne Win expressed his appreciation for that and also for the manner in which Air Commodore Ward conducted his affairs.[48] As he had to attend a reception at the Myanmar embassy, the plan to spend a day at the races at Sandown, a visit perhaps to the swan song of Betty Hutton at the Palladium, and a lengthy drive in the country, all had to be cancelled. Since Ne Win hated formality, official functions were limited and the initial visit to the UK was more of a social call, confirming existing arrangements, than anything else.[49]

The visit to the United States was more in the nature of exploring the possibility of a new relationship. Joined by the rest of his colleagues from the War Office, Ne Win flew to New York and Washington, D.C., where he commenced his round of meetings with the Deputy Assistant Secretary of State, U. Alexis Johnson. The discussions, described as cordial, did not concern arms purchases and Ne Win portrayed an air of confidence, noting that the insurgents were surrendering at the rate of 500 a month, up from 100 a month in 1950. Moreover, rice production was being maintained and the country was achieving stability.[50] Ne Win had originally planned to motor across the United States visiting various military bases, including Fort Leavenworth, but cut his visit short in order to attend to unspecified urgent business, possibly an offensive against the insurgents or the KMT.[51] He requested to meet with the three service chiefs of the army, navy and air force to discuss defence procurement. While he travelled on to London, his colleagues remained behind in Washington to finalize weapons purchases.[52] Though he wanted to send officers from the Burma army to America for training, he felt that he did not yet have men who were adequately prepared to do so.[53]

Ne Win's most substantive meeting was with the Office of Military Assistance in the Defence Department. There he was given rough estimates of the prices of weapons and equipment that he was interested in purchasing. The American side, taken aback by Ne Win's proposals, underscored that they were not seeking to undermine the British or replace their role as the lead weapons supplier to Burma and that no agreements could be reached until and unless the United States and Burmese governments entered into a government-to-government reimbursable aid agreement. Ne Win expressed the hope that he could persuade them to do so soon after his return.[54]

While in Washington, Ne Win hosted a dinner for all the defence people, and their wives, who had assisted his visit. Stopping over in New York on return, he attended the Army-Columbia football match and also viewed a game of ice hockey. Paul Yee, of Ameritex, who facilitated Ne Win's first trip to the United States in 1949, took Ne Win or perhaps U Thi Han to Macy's Department Store where substantial purchases were made. Colonel Davies, assigned as the liaison with Ne Win during his visit, reported that the General once said, "the British never give up any country they have held, pointing out that they supplied guns to the American Indians after our war of independence."[55]

Before Ne Win had unexpectedly cut short his visit to the United States and returned home via London, it was expected that he would stop by in Tokyo on his way back to Yangon. Though concerned that he would try to buy Japanese weapons with Burmese rice, which would irritate the British,[56] the Americans were keen for him to do so. Ambassador Sebald in Yangon thought it was important for Ne Win to better understand the American position on the Korean War and the future of East Asia.[57] In the end, however, the Americans considered it impolitic to press Ne Win over visiting Japan and desisted.[58]

A second-hand account of Ne Win's thoughts behind his visit to Washington was provided after the event in a memorandum based on a conversation between a State Department official and Colonel Davies, the American Military Attaché in Yangon, who apparently met with Ne Win frequently. According to Davies, Ne Win, who had control of half the national budget, wanted to build up to four divisions of troops, with half of the equipment for one division to be acquired from the United States. During his visit to the Office of Military Assistance, he created confusion when he presented a list of equipment he wanted to purchase even though no government-to-government agreement had yet been reached. In the course of a discussion about training, Ne Win averred that he was considering placing Brigadier Kyaw Zaw in charge and the Americans offered to show Ne Win or his delegation the American training facilities in Japan and Korea.[59]

On arrival in Myanmar after his short trip to New York and London, returning via Paris, his increasingly placid and cooperative relationship with the British and others continued. For whatever reason, after his return from New York, he was relaxing in Kalaw and Maymyo with the Indonesian Chiefs-of-Staff for five days from the end of November till early December. When Air Commodore Ward complained to Ne Win that the Commandant of the Burma Army Staff College at Kalaw, Colonel Hla Aung, was incompetent, Ne Win apparently agreed and undertook to remove him as he was making the work of the chief British instructor impossible.[60] En passant, Ne Win also expressed an interest in learning to fly.[61]

By December, Ne Win had produced a five-year plan for an expansion of the army element of the British Services Mission and the creation of a military academy based upon the model of Sandhurst.[62] In conversation with the American Ambassador, Ne Win was less forthcoming, indicating that he felt the current good relations with the BSM was being used as an excuse by some British officers "to feather their own nests". While Ne Win's attitude towards the United States had also modulated, even to the point of allowing the KMT to depart via Yangon, he made it clear that no formal request to purchase American equipment would be made until and unless the incoming Eisenhower administration ensured that such requests would be successful.[63] Rather than acting on the informal request, the Americans passed it to the British for approval.[64]

The interrelated issues of the futures of the KMT and the BMS dominated the first months of 1953. Much of the optimism and goodwill which were displayed by the United States and British governments towards Myanmar and its army quickly dissipated and options which seemed available the previous year, after the General's trips to the United States and England, began to close. Myanmar's fifth independence anniversary was marked by the formal notice of termination of the Let Ya–Freeman Agreement in a year's time, the occupation of Mong Hsu and the deposition of its Sawbwa by the KMT, and the launching of a major attack on the KMT south of Mawlamyine. Faced with a number of KMT attacks at the eastern border regions of Myanmar from the Chinese border to the far south, the army and the government moved together to attempt to resolve the issue. The army launched a major offensive, led by Brigadier Douglas Blake, in the Shan State in early March.[65] Against the continued urging of both the British and the United States governments, U Nu's government following a parliamentary debate on the issue finally took the matter to the United Nations on 25 March, charging the Nationalist Chinese government with aggression, as Ne Win had insisted upon for three years.

Five days before the introduction of the KMT issue in the UN, General Ne Win wrote to Lord Alexander, the British Minister for Defence, laying down his ideas for new terms to replace the Let Ya–Freeman Agreement. Apologizing for not writing sooner after his visit to London, Ne Win explained that he had been away from his desk for most of the previous four months, touring the country in preparation for the current offensive. While noting diplomatically that the Let Ya–Freeman Agreement was appropriate for the handover period from British to Burmese rule, the new agreement should have a training element composed of service attachés as an "Instructional Team". The weapons purchasing element of the present agreement would be dealt with separately from the "Instructional Team".

The remainder of the letter was largely in the nature of a series of complaints. The apparent understanding that Air Commodore Ward had reached the previous year on the dismissal of the Commandant of the Staff College would not be implemented. Ne Win would not concede to the dismissal of Colonel Hla Aung even under a threat that if he did not do so, three British officers would return to the United Kingdom.[66] He noted that Burma was allocated no staff training slots at the British Staff College at Camberley in 1953, though Thailand was offered places. In any event, Ne Win preferred to send his men to other Commonwealth countries for training. At that time, Burmese officers were going to Pakistan, India, Australia and New Zealand. Finally, he once more lamented the tardiness of the British in supplying the weapons ordered, despite Alexander's promises made during his London visit.[67]

Ne Win's private life faced a crisis at about the same time as he was concentrating on the KMT and the future training of the army officer corps and its foreign equipment sources. His father was taken ill and Ne Win brought him to Yangon to live near him. U Po Kha was sufficiently ill that Ne Win cancelled plans to accompany Malcolm MacDonald on another of his periodic visits to Myanmar, scheduled for 23 to 26 March. During the previous month, Ne Win had toured two days with the American Ambassador, William Sebald, and Air Commodore Ward, before arranging separate tours for them in and around Mandalay and Chauk.[68]

The Americans, faced with Burmese action in the United Nations, including a General Assembly resolution demanding the evacuation of the KMT from Myanmar, brought the Thai, Nationalist Chinese and Burmese governments together with U.S. negotiators in Bangkok and eventually agreed on a plan to resolve the issue. This was announced by the United States ambassador in Bangkok on 22 June. Earlier, at the time of the announcement that the government of Myanmar was to take the KMT issue to the United Nations, the government also announced the termination of the American Technical Cooperation Administration aid programme. Nonetheless, the Burma army in mid-year, following the apparent action by the new Eisenhower administration to resolve the KMT issue, though still without admitting complicity, requested the shipment of a large number of arms from the American government with no prior reference to the British Services Mission.[69] Ne Win was putting the British on notice. Even so, he ordered all available officers of the Burma army to attend a reception to mark the coronation of Queen Elizabeth II on 22 June.[70]

The Nu government approved a new draft defence agreement with the United Kingdom government on 22 July. As there had been no prior negotiations on the matter, and the only indication of its contents was in Ne Win's letter to Alexander in March, the British ambassador was more than a bit miffed. In his summary of its contents, Speaight noted that there was a complete divorce of the arms purchasing and training functions of the mission. Objectionable to him was also the omission of the two clauses which gave the Royal Navy and the Royal Air Force docking, fly over, and landing rights in Myanmar on an unlikely to be operationalized reciprocal basis. Furthermore, he felt the draft conditions of service for British personnel were unacceptable.[71] Nonetheless, he wanted an agreement to be reached after suitable negotiation in order to encourage the government and discourage "the hard left"; as Ne Win and Ward had "close personal relations"; and if there were no agreement, the Burmese would buy cheaper and more plentiful American weapons.[72]

Ne Win had been concerned about the lack of training for the army officer corps for sometime, but other pressing matters did not allow the development of the indigenous training required. At the 1953 commanders' conference, Ne Win noted the weakness of training, saying,

> the most serious weakness of the General Staff Office is the training area. Because of the weakness in training programmes, operational drawbacks become more and more common in battles. Difficulties in training programmes are lack of time and shortage of training materials — both manuals and equipment.... Because of the lack of skills in battlecraft and operations of weapons, fire power does not match enemy casualties. The war office has been trying hard to get materials for training. As we do not think the existing training facilities and schools are sufficient or of international standard, we plan to establish Combat Forces Schools and a Military Academy in the near future. The training programmes of these schools will determine the future course of the Tatmadaw. In order to run these training schools on our own, we have sent out trainees not only to England, India and Pakistan, as happened in the past, but also the United States, Australia and Yugoslavia.[73]

His key aids, Maung Maung and Aung Gyi, then spelled out the details of the steps to be made to improve the level of military knowledge of what up till then had been an army which had largely learned by doing and knew little military doctrine or theory.

Ne Win was without doubt exasperated with the British failure to live up to his expectations and their implicit promises, but probably more so with the Americans and also U Nu's government. As far as Ne Win was concerned, the Burmese government was going to demand at least 5,000 KMT troops to be expeditiously withdrawn and the Burmese ambassador to Thailand was instructed to demand this.[74] When the Nationalist Government would not agree to the demand that that number be withdrawn in three months and the remaining 7,000 within six months, it withdrew from further negotiations on 17 September. Conditions in the Shan State were clearly deteriorating and the military administration previously invoked was extended for another six months.[75] The Burma air force was ordered to bomb the KMT base in Mong Hsat. Ne Win and Home Minister Bo Khin Maung Gale were pressing U Nu to withdraw Myanmar from the United Nations,[76] while echoing Defence Minister U Ba Swe's earlier demand that the Chinese Nationalist government be expelled from the UN.

Faced with the military threat of the KMT as well as the continuing civil war amongst various indigenous groups, and the inability or unwillingness of the British and the Americans to supply what the army ordered, Myanmar turned to Yugoslavia. Communist Yugoslavia became one of the first places the Burmese looked to after Great Britain, India and the United States as a possible source of arms and training. Kyaw Nyein and other Socialist party leaders had visited Yugoslavia in 1947 and it was viewed as a model for Myanmar's socialist development. Kyaw Nyein led the army to seek Yugoslav assistance. Initially, Ne Win remained convinced that the army should pursue the possibility of purchasing American armaments despite their complicity with the KMT. Ba Swe and Kyaw Nyein disagreed. He and Kyaw Nyein argued so vehemently over whether to pursue the Yugoslav option that it was reported that Ne Win struck his Socialist colleague for a second time.[77]

However, the necessity of driving KMT out of the country before they could effectively link up with the Karen insurgents and open a sea route for supplies through Tanintharyi forced Ne Win, in September 1953, to turn finally to Yugoslavia and order mountain guns, various sizes of ammunition, mules, horses and ponies to prepare the army for a major offensive against the KMT the following year. In the next month, additional orders were placed for mortars, rocket launchers, flamethrowers, grenades and other equipment.[78] Apparently both the British and the American embassies were not informed about the Yugoslav weapons orders, for in January and February 1954, there were a flurry of telegrams between Rangoon, London and Washington expressing concern that the Burmese would turn either to other Communist governments or neutral Yugoslavia if their governments did not provide what was required. By then, of course, the deed had been done. According to Cavoski,

> General Ne Win expressed his gratitude for Yugoslavia's military assistance, and emphasised that "this was the very first time that one country sold them weapons without any postponement or complications." The guns had already been tested with excellent results and he was very pleased with them. Eventually, General Ne Win said, he was very interested in building an ammunition factory with Yugoslav assistance, but until that time "they would fully rely upon

procurements from our country." Yugoslavia had found another strong ally in Burma's ruling establishment.[79]

In a private conversation later with a British military official, Ne Win described Yugoslav equipment as "museum pieces".[80]

The rest of 1953 saw continued fighting with the KNDO and the KMT along the border, with government troops retaking the Mawchi mines and other important installations. With regards to the KMT issue, the Thai, American and Nationalist Chinese governments finally announced on 29 October that 2,000 KMTs would be withdrawn with their families. Before then, the army led by Brigadier Kyaw Zaw launched a large-scale attack to remove the KMT at Ne Win's order, apparently against the advice of members of the government, including Kyaw Nyein.[81] Between November and May the next year, three batches of KMT totalling nearly 6,000, consisting mainly of women, children and other non-combatants, withdrew from the Shan States to Chiang Mai and Lampang in northern Thailand for transit to Taiwan. They turned in only 1,323 weapons, many of no military value (Garver 1997, pp. 158–60; Lintner 1999, pp. 149–51). As the withdrawal of the KMT commenced, United States Vice President Richard M. Nixon arrived in Yangon on a three-day official visit. Though he discussed the KMT issue with Burmese ministers, there was still no admission of American complicity.[82] By then, however, Ne Win had been long convinced that the Americans were involved with the KMT and doubted the sincerity of their attempts to mediate a solution to the threat to Burma's sovereignty. He made that clear in a conversation with American military attachés three days before Christmas in 1953.[83]

By the end of the year there was no satisfactory solution to the KMT issue and despite the British ambassador's intentions, negotiations on a new Burma–Britain Defence Agreement were stalled. Ward and Ne Win had agreed in May that no new British personnel would be sent to Burma until an agreement was reached and the army side of the mission was now badly depleted. While relations between Ward and Ne Win were amicable, Ne Win and other officers ignored any advice and allowed the administrative and physical arrangements for the British personnel to deteriorate to an unsatisfactory level.[84]

As indicated a year earlier, the Let Ya–Freeman Agreement was allowed to expire on 4 January 1954. Nonetheless, the Mission remained in place for the time being with the hope, at least on the British side, that negotiations might be resumed to make its continued functioning possible.

In a lengthy conversation with Ward, Ne Win clearly dissembled when he claimed that the decision to end the BSM was not made by him only but by the National Defence Council, which comprised Prime Minister Nu and the Ministers for Defence, Home, and Foreign Affairs and himself, collectively. He emphasized that Burma would have to stand on its own two feet sometime and, as the Korean War boom in rice prices had ended, any expenditure had to be fully justified. Moreover, he expressed continued dissatisfaction with the army element of the mission, now headed by the euphonious Colonel Baker-Baker.[85]

Subsequently, an unofficial suggestion that the air force element of the Mission remain in place for another two years was vetoed by Ne Win.[86] The British government were willing to accept the Burmese draft agreement in order "to remain principal supplier of arms to Burma",[87] but Ne Win was not agreeable. With the KMT issue on the way to partial resolution, the British were concerned that the Americans would step into their role and the new Ambassador, Paul Gore-Booth, was keen to reassure the American ambassador that negotiations on a new agreement were continuing.[88] Despite the British hopes, the dismanting of the BSM continued as Burmese officers were keen to take possession of the superior quarters the British had remained in after independence. They also wished to purchase equipment that the British had been using. Despite the slow death of the BSM, cordial relations between Ne Win and Ward continued.[89]

In what amounted to a valedictory for the BSM, Ne Win and Ward met on 10 May for a reasonably lengthy discussion in which the General unusually revealed his political views and opinions to a foreign interlocutor. He had clearly come to trust and feel at ease with Air Commodore Ward. There were two items of business at the meeting: training and a military mission to Europe and the United States in the near future. As for training, Ne Win advanced the view that he did not have any suitable people to send on the courses available. As for the mission, Burma standing on its own feet militarily meant reaching out to other countries for arms and training. A search for sources was on. At the end of the agenda, they then discussed the problems of the Mission in the early years. Ne Win attributed these to interference in army affairs by General Temple and the pro-Karen attitude of him and other British officers. Finally, "We discussed politics and he told me that there was a certain amount of theory in communism with which he sympathised."[90] Had the germ of an idea been planted?

The success of the army against the KMT in the last quarter of 1953, and the arrival of new weaponry from Yugoslavia encouraged the army to launch "Operation Bayinnaung" to attempt finally to drive the KMT from the Shan State and remove any pretext for Chinese Communist intervention. In "Operation Bayinnaung", the army "proved itself an integrated fighting force: for the first time large-scale operations were carried out by an army and not by an assorted number of battalions" (Tinker 1967, p. 331). By now, having despaired of acquiring British weapons with which to defend the country, Ne Win indicated to a Yugoslav interlocutor that he "was very suspicious and implacable about military cooperation with Britain or India. He even expressed his hatred towards the British, due to their unfair treatment of the Burmese government and the army. With regards to India, he was open to political but not military cooperation" (Cavoski 2010, p. 24, fn. 89).

"Operation Bayinnaung" and related offensives drove the various insurgents to the Thai border and beyond, souring Burmese–Thai relations. Both Karen and Mon rebels had talks with the Thai military in March and were allowed to set up camps in the neighbouring country. The Americans put the blame on General Ne Win for his "antics" which allegedly "jeopardized" the success of the KMT evacuation at that time. These were said to include refusing to contribute to the cost of the evacuation, joining the Bangkok committee which comprised the United States, Thailand and Nationalist China, overseeing the evacuation, and refusing to cease military operations.[91] That he should object to paying to remove an invader armed and equipped by the United States and to cooperate with the facilitators of that invasion and its perpetuation seemed obvious to observers. Even the British ambassador expressed his sympathy for the position that Ne Win and the Burmese government had adopted.[92]

On 20 March, the Burma army retook Mong Hsat, the KMT headquarters, after heavy fighting in which the Yugoslav guns and mules played an important part.[93] Brigadier Kyaw Zaw, who was lionized by his men, took the opportunity of the victory to publicize his own role in the campaign. A number of high-ranking army officers flew from Yangon to Mong Hsat to celebrate the victory, but Ne Win was not amongst them. He remained in Yangon on "urgent business".[94] The following month, "Operation Hsinbyushin" was launched against the KNDO in the Papun area and KMT forces in Tanintharyi. Much of the recently formed Kayin state was thus brought under government control, but not Papun town itself. The following month KMT troops began evacuating Tanintharyi as well as the Shan State. Shortly after, "Operation Bandoola" was launched against the BCP to clear the Communists from the Pakkoku area of central Burma.

All of this fighting took place against the backdrop of the French defeat at the battle of Dien Bein Phu by the Vietnamese Communists, setting the stage for the Paris conference to end the French colonial presence in Southeast Asia but open up a new phase of American involvement. In the same month, East Pakistani officials finally arrested the *Mujahadin* leader Cassim that the Burmese had been confronting since 1947,[95] and Prime Minister U Nu opened the Sixth Buddhist Synod at the newly built Kaba Aye pagoda and the adjacent Great Cave, bringing Buddhist leaders from all the Theravada countries together for an expensive two-year reading of the fundamental Buddhist texts.

In the midst of many dramatic and distracting activities both at home and abroad, General Ne Win once more received Malcolm MacDonald who arrived in Yangon to attend the Buddhist Synod and meet various leaders, perhaps also having in mind the first Asian Socialist Conference that Kyaw Nyein and his colleagues were about to host at Kalaw. Ne Win "received him, as always, with great conviviality". The General indicated that he regretted the termination of the British Services Mission but the proposals the British put forward for renewal were unworkable, though some of his colleagues argued with him to the contrary. Consequently, he politely indicated that Burma might request British military advisers from time to time. Looking at the larger picture, he was optimistic that one more campaigning season would see the end of both the KMT and the KNDO and he was not particularly concerned about allegations of Chinese Communist infiltrators coming into Burmese territory.[96]

As Burma was reaching out to the world beyond the British Commonwealth and the United States to Yugoslavia, Israel,[97] and other countries, Communist China finally began to develop relations with its southern neighbour. Immediately after the revolution, China's foreign policy was critical of countries such as Burma and India, arguing that while they pretended to be neutral in the Cold War, there were only two camps — socialist and capitalist. In time the Chinese came to moderate their views. Having observed Myanmar's behaviour over the KMT issue with which they could find little to criticize and wishing to use Myanmar as a route out of China's isolation following the termination of the Korean War and the French defeat in Indochina, Chinese Premier and Foreign Minister Chou En-lai made the first of many visits to Yangon on his way to or from Beijing. Claiming that "revolution cannot be exported", he and Prime Minister Nu endorsed the five principles of peaceful coexistence.

During his approximately thirty-six hours in Yangon, Chou En-lai laid the basis of an ongoing relationship which was to last until 1967. Having previously stopped at Delhi where he and Prime Minister Nehru endorsed the same principles, Chou En-lai gave the Burmese leadership their first view of the new neighbour in the north. No longer would China be viewed through the prism of British or American Cold War perspectives. As Fan Hongwei has written, the visit marked the beginning of the "pauk phaw" (cousins) era in Burmese–Chinese relations (Fan 2009). During Chou En-lai's brief visit, the army was fighting the KMT which had launched an offensive against Mong Hkak, north of Kengtung. Order was being re-established in much of the Shan State despite the ongoing fighting and military rule was lifted in July.

The end of the year found the British once more speculating on the future of General Ne Win. The current military attaché, Air Commodore Ward and the BSM now departed, declared to a visiting colleague "that General Ne Win is a sick man, that his days of political influence are gone for good". Colonel Tonry also suggested, producing no evidence in support, that the army's purchase of transport equipment was handled only by Ne Win, who took a cut from Bo Set Kya with his car and truck agencies.[98] Whether his analytical powers were stronger than his predicative ones remain among the imponderables, but that Ne Win and Set Kya had fallen out earlier was in no doubt. Evidence for their coming together again was lacking. In any event, U Thi Han was Director of Military Procurement and Bo Tin Pe was Quarter Master General, both men with high reputations for probity of the kind that Ne Win insisted upon.

The Cold War in Southeast Asia was beginning to take on what became its semi-permanent structure by the middle of the 1950s. While the Burma army was still fighting the KMT in the Shan State and finally retook Papun from the KNDO, after seven years of siege, it pursued its neutralist foreign policy in the midst of neighbours increasingly involved in institutions which tied Southeast Asian politics to larger international ideological forces. Cold War politics permeated Burmese society as the ideological battle between capitalist "democracy" and Communist "egalitarianism" was waged. For example, Burmese *pwe* (traditional entertainment) attendees on Mandalay hill abandoned the performance to watch anti-Communist films presented by the United States Information Service (USIS). USIS was "everywhere in Burma". When this was noted by a visitor, her Burmese host replied, "America woos Burma because it feels that China woos India" (Mannin 1955, p. 120).

Neutralist Myanmar had its own friends, however, amongst the non-aligned with India, Indonesia and Yugoslavia being foremost among them. Marshall Tito made his first visit to Burma on 6 January 1955 and remained in the country for twelve days. During his visit he offered to equip a Burma army brigade. He, in turn, received a gift of rice.[99] West Germany, a reminder of the deep divisions the Cold War had brought to Europe, and the fragile environment that neutralist Yugoslavia persisted in, began during the same month as Tito's visit to search for suitable buildings for a West German legation in Yangon.[100]

The main institution of the Cold War in Southeast Asia, the American-inspired South East Asia Treaty Organisation (SEATO), was formally inaugurated on 19 February 1955 through the Manila Pact. Headquartered in Bangkok, it only had two Southeast Asian members, Thailand and the Philippines, with the other signatories being the United States, Great Britain, France, Australia, New Zealand, and Pakistan. Myanmar now had two neighbours, Pakistan and Thailand, formerly allied with the United States and the United Kingdom in an anti-Communist, anti-Chinese military alliance. It had to tread warily in its relations with all sides in the Cold War as it sought to maintain its integrity and independence. As the KMT affair and the *Mujahadin* issue had taught all who cared about Myanmar's independence, suspicions about the motives of one's neighbours extended not only to the supposedly aggressive Communist Chinese but also to the anti-Communist neighbours.

Following the inauguration of SEATO, the American Secretary of State, John Foster Dulles, visited Myanmar for one day. There were no substantive discussions and he made no attempt to persuade Myanmar to join SEATO.[101] In any event, Myanmar, along with India and Indonesia, had already made clear their misgivings about the establishment of military pacts and alliances in the region. In the end, SEATO may have been a "zoo of paper tigers", but no one knew that in 1955 (Cable 1986, p. 139). As Burma declined in British international concerns following the termination of the Let Ya–Freeman Agreement and Myanmar's growing multilateral diplomacy, British Secretary of State Anthony Eden gave even less time to the country than Dulles did. As the Bangkok meetings were brought forward a week or so over the original plans, he could only spare about an hour in Yangon to have his plane refuelled on his way back to London via Singapore.[102]

The British army, however, could still devote time to Yangon and General Sir Charles Loewin, the Canadian-born and Canadian-educated Commander-in-Chief of the British Far East Land Forces, visited Myanmar from 28 March to 5 April. He lunched with Ne Win and Daw Khin May Than on 29 March. The conversation, which lasted about as long as Eden's visit, was friendly, with Ne Win expanding on his views of the desirability of establishing a system of eighteen months of national service, something that no government had yet managed to introduce. He also felt that civilians should attend the new Defence Services Academy (DSA) so that the gap between soldiers and civilians could be narrowed, an idea which was tested in 1964.[103] The Defence Services Academy took in its first batch of candidates in June 1955. Disavowing any danger of a military coup, Ne Win also suggested that while the KMT had previously been supplied by the government of Thailand, among others, after a visit from Police General Phao Sriyanond, notorious for his connections with the American CIA and commander of the Thai occupation of Kengtung during the Second World War, such activities had ceased.[104]

Nonetheless, the army was still fighting against the KMT and during April–May, Brigadier Kyaw Zaw commanded "Operation Yangyiaung" against them. Fighting with the KNDO also continued and according to the United States embassy, despite allegations to the contrary, there was "no confirmation [of] indiscriminate burning [of] Karen villages although [the] Burma Army [was] known [to] burn barracks areas and immobile supplies after dispersing KNDO inhabitants". These methods were in line with the tactics that Ne Win had developed as early as "Operation Flush" and were designed to coax followers of the KNDO to join the government. From the American perspective, it was unreasonable to expect the government of Burma to accept the terms for peace that the KNDO were insisting upon. Now that the KNDO was cooperating with the Communists and the KMT were still active, the army had no choice but to maintain the offensive. The American embassy also found it "disturbing [that the] Thais [were] even contemplating clandestine assistance [to the] insurgents",[105] despite Ne Win's assertion that they had ceased doing so. Ne Win flew to the Thai border himself at the beginning of April to investigate whether the Burma air force had inadvertently bombed two Thai villages, as claimed by the Thai government.[106] The air force had been in pursuit of KMT troops and though the matter could have been easily settled, it became a cause of friction with the government of Pibul Songram after members of the *Pyithu Hluttaw* in Yangon made inflammatory remarks about Thai assistance to the KMT (Nu 1975, p. 270).

The Thai consideration of support for insurgents in Burma was apparently more than a thought. According to the U.S. embassy, reliable sources had informed them in June that the "KNDO in [the] border area [were] receiving new US-made weapons and ammunition from Thai army sources presumably without official Thai knowledge. Some weapons from deserted Thai Army Karen troops but intercepted radio messages indicate continuing supply including air drops coming from active Thai elements." The Burmese government was negotiating with the Thais to stop the practice,[107] but it continued into the 1980s. Meanwhile, new potential sources of ethnically labelled separatist activity were being contemplated. The 1947 Constitution of Burma provided, following elaborate procedures, that the Shan State and the Kayah State might opt to secede from Burma any time after 1958. Sao Shwe Thaik, Burma's first president and speaker of the Chamber of Nationalities, and his young wife, the Mahadevi of Yawnghwe, in a meeting with the British ambassador, vented their spleens against the Burmese and asked for British supervision of a plebiscite to ensure the Shan State could succeed through a three-step process. Meanwhile, Pakistan was not cooperating with Burma over the *Mujahadin* issue. Karachi refused to hand over Cassim after his arrest and complained that the settlement of Burmese in northern Rakhine was forcing Muslims into East Pakistan.[108]

Meanwhile, another block in the structure of the Cold War was being erected — the Bandung Conference of Afro-Asian nations. The Conference, attended by Egyptian President Gamal Abdel Nasser, Indian Prime Minister Jawaharlal Nehru, Chinese Premier Chou En-lai, and Burmese Prime Minister Nu, and hosted by Indonesian President Sukarno, launched the Non-Alignment Movement (NAM), with an endorsement of the Five Principles of Peaceful Coexistence which Nehru, Nu and Chou had agreed upon the previous year. The meeting created a multilateral forum for the non-aligned states in which Burma, U Nu believed, had to play a leading role (Westad 2007, pp. 99–106), but Ne Win tended to deprecate.

In September 1955, following the increasingly cordial relations between Chou En-lai and Nu, Ne Win led a powerful thirteen man delegation of senior military officials to China (Aung Myoe 2011, pp. 27–28). This visit was to have profound consequences for the General and Burma, unforeseen and unexpected at the time. Seven years after independence, most observers of Ne Win would have concurred with the British embassy's assessment that he had "become a cordial enigma". Though he had been suspected of political ambitions and had possibly considered taking over the government in 1949, he now seemed "to have abandoned all pretension to a political career" and was "firmly under the control of the Defence Minister, U Ba Swe". "Good looking, sport-loving, debonair, rather lazy and fond of a good time, he gives the impression of not liking serious business." His love of the Yangon Turf Club, first evidenced a quarter of a century earlier persisted, and he made his money at the races betting on the jockeys, not the horses, he claimed.[109] That strategy came to be extended to larger domains as well. The British embassy's assessment of the grip Defence Minister Ba Swe had on Ne Win, or indeed other top army officers, was vigorously disputed by others. Ba Swe, who rarely went to his office, and enjoyed drinking and poker, would sign any paper that Ne Win, Maung Maung or Aung Gyi put in front of him. In this way, the civilian government lost control over the army budget.[110]

If Ne Win had no political ambitions, a number of his subordinates allegedly did. At the Annual Commanders' Conference in September, Deputy Prime Minister Kyaw Nyein was allegedly heckled by the assembled officers for the government's poor economic performance and threatened with a coup if the government did not improve the economy. Moreover, they allegedly claimed that the police under the Home Ministry were hopeless and the army would have to take charge of village defence, and in this they were backed by Home Minister Khin Maung Gale. It was even claimed that Colonels Maung Maung and Aung Gyi would conduct any possible coup, but first Ne Win would be forced to retire and go abroad as an ambassador "to avoid bloodshed in the army".[111] Colonel Aung Gyi later denied this account, provided by an officer in attendance who was being removed from the army.[112] Nevertheless, it was widely believed that Aung Gyi was the driving force in the army as Ne Win was "too idle and pleasure loving" to dominate the scene.[113] Whatever the case, in November 1955, Ne Win went to Ba Swe's home and stated that the army would no longer involve itself in the affairs of the Socialist Party (Min Maung Maung 1995, pp. 112–13).

Before any such alleged threat to remove him could be acted upon, Ne Win left for China with thirteen senior colleagues, including Brigadiers Kyaw Win and Douglas Blake, Air Commodore Tommy Cliff, Vice Chief of Navy Lieutenant Commander Tin Thane Lu, and Colonels Chit Myaing and San Myint. Ne Win and Bo Khin Nyo would return after two weeks but the rest of the mission would continue touring for up to two months.[114]

The Chinese Communists apparently rolled out the red carpet in Beijing. Ne Win and his party spent a week in the capital, during which they met Premier Chou En-lai and senior military officials as well as being entertained handsomely. At the end of the week, Ne Win met Chairman Mao Tse-tung for the first time and dined with Marshall Chu Teh, head of the army and Vice-Chairman of the Republic. The second week was spent touring Chinese military installations outside the capital. In one of his speeches towards the end of his tour, Ne Win was reported to have said that before he came to China, he had misgivings about China and its intentions towards Myanmar, but after visiting, he felt reassured.[115] Whether this was dissembling of the kind that Ne Win had demonstrated in Bangkok, London and Washington, is, of course, unknown. At that time, there were reports of thirty members of the Chinese People's Liberation Army (PLA) crossing the border into the Wa territory in northern Shan State and clashing with Burmese troops (Lintner 1999, p. 442).

Whatever the case, Ne Win took an increasing interest in external affairs beyond the development of the army following his trip to China. Soon upon his return, he sought out the British Military Attaché, Colonel Oliver Berger, to discuss the current situation in Malaya where the "Emergency", the twelve-year long conflict between the British and the Malayan Communist Party, had entered its seventh year. There were discussions at that time of an amnesty for the Communists and he wanted to compare notes on a desire, he believed, by the Burma Communist Party for a negotiated settlement, but he would offer no amnesty. If the Communists surrendered without a settlement, they would be conceding guilt and would not be allowed back into the army. If they were allowed back into the army, that would lead to a coup, as had occurred in Syria and Argentina, because the army would not accept former comrades that had turned traitors.

Over three days of meetings, Ne Win and Berger discussed a number of topics. Noting that Burma was making no significant arms purchases, Ne Win averred that the country was short of foreign exchange and that there was no genuine external threat which would justify such expenditure. In time, he believed that the Burma army would be able to hold back any possible Chinese invasion in the far north of the country. In terms of government programmes and policies, he had been "stressing the need for a census since 1947". He once more brought up the idea of eighteen months of national service[116] and wanted to settle the Kachin and Shan veterans of the army in Hukaung Valley and the Shan States.[117]

Berger resumed his dialogue with Ne Win on 23 December, bringing along additional information on an amnesty in Malaya. The General expressed interest in the subject but indicated he thought it unfortunate that the Malayan leaders Tunku Abdul Rahman and David Marshall were meeting with the Communist leader Chin Peng.[118] He also told Berger that

> the [Burmese] Communist insurgent leaders were also trying to utilise the amnesty to increase their control over their rank and file and gain popular support for negotiations and for recognition for their party. He added that he was trying to separate the rank and file from the leaders by letting the former know that they were safe under the amnesty and that they were being kept in the jungle only by leaders who [were] themselves unwilling to surrender because the government had evidence against [them] that they had committed one of the three major crimes which debarred them from the protection of the amnesty.[119]

As was widely known, Ne Win was also unhappy about the agreement that Prime Minister Nu had entered into with the leaders of the Soviet Union, Nikita Khrushchev and Nikolai Bulganin, who had visited Myanmar for the first seven days of December (for the visit to South Asia by the two Soviet leaders, see Halle 1967, pp. 336–38). Ne Win concurred in Berger's opinion that Russian imperialism was an "imperialism of the mind" and Thakin Than Tun had also once used that expression. Turning to the Americans, the General said they were clumsy in attempting to offer more aid than the Soviet Union had done so soon after the visit.

> The General also told [Berger] that the KMT were still receiving arms and ammunition from what he called "American adventurers" through Thailand. The KNDO were also receiving arms including a few bazookas from the Philippines and from Borneo. These were also supplied by certain "adventurers".[120]

Foreigners and their activities in Myanmar was an issue that Ne Win considered frequently in the 1950s. Although accused by government ministers as well as foreign observers of being xenophobic, there was little evidence for such a claim when his behaviour is examined in detail. For example, after the British Services Mission was terminated, the army continued to hire British individuals to work in technical fields, such as in servicing Myanmar's second-hand Spitfires and other aircraft.[121] Ne Win got along well with British military and political figures, such as Air

Commodore Ward and Colonel Berger, who dealt with him directly and fairly. He told Berger about his plans to mount another campaign against the KMT following his discussions with visiting Thai Prime Minister Pibul and a forthcoming tour of the Shan States.[122] Pibul had given Ne Win "satisfactory assurances" that the Thai police would not allow fleeing KMT troops to enter Thailand.[123]

On the other hand, he often had reasons to be suspicious of foreigners meddling in Myanmar's internal conflicts, such as reports that four British ex-officers were training KNU fighters near Hlaingbwe prior to going to the Shan State to join the KMT.[124] Ne Win's suspicions about foreigners backing the government's insurgent opponents were not helped by antics such as the Assistant Military Attaché of the American embassy in Bangkok crossing the Thai–Myanmar border and spending a night in a KNU camp. Burmese liaison officers also reported truckloads of Americans being taken near the border. In the words of the British ambassador to Bangkok, "this is not the only recent evidence of dangerous United States contacts with Karens."[125] It was doubtful that an order by the American ambassador subsequent to these reports to avoid all contacts with KNU impressed Ne Win or anyone else in Myanmar.[126]

When the Russian security detail refused to rely on the arrangements of the Burmese Army for the safety of Khrushchev and Bulganin in 1955, affronts to the dignity and competence of the Burma Army obviously rankled the General. According to visiting former Governor Sir Hubert Rance, "Ne Win had been infuriated by the Russians", and there had been an actual clash between them and the army.[127] When Prime Minister Nu accepted a Russian offer to send agricultural advisers to Myanmar, Ne Win took this amiss. As the British ambassador wrote,

> General Ne Win, a close friend of U Nu, described to a member of the Embassy the embarrassment felt at U Nu's engagement of Russian experts to advise on agricultural development and his own determination severely to circumscribe their activities in the countryside.[128]

Ne Win's loyalty and friendship with U Nu was rewarded on 1 January 1956 when he was promoted to the rank of full General[129] and awarded the Thado Thiri Thudhamma honour three days later to upgrade his Maha Thiri Thudhamma status that was granted in 1949.

Though Ne Win was repeatedly described as lazy and indifferent towards his work, and preoccupied with family and personal affairs, he was often the indispensable man in an emergency, even in affairs not really his responsibility. For example, one afternoon, when five to six thousand persons rioted and, in the presence of the President of Burma, set fire to the Aung San stadium during a football match, Ne Win, who was meeting with Defence Minister U Ba Swe, and others were called to handle the matter. He intervened to order the release of seven persons arrested, and the rioters dispersed.[130] On another occasion, 150 members of the Myanmar air force ran amok in the Yangon Zoological Gardens, injuring 19 persons. Ne Win was notified, and abandoning his late afternoon tennis game, went to the zoo to restore order (Hopkins 1952, pp. 212–13).

There was no doubt, however, that he could be rude and discourteous as well as being the perfect host. He enjoyed drinking most evenings with the Americans and Europeans, as well as with his fellow Burmese, at the Union Club or the Lake Club on Kandawgyi Lake throughout the 1950s. However, when Ne Win was included in the plans for a forthcoming visit by Lord Mountbatten, he made it clear to Prime Minister Nu that he would be unavailable. When instructed to return, he refused. He also ignored a request to attend the parades and ceremonies on Independence Day to mark the visit of the Thai Prime Minister.[131]

His dislike of pomp and circumstances seemed to grow over the years. Though he was one of the most powerful men in the country, it was believed that he was "too indolent to make full use of this power". In the eyes of Colonel Berger, "the whole army therefore suffer[ed] from lack of direction and drive from the top". Berger did not share Count Tolstoy's views on the enforced idleness of military life.

> If man could find a state in which he felt that though he were idle he was fulfilling his duty, we would have found the conditions of man's primitive blessedness. And such a state of obligatory and irreproachable idleness is the lot of a whole class — the military. The chief attraction of military service has consisted and will consist of this compulsory and irreproachable idleness (Tolstoy 1997, p. 531).

On 27 April 1956, the second general election in Myanmar's independent history was held in much more peaceful circumstances than the first. The governing Anti-Fascist People's Freedom League (AFPFL) government of Prime Minister Nu won 55 per cent of the votes, while the opposition leftist National United Front (NUF), often referred to as the above-ground Communists, garnered nearly 37 per cent. The relatively narrow lead of the

League caused U Nu and his senior colleagues, particularly Kyaw Nyein and Ba Swe, to consider what their government could do to improve their standing with the public. Though the League was back in government, it was laying the groundwork for its own eventual split, which would be the next major challenge for Ne Win and the army.

In the meantime, however, Ne Win was preparing for a visit to the United States via Hong Kong and Japan, accompanied by his wife and Brigadier Maung Maung. From there, they would move on to London, then Yugoslavia and Israel.[132] The party left Yangon on 16 May and arrived in San Francisco on 23 May.[133] He was the official guest of General Maxwell Taylor, at that time Chief-of-Staff of the United States Army. He toured the major American army, navy and air force bases, visited Hoover Dam and Fort Knox, and, as in 1949, automobile assembly plants in Detroit. On 1 June, he was awarded the United States Legion of Merit by General Taylor and the official visit ended two weeks later.[134] The award of the Legion of Merit came as a surprise, as did the United States Air Force plane placed at the Burmese party's disposal. Ne Win was still looking to the United States as a major arms supplier, though none were purchased during the trip, and provider of training for the army officer corps, despite his concern about American "adventurers" and their links to the KMT and KNU. While he was in the United States, Prime Minister U Nu resigned in order to devote himself to his literary and religious desires and U Ba Swe took his place. Ne Win claimed to have known of the resignation a year before it happened.[135]

The British ambassador hoped to use the visit to improve relations between the Burma army and Britain as the army was turning towards Yugoslavia and Israel for the supply of arms. While in London, Ne Win had a follow-up sinus operation. During the 1955 visit, he spent an evening *a deux* with Lieutenant Colonel J.D. Fitzpatrick, then in the War Office, but previously a member of the British Services Mission in Myanmar. The Ne Win that Fitzpatrick met that evening was very different from the man he had known five years ago. He attributed this to Katy Ne Win whom, he believed, had "more or less domesticated" him. Fitzpatrick, though aware of the rumours that Ne Win no longer took any serious interest in military affairs, plied him for information on Myanmar officers whom he had worked with in the past. Fitzpatrick subsequently wrote,

> Most of these officers I mentioned were junior in rank and I felt that if he knew their whereabouts etc it would show that he was still interested.

He was, in fact, able to tell me not only their present jobs but all the appointments they had held since 1950. I was surprised at his detailed knowledge and the speed he brought it up.[136]

Part of his "domestication" appeared to be his abandonment of tennis for golf, a game he played several times while in the United Kingdom, including at St. Andrews.

Their conversation then turned to the procurement of arms and foreign policy issues. These were clearly on Ne Win's mind, but the current military mission in Czechoslovakia, he insisted, was on civil development project issues, and not military matters. In terms of relations with the United States, Fitzpatrick wrote,

> He appears to retain his dislike of American methods in many fields. Instances were:
>
> (a) The Americans were forcing Burma to trade with Communist countries because they are closing Burmese pre-war markets by giving the countries concerned aid in the form of arms and goods. He quoted rice as an example. India buys little from Burma now, he also says that Ceylon was likewise affected and was selling to China at far greater profit than in her previous markets.
>
> (b) Communist countries in order to wean Burma more than ready to barter goods in exchange, particularly machinery and weapons. He felt that Burma gained a great deal by this method of trading.
>
> (c) The Americans also attached too many strings to their aid and poked their noses into minor domestic matters on the score of aid.[137]

Turning to military matters, while he had great faith in Brigadier Kyaw Zaw as the northern commander, Ne Win felt that the military's progress of driving the KMT out of the Shan State was going too slowly, partly because of the difficult terrain. However, he left the impression with Fitzpatrick "that the Americans were not above suspicion however indirectly".[138] Expressing concerns for the leftward drift of Indonesian politics under Sukarno, Ne Win felt that the Indonesian army, which did not share those sentiments, would push in a neutral direction. Similarly, his forthcoming trip to China was to demonstrate to both the West and the Communist world that they would not know in advance toward which side he was leaning.[139]

During Ne Win's visit to Britain in 1956, Gore-Booth described him and Maung Maung as not really soldiers but politicians. He advised against taking Ne Win to military displays as he would find them boring. Ne Win arrived in London on 21 June and checked into a hospital the next day. His programme was very light, meeting the Chief of the Imperial General Staff, Field Marshall Sir Gerald Templer, former High Commissioner of Malaya and the Minister of Defence, Sir Walter Monckton, and attending a reception hosted by the Vice Chief of the Imperial General Staff at the Army and Navy Club. With the excuse of being under medical care, he turned down an invitation to the Queen's Garden Party, though he met with Monckton the same day. He attended a musical, lunched with Indian Prime Minister Nehru which Lord Mountbatten hosted, watched tennis at Wimbledon, and played a lot of golf, including during a tour of the Lake District. After drinks at the Cavalry and Guards Club and attendance at "La Plume de ma Tante", he was taken to the Mirabelle restaurant in Mayfair, but announced that he was tired and went home along with the Burmese guests.[140]

While in London, Ne Win attended a reception held in his honour at the Myanmar embassy. One of the guests was the writer and former colonial civil servant in Burma, Maurice Collis.[141] After the event, he wrote in his diary, "I found him [Ne Win] to be a pleasant, keen-looking youngish man. His wife was remarkably cosmopolitan for a Burmese woman, a good conversationalist, tactful and with natural flair." When Daw Khin May Than and Collis, along with an American Chinese friend of hers, lunched together the following month, his initial impression was confirmed (Collis 1970, pp. 154–55).

Ne Win and his party left London for Paris on 6 August by train, where he was the guest of the French army. From there he travelled to Yugoslavia and Israel where he visited military facilities. The party arrived in Belgrade on 13 August but Ne Win returned to London from Israel on 29 August without his wife and Brigadier Maung Maung and with just his ADC, Bo Lwin. He remained in London until 4 or 5 September and then returned directly to Yangon.[142] Altogether he was out of Myanmar for four full months. Upon his arrival back home, he met with the outgoing British ambassador. He indicated to Gore-Booth that he would attempt to get his British doctors to come to Burma the following year so that he would not have to travel abroad again to receive treatment. As for purchasing additional military equipment from the United Kingdom, he once more averred that the government had little money[143] and the army did not need heavy equipment. As for buying other things from the UK, he asserted that British cars and trucks were expensive and of poor quality although British airplanes were of a high standard. As to reports of clashes with and incursions by Chinese troops and the Burma army in the Wa territory of the Shan State, he implied that the area was worthless and people tended to exaggerate what they saw.[144]

During the six months U Nu was out of office, in his capacity as President of the ruling party, he commenced negotiations with the Chinese government on a border agreement which essentially recognized the British-bequeathed border, the line of actual control or the traditional border. In December 1956, Chinese Premier Chou En-lai and Vice Premier He Long visited Burma to discuss the border deal. The Chinese desire to open the issue may have been related to Chinese concerns that Burma was possibly aligning itself with the United States as a result of Ne Win's tour earlier in the year.[145] During their ten-day visit, Chou reviewed Burmese troops at Maymyo with General Ne Win and Marshall He Long, a veteran of the Chinese Communists' Long March and known as China's Robin Hood. Ne Win at that time extended an invitation for a Chinese military mission to visit Burma as he and his colleagues had visited China the previous year.[146] A little over two weeks later, a Chinese military mission led by Marshall Yeh Chien-ying, Deputy Chief-of-Staff and equivalent of Inspector General of the Army (Rice 1972, p. 533), arrived in Yangon and was received by General Ne Win.[147]

The Chinese mission, composed of nine officers from the army, navy and air force, remained in Myanmar for three weeks. They visited a number of military installations, including the northern and southern commands at Maymyo and Mingladon, the Yangon naval base, and Loikaw in the Kayah State. At a dinner hosted by Ne Win, according to the British, Marshall Yeh's speech was fulsome and advocated military cooperation between Burma and China. Ne Win's reply was less flattering, merely indicating that the Burma army was peaceful and he hoped that the Chinese were too.[148] The Soviet Union Defence Minister, Marshall Zhukov, followed the Chinese delegation less than two months later, and left an invitation for a Burmese military mission to visit his country but offered no military assistance.[149] Believing that Ne Win was about to make another visit to the United States in late 1957 for "medical treatment", Chinese General Staff Headquarters expressed the view that "in order to extend the civil war and resolve the problems of the Burmese forces' lack of equipment", Ne Win was about to make another trip to the United States despite the warming relations with China and continuing adherence to neutralism.[150]

Though the army was growing and security was increasingly being restored around the country, the situation was still fragile as the political situation was open to unpredictable ruptures and conflicts which had implications on the whole of society (Nash 1965, pp. 274–90; Callahan 1998, pp. 17–38). Moreover, the Shan Sawbwa and their political allies were increasingly mobilizing support for a separatist bid after 1958 (Lintner 1999, pp. 182–89). The secession question was very "far from dead" as twenty-nine of the fifty members of the Shan State Council favoured the move, only six short of the thirty-five required to implement the secession clauses of the constitution.[151] The following month, Sai Nwe founded the *Noom Suik Harn* (Brave Young Shan) insurgent group on the Thai border in cooperation with the KMT (Min Maung Maung 1995, pp. 132–33).

Despite being declared illegal, the White Flag and Red Flag Communist Parties remained powerful threats to the government and they both had their allies amongst the legal political elites in Yangon and around the country. The solidarity of the army after the splits of 1949 had since been maintained but appeared to be threatened in late 1956. Sometime during that year, papers which were seized from Communist Party headquarters by Colonel Kyi Win revealed that Brigadier Kyaw Zaw, the Northern Commander for the previous three years, was in contact with the illegal Communist Party, and perhaps even a member. Ne Win discussed the matter with Kyaw Zaw and other regional and brigade commanders at the Annual Commanders' Conference in September where he suggested to the Defence Minister to suspend Kyaw Zaw. Subsequently, Ne Win discussed the matter further with U Ba Swe and other civilians and, as a consequence, Kyaw Zaw was relieved of the Northern Command on 13 February 1957 and dismissed from the army on 7 June of the same year.[152]

Aware of the dangerous legacy that Aung San had left the army with when he insisted upon establishing ethnically segregated battalions in mid-1945, to which Mountbatten and the British government had conceded at the Kandy Conference, it was determined that the army should become ethnically integrated by 1951, with Burman officers and men mixed with the Shan, Kachin, Chin, Kayah, Kayin, and Gurkha battalions which were inherited from the British and had remained loyal to the Union. However, it was only in 1957 that the policy came into effect and though the ethnic names of the legacy battalions remained, Burman officers and men were henceforth mixed among them. By that time, nearly half the officers were from the major ethnic group, the Bamar.[153]

After a decade at the top of the army, General Ne Win's future in Myanmar's politics was often a point of speculation. It was believed that he had grown bored with army life and, having indifferent health, would possibly retire before long. The sinus trouble that had taken him twice to England for treatment recurred and his military bearing was showing obvious signs of decline. Though described as a close friend of Prime Minister Nu, the British military attaché believed him to be "little more than the mouthpiece of the AFPFL".[154] He was considered to be "lazy, selfish, and touchy and fundamentally dislikes all foreigners of any kind", though his friendship with Malcolm MacDonald, in contrast with General Temple, was noted.[155] Moreover, it was obvious that when foreigners were prepared to accept the Burmese way of life, he got on very well with them. An example was Colonel Ted Serong, the founder of Australia's jungle fighting centre, who came to Myanmar in mid-1957 to lecture. Serong and Ne Win became good friends (Selth 1990, p. 6). At the end of January 1958, Ne Win left Yangon for the United States to seek treatment for an unspecified bladder problem.[156]

Over a decade of independence, the army had grown and developed. Ne Win's apparent lackadaisical approach to his responsibilities was partly a facade and partly a consequence of the trust and confidence he placed in his key subordinates, particularly Brigadier Maung Maung and Colonel Aung Gyi, and until his exposure, Brigadier Kyaw Zaw, as well as Brigadiers Tin Pe and Aung Shwe, and partly due to his personality. Under Ne Win's supervision, Maung Maung was in charge of general staff work, including training and planning. Aung Gyi, who was an active Socialist and close to U Nu and the Socialists in the government, was in charge of organization and operations along with the northern and southern commands. The initiative for campaigns against the insurgents largely lay with the regional commanders. Ne Win took charge of intelligence and officer postings and promotions. He was always very well-informed of what his subordinates or various politicians were planning to do (Maung Maung n.p., p. 25). Mary Callahan, an authority on this period of the development of the Burma army, tends to discount Ne Win's role in the transformation of the army from a group of uncoordinated forces fighting many lesser, but still threatening forces, into the only organization in Myanmar which could move men and resources confidently across the country. She suggests that

Ne Win was too busy and distracted by personal scandals surrounding his social life to have had a role in what she believed was the key to the success of the army, the Military Planning Staff (MPS) which was the creation of Maung Maung and Aung Gyi.[157]

However, as noted above, Ne Win never shared fully the view that the country either required or could afford large-scale war fighting capabilities. While he perceived China as a threat, and had done so since 1948, his primary concern was containing and defeating insurgency within the country. At the army's annual officers conference in 1957, Ne Win once more emphasized the importance of military training along with moral and psychological warfare in order to deal politically as well as militarily with the country's continuing myriad insurgent movements. The opening of a National Defence College and a revamp of the curricula at the Command and General Staff College and other training centres were announced by the Commander-in-Chief. New thinking about military doctrine was taking place within the army (Aung Myoe 1999, p. 3). Old certainties were giving way to new realities and these were to test General Ne Win and those around him. The old order was about to change and soon unexpected political events would upset the routines that perhaps contributed to the view that Ne Win was lazy and bored with life.

Notes

1. Letter, Edward Hayward, Secretary, India, Pakistan and Burma Association, to J.D. Murray, 8 May 1950, enclosing Who's Who in Burma, FO371/83117.
2. Fourth Quarterly Report of the BSM by Temple, 10 January 1951, DEFE8/867.
3. Report of an interview between Major-General Temple, Head of the British Services Mission, and U Win, Minister for Defence, on 15 December 1950, enclosed with Letter, Temple to Permanent Secretary, Ministry of Defence, 10 January 1951, DEFE 8/867; also with Letter, Speaight to Secretary of State, 19 December 1950, FO371/83108.
4. Record of conversation letter, MacDonald and U Nu, 19 November 1951, FO371/92149.
5. Telegram, Speaight to FO, 20 January 1951, FO371/92148.
6. Telegrams, Speaight to FO, 21 January 1951, FO371/92148 and DEFE7/836. In an unrelated conversation, U Win claimed that there was "large scale weapons traffic in French and Italian arms in Burma", apparently related to corruption in the navy. Telegram, BSM to Ministry of Defence, 8 February 1951, DEFE 7/836. Four naval officers were subsequently suspended and the navy chief placed on leave for apparent corruption. Monthly Summary for February 1951, FO 371/93214.

7. Telegram, Speaight to FO, 23 January 1951, FO371/92148.
8. Letter, Speaight to MacDonald, 1 March 1951, FO371/92135.
9. Telegram, Rangoon to Secretary of State (SOS), 6 July 1951; Letter, Speaight to R.H. Scott, 7 July 1951, FCO 371/92149.
10. Letter, Macolm MacDonald to Herbert Morrison, 26 April 1951, FO371/92148.
11. MacDonald to Morrison, 26 April 1951, FO371/92148.
12. First Quarterly Report of BSM, Temple, 31 March 1951, DEFE 8/867.
13. Letter, Speaight to R. Scott, FO, 11 May 1951, FO371/92149. Similarly views can be found in "The Political, Economic and Military Problems of Burma", address given by G. Baker to the Imperial Defence College, 19 July 1952, FO371/92144.
14. Second Quarterly Report from BSM, Temple, 31 June 1951, DEFE 7/867.
15. Letter Speaight to R.H. Scott, 7 July 1951, FO371/92149.
16. Letter, MacDonald to Morrison, 26 April 1951, FO371/92148.
17. Letter, R. Whittington, Bangkok, to Speaight, 19 April 1951, FO371/92147.
18. Bo Setkya (U Aung Than) was apparently the agent for Ameritex, the American company that had facilitated his and Ne Win's 1949 trip to the United States. At that time, they were negotiating on the sale of two sugar mills, perhaps a steel rolling plant, cartridges and 5,000 .38 caliber pistols. Air Letter, Henry Day to Department of State, 21 July 1952, 790B/7-1141, Control 9492, No. 115.
19. Memo on General Ne Win's Leave of Absence by Col. Thomas H. Davies, 13 July 1951 (embassy papers). When Colonel Davies called on Ne Win at 10 a.m., he was in a meeting with the Chinese ambassador. That meeting went on for more than one hour.
20. Telegram, Key to SOS, 17 July 1951, 790B.00(W)/7-651, Control 3554, No. 17.
21. Telegram, Key to SOS, 14 July 1951, 790B.00(W)/7-1451, Control 7542, No. 56; Telegram, Speaight to FO, 17 July 1951, FO371/921149; Telegram, Rangoon to SOS, 21 July 1951, 790B.00(W)/7-2151, Control 11376, No. 76.
22. His brother-in-law, Daw Khin May Than's brother, George Ba Than, trained as a doctor in the United States and married an American woman.
23. Memo, Speaight to FO, 13 October 1951, FO371/92137.
24. See the papers in FO371/92155. For a detailed account of the American involvement in the KMT matter, see Kenton Clymer, "The United States and the Guomindang (KMT) Forces in Burma, 1949–1954: A Diplomatic Disaster", unpublished manuscript, 2012. For the role of the CIA air force in support of the KMT, see William M. Leary, *Perilous Missions: Civil Air Transport and CIA Covert Operations in Asia* (Washington and London: Smithsonian Institution Press, 2002), esp. pp. 129 and 195.

25. See Norman Lewis, *The Single Pilgrim* (London: Cape, 1953). Not a particularly good novel, it is obvious what Lewis was writing about. Lewis toured Burma in 1951, writing his perceptive travelogue *Golden Earth* (London: Cape, 1953). For Lewis' time in Myanmar, see Julian Evans, *The Semi-Visible Man: The Life of Norman Lewis* (London: Cape, 2008).

26. Conversations with Burma Leader, 11–20 November 1951 (by M. MacDonald), FO371/10133.

27. Stanton to SOS, 13 January 1953, Tel. 1301, 690B.9321/1-1353, RG59, CDF 1950–54, Box 2993, NAII.

28. Extract from Rangoon General letter of 22 February 1952, FO 371/101001. Kyaw Nyein had recently read a political biography of British Prime Minister Lloyd George and claimed to see an analogy between how Prime Minister Nu handled Ne Win and the Army, and Lloyd George and a recalcitrant British army during the First World War, particularly Lord Kitchener. The book was quite possibly Thomas Jones, *Lloyd George* (London: Geoffrey Cumberledge, Oxford University Press, 1951). In addition to difficult relations with Kitchener, Lloyd George "… neither sacked his C[hief]. I[mperial] G[eneral]. S[taff]. nor trusted him", p. 142. For further insights, see Hew Strachan, *The Politics of the British Army* (Oxford: Clarendon Press, 1997).

29. Telegram, Embassy to SOS, 18 February 1952.

30. Letter, Speaight to Eden, 14 January 1952, in 1st quarterly report for 1952, by Temple, DEFE 7/868.

31. Letter, Sir O. Franks to FO, 8 January 1952, FO371/101001, reporting a conversation with United States Secretary of State Dean Acheson.

32. Extract from Rangoon General letter of 22 February 1952, FO371/101001. Steel Brothers had proposed to sell the chummery to the National Planning Board for the use of the American consultancy firm Knappet-Tippett and Abbot but Ne Win objected. Eventually, it became the headquarters of the Myanmar Navy and is now the Yuzana Gardens Hotel. The Masonic Lodge was declared to be under permanent curfew and therefore inoperative. The latter was retailed to the author by the late U Hla Tun in 2005.

33. Letter, Speaight to R.H. Scott, 27 March 1952, FO371/101001.

34. Telegram, Commonwealth Relations Office to High Commissioners, 2 February 1952, FO371/101009; first telegraphed by Speaight to FO on 29 January 1952, FO371/101008.

35. Telegram, Speaight to FO, 22 February 1952, FO371/1010001.

36. Interview with U Than Nyunt, former journalist with *Myanmar Alin*. A more heroic version of the army's action is found in Maung Maung, *Grim War Against the KMT* (Rangoon: U Nu Yin Press, 1953).

37. British Services Mission Periodic Report, 1st Quarter 1952, 31 March 1952, WO32/15034.
38. Telegram, British Services Mission to Ministry of Defence, 24 April 1952, FO 371/101024; Telegram, Boothby to Ministry of Defence, 26 May 1952, FO 371/101024; Letter, E.D. Boothby to Anthony Eden, 31 May 1952, DEFE 7/838 or FO 371/101002.
39. Telegram, Day to SOS, 2 June 1952, 790B.00(W)/6-252, Control 222, No. 1155.
40. Record of Conversation between Air Commodore E.L.S. Ward and General Ne Win on 7 June 1952, FO 371/101025; Note for meeting on future policy toward British Services Mission, Ministry of Defence, 17 June 1952, DEFE 7/838.
41. Letter, Chancery, Rangoon, to SEAD, 24 May 1952, FO 371/101002.
42. Chiefs of Staff Committee, Supply of Equipment to Burma, FO Letter by R.H. Scott, 12 July 1952, DEFE 7/839. Bo Set Kya "had come into a fortune, nobody knows how". Edward Law-Yone, "Dr Ba Maw of Burma", in *Contributions to Asian Studies 16: Essays on Burma*, edited by John P. Ferguson (Leiden: E.J. Brill, 1981), p. 14. A biographical note prepared for the United States Secretary of State on 25 July 1949 states that Set Kya, who was alleged of part German ancestry and whose legal name was James Klusemann, had made his fortune as agent for the Socialist Party and in rice purchasing, import and export, and other business activities. By 1954, Bo Set Kya owned car agencies and the International Harvester Company franchise in Yangon. Anglo-Burmese Relations in Respect to the Supply of Arms by A. Goodwin, 20 December 1954, FO371/111990. Set Kya's wife, Daw Win Min Than, starred against Gregory Peck in "The Purple Plain", a movie released about a British pilot downed in Burma during the Second World War. Based on a novel of the same title by H.E. Bates (London: Michael Joseph, 1947), the screenplay was by Eric Ambler. Bo Set Kya left Yangon in 1962 and died in Bangkok in 1969 but will play an interesting role again in 1966, below.
43. BSM Periodic Report for April–July 1952 by Ward, DEFE 7/868; Report of Conversation between Head of British Services Mission and General Ne Win on 30 August 1952, DEFE 7/166 and FO 371/101025.
44. Telegram, Speaight to FO, 22 September 1952, DEFE 7/166.
45. Telegram, Rangoon to SOS, 12 September 1952, 790B.13/9-1250, Control 4524, No. 179.
46. Telegram, Gifford (London) to SOS, 7 October 1952, 790B.10-754, Control VR-390, No. 2025.
47. Letter, Foreign Office to Speaight, 7 November 1952, DEFE 7/166.
48. Telegram, Gifford (London) to SOS, 23 October 1952, 790B.00/10-2352, Control VR-1535, No. 2391.

49. Report of Conversation between General Ne Win and Wing Commander. E.L.S. Ward in the War Office on 13 September 1952, FO 371/101023; Letter, Speaight to J.G. Talhourdin, 20 September 1952, DEFE 7/166; Letter, Arthur Ringwalt to Robert Acly, Burma Affairs, State Department, 14 October 1952, 790B.5811/10-1452 CS/J.

50. Memorandum of Conversation, Courtesy Call of General Ne Win on Mr Johnson, 21 October 1952, 790B.5701-341.

51. Telegram, Gifford (London) to SOS, 23 October 1952, 790B.5701-554; telegram, Bruce to Rangoon, 22 October 1952, 790B.5602/10-290045.

52. Telegram, Rangoon to SOS, 12 September 1952, 790B.5204/10-270144.

53. Telegram, Bruce (Washington) to Rangoon, 6 November 1952, 790B.5811/11-352 01500.

54. Memorandum of Conversation, Lieutenant General Ne Win, U Sein Bwa, and U Alexis Johnson, 31 October 1952, 790B.00/10-3152.

55. Memorandum, by Henry Day, based on conversation with Col. Davies, 7 November 1952, 882008-343.

56. Telegram, Gifford (London) to SOS, 16 October 1952.

57. Telegram, Sebald to SOS, 22 October 1952, 790B.5811/10-2252, Control 9174, No. 653.

58. Telegram, Bruce to Rangoon, 22 October 1952, 790B.7832-4556, No. 301.

59. Memorandum, Henry Day, based on conversation with Colonel Davies, 7 November 1952 (embassy papers); Letter, H. Gresswell, MOD, or Ward, Rgn, 10 December 1952, DEFE 7/166.

60. As noted below, Hla Aung was demoted but there is no evidence of his dismissal. There is also apparent confusion or faulty memory involved, for the two accounts available of this affair do not tally. Ward indicates that Hla Aung's brother was one Lieutenant Colonel Smythe, but Callahan records Maung Maung as saying that Hla Aung and Smythe were the same person. Mary P. Callahan, *Making Enemies: War and State Building in Burma* (Ithaca: Cornell University Press; Singapore University Press, 2004), fn. 33, p. 248.

61. BSM Periodic Report for August–November 1952, Ward, 5 November 1952, DEFE 7/868 or WO32/15034.

62. Telegram, Gifford (London) to SOS, 12 December 1952, 790B.5/12-1252, Control VR-834, No. 3278.

63. Memorandum of Conversation between Lieutenant General Ne Win and Ambassador Sebald, 18 December 1952, 790B.00/12-1852.

64. British Military Mission Periodic Report, 1 August 1953 to 3 December 1953, WO 32/15034.

65. Blake was succeeded by Brigadier Kyaw Zaw and assumed Kyaw Zaw's former Southern Command post on 1 July. British Services Mission Period Report, 1 April 1953 to 31 July 1952, WO 32/15034.

66. Hla Aung, possibly an Anglo-Burmese, had been Superintendent of Land Records before the Second World War and joined the Burma National Army in 1943. He was apparently demoted by Maung Maung at the urging of Ne Win and Aung Gyi as Maung Maung suspected him of being a "plant" of Defence Minister U Win. Callahan, *Making Enemies*, p. 154 and fn. 33, p. 248.

67. Letter, Ne Win to Field Marshall Alexander, Minister of Defence, 20 March 1953, WO 32/15034.

68. British Services Mission, 1 December 1952 to 31 March 1953, 4 April 1953, WO 32/15034.

69. British Services Mission Period Report, 1 August 1953 to 3 December 1953, WO 32/15153.

70. British Services Mission Periodic Report, 1 April 1953 to 31 July 1953, WO 32/15034.

71. Letter Speaight to Marquess of Salisbury, 22 July 1953, WO 32/15153.

72. Telegram, Speaight to FO, 12 August 1953, WO 32/17153.

73. DR876, Defence Services Historical Museum and Research Institute, the 1953 Tatmadaw Conference, quoted in Aung Myoe, *Officer Education and Leadership Training in the Tatmadaw: A Survey*, ANU Working Paper no. 346 (Canberra: Strategic and Defence Studies Centre, Australian National University, May 2000), p. 2.

74. Telegram, Speaight to FO, 17 September 1953, FO371/106690.

75. At that time the Shan State was subjected to a number of insurgent forces as well as locally recruited forces raised by Sawbwa during the Second World War. Callahan, *Making Enemies*, p. 136.

76. Telegram, Washington to FO, 25 September 1953, FO371/101024.

77. Minutes of a conversation between the councillor of the Yugoslav embassy in Burma Comrade Simi and deputy commander of the Navy Tin Thein Lu, 13 September 1953, cited in Jovan Cavoski, *Arming Nonalignment: Yugoslavia's Relations with Burma and the Cold War in Asia (1950–1955)*, Wilson Center for Scholars International History Project Working Paper no. 61 (Washington, D.C.: Woodrow Wilson International Center for Scholars, April 2010), p. 29, fn. 112.

78. Ibid., p. 32.

79. Ibid., p. 33, citing Minutes of Conversation with Commander-in-Chief of the Burmese Army General Ne Win, 27 February 1954.

80. Report of Conversation between General Ne Win and the Military Attaché [Colonel Berger] on 22 and 23 November and 2 December 1956, DEFE 7/2093.

81. Telegram, Embassy to SOS, 13 November 1953, NARA, RG59. For the conflict itself during 1953, see Maung Maung, *Grim War Against the KMT*.

82. Letter, H.R. Oakeshott to Anthony Eden, 2 December 1953, FO 371/106683c.

83. Memorandum of Conversation between General Ne Win and the Army and Air Attachés of the American embassy in Burma, 22 December 1953 (embassy papers).

84. British Services Mission Periodic Report, 1 August 1953 to 3 December 1953, WO32/15034.

85. Report of Conversation with Air Commodore E.L.S. Ward, DFC, and General Ne Win on 2 January 1954, FO471/111983.

86. Monthly Summary for January 1954, by P.H. Gore Booth, 3 February 1954, FO371/111987.

87. Telegram, FO to Rangoon, 27 January 1954, FO 371/111984.

88. Telegram, Gore Booth to FO, 6 February 1954, also 9 February 1954, FO371/111987.

89. Letter, Ward to A.J. Newling, Ministry of Defence, 17 February 1954, FO371/111985.

90. Record of Conversation between Air Commodore E.L.S. Ward and General Ne Win on 10 May 1954, FO 371/101024.

91. Telegram, Washington to FO, 13 March 1954, FO 371/111967.

92. Telegram, Gore-Booth to FO, 16 March 1954, FO 371/111967.

93. On the fighting at Mong Hsat, see Maung Maung, "Destination Mong Hsat", *The Guardian* I, no. 6 (April 1954), pp. 18–20; reprinted in Robert H. Taylor, ed., *Dr Maung Maung: Gentleman, Scholar, Patriot* (Singapore: Institute of Southeast Asian Studies, 2008), pp. 402–7.

94. Letter, Gore-Booth to J.G. Tahourdin, 24 March 1954, FO371/111967.

95. Cassim succeeded Kawwal in 1950 after the latter's murder at the hand of rivals. At first, the Pakistan embassy in Yangon claimed that Cassim was killed but he was actually only under arrest. Pakistan, which had no extradition treaty with Myanmar, refused to return him for prosecution and he later lived in Chittagong. Moshe Yegar, *Between Integration and Secession: The Muslim Communities of the Southern Philippines, Southern Thailand, and Western Burma/Myanmar* (Lanham, Maryland: Lexington, 2002), p. 45. Cassim is also known as Kassem Raja, a Chittagonian who had fought with the British in the area against the Japanese during the Second World War. Kaiser Morshed, "Bangladesh-Burma Relations", in *Challenges to Democratization in Burma: Perspectives on Multilateral and Bilateral Responses*, by International Institute for Democracy and Electoral Assistance (Stockholm: International Institute for Democracy and Electoral Assistance, 2001), p. 58.

96. Memo No. 124, Gore Booth to Eden, 25 May 1954, WO15/15035. A month later, a naval attaché attached to the British embassies in Bangkok, Saigon and Rangoon paid his first visit to the Burma Navy. He found it "a class from [the much larger] easy going, muddled headed Siamese navy". In the course of his visit, he met with Ne Win who "chatted on many subjects

to do with his country for twenty minutes or so". Contrary to expectations, he was not shy. Note by C. Holmes, Naval Attaché, First Impressions of the Burma Navy, 23 June 1954, FO371/111900.

97. A Burmese delegation to Israel led by Colonel Aung Gyi and Commodore Than Pe visited Israel in June.

98. Anglo-Burmese Relations in Respect of the Supply of Arms by A. Goodwin, 20 December 1954, FO371/111990.

99. Monthly Summary for January 1955 by Paul Gore-Booth, 3 February 1955, FO371/117028.

100. Letter, Chancery to FO, 31 January 1955, FO371/117035.

101. Telegram, Sarrell to FO, 27 February 1955, FO371/117036.

102. Papers in DO 35/5947.

103. Seven "civilian cadets" were taken in that year. They had to pay tuition fees and underwent the same training as the military cadets. All seven opted to join the army and were duly commissioned. I am indebted to Dr Aung Myoe for this information.

104. Visit to Burma of General Sir Charles Loewin, Commander in Chief, Far East Land Forces, 28 March to 5 April 1955, FO371/117070.

105. Telegram, Rangoon to SOS, 1 April 1955, 790B.00/4-155, No. 934.

106. Telegram, Berkeley Gage, Bangkok, to Foreign Office, 1 April 1955, FO371/117038.

107. Telegram, Rangoon to SOS, 23 June 1955, 790B.00/6-2355, No. 1275.

108. Letter, K.R. Oakeshott to A.A.W. Ladymore, 7 June 1955, FO371/763977.

109. Leading Personalities in Burma, 27 June 1955, FO371/117027.

110. Interviews with Brigadier (retired) Maung Maung in the 1970s and 1980s, and U Thu Wei, 25 March 2010.

111. Copy of letter, C. Maxwell Lefroy to Mr W.E.-Eadie, 22 September 1955, FO371/11703.

112. Letter, R.F.G. Sarell to A.A.W. Ladymore, 19 October 1955, FO371/117030.

113. Letter, R.F.G. Sarell to A.A.W. Ladymore, 24 October 1955, DEFE7/2093.

114. Letter, R.G. Sarell to Harold Macmillan, 20 September 1955, FO371/111056.

115. Letter, J.M. Addis to Harold Macmillan, 21 November 1955, FO371/111056.

116. Maung Maung argues that Ne Win was not really in favour of a national service scheme. See Maung Maung, "Some Aspects of the 'Caretaker Government' 1958–1960: An Experiment in Democratic Process", unpublished manuscript, pp. 107–8, but there is ample evidence to the contrary.

117. Report of Conversation between General Ne Win and the Military Attaché [Colonel Berger] on 22 and 23 November and 2 December 1955, DEFE 7/2093.

118. The Balin Talks took place on 28 and 29 December 1955 in Kedah, following a series of earlier conversations establishing the parameters of the discussions.

119. Letter, Colonel Berger to Director of Military Intelligence, 23 December 1955, FO 371/123315.
120. Letter, Colonel Berger to Director of Military Intelligence, 23 December 1955, FO371/123315.
121. Letter, K.R. Oakeshott to A.A.W. Ladymore, 13 February 1956, FO371/123350.
122. Letter, K.R. Oakeshott to Chancery, 2 January 1956, FO371/123328.
123. Letter, Gore-Booth to Selwyn Lloyd, 2 January 1956, FO 371/123650.
124. Letter, Chancery Rangoon to Chancery Bangkok, 23 January 1956, FO371/123317. British officials believed they might be Anglo-Burmese; the source for the story was a British subject working in the Burmese Ministry of Defence.
125. Letter, Sir B. Gage, Bangkok, to FO, 20 February 1956, FO371/123324. The American admitted the act and claimed he did not understand its implication.
126. Telegram, Gage to FOI, 24 February 1956, FO371/123324.
127. Note by Lord Reading, 1 March 1956, FO371/123354. A Burmese soldier was struck by a Soviet security agent. Letter, R.H. Allan to Selwyn Lloyd, 1 June 1957, FO371/129404.
128. Letter, Gore-Booth to Selwyn Lloyd, 6 January 1956, FO371/123331.
129. *Thihmat Hpweya Koyei: AchetAlatmya* [Biographical Information for Recalling] (N.p.: N.p., N.d.).
130. *Sunday Nation* cutting, 27 November 1955, FO371/123650. Maung Maung, *The 1988 Uprising in Burma,* Southeast Asia Studies Monograph no. 49 (New Haven: Yale University Southeast Asia Studies, 1999), pp. 73–74.
131. Letter, Gore Booth to Selwyn Lloyd, 9 April 1956, FO371123330. Gore-Booth subsequently explained that Ne Win's reluctance to meet with Mountbatten at this time was perhaps due to a sense of "professional inadequacy" or a fear of appearing to be seen as of "lower status". Paul Gore-Booth, *With Great Trust and Respect* (London: Constable, 1974), pp. 220–21. Ne Win's frequent meetings with Mountbatten would seem to belie these assumptions.
132. German legation, Yangon, Kopf to AA, AA PA B 12 Bd. 1.218, 472.
133. Unfortunately, the author was unable to access the Japanese archives to discover what he did there.
134. Letter, British embassy in Washington, to South East Asia Department, 23 May 1956, DEFE7/2093.
135. Letter, Colonel Oliver Berger to unknown, 19 July 1956, Berger Papers, Kings College Library and Archives, London.
136. Untitled memo by Lieutenant Colonel J.D. Fitzpatrick, undated, with covering letter, indecipherable Evans (?) to G. Wheeler, Ministry of Defence, 10 August 1955, DEFE7/2095, p. 1.

137. Ibid., p. 2.

138. Ibid.

139. Ibid., p. 3.

140. Letter, W.D. Allen to Major W.F. Stanley, Ministry of Defence, 30 June 1956, FO371/123351; Letter, F.S. Tomlinson to Gore-Booth, 28 August 1956; Letter, Maung Nyun, Burmese embassy, to J.O. McCormick, 5 July 1956, FO371/123341; Letter, Colonel Oliver Berger, 19 July 1956, Berger Papers.

141. Collis was described by Michael Holroyd as someone who became "well known as an industrious non-fiction writer". "Bound Upon a Course: John Stewart Collis", in *Works on Paper: The Craft of Biography and Autobiography* (London: Little Brown, 2002), p. 121.

142. Letter, F.S. Tomlinson to Gore Booth, 28 August 1956, FO371/123341; Letter, F.S. Tomlinson to Gore Booth, 29 August 1945, FO 371/123341.

143. Defence expenditure at the height of the civil war had amounted to at least 40 per cent of all government spending. That percentage had declined to an average of about 33 per cent in subsequent years. However, total government expenditure was badly affected by the post-Korean war slump in commodity prices, the export of rice and timber being major income sources for the government. In the years 1955 and 1956, defence expenditure was less in real terms than in 1954. See Robert H. Taylor, "Burma: Defence Expenditure and Threat Perceptions", in *Defence Spending in Southeast Asia*, edited by Chin Kin Wah (Singapore: Institute of Southeast Asian Studies, 1987), pp. 252–80.

144. H.E.'s Farewell Call on General Ne Win, 20 September 1956, by F.G.W. Walshe, Military Attaché, FO371/123375.

145. According to some confidential conversations between Burmese officials and the Yugoslav Embassy in Rangoon, there were strong indications that the Chinese side reopened the border question in 1956 to foil any attempts made by General Ne Win to get economic or even military assistance during his visits to the U.S. and Great Britain. Telegram, Yugoslav embassy, Rangoon, 12 May 1956. The Chinese claimed the reverse, that the Burmese were using the Chinese border talks to get aid from the Americans. See Cavoski, *Arming Nonalignment*, fn 230, pp. 54–55.

146. BBC Monitoring Service, 13 December 1956, FO371/123322.

147. Papers in FO371/120899.

148. Letter, R.H.S. Allen to Selwyn Lloyd, 28 January 1957, FO371/1231294.

149. Letter, Rangoon Chancery to South East Asia Department, 4 March 1957, FO371/129008.

150. "Burmese Chief of General Staff Ne Win's Visit to US", Information Department, General Staff Headquarters, 7/10/1957–4/11/1957, 105-00810-02(1) [105-D0302].

151. Report of Visit to the Shan State by Peter Murray, 19 April 1958, FO643/145.

152. Kyaw Zaw eventually admitted that he had been in touch with the Communists and he eventually went to China as a senior Communist Party member. Aung Myoe, *Building the Tatmadaw: Myanmar Armed Forces Since 1948* (Singapore: Institute of Southeast Asian Studies, 2009), p. 55; Bertil Lintner, *Burma in Revolt: Opium and Insurgency since 1948*, 2nd ed. (Chiang Mai: Silkworm Books, 1999), p. 176.

153. In mid-1957, there were 5 Kachin battalions, 4 Chin, 1 Shan, 1 Kayah, 2 mainly Gurkha, 1 mostly Kayin, 14 minority designated battalions in all, and 38 predominantly Bamar battalions. Letter, Rangoon Chancery to South East Asia Department, 24 July 1957, FO371/129425.

154. Annual Appreciation of the Burma Army as at 30 September 1958, 14 October 1957, by Colonel F.G.W. Walshe, FO371/129425.

155. Letter, R.H.S. Allan to F.S. Tomlinson, 21 August 1957, DEFE7/2094.

156. Report by Colonel O.C. Berger on Colonel Aung Gyi's visit to London, 2 to 4 January 1958, FO371/135750.

157. Mary P. Callahan, "Building an Army: The Early Years of the Tatmadaw", *Burma Debate*, vol. IV, no. 3 (July/August 1997): 7–11. There can be no doubt that the first military doctrine of the army, that of strategic denial, and directed at defending the country against a Chinese invasion, was the brain child of Maung Maung. However, a Chinese invasion was not what the army was up against, and other than some of the campaigns against the KMT, it was indigenous guerrill warfare the army was confronting. Aung Myoe, *Military Doctrine and Strategy in Myanmar: A Historical Perspective*, Strategic and Defence Studies Centre, Working Paper no. 339 (Canberra: Australian National University, 1999), pp. 2–3.

7

REHEARSING AND REVIEWING
(April 1958 to February 1962)

Staff work, even of the most complex kind, can be learned by
civilians, for only a quick and accurate mind and a retentive memory
are needed. A commander can do with these attributes, but he
must add a quality easy to recognise but hard to define — a
strength of character, a determination with no obstinacy in it,
something that inspires, but does not arouse febrile excitement. He
needs wisdom rather than cleverness, thoughtfulness rather than
mental dexterity.

John Masters, *The Road Past Mandalay*, p. 207.

Events once more moved Ne Win's life in a different direction a decade
after Myanmar gained its independence. In 1958, he assumed the Prime
Ministership, the pinnacle of political power which he had refused to
grasp when it was first within his reach. How much he had a hand in
engineering the events that led to his elevation remains in dispute, but
the evidence, to the best it can be understood, is that he was at least a
willing participant in the politics which led to what U Nu subsequently
realized as his own irrational and petulant behaviour which allowed the
army to oust him from power. As Ne Win was the head of the army,
he might have taken measures to ensure a different result. In any event,
he did not stop the process which led to his first assumption of the reins
of government.

Burmese politics were changed irreparably when the ruling Anti-Fascist People's Freedom League (AFPFL) split into two factions at the end of April to the beginning of May 1958. The split had consequences not only for the country's political parties and its army, but also for the Buddhist monkhood, which was also fractured by the rupture (Mendelson 1975, p. 244). By 9 June, the split was absolute, but, in retrospect, it seemed to be inevitable after, if not before, the 1956 elections. The Socialists, led by Kyaw Nyein and Ba Swe, left the government at Prime Minister Nu's insistence, and he and his faction, now a minority in the *Pyithu Hluttaw*, could only continue in office with the support of minor parties, particular the largely pro-Communist National United Front (NUF) (the ur-manuscript on this is Sein Win 1959). There are various accounts of what happened next, but all of them ended with General Ne Win assuming the Prime Ministership for six months, subsequently extended to eighteen. Ne Win, though not the originator of the crisis which led to his becoming a "Caretaker" Prime Minister, was implicated at every turn, including in Nu's last minute bid to keep the AFPFL together by purging it of its corrupt and disloyal elements. Nu's proposed solution was a committee, a favourite device of his, comprised of himself, his key opponents, Kyaw Nyein and Ba Swe, with a fourth member, Ne Win. The idea got nowhere as Nu failed to consult any of the principals in advance.[1]

Nu told Ne Win of his final decision to split the League apparently before telling anyone else. He called Ne Win in and asked him not to moderate the dispute within the League and urged that the army not be involved. Ne Win went back to inform his colleagues in the General Staff headquarters about this information. He urged them not to dissuade Nu from his chosen course of action, but to assure the Prime Minister of their neutrality.[2] They did this but not without being drawn into a growing constitutional crisis eventually. The army officer corps was too deeply involved in party politics for that to happen, but even if it had not been so, the nature of the crisis would force the army to take a position, if merely for the sake of national defence and public tranquillity.

Ne Win was involved with, though not the originator of, another idea that contributed to the final split within the AFPFL. As noted in the last chapter, Nu had resigned from the Premiership after the 1956 election in order to meditate and pursue his writing career, but remained as President of the League. Consequently, major cabinet decisions were still put before him for approval, frequently delaying government business when he was out of town and incommunicado during one of his frequent periods of meditation. In early 1957, a proposal by Ne Win's old friend, Ambassador U Hla Maung, then posted to Beijing, was considered at a meeting at the residence of the then Prime Minister, U Ba Swe, at which Ne Win was present. Also present was U Kyaw Nyein. The proposal was that Nu should be elevated, rather like Mao Tse-tung, above internal politics and remain solely as President of the AFPFL.[3] All agreed to the idea and U Hla Maung then took the suggestion to Thakin Tin, Nu's ally, and explained it to him. Tin, who was in hospital, told Thakin Kyaw Tun of the idea. Kyaw Tun, in turn, gave Nu a version upon his return from a pilgrimage to Sri Lanka. He implied that the idea was a plot for Nu's permanent removal from power. Ne Win and Hla Maung had been tasked with telling Nu, but Kyaw Tun provided his version first, and their subsequent explanations were discounted by Nu. Seeing a plot to eliminate him, the ever-sensitive Nu believed the scheme was actually that of the crafty Kyaw Nyein, perhaps in collusion with the army.[4]

The day after Kyaw Tun told Nu of the proposal not to return him to the Prime Ministership, Ne Win came to see him. Nu writes in his memoirs, "He [i.e., Nu] had publicly stated he was retiring from politics in January 1957. Why then had they done this to him? And why had the army been brought in if not as a threat? He felt insulted. His ire rose." Ne Win, using the analogy of Mao Tse-tung, urged Nu to "remain president of the AFPFL and hold the strings of government". That was in fact the current position. Nu said he resented being coerced, and consequently, he was going to re-enter the government. Ba Swe willingly handed the prime minister's office back to Nu.

However, tension within the League redeveloped over a report from the army to the National Security Council about criminals being protected by leading politicians. The Kyaw Nyein faction, it was claimed, was pressuring the army and the police to take action against the Tin-Tun protégés, and Thakin Tin and Kyaw Tun objected. Nu conceded that the party would inevitably crack as these disputes kept occurring, and rather than remaining aloof and above the intrigue, he decided to join the Tin-Tun faction, dubbed the Clean AFPFL (Nu 1975, pp. 323–25). In his memoirs, Nu then elides over a number of other events in the crisis which reflect badly on him.

The matter might have rested with Nu reconfirmed as Prime Minister with a vote of confidence in early June in which he had the support of the majority of the ethnically designated minority political parties. However, the manner in which he hung on to power, and the passing of the 1958–59 government budget by presidential decree,[5] was unacceptable to many in the army. Nu had also made many offers to persons of doubtful loyalty, many recently released from prison. The machinery of government was winding down and crime was on the rise. Was Ne Win, therefore, originator of the army's threat to U Nu to leave office gracefully because of his dependence on the hard left and its consequences? Many accounts put the blame, or credit, on Brigadier Maung Maung and, to a lesser extent, Colonel Aung Gyi, nominal political allies of Ba Swe and Kyaw Nyein, and noted anti-Communists. While they were the principal actors on the army side, they neither originated the crisis nor made the first move within the army.

According to Maung Maung's account, written five decades after the event, and no doubt affected by his jaundiced views of Ne Win as well as his lack of regard for Nu, a number of field commanders and their deputies, all close to the Socialists, led by Brigadier Aung Shwe, then in charge of the Northern Command, met a number of times and conducted vague discussions about mounting a coup. When Maung Maung told Ne Win of this, he apparently did nothing to halt the coup.[6] When Nu forced the issue by passing the budget without referring it to the *Pyithu Hluttaw*, they pressed for a coup again. Maung Maung writes that Ne Win already knew of the plan for a coup when he was informed of this pressure.

> General Ne Win seemed always well informed. He felt it was wrong for the lower commanders, though comrades, to plan a military coup without even so much as indicating their respect for the G[eneral] S[taff]. He did not actually denounce the matter or suggest any action against such a venture. He merely said the GS comrades [meaning Maung Maung and Aung Gyi] should keep their eyes open, and take care that the situation did not develop into a dangerous state (Maung Maung n.p., p. 25).

According to Maung Maung, Ne Win and his colleague, Brigadier Tin Pe, were known to hold the Socialist leaders "in contempt for corrupt practices or for lack of political zeal or for drifting into what they considered 'right-wing' political programmes or ideological instability" (Maung Maung n.p., p. 4). Whether he sought to oust Nu or not, Ne Win was apparently being pressed to remove him by a faction of the army with which, unlike Maung Maung and Aung Gyi, he was not then in apparent political sympathy.

After the AFPFL split, the two factions, the Ba Swe–Kyaw Nyein group, known as the Stable AFPFL, and the Nu-Tin, the Clean AFPFL, sought to gather support from as many members of the *Hluttaw* as possible to either confirm or deny U Nu the majority he needed to maintain his government. If Ne Win left the cabinet in 1950 with a jaundiced view of politicians, the events of May-June confirmed this and his view became that of the army for the next fifty years. As *Guardian* Sein Win described, the two factions slung mud at each other's reputations and the former allies fought more bitterly than they did against their former political rivals.

> All means were used to mass parliamentary following. Ministerial positions were promised, money was lavishly used to buy up the MPs, autonomous States were bargained, and "special" concessions such as formation of racial battalions in the army, and removal of immigration and customs checks in smuggling areas, were promised. In short both factions tried to sell the country to serve their purposes; and only the price differed, one selling at a cheaper bargain than the other.[7]

Nu also called for elections to be held in November, more than a year earlier than constitutionally required.

Whatever the case, Ne Win insisted the army remain politically neutral,[8] and a conference of senior commanders at Mingaladon, led by Ne Win, was called to confirm that position on 23 June. There he said,

> There may be some of our comrades who find their personal attachments to some political leaders too strong. If they find their personal feelings in conflict with duty, then they should resign from the Tatmadaw [army]. We ourselves shall serve the people and uphold the constitution. We would work under any constitutionally established Government. We would also, on our part, request the leaders of the Government to respect the constitution, and call on us to render only those services which are in keeping with this.[9]

Ne Win also indicated that he did not wish to be Defence Minister in Nu's cabinet again but he would ensure that the Communists did not come to power.[10] Meanwhile, the affairs of state and the army continued, with an agreement being reached a few days later with the United States government to supply a sizeable amount of military equipment at greatly reduced prices. Ne Win's signature to the deal was required before 30 June. While the Burmese authorities wanted to keep the deal a secret, the Americans sought to publicize it.[11]

At the time of the split, it seemed likely that the army and the Union Military Police (UMP), under the Home Ministry controlled by Bo Min Gaung, might clash. UMP and other units had been called to the outskirts of Yangon. To help defuse the situation, on 30 July, Nu ordered Ne Win, Aung Gyi and Maung Maung to disband what many saw as the corrupt *pyusawhti*, or auxiliary police, loyal to the Socialists.[12] Nine days later, Ne Win held a meeting of Divisional Police Officers and Brigade Commanders and carried out the order (Myint Kyi and Naw 2007, pp. 68–69). This apparently alarmed the brigade commanders in the field as they relied on the *pyusawhti* to maintain order in some areas (Maung Maung n.p., p. 29). Not only did Ne Win obey Nu's order to disband the *pyusawhti*. Despite urgings, he also refused to "remonstrate with Nu even once". Nu made criticisms of the army in political speeches, which many commanders found offensive.

> He took U Nu's request not to intervene quite literally. At the same time he was watching the development of events, commenting to his staff about the deterioration going at a fast rate. The security position was badly compromised; Rangoon's outer defence had been penetrated by elements of Communists and White PVO forces (Maung Maung n.p., p. 30).

A month later, in preparation for elections which Nu had called for November, the Nu-Tin faction held a national convention in the Prime Minister's compound. There delegates from the districts made a number of allegations against individual army officers, accusing them of acting in the interests of the Swe-Nyein faction. They demanded these officers be transferred. "The delegate from Hanthawaddy declared the Army as Public Enemy Number One." For the men in the field who were being shot at by insurgents, this criticism stung and they complained again to their compatriots in the General Staff Office. Nu denied any knowledge of the allegations, which certainly left them incredulous as the damning words were broadcast by loudspeaker fifty yards from his room (Sein Win 1959, pp. 75–76).

Being aware of the pressure from the army on Nu to absolve his government of pandering to the hard left, and to deflect the army's criticism of him and his faction for ignoring the business of government, the Prime Minister made an effort to defuse the situation by inviting Ne Win, Aung Gyi, and Maung Maung into the cabinet.[13] Maung Maung and Aung Gyi, to whom the offer was made, were apparently shocked by what they saw as a brazen attempt to suborn them, which, if accepted, would have been looked upon by their regional command colleagues as bribes to keep them loyal. They reported Nu's proposition to Ne Win. He

> ... only smiled. He knew what would happen long ago. He was very good at working out the psychological reactions of an individual character. He can be called the best strategist in human reactions to specific situations. He specialised in it and studied the character, weaknesses and strengths, past and present activities, etc.; family relatives, attachments, friends, relaxations, strong indulgences, etc., everything about every individual he came across. He could remember all these data as well. His head was a memory bank for such details because he loved them (Maung Maung n.p., p. 35).

Rumours of a coup were rife as Maung Maung had ordered troops around Yangon in opposition to UMP. Home Minister Bo Min Gaung reported to U Nu that a coup was imminent. It looked increasingly as if the anti-Communist forces within the government were about to clash, thus prolonging and deepening the civil war. Nu called Ne Win, who denied the hearsay and then chastised Maung Maung and Aung Gyi for letting the rumours to be spread.[14]

The vote of confidence in U Nu as prime minister on 9 June was, according to *Guardian* Sein Win, "a remarkable chapter of appeasement and concessions to rebels (sic) unprecedented in the history of any country" (Sein Win 1959, p. 48). While Sein Win may have exaggerated, Nu was certainly trying very hard to convince the Communists rebels, particularly the White Flags and their supporters, to surrender and join with his government following the planned elections. He offered amnesties, released Communist supporters from prison, and encouraged all and sundry into his fold. For a while he seemed to be having success, and perhaps the country would finally achieve peace. However, when they were on the cusp of shared power, the Communists' position changed, and they began to make demands, including the legalization of their party and the absorption of their insurgent forces into the government army (Smith 1999, p. 177).

Nu was touring upcountry but returned on 22 September and held a cabinet meeting that day. Two ministers told the Prime Minister that the army was planning a coup that very night. Nu sent for Ne Win who could not be found, "being away at a party". The next day, Nu contacted Ne Win who promised to send someone to explain the situation to him. Ne Win sent Maung Maung (Sein Win 1959, pp. 79–82). The thought of the hard-left gaining a majority in the *Pyithu Hluttaw* was anathema to many Socialist-affiliated, anti-Communist officers such as Maung Maung and Aung Gyi, as well as to the regional commanders. In order to thwart Nu's plans, they raised the view that the country was too disturbed to hold a general election such as that held two years earlier. Instead, they proposed, initially to U Nu's idiosyncratic adviser, U Ohn, what they believed to be a compromise, the handing of power over to Ne Win who would hold elections in due course, and then return power to whoever won (Sein Win 1959, p. 36).

Nu had at least twenty-four hours to think about the imminent conflict between the anti-Communist forces, when Aung Gyi went with Maung Maung to see him again. Nu asked them to declare martial law and take over the government. They said they were not in favour of a coup and refused to do so. Apparently, it was that day or the next that Maung Maung put their proposition for a constitutional procedure in which Ne Win could take over the government and avoid a coup. Nu, in his account, implies that the idea of making Ne Win a Caretaker Prime Minister was his (Nu 1975, p. 327). Nu, realizing the folly of opposing the army further, convinced his supporters to go along with the plan and accepted the offer by Maung Maung and Aung Gyi. However, he insisted that elections be held within three months which the Colonels resisted on security grounds (Sein Win 1959, pp. 82–83).

On 25 September, the day that Maung Maung and Aung Gyi, together with Tin Pe, put their proposition to Nu and his adviser, U Ohn, word spread all over Yangon that something was up.[15] The army, navy and air force had imposed tight controls on the roads, waterways and airport of Yangon. The army sent back units of Union Military Police, some from nearly 300 miles from Yangon, though others had infiltrated the city in mufti. Insein was locked down by the army and, while the ministers' residential compound at Windermere was surrounded by the army, 400 armed supporters of Nu and his cabinet were present inside.

After Nu accepted the colonels' terms, Aung Gyi and Maung Maung reported back to Ne Win. Maung Maung remembers more than four decades later, "The first words by which Ne Win greeted Maung Maung was, 'Have all things been accomplished?' He meant the coup and was very, very disappointed", according to Maung Maung, "when Maung Maung said he had arranged a compromise solution in order that neither he, Ne Win, nor they, the army, would be accused by history of being traitors to the Government or their comrades, but rather helpers in salvaging the constitution." But this account is highly implausible. Ne Win would have known what the offer to Nu was in advance, even if, as Maung Maung asserts, he wanted "to run things completely without the encumbrances of the 1947 Constitution or further pandering to political parties and leaders" (Maung Maung n.p., pp. 38–39). The next day, U Nu made a broadcast announcing the cancellation of elections planned for November and the invitation for Ne Win to take over the government (Myint Kyi and Naw 2007, p. 124). Formally, Nu remained as the Prime Minister until the *Pyithu Hluttaw* met on 28 October, but in reality, power had already been passed from Nu's cabinet to the War Office.

According to an American observer of Myanmar politics then residing in Yangon, "During the week leading up to" the decision that Ne Win would assume the Prime Ministership from Nu,

> there was hardly a hint in the Burmese newspapers that such a dramatic development might be in the offing. Through the open channels of communication the public was informed only that U Nu had returned to Rangoon, radiant and elated, from a triumphant campaign tour of the dry zone, that the prospective election would be close, and that the competing "trade unions" representing each faction of the split AFPFL were not above using violence. The private and informed elements during the same period abounded with all manner of rumours; people in coffee shops were discussing whether SEATO troops might not have invaded the country and if it were true that the Chinese Communists had dispatched two divisions to assist the Burmese Communist insurgents. Then came the dramatic radio announcement by U Nu, consisting of only one sentence, informing the people that he was asking Ne Win to assume the responsibility of government. Since that date there has been no complete public report on all that happened in the action-filled week, and Burmese politics has continued without all of the participants sharing even a common understanding of the most dramatic and significant event of the postwar period (Pye 1962, p. 128).

On 26 September, Nu and Ne Win exchanged letters, the former offering, the latter accepting, an invitation to take over the government. Ne Win's letter is duly humble. As often in his remarks, he drew attention to "wrongful acts of violence on the part of some members of the armed forces" and promised to suppress such misdeeds as well as general lawlessness and crime. Promising to have a non-political, neutral administration, he pledged to hold elections by April 1959.[16] He eventually missed that target by ten months.

Western embassies were not disappointed by the military takeover, the West German ambassador drawing attention to reports in the Myanmar press comparing Ne Win's assumption of power to that of General de Gaulle in France that year. He urged a planned visit by the West German Minister for the Economy, Ludwig Erhard, to continue to take place as the situation was favourable to the anti-Communist forces with the army in power.[17] Quoting Goethe, the ambassador, when speculating on how the coup came about, thought that it might be "halfway she pulled him, halfway he fell for her".[18] The Germans also thought that the neighbouring Thai government was content with Ne Win's takeover as General Sarit and the other top Thai officials knew Ne Win and liked his anti-Communist posture.[19] The Chinese embassy, on the other hand, sniffed the hand of the United States in the coup, noting that U. Alexis Johnson, then U.S. ambassador to Thailand and formerly the Deputy Assistant Secretary of State whom Ne Win had met in Washington in 1952, was in Yangon for a week prior to the coup, and held two receptions, one for SEATO member states military attachés, and one for younger Burmese army officers.[20] The Soviet Union made no public comment on the ascension of the Caretaker Government, as it became known (Longmire 1989, p. 75).

When confirmed by the *Pyithu Hluttaw* as prime minister, Ne Win declared that the situation he had inherited "was approaching close to that sad spectacle of 1948–49".

> The effects of the political split spread throughout the country like a rampaging forest fire. People who used to work together before now viewed each other with deep suspicion. Former close comrades and colleagues became deadly enemies. Political splits in some areas became so serious as to lead to violence and killings. The split led to large increase in the activities of those elements who flout and violate the constitution of the Union of Burma, in their attempt to exploit the situation. Insurgents suffered intolerable damage, politically and military,

during the last 10 years, at the hands of the Government, and were in such sad shape that in late 1957 early 1958 began to admit that the rebellion was a mistake and to "enter the light" in increasing numbers. The Burma Communist Party (BCP) had made overture for peace. After the split, the BCP changes its tune and made new demands and put new pressures on the Government. Other insurgents too halted their steps when they were just about to emerge.

The situation became more and more confused. There was so much confusion that units of the Union Military Police, assigned to certain district areas began converging on Rangoon in large numbers, some in uniforms and some in civilian dress; and when the Inspector General of Police was asked the reason why such large numbers of UMP were being called to Rangoon, he replied quite honestly, that he did not know anything about the matter at all.

The situation was that much confused. The governmental machinery also deteriorated to its present weak condition. The rebels were increasing their activities, and the political pillar was collapsing. It was imperative that the Union should not drown in shallow waters as it nearly did in 1948–49. So it fell to the armed forces to perform their bounden duty to take all security measures to forestall and prevent a recurrence.[21]

Lest it be believed that this was just special pleading by a coup-maker, foreign commentators and analysts came much to the same conclusion (see, for example, Butwell 1963, p. 209; Walinsky 1962, pp. 568–69; Smith 1999, p. 175; Trager 1966, pp. 178–80).

Ne Win took his time to form a non-partisan civilian cabinet of respected persons, and even Maung Maung concedes that he was "quite scrupulous" (Maung Maung n.p., p. 38). He met with Maung Maung, Aung Gyi, and an American friend, Julian Licht,[22] to discuss the future direction of government policy and, according to Maung Maung, became frustrated with their refusal to push in a firm socialist direction. Ne Win allegedly said, "Close down all banks and nationalise them as well as all private businesses and bring in production, acquisition and distribution of consumers' goods by ration book method" (Maung Maung n.p., p. 40). This, of course, was the heart of the economic policy he did introduce after he took power a second time in 1962. After some discussion of economic policy, he told them to do what they liked and left for another meeting.

Subsequently, he met with the ministers for the ethnically designated states and confirmed their places, but did not announce the functional ministerial portfolios for more than two weeks after taking over the government.[23] None of them were from the political parties but all were chosen for their reputations for probity and competence. Included among them were U Thein Maung, a former Supreme Court judge; U Chan Htoon Aung, a former High Court judge; U Ka, a lecturer in Mathematics at Rangoon University; U Kyaw Nyein, not the politician but the Chairman of the Union Bank of Burma; U Khin Maung Hpyu, the Chief Secretary of the government and therefore top civil servant in the country; U San Nyun, a former Election Commissioner; U Chit Thoung, the government's Chemical Examiner; and U Ba Kaw, a retired judge.

Initially, Ne Win was the only member of the cabinet from the army, assuming not only the Prime Ministership, but also taking over the Defence and National Planning portfolios (Myint Kyi and Naw 2007, pp. 116–17; Maung Maung 1969, p. 252). He largely entrusted the responsibilities for the latter two, however, to Maung Maung and Aung Gyi respectively. Subsequently, Brigadier Tin Pe was made Minister of Mines, Minister of Labour, and Minister of Public Works, National Housing and Rehabilitation. Also, the civilian director of procurement in the War Office, U Thi Han, became Minister of Trade Development, Minister of Co-operatives and Commodity Distribution, and Minister of Industry. A total of 144 officers from the armed forces were assigned to assist the civilian ministers and to activate and motivate the civil service for various lengths of time during the next eighteen months of administrative reform.[24] This "stiffening" of the civil service produced a dramatic change in government efficiency. In Ne Win's address to the *Pyithu Hluttaw*, he reiterated points made in his letter to Nu, confirming that there would be no change in Myanmar's foreign policy, but that the government would deal firmly with businessmen who were involved in illegal operations.[25]

The Annual Commanders' Conference was held at Meiktila on 21 October. At this meeting the assumption of power by the army was explained to the regional commanders and others. U Nu also attended and provided his version of the split and subsequent developments. Maung Maung spoke about the course of events which led to the formation of the Caretaker Government. He put the blame not on the constitution, as he alleges Ne Win had done, but on "the immaturity of all of us: our political leaders and the people, but especially the men of the news media". He also gave a lengthy exhortation on the many failures of Communism (quoted in Maung Maung n.p., p. 39, exhortation, pp. 39–41). Maung Maung's analysis only accords to some degree with a paper written primarily by U Chit Hlaing, a civilian working for the army, at the behest of Colonel Ba Than and colleagues from the army's Directorate of Education and Psychological Warfare, which was circulated at the Commanders' Conference.

Maung Maung's comments and Chit Hlaing's paper differ particularly with regards to "misconstrued" provisions of the constitution concerning freedom of speech and association. The paper entitled, "Some Reflections on Our Constitution", discusses "the general apathy of the electorate", allowing themselves to be misled by the propaganda of rebels groups. The root of the constitutional crisis, therefore, lay in the immaturity and gullibility of the Burmese people. Constitutional revisions were perceived to be necessary to protect the country from being taken over by "gangster political movements, syndicalism, anarchism, and a totalitarian regime".[26]

The ideological statement, finally entitled, "The National Ideology and Our Pledge", was debated and agreed at the Meiktila Commanders' Conference.[27] The post-independence army, ten years after its birth in bloodshed and political rivalry, had developed a level of ideological coherence not previously achieved. A search for an army ideology had been under way since Ne Win called for one at the 1954 Commanders' Conference. Firmly articulating a strong anti-Communist posture, a second document, also written largely by U Chit Hlaing, was adopted at the 1960 Commanders' Conference prior to the national elections which saw U Nu returned to power. Entitled "The National Ideology and the Role of the Defence Services", this document insisted that democracy will only flourish when the "people respect the law and submit to the rule of law". It concluded,

> 45. Thus do the Defence Services hold the National Objectives of the Union to be, and adopt and give to themselves their Role and Attitude as set out above.
> In thus pursuing the aims of national politics, as distinct from party politics, the Defence Services pledge themselves to this adopted Role and Attitude:
> Peace and Rule of Law — First
> Democracy — Second
> Socialist Economy — Third

The distinction between "national politics" and "party politics" established a moral difference between the scheming politicians who, in *Guardian* Sein

Win's words, "would sell the country to serve their purposes", and the idealistic army which stood above such squalid behaviour. This document, summarized in Ne Win's speech to the annual commanders' conference in February 1960, prior to the election, became official army policy until 2 March 1962.[28] It was at the 1960 conference that Ne Win reiterated that the army and its officers should remain neutral in the election, despite their personal views and friendships.

At around this time, the army also began teaching what it referred to as "political science" to the officer corps. The Directorate of Education and Psychological Warfare undertook its first training course at the southern command headquarters at Mingaladon. The course was inaugurated by Ne Win who was reported to have said that "Members of the tatmadaw [army] should understand political science even though they must stay out of the activities of political parties. Also, they must safeguard the constitution." Several batches of officers, and later civil servants, were instructed in political theory, particularly Marxism-Leninism, propaganda techniques, economic policy making, and theories and applications of psychological warfare. Guest lecturers included the director of the World Buddhist University, journalists, and playwrights. U Chit Hlaing was the main instructor and crafter of the curriculum (Chit Hlaing n.d., p. 2). Though instruction was terminated at the end of the Caretaker Government, it was resumed in 1961 (Nakanishi 2013, p. 83, fn. 46).

Is Trust Vindicated? is the Caretaker Government's more than 500-page report on its achievements. It sets out in detail the major accomplishments of the first military-dominated government of Myanmar. By all accounts, it was an impressive government, cleaning up Yangon and other cities, lowering food prices, speeding up construction projects, developing entire new townships for persons previously squatting in squalor (Walinsky 1962, p. 367), and impressing foreign governments with the "can do" attitude of the Burma army.[29] Former ambassador Paul Gore-Booth subsequently wrote,

> When I revisited Burma in 1959, the ruling party had split and power had passed to General Ne Win. The General formed what might be called a technocratic government, efficient, authoritarian and not unimpressive. There was an atmosphere of shirt-sleeve activity and purpose; one only asked oneself whether the arrangement was temporary or would tend to become permanent (Gore-Booth 1974, p. 223).

Law and order was given particular attention. Maung Maung claimed to have been in charge of this area. Many leftists and others were arrested and detained for lengthy periods without trial. Interrogation centres and isolated prisons, where harsh methods were used to extract information from alleged Communists, were opened, including on Coco Gyun (Great Coco Island), the northernmost island of the Andaman chain.[30] Though the public were pleased with the improvement that the army government brought about, there was dislike in many quarters of its methods, thus contributing to the return of U Nu to power in 1960. Maung Maung proudly used the powers available to the government to halt what he considered violations of democratic rights in the form of criticism of the government in the press, which, of course, only fuelled journalistic antipathy towards the army once he was out of government (Maung Maung n.p., pp. 57–59).

Coping with the insurgent situation was one of the major problems the Caretaker Government faced. According to its statistics, it was estimated that there were approximately 9,000 insurgents, aided and abetted by another 5,000 sympathizers when it took power, though these figures fluctuated from time to time.[31] During the following fourteen months, the army launched 108 major and 323 local operations against the insurgents, losing 530 lives and causing 638 to be wounded. On the insurgents' part, 1,872 were killed, 1,959 wounded, and 1,238 captured. Another 3,618 surrendered, mainly Communists, and the government took 4,667 arms, both captured and surrendered, out of circulation. At the end of the Caretaker period, the army claimed that it had reduced insurgent numbers to fewer than 5,500, including an additional 1,000 KMT, the only group to increase during the period.[32] The government conducted a major round-up of illicit firearms, confiscating more than 14,000 rifles and other weapons in the first nine months of its existence. A number of private armies previously at the beck and call of politicians were consequently disbanded (Tinker 1967, p. 61).

The apparent corporate solidarity and harmony evinced by documents such as "The National Ideology and the Role of the Defence Services", conceal fissures within the officer corps which the following several years would expose. Just three months after the victorious Meiktila Commanders Conference, Brigadier Douglas Blake, the Anglo-Burmese officer in charge of the Southern Command, was forced to retire as Ne Win said he could no longer "protect" him. Ne Win had Blake moved to the Burmah Oil Company.[33] This was due to a severe feud between Blake and Maung

Maung, with the latter's temper and strong personality causing him to clash with others.[34]

In the eyes of many, Ne Win was the only person holding the army and the situation steady. However, he only entered into discussions with his subordinates when they disagreed amongst themselves.[35] When he had to be sedated for several hours for a urinary tract operation in late April 1959,[36] speculation immediately developed as to what would happen should he retire or be incapacitated. The British military attaché believed the result "would almost certainly cause dissension with the inevitable race for power in both the Army and the political spheres".[37] For the time being, however, Ne Win was very much in control and his behaviour drew even more praise. By September, his old friend Malcolm MacDonald wrote that he had "grown in stature" and was noted for his "unselfish patriotism and political prudence".[38]

Ne Win's pledge to reform and restore order to the country touched on all areas of government, including lifting the ban on the slaughter of cattle (Walinsky 1962, p. 5, fn. 3 and 394). He also discontinued the annual *balinista* (festival of *nats* [animistic spirits]) which Nu had made into a virtually official event.[39] The Caretaker government's insistence on enforcing rules and regulations also squeezed the private sector, including former Defence Minister Bo Let Ya's post-political business, the Martaban Company fishing fleet, which was forced to pay arrears on interest due on government loans (Walinsky 1962, pp. 318–19). There were implications of corrupt practices but, in the end, the government took no action against those involved (Nu 1975, pp. 328–29).

Ne Win did not hesitate to change the direction of government policy. While much of the detailed work was left to others under his supervision, some matters fell directly to him. He often felt swamped with decisions, many related to unfinished plans and projects of the former government (Maung Maung n.p., p. 46). An example was United States aid fund, $4.9 million dollars worth, which it was proposed to spend on the construction of rice and bran extraction mills. The deal for the rice meals, twelve in all, was already signed. When the contract for the twelve rice bran extraction mills came before Ne Win, he refused to sign on the grounds that it interfered with Myanmar's state sovereignty. The U.S. aid programme required the mills be sold to the private sector on completion. The real reason for Ne Win's refusal, however, was said to be that senior military officials involved in the project were quarrelling over which of their friends should get the contract (Walinsky 1962, pp. 531–32, fn. 11). The Ne Win government, in fact, refused both to apply for additional American government assistance on offer and scaled back on a number of projects, including a Yangon water supply and sewage project, ship building, dock expansion, and an extension to Yangon General Hospital. This was done on the grounds that the government was already financially extended and that previous aid money had been spent inefficiently (Walinsky 1962, pp. 530–31).

While reluctant to utilize or request additional loan money, the Ne Win government was willing to ask for American grant aid, i.e., gifts, for specific and highly desirable projects. While a number of lower-ranking officers in the military from time to time requested American grant aid for specific projects as there was no overall government request in place, these were ignored. However, in the early months of 1959, Ne Win sent the editor of *The Nation* newspaper, the OSS-trained Edward Law-Yone, as a special emissary to the President of the United States, requesting support for the construction of a modern, multi-lane highway from Yangon to Myitkyina via Mandalay, as well as residences for university students. In the event, Law-Yone failed to contact the Eisenhower White House and the government was forced to use conventional diplomatic approaches.[40] The United States government quickly agreed to the request and a feasibility study was undertaken. But by then, the Americans began to have second thoughts. Before negotiations could be completed, U Nu had returned to power and the project remained an outstanding issue in Myanmar–United States relations (Walinsky 1962, pp. 532–34).

The implications of the highway for Myanmar's relations with China were obvious. A modern, dual carriage motorway as a new Burma road would have a carrying capacity which would dwarf that of the pre-Second World War Burma Road. To be built by American contractors, probably the United States Army Corps of Engineers, at a cost of US$75 million dollars, the British believed that if the U.S. Government agreed, as they were being urged to do so by the American embassy, Burma would be "firmly in the American camp" in the Cold War.[41] To underscore the apparent pro-American direction in Burma's foreign policy at that time, it was noted that the Americans were advising on the setting up of a National Defence College, a project that Maung Maung was driving in order to achieve an early completion.[42] Maung Maung had also proposed to develop a four-division army that was to be equipped with American equipment and to act as a deterrent to a Chinese invasion. The U.S. Central Intelligence Agency (CIA) was advising on intelligence gathering methodologies, including perhaps on Coco Gyun or the Chinese border (Maung Maung n.p., p. 105).

During the Caretaker Government, Ne Win took a particular interest in Myanmar's rice export trade, a major source of government revenue. The export of agricultural products was put under the control of Lieutenant Colonel Mya Thaung but Colonel Aung Gyi also took a close interest. Ne Win, however, decided the prices of rice and which countries to send to, often looking for small buyers who would pay more than bulk buying rice deficit countries such as India or Pakistan. According to Maung Maung, "At that time Ne Win and everyone from defence services in government departments were thought to be above corruption; certainly Ne Win, Maung Maung and Aung Gyi were completely clean of it or favouritism or cronyism" (Maung Maung n.p., p. 78).

Ne Win often suspected others of corruption, however. As a counter-insurgency tool, Ne Win ordered Colonel Chit Myaing, who was in charge of the Ministry of Immigration, National Registration and Census, to register everyone in the country above the age of twelve. Each would be issued a registration card with a photograph. The monastic Sasana Purification Association favoured the policy but it was opposed by others in the monkhood (Smith 1965, pp. 216–17). The logistics effort to achieve this was significant and the country had none of the equipment required to achieve the task. Using Japanese wartime reparation funds, however, the government turned to Japan to purchase the requisites. But Ne Win suspected the government was being overcharged by the Japanese suppliers or Myanmar middlemen, so he instructed Chit Myaing to make the purchases in person, saying "You try to negotiate the purchase price and even if you go wrong, I know you are sincere, and if you make a mistake, don't worry. But if you take any bribes, I will kill you on your return" (Chit Myaing 1997, pp. 11–24).

Cabinet meetings in those days were held on Saturday mornings, and then in the afternoon the army officers attached to the ministries would discuss their problems with Maung Maung and Aung Gyi. Initially Ne Win attended the afternoon meetings, but as they dealt with details of administration, he soon stopped. He was briefed every morning at 8.30., however, by his subordinates on arrests, military actions and political developments (Maung Maung n.p., p. 84).

One issue he attempted to deal with was the thorny problem of the politicization of the student body at Rangoon University. For years, Communist and other political parties had agitated amongst the students, and indiscipline and corruption had led to a lowering of academic standards (Silverstein and Wohl 1964, p. 51). At his first address as Chancellor of the University, a week after assuming the role, Ne Win made it clear that his government would root out the political troublemakers amongst the student body.[43] He was encouraged by the press in this, with little comment evinced when left-wing politicians were arrested before the ceremony.[44] Soon after, Ne Win invited Dr Hla Myint, the noted Myanmar economist, then an Oxford lecturer, back to Myanmar to take charge of the University in order to restore discipline and the academic standards that U Nu's government had allowed, for reasons of political expediency, to erode.[45] Personally wired by Ne Win, Hla Myint was also asked to be an economic advisor to the government (Brown 2013, p. 127). He had to put up with much foul abuse by politically motivated students during his time at the university (Maung Maung n.p., p. 55).

The allegedly xenophobic Ne Win not only invited a noted Burmese economist who had taken British citizenship along with a British wife, but also other foreigners to advise him on various policy and technical matters while he headed the Caretaker Government. He called on a Briton, one Richard Leach, to advise him, as well as the American-Israeli, Julian Licht. Licht, an engineer and an associate of Dan Rose, who helped arrange Ne Win's first trip to the United States, was instrumental in terminating a contract between the British firm, Evans Medical Supplies, and the Burma Pharmaceutical Company of the government. He was often a house guest of Ne Win. Ne Win did terminate the contracts of Knappet Tippetts Abbott (KTA) Engineering consultants and Robert Nathan Associates, economic advisors, as well as the Soviet agricultural experts U Nu had invited several years earlier. In dismissing the American advisers that Nu had hired initially with money provided by a loan from the United States, and subsequently from government revenues, he was merely following the advice of a number of government secretaries who, like him, did not trust the foreigners to give objective advice.[46] As Gordon Luce wrote, "Burma was then flooded with advisors from foreign parts, who knew little or nothing about Burma, but had a Nostrum that had worked elsewhere."[47]

Ne Win met personally with Louis Walinsky, the chief economist from Robert Nathan Associates, to inform him of his government's decision. Amongst other things, Walinsky mentioned the indigenous reservoir of economic advice which the government might tap, including Dr Hla Myint. In terms of economic policies, Walinsky urged Ne Win to abandon a number of constraints and restrictions on the private market and, in particular, to use the economic talents of ethnic minorities, that is Chinese and Indians, more fully. The only alternative, he said, was to "either invite the foreigners to leave country, or else to treat them without discrimination". Ne Win, for his part, explained that the decision to end the Nathan contract was purely on economic grounds, implying that, in his view, the advisors were primary involved in generating expensive new projects which Burma could not afford. Walinsky felt that he did not understand their function adequately.[48]

Richard Leach advised Ne Win on minerals and mining. One day in 1958, L.A. Crozier poured out his problems as the manager of the loss-making Mawchi mine in Kayah State to Leach. The tin and tungsten mine, on the verge of closure, was beset by Karen, Kayah and other insurgents, as well as the corrupt Kayah state police, local amateur dacoits, and sometimes unhelpful army units, as well as infighting amongst the directors of the joint venture company on two boards in London and Yangon. Leach said he would arrange a meeting with Ne Win and a few days later, in Crozier's words,

> ... feeling like Daniel going into the lion's den, I was ushered into a room where General Ne Win and Leach were waiting, and I told him everything. The General was quite well informed and, in fact at one stage told me that the insurgents had requested me to put their case to SEATO. I said that I did not remember this and, in effect, denied it.
>
> "Oh yes," the General insisted, "we captured some documents in a Karen camp once."
>
> I gulped. Later I remembered the occasion, it had been during one of those meetings with [insurgent leaders] Daung Sein, Boh Special and one or two other notables. I had not passed on any request for help to SEATO, although I did mention the incident to one or two people. At my next meeting with General Ne Win, I told him that he had been quite right, but that I had forgotten the occasion and had not done anything about it.
>
> I explained as clearly as I could the complicated insurgent-Kayah State situation, the wished for succession to Thailand,[49] and how I had become involved in it. "What else could I have done?" I asked.
>
> The General nodded.
>
> I told him of our disappointment with the grade of ore at the mine, the falling metal prices, the fire that destroyed our stores just when the tide was turning for us, and my information as to who had

arranged for that fire. I told him of my trip to London, my return and — very bitterly — my income tax difficulties.

The General waved a hand, grinning. "I'll arrange that", he said.

I went on to tell him of the peace talks with the Karens and volunteered to meet the Karen insurgent leaders as an intermediary. The General said he appreciated the offer, but that contact would be have to be between the leaders and the army commanding officer of the area. I could hardly push the point as undoubtedly the General had seen a copy of the letter from [KNU leader] Saw Hunter [Thamwe] saying that they would only talk with me as an intermediary, so I merely said I would do anything I could to help.

The General was a good listener. My trepidation disappeared and my gratitude to Leach for arranging the meeting increased. It was the greatest relief just to speak to someone who understood those things, who could see the unavoidable involvements, who knew the mentalities and the loyalties of the people concerned and who, most of all, could understand motives. The conversation finished with the General asking me for photocopies of the documents I had described to him, which I promised to send. As he shook hands with me he grinned once more and said, "Let me know if you have any more trouble."

I left feeling greatly comforted and considerably impressed.[50]

Had the mine been able to reopen at that time, Ne Win's government would have wished for Crozier to return to manage it, but it was soon closed with the government paying off the liabilities.[51]

The Burmah Oil Company (BOC), the once highly profitable British-owned firm that, at its peak, supplied petroleum products from Suez to Tokyo and paid high dividends throughout the great depression, had long been a target for left-wing Burmese politicians for nationalization, though it was re-established in 1954 as a joint venture, with the government being a minority shareholder. The joint venture allowed the British-owned Burmah Oil to retain a majority share, with the government purchasing a third, and another nearly 12 per cent held by two smaller, largely Indian-owned firms. However, the government had resisted an outright takeover, much to the annoyance of Ne Win.[52] Various reasons were advanced for not nationalizing the firm, such as a shortage of capital and the technical knowledge of the oil industry. The Company, always under the threat of nationalization, had invested relatively little since the war in reconstruction or exploration for new oil and gas reserves (Corley 1988, p. 203).

There the matter rested unit the month of the election which led to Ne Win handing back power to U Nu. In February 1960, the government paid the final £1.4 million outstanding on a loan it had taken from Burmah Oil in 1954 with which to purchase its share of the business. Soon after, an article appeared in Law Yone's *The Nation* announcing that the government was soon to take 51 per cent of the shares. The wasting asset that was the old Burmah Oil Company was rapidly deteriorating in value. Though no one doubted Ne Win had engineered the announcement, it was apparently done on the advice of a visiting Canadian official on loan to the United Nations (Corley 1988, pp. 255-56).

Before then, however, there were other administrative matters and ceremonies of state which were in need of attention. One of the first major public events during the Caretaker period was the ceremony on 4 January 1959 to mark the 11th year of independence. Unlike in earlier years, this was an entirely military show. The parade was performed by the army, with the AFPFL being excluded. Ne Win took the salute with the President, Dr Ba U, a former minister in U Nu's government. U Nu also sat on the parade stand, next to Ne Win in full military uniform. Unlike some years when he did not bother to attend such events, Ne Win apparently enjoyed the day thoroughly, and in the eyes of the West German ambassador, intended to use the event to demonstrate his power.[53] Foreign affairs also started to take up Ne Win's time. Soon after the Independence Day celebrations, Marshall Tito of Yugoslavia arrived in Yangon harbour on his yacht for two days of talks with Ne Win, mainly on matters relating to economic cooperation.[54] They also touched on foreign policy issues with Tito giving his view of the posture non-aligned states like theirs should adopt.

> We think that it is correct that these countries maintain good relations with both the East and the West. Orientation toward only one side could be harmful. In our own interest, it is best to preserve certain balance in these relations. ... It is important for us to be fully aware what are their [i.e., the superpower's] true aims and not to let them succeed in their intentions.[55]

Ne Win made his first trip to Israel as Prime Minister. The previous year, the Chief-of-Staff of the Israeli Armed Forces, Moshe Dayan, had visited Burma with Shimon Peres, then Director General of the Israeli Ministry of Defence. They spent two weeks in the country, touring various areas and being lavishly entertained. In his memoirs, Peres writes,

Ne Win himself, a military man to his fingertips, accompanied us throughout our two-week stay. He was an extreme nationalist, determined not just to shore up his country's hard won independence but in effect sever Burma — which he increasingly and brutally did in later years — from much of the rest of the world. He said the only country he believed in was Israel. At that time, he seemed to us incorruptible in a country riddled with corruption. Despite his single-mindedness, not to say fanaticism, we built a close personal relationship. Later, Israel helped Burma develop its agriculture (Peres 1996, pp. 176–77).

Arriving in Tel Aviv on 8 June 1959 for meetings with Prime Minister David Ben Gurion, Ne Win was expected to discuss economic and military cooperation and to study the welfare systems developed for veterans of the Israeli army. Particularly of interest to him was the re-integration of disabled servicemen into civilian life.[56] The visit lasted a week, during which Ne Win made an excursion to a cement factory and an agricultural research and development centre at Lachish. At that time, eighty Myanmar soldiers and veterans were living and working at Ayelet Haschahar in Upper Galilee, studying collective agricultural methods on a kibbutz.

Ben Gurion and Ne Win had long private conversations but Ne Win made it clear that he would make no public statements on controversial international issues, especially on the Arab-Israeli conflict. According to a British report on the visit, Ben Gurion and Ne Win "took an immediate personal liking to each other"; "they talked with unusual candour of their respective and common problems"; "the General's natural simplicity and easy charm together with his gift of appearing to enjoy everything he did won hearts wherever he went."[57] After charming the Israelis, Ne Win flew to Rome for a two-day private visit before returning to Yangon.[58]

Important domestic matters had been on Ne Win's mind prior to his visit to Israel. One matter was how he could continue to remain as Prime Minister longer than the six months granted to him under the terms of the Constitution. Clause 116 specified that non-elected ministers could only serve up to that length of time. In February, the *Pyithu Hluttaw* voted to suspend the clause and allow Ne Win to remain in power until at least April 1960 when elections were planned.[59] Diplomatic opinion was that the decision was a popular one as the Caretaker Government, only four months into its task, had already greatly improved the situation.[60] While the West German ambassador believed that some of Ne Win's subordinates were keen to hold on to power, Ne Win, with his "responsible personality", would not seek to do so.[61] Soon after the extension of his term, Ne Win expanded his cabinet, appointing a deputy prime minister, U Lun Baw, and a new foreign minister, former Justice U Chan Htoon Aung, as well as a reshuffle of the ministers for the five ethnically named states.[62]

The other major domestic event was the abandonment by the Shan Sawbwa of their remaining legal powers. The reform of the Shan State government, and the ending of "feudalism" had long been a goal of the Socialist and other leaders of the AFPFL and steps had been taken in that direction earlier (Smith 1999, pp. 193–94). A ceremony to mark the introduction of full "democracy" in the Shan States would take place from 10 to 13 February 1959 and Ne Win particularly wanted the American ambassador, who had been planning to be abroad then, to be present.[63] Reflecting on the unresolved issue of the KMT and the role of the Central Intelligence Agency in the Laotian civil war, it seemed that Ne Win had a message for the United States government. The handover of their powers would remove the control the Sawbwa had previously held in the Shan State Council and this became a point of grievance between the government and the soon-to-be former Sawbwa.

On the day of the formal handover, Ne Win spoke of the compromise that Aung San had crafted at Panglong in order to coax the hill peoples' leaders to join with the rest of Burma in gaining independence. Noting also that the constitution of Burma stated the country was to be a democracy, the anomaly between that aspiration and the remaining autocratic powers of the Sawbwa, had lead Aung San and his successors to expect the Sawbwa would willingly abandon their historic rights in time. In this they were not disappointed even if the abandonment of "traditional rights" was given grudgingly. On 29 April 1959, Ne Win said,

> Formerly certain discreditable features of feudal rule and the shortcomings and indiscretions of some of the Chiefs had influenced my attitude towards them. But after witnessing the wholehearted and sincere way in which the Chiefs had set about divesting themselves of their rights and prerogatives, I cannot but entertain great admiration for their spirit. For one thing, had the Chiefs decided differently, various administrative as well as political problems with both administrative and political implications would have cropped up to poison the relations between the Shan State and the rest of the Union.[64]

Having failed in their earlier plan to implement the secession clause of the Constitution, the Sawbwa were now abandoning their remaining powers in exchange for a state pension and, of course, residual power which stemmed from their rank in traditional society. Ne Win was not alone in harbouring feelings of distain for the "feudal privileges" of the Sawbwas' rule (Sanda 2008, p. 240). Despite his public praise for the selflessness of the Sawbwa, Ne Win believed that some of them, at least, were planning to revolt. At a dinner with American diplomats a few days prior to the handover of power, both Ne Win and Maung Maung mentioned possible American involvement coming from Chiang Mai in Thailand and directed by one Sao Hkun Suik, an uncle of the former Sawbwa of Kengtung. Sao Hkun Suik was said not only to have visited the American consulate in Chiang Mai, but was also armed with American weapons.[65] Kengtung was still the scene of government military campaigns against the KMT.

At about the same time, Ne Win reviewed the discussions that U Nu had initiated with Chou En-lai in 1956 on the subject of the Burma–China border. He did this after discussions with both factions of the AFPFL and also with politically important people in the Shan and Kachin States. He then wrote to the Chinese, proposing to reopen the border negotiations. The Chinese replied on 24 September (Woodman 1962, pp. 535–36), just days before he was to make a trip to India, Pakistan and Egypt. Six days later, and for the first time, a telegram from the Burma Communist Party to Beijing to mark the 10th anniversary of the Communist revolution was published in *The People's Daily*, giving the BCP recognition not previously displayed (Steinberg and Fan 2012, p. 393). This was viewed as an unfriendly act by the Myanmar government and raised fears about future Chinese attitudes towards the country. Ne Win's suspicions about the Americans and the Shan Sawbwa were matched by his concerns for the Chinese and the BCP.

Before he could turn his attention to the border question, perhaps the most important issue in the foreign relations of Myanmar then, Ne Win first had to conclude his trip to the Middle East and South Asia. He was in Egypt for ten days, touring and holding discussions with senior figures in the United Arab Republic government, including two sessions with President Nasser. The tour included visits to military bases and agricultural projects. Ne Win used the opportunity to explain Myanmar's close ties with Israel which he said grew out of their trade relations. The joint communiqué issued at the end of the visit was the usual boilerplate about the need for economic and social development in the Afro-Asian world and the importance of the Bandung principles, as well as the need for world leaders to get to know each other on a personal basis.[66] The Arab-Israeli conflict was ignored.

From Cairo, Ne Win flew to Karachi where, over two days, he conducted substantive talks on the problem of the Myanmar border with East Pakistan under the military government of Field Marshall Ayub Khan. Khan had conducted a coup and seized power at about the time that Ne Win became Myanmar's prime minister. The Pakistanis complained that Muslims, some of whom claimed they were Myanmar citizens, were being forced back into their territory. The Myanmar government was, on the other hand, under pressure, particularly from Rakhine Buddhist monks, to resist Pakistani military forces which were said to be crossing the border into Myanmar territory (Mendelson 1975, p. 338). The two sides agreed to establish a "high level" commission to investigate the border situation.[67] Incursions from East Pakistan by both illegal immigrants and Pakistani troops were said to have declined after Ne Win's visit. On his return to Yangon, Ne Win briefed Maung Maung and Aung Gyi on his trip and allegedly claimed that both Nasser and Khan urged him not to return power after the election but to retain office. Ne Win told them that he did not enjoy the detailed work of day-to-day government management and the domestic and international criticism which came with the job (Maung Maung n.p., pp. 119–21).

From Karachi, Ne Win and his party of four flew to Delhi where talks with Prime Minister Nehru commenced almost as soon as he touched down. Though expected to make speeches on his arrival, at a dinner later that same day, and on his departure, Ne Win uttered not a single word in public. Nor, as per normal after such a visit, was a joint communiqué issued at the conclusion of the meetings. On his return to Yangon, Ne Win said that there was no need for a joint communiqué as relations with India were cordial.[68] Without doubt the key issue they discussed was their mutual border issues with China. After Ne Win departed, the Myanmar ambassador to India took pains to explain to his West German counterpart the differences in the way the Burma–China border and the China–India border issues were perceived. As far as he and his government were concerned, China had recognized the existing line of control, except for the territory around three villages, Hpimaw, Fawlam and Kangfang, which the Chinese had assigned to British Burma.[69]

However, the Chinese did not refer to the border as the MacMahon Line or the British-drawn line but the traditional line of control. Except for some local political issues in the Kachin State, the border issue was actually resolved, unlike the situation of the India–China border.[70] Ne Win also advised Nehru to keep the Dalai Lama and the Tibetan issue out of the equation. Nehru was said to have got on well with Ne Win, despite his aversion to generals who seized power; as Ne Win had done the deed to preserve the constitution, his action was laudatory in Nehru's eyes.[71]

Soon after Ne Win's return from India, he received the newly arrived Soviet ambassador. After his call, the ambassador went to the Chinese embassy and reported on his conversation with Ne Win. According to the Chinese version of that meeting, Nehru had asked Ne Win to mediate between China and India over their border dispute. Ne Win suggested to Nehru that China's behaviour over the border was proper and if there were faults in the negotiations between Burma and China, some of the problems must be from the Burmese side. Ne Win also asked the Soviet ambassador to inform his Chinese counterpart of his discussions with Nehru. He mentioned that Pakistan had proposed a military agreement with Myanmar, which the latter had cautiously accepted.[72]

Just as Chinese domestic politics contributed to Myanmar's problems with China in the KMT affair, so did Chairman Mao's "Great Leap Forward". The Rangoon *Nation* newspaper published an article on 7 November claiming that 30,915 persons had fled across their common border, presumably fleeing from the exactions of the Great Leap. Most, if not all of the immigrants were ethnically Shan, Kachin or other local linguistic groups, rather than ethnic Han. The refugees were being cared for both by the army and local communities.[73] In the meantime, there had been a further exchange of notes between Chou En-lai and Ne Win, ending with an invitation for Ne Win to visit Beijing the following year (Woodman 1962, p. 536).

Ne Win was in Beijing from 24 to 29 January 1960. Following discussions, he and Chou En-lai signed two agreements, a treaty of mutual non-aggression and a border agreement. Opposition to the border deal in the Kachin state was ignored in order that Ne Win could sign the agreement prior to forthcoming elections which would see the termination of his government. The affected areas of the border were then under the control of the central government's Frontier Areas Administration, having been removed from the control of the Shan and Kachin State governments. No representatives from those regions were members of Ne Win's delegation to China. The terms finally agreed upon were probably as favourable to Myanmar's interests as possible. Very little of what the Chinese had initially claimed was conceded, and Myanmar was able to get an agreed demarcated border with its powerful neighbour for the first time in history.[74] Apart from some minor alterations, amounting to less than fifty square miles in total, "the Chinese accepted in essence, the British-defined boundaries" (Whittam 1961, pp. 174–83, quotation on p. 181). So pleased was Ne Win with the results that he described the relationship as that of brothers (nyi-ako) at a concluding banquet after Chou En-lai praised the "pauk-phaw" (cousinly) relationship of the two neighbours (Aung Myoe 2011, p. 47). By October, despite the difficult terrain and the monsoon weather, joint Chinese–Burmese army survey teams had demarcated the border on the ground.

During February and March, when Ne Win was in effect a "lame duck" Prime Minister, he was busy receiving foreign visitors, including the Prime Minister of Nepal, succeeded by the King and Queen of Thailand,[75] and Soviet Premier Nikita Khrushchev. Prince Philip, the Duke of Edinburgh, also stopped over for a week and met frequently with Ne Win. Nepalese Prime Minister Koirala stayed for several days and had lengthy discussions with Ne Win on the border agreement with China.[76] Koirala was on his way to Beijing for discussions on the Nepalese–Chinese border. Subsequently, the Secretary of the Ministry of Foreign Affairs of Nepal told a British official that "General Ne Win advised them to take a tough line and to stick to their positions to the very last — the Chinese wanted agreement and would give it. This they found to be true, and they are very grateful for the General's advice."[77] Ne Win urged the Thai government to "co-operate in dealing with (or rather in not giving assistance to) the Shan rebels" but they would only offer "closer liaison at the local level".[78]

As the prospects for new elections to see a return to civilian government loomed, there is evidence that some in the army considered ways to resist that possibility, contrary to Ne Win's order on 22 December 1959 that the army, police and civil service were to be impartial in the conduct of the elections (Min Maung Maung 1995, p. 135). A number of field commanders met at Colonel Chit Khaing's house to consider contingency plans in the event that the Nu-Tin Union Party came to power (Callahan 2004, p. 196). However, they did nothing, though some local units apparently interfered with ballot boxes to ensure the victory of the Swe-Nyein AFPFL candidate. Despite the apparent desire by many in the army to see the defeat of Nu's Union Party, Nu returned to power with a clear majority in the Pyithu Hluttaw (Bigelow 1960, pp. 70–74; Butwell and von der Mehden 1960, pp. 144–57). At the end of the Caretaker Government, Ne Win organized a celebratory lunch at his residence on Inya Lake.

According to Colonel Chit Myaing, he took his guests, all army officers except for *Nation* editor Law-Yone, to his boat house after lunch. There he began scolding them for their interference in the elections in support of Kyaw Nyein and Ba Swe's party. "You fools", he said, "you bet on the wrong horse."[79]

The return to civilian government was internationally attributed to Ne Win who was praised around the world for holding elections and leading his troops back to the barracks. He was awarded the Magsaysay Award but refused to accept it, presumably because of Magsaysay's close connections with the American Central Intelligence Agency and the general pro-Western tone of the award,[80] though the public explanation was that he was merely carrying out his duty.[81] Ne Win certainly had reservations about returning power to Nu. His promised policies on making Buddhism the state religion and the granting of additional ethnically designated states boded ill for the future. Just a month before turning the government over to Nu, Ne Win described him as "dangerous", "not quite sane", "mentally vague", "petulant", and "duplicitous" in a conversation with the United States ambassador.[82]

Nu's return to power led to changes in the political institutions of Myanmar which would undo his electoral triumph in the not too distant future. Among the promises he had made was that Buddhism would be declared the state religion. When a constitutional amendment to that effect was passed in 1961, effectively changing nothing as the constitution and government already provided the religion of the majority financial and institutional support, followers of other religions protested at the implications for religious freedom of an official religion. He then passed a constitutional amendment guaranteeing freedom of religion to appease the Christians, Muslims and animists, in turn irritating the Buddhist monkhood. He also offered further steps towards the semi-devolution of government powers to states, putative and real, in an emerging federal constitution, implying replacement of the hybrid, "union", constitution granting greater powers to the ethnically designated states.

Nu's personal views on Buddhism, and his use of the faith for political purposes, were well known. That he saw himself as a modern bodhisattva, an emergent Buddha, was also well known and part of his electoral appeal. His piety spread from the personal to the public arena, with his ban on the slaughter of cattle, and his use of public funds to build pagodas and host the Sixth Buddhist Conference. Ne Win's views on Nu's religiosity were unknown, but one can speculate. Ne Win had no particular affinity with Buddhism and its practices and traditions that were ostentatiously displayed by Nu and his followers. Though he entered monkhood as a young novice, he had no wish to carry on Buddhist rituals from his youth (Maung Maung 1969, p. 306). His family was perhaps one of the few in Yangon, if not the country, of persons not declared Christians or Muslims (and even some of them), without a Buddha image or shrine. He used to ridicule the Buddha, who he referred to as "kala galay" (Indian boy), and stated he did not think "that Indian fellow ever came here". He also made fun of the Pope, telling the devoutly Catholic Maung Maung about Pope Joan, the female pope, and used to discuss allegations of sodomy amongst the Buddhist monkhood. Most of the time, however, he kept his views on religion to himself.[83]

Whatever Ne Win's personal views on Buddhism and other religious traditions were, in 1958 his government had inherited a number of problems regarding religion from its civilian predecessors. Factionalism in the monkhood was a major problem which the politicians, including U Nu, both made use of and feared. The solution they saw was a two-prong effort to organize and control monkhood. This involved forming a Sangha (monkhood) Parliament composed of monks elected by the entirety of the monkhood. Both were resisted by the most powerful monastic institutions as an attempt to undermine their autonomy as had happened to the Thai monkhood nearly sixty years earlier. The Caretaker Government, however, thought it saw an opportunity to register the monkhood and form the Parliament as a parallel effort to provide national identity and registration cards for all citizens over the age of twelve. Rather than taking on the issue of organizing the monkhood, the government would first register it (Mendelson 1975, p. 341).

While some of the monkhood were willing to cooperate with the government, many were not. The Myanmar sangha, lacking the control that the Thai state had achieved at the start of the twentieth century, was deeply involved in politics, contrary to its other-worldly purpose. Earlier, Myanmar kings, including the reformist Mindon, attempted to regulate the monkhood in order to preserve its role as a strictly religious body, with little success (Myo Myint 2012, pp. 202–12). The registration of monks, nuns, and koyin (novices) had been authorized by law in 1949 for four purposes: (1) population statistics, (2) identifying law breakers, (3) preventing impersonations at elections, and (4) tracing absconders. As the government was also concerned about Communists and other insurgents cloaking themselves as monks, bringing monkhood into the registration process was essential. Early in its period of rule, the Caretaker Government had raided several monasteries in Yangon and found arms hidden in drains and under prayer rooms. Ne Win's government halted the propitiation of *nat*, local spirits, which Nu had revived, on the advice given by a group of senior monks (Smith 1965, pp. 174–75). Nu brought back the practice on returning to power, to the point of ordering the construction of two State Nat Shrines, despite the belief by many Buddhists that such superstitious activities were bogus (Smith 1965, p. 177).

As the registration of the laity was nearly complete, registration of monkhood was now in order. However, many monks objected, partly because they saw registration as a first step towards a Sangha Parliament, and partly because they objected to the questions and the form for registration, which were identical to that for laypersons. Colonel Chit Myaing backed down on the registration form issue and agreed to use revised cards for monks, and again denied that registration was a prelude to a Sangha Parliament. His efforts at appeasement failed. The monks further objected to a requirement upon registration that they report to the local authorities if they were to be away from the place of registration for more than a month. At this point, the military was on the point of handing power back to Nu and the matter ended, once more a victory for the anti-registration, anti-state sanctioned organization monks (Mendelson 1975, pp. 344–47). Though making Buddhism the official state religion provided Nu further justification for registering the monkhood, he made no serious attempt to do so.

Having handed the reins of government back to the obscurantist Nu, Ne Win departed for England and then travelled to the United States before returning to London again on 30 June. Apparently, his time in the United States of approximately a month was mostly spent at the university hospital in Minneapolis, Minnesota, receiving treatment for the bladder or urinary problem for which he was sedated in Yangon in 1959. From his perspective, the trip was marred, however, when the United States Customs officials insisted on searching his luggage on arrival in New York and other slights on the visits as they failed to recognize he and Daw Khin May Than. As with his visit to the United States, Ne Win's British visit was also a private affair but, nonetheless, he had a number of official engagements. On 4 July, Prime Minister and Lady MacMillan hosted a lunch for him and Daw Khin May Than, along with Lord Mountbatten and a number of diplomats connected with Myanmar, particularly the Gore-Booths. On the 12th, he lunched with Field Marshall Sir Francis Festing, whom Ne Win had met in 1956 when he visited Yangon as Commander of the Far East

Land Forces. The next day, he had lunch with Her Majesty, the Queen, followed by another engagement with Mountbatten the following day.[84] He also received some undisclosed medical treatment in London.

Upon leaving England, Ne Win made his first of what became many trips to the Federal Republic of Germany. According to the Yangon representative of the state-owned Fritz-Werner Company, which had contracts with the Defence Services Institute (DSI), the army-owned holding company run by Brigadier Aung Gyi, Ne Win was keen to know more about Germany and to have talks with Fritz-Werner officials. Fritz-Werner constructed factories were supplying the Myanmar army and Ne Win and his colleagues were very happy with the relationship. The company's director, a Dr Meyer, was well known to Ne Win (Zollner 1994, pp. 197–204). While in Germany, he wanted to visit dockyards for discussions on ordering new ships for the Burma Five Star Line and also the development of a new rifle. He also expressed an interest in meeting senior German military leaders and cabinet ministers.[85] As to what actually happened on the visit, there is no available record.

The year 1960 was another of extensive travels for Ne Win. After his trip to the United States, Great Britain and West Germany, he was soon off to Beijing for the second time that year, this time as a member of Prime Minister Nu's large delegation formally to sign the border agreement on Chinese National Day, 1 October. Chou En-lai, in turn, came to Yangon in early January 1961 to exchange instruments of ratification of the border agreement and, in addition, offered a thirty million pound loan over six years.

The end of the year saw increased cooperation between China and Myanmar on the border agreement. Twice between 22 December 1960 and 9 February 1961, People's Liberation Army (PLA) forces entered Myanmar territory and attacked, in conjunction with the Myanmar army, the remaining KMT. The KMT headquarters was destroyed as a consequence. While it was reported that more than 4,300 KMTs departed for Taiwan subsequently, the remainder gathered along the Laotian and Thai borders of Myanmar (Steinberg and Fan 2012, p. 393; Lintner 1999, p. 445). On the first day of the PLA operations within Myanmar, the British presented their assessment of political conditions in the former colony at a South East Asia Treaty Organisation (SEATO) Council meeting, asserting that Nu was firmly in control and that the people were tired of the army. The Australian representative added that Nu and Ne Win were getting along well and the situation for the new government was set fair. It was Ne Win's subordinates, however, especially Brigadier Maung Maung, who were said to be politically ambitious.[86]

On 1 February 1961, Brigadier Maung Maung was unexpectedly dismissed from the army and sent abroad as ambassador to Israel, a country he had often visited. Speculation as to the cause of Maung Maung's dismissal hinges on his close links with the American CIA, including using CIA advice to develop a counter-intelligence capacity, and his firm anti-Communist stance.[87] Bo Lwin, then head of army intelligence and having direct access to Ne Win, viewed Maung Maung's operation as a threat to his position and an entree by the CIA into the army. Also, at that time, as Myanmar was enjoying improved relations with China, anti-Communism was out of favour amongst many in Yangon.[88] Anti-Americanism was strong, however, especially after a Burma Air Force plane was shot down in a clash with an unmarked B-24 airplane supplying the KMT in the Shan State. Flight Lieutenant Peter's death, prominently displayed at the Army museum in Yangon and now Naypyitaw, was the result of a clash with an American-built plane contracted to the American Central Intelligence Agency. The event led to demonstrations in Yangon (Min Maung Maung 1995, pp. 152–53; Hilsman 1964, 1967, pp. 304–5).

Six days after Maung Maung's dismissal, as Ne Win was convening the Annual Commanders' Conference in the capital, the press announced the dismissal of ten other senior officers, nine brigade commanders and the person in charge of the Southern Command, Brigadier Aung Shwe. They either retired from the army or were sent abroad as military attachés, with Aung Shwe becoming ambassador to Australia.[89] Though there was much speculation as to what lay behind the purge, the official reason for the most significant shake-up of the armed forces since the purge of Brigadier Kyaw Zaw was the alleged interference of these men in the 1960 elections (Callahan 2004, pp. 200–1). What took place between Nu and Ne Win prior to the purges remains to be discovered.

Ne Win and Aung Gyi, as the remaining senior staff officers, took advantage of the purge to reorganize the army and its command structure. The powerful Northern and Southern Commands created by the British in 1947 were dissolved, and in their stead five divisional commands with four independent brigades located in border-security trouble spots, the Rakhine, Kachin, Naga, and Chin regions, covering the borders with East Pakistan, India, and China were created. The brigades and three of the divisional commands were heavily involved in counter-insurgency warfare at the time, dealing particularly with Karen, Shan, and Kachin separatists and the KMT. The new and much reduced Northwestern and Central Commands, strategically located for security duties, and facing significant Communist forces, were placed under Ne Win loyalists, Brigadiers Sein Win and San Yu (Callahan 2004, pp. 201–2).

When Ne Win met again with Chou En-lai and Luo Ruiqing at the end of March 1961, he explained that the purge of Brigadier Maung Maung and the other ten senior officers was an action he had taken after visiting the Chinese border area the preceding January. According to the Chinese, "Ne Win said that after he had met Vice Premiers Luo and Chen in January he had gone to the front line to review the clearing of the Chiang bandits' nest, and on returning to Rangoon had cleared out some bad elements in the armed forces."[90] At the January meeting, the issue of American involvement in Laos was one of the key topics for discussion. On 5 January 1961, according to Qiang Zhai,

> Zhou Enlai stated that although the Soviet Union and North Vietnam had provided indirect assistance to Souvanna Phouma's [neutralist] government, the United States not only had assisted the Boun Oum [rightist] regime but also had sent U.S. troops to Laos. The United States "had thus lost justification" for its actions and had to consider the possibility of a direct confrontation from the Soviet Union if it decided to dispatch troops on a larger scale. Calling Sihanouk's proposal for an enlarged Geneva Conference on Laos "excellent". Zhou went on to point out that China opposed the presentation of the Laos question to the United Nations and objected to the international organisations intervention. While condemning the dispatch of U.S. troops to Laos, Zhou said nothing about the presence of North Vietnamese soldiers in Pathet Lao-controlled territory (Zhai 2000, pp. 96–97).

Luo praised Ne Win and said that "splittist elements" had to be severely dealt with, to which Ne Win responded by saying he had offered to those removed an opportunity to reform but that had failed. They "had committed the crime of treason".

Rather than observing how Nu governed, Ne Win was soon off on his travels again. In March, as noted above, he visited China and held two days of meetings with Chinese Premier Chou En-lai and Vice Premier Luo Ruiqing, who was also head of the People's Liberation Army General Staff Department. Their discussions ranged widely from the situation in Laos, the purge of the Myanmar army, oil exploration and development, and a possible second Afro-Asian Bandung-type conference. Regarding Laos, Ne Win expressed the view that the United States intended to start a small-scale war in the country, which was being resisted by France and Britain. The KMT who had fled from Myanmar had joined in the conflict in Laos. Though British Prime Minister MacMillan had convinced President Kennedy to agree to a ceasefire, in the long run the Americans wanted a war in Laos. Ne Win was concerned that the KMT, then involved in the fighting in Laos, would link up with Shan rebels in Burma and the war would spread to the entire region.[91] As Premier Chou made clear the previous year, the Chinese side did not dissent from Ne Win's analysis and praised the Burma army for how it handled the KMT issue (Steinberg and Fan 2012, p. 50). As Ne Win and Chou were sharing their deep concerns about Laos and American intentions there, so also in Washington "in the early 1960s, Laos was no sideshow" (Jacobs 2012, p. 4).

Ne Win, in turn, thanked the PLA for its assistance in dealing with the KMT. He also made it clear to the United States ambassador in Myanmar that whatever the Americans claimed, the Burmese were not deceived. Furthermore, Aung Gyi had discussed the border issue with the Thai military and the Myanmar side was well aware of the assistance that Thailand was providing the KMT, whom the Chinese referred to as "Chiang's bandits". The Myanmar army, due to logistical problems, were often forced to purchase supplies in Thailand for the troops in the Shan State, but when the army attacked the KMT, the Thai military cut off those sources of supply. This unfriendly attitude was noted.[92] Just a month earlier in February 1961, the new Kennedy administration had proposed the involvement of Myanmar in Laotian affairs as part of a three-nation commission, along with Cambodia and Malaya, to bring a resolution to the civil war there. Nu's government had promptly rejected the idea, as ventriloquized by the King of Laos, as a scheme to bolster the rightist forces. Ne Win would have known of the implausible ploy (Oberdorfer 2003, pp. 162–63).

Ne Win then discussed the unwillingness of U Nu's government to complete the nationalization of the Burmah Oil Company which remained as a joint venture. This made Ne Win angry and he was quoted as saying, "No patriot should agree to this." He indicated that after his forthcoming visit to the Soviet Union, Eastern Europe, and West Germany, during which he would be studying the oil industry, he was likely to proceed to England for discussions on the future of Burmah Oil. As for a second Bandung conference, Ne Win "suggested that the meeting should expose the cheating and manipulation practiced by Western nations on the Asian and African nations".[93] Ne Win's admiration for Marxist theory seemed to be maturing and the progress he saw China making economically, in contrast to the pace of development in Myanmar, encouraged him further in that direction (Chit Hlaing n.d., p. 5).

Indeed, the issue of the future of the Burmah Oil Company arose again after Ne Win returned to Myanmar following his trip to Europe. After Nu resumed the Prime Ministerial post, he announced that his government would undertake no more nationalizations of private businesses. Moreover, the former Minister for Mines, M.A. Rashid, returned to that office, apparently ensuring continuity. Soon, however, the government began to discuss a 50–50 arrangement but talks on that were terminated, but a demand for a 51 per cent government ownership was on the table. This was agreed but then the government dawdled at implementing the agreement. A year after stepping down as Prime Minister, Ne Win once more declared his interest in the oil industry and demanded to see documents related to the proposed takeover. "That request", in the words of the official historian of Burmah Oil, "clearly embarrassed ministers, but they could hardly tell the general to mind his own business" (Corley 1988, p. 259). Aung Gyi also started to take an interest in the matter and government ministers began to act. In particular, when Ne Win and Aung Gyi saw the relevant documents, they took exception to an agreement that the government would take no further share of the company for at least fifteen years. By then nearly two years had transpired, and the matter was about to be resolved, but that requires another chapter for the telling.

From Beijing, Ne Win flew to Moscow where he was received as a guest of Premier Khrushchev. As the political situation in Myanmar continued to deteriorate, with a split rather like that of 1958 in Nu's new Union Party, and the growth of new anti-Yangon guerrilla armies amongst Kachin and Shan groups opposed to Nu's state religion policy and the forcing from power of the Sawbwa,[94] the world was courting Ne Win as the man most likely to inherit the mess. The international situation at that time was particularly fraught. Civil wars, with great power involvement, were developing in the Congo and Laos, there was continuing conflict in Vietnam, and growing tensions over Berlin made frequent headlines. The Bay of Pigs invasion by CIA-backed Cubans, a failed attempt to topple the Communist government of Fidel Castro, and authorized by the new United States President, John F. Kennedy, was not far off.

There was no indication of what role, if any, Ne Win played in one of the minor dramas of the Cold War that occurred during his time as

Prime Minister. On 23 June 1959, a young official responsible for spreading Communist propaganda in Myanmar, Aleksandr Kaznacheev, defected from the Soviet legation to the United States embassy. In his account, it was his growing doubts about Communism which led him to defect, though Myanmar friends also believed it was because of an automobile accident in which he and his Burmese girlfriend were involved. In any event, with the obvious cooperation of the Myanmar authorities, Kaznacheev was flown out of Mingaladon airport in a special U.S. government plane after meeting with officials from the Soviet embassy for thirty minutes. His last meeting with his employers was arranged to demonstrate that he was not being forcibly taken to the West. Kaznacheev's account of training and experiences, however, was noteworthy at the time as one of the first indications of Chinese–Soviet conflict over Southeast Asia. Ne Win would have been aware of the incident, as well as an earlier failed defection of a Soviet military attaché who was flown out in a Chinese plane, allegedly annoying the Myanmar authorities.[95]

Ne Win intended to remain in the Soviet Union for twenty-three days and then move on to Poland, Rumania, the German Democratic Republic, and Czechoslovakia before entraining to Frankfurt and then Bonn. He sought an invitation to visit West Germany again which was immediately extended. Visits to West Berlin and Hamburg were sought, as well as learning about German military, industrial and medical developments.[96] However, in late April or early May, Ne Win became ill with ear and sinus troubles, and postponed his Eastern European trip to fly to London for medical treatment.[97]

He remained in the London Clinic until 22 May and had lunch with Prime Minister MacMillan again the following week, having been received by Princess Alexandra as well as Malcolm MacDonald and Lord Mountbatten.[98] At the lunch, the other guests included the notorious British Defence Minister, John Profumo, Field Marshall Festing, and Ne Win's old friend, U Hla Maung, now ambassador in London.[99] MacMillan was advised not to discuss the old saw about Burma joining the Commonwealth and to note Ne Win's concern that American intelligence and other agencies would not tolerate President Kennedy's acceptance of neutralism as a valid foreign policy posture.[100]

While in London in August, Ne Win was staying in a small flat off Kensington Gardens where he received the brother of the former Mawchi Mines manager, the noted journalist on Southeast Asia, Brian Crozier. In a remarkably informal atmosphere, Ne Win discussed with Crozier his concerns about the political conditions in Myanmar, leaving the impression that if events were "to drift once more towards ruin and disunity", he would take power again.

> One sensed a deep-seated conflict within him, however, which arose from a sincere horror of the political game, allied with a genuine reluctance to adopt unconstitutional means. While he had been Premier, he told me, the politicians of both factions of the AFPFL had asked him to form and lead a new national party, "but I sent them away. What would be the use of forming another party? I had to stay outside politics to make sure the next elections would be fair. In Burma a political party can't win an election without being corrupt. If I had accepted the offer to form a political party of my own I would have had to become corrupt myself, and I am not prepared to do this.

Ne Win also discussed the need for constitutional continuity and criticized other military leaders, such as Egypt's Gamal Abdel Nasser and Iraq's Abd al-Karim Qasim, for creating a political vacuum after they seized power. During the Caretaker period, he insisted on consulting the two main political leaders, U Nu and U Ba Swe, on proposed legislation in order to ensure continuity in government (Crozier 1963, pp. 73–74).

While Ne Win was travelling the world, there was speculation back in Yangon about individuals plotting to succeed him. Brigadier Aung Gyi was now the butt of confection for taking over, following the dismissal of the pro-American Maung Maung and other senior officers. They were said to be resistance to the policy of friendship towards China that Nu and Ne Win had developed in the previous few years in the process of resolving the border dispute. The notion that Ne Win wished to become President, a largely ceremonial post, when the position became vacant in 1962, was also in the air.[101]

As noted above, in October 1961, Ne Win accompanied Prime Minister U Nu to China for another official visit and Israeli Prime Minister David Ben Gurion visited Myanmar in December for seventeen days, nine of which were spent studying meditation at Nu's residence.[102] In between these events, President John F. Kennedy gave the order to send the first American combat troops to shore up the South Vietnamese government in the foreign-sponsored civil war. The political scene in Myanmar was clearly getting fraught, and tensions abounded at this time. Brigadier Aung Gyi postponed a planned trip to Britain because of problems with the

Prime Minister. He tried to visit London, and possibly West Germany, in February, but once more he had to postpone.[103] The visit never took place, even though it was rescheduled from February to March and then early April.[104] Relations were strained at that time with Thailand, which was providing no cooperation in dealing with the KMT along their common border.[105]

On 3 January 1962, Nu's government agreed to the upgrade of the East German trade office to a full embassy. The government had resisted the move for some time, but in the eyes of the Communist nations, this put Myanmar's neutrality in the Cold War in question.[106] How could good relations with West Germany be justified if there were no good relations with East Germany?

On 25 February, a federal seminar was convened in Yangon with the purpose of putting forth ideas on revising the Myanmar constitution to give greater powers to the ethnically designated border states. This had U Nu's blessing, having been preceded by a conference of ethnic leaders at Taunggyi at which three government ministers attended.[107] Ne Win, who had attended some of the sessions of the seminar, later said he had overheard "extremist" comments which led him to believe that a rebellion was being plotted in the Shan State.[108] On the evening of 1 March, Ne Win and Daw Khin May Than attended a performance of a Chinese musical troupe that was visiting Myanmar. He had an altercation with youths sitting behind them who put their feet on their chairs. At the end of the performance, he went on stage to congratulate and thank the performers. Later that night, Ne Win took power in a coup. That coup, unlike the military takeover of the government in 1958, was complete and nationwide. "Units took up strategic positions not only around Rangoon but in key upcountry locations as well. This was a coup which bore the stamp of a unified, bureaucratized military, in which orders were followed with remarkable regularity throughout the territory" (Callahan 2004, p. 203). Ne Win was in command.

Notes

1. Maung Maung, "Some Aspects of the 'Caretaker Government' 1958–1960: An Experiment in Democratic Process", unpublished manuscript, p. 2. As U Maung Maung did not have a chance to edit the manuscript for publication, the author has taken the liberty of making minor corrections to the spelling or grammar to aid readability.

2. Ibid., p. 3.

3. A similar idea had also been floated at the residence of Prime Minister Ba Swe by Colonel Kyi Win, Ba Swe's cousin, again, in early 1957. Present at that meeting were a number of senior cabinet ministers, including Kyaw Nyein, and members of the General Staff and field commanders, but not Ne Win. Ibid., p. 27.

4. Sein Win, *The Split Story: An Account of Recent Political Upheaval in Burma: With Emphasis on AFPFL* (Rangoon: The Guardian, 1959), pp. 20–21. In Maung Maung's somewhat garbled version of events, Thakin Tin and Thakin Kyaw Dun (or Tun) later related a version of the alleged plot to remove Nu, which included army collusion. Maung Maung, "Caretaker Government", p. 28. Also, Thakin Nu, *U Nu — Saturday's Son*, translated by Law-Yone and edited by Kyaw Win (New Haven and London: Yale University Press, 1975), p. 322.

5. For the passage of the 1958–59 budget by Presidential Ordinance, see Sein Win, *Split Story*, pp. 55–63.

6. Mary P. Callahan, *Making Enemies: War and State Building in Burma* (Ithaca: Cornell University Press; Singapore University Press, 2004), p. 186. In his account of the 1958 coup, Yoshihiro Nakanishi makes much more of the pressure from Aung Shwe and the Northern Command to conduct a coup. He suggests that if it were not because of Maung Maung and Brigadier Ba Lay (sic, Blake), the opposition of the idea of a coup by the Southern Commander, and the handover to Ne Win by Maung Maung, the constitution would have been preserved. This strikes me as implausible, given Maung Maung's, Nu's, and *Guardian* Sein Win's accounts of what transpired. See Yoshihiro Nakanishi, *Strong Soldiers, Failed Revolution: The State and Military in Burma, 1962–88* (Kyoto: Kyoto University Press, 2013), pp. 84–88.

7. Sein Win, *Split Story*, p. 37. Maung Maung even suggests "ladies of pleasure" and cash bribes were offered. Maung Maung, "Caretaker Government", p. 16.

8. Elgar van Randow to AA, 3 June 1958, AA PA B 12 Bd. 1.192, 485–87. Sein Win, *Split Story*, p. 69.

9. Reported in *The Guardian Daily*, 24 June 1958, and quoted in Maung Maung, *Burma and General Ne Win* (London: Asia Publishing House, 1969), pp. 242–43.

10. Letter, Peter Murray to Selwyn Lloyd, 15 July 1958, FO371/135729.

11. Letter, A.J. de la Mare, Washington, to F.S. Tomlison, 26 May 1958, DEFE7/2094; Telegram, Murray to Foreign Office, 25 June 1958, DEFE7/2094.

12. Formed when the former sitwundan were absorbed into the army in 1956, Dr Callahan describes the pyusawhti as "a party army". Callahan, *Making Enemies*, p. 143.

13. Dr Callahan adds Colonel Tin Pe to the list of those to be included in the cabinet under the Nu offer. Callahan, *Making Enemies*, pp. 186–87. In Maung Maung's version of the coup, as told to Dr Callahan, he created the coup to stop the regional commanders from mounting their own putative coup. As there is no other evidence to support this thesis, and he does not repeat it in his own manuscript, the question remains open as to the accuracy of his account as retold by her. Sein Win, *Split Story*, p. 188. For counter-evidence, see the comments by Colonel Hla Maw, Sein Win, *Split Story*, p. 190.

14. Maung Maung, "Caretaker Government", p. 35. Maung Maung claims that at this time Ne Win had discussed with his subordinates about establishing a communist-like system with himself as the head. The parliamentary system had demonstrated that it could not resolve the country's issues. The validity of this claim is hard to verify. There may have been some truth in it, but the fact that Ne Win waited four more years before taking actions to change the system suggests that he may have been merely thinking aloud, with no intention of any action or did not feel confident that he would succeed. Maung Maung, "Caretaker Government", p. 31.

15. Telegram, Rangoon to Secretary of State, 25 September 1958, 790B.00/9-2558, No. 277.

16. Ne Win's letter to U Nu, 16 September 1958, FO371/135729; the exchange is also reprinted in Sein Win, *Split Story*, pp. 84–89 and Appendix 3 of *Is Trust Vindicated? The Chronicle of Trust, Striving and Triumph: Being an Account of the Accomplishments of the Government of the Union of Burma: November 1, 1958–February 4, 1960* (Rangoon: Director of Information, Government of the Union of Burma, 1960), pp. 543–44. Maung Maung claims that he drafted the letters; Sein Win states that U Nu drafted both his letter and Ne Win's. Sein Win, *Split Story*, p. 90.

17. Von Randow to AA, 27 September 1958, AA PA B 12 Bd. 1.192, 488–89.

18. Von Randow to AA, 29 September 1958, AA PA B 12 Bd. 1.192, 490.

19. German Mission to AA, 2 October 1984, AA PA B 12 Bd.1.192, 498–99.

20. "The Political Situation in Burma", Embassy in Burma, 2300 hrs, 29 September 1958, 105-00559-02(01) [105-C0515].

21. Quoted in Maung Maung, *Burma and General Ne Win*, pp. 247–48. The speech in its entirety is reprinted as Appendix 4, in *Is Trust Vindicated*, pp. 545–49.

22. Licht, a friend of Ne Win, had managed industrial projects in the United States and Europe, and was on a year's leave as a general manager of a factory producing spare parts for the United States Army. Ne Win and Licht apparently met in 1949 while Ne Win and Set Kya, with others, were negotiating a small arms deal with the Italians. Maung Maung, "Caretaker Government", p. 42 and p. 146, fn. 27. It was apparently based on advice from Licht that led Aung Gyi successfully to turn the army canteen services

into the Defense Services Institute, the largest economic holding company in Myanmar by 1960. Maung Maung, "Caretaker Government", p. 54. State and army owned banks, despite Aung Gyi's and Licht's advocacy of the private sector, enjoyed a "bonanza" during the Caretaker period. Sean Turnell, *Fiery Dragons: Banks, Moneylenders and Microfinance in Burma* (Copenhagen: NIAS Press, 2009), pp. 216–18. Ne Win apparently also took economic advice from another American, Mr Tommy Davis, who was an OSS friend of Edward Law-Yone. For an account of how the Davis became a non-guest in Ne Win's residence, see Wendy Law-Yone, *Goldern Parasol: A Daughter's Memoir of Burma* (London: Chatto and Windus, 2013), pp. 134–35.

23. When the state councils met, they made their own nominations for their respective chief ministers and Ne Win, contrary to previous practice, accepted the nominations automatically. For Shan State, they were Sao Hom Hpa; Kachin, Duwa Zau Lawn; Chin, U Ral Hmung; Kayin, Dr Saw Hla Tun; Kayah, Saw Wunna.

24. A list of officers attached to the relevant ministries is printed as Appendix 9 of *Is Trust Vindicated*, pp. 561–67.

25. For an overall assessment of the performance of the Caretaker Government, see Louis J. Walinsky, *Economic Development in Burma, 1951–1960* (New York: Twentieth Century Fund, 1962), pp. 252–66.

26. The paper is analysed in Callahan, *Making Enemies*, p. 189.

27. Printed as part of Appendix 1 of *Is Trust Vindicated*, p. 534. This section also includes a brief historical indication of how the document came to be produced. "The National Ideology and the Role of the Defence Services" is reprinted on pp. 536–41.

28. Ibid., p. 3.

29. The role of the Myanmar army during the Caretaker period was one of the arguments that was used by American political scientists in the 1960s to justify military governments in developing countries. See J.J. Johnson, ed., *The Role of the Military in Developing Countries* (Princeton: Princeton University Press, 1962), particularly the chapter on Burma by Lucian W. Pye. Pye lived in Myanmar during the period of the military government and developed his theory of so-called "Burmese political culture" which was mentioned in his book, *Politics, Personality and Nation-Building: Burma's Search for Identity* (New Haven: Yale University Press, 1962).

30. The author met with several former Communists who showed him the scares on their legs as a result of broken bones caused during interrogations on Coco Gyun. Maung Maung explains that the use of Coco Gyun was to send people "for an undetermined period separated from family and friends but especially from the occupation", presumably left-wing politics. Maung Maung, "Caretaker Government", pp. 40–41. A total of 432 "trouble making politicians were arrested and 153 banished to Coco Gyun". Hugh

Tinker, *The Union of Burma: A Study of the First Years of Independence*, 4th ed. (London: Oxford University Press, 1967), p. 61. For the history of the island and its neighbours, see Andrew Selth, "Burma's Mythical Isle", *AQ-Australia Quarterly*, vol. 80, no. 6 (November–December 2008): 24–28 and 40.

31. White Flag Communists, 3,050; Red Flag Communists, 750; Karen National Defence Organisation, 3,700; Mon National Defence Organisation, 50; Mujahids, 120; Chinese Nationalists (KMT), 1,350; and an unknown number of Shan insurgents, estimated at 500 to 1,500 strong. *Is Trust Vindicated*, p. 19.

32. Remaining insurgents number 700 White Flag Communists; 209 Red Flag Communists; 1,695 KNDO; 274 Shan insurgents; 2,317 KMT; and 290 Mujahid. Ibid., pp. 31, 43.

33. Letter, Douglas Blake to the author, 20 June 2008.

34. Telegram, Allen to Foreign Office, 7 February 1959, FO371/143888.

35. Notes on Burma Army Personnel, 20 June 1959, FO371/143888.

36. Letter, R.H. Allen to Selwyn Lloyd, 30 April 1959, FO371/143887.

37. Annual Appraisal of the Burma Armed Forces for the Period 1st June 1958 to 30th April 1959, by H.M. Military Attaché, FO371/143887.

38. Note by Malcolm MacDonald on trip to Rangoon, 21 to 24 September 1959, FO371/143861.

39. Richard Butwell, *U Nu of Burma* (Stanford, California: Stanford University Press, 1963), p. 71. U Nu, according to Ingrid Jordt, was going to reintroduce the ban prior to 1962 in which Ne Win seized power. She writes that Nu offered to allow Ne Win to sign the bill making animal slaughter illegal in order to earn merit but Ne Win declined. She provides no sources for this and it is difficult to understand what legal status Ne Win could have had prior to the coup which would allow him to sign into law legislation. That was the constitutional responsibility of the President. Ingrid Jordt, *Burma's Mass Lay Meditation Movement: Buddhism and the Cultural Construction of Power* (Athens: Ohio University Press, 2007), pp. 197–98.

40. Maung Maung writes that the highway idea was his and agreed by Ne Win because of the corruption and inadequate carrying capacity of the Inland Water Transport flotilla and the Burma railways for commercial, not military, goods. Maung Maung, "Caretaker Government", pp. 116–19.

41. Letter, R.H.S. Allen to R.P. Heppel, 20 May 1959, FO371/143865.

42. Letter, R.H.S. Allen to R.P. Heppel, 18 August 1959, FO371/143887.

43. This speech and that given the following year at the University are reproduced as Appendices 6 and 8 in *Is Trust Vindicated?*, pp. 555–57 and 560.

44. Von Randow to AA, 8 December 1958, AA PA B 12 Bd.1.191, 20–21.

45. Letter, Allen to R.P. Heppel, 31 January 1959, FO371/143865; Silverstein and Wohl, "University Students and Politics", p. 53.

46. Letter, R.H.S. Allen to R.P. Heppel, 31 January 1959, FO371/143865. Maung Maung, "Caretaker Government", p. 46; Thet Tun, "A Critique of Louis J. Walinsky's *Economic Development in Burma, 1951–1960*", *Journal of the Burma Research Society*, vol. XLVII, part 1 (June 1964): 173–82.

47. From John Seabury Thompson, "A Second Chance for Burma: The Interim Government and the 1960 Election" supplement to J.S. Furnivall, *The Governance of Modern Burma* (New York: International Secretariat, Institute of Pacific Relations, 1960), p. 145, fn. 31, quoting G.H. Luce's obituary of Furnivall in *The Nation*, 13 July 1960.

48. Louis Walinsky, Meeting with the Honourable Prime Minister, 17 December 1958, written on 19 December 1958, Louis Walinsky Papers, Cornell University Library, Collection Number 4874, Box 5, Folder 4.

49. Even the Minister for the Kayah State, Saw Wunna, had had ambitions since before 1958 "to secede from the Union of Burma, join up with Thailand and run the Kayah State — with the mine at Mawchi — as his private empire". L.A. Crozier, *Mawchi: Mining, War and Insurgency in Burma*, Australians in Asia Series 11 (Brisbane: Centre for the Study of Australia-Asia Relations, Griffith University, March 1994), p. 31. In 1956, at his home in Yangon, and with a "nattily dressed in tweed jacket and grey slacks" Shan Sawbwa present, Saw Wunna told Crozier that the Kayah State, and by implication, the Shan State, were going to secede and join with Thailand. Ibid., pp. 37–38.

50. Ibid., pp. 104–5.

51. Ibid., pp. 108–9.

52. Notes from Thein Nyunt, "U Ne Win Akyaung Thi Kaung Saya Akyetalet Akyou" [Some Information About Ne Win], photocopied typescript, unpublished paper (n.p., n.d.).

53. Von Randow to AA, AA PA B 12 Bd.1.216, 57–60.

54. *The Times*, 8 January 1959; FR German Mission to NATO, Paris, Wickert to AA, 23 January 1959, AA PA B 12 Bd.1.215, 141.

55. AJBT, KPR, I-2/11-3, pp. 8–9; quoted in Jovan Cavoski, *Arming Nonalignment: Yugoslavia's Relations with Burma and the Cold War in Asia (1950–1955)*, Cold War International History Project Working Paper no. 61 (Washington, D.C.: Woodrow Wilson International Center for Scholars, April 2010), p. 58, fn. 231. According to Cavoski, Yugoslav officials concluded over time that Ne Win was the most important person in Yugoslavia's relations with Burma. Ibid., pp. 51–52. Ne Win also met with the visiting head of the British Navy in East Asia in April, but the talks were without substance. Letter, R.H. Allen to Selwyn Lloyd, 30 April 1959, FO371/143887.

56. Von Randow to AA, 25 May 1959, AA PA B 12 Bd.1.215, 241.

57. Letter, B. Latt, Tel Aviv to Selwyn Lloyd, 19 June 1959, FO 371/142300. Maung Maung notes the positive impression made upon Ne Win by his visit to Israel, as opposed to the negative reaction he had to his visits with

fellow generals Nasser of Egypt and Ayub Khan of Pakistan later in the year. Both Nasser and Ayub Khan tried to get him to severe relations with Israel. Maung Maung, "Caretaker Government", p. 121.

58. BBC telex, no date, reached the Foreign Office on 22 June 1959, FO371/142300; Racky, Yangon to AA, 27 June 1959, AA PA B 12 Bd.1.215, 144–45. The Germans believed there were 150, not 80, Burmese studying and working in Israel.

59. For the finessing of this decision, see Maung Maung, "Section 116 of the Constitution", *The Guardian*, vol. VI, no. 3 (March 1959): 11–12; reprinted in Robert H. Taylor, ed., *Dr Maung Maung: Gentleman, Scholar, Patriot* (Singapore: Institute of Southeast Asian Studies, 2008), pp. 488–92.

60. Von Randow to AA, 17 February 1959, AA PA B 12 Bd.1.193, 501.

61. Von Randow to AA, 5 March 1959, AA PA B 12 Bd.1.193, 504–7.

62. Von Randow to AA, 28 February 1959, AA PA B 12 Bd.1.193, 502.

63. Memorandum of conversation, Ne Win and McConaughy, 13 January 1959. No. 360.

64. The speech is printed as Appendix 7 in *Is Trust Vindicated?*, pp. 558–59, quotation on p. 559.

65. Telegram, Rangoon to Secretary of State, 24 April 1959, 790B.00/4-2459, Control 16027, No. 909.

66. German embassy, Cairo to AA, 9 October 1959, AA PA B 12 Bd.1.125, 149–51; Egypt embassy, Cairo to Weber, AA, AA PA B 12 Bd.1.207, 427; Letter, C.T. Crowe to Selwyn Lloyd, 10 October 1959, FO371/143863. The British believed the talks were less lengthy but equally useless.

67. Letter, L.B. Walsh-Atkins to Earl of Home, 16 October 1959, FO371/143867.

68. Ne Win's visit to India, Chinese embassy in India, 9 October 1959. A Brief Account of Ne Win's Visit to India, Chinese Embassy in India, 10 October 1959. Ne Win's Visit to the Arab League, India and Pakistan, Chinese Embassy in Burma, 14 October 1959, 105-00912(1) [105-D0427].

69. China's insistence on the return of the three villages angered many in Myanmar and was used by the press to criticize the government for not being tough with China and getting few concessions for all that the government had done for the Communists in the United Nations and in other ways.

70. German embassy in New Delhi, to AA, 20 October 1959, AA PA B 12 Bd.1.215, 154–56.

71. Letter, High Commission, New Delhi, to South East Asian Department, 29 October 1959, FO371/143866.

72. The Soviet Ambassador's discussions with Ne Win, Embassy in Burma, 18 October 1959, 105-00912(1) [105-D0427].

73. Von Randow to AA, 13 November 1959, AA PA B 12 Bd.1.207, 428–29.

74. Telegram, von Randow to AA, 24 January 1960, AA PA B 12 Bd.1.215, 158–62.

75. Ne Win and the King apparently became quite friendly, playing tennis together twice a day. Maung Maung, "Caretaker Government", p. 122.

76. Letter, R.H.S. Allen to Selwyn Lloyd, 17 March 1960, FO371/152558.

77. Letter, R.R. (indecipherable), Katmandu, to Selwyn Lloyd, 11 April 1960, FO371/152558.

78. Letter, Bangkok embassy to Chancery, 18 March 1969, FO371/152645.

79. Chit Myaing, "In His Own Words", *Burma Debate*, vol. IV, no. 3 (July/August 1997): 11–24. Chit Hlaing provides a different version. He states that the meeting took place at the War Office and Ne Win furiously declared, after ordering the attendees to stand up as he entered the room, "You are all stupid. You don't know what you should do or what you should not do. You must all resign." Chit Hlaing, "The Tatmadaw and My Political Career", unpublished paper, translated by Kyaw Yin Hlaing, p. 4. Chit Hlaing may have confused the post-election dinner and the dismissal of the officers later in the year.

80. See Ne Win entry in *Who's Who in Burma 1961* (Rangoon: People's Literature Committee and House, 1961) and Foreign Office Memo by C.W. Squire, 8 August 1960, FO371/152253.

81. Thompson, in Furnivall, *Governance of Modern Burma*, fn. 50, p. 153, citing *The Nation*, 4 August 1960.

82. Rangoon to Secretary of State, 9 March 1960, 790B.00/3-960, CDF, Box 2103, RG59.

83. Maung Maung, "Caretaker Government", p. 104. Much of my understanding of Ne Win and his religion stems from discussions with many ministers and/ or army officers, who knew him well, having lived and work closely with him over a number of years.

84. Papers in PREM11/4650.

85. Message, von Radow to AA, 13 July 1960, AA PA B 12 Bd.1.203, 102–4.

86. Notes from Restricted Session, SEATO Council Discussions, 22 December 1960, FO371/166621.

87. Aung Myoe, *Building the Tatmadaw: The Organisational Development of the Armed Forces in Myanmar, 1948–58*, Strategic and Defence Studies Centre, Working Paper no. 327 (Canberra: Australian National University, November 1998), fn. 54, p. 35. Maung Maung attributes some of the reasons for his dismissal to tales the Marxist member of the *Pyithu Hluttaw*, Widura Chit Maung, told to Ne Win. Maung Maung, "Caretaker Government", pp. 56–57. See also, Butwell, *U Nu of Burma*, pp. 232–33.

88. Callahan, *Making Enemies*, pp. 198–99. Nakanishi also suggests, but provides no source, that Maung Maung may have allowed the CIA to construct "espionage related facilities in the border area with China" which the Chinese had learned about. Nakanishi, *Strong Soldiers, Failed Revolution*, p. 89, fn. 57. Maung Maung, in his writings and the author's many conversations with him in the 1980s never made any reference to this, though he did

discuss the detention and interrogation facility established on Coco Gyun.

89. During the next fourteen years, he was also ambassador to Egypt, France and Spain. During the 1990s and 2000s, he was head of the National League for Democracy, for which he was never detained, as were other party leaders, such as former General Tin U and Daw Aung San Suu Kyi.

90. Main points of the discussion between Premier Chou, Vice Premier Luo Ruiqing, and General Ne Win, 20 and 30 March 1961, 105-0176-04 [105-Y0291].

91.   When in 1961, the Burmese Government used force to dislodge them [i.e. KMT troops], several thousand of these armed men drifted eastward into Thailand and Laos. No one knew exactly how many there were or what their movements were. On 14 March 1961, however, Lucien Coudoux, a journalist, saw approximately 1,200 of these irregulars at Ban Hoei Sai, on the Laos side of the Mekong, crossing the river into Thailand; they carried American rifles, machine guns, mortars and bazooka. A month later, an official of the Chinese Nationalist Consulate in Vientiane reported that Nationalist aircraft had airlifted 4,000 Kuomintang

to Laos. Arthur J. Dommen, *Confict in Laos: The Politics of Neutralization* (New York: Praeger, revised edition, 1971), p. 193.

92. Main points of the discussions between Premier Chou, Vice Premier Luo Ruiqing, and General Ne Win, 20 and 30 March 1961, 105-0176-04 [105-Y0291]. The uncooperative Thai attitude was confirmed by the British air attaché in Yangon following a trip to Chiang Mai in December 1961. Letter, Air Attaché, Rangoon, Group Captain P.W. Cook, to Air Ministry, 29 December 1961, FO371/166621.

93. Main points of the discussions between Premier Chou, Vice Premier Luo Ruiqing, and General Ne Win, 20 and 30 March 1961, 105-0176-04 [105-Y0291].

94. For details, see Butwell, "A Second Chance", in *U Nu of Burma*, pp. 224–41; Martin Smith, *Burma: Insurgency and the Politics of Ethnicity*, 2nd ed. (London: Zed Books, 1999), pp. 186–95; Kyaw Win, Mya Han, and Thein Hlaing, *Myanmar Politics 1958–1962*, Volume III, translated by Hla Shein (Yangon: Win Aung, April 2011), Chapters X through XII, pp. 1–286.

95. Aleksandr Kaznacheev, *Inside a Soviet Embassy: Experiences of a Russian Diplomat in Burma*, edited by Simon Wolin (London: Robert Hale, 1962). Interviews with Arthur W. Hummel, Jr., Public Affairs Officer, USIS, Rangoon (1957–61), pp. 22–23; and Cliff Forster, Information Officer, USIS, Rangoon (1958–60), p. 30.

96. Messages, von Randow to AA, 17 and 23 March 1961, AA PA B 12 Bd.1.203, 105, 107–8. Probably an internal AA report, 20 April 1961, AA PA Bd. 1.203, 123–26.

97. Northe reports to GER legation, Yangon, 2 May 1961, AA PA B 12 BA.1.203, 128; Germany Ministry of Defence, Bonn, Col. Buksch to Military Attaché, London, 3 May 1961, AA PA B 12 Bd.1.203, 96; AA internal Vocke, AA Pa NB 12 Bd.1.2100, 442.

98. *The Times*, 30 May 1961.

99. PREM 11/4650

100. Note from the Foreign Secretary to the Prime Minister, 26 May 1961, PREM 11/4650.

101. Message, von Randow to AA, 5 April 1961, AA PA B 12 Bd.1.203, 111–14.

102. Letter, Richard Allen to Earl of Home, 27 December 1961, FO371/164305.

103. Letter, Richard Allen to F.A. Warren, 19 December 1961, FO371/1664404.

104. Letter, A.R.K. MacKenzie to F.A. Warren, 28 February 1961, FO371/166404.

105. Letter, Air Attaché, Rangoon, Group Captain P.W. Cook, to Air Ministry, 29 December 1961, FO371/166621.

106. Hoffmann to AA, AA PA B 12 Bd.1198, 385–86.

107. Mya Han and Thein Hlaing, *Myanmar Politics 1958–1962*, Volume IV, translated by Sai Aung Tun (Yangon: U Win Aung, April 2011), Chapter XIV, "The Federal Principle", Chapter XV, "The Taunggyi All-States Conference" and Chapter XVI, "The Union Government and the Federal Principle", pp. 1–163.

108. Nakanishi, *Strong Soldiers, Failed Revolution*, p. 95, fn. 86. Nakanishi dismisses Ne Win's comments given at the first commanders conference after the coup, claiming that there was no discussion of secession at the federal seminar. However, what was overheard in the tea breaks of the meetings could be something else. Moreover, the discontent of the leading figures in the Shan States, including former Sawbwa, was well known. The turmoil in neighbouring Laos and the involvement of the United States in both Laos and Thailand at that time could easily lead a cautious assessor of what was being planned to draw the conclusion that pre-emptive measures were necessary.

8

COUP D'ETAT AND REVOLUTION
(March 1962 to February 1964)

> When you come into the presence of a leader of men, you know you have come into the presence of fire — that it is best not incautiously to touch that man — that there is something that makes it dangerous to cross him.
>
> *Woodrow Wilson*

General Ne Win's assumption of power on 2 March 1962, while not unexpected, was nonetheless a surprise to many. It was executed in secrecy, and apparently even the deputy commander of the armed forces, Brigadier General Aung Gyi, was not informed until the next morning, though he must have been expecting it as early as November 1961, when he raised the prospect with colleagues. Others in the army, including Brigadier General Tin Pe, had been urging Ne Win to halt what they saw as a drift towards the dissolution of the Union of Burma. U Nu's cooperation with the Shan and Kayah traditional leaders in the Federal Seminar, and growing discontent in other minority areas caused by Nu's constitutional amendment making Buddhism the state religion, were creating political forces which many in the army felt the increasingly fractious Union Party government could not resist.[1] Kachin Christians, led by former students fired by zeal for "Kachin national culture", resented the installation of Buddhism as the state religion and the Shan Sawbwa, in the name of Shan "national determination", were beginning to organize armed opposition to the government. The possibility of the Union Party splitting, as the AFPFL had done in 1958, became ever more likely, especially after Nu, the only person holding the party together, announced he would not run for office again after the next elections due two years hence (Silverstein 1977, p. 66). Planning for the corp commenced on 24 February, and twenty-eight officers were instructed as to what to do when the order for the coup was given. However, the date remained unknown until Ne Win gave the order (Mya Han and Thein Hlaing 2001, pp. 164–65).

Nu who was held incommunicado at Mingaladon from the middle of the night, initially believed that his detention was engineered by junior officers and soon Ne Win would come to his rescue (Nu 1975, pp. 141–44). He, like many others, had false expectations, believing the past would be a guide to the future. Those who learned of the overnight coup, particularly amongst the Western diplomatic community, were not particularly concerned about its consequences. Ne Win, as seen by the United States ambassador, could be trusted once more to clean up the mess and restore order (Everton 1964, p. 6), a view shared by his West German counterpart.[2] Five days after the coup, the Chinese government recognized the Ne Win government, the fourth state to do so. Two days later, the Soviet Union did the same (Longmire 1989, p. 75). Part of the reason for the lack of concern by foreign governments about the coup was the reassurance that Myanmar's foreign policy, emphasizing non-aligned and neutrality, would not change.[3]

Other than the family of Sao Shwe Thaik whose teenage son was killed while challenging troops which came in the night to detain his father,[4] and the thirty-five or forty other politicians incarcerated, including five cabinet ministers, the President, the Chief Justice, and leading Shan and Kayah figures attending the Federal Seminar, life for the remainder of the country continued largely unconcerned about the change of regime. Most of those arrested were first detained at the Myanmar Athan building where the Federal Seminar had been held the day before and then taken at dawn to the Yan Gyi Aung Garrison Cinema Hall at Mingaladon. There they were served nam roti and tea. President Win Maung, Prime Minister Nu, Chief Justice Myint Thein, and Ministers Thakin Tin, Sao Hkun Hkio, U Rashid and Sao Wunna were isolated from the rest (Mya Han and Thein Hlaing 2001, p. 169).

There were no public protests against the coup and the media remained non-committal on the end of Nu's cabinet. Even a statement issued by the leftist Rangoon University Students Union (RUSU) denouncing the army's anti-democratic methods, was repudiated by the majority of the students (Silverstein and Wohl 1964, p. 62).

The next few days and weeks were unusually busy for Ne Win. The lack of pre-planning and absence of thought about future policy direction created a significant policy vacuum which Ne Win was quick to fill. He had put forth ideas to his colleagues on the political side from time to time in the past, but these had been rejected. On land reform and agricultural policy, his ideas to compete with the Communists with a policy that would appeal to peasant interests had been rejected by U Nu's government during the civil war. His ideas on creating a socialist economy, including the "ration book" system, which were discussed with Maung Maung, Aung Gyi and Julian Licht in 1958, had been rebuffed then, and he subsequently let them get on with managing the economy while he saw to other government business. Now, however, he could put his ideas into effect, but he needed an explanation of those ideas rooted in an ideology which would appeal to the overwhelmingly Buddhist population. His audience were familiar with Buddhist concepts and had listened to Marxist socialist rhetoric from their politicians for years. Like U Ba Swe and U Nu before him, he needed to show how his version of socialism was ideationally compatible with the philosophical outlook of the majority of the population. He had a lot of work to do.

Unlike the Caretaker Government, for which Ne Win and his colleagues in the General Staff office had several weeks to plan, now decisions had to be made on the spot, without significant consideration or consultation. Like the army in the midst of the civil war, policy was made "on the go", as it were, but now only one man determined the direction of events, Ne Win. Number One, at the age of fifty-two, had emerged and ideas which he had harboured for more than a decade now came to be implemented under the name of socialism, a Burmese, self-reliant, form of socialism. Though Ne Win set out to change Myanmar through his own version of *towhlanyei* (revolution),[5] as an individual, he did not change. Four-and-a-half months after the coup, on 13 July, he flew off to Vienna, Austria to seek medical treatment for himself and his wife and then commenced a three-month holiday in Europe and Great Britain.

Ne Win arrived unusually early at the War Office on the morning of 2 March at 6:30 a.m. He was met by Colonel Than Sein and Colonel Kyaw Soe, the two officers ordered to execute the removal of the old regime. When it was explained that the teenage son of Sao Shwe Thaik had been shot dead after the former President's security guards began firing on the army unit which had come to arrest his father, Ne Win expressed regret. Later, he sent a message to Sao Shwe Thaik who was in detention at Mingaladon, and the Mahadevi of Yawngwe, then in London, via Colonel Saw Myint. It stated,

> I understand your son Saw Myee Myee lost his life at dawn on March 2 when Army personnel arrived at your residence to perform their duties as directed by the Revolutionary Council. For this unexpected tragedy, members of the Council as well as myself are deeply sorry.[6]

He also visited seven persons briefly, including U Zahre Lian and Saw Mahn Hpa, who had been detained by mistake. He apologized to them and assured them of their freedom.[7]

However, he first ordered that an announcement of the coup be written, and at the suggestion of Brigadier Aung Gyi, former head of the Directorate of Education and Psychological Warfare, Colonel Ba Than, who was sleeping nearby in an army guesthouse, was requested to prepare a statement. Ne Win found Ba Than's draft too lengthy and ordered another, prepared by Colonel Saw Myint, after Ne Win dictated the few points to be included. This was very terse and provided no hint of what was to come. The thrust of the message was the army was forced to retake control because of the continuing disintegration of the country. Nothing was said about socialism, self-reliance, or other revolutionary intentions, perhaps still at the back of Ne Win's mind. Ne Win recorded the text and it was broadcast to the nation by Myanmar Athan (Myanmar radio) at 8:25 a.m. (Chit Hlaing n.d., p. 9).

> ... In order to put a stop to the extremely grave situation that has befallen the Union, the Armed Forces had taken over the government.
>
>   The people of the country should not feel disturbed but should continue to carry on with their work normally and peacefully.
>
>   The government employees should also continue to do their duties as before. Education officers and students especially should not allow the present development to interfere with their work, but should go ahead with the examinations which are being held.
>
>   We promise to do our best for the health and prosperity of the people (quoted in Mya Han and Thein Hlaing 2001, p. 170).

In the meantime, senior military officers had begun to join Ne Win and Aung Gyi in the War Room of the Defence Ministry. Indicating that this government was going to be unlike the previous Caretaker Regime, Ne Win immediately formed both the Revolutionary Council with sixteen senior military officers and the Revolutionary Government Cabinet with

TABLE 8.1

Initial Members of the Revolutionary Council

General Ne Win, Chairman

Brigadier General Aung Gyi

Commodore Than Pe

Brigadier General T. Clift

Brigadier General Tin Pe

Brigadier General San Yu

Brigadier General Sein Win

Colonel Thaung Kyi

Colonel Kyi Maung

Colonel Maung Shwe

Colonel Than Sein

Colonel Kyaw Soe

Colonel Saw Myint

Colonel Chit Myaing

Colonel Khin Nyo

Colonel Hla Han

Colonel Tan Yu Sang

U Thi Han and seven senior military officers from the Revolutionary Council. On average, the members of the Revolutionary Council were about a decade younger than Ne Win. Ne Win chaired both groups. Members posted outside Yangon learned of their appointments via radio broadcasts of the news. The next day the major organs of state established by the 1947 Constitution were abolished, including the two houses of the *Hluttaw* and the putative state councils and governments. New state governments were then formed with stalwart Shan nationalist, but anti-Sawbwa egalitarian U Tun Aye (Nam Kham), made chairman of the Shan State. As Ne Win appointed Tun Aye, he told him,

> You've never had a chance to show what you can do. I am now giving you the opportunity to serve your country by making you Chairman of the Revolutionary Council of the Shan State. Go and do your best. If you fail, just hang yourself.[8]

Two days later, Ne Win assumed all executive, legislative and judicial authority as Chairman of the Revolutionary Council. While the institutions of the 1947 Constitution were dismantled, so were the policies and activities of foreign institutions. No explanation was provided, however.

In April, the British Council was ordered to stop offering scholarships directly to students. In future, all scholarships would have to be channelled though the government. Similarly, English language lessons at the British Council were halted as were the activities of the Ford and Asia Foundations and the United States government's Fulbright scholarship programme. The well-paid and cosseted Westerners that Ne Win had ousted in 1958 were now joined by others whom Ne Win saw as undermining Burma's bid for self-reliance. When the American embassy tried to raise the question of the proposed American-built highway between Yangon and Myitkyina, an official at the Foreign Ministry demurred, not wishing to bring the subject up with Ne Win as it would be linked to the closure of the foundations and Fulbright operations.[9] In mid-May, the government took direct control of the country's universities and abolished the Buddhist Sasana Council that Nu had established to propagate the now former state religion.

At 10 a.m. on 4 March, Ne Win met with leaders of the country's legal political parties not under arrest. Members of the AFPFL, the Ba Swe–Kyaw Nyein faction having retained the name, Nu's Union Party, and the leftist National United Front (NUF), met with Ne Win at the army's Dagon Guest House. Outlining the weaknesses of the 1947 Constitution, he called for suggestions from the party leaders as well as their cooperation in establishing a new socialist regime in Myanmar. By then, the Psychological Warfare Unit had been put on notice that it would be required to undertake some work on behalf of the Revolutionary Council. The next evening, Brigadier Aung Gyi briefed the three key members of the unit, and indicated that General Ne Win would meet with them on the 6th.

The key members of the Psychological Warfare Unit, Colonel Saw Myint, U Saw Oo, and U Chit Hlaing,[10] met with Ne Win in his office as scheduled. As recalled by Chit Hlaing, Ne Win explained that the purpose of the Revolutionary Government was to "rebuild the country properly". Ne Win went on to say that they would "have to modify the anti-Communist lectures and literature we had produced during the period of psychological warfare" for they were "planning to establish a leftist political system". Even if they were called Communists, they would persist and implement a plan for the betterment of the country.[11] The reference to earlier psychological warfare work was to the programmes that had been carried out under former Brigadier Maung Maung during and after the Caretaker Government period. This had included a campaign declaring that the Buddhist Dhamma (or Law) was in danger from anti-religious Communists and the formation of an anti-leftist National Solidarity Organisation mass mobilization movement under army sponsorship.

Ne Win went on to explain what he wanted from his three subordinates, as subsequently remembered by Chit Hlaing:

> We have formed the Revolutionary Council. We now need to present our policies to the country. I will tell you the main points I want included in the policies. The most important thing is the economy. The state will have to nationalise all big businesses. We will allow private enterprises in some sectors. We will try to run cooperatives more properly. In this way, we will try to establish the Socialist system step by step. With regard to political matters, we will have to consult with existing political parties. If we can find a way to work together, we will work with all of them. We will institute a one-party system. This is the only option left to us. We will not get very far if we are stuck with the parliamentary system where several political parties compete for power. Other people might call our system the Eastern democracy or proletarian dictatorship. We will have to try it in the interests of the peasants, workers and the general public. Since the majority of the population in our country are peasants, we will have to give them priority. Unlike Communists, we cannot simply give priority to the workers. Well, we will work with not just peasants and workers but anybody who is willing to work for the interests of the country.[12]

As Ne Win and the three men were discussing what he had said, and what to do with the problem of corruption or how, if their plans failed, they would have to revise their programmes in future, a message of congratulations to Ne Win on conducting the coup arrived from General Phoumi Nosavan, the right-wing, United States Central Intelligence Agency (CIA)-backed, drug-dealing, semi-warlord figure of neighbouring Laos, then under the control of various warring Communist and anti-Communist military and royalist factions. Ne Win, on reading the message, laughed loudly and said, "this guy Phoumi is congratulating me. This is worse than being hit in the face with a bag of shit. We are different from him."[13] Brigadier General Aung Gyi then entered, and after telling Ne Win that he was to hold the first of several press conferences, asked how far he should describe what was planned. Ne Win told him not to be precise as they were still discussing the details. He should just say that they were going to pursue "practical socialism" (Chit Hlaing n.d., p. 12).

Chit Hlaing was asked to prepare the first draft of the Revolutionary Council policy paper as Colonel Saw Myint and U Saw Oo were busy with other duties.[14] Saw Myint was secretary of the Revolutionary Council and Minister for Information and Saw Oo was busy at the Myanmar news agency. On 21 March, Chit Hlaing prepared a draft which Ne Win discussed with him, Saw Oo and Saw Myint on 8 April, prior to submitting it to the entire Revolutionary Council. Noting the attention to the poor working class as the key feature of the socialist programme, Chit Hlaing recalled that Ne Win observed that the socialism they were to establish should be to the benefit of all people.

> He said that although workers and peasants were the majority in number, the Revolutionary Council would work with anyone of any social class so long as he believed in the system the Revolutionary Council was planning to establish. The General also noted that what Brigadier Aung Gyi said about the business class at the press conference before was not complete. He said, "We will create a place for them within two years. Unlike Communists, we don't regard them as enemies. If they support us, we will work with them. They will be allowed to engage in the distribution of goods together with us. If we explain this to the traders in advance, they will have a clear understanding of their future."

Ne Win went on to explain that, unlike Communists such as Thakin Soe, the Revolutionary Council had no intention of liquidating the assets of the prosperous.

> We will have to keep the rich people where they are. However, rich people will have to allow the lives of poor people to improve. In that process, the bourgeoisie might become less wealthy than they were, but they won't become poor people.

However, he opposed selfish and self-righteous behaviour on the part of the rich and also thought that Buddhist monks and other religious figures should constrain their activities and avoid politics. After criticizing parliamentary democracy as a political system which benefitted the rich, he urged them to avoid using the word "imperialism" too frequently in the policy paper. What they needed to do was to strike a balance between capitalism and Eastern European style socialism. The system he wanted to establish was one in which "each and everyone in the country can fill their stomachs" (Chit Hlaing n.d., pp. 13–14).

After further redrafting, Ne Win approved the draft paper at a meeting at the president's residence and ordered it printed and distributed for discussion at a two-day meeting of the Revolutionary Council commencing on 24 April. In the meantime, however, Brigadier Aung Gyi, perhaps believing Ne Win no longer wanted him in the Revolutionary Council after his comments at the press conference were strongly contradicted by Ne Win, went into internal exile, flying to Machanbaw in the far north of the Kachin State. In outlining the kind of socialist regime the Revolutionary Council had in mind, Aung Gyi proposed a continuing role for the private sector as a complement to the public sector. Ne Win sent Colonel Saw Myint and U Chit Hlaing to ask Aung Gyi to return to Yangon, and together with the regional commander, Colonel Lun Tin, they convinced him to do so. Aung Gyi was obviously pleased to be asked to come back as part of the Revolutionary Council by Ne Win, his old colleague in arms.

The two-day Revolutionary Council meeting was taken up with a reading, paragraph by paragraph, and discussions of the document which became "The Burmese Way to Socialism". Though the discussions were said to have been frank, there was no significant controversy until they came to the section on the role of private businesses in the economy. Here, not unexpectedly, Brigadiers Tin Pe and Aung Gyi differed. Aung Gyi argued for a role for the private sector, while Tin Pe urged speedy and full nationalization of the economy to achieve socialism. The majority seemed to agree with Aung Gyi but Tin Pe held his ground. Ne Win appeared to agree with both of them, seeking a speedy way to socialism but acknowledging a role for indigenous business. Aung Gyi called for a vote on the matter to end the debate. The meeting went silent since votes were unknown in army gatherings. Ne Win then interjected, "Come on men, we shouldn't be arguing over this matter. We will have to make the policy in accordance with the prevailing conditions." Turning to Tin Pe, he said in English, "hey, Ko Tin Pe, why can't you agree on this point?" Tin Pe then conceded and the meeting moved on (Chit Hlaing n.d., p. 16).

The agreed text, duly printed and marked "Top Secret" of "The Burmese Way to Socialism" was presented next to a Commanding Officers Conference held on 29 and 30 April at which Ne Win presided. After Ne Win explained the policy of the Revolutionary Council, the document was read out. On the second day of the conference, there was much discussion about the danger of left-wing politicians, many of whom had been involved in the Communist insurgencies and might be able to manipulate the new socialist programme to their advantage. Ne Win attempted to reassure them that this would not happen. At the conference, the catchphrase "*ayinshin ayinshinn*" (Clean Out the Capitalists) was said to have been coined by Colonel Tin U.[15] With the approval of the Commanders' Conference, Saw Myint read "The Burmese Way to Socialism" over Myanmar Athan and Ne Win presented copies of the document to the leaders of the legal political parties on 7 May. He urged them to read and study the document prior to his next meeting with them.[16]

Ne Win also instructed Saw Myint, Saw Oo and Chit Hlaing to draft a constitution for a political party and the socialist principles that the party should adopt, in consultation with Colonels Than Sein, Kyaw Soe, Hla Han, and Brigadier Tin Pe. The absence of Brigadier Aung Gyi from the list would not have been lost on him and others. On 17 May, Ne Win met for a third and final time with the leaders of the extant political parties. Unsurprisingly, they were unwilling to endorse the "Burmese Way to Socialism" as presented to them. Whether the party leaders felt that Ne Win would eventually return power to them, as he had done in 1960, is much speculated upon. The AFPFL may have felt that Ne Win would share power with them, given the army's affinity with the party in earlier years. The NUF felt the programme was insufficiently Marxist, though it had some positive aspects. In any event, they rejected Ne Win's invitation to follow him and from that meeting onward, the die was cast. After six weeks of frantic party building, the formation of the Burmese Socialist Programme Party as a cadre party was announced on 4 July (Chit Hlaing n.d., pp. 17–18). On the same day, General Ne Win's wife, Daw Khin May Than, flew to Vienna for medical treatment.

Two days later, two of the Party's top committees, the Party Central Organising Committee and the Party Discipline Committee, were formed, both composed of officers from the Revolutionary Council. Perhaps as a result of the differences in opinion within the Council, the third top committee of the Party, the Socialist Economy Planning Committee, was not formed yet.[17] In the announcement of the formation of the party by the Revolutionary Council, it was noted that "quality above quantity" was desired and therefore it would be organized initially as a cadre party. The existing political parties were encouraged to offer "sincere and constructive criticisms, but the Revolutionary Council urged them to refrain from indulging in destructive measures".[18]

The first foreign visitors received after the coup were Singapore's Prime Minister Lee Kuan Yew and his wife. The Ne Wins hosted them for lunch at their home, which Lee described as a medium-sized bungalow in the suburbs disconcertingly surrounded by guns and tanks. Over lunch, Ne Win was inattentive to Lee's explanation of Indonesian President Sukarno's opposition to the forthcoming formation of Malaysia, initially including Singapore. His mind was clearly elsewhere (Lee 2000, p. 359).

In the intervening six weeks, on 23 May, Ne Win received his first foreign head of government, Prince Souvanna Phouma, leader of the neutralist camp in the ongoing Laotian political crisis, and recently re-appointed Prime Minister. Little came from the meeting, though the newly appointed Myanmar Foreign Minister, U Thi Han, was about to fly to Geneva to attend the thirteen-nation conference which led to the so-called "neutralization" of Laos, in an attempt by the British and French to avoid expanding the Laotian civil war into an international conflict further drawing in the United States, Communist China and North Vietnam. The internationalization of the war in Laos was an important backdrop to Ne Win's 2 March coup. The fear of most of the participating governments in the conference was that the United States would involve itself more deeply in the fighting, in support of the deeply factionalized Royal Lao Government against the Communist Pathet Lao, in what up until then had been an American shadow war, and that this would inevitably draw not only North Vietnam but also China into war with the United States. According to an official in the Kennedy administration, the Central Intelligence Agency was dominating American policy in Laos. As he wrote, "The CIA's basic assumption seemed to be that Laos was sooner or later to become a major battleground in the military sense between the East and the West, and the programs they conceived and pushed through in Washington were based on this assumption" (Hilsman 1964, 1967, p. 115). As the Sino–Soviet split was not yet then fully apparent, such a conflict would have drawn the two ideological blocs in the Cold War, the East and the West, into the kind of mortal combat which had occurred the previous decade on the Korean peninsula. If such an expanded war were to occur, there is no way that Myanmar could not have been involved, with horrific consequences for the Myanmar people.[19]

Earlier, on 10 May, Ne Win had received the letters of accreditation of the newly appointed Philippine, Canadian and West German ambassadors.

Herr Bottler, the West German Ambassador, raised the question of divided Germany in the Cold War when they met and Ne Win responded by discussing divided Vietnam and Korea. He said the current situation was unjust and the only peaceful solution could come through an international commission. Turning to domestic matters, Ne Win thanked the Ambassador for suggesting that West Germany would be willing to assist in Myanmar's economic development and emphasized that he wished to rule through political institutions but was forced by necessity to rely on the army.[20] According to the Ambassador, Ne Win, who kept protocol to a minimum, looked stressed. Receiving the Ambassador's credentials while sitting down, he only became animated when the question of divided countries in the Cold War was raised.[21] By June, the pattern of relations between the government and the diplomatic community which was to persist for the next twenty-six years and more, was established. Top officials rarely attended public functions or accepted invitations to dinners or receptions. Relations became largely limited to interactions with officials in the Ministry of Foreign Affairs whose normal response was to refer the matter to higher authorities.[22]

The academic year commenced in early June with new and much stricter rules being imposed on the student body in an attempt to halt the persistent demonstrations by a small but vocal, largely Communist-inspired, group of students. They proceeded to demonstrate against the new rules on 10 June.[23] Demonstrations continued into July, when the students took possession of the Rangoon University Students Union building. This became the centre of opposition to the new regime. Eventually, on 7 July, the army was called in to retake the campus. Finally the students "provoked the army to shoot into the crowd, killing at least fifteen people, destroying the Rangoon University Student Union building, and closing the university for a temporary period" (Silverstein and Wohl 1964, p. 50). Ne Win, in a radio broadcast after the event, accused the students of being manipulated by Communist forces and justified the action of the army on the 7 and 8 July, when the Union building was blown up, in terms of reoccupying territory being denied to legally constituted authorities. It was a strong speech and one phrase, that the army would fight "sword with sword and spear with spear", became part of student and leftist lore.[24]

In the army's view of the affair, the demonstrations leading up to the destruction of the union building was a Communist probe of the new military government (Min Maung Maung 1995, p. 170). Who gave the order to blow the building then became a point of dispute within the

Revolutionary Council. Ne Win believed Aung Gyi was responsible, but he denied that he was to blame, putting the onus instead on then Lieutenant Colonel Sein Lwin.[25] Yangon and Mandalay universities remained closed until 27 August, with students returning to their hostels from the 22nd. Under the new regime which was overseen by Education Minster Colonel Hla Han, university staff were enjoined to create discipline on the campus and ensure students eschewed partisan politics. Education was to facilitate the building of socialism in future and priority would be given to scientific, technical and vocational subjects.[26] Relations between the army and leftist students remained tense for a number of months thereafter. On one occasion, two officers drove their Volkswagen on to the campus, but had to flee an attacking mob of students who then burned the vehicle. Ne Win's relations with the university also remained strained for many years following his assault on two physics lecturers a few years later who allegedly spat on his wife at a dinner he hosted for the teachers. He recalled the incident twenty years later (Tin Aung n.p., circa 2000, p. 29).

Despite the unfortunate events that marked the first months of the Revolutionary government, including the death of Sao Shwe Thaik's son, the students' demonstrations at the university, and the unwillingness of political party leaders to accept Ne Win's socialist vision, there were still events to cheer Ne Win and assure him that what he was undertaking was the right way to unify and stabilize Myanmar's fractious politics. The idea of "Leftist Unity" which had once inspired U Nu, and had been encouraged by Ne Win at the height of the civil war in 1948–49, would have been on his mind when he met with U Htein Lin and his wife, Daw Saw Mya, on 7 July. Htein Lin and Saw Mya had been left-wing activists in the anti-Japanese resistance and after independence had joined with the pro-Communist White Flag People's Volunteer Organisation (PVO).[27] Htein Lin and Saw Mya, then members of Thakin Soe's Red Flag Communist Party, had left the party after Ne Win seized power and had decided to support his government. Some of his old comrades from the left, at least, understood and supported his cause (Chit Hlaing n.d., p. 20).

After Htein Lin and Saw Mya left, Ne Win discussed with Chit Hlaing his ideas about a philosophy or guiding principles of the new Burma Socialist Programme Party. He indicated that he thought perhaps Chit Hlaing could draft such a document. Chit Hlaing said the philosophical part had been worked out in a pamphlet he had used in his teachings during the Caretaker Government period, and that he could combine that with the socialist goals of the Revolutionary Council and update it quickly. Ne Win recalled the pamphlet and urged Chit Hlaing to take his time and work out a new document based on the original. Whatever he included in the document, Ne Win urged him not to "undermine national, religious and cultural values, and that it should be sophisticated and pragmatic at the same time" (Chit Hlaing n.d., p. 21).

On 11 July, Ne Win appointed Dr Maung Maung as the Chief Justice of the Union. Maung Maung who graduated from the Japanese-era military academy before returning to civilian studies recently completed a fellowship at Yale University. Ne Win knew Maung Maung well and they became close confidants. Ne Win respected Maung Maung's education and his quiet, contemplative nature. He insisted that he, and the Attorney General, U Ba Sein, a Christian who knew Maung Maung well, were given free reign in the application of the law, and that Ne Win never instructed him in reaching any decision (Maung Maung 1999, pp. 56–57). Nevertheless, he was aware of the direction of policy that the Revolutionary Council was pursuing and understood the outlook of his fellow party colleagues. His party membership number was sixty with Ne Win being number one.

Ne Win's departure for Europe five days after the destruction of the Students Union Building was apparently prompted by his wife's departure the previous week. Leaving Aung Gyi nominally in charge of the Revolutionary Council, no public announcement of his journey or temporary successor was made.[28] The purpose of their European trips, coming so soon after such dramatic developments, led to much speculation among the diplomatic community in Yangon. The British initially believed Daw Khin May Than was departing in order to study how the healthcare systems of Austria and the United Kingdom functioned, presumably in preparation for developing a new healthcare system in socialist Burma. Where she was staying in Vienna remained a secret, as there was no record of her stay at any of the leading hotels.[29] When Ne Win left on 13 July, the British embassy speculated that he was on the verge of a nervous breakdown and would be staying in Vienna for at least six weeks. However, there was further speculation that it was perhaps due to Daw Khin May Than who required treatment for an undisclosed nervous disorder.[30] The West Germans believed that the Vienna trip was for the treatment of Ne Win's recurring sinus troubles.[31] What is known is that Ne Win was treated for a severe case of tennis elbow by Dr Hans Hoff, the Director of the Vienna University Neuro-Psychiatric Hospital.[32] Ne Win had had an injury to his neck during the war and the old injury worsened as a result of playing tennis.[33] Earlier, Ne Win had tried Chinese medicine including acupuncture for his elbow, as advised by Chou En-lai.[34] The speculation by the West German embassy in Vienna came nearest to the apparent purpose of the visit. He was seeking treatment for "an acute bone disease", i.e., his tennis elbow.[35]

In addition to seeking medical attention in Vienna, and eventually giving up tennis to devote himself to golf on Dr Hoff's suggestion, Ne Win also attended to international affairs. On 17 July, W. Averill Harriman, the United States Assistant Secretary of State for Far Eastern Affairs, flew to Vienna to meet with Ne Win in order to explain the approach of the Kennedy administration towards neutralism.[36] Hoping to differentiate the Kennedy line from that taken by the Secretary of State John Foster Dulles during the Eisenhower government, he explained that neutralism was no longer perceived as a strategic error, or immoral, by the new President who had assumed office that year. Ne Win responded by saying that his not going to Washington, D.C. at that time should not be interpreted as a snub directed at the American administration, and that his first trip abroad since taking over the reins of power was to Vienna for treatment of his wife's mental condition.[37] Harriman then returned to the Geneva Conference which formally neutralized Laos, but that did not halt the American shadow war. The United States soon commenced a secret war there using ethnic Hmong Laotians as well as Shan, Lahu and Wa guerrillas from Burma along with KMT troops from Burma and Thailand.

Following their medical treatment in Vienna, Ne Win and Daw Khin May Than travelled informally and unofficially for six days in Germany from the end of August to the beginning of September. Driving from Vienna, they set out to Passau. Somewhere on their journey they were met by Dr Meyer of the Fritz Werner Company and had dinner with the former German ambassador to Myanmar, Mr Randow, on 2 September. The dinner was apparently a happy, relaxed affair, and Ne Win was reported to be very pleased with the treatment for his tennis elbow.[38]

In England, Ne Win and his wife had a fairly leisurely programme of activities.[39] On 18 September he met the Foreign Secretary, Alec Douglas-Hume, at the Myanmar embassy. Three days later, after being received by Her Majesty, Queen Elizabeth II, Ne Win and Prime Minister Harold MacMillan lunched together at Admiralty House. Ne Win complained of being tired and having lost the use of the muscles in his right hand, probably as a result of his problematic tennis elbow. He was therefore returning to Vienna for further treatment, but was unconcerned about events back in Myanmar.

Covering a range of world concerns at that time, Ne Win revealed that he did not trust Prince Sihanouk and never met persons like him alone. He put down the success of the Caretaker Government in reaching a border agreement with China to the conflict between China and India over their mutual border. As for the Communist problem in Myanmar, Ne Win was not particularly concerned, for having four Communist parties and both Chinese and Soviet embassies in Yangon meant that the Communists largely fought amongst themselves.[40] Subsequent to the lunch, Ne Win wrote to Macmillan, noting that he and Daw Khin May Than had visited London in each of the past three years, and inviting the British Prime Minister to Yangon. Several weeks later, MacMillan wrote back to decline the invitation.[41] How the Ne Wins passed their time in Great Britain and Europe was unknown, but presumably as in the past, he attended the races and played golf. He apparently met very few people.

On 16 October, Ne Win and Daw Khin May Than returned to Yangon, looking healthy and happy. The press reported nothing of his time in Austria and Germany, but pictures of his meetings with the Queen and the British Prime Minister were published. On arrival, Ne Win said nothing to the waiting journalists and went straight to his office. While he had been away, Tin Pe and Aung Gyi, the architects of divergent economic strategies, had both been ill and were hospitalized. However, both remained in the public eye, though Tin Pe's health required him to spend some time at Walter Reed Army Hospital in Washington, D.C.[42]

Soon after his return, Ne Win began making plans for further trips abroad, even as he was receiving foreign guests. The President of Rumania, Chivu Stoica, visited from 20 to 22 October. Rumania was one of the countries, together with Israel and the Soviet Union, which was interested in becoming involved in Burma's oil industry at that time. On 30 November, a delegation from the United States Senate Foreign Relations Committee visited Yangon. Ne Win met with Senators Mansfield, Boggs, Pell and Smith for more than an hour of "friendly, animated and gracious" conversation. In the Senators' subsequent report on their Southeast Asian tour, they noted the sensitivity of the Burmese to foreign influence and commented that it was probably a good thing that the United States had no economic assistance programme in Myanmar. They recommended the removal of the single American aid official as he was "superfluous" and misleading, implying that the United States sought an aid-driven relationship.[43] Afterwards, Foreign Minister U Thi Han attended a Thanksgiving Day dinner at the American embassy after hosting a reception for the Senators.[44] Five days later, the

Chief-of-Staff of the Israeli Army and the Director General of the Israeli Ministry of Defence also arrived for an eight-day visit.[45]

No sooner had the Rumanian President departed than Ne Win commenced one of his many tours of the country to make field inspections of government development projects and military camps. Accompanied by the commander of the North West Command, Brigadier San Yu, Director of Military Intelligence, Lieutenant Colonel Lwin, the Secretary of the Revolutionary Council, Lieutenant Colonel Ko Ko, and Lieutenant Colonel Gwan Shein, he arrived at Myitkyina on 24 October. After discussing Kachin state affairs for a day, he next went to Katha where he met with the members of the local Security and Administration Committee (SAC), the army-dominated bodies but including civilian officials and the police, established at all levels below the Revolutionary Council as the key coordinating body for government affairs. From there he went to Shwebo and then Mandalay, addressing local military units as well as government officials and encouraging them to work together to develop the economy and raise local living standards. On 28 October, Ne Win cut short his trip to return to Yangon to deal with correspondence regarding the growing danger of war between China and India, having been written to by Indian Prime Minister Pandit Nehru, Chinese Prime Minister Chou En-lai, and Egyptian President Gamal Abdul Nasser. Two days later, he resumed touring, visiting Taunggyi in the Shan State and Loikaw in Kayah.[46]

Former President and Speaker of the Chamber of Nationalities Sao Shwe Thaik, who had been detained along with U Nu and others at Insein Prison since 2 March, passed away on 21 November 1962 at age 68. The five-times-married Sawbwa of Yawnghwe for fifty years, he was given a formal funeral after his body was brought back to Yawnghwe, and despite Ne Win's aversion to Myanmar royalty, "with the honour and pageantry of a royal occasion", with the cooperation of the army and local government authorities (Aye 2009, p. 102; Elliott 1999, pp. 318–21; Sanda 2008, pp. 272–73).

From 5 to 11 December, Ne Win and a delegation of ten others, including U Thi Han and the Myanmar ambassadors to India and China, Daw Khin Kyi[47] and U Kyaw Win, were in Sri Lanka to participate in the first and only international conference of his career.[48] Held in Colombo from 10 to 12 December and hosted by the Sri Lanka government, the purpose of the six-nation conference of neutral Afro-Asian states[49] was to put an end to the Chinese–Indian border dispute which had led to a brief war between the two Asian giants in October and November 1962. Ne

Win, who spoke at the initial session about the need to preserve Burma's status as a friendly third party to both of the disputants, apparently became disenchanted with the proceedings as some of the delegates, which included Prince Sihanouk, appeared to be partisan in their approach. He did not speak again, leaving the conference before it concluded, and delegating Foreign Minister Thi Han to make the final statement for Myanmar.[50]

From Sri Lanka, Ne Win went to Bangkok, a city he had visited several times in the past. He remained in Thailand for a week, the first three days as a guest of the King and Queen, and then as a private guest of the head of the Thai military government and old acquaintance of Ne Win, Field Marshall Sarit Thanarat.[51] What was discussed in their meetings remains unknown. That Ne Win would have been suspicious of Thai complicity with Shan, Karen and other insurgents along their mutual borders would seem entirely reasonable as he believed that the Americans were still supporting the KMT troops in the Shan State and Laos.

In the midst of these international affairs, the socialist and administrative revolution in Myanmar proceeded apace, as an analyst wrote, in "a systematic, if not spectacular, manner" (Badgley 1962, p. 24). The small cabinet, with each member referred to as "in charge" rather than minister and responsible for several ministries, was hard pressed and despite working long hours, to many on the receiving end, the revolution looked more chaotic than systematic. Ne Win, together with Aung Gyi, other times with Tin Pe, and sometimes with both, toured the country incessantly, inspecting agricultural and industrial projects, and meeting large numbers of persons. Ne Win attended the Revolutionary Council's second "Peasant Seminar" which was held at Ohndaw from 30 December 1962 to 1 January 1963.[52] These "seminars", which brought peasants and government officials from the surrounding areas together, were a combination of festival and peasant political-mobilization campaigns designed to encourage support for the new government. Having missed the first seminar held at Myinmu, Sagaing Township, because of his international travels, Ne Win spent several days at the second, and addressed the 100,000 persons at Ohndaw. All of the top leaders of the Revolutionary Council were also present, including Aung Gyi and Tin Pe.[53] Other such "seminars", with Ne Win normally in attendance, were held subsequently at Duya (31 January 1963), Daik-U (8 May 1963), Popa (2 June 1963 and 30 January 1964), Toungoo (3 March 1964), and Yangon (7 March 1966 and 1 March 1968).

The policies and rhetoric of the Revolutionary Government and the Burma Socialist Programme Party increasingly came to be seen as identical with Communism, at least in the minds of many commentators and journalists. In order to assuage such accusations, Ne Win sought a meeting with his old university history tutor, Professor B.R. Pearn. Given the rarity of such an event, it was assumed by Western diplomats that Ne Win organized the meeting in order to deliver a message to their respective governments. Pearn, who joined the British Foreign Office after his academic career was terminated by the Second World War, reported that Ne Win argued that the West was wrong in its appraisal of him and his policies. Ne Win "repeatedly stressed 'he was not a communist, never has been a communist and never will be a communist'".[54]

Despite the favourable coverage given to the policies of the Revolutionary Council in the Soviet press (Longmire 1989, p. 75), Nikita Khrushchev felt that perhaps Ne Win was proceeding too fast with his rush to socialism. He sent an emissary with a personal letter to Ne Win. The emissary was one Ulanovsky, most likely Rostilav Ulanovsky, a leading Soviet theorist on political developments in Asia, Africa and Latin America. His publications included *National Liberation* which devoted space to a discussion of the Burmese Way to Socialism.[55] Chairman Khrushchev advised Ne Win that in order to avoid inflation, unemployment and shortages of consumer goods, he should follow caution in the nationalization of the economy, implying allowing small businesses to remain in the hands of the private sector. He also advised Ne Win to study the mistakes that had been made in the Soviet experience of introducing socialism. Ne Win apparently thanked, through Ulanovsky, Khrushchev for his advice and then ignored it (Chit Hlaing n.d., p. 31). Chou En-lai's visit to Yangon in July 1964, discussed in the following chapter, was intended to convey a similar message. Apparently Mao Tse-tung became concerned about reports from the Chinese embassy in Yangon about the decline in the economy and sought to encourage Ne Win to lessen his socialist ardour.[56]

On 1 January 1963, Ne Win's long cherished goal to nationalize the Myanmar oil industry was finally achieved, with the government taking over both the Burmah Oil Company (1954) (BOC) and the Indo-Burma Oil Company.[57] The nationalization of the oil industry was one of the points upon which Ne Win and his deputy, Aung Gyi, came into conflict. At one of his post-coup press conferences, when asked about the future of BOC, Aung Gyi replied that he had not become the Minister for Trade and Industry in order "to be another Mossadeq", referring to the Iranian prime minister who was ousted in 1953 by the CIA and British Secret Intelligence Service (MI6) after attempting to nationalize the Anglo-Iranian

Oil Company. Ne Win reportedly rebuked Aung Gyi for doing so. William Eadie, then Chairman of Burmah Oil and well informed about developments within the Revolutionary Council, sent Ne Win good wishes on the tasks that he had undertaken twenty days after the coup. Convinced that Ne Win was so tied down with paperwork and bogged down by petty detail, including reading more than 200 anonymous letters every day from which he was alleged to take policy guidance, he believed Ne Win to be harassed and irritable. Eadie therefore hoped that he would not have time to get around to looking again at BOC (Corley 1988, p. 262).

Ne Win complained not long after receiving Eadie's note to the British Ambassador about the 1960 deal done between the government and BOC. He was reported to have said, "As usual, clever British business had taken advantage of the inexperienced Burmese." When the ambassador pointed out that it was the legal government of Burma, then under U Nu and U Rashid, which had concluded the deal, Ne Win "retorted, 'that was why members of that government were behind bars!'". John Dewhurst, the manager of BOC in Burma, attempted, without success, to discuss the future of the company with Aung Gyi, but he too was tied up in detailed work and failed to make appointments for them to meet. Malcolm MacDonald, who visited Ne Win in May, raised the future of BOC but the discussion was elusive (Corley 1988, p. 263).

The Board of Directors of BOC (1954) in Myanmar had three Burmese and two British members. While Ne Win was away in London in August, two new Burmese members of the board were appointed. They promptly marched into the company's offices and called a meeting of the Burmese employees. Explaining that nationalization was in the air and that cuts in pay would follow, they threw their weight about. When later confronted by one of the British directors about their high-handed behaviour, the two Burmese directors apologized and the matter was left to rest. On 6 October, the government announced that the army-owned Burma Economic Development Corporation (BEDC) would henceforth monopolize the import of oil products, a business previously handled by a subsidiary of BOC. At about this time, reports began appearing in the Rangoon papers that the now greatly weakened downstream distribution company owned by BOC would be nationalized. The days of BOC (1954) were clearly numbered (Corley 1988, p. 265).

While negotiating the sale of the remaining assets of the company to the Burmese government, Aung Gyi explained to a BOC board member that the reason the 1960 agreement between the company and Nu's government rankled Ne Win so much was that it was not shown to him before being approved. When he pointed out that Ne Win was not then part of the government, he was "told sharply that the general was the most important person in Burma and should as a matter of course have been consulted" (Corley 1988, p. 267). After several months of negotiations, a deal was finally struck and the entirety of BOC's assets were passed to the government in exchange for £4.7 million in two instalments, paying 3.5 per cent interest on the outstanding balance free of Burmese tax.[58] The two instalments were paid in 1963, encouraging other foreign companies facing nationalization to attempt similar deals. The Burma Corporation, Unilever, the Bombay Burmah Trading Corporation, Chartered Bank of India, and others, however, were not as favoured and have yet to be compensated (Corley 1988, p. 270).

In his first Independence Day broadcast since seizing power, Ne Win admonished the population not to squander their wealth and go into debt in order to undertake showy or pretentious exhibitions when making donations to the Buddhist monkhood or other acts of charity. Frugality and self-reliance were called for. As for those who opposed the Burmese Way to Socialism, he claimed they were just a minority who exploited the farmers via loans and enjoyed special rights which would soon be removed. However, as they were nationals, they would not be liquidated but would be forced to find honourable and justifiable occupations in future. His government would "have to reform by gentle, persuasive methods as far as possible any element of our society who goes counter to this declared policy". Ne Win concluded by noting what he called the "deterioration of the traditional social and cultural values of all races in the country — the Burmese, Shans, Karens, Kachins, Chins, Kayahs, etc." This "moral degeneration" had led to a decline in mutual assistance in society and the deterioration of relations between parents and teachers, teachers and students, husbands and wives.

> This unhappy state of affairs however is the outcome of the slow and clever process of repression which Burmese culture and traditions had suffered during the days of the colonial regime. The object of the colonial power was to prolong its rule with the minimum of resistance on the part of the governed. The first clever step it took was therefore to suppress all literature likely to inspire patriotism in the people, and to undermine the national culture which would preserve the unity and strength of the people. It introduced school-books designed to achieve its purpose unobtrusively, and when it was assisted by missionaries

accompanying it into Burma, the fate of Burmese national culture and traditions was sealed. Our country is still suffering from the lingering ill-effects of the colonial regime. Hence, our Education and Union Culture Ministries are taking necessary measures to put things right as quickly as possible. The economic deterioration shall be corrected economically, and the moral degeneration among the people shall be similarly checked by a revival of our traditional observance of moral and social rules of conduct. I would therefore appeal to you all to play your part in bringing about a general rejuvenation in the moral and cultural life of the nation and thereby help the country in the march forward to national prosperity.[59]

The Burmese Way to Socialism was gaining seemingly irresistible momentum after nine months. On 17 January 1963, *The System of Correlation of Man and His Environment*, the BSPP's ideological and philosophical justification, drafted by U Chit Hlaing, was adopted and published.[60] Twenty-one months later, the Revolutionary Council published the *Specific Characteristics of the Myanmar Socialist Programme Party* as a clarification to *The System of Correlation of Man and His Environment* after it was criticized, particularly by anti-Communist monks and supporters of U Nu for being Communist and anti-religious.[61] The charge that the Revolutionary Council's policies were the same as those of the Communists was one Ne Win and his colleagues had continually to refute. It was a fruitless attempt, however, for if the re-establishment of the goal of Leftist Unity as perceived in 1948–49 was to be achieved, the government had to reach out to supporters of the Communist Parties, if not to the leaders themselves.

At the end of January, Czechoslovakian President Antonin Novotny and his wife made a state visit to Burma. Ties with the socialist bloc countries, especially in Eastern Europe, were important for establishing the credentials of the Revolutionary Council and Ne Win as revolutionary socialists, if not Communists. The Novotnys remained in the country for three days and were taken by Ne Win and Daw Khin May Than to Mandalay and Bagan. This visit began Myanmar's long connection with Czech-built, and eventually Myanmar-assembled, Zetor tractors which were used on state farms and on the streets of Myanmar's cities for many years. It was agreed that 2,000 tractors would be purchased each year.[62]

The momentum of the Revolutionary Council in a leftward direction finally became too much for the moderate socialist Brigadier Aung Gyi. He resigned, or was fired,[63] from the Council and his post as Minister for Trade and Industries on 8 February and soon went into internal exile again, just as he had done the previous year. This time, however, Ne Win sent no emissaries to Machanbaw to sweet talk him back into the government. Aung Gyi apparently felt that his position as Ne Win's deputy had been undermined by criticism levelled at him by Tin Pe and others in the Council during the three months he had acted for Ne Win the previous year.[64] Whether it was primarily from ideological position, policy differences, or personal pique, Aung Gyi, nonetheless, in his resignation statement, pledged his loyalty to Ne Win. The equally moderate, but less well-known, Colonel Chit Myaing succeeded Aung Gyi in his ministerial post,[65] and Brigadier San Yu rose to take the post of Vice Chief-of-Staff (Army), thus becoming Ne Win's deputy, a position he would hold for the next twenty-five years. Ne Win now had few, if any, in his inner circle with the temerity, or experience, to challenge his views.

As head of state, Ne Win had to make many statements of public policy, especially during major state occasions, a practice he had previously abhorred. He now used these occasions to announce the direction of policy under the new regime. The first Union Day occasion, marking the sixteen years since the signing of the Panglong Agreement, was one such example. Though the Panglong Agreement was merely a document whereby the British recognized leaders of the area referred to as the Frontier Areas and the Shan States agreed to merge their territories with what was known until then as "Burma proper", it had become a document filled with new meanings for politicians pursuing ethnic politics. Union Day had always been a day to champion the ethnic diversity of Myanmar, with music and dancing by various so-called National Races, particularly the "big eight" — Bamar, Shan, Kayin, Kachin, Kayah, Mon, Rakhine, and Chin — which incorporated many smaller identities. The 16th celebration which Ne Win attended at Loikaw, the capital of Kayah State, was no exception. At the celebration, Ne Win presented the "Revolutionary Council's Declaration of Faith in Respect of Indigenous Peoples".[66]

However, while the message behind the music and dance was ethnic diversity, the message of the General's terse remarks was that of human equality. Explaining that it was the championing of alleged ethnic group rights against the unity of the nation-state that had forced the army to seize power, Ne Win pledged that his government would treat all citizens equally.[67] This egalitarian doctrine was, of course, criticized as Burmanization by politicians claiming to speak for particular minorities. Just as the Burmese Way to Socialism had given the impression of communism, yet not being Communist, the government's ethnic policy also both championed and denied the relevance of ethnicity in public policy in favour of majority rule and equality of esteem.

The Revolutionary government quickly undertook a number of policy innovations designed to better integrate the minority ethnic border regions with the core of the country. As the army felt itself to be a multi-ethnic institution, so that ideal became a goal for the country. Schools, public and not yet nationalized private and missionary schools, were required to teach in the national language, Burmese. Army veterans, emulating Israeli kibbutz, were resettled in border areas. Children from the minority ethnic-designated states were taken on tours to other parts of the country. On 20 October 1964, the government opened the Academy for the Development of National Groups at Ywathitkyi, Sagaing Division. At the academy, students from various linguistic backgrounds were taught other "national languages" before being despatched to teach in various parts of the country the lessons they learned while living and studying with members of other linguistic communities. The effort to integrate the population in the name of socialism and egalitarianism encouraged ethnically designated minority political leaders to increase their support for insurgents resisting national integration (Badgley 1963, pp. 93–94).

However, Ne Win believed that the state, while it should encourage the maintenance of traditions, should not be involved in perpetuating religious practices. At about this time, the government abolished U Nu's practice of using Buddhist monasteries as substitutes for public schools, teaching the religion side by side with secular subjects, all taught by monks. He also abolished the Pali University system and the Sasana University, both established by Nu after independence. The latter institution, which was not supported by much of the monkhood, was primarily concerned with education in English as a missionary enterprise to spread Buddhism and had graduated only one group of students before it was closed (Khammai Dhammasami 2007, pp. 14 and 20). Soon after the coup, the policy of undermining nat worship begun during the Caretaker period was revived (Smith 1965, pp. 296–97). Ne Win halted Nu's projects to build two State Nat Shrines, a move favoured by many who saw Buddhism as a religion of reason (Smith 1965, p. 77). As Smith notes, Ne Win had two desires. One was the separation of the state from religion; the other was to eliminate non-rational practices which inhibited the development of an advanced society. The popularity of Myanmar's mass lay meditation movement surged, according to Ingrid Jordt, thanks to Ne Win's attempt to separate the monkhood from the state and its politics (Jordt 2007, p. 4). As during the colonial period when there was no government to take responsibility for the faith, it fell to the laity to help preserve the religion, although other factors were also at work (Jordt 2007, p. 213).

Ne Win's approach to the responsibilities he had assumed on 2 March 1962 became clearer in a speech he gave to a meeting of top officials from all levels of government at a conference of the Central Security and Affairs Committee held on 2 April 1963.[68] He explained that the General Amnesty Order of 1963, issued the previous day, was designed out of a desire to unite the entire country. By annulling all crimes and illegal acts, other than rape or murder, committed prior to the order, not only by insurgents but also including corrupt acts by civil servants, the intention was to start afresh, abandoning old views and working with a greater sense of responsibility in future. In any event, Ne Win explained that the amnesty also recognized that in the past many who should have been punished were not. Justice, like the *Paukkhrawattha* rain, the rain mentioned in Buddhist scriptures which only falls on those who wish to be wet, only gathered in some guilty of crimes and misdemeanours. However, those caught violating the law in the future would be dealt with severely. The B-class prisons of the past were to be abolished and a much harsher regime would apply in future. The moral deterioration of the country, which had affected all elements including the armed forces, had to be addressed. Rules which were impossible to abide by, such as that civil servants should not participate in political activities, would also be abolished, hence permitting them to join the BSPP.

Concerning the establishment of the Party, Ne Win drew attention to the fact that government personnel were involved, in contrast to the old system whereby the civil service and the army were barred from political activities. He noted the hollowness of this contention, stating:

> everything is connected indirectly. If a government liked by the military is in power, it will straight away do exactly what the government asks. If a government not of the same mind with the leaders of the military is in power, then even though orders are given from above, the person below slips away cleverly, without obvious fault. This is what is happening in other countries.

Discussing the link between domestic politics and international relations, Ne Win reiterated his often heard aphorism to the effect that "the strength of the country is in the country". Those who seek to love the Aunty outside rather than the Mother of their own are in danger of selling out their country for purposes other than those for the good of the country. "When the outside people give, they have their own motives. They create the bush (to catch it) as they see the rabbit."

Ne Win reiterated that Burma would continue to follow a foreign policy of strict neutrality. Perhaps still stung by his experience at Colombo and concerned over the deterioration of the political situation in neighbouring Laos and Vietnam, he made clear his unswerving dedication to non-alignment. However, reiterating the link between international affairs and the domestic opposition to his government, he warned his opponents to halt their search for support abroad. Noting that a foreign submarine had been spotted in Myanmar territorial waters the previous Sunday near the Myeik islands, he called on all to be wary of external influences. The Revolutionary Government was not afraid of outside enemies, but the danger of fifth columnists and internal spies was all too obvious. They would be found and their activities halted before they could sell out their country. The amnesty was an effort to start anew, but the message was that in future, harsh measures would be taken against enemies of the state, whoever they might be.

He dismissed the criticism his government was receiving from home and abroad. "The outside does not care for us one bit. We also are not working for their affection." As to the accusation that the Revolutionary Council was overwhelmed with work and could not cope with its responsibilities, Ne Win conceded that this was true. However, drawing on the analogy of the condition of the army and the government at the height of the civil war in 1948 when they could barely control Yangon, he indicated that they fought back "little by little" then. "Therefore, for us also, while we are taking responsibility for both military and political affairs, if, by any chance, we are ganged up upon, we can survive, with the strength we can muster, creating a base and shoring up."

At a ceremony marking the opening of a cooperative village at Daik-U in Bago Division on 8 May, Ne Win made another of his typical speeches, sometimes redundant, often laced with anecdotes from his personal experience.[69] The cooperative village was planned as an experiment, and if successful, would have been replicated in order to provide land to the estimated two million landless labourers in the country. Ne Win began by explaining that his Council and government were giving priority to matters pertaining to farmers and workers because they made up the overwhelming majority of the population, 95 per cent, with the farmers accounting for 80 per cent and the intelligentsia amounting to just 5 per cent. He admitted that his government still did not have a settled agricultural policy as they were studying the different kinds and problems of agriculture in the various regions of the country, from the Delta to *taungya* (so-called slash and burn) in the hills of the border regions.

Ne Win explained several times that he only became aware of the poverty of landless labourers at the peasant seminar held earlier in the year at Duya and, as a result, his government was going to distribute paddy land to the landless, many of whom lost their fields during and after the Second World War. "Please remember", he added, "however, that the success or failure of our good intentions depends on you."

> During my younger days, in about 1924 or 1925, there were no sharp distinctions in the economic levels of villagers. In the Pyay District, where I come from, however poor a villager might be, he usually owned a cart and a pair of bullocks and five or six acres of land. Besides, he could rent an equivalent area. At transplanting and harvesting time, all the womenfolk in the village lent a hand. What joyous occasions those were, each helping the other.
>
> Farm coolies came into existence only later, following the unequal distribution of wealth in the villages. All they have is their physical strength, and none of them own a cart and a yoke of oxen. ... Now we are giving priority to improving their lot.

Hence, the cooperative village was established. The loans the government had provided the farmers to get started in their agricultural work, he urged, should be used wisely and they must accept that austerity would be essential until they have gotten through two or three seasons, assuming the weather was favourable. Noting that the farmers were expected to repay the loans extended within three years, weather and crops permitting, Ne Win reminded them that their responsibilities were as heavy as those of the government in making the cooperative village project a success.

Ne Win, who was not a great reader of books, might well have contemplated the words of Alexis de Tocqueville, when considering the peasants to whom he was directing his remarks:

> Actually it was to these very conditions that our peasantry owe some of their outstanding qualities. Long enfranchised and owning some of the land he worked, the French peasant was largely independent and had developed a healthy pride and much common sense. Inured to hardships, he was indifferent to the amenities of life, intrepid in the face of danger, and faced misfortune stoically. It was from this simple, virile race of men that those great armies were raised which were to dominate for many years the European scene. But their very virtues made them dangerous masters. During the many centuries in which these men had borne the brunt of nation-wide misgovernment and lived as a class apart, they had nursed in secret their grievances,

jealousies, and rancors and, having learned toughness in a hard school, had become capable of enduring or inflicting the very worst (Tocqueville 1955, p. 207).

As indicated in his Independence Day address after the coup, culture, national culture, was a central aspect of the revolution Ne Win was attempting to orchestrate. On 23 May 1963, he made a major address on the subject at a seminar for theatrical artistes in Yangon at the Kyaikkason Ground, as the former Rangoon Turf Club that Ne Win knew so well but closed after gambling had been banned by his government the previous year.[70] Though defining theatrical artistes widely, he was mainly addressing the interests of the itinerant road shows that travelled the country putting on pwes[71] for villagers. He argued that people did not adequately appreciate the fine arts in Myanmar, in part because they were not encouraged by the British. Moreover, the actors were selfish, competing with each other, but at the same time exploited by moneylenders. They had a hard life and like all but a small minority, enjoyed no economic security in old age. He went on, in the rather rambling style of his speeches,

> Regarding responsibilities, it is most important that we should preserve our Burmese traditional forms of cultural arts from disappearing altogether. I am advocating for the preservation of our cultural heritage because of the current trend is that people in towns including myself do not know even how to speak Burmese well. Those who can speak Burmese accurately can be found only in the countryside; and among the people in urban areas only those belonging to the theatrical world can speak correctly Burmese. Not only that, they have better mastery of the Burmese classical melodies such as *patpyo*, *kyo*, *yadya*, *bwe radu*, *rakan*, *egyin* and *ainggyin*. How they are composed and in what manner they should be rendered, I confess I have very little knowledge. These classical melodies, of course, exist in books but the correct methods of rendering them are nearly disappeared. We wish to revive and preserve our Burmese literature including classical songs in their original form, and in implementing this project the responsibilities of dramatists and stage artistes are by no means small. Regarding classical melodies, at present there is a divergence of views on how they should be rendered. This is because our classical songs have not been originally set in notations as in Western countries but handed over from generation to generation by ear only. So, instead of each insisting that his particular version or rendition is authentic, musical scholars will have to compare notes, resolve their differences and agreed to leave standardised versions for posterity.

Similarly, he called on musical instruments and the Burmese language to be preserved. A new dictionary was required to illustrate instruments and words that people did not understand or know the meaning of, while they understood new foreign words like "rocket".

In terms of their performances, Ne Win drew his audience's attention to what he saw as the tendency of artistic troops to play to the mass love of tragedy, often distorting the *Jakata* and other tales in order to increase the quality and quantity of pathos. "And in their place, dramatists should portray, in keeping with the needs of the new era, more scenes calculated to foster patriotism, promote physical and moral courage as well as a capacity to evaluate intellectual and physical labour." Patriotism and the love of work and the dignity of labour were themes to take up from Burmese history. In this, the artistes would have to rely on their own efforts. He concluded,

> It is an incorrigible habit among our people to be always relying on the Government for the solution of any problem. The Government can offer advice and extend material help to a certain limit only. The real work of resolving problems rests with the people themselves. I shall conclude with an appeal to you all to sink your personal differences and pride, practise mutual help and work with unity to resolve common problems, and to co-operate with the Government to turn our country into an "Edifice of Knowledge".

Despite his call not to rely on the government, the government continued to take on more and more responsibilities. Contradictions or not, the revolution rolled on, with the announcement on 15 February that the state was to nationalize industrial production, distribution, and imports and exports. The private sector would be limited to retail trade. Ne Win explained this to a hastily gathered group of 150 leading business persons in Yangon. Aung Gyi's Burma Economic Development Company, which he had set up initially as an economic auxiliary of the army, became the economy's largest entity during the Caretaker period and was now broken up and subsumed into the government trade corporations which emerged to replace the private sector. Four days later, the government made a partial retreat and indicated that the process of socialization would take longer than anticipated.

Criticism of and resistance to the Revolutionary Council's socialist lurch began to emerge in 1963 as the army appeared to have taken on greater responsibilities than it had the capability to manage. Aung Gyi's departure was seen as culminating the obvious growth of the influence of the radical socialists Tin Pe, Ba Nyein[72] and Kyaw Soe on Ne Win's thinking.[73] On 23 February, the government nationalized all thirty-one banks, both foreign and local, and public and private.[74] From then until their departure from the government, Tin Pe and Ba Nyein pushed the socialist revolution on Ne Win's behalf.

If the army was hard-pressed to manage all of the economic responsibilities it had assumed, it had other tasks to handle as well. One was the development of the Burma Socialist Programme Party (BSPP) from being just the members of the Revolutionary Council to becoming a proper party capable of playing a role in the governance of the country and mobilizing popular support for its policies. On the anniversary of the coup on 2 March, invitations were sent for candidate members of the party. Party building had begun, but invitations were sent only to members of the armed forces.[75] The army also faced continuing or renewed insurgent threats. The day after the coup anniversary, rebels in Kachin State attacked the Mohnyin town police station, making off with 150 rifles, and one Mohammed Jafar Habib established a new group, the Rohingya Independence Force (RIF), on the border with East Pakistan (Lintner 1999, p. 447).

Ne Win, while supervising all of these activities, also had the affairs of state to manage, including a visit by the King of Laos.[76] The joint communiqué issued at the end of the King's visit emphasized the desire of Ne Win for Laos to become truly independent, which it clearly was not in 1963.[77] A few days later, at a dinner for the Vice Foreign Minister of Japan who had come to sign a wartime reparations agreement,[78] Ne Win dominated the conversation and left the impression with one of the Japanese present that the United States was the only country being unfriendly towards Myanmar.[79] Aung Gyi, who had negotiated the deal, would have been missed on that occasion and others. If the Japanese, Germans and others were baffled by Ne Win's revolution, so were the Chinese. On 12 March, the Chinese foreign ministry instructed its embassy in Yangon to make no comments on Myanmar politics or the Burmese Way to Socialism either privately or publicly (Steinberg and Fan 2012, p. 394).

The move to the left took another step on 1 April 1963. As noted above, on that day the government issued a general amnesty offer to all rebels and other perpetrators of crimes. If they turned in their weapons and abandoned their insurgent colleagues by 1 July, they would face no punishment and would be accepted back into the legal fold.[80] As part of the amnesty, a number of prisoners were released, perhaps as many as 12,000. Many were members of the left-wing NUF or students arrested the previous year. Former civil servants among the prisoners were encouraged to return to their old posts, with half of their salaries paid to them while they were in detention. To demonstrate his sincerity in issuing the amnesty, Ne Win personally went to the old Rangoon prison to address the inmates. He told them,

> You are free to go home. We shall try to remove the root causes, the economic ills that brought you here. But those of you of criminal habits must mend your ways, too. Don't come back.

According to Maung Maung, many were back within weeks (Maung Maung 1999, p. 74).

Few insurgents immediately took up the offer made in the general amnesty.[81] The attempt to tempt leftist and other insurgents to join the Revolutionary Council government, however, received a fillip from the visit of the Chinese Communist President to Yangon from 20 to 23 April.[82] Liu Shao-chi proposed to Ne Win as they were being driven to the airport at the end of his visit that the Burmese Communists, being genuine patriots, merely wanted peace and encouraged Ne Win to open peace talks with them. Ne Win remained non-committal but remarked that he would discuss the possibility with his colleagues (Steinberg and Fan 2012, p. 73).

On May Day, the Revolutionary Council announced its thirteen-point programme on Workers Affairs and established the Working People's Councils.[83] On that occasion, Ne Win made another lengthy speech at the Kyaikkasan Grounds.[84] As in many of his speeches, he did not promise his audience anything other than fairness as they advanced together towards the goal of socialism. He admonished the workers to be reasonable and to work hard, while encouraging business owners, as they waited to be nationalized, and already nationalized industry's managers, to end artificial distinctions between labourers and managers. Calling for self-reliance, he also insisted that people acknowledge and respond in kind to the sacrifices and expenditures that the state was making to build socialism and improve their lives. They should not, he admonished, drive tractors like racing cars as they were expensive and cost foreign exchange. Similarly, the farmers in the audience were reminded not to treat the loans the government provided them as gifts, but as debts that they were enjoined to repay.

An insight into Ne Win's thinking more than a year after the coup was provided in an interview that he gave the outgoing United States ambassador, John Scott Everton. Ne Win, who said that he was working sixteen hours a day as Burma was "too backward" for a forty-hour week, was apparently cheerful, but tired and strained. He was clearly preoccupied with domestic affairs and only discussed foreign affairs when prompted. He advanced that the agricultural policies he was going to pursue were those he had proposed to the government in 1950 but had been rejected then. Burmese farmers, he argued, were very conservative and hard to change but they had to do so, in order that the agricultural diversity and self-sufficiency that the country required could be achieved. Similarly, self-sufficiency would be sought through import-substitution industrialization strategies. Because of the country's lack of skilled technicians, the available natural resources remained untouched. The lack of technical skills was because colonialism had left Burma a nation of clerks and technical training in the West was useless because those who were sent abroad came back as misfits in Myanmar.[85] Turning to foreign affairs, he felt that while Myanmar had an interest in what happened in the civil war in neighbouring Laos, it could do little about it. He said, "it all depends on the giants: Russia, the United States and China." Burma was just a small country. Noting that there were no outstanding issues in U.S.–Burma relations, he did not relish the development of regional groupings as Malaya and other governments in the region were then discussing, while Indonesia was pursuing its confrontation policy over the formation of Malaysia from the remaining British colonies in Southeast Asia. He reiterated, "We are only a small country and we can only take care of our own problems." Asked if he were concerned by criticism in the foreign press of him and his government, he replied, "It doesn't matter to us what the press prints."[86]

These views were reiterated in a meeting between Ne Win and a visiting Philippine trade minister who came to Burma to buy rice for the Philippine army. In the meeting, which included Colonel Chit Myaing, the normally abstemious Ne Win had five drinks. When the visiting minister suggested that Burma send people to the Philippines for training, Ne Win again replied that the training given abroad was often inappropriate. As for opening an embassy in Manila, he replied that Burma could not afford all of the embassies it would like to have.[87]

The radical socialist direction that Ne Win took, and the obvious exclusion from power of those who refused to join with Ne Win in his new single-party organization, finally prompted discussions on how to oust him from power. According to a source who reported to the American embassy, he had stumbled upon a meeting around mid-April 1963 of a conspiratorial group who met at the home of a businessman, one U Tin Oo. Those present included former Defence Minister U Win, former Minister and Thirty Comrade Bo Min Gaung, former Prime Minister U Ba Swe, and former Deputy Prime Minister U Kyaw Nyein. Known as a "Committee of 19", they planned to move against Ne Win before the end of May and believed that they had the support of "Aung Gyi's faction" in the army.[88] Whether such a faction existed was never demonstrated. Perhaps getting an inkling of plotting against him by former colleagues, Ne Win closed down Edward Law-Yone's *The Nation* newspaper on 18 May. Ba Swe, Law-Yone, Kyaw Nyein and at least six others were arrested on and around 9 August, while Thakin Tin, Bohmu Aung and Thakin Tin Maung, ministers in the former government, were released from detention.[89] Bo Let Ya's arrest followed in December (Law-Yone 1981, p. 17). And then his brother, U Mya Hlaing, the former editor of *Myawaddy*, the army-sponsored journal in which U Chit Hlaing had published his initial ruminations which became the Burmese Way to Socialism, was arrested in July the next year.[90]

Plotting against Ne Win was obviously rife, but equally inept. Both U Kyaw Nyein and Bo Setkya had conversations in May with officials, including the Ambassador at the American embassy, as to how to thwart Ne Win's ambitions. The plotting, which included both former members of the Thirty Comrades and various former political party leaders, was uncoordinated.[91] The only person who might have been able to get both civilian political and army support was former Brigadier, now U, Aung Gyi. He had removed himself from Yangon after his resignation in February, and, as he had done the previous year, took himself off to the northernmost town in Myanmar. He remained there for three-and-a-half months. At the end of May, he returned to Yangon and declared he was ready to oppose Ne Win and his socialist policies. However, he first returned to Paungde, his hometown south of Pyay, to meditate.[92]

Rumours of increasing armed, as well as elite resistance, to Ne Win's rule came at mid-year. The American embassy was "reliably informed" that Dr Aung Than, a dentist and Daw Khin May Than's brother-in-law, had been asked by Ne Win to tour the Shan State and report back on what he saw. He allegedly reported that new and modern American- or Thai-supplied, perhaps via SEATO, weapons were being used by insurgent forces.[93] Militant monks, in the form of the Yahan Pyo League, previously affiliated with the AFPFL and thought to be in support of U Kyaw Nyein, approached the American embassy at about the same time, hinting that they would like to be supplied with arms as they believed the Americans were providing Shan and Kachin insurgents.[94] Monks in Mandalay did more than dream of revolting. According to *Botataung*, U Thein Pe Myint's newspaper, 10,000 monks attended an anti-Revolutionary Council rally, where a leading monk, U Kethaya, sometimes referred to as the "American *pongyi*" (Smith 1965, pp. 301–3), predicted Ne Win would be assassinated because of his attachment to Communism.[95] The protesting monks were possibly assisted in their demonstrations by the United States consulate in Mandalay.[96] In 1963, the government had to back down on a largely symbolic plan to place control of the maintenance of ancient sites, including pagodas, under the archaeology department following monastic opposition (Smith 1965, pp. 299–300).

Elaborate, and scarcely creditable, rumours of plotting and ill will within the Revolutionary Council also circulated in Yangon. An unnamed source told the American embassy in June 1963 that Brigadier Tin Pe needed urgent medical attention abroad and would prefer to have it in either the United Kingdom or the United States. In any event, he was worried about "death by injection". Ne Win would not let him go to Vienna for treatment as Colonel Kyaw Soe was receiving treatment there and they might plot against him. That Tin Pe required medical treatment, however, was firmly denied by Colonel Hla Han who was "in charge" of not only education but also health in the Revolutionary Government.[97] Several years later, Brigadier Tin Pe did go to Vienna for medical treatment.[98]

Ne Win had his own medical issues around that time. When his uncle, Thakin Ba Sein, the veteran leader of the *Dobama Asiayon* and leader of a number of lost right-wing causes in the 1950s, passed away, Ne Win called at his home on the morning of his funeral, 19 June 1963 (Sein Tin 2011, p. 225), having just risen from his own bed to which he had been confined for a week with a recurring bladder complaint. Rumour had it, however, that he had venereal disease.[99] Rumours of Ne Win's imminent demise were often heard over the next four decades until when the event actually occurred, some refused to believe the news.

Party building took up much of Ne Win's time in early July. On 1 July, he opened the Central School of Political Science which was designed to train party cadres to develop the party from a cadre to a mass organization. Ne Win addressed the first batch of 266 trainees on 19 September, explaining that the coup had been necessary to end inequality; that inequality was the cause of ethnic and class conflict; and ending conflict would result in peace.[100] During the first year of its existence, the Revolutionary Council had lost two members in addition to Aung Gyi. Commodore Than Pe had died and Colonel Kyi Maung, a close associate of Aung Gyi, had resigned. Others, such as Tommy Clift, the head of the air force, had made their dislike of the General's policies obvious by rarely attending meetings. Clift, an Anglo-Shan with a British wife, was dismissed by Ne Win on 27 November.[101] In order to fill the vacant seats on the Council, regional commanders were brought on with no ministerial responsibilities.[102]

Ne Win's concerns about domestic politics and the revolution, of course, had international implications. On 2 September 1963, he addressed a conference of Burmese ambassadors in Yangon. There he declared:

> We have to accept the existence of two opposing power blocs, the Eastern and the Western bloc. Though we may wish to keep aloof from bloc politics, we cannot do so; it has repercussions on us every now and then. Nevertheless, we should keep aloof as best we can. At this point I wish to say something about countries taking foreign aid; it isn't quite proper to mention the names of these countries. Some of these recipient countries, though they can do without foreign aid, consider it a good thing to take from others. Some others are small, newly independent countries faced with serious economic problems, and they cannot possibly do without foreign aid. These countries, of course, deserve sympathy and understanding. Having foreseen all these, we have not taken foreign aid. We can after all carry on by ourselves. In fact, we have been getting on by ourselves. In fact, we have been getting along on our own, practicing strict economy. All this is now becoming evident. You have, no doubt, seen what has happened to those recipient countries. What I am saying now relates to the over-all economic and political situation of the whole country. In addition, we devote much of our attention to domestic politics. Here we place our reliance on the masses in our country.
>
> How can a man who becomes the leader of his country through outside help and influence just as the cheeks become radiant because of diamond ear-rings, as the Burmese saying goes, hope to be able to do much for his country?[103]

These views clearly reveal how Ne Win felt that domestic politics and national independence required economic austerity and self-reliance. These were themes often reiterated over the next twenty-five years. "The strength of the country lies in the country."

Ne Win, in the words of an American embassy report, was "running a one man show and is not seeking advice". The rumour mill was churning out lurid and implausible stories in the absence of real information. Ne Win, now permanently residing in the old Governor's mansion, always travelled in a "convoy with police radio cars stationed along his route". He was said to be "morbidly preoccupied with the possibility of assassination".[104]

Certainly there was plotting to oust Ne Win, if not to assassinate him. His former colleague in the Thirty Comrades, travelling companion and possible business partner, Bo Set Kya (U Aung Than) was known in mid-October 1963 to be in Bangkok on a mission to buy arms to ship to Tachilek on the Shan State–Thai border.[105] From Bangkok, Set Kya had apparently travelled to London, seeking support for a move of some sort against Ne Win and the Revolutionary Council. Having been spurned by Mr Schnee and Mr Dexter of the American embassy in Rangoon when he and U Kyaw Nyein had approached them for American support against Ne Win, Set Kya sought out Louis Walinsky, former Chief economist with Robert Nathan Associates whom Ne Win had dismissed in 1958. Set Kya, who claimed he had walked but had actually flown out of the country in August, was spotted by Myanmar intelligence agents in Bangkok. He did not believe they knew he was now in Washington. Set Kya indicated he no longer sought American support but hoped the State Department would not interfere with his efforts to find support "from other sources". Walinsky, who thought Ne Win was "essentially a stupid and dangerous man", sought to support Set Kya in his quest for assistance. He believed that if only a creditable leader could be found, the army would desert Ne Win.[106]

In a partial and carefully engineered exception to Ne Win's normal spurning of contacts with foreign diplomats, the new American ambassador eventually saw a great deal of the chairman. Henry A. Byroade, a West Point graduate and the youngest general in the U.S. Army at the end of the Second World War, known to be a "ladies man", got on very well with Ne Win once they became acquainted.[107] Given Byroade's military background and work in Germany, Egypt and other Cold War trouble spots, Burmese intelligence was wary of the new Ambassador, perhaps reflecting the suspicions of their leader. Byroade, who was described as "not one of the world's workaholics by any means", purchased Edward Law-Yone's 1935 Rolls Royce (for Law-Yone's acquisition, see Law-Yone 2013, p. 239) and spent most of his days dismantling and rebuilding the car, including leopard skin seats and teak panelling. Gradually, the suspicion that he was up to something nefarious dissipated and he then turned his psychological powers on Daw Khin May Than. A saying amongst the diplomatic community developed that "when the British Ambassador or the Chinese Ambassador talked to Kitty Ne Win they were talking to the wife of the Head of State. When Byroade talked to her, he was talking to a woman and she knew it."[108] They apparently became fast friends.

Byroade presented his credentials on 7 October 1963.[109] Their half-hour meeting, during which he found Ne Win "quite likeable personally", began a relationship which grew to become one of apparent rapport and secret informal social engagements. Byroade began by indicating President Kennedy's regret at the difficulties Ne Win faced with American immigration and customs officials on his last visit to New York. Passing on Kennedy's comments, Byroade further remarked,

> The President continued that in view of Burma's neutrality it would obviously be inappropriate for the US to make a commitment to any specific military measure in some undefined future contingency. Nevertheless there should be no doubt of the willingness of US to take all feasible measures to support Burmese resistance against foreign aggression, direct or indirect, or against other foreign threats to Burma's independence.

Kennedy's words implied a shift not only in United States policy towards neutralism as a foreign policy option but also an expansion of American commitments to assist countries threatened by its Cold War enemies. The Eisenhower administration, under Secretary of State John Foster Dulles, had insisted that before U.S. assistance could be provided, a prior treaty commitment was essential (Porter 2005, pp. 72 and 84).

Ne Win made no comment on these obviously significant remarks but apparently appeared pleased by Kennedy's words, as reported by Byroade, and the President's apparent personal interest in Burma. According to Byroade,

> He said he thought the Kennedy administration had changed the US understanding of neutral nations and their problems. He supposed [the] President might well be confused about what is happening in Burma. This would not seem unusual as he felt sure even many Burmese

were not really aware of what he was trying to do. He hoped things would clear up in [the] future and everyone would see that he [was] on the right path. Burma had a great desire to be left alone with her problems at the moment although he knew that no nation, as no individual, could really stand along [sic] for very long. The story had proven however that Burma must be aware of [a] seeming friend who let her down.[110]

When pressed to indicate if the United States was the "seeming friend who let her down", Ne Win's

reaction was immediate and he spoke with feeling, saying he would tell of one of [the] past grievances. He related the great sense of personal loss he had felt when he found that some of his closest friends in the officer corps had been subverted by us and were vrur [sic] agents.

Byroade believed he was speaking of Brigadier Maung Maung. Byroade pledged that such a thing, if true, would not happen again while he was ambassador. They went on to discuss how Kennedy was trying to bring the CIA under control using methods that Ne Win had once told Averill Harriman he used to control an over-powerful minister in his government (for the policies toward the CIA by President Kennedy, see Hilsman 1964, 1967, pp. 63–89). Ne Win indicated that he would like to meet with President Kennedy personally but Byroade was convinced the President would not have the time to accept such an invitation since his visits to India, Pakistan and Ceylon were still pending. The two parted amicably, with Byroade requesting that they meet occasionally. At their farewell, they mutually agreed that they "would have had [a] less troubled life had" they remained in the army.[111]

Subsequently, Byroade recalled that he also discussed the KMT intervention of the early 1950s. Having been told in Washington that the United States ambassadors continued to deny the story long after it was publicly documented, prompting Ne Win to remark to one hapless follower of the State Department line, before walking away, "Why don't you just go home?" When Byroade refused to deny the United States involvement in the KMT affair, and put it in the context of the Korean conflict, Ne Win never mentioned the matter again.[112] Byroade certainly, for all of his apparent candour, did not tell Ne Win about the unauthorized overflight of Myanmar territory by CIA planes supplying anti-Communist Tibetan insurgents (Conboy and Morrison 2002). Nor was it likely they discussed the CIA-engineered assassination of South Vietnamese President Ngo Dinh Diem on 2 November (on Diem's assassination, see Jacobs 2006).

The second half of 1963 was dominated by peace talks that the government entered into with all the country's insurgent groups, Communist and ethnically labelled. Invitations to the peace talks were issued on 11 June.[113]

Overture Made to All Underground Armed Organisations by The Revolutionary Council

1.   The Revolutionary Council, being earnestly desirous of restoring total peace in the Union, makes this overture to all organisations underground, which are up in arms for political or racial causes, to come forth and construct together in a practical way the yearned-for edifice of peace.

2.   If the underground armed organisations, while wishing to restore peace even as the Revolutionary Council does, hold the [General] Amnesty [Order of 1 April] inadequate or are held back by other reasons, the Revolutionary Council extends this overture to parley and help resolve their various problems.

3.   The Revolutionary Council considers that hard and fast conditions exacted before the parleys begin serve only as evidence of tension and to confine the parleys within narrow and rigid areas so that they may well frustrate, rather than promote, the cause of peace.

4.   The Revolutionary Council announces its readiness to parley with any underground armed organisation, regardless of whether it is in arms for a political cause or a racial cause, if such an organisation comes to the parley free from hard and fast conditions, to discuss and sincerely search for solutions to outstanding problems in a practical way with the real situation of the country in full view.

5.   The Revolutionary Council will carry to the parleys the basic attitude that no useful purpose will be served by heaping mutual blame for what has happened in the past and that these parleys are not designed for exploitation, but their high and constant aim should be to promote the welfare of the peasants, the workers and the working citizens of our nation.

6.   The Revolutionary Council offers safe passage to delegates of underground armed organisations proceeding to or from the parleys. Should the parleys fail the delegates shall receive not only safe conduct to the underground where they may wish to return but also three days' immunity from arrest or hostile action.[114]

Two weeks later, the leader of the Burma Communist Party in exile in China, Thakin Ba Thein Tin, met with the Burmese ambassador in Beijing, U Kyaw Win (Steinberg and Fan 2012, p. 394). Negotiations with the insurgents commenced in Yangon on 11 July, one month later. The first group of BCP exiles arrived the next day, a second group ten days later. Ne Win became personally involved in the talks from 28 October.[115] Typical of the attitude of some of the ethnic minority insurgent leaders, if not the Communists, was a belief that the Revolutionary Council had proposed the talks because the army was about to collapse. A split within the Shan State Independence Army (SSIA) group, and the strategy they adopted in the talks, is illustrative. The SSIA exiles from Thailand assumed that the peace talks were called because the army was desperate for a deal and therefore they should press their maximum demands for "federalism". The internal group, led by Chao Tzang Yawnghwe, a son of the late Sao Shwe Thaik, Sawbwa of Yawnghwe, was less sanguine and felt they should approach the talks more cautiously. Though the exiled SSIA leader opened with maximum demands, which were firmly rejected by Ne Win who was apparently not in a mood to compromise, the SSIA wanted to keep the talks going as long as possible in order to gain favourable attention (Chao 1987, p. 15).

As Martin Smith explains, the peace talks became part of both the insurgent's and government's "set-piece histories, each side continuing to repeat its own well-rehearsed version of events" (Smith 1999, p. 206). However, as he also explains, Ne Win did genuinely appear to be hoping that the talks might lead to an end to the civil war. He personally wrote to the Karen National Union military strategist Mahn Ba Zan and leaders of the Karen National United Party (KNUP) about the tragedy of the fourteen-year-long civil war for the country and appealed for their assistance, penning "I've taken hold of the tiger's tail, and can't let go."[207] Not only did the Chinese government support the talks, but their ideological rival, the Soviet Union also encouraged the Communists to reach a compromise with the government (Longmire 1989, p. 75).

The talks with Thakin Soe's Red Flag Communists, who denounced both China and Russia, broke down early and they were flown back to the jungle in Rakhine. In addition to Soe's Communists and the major Communist party, which included delegates from both China and from within the country, other delegations represented the SSIA, the Shan Nationalities United Front, *Noom Suik Harn* (Brave Young Shan), Tailand National Army, Kachin Independence Organisation, Communist Party of Arakan, as well as members of the then Communist-aligned National

Democratic United Front, Karenni National Progressive Party, New Mon State Party, and the Chin National Vanguard Party. However, on 15 November, talks with the Communists were declared a failure and the insurgents were given free passage to return to their bases or back into exile in China. The United States ambassador felt the failure of the talks with the Communists was in the U.S. interest.[116] The talks with the SSIA rebels continued until 18 December (Lintner 1999, p. 447).

The non-Communist ethnic groups put forward demands such as the establishment of autonomous states with the right of secession and similar demands which the government had previously rejected. Similarly, the Communist and Communist-aligned groups insisted on maintaining control of their own armed forces and territories they dominated. From the government's perspective, these demands amounted to "the balkanization" of Myanmar. Any such divisions could lead to outside intervention and the country could become divided and used as a Cold War pawn as were Laos, Vietnam, Korea, Germany, and the Congo.[117] Unsurprisingly, despite the optimism that surrounded the start of the talks, they concluded in failure except for the small success of the surrender of the veteran Karen leader Hunter Thamwe's splinter insurgent force.[118] However, even his forces would only follow their leader in surrendering after Ne Win sent a delegation to them in the jungle assuring them of the government's good intentions. A few months after the failure of the talks with the Shan groups, two of them, the Shan State Independence Army and the Shan United Nationalities Front, joined their miniscule forces under the leadership of the widow of Myanmar's first President, the Mahadevi of Yawnghwe. She was provided with assistance by Thai intelligence agents in her operations in Chiang Mai (Elliott 1999, pp. 347–53).

A week after the government concluded the peace talks with the Communists and most of the other groups, United States President Kennedy was assassinated. On being informed of the news in the middle of the night, Ambassador Byroade sent Ne Win a handwritten message conveying the news.[119] The Myanmar Foreign Minister did not come to the American embassy to sign the book of condolence. As claimed to be customary, only the Chief of Protocol signed the book and attended a memorial service with the Chief of the Political Division of the Foreign Ministry.[120]

On Ne Win's mind the day after Kennedy's assassination was how the Chinese government would respond to the failure of the peace talks with the Burma Communist Party. Up until then, the BCP had received no material assistance from the Chinese Communists, and their main area of operation was in the Bago Yoma, far from the Chinese border. Nonetheless, the Chinese were obviously interested in the fate of the Burmese Communists and maintained the party elite in exile in Beijing, to which Thakin Ba Thein Tin and others returned after the talks in Yangon ended in stalemate. Consequently, at the first opportunity, Ne Win sent a personal message to Beijing. When the Chinese Vice-President, Marshall He Long, stopped over at Yangon airport on his way to Indonesia on 23 November, Ne Win asked him to send word to Beijing that the failure of the peace talks was an internal affair and did not have any impact on the bilateral relations between the two neighbours (Steinberg and Fan 2012, p. 395). The same point was certainly made when Ne Win hosted a dinner when Chinese Premier Chou En-lai stopped at Yangon again on 13 December. Also at the dinner, along with the Chinese Ambassador and Foreign Minister Thi Han, was Health and Education Minister Hla Han. He had headed the Council team that negotiated with the White Flag Communists.[121]

The talks with the insurgents had apparently gone on in parallel with some feelers to the government from the remaining AFPFL leader, acting president U Tun Win. Tun Win allegedly met with Ne Win on 7 October when they discussed how the party might be able to cooperate with the Revolutionary Council. Ne Win reportedly claimed that he could not release the arrested AFPFL leaders at that time as it would be misunderstood and perhaps lead to armed conflict. He was also concerned that Kyaw Nyein, if released, would attempt to assassinate him but he could work with Ba Swe or Nu because they were honest and straightforward. He advised the party not to try to get their members released from prison via the courts because, as Ne Win was reported to have said, "the members of the court would be handpicked by me and they would have no chance."[122]

The first months of 1964 saw further policy measures designed to ensure the isolation of the country from the outside world. New visa rules were introduced in January. Tourist visas were suspended and only twenty-four hour transit visas were issued. The West German ambassador thought that this was to stop journalists from coming to write negative stories about the Burmese Way to Socialism.[123] Whatever the case, Myanmar under Ne Win was increasingly gaining the reputation of an isolated nation. Though occasional scholars, official aid workers, United Nations staff, and foreign diplomats came and went, the number was small and the nightlife and restaurant scene that had once played to the expatriate population soon closed down. Visas to journalists in future were issued for reasons of state, not to entertain or titillate international audiences.

Ne Win gave a lengthy address at the Peasants Seminar at Mount Popa on 2 January 1964. In his speech, he criticized the farmers who, for untenable reasons, claimed to be unable to repay the loans the government had advanced them. The government had loaned out Kt 700 million the previous year, but in its second year it could only provide Kt 400 million because of a shortfall in repayments. For a variety of reasons, the agricultural sector was clearly faltering, with a decline in rice production of 10 per cent over the peak production in 1962 (Badgley 1965, pp. 56–57). Ne Win also defended the inability of the government to quickly resolve the problem of tenancy and usufruct, saying that every government faced the same problem and asking for patience. Aware of the plotting against his government during the previous year, and the attempts by his enemies to seek foreign support, he called on his audience of 20,000 from the northern and central reaches of the country to remain loyal.[124] Two days later, he hosted a garden party at his residence for 1,000 persons, including peasants and workers as well as intellectuals and "the widows of the nation's fallen leaders".[125]

Rumours of Bo Set Kya's activities in Bangkok, London and Washington to generate support for a movement to oust Ne Win was rife in Yangon by January. Dr Ba Maw, the former Adipati Ashin Mingyi, and now grand old man of Burmese politics, explained to an official of the American embassy, in what appeared to have been a slightly fanciful set of stories, that Thakin Tha Khin was also assisting Bo Set Kya. Ba Maw's son, Zali Maw, was Set Kya's legal advisor. Ba Maw claimed that Set Kya was broadcasting demands that Ne Win step down and restore democracy from Thailand by 31 January or he would invade with his "Forty Comrades". Neither Ba Maw nor any American listening agency had heard these broadcasts, but he was convinced they were being made.[126] Ne Win had also got wind of Set Kya's plotting and believed that he was trying to organize the dwindling Burmese business community to move against him, including his assassination, according to Lord Louis Mountbatten.[127] A number of arrests were made of persons thought to be implicated in the Set Kya plotting, which was said to have included Bo Let Ya.[128]

Apparently, Ne Win and Daw Khin May Than had an informal three-hour discussion with a leading educator and his wife on 25 January. According to the wife, who reported to the American embassy, Ne Win admitted that he "... had made a mistake dealing with university students; would have been better to treat them like a father". He also complained of his officers keeping information from him, such as a recent shortage of cooking oil in the markets. He also expressed his dislike of foreign embassies and of Burmese who hung around them seeking favours. He particularly disliked the Russians for their heavy drinking and encouraging

Burmese students to do the same. The wife felt that security around Ne Win had been tightened even further following the assassination of President Kennedy.[129]

At the end of January 1964, Lord Mountbatten made the first of several trips to Myanmar to meet with Ne Win informally. On this occasion, they spent a day together at the beach resort of Ngapali on the Rakhine coast at the state guest house where, as Mountbatten wrote in his diary, Ne Win was "so alone and aloof that he has absolutely nobody in whom he can confide" (Ziegler 1989, p. 89). Lord Mountbatten told General Ne Win that, "in spite of his Socialisation laws, the British Government backed him to the full, not only because they believed in him personally, but because clearly he could be a stabilising factor in the very unstable world of South-East Asia."[130]

"On the insurgency", according to notes on their discussions made by the British,

> General Ne Win indicated ... that the day, January 31, would see the expiry of the General Amnesty; from then on he would launch an all-out offensive against the insurgents. It was out of the question that he should have any further truck with the Red Flag, White Flag or any other Communist insurgent group. He was determined to crush insurgency and proposed to do so partly by military means — the army had hitherto only deployed part of its strength but would now bring its full force to bear — and partly by economic means. As to the latter, he pinned great hopes upon the system of Government agricultural loans to paddy farmers. Of the loans occasionally granted by the previous civil administrations, only half had reached the farmers, the rest having been pocketed by the politicians. As a result of his reforms the farmer was assured of loans at low rates of interest and also of getting the full amount.

As for the future, Ne Win did not trust the old politicians or civil servants, but when the insurgency problem had been resolved, he might make some conciliatory moves, perhaps releasing U Nu and his ministers rather than putting them on trial for "corruption and other misdemeanours". He also believed he could put the former Chief Justice, U Myint Thein, on trial for advising the Shan Sawbwa on how they could implement the secession clause of the former constitution. Turning to foreign affairs, the name of Ambassador Byroade arose. Byroade had been a liaison officer at Mountbatten's Kandy headquarters during the Second World War. With regards to American policy, the only remark of substance volunteered by Ne Win was that the United States "was trying to buy friends in South-East Asia". When asked of his views on the Britain-Burma Society in London of which Mountbatten had been founding patron in 1957, Ne Win indicated he had no objection as there were many Burma-Soviet Society branches across Myanmar.[131]

At the end of the first two years of his rule, Ne Win might have concluded that despite ongoing problems, he was managing things fairly well. In terms of domestic politics, as to be expected, the old elite, represented by Bo Set Kya and Bo Let Ya and their ilk, opposed him but they could be easily locked up and put aside as needs be. Soon, all political parties other than the BSPP would be made illegal.[132] On the downside, however, the failure of the peace talks had closed off the possibility of rebuilding the leftist unity of the past, but it had cleared the air and now he could prosecute the war against the Communists and other insurgents both militarily and with economic policies designed to mobilize the peasants and workers to support the government. The capitalists were on the run and despite problems of implementation in the early days, the Burmese Way to Socialism looked to be getting under way. While ethnic insurgencies persisted, and some were receiving training in Thailand,[133] the army would be able to cope eventually and in the meantime, they would be contained.

Similarly, in terms of foreign relations, Ne Win could sleep well at night despite the threats of assassination from his opponents. Both the British and American governments had sent high-level emissaries to assure Ne Win, despite their dissatisfaction with his socialist policies, when push came to shove, they would back Burma and its independence against any outside power. Nearer neighbours, bigger and more powerful than Burma, had indicated that they had no outstanding problems in their relations with the Ne Win government. The General and his wife departed on 8 February for a two-day visit to New Delhi for two cordial meetings with the ailing Prime Minister Nehru.[134] A few days later, Chinese Premier Chou En-lai and Marshall Chen Yi, both of whom knew Ne Win well from earlier encounters, came to Yangon for a four-day visit. On their departure on 18 February, a joint communiqué was issued reaffirming the communiqué issued at the end of Liu Shao-chi's visit in the previous year in regard to non-interference in domestic affairs.[135]

Casting his mind back further in Myanmar's recent history, and his place in it, Ne Win might well have agreed with Count de Tocqueville when he wrote,

But when the virile generation which had launched the Revolution had perished or (as usually befalls a generation engaging in such ventures) its first fine energy had dwindled; and when, as was but to be expected after a spell of anarchy and "popular" dictatorship, the ideal of freedom had lost much of its appeal and the nation, at a loss where to turn, began to cast round for a master — under these conditions the state was set for a return to one-man government. Indeed, never had conditions been more favourable for its establishment and consolidation, and the man of genius destined at once to carry on and to abolish the Revolution was quick to turn them to account (Tocqueville 1955, pp. 208–9).

In the name of Revolution, Ne Win did not intend to put an end to it, but he had set himself on a course which was to construct a regime which would shape the future of his country long after his death. Over time that regime would become incapable of foreseeing the challenges that the present and future would create. When faced with new realities, it knew not how to respond. Looking backward, he did not look forward, but that was still decades away.

Notes

1. Chit Hlaing, "The Tatmadaw and My Political Career", unpublished paper, translated by Kyaw Yin Hlaing, p. 5. Moderate elements in the army shared the view that the coup was prompted by both Nu's establishing Buddhism as the state religion and the threat of the Shan States seceding under the auspices of the Sawbwa. See Colonel Chit Myaing, "In His Own Words", *Burma Debate*, vol. IV, no. 3 (July/August 1997): 11–24.
2. Dr Borneman report, 3 March 1962, AA PA B 12 Bd. 1, 190, 238–39.
3. On the day of the coup, the Revolutionary Council issued a statement to that effect. See Burma Socialist Programme Party Central Organising Committee, *Foreign Policy of the Revolutionary Government of the Union of Burma* (Yangon: Burma Socialist Programme Party, 1968), pp. 5–6.
4. For a view of the coup by the daughter of Sao Shwe Thaik, who was then in Laos with her British journalist husband covering talks of the Laotian civil war, see Sanda, The *Moon Princess: Memories of the Shan States* (Bangkok: River Books, 2008), pp. 261–64.
5. As opposed to U Nu's notion of revolution, *ayeidawbon*. Robert H. Taylor, "The Burmese Concept of Revolution", in *Context, Meaning and Power in Southeast Asia*, edited by Mark Hobart and Robert H. Taylor (Ithaca, New York: Cornell University Southeast Asia Program, 1986), pp. 79–92.
6. Quoted in Mya Han and Thein Hlaing, *Myanmar Politics 1958–1962, Volume IV*, translated by Sai Aung Tun (Yangon: U Win Aung, April 2001), p. 165, quoting *The Nation*, 4 March 1962.

7. Ibid., p. 169.
8. Mya Han and Thein Hlaing, *Myanmar Politics 1958–1962, Volume IV*, p. 174, quoting *The Nation*, 4 March 1962.
9. Telegram, Rangoon to Secretary of State, 3 May 1962, Rangoon 824 790b.00/5-362 XR 611.70b41, Control 2524, No. 824.
10. Saw Oo and Chit Hlaing were both former members of the Myanmar Communist parties, White Flag and Red Flag, respectively.
11. Chit Hlaing, "The Tatmadaw and My Political Career", p. 11. A similar version of Chit Hlaing's life and his involvement in the writing of the ideology of the BSPP is found in Part III. U Chit Hlaing, "A Short Note on My Involvement in the Burma Socialist Programme Party (Unrevised Version)", in *Soe, Socialism and Chit Hlaing, Memories*, edited by Hans-Bernd Zollner, Myanmar Literature Project, Working Paper no. 10:10 (Passau: Passau University, n.d.), pp. 114–61.
12. Ibid., pp. 11–12.
13. Phoumi, a cousin of then Thai Prime Minister Sarit Thanarat, often attracted scatological references. President John F. Kennedy referred to him as a "total shit". Seth Jacobs, *The Universe Unraveling: American Foreign Policy in Cold War Laos* (Ithaca and London: Cornell University Press, 2012), pp. 5 and 7.
14. Yoshihiro Nakanishi, *Strong Soldiers, Failed Revolution: The State and Military in Burma, 1962–88* (Kyoto: Kyoto University Press, 2013), pp. 79–84 and 91–95, provides a useful discussion of the evolution of the thinking of Chit Hlaing during his student revolutionary days in the 1940s, his period in Europe in the 1950s, and his joining the Department of Psychological Warfare. He, however, is misleading when he makes a distinction between Chit Hlaing's writings as "propaganda" and his preparation of the "ideology" of the Revolutionary Council. The line between ideology and propaganda is a thin one, if it exists at all. That Chit Hlaing believed what he wrote at the time to have been true is undeniable, though after 1988 he repudiated his earlier views. As Emerson wrote, "a foolish consistency is the hobgoblin of little minds". Chit Hlaing was not narrow minded. For more on Chit Hlaing's thought, see "Part One: Maung Chit Hlaing's Man's World View", in *Red Peacocks: Commentaries on Burmese Socialist Nationalism*, edited by John H. Badgeley and Aye Kyaw (New Delhi: Readworthy, 2009), pp. 1–94.
15. This was the Colonel Tin U who became chairman of the National League for Democracy in 1988. Interview with U Shwe Than, 3 March 2007.
16. Ibid., p. 17; *Towhlanyei Kaungsi ei Hluthsaungchet Thamaing Akyinchut* [Concise History of the Actions of the Revolutionary Council] (Rangoon: Printing and Publishing Corporation, 2 March 1974), p. 12.
17. *Forward*, vol. 1, no. 2 (22 August 1962): 2.
18. "The Revolutionary Council Announcement on Formation of a Political Party", *Forward*, vol. 1, no. 1 (7 August 1962): 5.
19. The United State government, believing in the so-called "domino theory" which asserted that "if Laos should fall to the Communists, then it would

just be a question of time until South Vietnam, Cambodia, Thailand and Burma would collapse". "Laos was the key to the entire area of Southeast Asia". "Memorandum of Conference on January 19, 1961 between President Eisenhower and President-Elect Kennedy on the Subject of Laos", Memorandum from Clark Clifford to President Johnson, 29 September 1967. *The Pentagon Papers: The Defense Department History of United States Decision-making on Vietnam (The Senator Gravel Edition)*, Vol. II (Boston: Beacon Press, n.d.), pp. 635–37.

20. Ger Emb Amb Bottler to AA, 10 May 1962, AA PA B 12 Bd. 1 190, 232; also AA PA B 12, Bd.1.198, 387.

21. Ger Emb Amb Bottler to AA, 12 May 1962, AA PA B 12 Bd.1.198, 388–91.

22. Ger Emb Amb Bottler to AA, 8 June 1962, AA PA B 12, Bd.1.190, 260–67.

23. *Towhlanyei Kaungsi ei Hluthsaungchet Thamaing Akyinchut*, p. 17.

24. Ger Emb Amb Bottler to AA, 13 July 1962, AA PA B 12 Bd.1.190, 268–72. He made the same point later in July to the United States Undersecretary of State W. Averill Harriman in Vienna. Memorandum of Conversation, General Ne Win and Ambassador W. Averill Harriman, 9 September 1966.

25. See discussion in Chapter 13, pp. 538–39.

26. *Forward*, vol. 1, no. 2 (22 August 1962): 3

27. See Maung Maung, "Htain Lin, A Young PVO Insurgent", originally published in *The Guardian* in December 1955 and reprinted in *Dr Maung Maung: Gentleman, Scholar, Patriot*, edited by Robert H. Taylor (Singapore: Institute of Southeast Asian Studies, 2008), pp. 183–89.

28. Ger Emb Yan, Amb Bottler to AA, 13 July 1962, AA BA B 12 Bd. 1.212, 577.

29. Telegram, Allen to FCO, 4 July 1962, FO 371/166404.

30. PREM 11/4650; Telegram, Allen to FO, 9 July 1962, FO 371/166404.

31. Ger Emb YGB Amb Bottler to AA, 14 July 1962, AA BA B Bd.1.212, 579.

32. Interview, Dr Franz Gerstenbrand, Vienna; Dr Hans Hoff, 1897–1969, was successor at the University of Vienna to the professorship once held by Sigmund Freud. Unlike Freud, he used drugs as an aid to treatment. See memoriam to Dr Hoff by Andrew K. Bernath, M.D., in *The American Journal of Psychiatry*, vol. 128, no. 8 (1 February 1970): 1178.

33. Interview with University Professor Dr H.C. Mult. Franz Gerstenbrand, Vienna, 14 September 2008.

34. Telegram, Allen to FO, 9 July 1962, FO 371/166404.

35. Ger Emb Vienna, Hoffmann to AA, 18 July 1962, AA BA B 12 Bd.1.212, 580.

36. Memorandum of Conversation, General Ne Win and Ambassador W. Averill Harriman, 9 September 1966.

37. Telegram, Geneva to Secretary of State, 18 July 1962, 7908.00/7-1862, Control 12670, No. 49.

38. AA Randow reports, 3 September 1962, AA PA B 12 Bd.1.203, 135–36; Sante reports, 3 September 1962, AA PA B 12, Bd.1203, 138.

39. Papers in FO 371/166405.

40. Record of Conversation, 21 September 1962, PREM 11/4650; FO371/ 166405.

41. Prem 11/4650

42. Telegram, Ger Emb Ygn Amb Bottler to AA, 16 October 1962, AA BA B 12 Bd.1.212, 581–83.

43. *Viet Nam and Southeast Asia: Report of Senators Mike Mansfield, J. Caleb Boggs, Claiborne Pell, and Benjamin A. Smith to the Committee on Foreign Relations, United States Senate* (Washington, D.C.: U.S. Government Printing Office, 1963), pp. 15–16. This reiterated the same point made by Mansfield when reporting on a trip to Southeast Asia to President Kennedy in December 1962. Noting that the United States had a minimal commitment to both Malaya and Burma, he wrote, "In the case of Burma, this fortuitous state of affairs would appear to be largely one of Burmese choice." *Two Reports on Vietnam and Southeast Asia to the President of the United States by Senator Mike Mansfield* (Washington, D.C.: U.S. Government Printing Office, 1973, reprinted report of 18 December 1962), p. 13.

44. Telegram, Rangoon to Secretary of State, 30 November 1962, 120.1500/11-3062 XR 6/611.90b.

45. Letter, S.B. Hebblethwaite to F.A. Warren, 28 December 1962, FO371/ 170528.

46. *Forward*, vol. 1, no. 8 (7 November 1962): 3.

47. The widow of General Aung San and mother of National League for Democracy Chairperson Daw Aung San Suu Kyi, whom U Nu had appointed ambassador to India in 1960 following her support for him in the elections that year, stayed on as Ne Win's representative until 1967.

48. *Towhlanyei Kaungsi ei Hluthsaungchet Thamaing Akyinchut*, p. 218.

49. Indonesia, Burma, Cambodia, Sri Lanka, Egypt, and Ghana attended.

50. Despatch No. 3, Colombo Conference, DO 196/182; Pamphlet entitled Conference of Six Afro-Asian Non-Aligned Countries, Colombo, 10–12 December 1962, DO196/183.

51. Letter, T.T. Gatty, Bangkok, to C.J. Howells, 28 December 1962, FO371/166621; *Towhlanyei Kaungsi ei Hluthsaungchet Thamaing Akyinchut*, p. 218.

52. *Towhlanyei Kaungsi ei Hluthsaungchet Thamaing Akyinchut*, p. 22.

53. *Forward*, vol. 1, no. 2 (7 January 1963): 21.

54. Telegram, Schnee to Secretary of State (SOS), 10 December 1963, Rangoon 390 Pol 15-1, Burma Control 6222, No. 390.

55. Moscow: Progress Publishers, 1978.

56. Interview by Tang Shuyi, "Former Chinese Ambassador to Myanmar Cheng Ruisheng's Narration", *International Herald Leader* (Beijing), 26 December 2003. I am indebted to Professor Fan Hongwei for the reference.

57. *Towhlanyei Kaungsi ei Hluthsaungchet Thamaing Akyinchut*, p. 40.

58. A new board of directors then took over the company, chaired by Brigadier Aung Gyi and including amongst its seven members, Brigadier Tin Pe and Foreign Minister U Thi Han. *Forward*, vol. 1, no. 2 (7 January 1963): 24.

59. "Independence Day Message", *Forward*, vol. 1, no. 12 (22 January 1963): 9–10, quotation from p. 10.

60. *Towhlanyei Kaungsi ei Hluthsaungchet Thamaing Akyinchut*, p. 10.

61. Pyihtaungsu Myanmar Naingngan Towhlanyei Kaungsi [Union of Myanmar Revolutionary Council], *Myanmar Hsoshelit Lansin Pati ei Witheitha Latkangmya* [Specific Characteristics of the Myanmar Socialist Programme Party] (Yangon: Myanmar Socialist Programme Party, Party Affairs Central Committee, 4 September 1964). For a fuller discussion of the ideology of the BSPP, see Robert H. Taylor, *The State in Myanmar* (London: Hurst; Honolulu: University of Hawaii Press; Singapore: NUS Press, 2009), pp. 298–300 and 361–65.

62. *Towhlanyei Kaungsi ei Hluthsaungchet Thamaing Akyinchut*, p. 224; Letter, G.C. Whitteredge to Earl of Home, 7 February 1963. FO 371/1588.

63. According to Colonel Chit Myaing, "In His Own Words", pp. 11–24.

64. Interview with Brigadier General (retired) Aung Gyi, 9 March 2006.

65. For Chit Myaing's account of Aung Gyi's conflict with Tin Pe, see Colonel Chit Myaing, "In His Own Words", pp. 11–24.

66. *Towhlanyei Kaungsi ei Hluthsaungchet Thamaing Akyinchut*, p. 14.

67. "Pyi Htaungsu Nei Mein Hkwan" (Union Day Speech), *Myanmar Hsoshelit Lansin Pati Ukkatakyi ei Hkit Pyaung Towhlanyei Thamaing Mein Kwan Paung Hkyut* [Collected Era Changing Historical Speeches by the Chairman of the Myanmar Socialist Programme Party], Volume 2 (Yangon: Myanmar Hsoshelit Lansin Pati Central Committee Headquarters, 1985), pp. 17–18.

68. *Hkit Pyaung Tawhlanyei Thamaing Win Meinhkun Paungkyut*, Vol. 2, pp. 316–28.

69. Ibid., pp. 74–83; translated as "Living and Working Together", *Forward*, vol. 1, no. 20 (22 May 1963): 12–13.

70. *Hkit Pyaung Tawhlanyei Thamaing Win Meinhkun Paungkyut*, Vol. 2, pp. 370–75; translated at "Preserving and Enriching National Culture", *Forward*, vol. 1, no. 21 (7 June 1963): 6–7.

71. All night performances of the Jataka tales with singers, dancers and puppeteers. Villages would collectively raise the funds to pay the itinerant performers.

72. Ba Nyein had been a member of top rank Burma Civil Service but resigned in order to join the Burma Workers' and Peasants' Party and subsequently the National United Front. He became financial advisor to the Revolutionary Government and later Vice Chairman of the Worker's Council. N. Nyun-Han, "Burma's Experiment with Socialism" (unpublished PhD dissertation, University of Colorado, 1970), p. 45, fn. 1. Ne Win was said to have had

a high regard for Ba Nyein for the sacrifice he made in resigning from the prestigious top civil service to devote himself to politics in a cause then unlikely to succeed. However, at about the time Ba Nyein was joining the NUF's predecessor, the Burma Workers' and Peasants' Party, Ne Win was accusing the party of double-crossing him. See Chapter 5, pp. 107–58.

73. Ger Emb Ygn Amb Bottler to AA, 18 March 1963, AA PA B 37, Bd. 24, 762–67.
74. *Towhlanyei Kaungsi ei Hluthsaungchet Thamaing Akyinchut*, p. 40.
75. Ibid., p. 19.
76. *Towhlanyei Kaungsi ei Hluthsaungchet Thamaing Akyinchut*, p. 22.
77. Excerpted in Burma Socialist Programme Party Central Organising Committee, *Foreign Policy of the Revolutionary Government of the Union of Burma* (Yangon: Burma Socialist Programme Party, 1968), p. 25.
78. Airgram, Yangon to SOS, 30 March 1963, POL-Burma, Control 2765.
79. Airgram, James V. Martin to Department of State, 5 April 1963, Pol 17-4 Burma Jap No. A-537.
80. *Towhlanyei Kaungsi ei Hluthsaungchet Thamaing Akyinchut*, p. 144.
81. Ger Emb Ygn Hillegart to AA, 8 April 1963, AA PA B 37, Bd. 24, 777–79.
82. *Towhlanyei Kaungsi ei Hluthsaungchet Thamaing Akyinchut*, p. 220.
83. *Towhlanyei Kaungsi ei Hluthsaungchet Thamaing Akyinchut*, p. 21.
84. *Hkit Pyaung Tawhlanyei Thamaing Win Meinhkun Paungkyut*, Vol. 2, pp. 201–11; translated in *Forward*, vol. 1, no. 19 (7 May 1963): 24.
85. Airgram, Memorandum of Conversation with General Ne Win by Amb. John Scott Everton, 10 May 1963, Pol Burma U.S. No. A-587; Telegram, Everton to SOS, 4 May 1963, Rangoon 597 Pol Burma U.S. Control 2875, No. 597.
86. Ibid.
87. Airgram, Rangoon to SOS, conversation with Philippine Trade Minister, 21 May 1963, E.5 Burma XR Inco Rice Burma XR Pol Burma-Phil.
88. Telegram, Rangoon to SOS, 15 April 1963, Pol 26 Control 1016, No. 568.
89. Bertil Lintner, *Burma in Revolt: Opium and Insurgency since 1948*, 2nd ed. (Chiang Mai. Silkworm Books, 1999), p. 447; Josef Silverstein, "First Steps on the Burmese Road to Socialism", *Asian Survey*, vol. IV, no. 2 (February 1964): 721. Law-Yone told the story years later that he was arrested for having an affair with Daw Khin May Than. See Wendy Law-Yone, *Golden Parasol: A Daughter's Memoir of Burma* (London: Chatto and Windus, 2013), pp. 249–53.
90. Telegram, Byroade to SOS, 31 July 1964, LBJ Library, Box 235, Burma Cables Vol. 7/64-12/68.
91. Airgram, Rangoon to SOS, 24 May 1963, Pol 26, No. A-640.
92. Telegram, Rangoon to SOS, 30 May 1963, Pol 6, Control 24198, No. 652.
93. Telegram, Rangoon to SOS, 7 June 1963, Pol 26, Control 5359, No. 667.
94. Airgram, Rangoon to SOS, 19 June 1963, Pol 26 Burma A-62.
95. Airgram, Rangoon to SOS, 27 September 1963, Pol 26 Burma XR SOC 12-1 Burma.

96. Equipment was provided to anti-Communist monks in Mandalay at about that time or earlier by the United States consulate, according to an interview with Ruth McLendon, Political/Consular Officer, Rangoon (1962–66), but when she and Ambassador Byroade were approached directly by a leading anti-Communist monk, they denied him support. Association for Diplomatic Studies and Training, 2012, Burma, pp. 57–58.

97. Telegram, Schnee to SOS, 11 June 1963, Pol 6, Control 8443, No. 869.

98. Interview with Dr Franz Gerstandbrand, 8 September 2008, Vienna.

99. Letter, S.H. Hepplethwaite to F.A. Warner, 26 June 1963, FO372/169784.

100. Telegram, Rangoon to SOS, 20 September 1963, Rangoon 189 Pol 12-9 Burma Control 15547, No. 189.

101. Telegram, Byroade to SOS, 27 November 1963, Rangoon 354 Pol 27 Burma Control 17688, No. 354. Though often speculated that Ne Win did not like or trust Clift, there is no evidence that his dismissal was due to fact that he was an Anglo-Burmese with a British wife. Third in command of the Air Force, Lieutenant Colonel Thaung Dan, who had been instrumental in the peace talks with the Communists, at personal risk to himself, presumably deserved a promotion and Clift was known to have had clashes with others in the Revolutionary Council, though not Ne Win. Ibid.

102. Airgram, Embassy Rangoon to SOS on Subject: The Union Revolutionary Council and Leadership in Burma, 12 July 1963, Pol 15 Burma A-16.

103. Burma Socialist Programme Party Central Organising Committee, *Foreign Policy of the Revolutionary Government of the Union of Burma* (Yangon: Burma Socialist Programme Party, 1968), pp. 108–9.

104. Airgram, James V. Martin to Department of State, 20 September 1963, Pol 15 Burma No. A-124.

105. Telegram, Rangoon to SOS, 16 October 1963, Pol 26 Burma, Control 13057, No. 266.

106. Memorandum of Conversation: The Efforts of Bo Setkya to Gain Support for a Coup in Burma, Louis Walinsky and John Seabury Thompson, 23 November 1963, Pol 26 Burma.

107. Byroade, born in 1913, became head of German Affairs in the U.S. State Department under Secretary of State Dean Acheson, having been "loaned 'at a cocktail party'". With an advanced engineering degree from Cornell University, Byroade "because of his military background, sleek dress, and reputation as a 'ladies' man' with 'playboy instincts', he cut a colorful swath … and gained Acheson's admiration as a shrew analyst". After working on the transition of Germany from military to civilian rule, Byroade turned his analytical skills to the Middle East, focusing particularly on Arab relations with Israel. Robert L. Beisner, *Dean Acheson: A Life in the Cold War* (Oxford: Oxford University Press, 2006), p. 116. Someone who worked with him said that he had divorced his first wife to take the wife of a member of his staff at his previous post. He was attentive to the ladies but never

improper. Interview, Robert S. Steven, Economic Officer, Rangoon (1962–64), Association for Diplomatic Studies and Training, 2012, Burma, p. 49. Prior to Burma, Byroade has been ambassador to Egypt, South Africa, and Afghanistan.

108. Interview, Edward C. Ingraham, Political Counselor, Rangoon (1967–70), Association for Diplomatic Studies and Training, 2012, Burma, p. 82.

109. Byroade was thoroughly briefed and prepared for the interview. See interview with Ruth McLendon, Political/Consular Officer, Rangoon (1962–66), Association for Diplomatic Studies and Training, 2012, Burma, p. 61.

110. Byroade to SOS, 7 October 1963, Rangoon 245 Pol Burma-U.S. Control 4856, No. 245.

111. Second telegram, section two of two, Byroade to SOS, 7 October 1962, Rangoon 245 Pol Burma-U.S. Control 4856, No. 246.

112. Interview with Henry Byroade, Ambassador, Burma (1963–69), Association for Diplomatic Studies and Training, 2012, Burma, p. 68.

113. *Towhlanyei Kaungsi ei Hluthsaungchet Thamaing Akyinchut*, p. 12.

114. *Forward*, vol. 1, no. 10 (22 June 1963): 2.

115. *Towhlanyei Kaungsi ei Hluthsaungchet Thamaing Akyinchut*, p. 13.

116. Telegram, Rangoon to SOS, Harriman from Byroade, 5 December 1963, Rangoon 277 Pol 27 Burma Control 3639, No. 377.

117. A view shared by others as well. See Thein Pe Myint, *Kyaw Nyein* (Yangon: Pyithu Sapei Taik, 1962) and the same author's *Critique of the Communist Movement in Burma*, mimeographed, circa 1967, pp. 32–33.

118. He was eventually sent as ambassador to Israel. Smith notes that intercepted signals between the KNU headquarters and the KNU delegation on their way to Yangon for the peace talks allowed the government to split the KNU delegation, facilitating his defection. Martin Smith, *Burma: Insurgency and the Politics of Ethnicity*, 2nd ed. (London: Zed Books, 1999), p. 217.

119. Byroade sent a personal handwritten note to Ne Win's residence as soon as he was informed of Kennedy's death. Interview, Robert S. Steven, Economic Officer, Rangoon (1962–64), Association for Diplomatic Studies and Training, 2012, Burma, p. 48.

120. Telegram, Byroade to SOS, 27 November 1963, Rangoon 354 Pol 27 Burma, Control 17668, No. 354.

121. Telegram, Schnee to SOS, 23 December 1963, Rangoon 423 Pol 7 Chicom Pol 7 Burma-Chicom.

122. Memorandum of Conversation: U Hla Htway Explains AFPFL Policies, U Hla Htway, sub-editor of *The Nation* and Robert W. Mount, USIS, 14 November 1963, Enclosure No. 1 A-218 from Rangoon. Tun Win, former editor of the *Mandaing* daily newspaper, the organ of the AFPFL, lived quietly in Yangon until he was nominated as Burma's ambassador to the United States in January 1966. Letter, Dean Rusk to President Johnson, 3 January 1966, LBJ Library, Box 235, Burma Cables Vol. I. 7/64-

12/68. On how the Revolutionary Council removed the independence of the judiciary in politically significant cases, see Nicholas Cheesman, "How an Authoritarian Regime in Burma Used Special Courts to Defeat Judicial Independence", *Law and Society Review*, vol. 45, no. 4 (2011): 801–26.

123. Ger Emb Ygn Amb Bottler to AA, 9 January 1964, AA PA B 37, Bd. 24, 785.

124. *Hkit Pyaung Tawhlanyei Thamaing Win Meinhkun Paungkyut*, vol. 2, pp. 83–90.

125. *Forward*, vol. 2, no. 2 (7 January 1964): 2.

126. Byroade to SOS, 24 January 1963, Pol Burma 24.

127. Confidential extracts from the record of the meeting between Lord Mountbatten, Chief of the Defence Staff, and General Ne Win, Chairman of the Revolutionary Council of the Union of Burma on 30 and 31 January 1964. Around this time, Bo Let Ya disappeared and Saw Kya Doe, who was General Manager of Let Ya and Company, soon followed. See the account by an employee of Let Ya and Company in Spencer Zan, *Life's Journey in Faith: Burma, from Riches to Rags* (Bloomington, Indiana: Author House, 2007), pp. 173–74. This group often met at the student hostel for American missionary children in Bangkok which was managed by Spencer Zan. When he advised them to seek talks with Ne Win before attempting to organize an army to remove him, they replied, "We'll kill the son-of-a-bitch". The Mahadevi of Yawnghwe was involved in the talks and Zan had frequent calls from the American embassy which he assumed were from CIA agents. He and the others were often followed by persons suspected of being Myanmar Military Intelligence officers in Bangkok. Ibid., pp. 238–39 and 248, and *passim*.

128. Airgram, Rangoon to SOS, Continued Reverberations from Bo Letya-Bo Setkya Plots, 27 January 1964, Pol 23-9 Burma No. A-326.

129. Telegram, Rangoon to SOS, 31 January 1964, Rangoon 505 Pol Burma Control 23991.

130. Confidential extracts from the record of the meeting between Lord Mountbatten, Chief of the Defence Staff, and General Ne Win, Chairman of the Revolutionary Council of the Union of Burma on 30 and 31 January 1964.

131. Ibid.

132. Under the Law to Protect National Unity or the National Unity Protection Law which was promulgated on 28 March 1964.

133. Letter, P.H.R. Marshall to R.H. Hanbury-Tenison, SEAD, 5 March 1964, FO371/175349.

134. Papers in DO 196/332.

135. *Towhlanyei Kaungsi ei Hluthsaungchet Thamaing Akyinchut*, p. 220; David I. Steinberg and Fan Hongwei, *Modern China-Myanmar Relations: Dilemmas of Mutual Dependence* (Copenhagen: NIAS Press, 2012), p. 395.

9

COLD WAR GENERAL
(March 1964 to February 1967)

Sympathy for the favourite nation, facilitating the illusion of an imaginary common interest in cases where no real common interest exists, and infusing into one the enmities of the other, betrays the former into a participation of the quarrels and wars of the latter without adequate inducement or justification.

President George Washington's Farewell Address

Two years after seizing power, Ne Win had settled into the job he had created for himself. There was no going back to the old parliamentary system. The die was cast. National unity and preservation of the state depended upon him, he concluded, and the tools he had available to him, primarily the army. But Ne Win saw himself as a political figure, not just a military leader, and therefore developing the Party became part of his plans for building a new, socialist, secure Myanmar in a hostile environment. That hostile environment included not only foreign states with, if not designs on Myanmar, at least a keen interest in what happened in the country. It also included personal enemies that he had made not only as the general who led the army in the civil war but also as the political figure who had decided his old colleagues were not up to the tasks they were given.

Ne Win and Daw Khin May Than had taken no medical treatment or foreign trip in 1963, but in 1964 they were able to take a two-month holiday. Busy as he was with governmental affairs, his life, while hectic, began to settle to a routine. He called fewer and fewer meetings of the Revolutionary Council, often deciding matters directly with the relevant ministers or officials on his own. He encouraged ministers not to interfere in the work of other ministers but to stick to their own affairs. Mired in much detail, he was unable to keep track of the activities of some of his colleagues, particularly Brigadier Tin Pe and Colonel Than Sein, who were responsible for economic affairs.[1] When he was in Yangon, his day normally began at about 6:30 in the morning. Daw Khin May Than rose before him to read the newspapers and listen to the English and Burmese services of the BBC as well as Myanmar Athan. He also read the Burmese newspapers before they met for breakfast at 8:15 Daw Khin May Than would then brief him on world news. At nine, he went across to a separate building opposite the Presidential residence and worked until mid-afternoon, after which he would depart for a round of golf. After dinner and a few pegs of whisky, normally no more than three, he retired to bed around 10 p.m. During the course of the evening, Daw Khin May Than would read to him news reports from rolls provided by News Agency Burma (NAB). She would read off the title of a topic and he would decide whether he wanted to hear the full report.[2] Always a family man, though not, because of his heavy responsibilities, closely involved in his children's upbringing. He provided a home for a learned monk, the head of a monastery at Paukkaung and a relative of his father, in a modest house built by a previous president in the Presidential compound.[3]

The third year of the revolution continued on much as the first and second, though with more routine and fewer surprise moves. The moderate Colonel Chit Myaing, a close ally of Brigadier Aung Gyi, resigned from the Revolutionary Council on 1 April 1964, and was briefly detained in prison. However, as became customary when Ne Win's old friends were asked or forced to stand aside, another post was found for him. In his case, U Chit Myaing became ambassador to Belgrade and eventually, London. U Aung Gyi, after a few years, opened a tea shop which was always ensured of getting supplies from the state stores at favourable prices. Those in the Western diplomatic community who speculated on Ne Win's programmes and policies became increasingly cut off from contact with him and his government. Believing Ne Win was surrounded by ill-educated men who kept bad news from him, Ambassador Byroade wrote at the end of April 1964:

> One of the most dangerous aspects of the General's present habits has been an increasing isolation from all contacts that could give him a true picture of what his lackeys are daily administering upon the people of Burma. Reportedly his irritability and increasing tendency to rant and rave have caused those still around him with some moderation and objectivity to remain silent. We hear that seldom anyone volunteers advice or information to him except the leftists who still implant their own seeds (often against the U.S.) for this own obvious purpose. His isolation apparently embraces a lack of interest in foreign affairs to the point where even communications from other heads of state are ignored and left unanswered.

Discounting the American ambassador's concerns about "leftist advisors", Byroade nonetheless felt that it was in the interest of the United States not to interfere in Myanmar's domestic politics, as the United States could not cope with another trouble spot in Southeast Asia if it were to do so. And besides, Ne Win was anti-Chinese and anti-Communist.[4] What the ambassador failed to recognize was that, despite his belief that Ne Win was not being appropriately informed of what his subordinates were doing, he could see the bigger picture and, moreover, though few would recognize it now, many people, particularly amongst the farmers and workers, were enthusiastic about the socialist revolution then.

Those who spoke English and had contacts with Western embassies were amongst those who lost out most from the policies of the Revolutionary Council. Also, among those losing out were the Indian business community, as their factories and shops were nationalized and approximately one-third of the Indian community left Myanmar, often having all of their assets confiscated, including gold and jewellery removed at the airport or wharves on departure. By April 1963, all foreign trade had been nationalized and more than 13,500 local shops were taken over by twenty-two trade corporations (Tin Maung Maung Than 2006, p. 147, fn. 27). Though the departure of the Indian business community was often called an "expulsion", this was denied by a British official in India. As they could no longer pursue their trades, they were leaving "voluntarily", "and indeed some of them originally complained about the difficulty of getting out".[5] Nationalization had the same effect as expulsion, even if the justification was made not in ethnic, but in economic policy, terms.

The opposition to the regime, however, remained slight and it was realized by realists that unless the army would turn against their chief, stopping Ne Win appeared to be impossible. His armed opponents, the

Communists and ethnic separatists, now back in the field, were seen to be even worse than his egalitarian economic policies. Dreamers of mounting a countercoup to Ne Win in 1964, like former Colonel Kyi Maung, and perhaps U Aung Gyi, sought the views of former colleagues in the army who were busy fighting the insurgents, such as Colonel Lun Tin who was in charge of the Northwest Command. Even if found favourable, they still felt they needed the support of the United States for such a move.[6] They did not get it.

Despite its alleged heavy-handedness, the Revolutionary government was not able to impose its will wherever it wanted. An order in mid-April that all Buddhist organizations had to register with the appropriate authorities was rescinded two weeks later in the face of monastic opposition. However, just as the demolition of the Rangoon University Students Union building dealt a serious blow against the reputation of the regime, so too did the government's demonetization of the kyat. Via Revolutionary Council Law 7 of 1964, enacted on 17 May, all 50 and 100 kyat notes had to be turned in.[7] Three reasons were given for an action which removed more than half of the economy's money in circulation, all related to what were seen as attempts to avoid the consequences of the socialist revolution by manipulating the currency and markets. These included (1) heavy withdrawals of cash at the time of bank nationalization, (2) dumping of goods on the market on the cusp of the nationalization of enterprises, and (3) smuggling abroad and selling kyat at discounted prices. However, it was only the rich who had 50 and 100 kyat notes who would suffer. For the few honest working people who were left holding the now worthless cash, they could redeem a small amount once it was demonstrated that the money was honestly earned, so it was claimed.[8] One of the chief victims of the demonetization was Colonel Saw Myint, the Minister for Information, whose wife, having received advanced warning of what was to come, took steps to protect the family's monetary assets. He was forced to resign and subsequently given life imprisonment, though he was released fourteen years later following an amnesty order (Chit Hlaing n.d., pp. 22–23).

Resistance to the effects of the regime's policies affected Ne Win's immediate family. His brother-in-law, Dr George Kyaw Than, brother of Daw Khin May Than, and a urologist with an American wife, met with the General and his wife in late June. Dr Kyaw Than requested a passport in order to migrate to the United States where he had been offered a medical appointment. Apparently a row developed, with Ne Win shouting and Daw Khin May Than in tears. After the discussion had calmed down,

Ne Win indicated that he would have to discuss the matter with the "boys". This and other matters suggested to the United States embassy staff that Ne Win was losing his independence within the Revolutionary Council.[9]

The following week, another source, a retired army officer, told American embassy staff that the Revolutionary Council had voted seven to five, Ne Win with the majority, to abandon socialism and slowly return power to a civilian constitutional government.[10] It was not to be, though a year later, Ne Win did ask U Chan Aye and U Ba Nyein to present alternative economic strategies for the country. Chan Aye and his colleagues, U Thet Tun, Dr Aye Hlaing, and Dr Ronald Findlay, presented a plan designed to increase incentives for farmers to produce for export, rather than for self-sufficiency. Ne Win, on being presented the report, said that the strategy "would put the country into the hands of the CIA [US Central Intelligence Agency]", and Ba Nyein's plan became unquestioned orthodoxy for the next six years, until Tin Pe's departure from the government.[11]

Though Ne Win met with few diplomats, he did set aside an evening for dinner with Professor Frank Trager and his wife on 30 June, the same day that General Ne Win's father, U Po Kha, passed away and was given a simple Buddhist cremation ceremony (Maung Maung 1969, p. 306, fn. 8). Trager, a professor at New York University and the author of a number of books and articles on Myanmar politics, had previously been an administrator in the American aid programme in the early 1950s, and was believed to work with at least one American intelligence agency. A former Marxist and socialist, like his mentor Sidney Hook and others, he had moved to the right politically and was a dedicated anti-Communist. Trager, who also dined with Dr Maung Maung and Professor Kyaw Thet, and their wives, retailed the evening to Ambassador Byroade, who informed Washington as follows:

> Greatest surprise for us was role played by Kitty Ne Win who may be more of factor than we had realised. Trager reports she dominated entire evening giving every impression she visualised herself in role of the historically powerful Burmese queen. Ne Win interrupted her only twice in an evening in which she portrayed herself as bitterly anti-American, voicing primarily commie-like slogans and clichés, and attempting to avoid deeper discussion of her allegations. She bragged that General kept abreast world events largely through her reading to him in bedroom and it obvious her selection of items quite biased. Her most frequent quotes were from book "Bay of Pigs".

The Tragers thought Daw Khin May Than had changed dramatically since they last met and wondered whether she would become a Madame Nhu of Burma — Madame Nhu being the powerful sister-in-law of South Vietnamese President Ngo Dinh Diem.

> Ne Win by contrast somewhat more conservative but took general line that U.S. should leave Southeast Asia alone. At one time he said that all that was wrong with the world was the struggle between the "eagle" and the "bear". ... Both the Ne Wins took general line they did not distrust intentions Communist China. Kitty started off discussion international affairs by referring to start of Korean conflict as U.S. attack on North Korea.
>
> Both Ne Wins were scalding in their frequent references to CIA. Ne Win at one point said quite seriously he personally convinced CIA killed President Kennedy. Trager replied, "nonsense", whereupon Ne Win said, "prove it."

When Trager brought up the treatment of Indians departing from Yangon airport in recent months, "Ne Win snapped, 'Your country taught me', in obvious reference to his treatment by U.S. customs officials on his ill-fated trip to Washington in June, 1960." Daw Khin May Than also made reference to the problem with the United States customs and both indicated no sympathy with the exiting Indians. It was once averred that neighbouring Thailand was a "country under military occupation by US". In general, Ne Win seemed optimistic and positive towards current internal developments, including socialism and the nationalization of the economy. As for the insurgency, he seemed relaxed as well, believing apparently that the ethnic insurgents would eventually join the Burmese Way to Socialism as it benefitted the working people. With regards to the Kachin insurgency, it merely required a holding operation until it died a natural death.[12]

As a follow-up to the report on the Trager–Ne Win encounter, a second secretary of the United States embassy reported a conversation she had with a high official near the Revolutionary Council. Confirming the views expressed to the Tragers,

> General Ne Win's basic motivation in organising the revolution was his determination to prevent Burma from being either a cold-war battlefield like Laos or Vietnam or a puppet of either of the major protagonists. He is convinced that only an authoritarian socialist government can push through the economic and social revolution which is needed to unite the people and give them the will and ability to resist both attack from outside and subversion from within. He defends the disruptive

speed of his economic revolution on the grounds that Burma has no time to lose if she is to save herself, and considers the class war a distasteful but necessary method of distracting the people from the ethnic and political quarrels by persuading them of the need for all working people to unite against the "exploiting class" and "foreign imperialists".[13]

While Ne Win and his colleagues may have felt their Way to Socialism was the salvation of Myanmar in a cruel and dangerous world, their views on life could not have been more different from those of some of their Western interlocutors. When Lord Carrington, then Minister without Portfolio in the British government, visited Yangon briefly, he encouraged the Minister for Information, Colonel Saw Myint, to accept invitations from both the British Broadcasting Corporation and Reuters. After his encounter, he commented "that talking to the Burmese is like talking to a sponge".[14] Carrington did not meet with Ne Win but was reported to take the view that "Burma is now a Communist state." He claimed that he detected "xenophobia" amongst officials and thought the top Ministry of Foreign Affairs personnel he met were "almost pathological in their attitude toward SEATO and the US and UK". Their attitude could be summarized as, "Can't you just leave us alone?"[15]

Foreign leaders who met with Ne Win personally, however, came away with a different impression of Myanmar and his government's intention than did Carrington. Like Ambassador Byroade, the Australian External Affairs Minister Paul Hasluck was impressed by Ne Win's political shrewdness after an hour meeting on 4 June. According to Byroade, "Hasluck got the feeling Ne Win was hipped on the subject of corruption", following a discussion in which Ne Win said that one of the results of foreign aid was graft and corruption. Though Ne Win was anti-American, he was also anti-Chinese and, all-in-all, in Hasluck's view, a good thing for Myanmar. He extended an invitation to Ne Win to visit Australia, but Ne Win, though pleased, demurred as he had other pressing foreign trips to make.[16]

Soon after the Ne Wins' apparent tirade at the United States, as recounted by the Tragers, they were visited by a top "bear". The Soviet Deputy Prime Minister briefly visited Burma on 2 July. Despite trying to isolate itself, the government of Ne Win was increasingly being courted. Chinese Premier Chou En-lai arrived in Yangon a week or so later and held three separate meetings with Ne Win, as noted in the previous chapter, and despite concern about the pace of socialism in Burma, he confirmed China's continuing support for his government.[17] At one of the meetings, on 10 July 1964, Chou said that China had to be prepared to fight a Korean-style war as a result of the American escalation of their military support for the anti-Communist forces in Laos and Vietnam (Zhai 2000, p. 131). In one of their meetings, Chou En-lai discussed at length China's admiration and respect for Burma's "policy of independence, autonomy and peaceful neutrality, and friendly relations with neighbours". Apparently the previous day they had touched on Burma's relationship with Thailand. Chou extolled this policy. Although Thailand was allied with the United States,

> ... Burma still maintains a policy of winning it over. Burma will not counter attack unless Thailand follows the US and conducts direct sabotage against Burma. If this happens, when their sabotage activities are defeated, you still want them to be an Asian country and will continue to win them over.

At their second meeting, Ne Win explained his economic policy and current problems. He began by saying, "Once we had decided our objectives, if we moved too fast we would not succeed and if we moved too slowly we would not succeed either." In terms of Myanmar's internal affairs, Chou said that it was not their policy to discuss or interfere. However, as they had discussed in the morning, he felt that in terms of what had been explained of the country's three major problems, or three opponents to the government's policy — imperialism, feudalism, and the capitalist class and profiteers — they were not independent but interconnected. In China's experience, there were always foreign forces and persons in the country who had to be confronted, but they were few. "Patriotic national industrialists and businessmen" were in a different category.

Ne Win then raised two points. One was a query about China's experience in the "utilization of the national bourgeoisie". Here Chou said they were "used" but had to be closely controlled because "capitalists are capitalists". The second point concerned the joint communiqué they were about to issue. He went on,

> The US is currently adopting all sorts of hostile activities directed at Burma. The situation in Laos is very tense. The US will certainly speculate a lot about your visit to Burma and may suspect that we have reached some agreement to take some action, and will thus intensify its sabotage of Burma. If it does, Burma is likely to suffer

losses. To resolve this problem we suggest adding a paragraph to the joint communiqué. This is not something we have discussed but is in the Chinese-Burmese mutual non-aggression agreement.

Ne Win then proposed adding a sentence: "China and Burma will not allow any foreign country to establish bases or cross their border, and commit acts of sabotage", to which Chou replied, "I completely agree." They then undertook a lengthy exchange about what the communiqué should say about Laos. Ne Win wanted to ensure that any statement on the Laotian situation would not put Myanmar in an uncomfortable position. Chou agreed and left the wording to the officials.

The meeting ended on a curious note. There were rumours that the Chinese delegation had got wind that Ne Win would not accompany them to the airport on departure. This was because there were reports that an attempt would be made on Ne Win's life. Ne Win insisted "they are just rumours, we are taking measures". Both Chou and Vice Premier Chen Yi expressed concern that Ne Win should not put his life in danger. Whereas their party was large and they could easily be replaced, he was irreplaceable. Ne Win complained, however, that his colleagues would "not allow [him] to go anywhere. It is like being in a cage." After Chou remarked that both Chairman Mao and President Liu were concerned about Ne Win's safety, as all who stood up against imperialism were at risk, the following exchange took place:

Ne Win: The particular problem is US foreign policy.

Chou: The CIA.

Ne Win: They behave like robbers. I have seen reports in the press that some of the important people ... are indifferent about war with China.

Chou: It is as if there are two wings, both separate and united. When their nerve is weak then they are afraid, when they feel strong then they are not.

Ne Win: The most problematic is the CIA.

Chou: They are not a big problem. They can only cause small troubles.

Ne Win: The CIA acted on its own without going through the President or the State Department to attack Cuba.

Chou: They thought they were going to win. After they were defeated the President reorganised them and McNamara took over the Department of Defence and does not allow the CIA to act independently. Thus the President's power has been somewhat increased and centralised. It is said the CIA is implicated in Kennedy's assassination. The case is unlikely to be solved for a long time.

Ne Win: But some traces have been found.

Chou: They cannot say anything now, but perhaps after several years internal news will leak out.

Ne Win: The CIA is like a government that overrides the legal government.

Chou: If they cannot do anything big then they make small trouble. Major issues have to go through the State Department.[18]

Despite Chou's comments in July that the Chinese government did not interfere in or even comment on the internal affairs of other countries, on the 15th anniversary of the establishment of the Chinese Communist regime on 1 October, a statement of congratulations from the Burma Communist Party was reprinted in the *People's Daily* newspaper and broadcast on Beijing radio. It put the blame on the failure of the peace talks the previous year on "the sabotage of the imperialists, domestic reactionaries, and revisionists" (Steinberg and Fan 2012, p. 395).

Whether due to an intervention by Frank Trager,[19] or Ne Win's feeling of a need to balance his relations with the visiting Russians and Chinese, or Byroade's hours of reassembling Law-Yone's Roll-Royce had had an effect, Ne Win devoted an hour and a half to a conversation with the American ambassador on 30 July.[20] Foreign Minister Thi Han suggested to Byroade that a meeting might be arranged, but the ambassador was warned that Ne Win was "a very blunt man and they never could tell what his mood might be like". He might be "very busy" and "irritated" by something contained in a three-letter deletion of text by a censor in the United States National Archives from Byroade's telegram reporting the meeting. The censored three letters are most probably "CIA". Drawing attention to a recent book by Robert Trumbull, *Scrutable East* (1964), U Ohn Khin of the Ministry of Foreign Affairs reminded Byroade that the last three U.S. ambassadors had also claimed that they controlled the agency but no one believed them.[21]

Byroade commenced his meeting with Ne Win with a *tour d'horizon* of Southeast Asia and U.S. objectives therein. Ne Win replied briefly that Burma "would remain completely aloof and did not wish to be forced to take sides". He said that he told Chou En-lai the same thing. Reiterating the late President Kennedy's message to Ne Win, and indicating that the new President, Lyndon Johnson, took the same view of Burma, Byroade expressed disappointment that Burmese officials were still suspicious of American intentions. Ne Win had little to offer on that or other points.

With regards to bilateral matters, Ne Win was not interested in any new aid projects but was concerned about the high cost of maintenance of the military equipment being purchased under the ten-year U.S. defence arrangement. When mention was made of the possibility of reopening the U.S. Information Service library in Yangon, Ne Win indicated that there was no need for that as the country had to develop its own intellectual class.

> Ne Win shook his head and said that they could not reopen. He said that after colonialisation, Burma had been left without any resources of its own. Its educational and health structures, to give examples, had been left entirely dependent upon foreign methods and even materials. Again he went off into unimportant details. He said it would be just too much effort and take too much time of men and machines to go through all the foreign books and weed out those unsuited for present day Burma. He ended with a query as to whether I did not think it the duty of the state to correct library deficiencies. Burma, he reiterated, must learn to stand on its own feet and become independent of foreigners; until that day arrived, Burmese could not really feel independent.

Amongst the many visitors to Myanmar in 1964 was U Thant, U Nu's former Secretary and then Secretary-General of the United Nations. During the northern summer of that year, he had toured world capitals seeking a solution to the war in Vietnam. According to him, he was particularly encouraged to do so by Soviet Premier Nikita Khrushchev and General Ne Win. During Thant's visit to Yangon, Ne Win organized a dinner in his honour,[22] and Foreign Minister Thi Han organized a reception at which the Chinese ambassador attended but talks to end the war progressed no further until the following January. The fact that Yangon was one of the five capitals in the world in which both the United

States and North Vietnam had diplomatic representation, and top State
Department Cold Warrior Byroade was U.S. Ambassador, made Ne Win's
capital an advantageous site for talks. The following January, when Adlai
Stevenson, the United States Permanent Representative at the UN, and
Thant discussed possible venues for secret talks between the United States
and the government of North Vietnam, Thant proposed Yangon and
Stevenson asked him if it could be arranged. On 18 January, assurance
from Yangon came that the secret talks would be facilitated there.
However, the possibility was ended when President Johnson ordered the
escalation of bombing of northern Vietnam on 7 February (Thant 1977,
pp. 62–66).

After his spate of discussions with foreigners, Ne Win devoted the
next few months to party and government matters, as well as sending
condolences on the death of veteran socialist and nationalist writer, Thakin
Kodaw Hmaing, who died on 23 July, and making a contribution to the
cost of an elaborate funeral and entombment at the foot of the Shwe
Dagon Pagoda.[23] Amongst other things, he addressed military personnel
and BSPP cadres undergoing training at the Central School of Political
Science on the differences between the Burmese Way to Socialism and
communism,[24] a point he had made in his meeting with the American
ambassador the previous month. He supervised the nationalization of
the remaining newspapers and magazines, allowing only official Burmese
language and two official English language newspapers to continue. While
any hint of freedom of the press was finally eliminated, so too were all
of the other foreign language newspapers, the Chinese press, both
Communist and Nationalist, being closed. On 12 September, the
Revolutionary Council gained five new members, including Brigadier
Thaung Dan, Colonel Tin U[25] and Colonel Maung Lwin, and on
17 September the Revolutionary Council announced an expanded cabinet.
Amongst its fourteen members, Brigadier Tin Pe became Minister for
Supply and Cooperatives and Trade Development and Brigadier San Yu
became Deputy Commander in Chief. The day before, General Ne Win
arrived in London.[26]

Five days later, he checked into the London Clinic. On 23 September,
with a British election three weeks off, Ne Win accepted an invitation to
luncheon with Sir Alec Douglas-Home, then the Prime Minister.[27] Despite
Home's electoral concerns, the lunch with Ne Win and Daw Khin May
Than took place on 8 October. Amongst the guests was Mr Strain of the
Burmah Oil Company who, despite the troubles between the Burmese

government and the oil company, had always remained friendly. Talking points for the lunch were good relations, economic assistance via the Colombo Plan, and the release of UK assets and compassionate cases, that is to say, retrieving the chattel and monies seized in the widespread nationalization of the previous three-and-a-half years.[28] Over the course of lunch, Sir Alec agreed with Daw Khin May Than when she opined that democracy did not really work in Burma at that time.[29] Apparently democracy still worked in Britain and three weeks later the Ne Wins had a second lunch with a newly elected Prime Minister, Harold Wilson.[30]

After Ne Win's brief spell at the London Clinic, the bulk of his and his wife's time seems to have been devoted to holiday. On 5 November, Daw Khin May Than lunched with former ICS officer and author of a number of books on his experiences in Burma as well as Burmese and Asian history, Maurice Collis, and Noel Whiting.[31] She indicated that Ne Win was seeing no one while in London but "was very tired" and "suffering from sinus trouble" which she believed "was partly nervous". He needed rest as psychiatrists were not effective at finding a cure. Denying that the Ne Win regime was Communist, she talked at some length about the desire to develop the country equitably and discoursed on the wasteful and self-seeking American aid officials for which they now had no use (Collis 1977, pp. 171–72).

One of Ne Win's accomplishments from his London stay was the return of "the Mandalay Regalia", a trove of valuable historic objects, including King Alaungpaya's sword, seized by the British when King Thibaw was ousted from the throne in 1885. Ne Win was seen brandishing the sword on his return from London on 16 November after a two-month stay abroad. The royal objects were then placed on display at the National Museum, an elegant British-era colonial office building on Pansodan Street, near Strand Road (Shah 2012, p. 308).

Upon Ne Win's return to Myanmar, he was once more being wooed by competing sides in the Cold War. Marshall Chen Yi, Vice-Premier of China, and Ne Win met twice for two days in early December. Before that, the Chinese ambassador assessed Ne Win's visit to Britain, concluding that his socialism was sincere and that the United States was trying to destabilize the situation.[32] After discussing Ne Win's return with the Mandalay palace court regalia, and Ne Win's haemorrhoids, Chen Yi mentioned the Soviet Union. Ne Win expressed the hope that China and the Soviets would resolve their differences. Also on their agenda were developments in Vietnam and the formation of Malaysia, as well as the testing of nuclear weapons and who should be allowed to attend the second Afro-Asian conference. The conversations were relaxed and largely informal.[33]

The Chairman of the Democratic Republic of Korea, Kim Il-Sung, also visited Myanmar for one day in mid-December. He cut short his visit and Ne Win, according to Foreign Minister Thi Han, found their conversation surprisingly business-like and bereft of the ideologically stilted conversations he had had with the Chinese and other Communists.[34] Kim was soon followed by the Foreign Minister, and subsequent Prime Minister, of Pakistan, Zulfiqar Ali Bhutto. Bhutto also raised the issue of holding a second Afro-Asian conference with Ne Win. "The General indicated his dislike of conferences, saying that he had 'burnt his fingers' at the Colombo Conference on the Sino-Indian conflict in 1962." His foreign policy from then on was to "avoid giving offence to any country and, in short, keep himself to himself". A conference would merely be an opportunity to "indulge in polemics" over Kashmir, Indonesia's *Konfrontasi* with Malaysia, and the like. On the Konfrontasi question, Ne Win went out of his way to be non-committal as seen in a meeting with Indonesia foreign minister Subandrio in January 1965.[35]

Ne Win, who very much steered Myanmar's foreign relations throughout his time in power, entrusting the details to his aide U Thi Han and succeeding foreign ministers, set out in February 1965 to shore up relations with India and Pakistan. These were his first formal visits abroad since taking power, though he had flown briefly to India in 1964 on a private visit to see the ailing Pandit Nehru. The nationalization of the assets and the subsequent departure of large numbers of Indians and Pakistanis from Myanmar had become a small domestic political problem for both governments, but neither chose to make it an issue. Accompanied by his wife, Thi Han, and Brigadier Sein Win, Ne Win departed for New Delhi on 5 February. After three days there, he also visited Agra, Bangalore, Poona and Bombay, before leaving a week later for Pakistan.[36] Ne Win met with Prime Minister Lal Bahadur Shastri on three occasions, including a state banquet hosted by the Indian president. He also played two rounds of golf.[37]

The visit to Pakistan from 12 to 19 February included meeting twice with President Ayub Khan, and visits to Lahore, the Khyber Pass, as well as Karachi. The main topic of discussion was the border between East Pakistan and Rakhine State and the related problem of what the Myanmar government saw as Bangladeshi illegal immigrants into Myanmar. It was believed there were as many as 250,000 such immigrants in 1965. Both governments wanted to keep the issue from becoming politicized. As generals who had fought on opposite sides in the Second World War, Ne Win and Ayub Khan were quite relaxed with each other.[38]

In the midst of rounds of international diplomacy, death continued to take its toll. Despite the nationalization of schools and hospitals, Ne Win's old nemesis, Dr Gordon Seagrave, had continued operating at Namhkan under nominal government control.[39] Seagrave, however, passed away in March and was buried on the 31st. Two of his sons, Sterling and John, were present, having been permitted to visit the area under strict conditions following an intervention with Ne Win by the American Ambassador, Henry Byroade (Newhall 1969, pp. 217–25, a less accurate version is Aye 2009, pp. 110–11). Byroade probably found intervening on behalf of the sons unhelpful to his strategy of getting close to Ne Win and the Burmese government. Shortly after Seagrave's death, he discouraged attempts by his predecessor, John Scott Everton, a Baptist educator and Ford Foundation researcher, from visiting Namhkan, as he had often attempted to do while serving in Rangoon.[40]

Amongst the topics discussed by Ne Win in India and Pakistan in February was the increasing involvement of the United States in the war in Vietnam, including the bombing of North Vietnam. Also, Ne Win assured the Indian government that the Revolutionary Council's nationalization policy was non-discriminatory and that Indians and others of South Asian descent could play a role in Myanmar's social life. Shastri apparently accepted his statements at face value (Liang 1990, p. 133). Ne Win discussed the war in Vietnam with North Korean leader Kim Il-sung who paid a second brief visit to Myanmar, issuing an invitation that Ne Win visit his country.[41]

Chinese Premier Chou En-lai once more stopped in Yangon for meetings with Ne Win on 3–4 April. In the first of their meetings, Ne Win and Chou agreed that the United States government could not be trusted as their words were belied by their actions. Moreover, while the previous Conservative government in Britain had attempted to constrain the actions of the United States in Southeast Asia, the Wilson Labour government was just following the U.S. lead, in Ne Win's view, because of its need for American support in order to receive financial assistance from the International Monetary Fund.

Ne Win then explained why Myanmar had not publicly responded to the call by the government of Yugoslavia to the members of the Non-Aligned Movement to publicly denounce the American escalation of their attacks on North Vietnam after the Gulf of Tonkin incident when the Americans claimed that a U.S. navy ship had been attacked.

We think that the US has long ago decided on its move and has proclaimed it to many countries. It does not listen to the views of other countries. The US has sent troops to South Vietnam as reinforcements and is bombing North Vietnam. They continue to do as they like regardless of world public opinion. They originally used the excuse for the bombing that Americans had been killed. Why was this excuse used? We think it was aimed at the US public in order to mobilise the people to support the government.

After the Gulf of Tonkin incident, some US Congressmen criticised the US government, as did some of the press. In order to win victory in the election the Johnson government had to criticise the proposal to win votes. Of course, everyone was in fact planning at that stage to expand the war. The war began to be implemented after Johnson's victory. The US is moving troops from Japan, South Korea and Okinawa in preparation for a major fight. In order to avoid the people blaming him for saying different things before and after the election, Johnson was bound to use the excuse of US casualties in South Vietnam. Of course, some such as the *New York Times* continue to criticise the government, while the Republicans support it completely.

However, in implementing its plan to expand the war, the US does not have a complete grip on public opinion in the US. The US is a rich country, and most people do not want war. If the Pentagon and the party in power want to fight, they must find a way to stir the feelings of the US people. At the beginning of World War II, Roosevelt did a lot of work on this. It is said that he had information about the Pearl Harbour attack before it happened, but deliberately did not take preventive measures in order to incite the US people. This method has become the US tradition.

The US government and the Pentagon are currently using any excuse to mobilise the masses. They say they will not fight China, but this cannot be believed. The US is facing problems in Africa and the Middle East, and more importantly with the black people in the US. Its economic situation is in turmoil. In general, it has a lot of problems at home and so should not cause trouble abroad, but it is possible that because of its domestic problems it will cause trouble abroad to distract its people. We must make sufficient preparations for this.

The US is becoming worse and worse. It has used poison gas in South Vietnam. It may do even worse things such as use tactical nuclear weapons. The possibility exists and we must make plans for the worse.

Following this lengthy analysis of how the Johnson administration was pursuing the war in Vietnam, Ne Win, after noting some recent developments, explained that his government had put up similar notes to both China and the United States making the same point, "namely a peaceful resolution through negotiations". The Myanmar ambassador in Washington had made this point, but as far as responding to a Non-Aligned Movement (NAM) call was concerned, his government thought it a waste of time as the Americans had already made up their minds to fight. However, as the Americans had now responded to the NAM call, perhaps Myanmar was wrong. In Ne Win's words, "If it really is thinking of responding to the appeal, then our original estimate was wrong. But if it is just playing games, then Burma was right."

He continued:

> The fighting in Vietnam is serious, but it has not yet reached the decisive point. Burma opposes imperialism, colonialism and economic exploitation. But we are not prepared to confront the US openly until the decisive point is reached. We must choose our moment. When the decisive moment comes we will take action. Now everyone is censuring the US and there is no point in Burma doing so, but we are using tactful language to let the US know we are not happy with it.[42]

In their second meeting the next day, they covered much the same ground. Amongst the diplomatic community in Yangon, it was believed that Chou wished to encourage Ne Win to attend the anniversary celebrations of the Bandung conference in Indonesia but Ne Win declined as he was too busy.[43] According to an Egyptian diplomat, Ne Win also resisted pressure to speak out more forcefully on the question of the anti-imperialist struggle.[44]

The spate of foreign visitors to Yangon continued in April, with Chou En-lai returning again twice, on his way to and from the Bandung celebrations, and had more meetings with Ne Win. The meeting on 16 April was fleeting, but those on 26 and 27 April were more detailed, sometimes covering topics previously discussed. Much of the other discussion touched on China's technical and economic assistance to Myanmar, and the issue of how the government of Myanmar was dealing with monks who were protesting at the new government registration requirements.[45]

Chou and Ne Win discussed the arrest of what Ne Win called "fake monks" for some time. He explained that raids had been conducted throughout the country and some monks were arrested in bed with women. A total of 80 to 90 were brought in. They were using presses provided by an American foundation some years before and had extensive overseas connections, from Bangkok to France and the United States. The Thai World Buddhist group was one of their contacts. Separating the good monks from the bad was a big problem, as was factionalism amongst the monkhood which had become politicized under the regime of U Nu. The King of Nepal was in Yangon on the same day but Ne Win told him nothing of the arrests of the monks because the news had not yet been released.[46]

Chou En-lai's frequent visits to Yangon were apparently starting to wear on Ne Win. His temper was apparently short, and in an unrelated event three days before Chou's third visit in April, Ne Win allegedly had a physical altercation with a man he met on the Maymyo golf course during Myanmar New Year's celebrations.[47] Amongst the other delegates to the Bandung meeting passing through Yangon was North Vietnamese Prime Minister Pham Van Dong. According to a report from Ambassador Byroade after a meeting with Myanmar foreign minister U Thi Han, during a session with Pham Van Dong,

> At one point Ne Win asked point blank if his government had taken fully into account immense strength of US. Pham Van Dong replied immediately and curtly that they had naturally given consideration to and taken into account all aspects of situation. Later on he made a statement that the only reason US had not bombed Hanoi up to now was position taken by Afro-Asian nations. This seemed a bit too much for Ne Win who shielded his face with his hands and gave Thi Han a wink and a broad grin.[48]

Another conversation was reported to Byroade by a Burmese friend, who claimed he had been in Ne Win's house when he returned from a three-hour meeting with Chou En-lai. Ne Win supposedly said, "That bastard. He thinks he can drop in here every two weeks and that I should be at his beck and call."[49] Ne Win also indicated that the escalation of the war which the Americans were then undertaking was changing the situation. The Chinese and the North Vietnamese would be hard pressed to defeat the United States in the kind of war being envisaged, and that, in the long run, would be to the advantage of Burma.[50]

Ne Win met with British as well as Asian leaders during April. Patrick Gordon Walker, a Labour politician then out of office but sent on a tour of Southeast Asia in an attempt by the Wilson government to encourage peace talks on Vietnam (Zhai 2000, p. 158), told the American ambassador that Ne Win had told the Chinese that they were responsible for keeping a "close eye" on the Burmese Communists in China. In terms of the insurgencies, while the ethnically nominated rebels were a problem in the border areas, the real problem was the White Flag Communists. Ne Win refused to be drawn by Walker to discuss either the situation in Laos or Vietnam, or President Johnson's speech of 7 April at Johns Hopkins University in Baltimore in which he justified the escalation of the war in terms of defending the right of South Vietnam, and all independent states, to chose self-determination.[51]

Dreams of overthrowing Ne Win continued not only to be planned but also attempted, in May, following the spate of foreign dignitaries passing through Yangon, particularly to and from Communist countries on their way to the non-aligned world. Dr Ba Maw's daughter, Mrs Thida Sturtevant, who had married an American diplomat, and was then living in a Washington, D.C. suburb, asked to see Mr Schnee, former Deputy Head of Mission in Yangon, on 1 May 1965. He had discussed with her the previous year about the plan of Dr Ba Maw and her brother-in-law, Thirty Comrade Bo Yan Naing, to overthrow the Ne Win regime with American assistance, if possible. As he told her the year before, this was unlikely but, nonetheless, they were hoping that when they came to power the Americans would be sympathetic, especially since Myanmar might join SEATO. Schnee noted that the Chinese would not appreciate that, and left her with the impression that the U.S. government did not support the scheme.[52]

Nonetheless, Bo Yan Naing and five others slipped out of Myanmar into Thailand in late May, claiming they had 400 troops already trained there. The plan, as Mrs Sturtevant had told Schnee, was to establish a redoubt east of Mawlamyine where others would join them, including former Brigadier Saw Kya Doe. Before departing, and confident of support from the Mon people as Dr Ba Maw currently claimed to be a Mon, Bo Yan Naing left a "Manifesto of the National Liberation Army",[53] which had been written by Zali Maw for an American audience at the American embassy. According to Roland Ye Htun, another of Bo Yan Naing's brothers-in-law, he had met with the head of Military Intelligence, Colonel Lwin, who allegedly knew nothing of the Bo Yan Naing scheme. Nonetheless, he expected that Dr Ba Maw would be arrested and so would he, therefore he was going to escape to Thailand too.[54] Whether he was implicated in the Ba Maw family scheme or not, former Brigadier Aung Gyi was arrested and imprisoned on 15 June. The National Liberation Army provided the American embassy later in the year with a document claiming that it had 500 members plus the support of four to five thousand "right wing" Karens. In addition to Bo Yan Naing, Saw Kya Doe, and Zali Maw, one Captain Kyaw Zwa Myint, allegedly one of Ne Win's personal staff and a member of Military Intelligence, was providing leadership to the group. Tommy Clift was also claimed to be involved, having remained in Thailand rather than going to England as he said he was going to do.[55]

Foreign relations, particularly with China, continued to occupy much of Ne Win's time. In May 1965, Singapore's Lee Kuan Yew paid his second visit to Yangon. According to Lee, Ne Win liked it when he, replying to a toast, said,

> "If we approach Asian problems of poverty and underdevelopment through the rose coloured spectacles of the Western European socialists we are sure to fail." I did not realise at that time how determined he was to be self-sufficient, to have little to do with the outside world and to return to a romantic, idyllic past when Burma was rich and self-sufficient.

Ne Win and Lee played a round of golf together. Lee found the security precautions extraordinary, with troops along the fairways facing out and Ne Win wearing a helmet when he was not swinging a club. The threats of assassination were taken seriously (Lee 2000, pp. 360–61).

Ne Win travelled to Beijing again on 24 July, commencing a one-week official visit confirming the more informal discussions he had in Yangon with Chou and others. At the banquets and in a joint communiqué, the two sides reiterated their adherence to the five principles of peaceful coexistence and opposition to the recognition of two Chinas. Myanmar also reaffirmed its advocacy of a United Nations seat for Beijing but refused to be drawn, as the Chinese certainly wished, further into China's conflict with the Soviet Union or other general, anti-imperialist, i.e., anti-American, rhetoric, including on the conflict in Vietnam.[56] Nonetheless, despite the different views of the two governments, when Chairman Mao Tse-tung received Ne Win at the Great Hall of the People in Beijing, they had a pleasant conversation. Mao led Ne Win in and out of the Great Hall hand in hand.[57]

On 22 August 1965, Vice Premier Chen Yi once more stopped over in Yangon, this time returning from a visit to President Sukarno of Indonesia. Sukarno had just announced the formation of a Jakarta–Phnom Penh–Hanoi–Peking–Pyongyang axis and Indonesia's withdrawal from the United Nations, the International Monetary Fund, and the World Bank. Sukarno's public posturing was of a kind which did not appeal to the undemonstrative Ne Win. While not drawn by Chen Yi on Ne Win's views of Sukarno's announcement, he did confirm that he told his Indonesian colleagues in 1955 or 1956 that in regard to U.S. aid, "the more you take the more poisonous it is". They then turned to discuss Ne Win's meeting the previous day with Algerian President Ahmed Ben Bella, an idiosyncratic former general who was soon ousted in a military coup. Other than indicating their talks were "very frank", Ne Win would again not be drawn to comment on Ben Bella and when Chen Yi tried to do so, Ne Win replied by saying he was going to visit the Soviet Union before long, although he later indicated an invitation to visit Algeria had been extended.

Ne Win and Chen Yi had a lengthy and amiable discussion about peasant behaviour in both China and Myanmar. Peasants liked to store rice and this cut back on the rice available for export, which was a particular problem for Myanmar that year. Also, the peasants were "frittering away government agricultural loans". China had experienced the same problem. Chen Yi said, "Peasant psychology is always the same. They are happy when they have stored grain and unhappy when they have no stores."[58]

In early September 1965, Ne Win made his second visit to the Soviet Union, touring Tashkent, Zaparozhe, Rostov-on-Don, and Tbilisi, as well as meeting senior party and government leaders. Soviet credit was granted for the purchase of agricultural equipment and spare parts (Longmire 1989, p. 76). Ne Win had now called on all his neighbours and the major players in the Cold War except the United States. Little came of the visit to Moscow, though the West German diplomatic corps was pleased that Ne Win would not be drawn to comment on the question of divided Germany, the Burmese maintaining that it was a German question to resolve.[59]

The flow of foreigners through Yangon must have seemed endless. Ne Win gave a formal banquet to Prince Sihanouk on 16 September, and met and saw him off at the airport on his way to Beijing. Sihanouk gave a characteristic anti-American and anti-Soviet speech to which Ne Win remained, in his remarks, non-committal.[60] The following month, Ne Win was much more fulsome in his comments at a meeting with a visiting delegation of five members of the United States Senate Foreign Relations Committee led by Senator Mike Mansfield.[61]

According to the American account of their forty-minute meeting, Ne Win, who did all the talking on the Burmese side, knew nothing of possible talks in Yangon between the Americans and North Vietnamese, but as he had indicated via U Thi Han the previous year, he would be happy if U Thant, the UN Secretary General, could arrange them. He said

> ... the situation in Vietnam was of great concern to Burma but he believed that the best role for Burma was strict neutrality. He felt that condemnation of either side could serve no useful purpose. He said Burma had been under considerable pressure to take sides on this issue and denounce the United States but that they had steered clear of such a position.

When Mansfield mentioned that the Senate committee had made a tour of European capitals, Ne Win was quick to enquire on the views of the European Communist governments. All were pro-Hanoi, though Poland was helpful, he was told. Mansfield drew attention to the wording of the communiqués issued after Ne Win's recent visits to China and the Soviet Union. Ne Win indicated that they had to hold firmly to their position despite opposition from their Communist hosts.

Throughout the discussions Ne Win clearly chose his words carefully, refusing to comment on the India–China border dispute or to volunteer to be a mediator between the warring sides in Vietnam. He discounted the anti-war demonstrations in the United States, saying it was easy to get people to march and chant. Lunch followed, with the Senators' wives and Daw Khin May Than. "Madame Ne Win and the General as hosts were charming and entertaining, and seemed to enjoy the occasion themselves."[62] Reporting on the U.S. Senators' visit, West German Ambassador Bottler advanced the view that the inner circle of the Ne Win administration were of the opinion that the U.S. presence was a stabilizing influence on the situation in Southeast Asia and without it the Chinese would become aggressive, but no one would say that publicly.[63] This is indeed plausible but unproven. Ne Win's Burma was willing to stand up to China on some issues, including signing the nuclear test ban treaty and opposing China's position on nuclear weapons, together with India, Yugoslavia, and Egypt at the Cairo Non-Aligned Conference in October 1964 (Badgley 1965, p. 60).

In a subsequent report to President Johnson by Senator Mike Mansfield on their meetings with Ne Win and others, Mansfield noted that they "were at all times correctly and courteously received and, on occasion, as in Cambodia and Burma we were received with very great warmth".[64] Otherwise, the report made no specific reference to Burma, but generally noted that the American "engagement in Viet Nam" would "probably continued to be regarded as tolerable as long as it" remained an American problem. By implication, any spreading of the conflict was anathema to the entire region.[65] Ne Win was unlikely to have demurred from this position.

Setting aside the fraught international atmosphere in and around Southeast Asia which had consumed much of his time and energy during 1965, Ne Win dedicated himself to domestic affairs, speaking four times in the space of two weeks in the middle of the year. He both opened and closed a Commanding Officers' Conference, the second of the year[66] which lasted nearly a week, and the BSPP's first seminar, which was convened two days later and included many of the same persons. The four-day seminar resulted in little change in policy or personnel, but served as an opportunity to review the work of the Revolutionary Council over the previous three-and-a-half years. Several hundred delegates were present, coming from throughout the country. In opening the conference, Ne Win began by saying he was in the position of a "commander of a military unit in disarray" as he was "faced with the problem of how to mobilise and regroup the people in order to set up an organisation that will serve the interests of the country in a spirit of unity".[67]

Admitting that many applicants for party membership were not sincere believers in socialism, but rather saboteurs, self-seekers, or persons dogged with "old thinking and erroneous attitudes and instincts", they still had to be accepted for the sake of national unity. Speaking of "things as they are", pointedly calling his listeners "the audience", rather than colleagues or comrades, Ne Win expressed his dissatisfaction with the development of the party up till then. However, he had to work with people as he found them and hoped that in time they would change. Alluding to those in the party who criticized it for not being as radically socialist as they wished, as well as the opportunists among them, he drew attention to the party discipline rules which were to guard against the plague of factionalism which, of course, had undermined political parties in Myanmar in the past. With all the attention he had been devoting during the year to the Cold War, Ne Win spent a reasonable amount of time discussing the Eastern and Western blocs and how adherents of one or the other in Myanmar led to factionalism in the party. Just as Myanmar avoided taking sides in the Cold War, so persons in the country and the party should do the same.

Writing more than half a century after these events, and knowing the ultimate failure of the Burma Socialist Programme Party and the revolution Ne Win steered, it is difficult to recall the enthusiasm that many felt at that time. Writer and lawyer U Chan Aye recalled in 2006,

> I also joined the party. I thought I could do something good for the country. Many people, at that time, felt that it was a good opportunity for us to do for the country. On the one hand, we thought that military officers did not really understand socialism. We understood socialism better than they did. Many people now like to highlight only the negative aspect of the coup. In those days, many people were excited about the future of the country. It was hard to resist the pressure and persuasion of the moment. We were pressured to do something. We also felt persuaded by what the military said it would try to achieve.[68]

The flavour of Ne Win's rather ambiguous and rambling speech, weaving Myanmar history with the Cold War and factionalism in the party and lack of unity in the country, is captured perhaps most clearly in this paragraph:

> When it comes to ourselves we must have relations as between brothers and sisters so that we may never be divided. If it is asked whether this could be possible I should refer you to the fact that even a single person is likely to have differences with himself. Two persons might have two sets of likes and dislikes. In that case the two should undertake common tasks together. But neither should do what the other dislikes. Yet if this principle were to be observed the interest of both might suffer. In that case even what is not liked may have to be done. These exceptions must be permitted. Rules should not form a rigid system. This is the meaning of the middle way. The middle path must be taken to permit flexibility. We cannot be dogmatic. It is the same with this treatise. It should not be inflexible. We will do certain things at one moment. When necessary we must change. When should we change? In our studies we will find both rewarding and unrewarding elements in the programmes of others. After such studies we will undertake to do things in unity.[69]

Perhaps alluding to the implicit promises of support and understanding that he had received since the time of the coup from the United States, Great Britain, India, and China of assistance in time of need, Ne Win underscored that though the country would "have to depend on ourselves", "naturally there will be help of some sorts". However, "assistance will be measured". Hence, in his repeated urging in his public speeches, he said that "solidarity lies with us, that our strength lies within the country".[70] And party solidarity had to be built in order to build national solidarity.

After repeating himself several times, Ne Win finished his speech promptly, drawing attention to the disparity in pay rates for army personnel seconded to the Party and civilians who received, not salaries, but emoluments as they were on probation. This created ill will and opened the route to corruption. Though he had addressed these problems in specific plans, overall there was still much to do. To military personnel in the party, he urged them to be disciplined and vigilant. He also urged civilian members returning to their towns and villages to be vigilant as well since the Party's armed enemies were liable to attack them and the police and army could not always provide protection. Indeed, the police sometimes might be the ones who harmed them.

Unlike his opening remarks, his concluding speech concerned policy matters, particularly economic and social affairs, as well as the theme of national solidarity. He commenced with a disquisition on the current world economy and the problems then faced by both Western and Eastern economies. He also deviated to essay on the great depression of 1929–30 and how the Austrian banks fell and the rise of Hitler. En passant, he referred to the economic policies his revolutionary government had introduced. Facing the accusation straight on that those policies had been cruel, he noted how the Kennedy administration had faced down the U.S. steel industry when it put up prices contrary to government wishes. It was threatened with audits of its tax returns and other measures.

> We are accused of being dictatorial and harsh but when a crisis comes didn't they also act likewise? It is not possible to hoodwink someone who follows history closely. When conditions are good we must act in accordance with those conditions. They acted in that manner when conditions were difficult in that period.[71]

Turning to Myanmar's current economic condition, Ne Win began by lamenting on the absence of accurate statistics. Students were being used to fill the gap by conducting surveys, but these had so far been inadequate. He was aware of the advice received from many quarters about mistakes in implementing socialism in other countries, particularly in making haste. Ne Win described the "notorious People's Stores Corporation" (PSC) which had replaced the private sector retail traders as "like rain on the river they send oil to Magwe". Oil-rich Magwe must have received the oil "due to dishonest intentions or to lack of skill". Few had the skills needed for the rice market. "The problem was in commodity exchange and problems of transportation, infrastructure and communication." When ingredients were not available because the planning system had let down the distribution system, there were complaints that affected the entire household. "Major Ko Ko Gyi told me that it is difficult to mobilise even his housewife. This is probably so", Ne Win lamented.

He admitted that the military personnel and leftist politicians whom the government was using to run the economy did not have the knowledge required for their tasks. But had they not taken on tasks for which they, including himself, he admitted, were not qualified to undertake, they would never achieve socialism. Even Myanmar's former capitalist class did not know what they were doing and had to rely on Chinese, Indian and English merchants to handle their transactions.

> We are unskilled people assembled. The skilled people we ask to help are not really that skilled. They do not know how to deal in foreign trade. …
>
> [Skilled indigenous capitalists asked to help the regime] … I should like to ask whether what they are skilled in is theft. They may understand how to steal but do not know how to handle international trade and are ignorant of international prices.
>
> Unskilled people are having to handle these matters. There is no one to teach these people, so how should they learn? PSC salesgirls are haughty and unmannered in speech. Some may do these things deliberately. Others do not know better. They see others being haughty and think that is what should be done. This is the fashion.
>
> Even the man with goodwill does not know how to deal with the customer, how can the one who has no goodwill behave? We had to take over the former employees of the Cooperatives because we did not wish them to lose their jobs.
>
> The Cooperative employees too are not skilled. They take out 100 cases of condensed milk from the Supplies. They sell 20 cases across the counter. The other 80 cases are put out to the black market. There are men of good will as well as of ill will in the Cooperatives.

> We took over all the employees of the BEDC [Burma Economic Development Company]. But because there were no trained people in the Cooperatives and BEDC we ran into difficulties. Neither they nor we were skilled.
>
> But we are fortunate. Because we had a large supply of food commodities if we could not get a certain commodity we could at least get another. We will not die of hunger.[72]

Defending the manner in which nationalization took place, Ne Win said that it was done systematically, starting in Yangon, but as the headquarters of firms were in Yangon, the district shops became laws unto themselves and once more "it was like having caught hold of the tiger's tail".[73] However, through experience, they would learn how to manage and the system would improve. Ne Win then turned to anecdote to discuss how they would have to live through the transitional period until the socialist system worked adequately. Recalling how things were tough financially in the early 1950s, he explained that there were shortages of things including nipples for baby bottles for his three bottle-feeding children. His wife approached a wealthy Indian who offered her assistance. Ne Win insisted, however, on feeding the babies with spoons and, after a week of screaming children, peace was restored at home.

He then went on to discuss at length how the market after independence had been manipulated by foreigners, mainly Indian ("Chulia", i.e., Tamil) traders, who squeezed maximum profits and corrupted members of the civil service, including the police and the army. The government's priorities were the people's welfare, particularly food, clothing and shelter. The transitional period from the market economy to the socialist economy would take as long as it takes. "Lack of know-how may be a handicap for us, but we shall acquire that know-how some day through trial and error. But how people grumble and complain, and how cunningly the mischief-makers fan the fires."[74] Two other problems, he noted in passing, were the inadequacies of the rationing system the government had developed and the problem of finding workers who would work hard enough to fulfil their responsibilities. The government had resolved the former by counting the number of persons per family, rather than treating every family as if it were an identical unit. However, the labour problem would only be solved, he implied, by imposing more labour discipline. Otherwise, the Indian shopkeepers would keep all the business, as even the government had been using them until recently. His point was that "workers and peasants must not be pampered and spoiled".[75]

He concluded the economic section of his remarks by discussing problems in calculating the amount of rice available for export, as opposed to what was believed to be in domestic stores. He conceded that their statistics were woefully inadequate and he was given wildly differing statistics from time to time. Moreover, peasants were undermining the socialist system by selling their rice to the government and then buying it back at a lower price. He put down the problems in the rice trade again to the lack of knowledge on the part of his colleagues. The result was that "they get cheated right and left. I feel my head, sometimes, and there are those scars, and I say, 'No more, no more being hit on the head.' So much for the economy."[76]

Turning to social affairs, Ne Win admonished his audience to avoid mixing religion with Party activities. As Myanmar had adherents of different faiths, the Party should avoid appearing to favour one over another. Besides, the country had freedom of religion and when people tried to use religion in other activities, such as in schools, it could lead to conflict. "These may look like small things, but they are not. The manipulators are still active. So, in brief, do not use or be used by religion or religious groups."[77] After further discussion of the need for religious and political doctrines to change in keeping with the times, making several references to the then current Vatican Council, and then a discussion of the problems of evidence and reporting in the press and courts, Ne Win concluded with a call for national unity and unity within the party.

In his assessment of Ne Win's two speeches at the Party Seminar, the West German Ambassador remarked that the party had not been able to consolidate itself either organizationally or ideologically after three-and-a-half years of existence. He put this failure down to the backwardness of the mass of the people and also to the humane methods used by Ne Win's government. These methods were confined to economic pressure and protective custody. To Herr Bottler, Ne Win did not "appear like the typical rough dictator", but as someone willing to refine his methods in order to achieve justice and the welfare of the people.[78]

The charitable ambassador had overlooked a large part of Ne Win's speech, that dealing with the economy. From the beginning of the Revolutionary Council government, Ne Win knew that the economy was the key to success. More than three years after the launch of the socialist road, Ne Win had to admit that little had been achieved, except the creation of economic confusion and new methods of distorting prices. What was

Ne Win's solution then? More of the same. Ne Win believed that people could learn "on the job", just like he did, and this was perhaps his biggest mistake. Certainly people could learn by doing, but it takes more time than politics allows. However, Ne Win felt that no matter how big a mess his government had created, it would eventually be resolved, and in the meantime no one would starve. In time, the economy did come to be managed more effectively, but managing for self-sufficiency was not the way to develop a strong economy and a resilient nation. It took several more decades to demonstrate that economic management is not as easy as containing a civil war.

Ne Win rounded off international business at the end of 1965 with a brief visit by the new Indian Prime Minister, Lal Bahadur Shastri, who was under political pressure at home over the nationalization of Indian-owned businesses. By the beginning of December, 129,575 Indians were reported to have been repatriated, with another 52,000 placed on a waiting list. Despite this problem, the talks between Shastri and Ne Win were reportedly most cordial.[79] At the end of the year, Mr Clifford Naunton Morgan, Vice President of the Royal College of Surgeons,[80] and his family came to Yangon as Ne Win's private guests, unknown to the British embassy. Morgan conducted some minor surgery on Ne Win during his visit.[81] The allegedly xenophobic Ne Win also entertained Mr J.C. Irwin, the Keeper of the Victoria and Albert Museum, and his wife, for two weeks in January, including a lunch at the presidential residence.[82]

The year's diplomatic rounds began in February, with Ne Win making a six-day visit to Sri Lanka,[83] his first such visit since the ill-fated Colombo conference of late 1962. Whether at Ne Win's behest or that of the Sri Lankan government, at the state banquet which followed the talks between the two governments, the North Vietnamese, North Korean and East German ambassadors were not invited. Ne Win was apparently most affable with the West German ambassador, recalling his warm relations with the former and current Federal ambassadors in Yangon. Apparently, much of the trip was devoted to visits to Buddhist sites, to which Ne Win made significant donations, but given the separation between religion and the state in Myanmar, in contrast to Sri Lanka, monks were excluded from the delegation or ceremonies.[84]

Though Ne Win had been careful not to compromise Myanmar's neutrality over any major international conflict, the escalation of American involvement in Vietnam finally drove him to write to President Ho Chi Minh on 21 February 1966. His letter stated,

As a nation which has experienced both the indignities of foreign domination and rigours and ravages of war on our soil, the Burmese Government and the Burmese people have great sympathy for the Vietnamese people, particularly the people of South Vietnam who have been subjected continuously to untold misery and suffering for the last twenty years. It distresses us particularly that the situation in South Vietnam today should be so far removed from the peaceful, political settlement envisaged for Vietnam under the terms of the Geneva Agreement of 1954.

It would like to venture the thought, Excellency, that perhaps it would still be possible for the entire Vietnamese people, irrespective of their particular persuasions, to resolve peacefully the problem which faces Vietnam today — a problem which initially was caused by foreign domination and foreign interference.

As a sympathetic and near neighbour of Vietnam, I may be permitted to express the sincere hope that it should be possible to achieve a truly independent, democratic and sovereign Vietnam, as envisaged in the Geneva Agreement, by some other way than through the continued suffering of the people of Vietnam.[85]

Reliance on the terms of the 1954 Geneva Agreement on Indochina, which had they been followed by all the parties at the conference, including the United States which refused to sign the agreement, might have led to the relatively peaceful unification of Vietnam in the 1950s. This was a cardinal point in Myanmar's international position, reiterated in many joint communiqués that were issued following Ne Win's exercising of personal diplomacy in the mid-1960s. Though Ne Win disapproved of the American intervention in Vietnam, he never condemned it outright in public. His views on American power in Southeast Asia were clearly ambivalent, wanting a U.S. balance for China, but in a way which did not interfere in domestic affairs. From experience, he knew that to be impossible.

Immediately on Ne Win's return to Yangon from Sri Lanka, Communist cells within the army were exposed and approximately 100 arrests were made (Lintner 1999, p. 449). Meanwhile, the socialist revolution continued to unfold, with the government declaring monopolies over more trade items,[86] only to be reversed seven months later, and all private schools, including Christian missionary and those owned by the Chinese and Indian communities, were nationalized. Thirty-nine thousand students were at that time attending 209 Chinese language schools. The domestic revolution, however, was in the hands of the ministers, for Ne Win seemed to devote more and more time to international relations. At about the same time, the Revolutionary Council articulated a plan to abandon English as a medium of instruction. Indigenous minority languages would continue to be taught in schools up to the second standard and indigenous "minority groups could develop and promote their respective culture freely as long as their cultural activities did not negatively affect the national unity and the RC [Revolutionary Council's] socialist projects" (Kyaw Yin Hlaing 2007, p. 161). Over the next decade, the government published elementary readers in Hakka Chin, Kachin, Mon, Po Karen, Sgaw Karen, and Shan (Kyaw Yin Hlaing 2007, p. 179).

The month of April saw two high-level delegations visit Yangon. The Thai Foreign Minister, Thanat Khoman, accompanied by the Deputy Minister for Defence, Air Marshall Dawee Chullasap, conducted talks largely concerning the various exiles in Thailand who were attempting to overthrow Ne Win's government. Amongst those mentioned were Bo Yan Naing and his so-called National Liberation Army, who had been joined by former Air Force chief Tommy Clift and former Burma National Army member Saw Kya Doe, as well as the widow of Sao Shwe Thaik, the Maha Devi of Yawnghwe, Sao Hearn Kham, who was attempting to lead Shan insurgents from Chiang Mai in northern Thailand.[87] Doubtlessly, the talks were not satisfactory from the Burmese perspective, with Thailand harbouring, if not assisting, anti-regime elements. Marshall Dawee was said to have described Ne Win as "mad" for pursuing socialism.[88]

Also in April, Chinese President Liu Shao-chi, accompanied by Vice Premier and Foreign Minister Chen Yi, once more visited Yangon for two days of talks.[89] Once more they pressured Ne Win to take a more public stand in opposition to the American war in Vietnam, and once more they were frustrated (Steinberg and Fan 2012, p. 396). While Ne Win was dealing with the Chinese, Indian and other foreign relations issues that his government faced, he was also in conversation with the American ambassador about a possible state visit to the United States. Ne Win's patience with the Chinese was growing thin and he poured out his frustration to Henry Byroade when they met on 2 May to discuss a forthcoming visit to the White House in Washington. According to Byroade's account, before Ne Win's visit to China in July 1965,

> He had stated his desire for simplicity frankly to them prior to his visit yet extent of their welcome made him ashamed and angry. Thousands and thousands of people who obviously cared little for him had been ordered to line the streets. He said maybe they had a lot of unemployed around Peking but he still didn't like it. He had sat

through dozens of interminable speeches and had finally told them he would not reply anymore. At each stop, mayors, military commanders, and political commissars had each made pointed speeches to which he was supposed to reply.[90]

Ne Win indicated that he and Liu Shao-chi had had little to discuss during the Chinese President's most recent visit. Clearly, the fall of President Sukarno and the massacre of thousands of members of the Indonesian Communist Party since they last met had been a loss for China, Liu averred, but Vietnam was the bigger problem they faced. They apparently agreed that the Vietnamese Buddhist monk, Thich Tri Quang, who was leading opposition to the military government in Saigon, was no match against the Communists.[91]

Ne Win soon departed on 7 May 1966 for a four-day visit to Pakistan. There he signed a treaty marking the middle of the River Naaf as the official border. He also played several rounds of golf.[92] Troublesome as the border issue with East Pakistan was and would remain, an even bigger problem for Ne Win and Myanmar was about to commence on the other side of the country's border with China. On 16 May, Chairman Mao issued letters calling for a cleansing of the Communist Party and the Cultural Revolution was launched. Ne Win, like the rest of the world, was unaware of the implications of that move until sometime later.

In Myanmar, the army was gearing itself up to take the fight to the Communist and other insurgents two years after Ne Win had said they would now use greater force than in the past, and organized its first mobile infantry division in June. The 77th Light Infantry Division (LID), based at Hwambi, north of Mingaladon, at the bottom of the Bago Yomas, was under the control of the Chief of Staff, rather than the territorial military commanders and could be used as a mobile reserve. Two more LIDs were raised the following year (Tin Maung Maung Than 1989, p. 45). The army was gearing up not only to garrison the country but also to confront the insurgents. The twin burdens of garrisoning the country and taking on the insurgents, and administering the increasingly complex and faltering socialist economy and society, was putting a heavy strain on army resources. Nearly two-and-a-half years after the coup, the Ministry of Defence ordered that army personnel serving on the Security and Administration Committees at various levels should be relieved of military duties in order to devote themselves entirely to their civilian responsibilities.[93]

In the meantime, Ne Win set off on 20 June on a trip around the world, only to return to Myanmar more than three months later. The first stop was Czechoslovakia, repaying the visit of the Czechoslovak president soon after the coup four years earlier. After a four-day visit from 21 to 24 June 1966, he made an official visit to Rumania from 24 to 27 June.[94] While there, he visited a petrochemical works and oilfields and made a courtesy call on the General Secretary of the Rumanian Communist Party, Nicolai Ceausescu. Travelling in a private plane with an entourage of thirty-six, Ne Win departed for Vienna for a private visit. A medical check-up with Professor Dr Hoff was arranged. He was slated to leave Vienna on 30 June,[95] but there was no record available of his travels from then until 22 July when he arrived in London for a six-week visit.[96] Most probably he had spent seven weeks holidaying in West Germany and perhaps Italy and Switzerland. By then the government had opened a jewellery outlet in Zurich.[97]

In London, Ne Win lunched again with Prime Minister Harold Wilson on 8 August. At the lunch, there was mentioned a proposal that Ne Win's deputy, Brigadier San Yu, should visit Britain as the guest of the Chief of Defence Staff, Field Marshall Sir Richard Hull.[98] The invitation had been put directly to San Yu on 20 June, who refused, explaining that it would be too cold to visit in winter. When it was put to San Yu that Ne Win often visited England in winter, he replied that Ne Win was "not like the rest of us". He did not mind getting cold and wet.[99] At some point in the London stopover, Ne Win also met the Queen. Three days later, he lunched with Maurice Collis, along with Noel Whiting, and called at his home ten days later on 21 August.

Over pre-prandial drinks on 11 August, Collis remarked to Ne Win that he had seen a rumour in *The Daily Mail* on his way to lunch that U Thant was going to step down as Secretary General of the United Nations. This was the first time that Ne Win had heard of this, and "a curious expression flitted across his face for an instant, as if the news was not altogether agreeable to him". Over lunch, Ne Win conceded that he was still suffering from sinus trouble. Turning to politics, Collis reported that he asked Ne Win, "What, in a word, was his aim?" He replied,

> "I want to give the Burmese people back their country." They had been given back the country in a political sense, but they could not use political freedom if the West held them in an economic and financial grip. His policy was to loosen that grip. The Burmese must get on

without foreign aid, especially loans. They must work out their own salvation. Madame interjected: "The difficulty is that the Burmese are lazy." They have to be forced to reassume control of their destiny. The General's aim is to oblige them to become, as they once were, complete masters of their dominion.[100]

When Collis mentioned Chiang Kai-shek, Ne Win remarked, "The Taiwanese people give us nothing but trouble." He also did not like American puppets who "had taken up the American way of life" (Collis 1977, p. 190). The lunch apparently took place at a guest house owned by the Myanmar government where Ne Win frequently stayed. It was at 83 Victoria Drive, Wimbledon, near the military attache's residence. Ten days later, after a call from Daw Khin May Than, she and Ne Win, along with bodyguards, arrived at Collis' Maidenhead home after lunching with one of Ne Win's doctors at Newbury. Ne Win invited Collis to return to Burma to assist in the excavation of an old capital at Taungdwingyi, but Collis, nearly 80 years of age, begged off. When he suggested to the General that he should have his portrait painted by Fileks Topolski, the Polish impressionist in London, Daw Khin May Than immediately endorsed the idea, but Ne Win was firmly against it (Collis 1977, pp. 196–98).

Ne Win and his party arrived at the United States on 7 September, and after touring historic Williamsburg in Virginia, reached Washington on 8 September. Prior to that, much work was undertaken to ensure that the visit was a success. Ne Win had explained, after his Chinese visit the previous year, that he hoped for as informal an atmosphere as possible. He did not want to remain in the United States for long, but perhaps a stopover in Hawaii after Washington to play golf would be in order. "He did not wish to be difficult on protocol matters and would accept whatever we thought should be done." However, he did not "like big and dressy affairs which seemed to him rather pointless as it would not be possible for him to communicate with many of the guests in any event".[101] Protocol matters were, however, to tie the White House into some knots, with the First Lady, Mrs Johnson, getting rather knotted about the subject.[102] Ne Win knew that wearing a military uniform would not look good in the eyes of the American press. He also knew that wearing the traditional Burmese dress of silk *longyi*, *eingyi* jacket and *kaung baung* would lead to ridicule amongst the philistine Americans. However, he abhorred white tie and tails, and had even gained permission to be received by the Japanese emperor in a simple business suit. Mrs Johnson insisted on something more formal, so that ladies could wear long dresses. Eventually it was agreed that the dinner would be a simple affair in the family quarters upstairs. Johnson enjoyed the relaxed atmosphere so much that it became his style until the end of his presidency.[103]

Before protocol matters could test the friendly relations, another problem arose — Bo Set Kya, or U Aung Than, Ne Win's old associate from the Thirty Comrades and Thakin Ba Sein's faction of the *Dobama Asiayon*. As William P. Bundy, Assistant Secretary of State for East Asian and Pacific Affairs wrote to President Johnson on 28 August, despite U.S. government attempts to forestall him, Set Kya, then a rabid opponent of Ne Win, had attempted to reach Washington before Ne Win arrived. Though living in Paris, Set Kya had extensive links in the United States, having been an agent at one time for Kaiser-Frazer Corporation, the manufacturers of the Jeep,[104] and was in contact with Louis Walinsky of Robert Nathan Associates. Set Kya had been stopped from taking a 7 p.m. shuttle flight from New York to Washington and was under tight surveillance by U.S. government agents, having been found in a small hotel following a "dragnet". Set Kya was subsequently served with a document that stated, probably illegally, that his visa was invalid, having been issued on an illegal passport, and he had one week to leave the United States.[105] The matter was made even more difficult because Walinsky's son was on the staff of Senator Robert Kennedy, Johnson's arch political rival.[106]

Walinsky had been involved in a public dispute over the Ne Win state visit, he being adamantly opposed and under the belief that the primary reason for his coming was to ask for aid in order to forestall a "popular rising" against his government.[107] Walinsky resigned from the Asia Society after its council voted to extend hospitality to Ne Win to try to make up for the shoddy treatment he had received at the hands of U.S. officials in 1960.[108] His correspondence against the Ne Win visit continued into September when U Nu's biographer wrote in *The New Republic* that Burma did not seek aid from the United States.[109] Walinsky was up against powerful interests in the United States government and Ne Win had done a good job in creating a favourable impression in the United States press before his arrival.

In June 1966, Harrison E. Salisbury, the assistant managing editor of *The New York Times*, was given an exclusive private tour of Burma in Ne Win's personal airplane. His articles discussed the alleged "unusual loans" being given by Chinese pawnshops and opium dens in Burma which were interpreted as a form of Communist infiltration. At one point in a interview with Salisbury, Ne Win apparently said, while looking at a map of Asia, "I wish I had a pair of atomic scissors and I could cut us right out of there and move us out in the ocean."[100] In his articles, he described, in melodramatic language, the plucky Burmese army, outgunned but full of courage, taking on the Communists whom most Americans believed at that time would take over all of Southeast Asia. Ne Win was dubbed "Asia's Cromwell".[111] In a private dinner with Ne Win at the former British governor's residence, then surrounded by barbed wire and bright lights, the Chairman told the story of how he beat men under his command during the Second World War who had cut down a tree in order to get him an orchid he coveted. "I wanted the orchid but I did not want to take the life of the tree." "I beat the men", he said. "It was necessary." Salisbury believed Ne Win would beat his country "if he thought it was necessary for its own good", for, he concluded, "He was a man of many faults, but lack of bravery, patriotism and dedication to his cause was not in him" (Salisbury 1967, p. 96).

Salisbury was impressed with much of what he found in Burma, especially the resolute attitude of the army officers with whom he spoke. One was convinced that white men could never win a war in Asia and that was why the Americans were doomed to failure in Vietnam. They were in danger of making the same mistake in Thailand but Ne Win's go-it-alone policy was a viable alternative. The American journalist was also struck by the honesty of the government which he believed to be unique in Asia. Ne Win said to him that "Unless we Burmese learn to run our own country, we shall lose it. Of course there are hardships, but we must put our house in order." Aid merely crippled and paralysed recipient nations and Burma did not want to experience a deluge of foreign money as was afflicting neighbouring countries (Salisbury 1967, p. 91). Above all, Salisbury was struck by the anti-Chinese, as well as anti-Communist, tone of what he found in Myanmar.

Ambassador Byroade travelled to London to join Ne Win for his trip to the United States. They met on 30 August, and discussed the Set Kya affair for about forty-five minutes before dinner. Ne Win "showed a surprising knowledge of the problems our government could face in the deportation of an alien". Ne Win did not seem to blame the U.S. government for complicity in Set Kya's arrival but then asked, "But who in America supports and helps this man?" To that Byroade eventually replied, according to his account, he did not know but that "it was no secret to him [i.e., Ne Win] that there were private individuals in America who considered themselves Burmese experts and who were not happy about him and his government." Byroade and Ne Win then agreed that these individuals had no substantive influence on U.S. policy towards Burma. Ne Win "apologised for his display of annoyance towards certain American individuals, and asked that I forget it".[112]

In Secretary of State Dean Rusk's briefing document on the Ne Win visit to the President, he stated the purpose of the visit was

> ... as a gesture of support for his efforts to maintain Burma's non-alignment and independence and a reaffirmation of our willingness to accept true neutrality in a Southeast Asian State. This visit is also intended to dispel suspicious which Ne Win has long held that the United States is hostile to his government and help improve the atmosphere of our relations with Burma.[113]

Ne Win had in the past "indicated awareness of the importance of an American presence in Southeast Asia to permitting Burma to preserve its independence". There were no bilateral issues to discuss, but topics of conversation included Vietnam, Southeast Asian regional development, and Communist China, a country Ne Win had visited frequently.

Accompanying the Rusk memorandum was a copy of a telegram from Ambassador Byroade setting forth his views on the visit. As far as he was concerned, Ne Win's primary purpose was to use the visit to "prove his continuing neutrality". He went on, "He does not want us to lose in Vietnam, but he worries that escalation may involve Burma. He desperately wants to stay out of this conflict because he is painfully aware of the great destruction past wars have wrought upon Burma." He urged the President to impress upon Ne Win that he should have no fear that the United States would support his various ethnic or anti-socialist opponents, despite his having "been obsessed in part with fear of CIA". Ne Win's personal knowledge of China's leadership was something the President might like to probe, though he might not be too forthcoming, being of the belief that no one in Washington could keep a secret.

Ne Win was unlikely, Byroade thought, to raise the question of aid, but if the subject came up, "he is capable of giving a quite refreshing viewpoint as to how nations must learn to stand on their own feet." Much to the relief of the State Department, the government cancelled the proposed Yangon–Myitkyina highway project prior to Ne Win's trip. Like other Burmese, he believed that American aid programmes were far too bureaucratic and involved too many technicalities. In regard to the U.S. military assistance agreement which had been in place for ten years since 1958, this had provided assistance in Myanmar currency for cut-rate equipment valued at $35 million and though small in comparative terms, made the U.S. the largest supplier of arms to Burma. It was in their mutual interest that this arrangement continue and Ne Win was furious that UN Secretary General U Thant had mentioned the arms aid programme recently. He need not have been, as the question of renewing the agreement was publicly discussed in an article by Selig S. Harrison in the *Washington Post* on the day of Ne Win's departure from Washington.

It was not known by Foreign Minister Thi Han or other Burmese officials whether Johnson and Ne Win discussed U.S. military assistance to Burma, but the subject did come up in a meeting between Thi Han and the U.S. Secretary of State shortly after Ne Win's return to Yangon. Rusk, who did not meet with Ne Win in September because of ill health, indicated in October that the U.S. was willing to continue the assistance despite the inability of Myanmar to purchase large quantities because of budgetary problems. As long as the programme remained largely a secret, it satisfied both sides.[114] Of course, like the American "secret war" then under way in Laos, to those who followed Asian international affairs closely, it was far from secret (for the American secret war in Laos, see Rust 2012 and Jacobs 2012). The continuation of American assistance would have been particularly noted in Beijing, even if it was not discussed.

Going on at length, Byroade advised the President not to deny the KMT episode and try to avoid discussing the Thais, or U Nu and other detainees. On the positive side, he wrote,

> Burma is one of the few countries in the world that does not, publicly or privately, keep telling the U.S. how to manage its foreign affairs. Soon after he was invited on this visit, Ne Win reportedly said, "Maybe the Americans are finally going to appreciate a guy who can keep his mouth shut". (This was done in the context which suggested he was thinking of Sukarno, Sihanouk, etc.) They could be frank. "There will be no danger whatsoever of any leak from him, or his staff, to the press." Toasts and speeches criticising third parties should be avoided as they embarrass him, as happened in Eastern bloc countries.[115]

Byroade concluded that his advice was based on his belief

... that Ne Win, with all his shortcoming, remains our best bet in Burma today. The majority of his Burmese critics do not want him replaced. They are furthermore glad he is going to the U.S. as they see in this a sign of a future more to their liking. My advice is also based upon the conviction that we want above all a stable, independent Burma which can manage to stay out of Southeast Asian conflict, and whose relations with us continue, in a slow and undramatic way, to improve up to the point of neutrality leaning slightly — but not too much — on our side.[116]

A third briefing document supplied to the President provided him with a brief biography of Ne Win and Daw Khin May Than as well as the other members of their encourage. Ne Win ran a one-man government with an unquestioned record as a patriot but his "domestic accomplishments [were] widely challenged". She did not like 'do-gooder' American women.[117]

The official visit was from 8 to 10 September.[118] On the first day, the two heads of state stood side by side in the Rose Garden of the White House and made short speeches, before retiring inside for talks. Johnson and Ne Win spoke together alone for over an hour while their staff waited in the cabinet room near the President's office. Later in the evening, the President and Mrs Johnson hosted an informal dinner for Ne Win and selected members of his party. The second day, Ne Win was taken for lunch at the men-only Burning Tree Golf Club in suburban Bethesda, Maryland, where he met with the famous American golfer Gene Sarazen, then in his mid-60s. In the afternoon, he had brief meetings with W. Averill Harriman and Under Secretary of State George Ball between 4 and 5 p.m., before meeting the President again. In the evening, Ne Win hosted a reception at Blair House which the President attended along with members of Congress and official Washington.[119]

The note on Ne Win's meeting with Harriman provides the clearest insight into some of the discussions they had in Washington. After reviewing their meeting four years ago in Vienna, Ball raised the subject of the Cultural Revolution which was getting under way in Beijing and the emergence of General Lin Biao as a leading figure. Ne Win said that he had not met Marshall Lin on his visit to China in 1965, but they had met in 1961 or 1962 when Lin was not in good health. Mao, on the other hand, was in fine form when they met in 1965. Ne Win believed the recent purge of the mayor of Beijing, Peng Chen, in June, was just the beginning of what would become the turbulence which would mark Chinese domestic politics and foreign policy for the next five or six years.

"He did not interpret Lin Biao's present pre-eminence as indicating that the Army had more influence than the Party. He pointed out that Mao Tse-tung appeared to be as suspicious of the Army leadership as of the Party leadership", perhaps also reflecting his own views. Ne Win believed that both Chairman Liu Shao-chi and Premier Chou En-lai were then not as influential as they had been. On the subject of the war in Vietnam, Ne Win was of the opinion that while Moscow was trying to use its influence to end the war, the Chinese were keen on keeping it going. Ne Win seemed genuinely to accept what President Johnson had told him about the U.S. position and expressed regret that he was unable to help or offer any useful advice on how to end the war.[120]

Reverting to Laos, Harriman reminded Ne Win that he (i.e., Harriman) had met with Prince Souvana Phouma, the neutralist Prime Minister of that country, in Yangon. That meeting had been important in achieving the neutralization of Laos. Perhaps, Harriman suggested, Yangon could become the Geneva of the Far East. Ne Win demurred, saying that "Burma was too weak" to play such a role. Turning to other current Asian topics such as Indonesia, which Ne Win had not visited since 1951, he referred to the bloodbath that was taking place with the elimination of thousands of alleged communists, saying that "the Indonesians were quite violent people".[121]

In Ne Win's conversation with Ball on the second day, the only matter of substance was the presence of Bo Set Kya in the United States. Ne Win indicated that he had no objection to Set Kya being given permission to remain or being granted asylum in the United States. "Setkya was after all a human being and had to live in some country." However, he did not want him to be allowed "to use the United States as a base to try to harm his country". Ball assured Ne Win that Set Kya and those who supported him in the United States would get no cooperation from the government.[122] At the second meeting with Johnson, as with the first, Johnson and Ne Win engaged in an intimate conversation without their aides having a chance to hear their private views.[123]

At the press conference at the end of Ne Win's visit, Walter W. Rostow, the President's Special Assistant for National Security Affairs, when asked whether the administration had discussed the future of U Thant or the detention of U Nu, he indicated not. Rostow went on to say, "When the Chairman and the President were talking privately, we had an interesting discussion of Burmese economic development, the world food problem, their plans to develop their agriculture." "The question of economic assistance didn't arise." While they discussed the ongoing war in Vietnam, with Johnson outlining the American position, Ne Win offered no assistance or advice as to how to end the war. Denying at several points in the press conference that relations with China were discussed, Rostow concluded by saying,

> The President did express to us, and privately, his satisfaction at having had a chance to talk directly with the Chairman. It was perfectly clear to all of us as they came into the Cabinet Room that they really had communicated.
>
> I know our President, just a few minutes ago, expressed really his satisfaction at this meeting and his feeling that it was a success. I must say that the reception at the family dinner last night was a remarkably pleasant and lively affair; truly a family affair.[124]

After departing from Washington on the 10th, the Chairman and his party stopped off in Hawaii for a one-week holiday. In his report to the President on their departure, Ambassador Byroade wrote that he felt "the discussions with the President alone apparently did more in two hours to accomplish our modest objectives re Burma than we could have done in two years at lesser levels." Byroade was particularly pleased in the changed attitude of Daw Khin May Than who talked with him "quite openly about their past worries about America", but was now in "obvious relief that these worries are now gone".[125] After the state visit to Washington, the Byroades and Ne Wins visited each other frequently, including one Christmas dinner at the Ne Win residence. Ne Win's children remember Mrs Byroade bringing them ice-cream, a rare treat in Myanmar in the 1960s.

From Hawaii, Ne Win then went on an official one-week visit to Japan,[126] where he was received by the Emperor and discussed economic matters with Prime Minister Eisaku Sato. Sato offered assistance in the development of Myanmar's agriculture, as food security was a high priority in Japanese foreign policy. They also shared similar views on the growing war in Vietnam (Liang 1990, p. 151). This was followed by a few days stay in Thailand where he met with some junior members of the Thai royal family and Prime Minister Field Marshall Thanom Kittakachorn, and played golf. In the few meetings he attended, Ne Win appeared relaxed.[127] One was with the Minister of Interior and second-most-powerful man in the Thai military government, General Prapas Charusathien. The two apparently discussed the Burmese refugees in northern Thailand but

Ne Win avoided creating a diplomatic issue that would cause a rift in Burmese–Thai relations by bringing up the lack of constraint on the behaviour of anti-government politicians and insurgent leaders such as Bo Yan Naing or the Maha Devi of Yawnghwe.[128]

Ne Win was sufficiently relaxed after he got back to Yangon that he ordered the release from detention of both U Nu and U Ba Swe on 27 October, but not Kyaw Nyein and others whom he apparently believed wished to assassinate him. Ne Win personally greeted Nu and Ba Swe and indicated to them that they were free to go abroad for medical treatment or on Buddhist pilgrimage.[129] The day before, Burma had withdrawn from the Sterling Area, giving the reason of a desire "to secure freedom on action" in protecting its "foreign exchange reserves in the face of a weakening pound".[130] Because Dean Rusk had been unable to meet Ne Win in September, U Thi Han urged him to come to Yangon later in the year. However, Ne Win told Thi Han when he returned to Yangon from the UN General Assembly that it would not be appropriate for Rusk to come, particularly from a SEATO meeting in Bangkok.[131]

After Ne Win's brief unofficial stop in Bangkok in October, Thai Prime Minister Thanom and a party of thirty-five visited Myanmar from 10 to 12 November. This came at a particularly busy time for Ne Win who was also involved in the Annual Commanders' Conference, as well as preparations for a second seminar of the Burma Socialist Programme Party, held from 14 to 17 November. Nevertheless, he met Thanom at the airport, attended receptions in his honour and continued the discussions they had had in Bangkok. Ne Win gave no indication publicly that he was concerned about the anti-regime activities in Thailand.[132] Never one to sit still for long in those days, Ne Win went on a state visit to Nepal from 30 November to 3 December.[133]

Ne Win's apparent fascination with royalty, particularly the British royal family, received a fillip when Princess Alexandra and her husband, Sir Angus Ogilvy, visited Myanmar from 10 to 17 February 1967 as his personal guests. Uncharacteristically for the royal princess, Ne Win and all of the Revolutionary Council members, bar two, attended a reception held in her honour by the British ambassador. The Olgilvys were shown around Bagan by Ne Win and taken to his guest house at Ngapali. Princess Alexandra also met with the wife of the Sawbwa of Mongmit, Sao Hkun Hkio, despite the fact that the former foreign minister was in detention. The doughty daughter of an East London greengrocer, the Mahadevi of Mongmit doubtlessly gave the Princess another view of Ne Win's Burma than he would have liked. Security for the royal visit was very tight and even the British ambassador had difficulty finding out where the royal party was and what they were doing.[134]

Lord Mountbatten visited Myanmar from 21 February to 3 March, mainly as part of a Southeast Asian tour to make a television series about his life. When he arrived in Yangon, he wanted to be filmed entering the country but was persuaded by the British ambassador not to send his cameraman out in front of him upon arrival at the airport. When he did descend the steps of his plane, he realized why. General Ne Win was waiting to receive him. He was promptly whisked away in Ne Win's Mercedes with a Tommy gun[135] at his feet and two more in the front seat (Ziegler 1989, p. 151). On this occasion, his hour of gossip and lunch with Ne Win, however, revealed no information of note (Ziegler 1989, pp. 152–53).

Balancing the demands of running Myanmar's difficult tightrope walk of neutrality between China, the Soviet Union and the United States would have been a challenging task for any individual. At the same time, building a political party from scratch, managing a dysfunctional economy, and an ongoing insurgency might be overwhelming for most men. Despite attacks on his health and perceived threats to his life, Ne Win seemed to thrive on these multiple challenges. He showed no signs of wilting and his zest for life seemed as strong as ever. As General San Yu said, he was different.

Notes

1. Airgram, James V. Martin to Department of State, reporting on a conversation with *Guardian* Sein Win, 4 June 1963; Memorandum of Conversation: Current Political Situation, U Sein Win and Mr Morton Smith, USIS, 3 June 1963 (embassy papers).
2. Interview with Dr Soe Lwin, 12 August 2012.
3. Interview with Dr Soe Lwin and U Ngwe Thein, 12 August 2012.
4. Telegram, Byroade to Secretary of State (SOS), 28 April 1964, LBJ Library, Box 235, Burma.
5. Letter, J.G. Walmsley, New Delhi, to B.L. Simmonds, DO 196/132.
6. Telegram, Rangoon to SOS, 8 May 1964, Pol 2 Burma, No. 469.
7. *Towhlanyei Kaungsi ei Hluthsaungchet Thamaing Akyinchut* [Concise History of the Actions of the Revolutionary Council] (Rangoon: Printing and Publishing Corporation, 2 March 1974), p. 42.
8. *Forward*, vol. II, no. 20 (22 May 1964): 3.

9. Memorandum of Conversation, George Kyaw Than and Ralph F.W. Eye, 24 June 1964 and Airgram, Martin to SOS, 4 July 1964, Pol 23 Burma.

10. Telegram, Embassy, Rangoon to SOS, 3 July 1964, Pol 15 Burma, No. 002720.

11. Ian Brown, *Burma's Economy in the Twentieth Century* (Cambridge: Cambridge University Press, 2013), p. 139, drawing on Thet Tun, *Waves of Influence* (Yangon: Thin Sapay, 2011), pp. 173–75 and 185–86; Brown's interview with U Thet Tun, Yangon, 25 January 2012; personal communication with Brown from Ronald Findlay, 21 February 2012.

12. Telegram, Byroade to SOS, 30 June 1964, Rangoon 797 Pol 15-1 Burma, No. 29065.

13. Airgram, Ruth A. McLendon, 2nd Secretary, to SOS on leadership, 10 July 1964, Pol 15 Burma, No. A-11.

14. Letter, J.E. Cable to S.H. Hebblethwaite, Rangoon, 13 July 1964, DO 196/334.

15. Memorandum of Conversation between Secretary of State and Lord Carrington, British Minister without Portfolio, American embassy in Manila, during 9th Council Meeting of SEATO, 13 April 1964, SEATO 3 XR Pol Burma.

16. Telegram, Byroade to SOS, 4 June 1965, Canberra 868 Pol 1 Burma xr AID Burma.

17. *Towhlanyei Kaungsi ei Hluthsaungchet Thamaing Akyinchut*, p. 220; Tang Shuyi, "Former Ambassador to Myanmar Chen Ruisheng's Narration", *International Herald Leader* (Beijing) 26 December 2003.

18. Record of Premier Chou En-lai's Talks with Chairman of Burmese Revolutionary Council Ne Win, 10 and 11 July 1964, CAMFA 106-0144805.

19. Never one to hide behind false modesty, Trager wrote to Secretary of State Dean Rusk on 17 September 1964 that his two weeks in Burma were a first for an American that year. He believed he smoothed communications between Ambassador Byroade and Ne Win. Letter, Frank Trager to Dean Rusk, Pol Burma 13249.

20. This summary of the meeting is based on Telegrams, Byroade to SOS, 30 July 1964 and 31 July 1964, LBJ Library, Box 235, Burma Cables Vol. 7/64-12/68.J.

21. Telegram, Byroade to SOS, 24 July 1964, LBJ Library, Box 235, Burma Cables Vol. 7/64-12/68. Following the Bay of Pigs failure in the early days of the Kennedy administration, the President did order, on 29 May 1961, that all agencies operating in a country do so under the control of the ambassador. This was done to stiffen control over the CIA. See Timothy N. Castle, *At War in the Shadow of Vietnam: U.S. Military Aid to the Royal Lao Government 1955–1975* (New York: Columbia University Press, 1992), p. 54.

22. Telegram, Byroade to SOS, 31 July 1964, LBJ Library, Box 235, Burma Cables, Vol. 7/64-12/68.

23. Telegram, Byroade to SOS, 31 July 1964, LBJ Library, Box 235, Burma Cables, Vol. 7/64-12/68.

24. Telegram, Rangoon to SOS, 24 August 1964, Rangoon 123 Pol 1 Burma, No. 019699.

25. Tin U was made Commander of the Central Command in 1964 in succession to Brigadier San Yu.

26. Note to the Prime Minister, 16 September 1964, PREM 11/4660.

27. Letter, Ne Win to Alec Douglas-Home, 23 September 1964, PREM 11/4650.

28. Note to the Prime Minister before lunch, 7 October 1964, PREM 11/4650.

29. Letter, J.O. Wright to N.M. Fenn, 8 October 1964, PREM 11/4650 and PREM 13/3071.

30. PREM 13/3071 and DO 196/334.

31. Whiting had apparently lived in Rangoon and spoke fluent Burmese, though he was not a government official. He met with Queen Supayalat after her return from exile at Ratnagiri and was apparently a source for Collis' *She was a Queen* (London: Faber and Faber, 1937); I am indebted to Dr Elizabeth Moore, and through her, U Than Swe (Dawei), Deputy Minister of Culture, Myanmar in 2012.

32. Burmese President Ne Win's visit to the UK and Burmese-British Relations, 17 November 1964, 105-01601-04.

33. Record of Vice Premier Chen Yi's discussions with Chairman Ne Win (1), 4 December 1964, and (2) 5 December 1964. 203-05594-01.

34. *Towhlanyei Kaungsi ei Hluthsaungchet Thamaing Akyinchut*, p. 220; Byroade to SOS, 27 April 1965, Rangoon 576, Pol 15-1, Burma 22264.

35. Telegram, Byroade to SOS, 23 January 1965, LBJ Library, Box 235, Burma Cables Vol. 7/64-12/68.

36. Telegram Rangoon to SOS, 5 February 1965, Box 235, Burma Cables, Vol. 77/64-12/68, LBJ Library.

37. German embassy in Yangon, Dr Jungfleisch to AA, 8 February 1965, AA PA B 37 Bd. 140, 433–34; German embassy in India, to AA, AA PA B 37 Bd. 140, 433–34.

38. German embassy in Karachi, Scholl to AA, 22 February 1965, AA PA B 37, Bd. 140, 437–40.

39. In 1965, the Directorate of Health Services, in an effort to get services delivered to rural areas and carry out other reforms, decentralized administration to the divisional and township health officers with funding centralized under the Ministry of Health, replacing the mixed funding system which tended to privilege urban health care. See Myanmar Department of Health, Myanmar Health Care System, "Health in Myanmar 2011", Naypyitaw, 2011, pp. 1–5.

40. Telegram, Byroade to SOS, 16 April 1965. Byoade was concerned about the plans of Seagrave's son, Sterling, to join the Shan insurgency against the Ne Win government. Telegram, Byroade to SOS, 5 April 1965, all in LBJ Library, Box 235, Burma Cables Vol. 7/64-12/68.
41. *Towhlanyei Kaungsi ei Hluthsaungchet Thamaing Akyinchut*, p. 220.
42. Record of Premier Zhou Enlai's talks with Burmese Chairman Ne Win, 3 April 1965, CAMFA 203-00654-02.
43. Record of Premier Zhou's discussions with Ne Win (2), 4 April 1965, CAMFA 106-12266-07.
44. Telegram, Rangoon to SOS, 9 April 1965, Rangoon 540 Pol 2-1 Burma.
45. Record of Premier Zhou Enlai's one-on-one discussions with Chairman Ne Win, 27 April 1965, CAMFA 105-01900-01.
46. Ibid.
47. Telegram, Rangoon to SOS, 24 April 1965, Pol 2 Burma, No. A-353.
48. Telegram, Byroade to SOS, 27 April 1965, Box 235, Burma Cables, Vol. 7/64-12/68, LBJ Library. Thi Han gave a similar version of the conversation to U.S. Secretary of State Dean Rusk at the United Nations in September, Memo to Mr Bundy and Richard T. Ewing by J.M. Kane, 8 October 1965, Box 235, correspondence, 1965, LBJ Libary.
49. Ne Win had confirmed his displeasure at Chou's frequent and secretive visits to Yangon in a conversation with the American ambassador on 30 July 1964. Telegram, Byroade to SOS, 31 July 1964, Box 235, Burma Cables Vol. 7/64-12/68, LBJ Library.
50. Telegram, Byroade to SOS, 19 April 1965, Box 235, Burma Cables Vol. 7/64-12/68, LBJ Library.
51. Telegram, Byroade to SOS, 22 April 1965, LBJ Library, Box 235, Burma Cables Vol. 7/64-12/68.
52. Memorandum of Conversation between Mrs Thida Sturtevant, daughter of Dr Ba Maw, and Alexander Schnee, formerly DCM Rangoon, 1 May 1965, Pol 2 Burma and Pol 23-8 Burma.
53. Telegram, Rangoon to SOS, 28 May 1965, Rangoon 642 Pol 33-9 Burma.
54. Memorandum with Roland Ye Htun and Kingdon W. Swayne, First Secretary, American embassy in Rangoon, 31 May 1965, Pol 23-9 Burma.
55. Burma: National Liberation Army (unsigned but in handwriting says PIB No. 21), NARA.
56. German embassy in Yangon, Ambassador Bottler to AA, 27 July 1965, AA PA B 37, Bd. 140, 437–40; German General Consulate Hong Kong to AA, 11 August 1965, AA PA B 37, Bd. 140, 455–57; German embassy in Yangon, Ambassador Bottler to AA, 17 August 1965, AA PA B 37, Bd. 140, 462–64.
57. Hong Junjie, "Interview with Burmese Language Interpreter for Chairman Mao and Premier Zhou, Cheng Ruisheng", *Liberation Daily*, 27 June 2011. I am indebted to Fan Hongwei for this reference.

58. Vice Premier Chen Yi's meeting with Ne Win in Rangoon on his way back to China from Indonesia, 22 August 1965, CAMFA 105-01901-01.

59. German embassy Ambassador Bottler to AA, 11 September 1965, AA PA B 37, Bd. 140, 471 and 28 September 1965, AA PA 37, Bd. 140, 475–77.

60. Letter, W.I. Combs to D.F. Murray, 19 October 1965, FO371/180476.

61. The other senators were George Aiken, Hale Boggs, Daniel Inouye and Edmund Muskie. They were accompanied by Ambassador Byroade. On the Myanmar side, those present were U Thi Han, Colonel Hla Han, and Colonel Maung Lwin.

62. Secret Memorandum of Conversation, 26 November 1965 (embassy papers).

63. German embassy, Ambassador Bottler, 30 November 1965, to AA, AA PA B 37 Bd. 140, 492–93.

64. *Two Reports on Vietnam and Southeast Asia to the President of the United States by Senator Mike Mansfield* (Washington, D.C.: U.S. Government Printing Office, 1973, reprinted report of 18 December 1962), p. 17.

65. Ibid., pp. 28–29.

66. The first being in July when Ne Win spoke for three-and-a-half hours, mainly on the subject of the BSPP socialist ideology. *Forward*, vol. II, no. 24 (1 August 1964): 2.

67. Burma Socialist Programme Party Central Organising Committee, *Party Seminar 1965: Speeches of Chairman Ne Win and Political Report of the General Secretary* (Yangon: Burma Socialist Programme Party, February 1966), pp. 9–10.

68. Interview with U Chan Aye, March 2006.

69. *Party Seminar 1965: Speeches of Chairman Ne Win*, p. 17.

70. Ibid.

71. Ibid., p. 188.

72. Ibid., pp. 192–93.

73. Ibid., p. 193.

74. Ibid., p. 197.

75. Ibid., p. 200.

76. Ibid., p. 203.

77. Ibid., p. 204.

78. German embassy in Yangon, Ambassador Bottler to AA, 16 December 1965, AA PA B 37, Bd. 138, 1030–35.

79. Papers in DO 196/332 and DO 196/335, particularly 6 December 1965 question in the Lak Sabha (Indian parliament) to the Minister of Foreign Affairs. Foreign observers put the number at 300,000. John Badgley, "Burma's Zealot Wungyis: Maoists or St. Simonists?", *Asian Survey*, vol. V, no. 1 (January 1965): 55.

80. Obituary, Sir Clifford Naunton Morgan, *British Medical Journal*, vol. 292 (15 March 1986): 772.

81. Letter, W.I. Combs to D.F. Murray, 28 December 1965, FO371/185974.
82. Letter, D.A. MacLeod to D. Tonkin, 1 February 1966, FO371/185974.
83. *Towhlanyei Kaungsi ei Hluthsaungchet Thamaing Akyinchut*, p. 218.
84. German embassy in Colombo, illegible to AA, 17 February 1966, AA PA B 37 Bd. 140, 487–89.
85. Burma Socialist Programme Party Central Organising Committee, *Foreign Policy of the Revolutionary Government of the Union of Burma* (Yangon: Burma Socialist Programme Party, 1968), pp. 88–89.
86. *Towhlanyei Kaungsi ei Hluthsaungchet Thamaing Akyinchut*, p. 218.
87. Letter, Sir A. Rumbold to FO, 12 April 1966, FO371/186159.
88. Letter, L.J.D. Wakely to D.F. Murray, 12 April 1966, FO371/186159.
89. *Towhlanyei Kaungsi ei Hluthsaungchet Thamaing Akyinchut*, pp. 220 and 261.
90. Telegram, Byroade to SOS, 2 May 1966, Rangoon 556 Pol 7 Burma.
91. Ibid.
92. *Towhlanyei Kaungsi ei Hluthsaungchet Thamaing Akyinchut*, pp. 261 and 218; Letter, R.J. Stratton to V.C. Martin, Commonwealth Relations Department, 18 May 1966, DO 196/333.
93. GDR GC YGN Resch to Deputy Minister, MFAA, 24 August 1966, AA PA MFAA C 161, 1060–63.
94. *Towhlanyei Kaungsi ei Hluthsaungchet Thamaing Akyinchut*, p. 223; FO371/185948.
95. Telegram, Bucharest to SOS, 28 June 1966, Bucharest Tel 1223, Pol 7 Burma, No. 27675.
96. PREM 13/3071; FO371/185948
97. Interview with former Colonel Ko Ko Gyi, London, June 2005.
98. Letter, R.A. Fyjis-Walker to illegible, 8 August 1966, FO371/185975.
99. Letter, L.J.B. Wakely to D.F. Murray, 24 June 1966, FO371/185975.
100. Maurice Collis, *Diaries: 1949–1969*, edited and introduced by Louise Collis (London: Heinemann, 1977), p. 189. Daw Khin May Than's reference to the Burmese being lazy is echoed in many European writings on colonial Burma. See the discussion in Jonathan Saha, *Law, Disorder and the Colonial State: Corruption in Burma c. 1900* (London: Palgrave Macmillan, 2013). George MacDonald Fraser provides a view in his wartime memoir of Burma as follows:

> The Burmese of the south had discovered a dimension of leisure unknown to the West; they lived in their bashas, planted their rice, ate mangoes and bananas, sat on their verandahs and smoked by way of exercise, and enjoyed an existence of complete tranquility which even a full-scale war seldom disturbed. Probably no people on earth moved so slowly, or so infrequently.

Quartered Safe Out Here: A Recollection of the War in Burma (London: Harper Collins, 2000), p. 157. However, other Southeast Asians shared these views of their fellow countrymen. As Prince Souphanouvong, the so-called Red Prince who eventually became President of his country after its long civil war wrote in 1956,

> As long as the Lao will not rid themselves of their disastrous inclination to make the least effort, you may be certain that they will never have any other profession, craft, or livelihood than those of the low wage-earner, the artisan, the coolie, and the debtor. In the end, they will not enjoy a single liberty on their own soil.

Quoted in William J. Rust, *Before the Quagmire: American Intervention in Laos, 1954–1961* (Lexington: University Press of Kentucky, 2012), p. 47.

101. Telegram, Byroade to SOS, 2 May 1966.
102. Memorandum to the President, 12 August 1966, "Where do we stand vis-à-vis the Ne Win dinner at the White House", LBJ Library, Box 235, Ne Win Briefing Book.
103. Interview, Ruth A. McLendon, Political/Consular Officer, Rangoon, 1962–66, Association for Diplomatic Studies and Training, 2012, Burma, p. 62.
104. He had also been an agent for Timken Roller Bearing Company, Harnischfeger Corporation, the Galion Iron Works and Manufacturing Company, and Iowa Manufacturing Company, among other United States companies. At one time Daniel Rose, who helped arrange Ne Win's first trip to the United States with Bo Set Kya, was a partner in Setkya Motors. Telegram, Rangoon to SOS, 22 August 1966, LBJ Library, Box 235, Burma, Ne Win Visit Briefing Book.
105. Set Kya then acquired the legal services of the liberal civil rights lawyer Joseph Rauh's law firm and did a deal with the federal authorities in New York. In order to avoid the publicity of his contesting his deportation order, he agreed to enter a hospital in New York immediately for minor surgery. The United States government agreed to pay the costs of his treatment as he managed to convince them that he was "indigent or virtually so". He remained under tight surveillance. W.P. Bundy, "For the President's Evening Reading", 27 August 1966, Ne Win Briefing Book, Box 235, LBJ Library.
106. Memorandum for the President from W.P. Bundy, 28 August 1966, Box 235, LBJ Library. For the Kennedy-Johnson relationship, see Robert A. Caro, *The Years of Lyndon Johnson: The Passage of Power* (New York: Alfred A. Knopf, 2012), *passim*.
107. Letter to the Editor, *The Washington Post*, 10 April 1966, from Louis J. Walinsky, Walinsky Papers, Box 6, File 15.
108. Letter to Porter McKeever, Chairman, Burma Council, The Asia Society, 31 May 1966, Walinsky Papers, Vox 10, File 4.
109. Richard Butwell, "Burma Doesn't Want Aid", *The New Republic*, 3 September 1966, pp. 14–15 and correspondence from Walinsky to Butwell, 12 September, in Walinsky Papers, Box 6, File 15.

110. Interview, Ruth A. McLendon, Political/Consular Officer, Rangoon, 1962–66, Association for Diplomatic Studies and Training, 2012, Burma, p. 67.

111. He later brought his experiences in Burma together in a book, *Orbit of China* (London: Secker and Warburg, 1967), pp. 83–96.

112. Telegram, Bryoade, London, to SOS, 31 August 1966, London 1693 Pol 7 Burma London 1693.

113. Ne Win Briefing Book, Box 235, LBJ Library.

114. Memorandum of Conversation at 21st UNGA, 8 October 1966, Pol Burma-U.S. XR REF 19-U.S.-Burma.

115. Ne Win Briefing Book, Box 235, LBJ Library.

116. Ambassador Byroade's Cable of August 18 on Meeting with General Ne Win undated accompanied Rusk Memo to President in ibid.

117. Biographic report attached to briefing paper to the President on Ne Win and his wife in ibid.

118. *Towhlanyei Kaungsi ei Hluthsaungchet Thamaing Akyinchut*, p. 223.

119. Telegram, Byroade to Ranard, Rangoon, 9 September 1966, Pol 7 Burma, No. 43581.

120. General Ne Win's son, Pyo, recalls his father telling him subsequently that President Johnson asked his opinion on the Vietnam situation and he replied that the United States should withdraw soon. Email communication, 25 January 2015.

121. Memorandum of Conversation, General Ne Win and Ambassador W. Averill Harriman, 9 September 1966, Pol 7 Burma.

122. Memorandum of Conversation, The Undersecretary's Call on General Ne Win, 9 September 1966, Pol 7 Burma xr Pol Burma 15-1 Pol 30 Burma, No. 13998.

123. Telegram, Richard T. Ewing to American embassy in Rangoon, 11 September 1966, Pol 7 Burma, No. 009166.

124. News Conference transcript, 9 September 1966, "Diary Backup for collection, President's Appointment File", Box 44, LBJ Library.

125. Telegram, Byroade to President and Secretary of State, 18 September 1966, Defense Dept Pol 7 Burma, No. 015968.

126. *Towhlanyei Kaungsi ei Hluthsaungchet Thamaing Akyinchut*, p. 218; FO371/185948.

127. Airgram, Embassy Bangkok to SOS, 7 October 1966, DEF 7 Burma Pol Burma-Thai No. A-292; also FO371/185948; *Towhlanyei Kaungsi ei Hluthsaungchet Thamaing Akyinchut*, p. 218.

128. Airgram, Embassy Bangkok to SOS, 7 October 1966, DEF 7 Burma Pol Burma-Thai, No. A-292.

129. *Forward*, vol. 5, no. 7 (15 November 1966): 2.

130. "Morning News" of India, 17 October 1966, DO 196/334. Tin Maung Maung Than, *State Dominance in Myanmar: The Political Economy of Industrialisation* (Singapore: Institute of Southeast Asian Studies, 2007), p. 132. Burma was

the only non-Commonwealth country in the sterling bloc in South and Southeast Asia.

131. Telegram, Rangoon to SOS, 17 October 1966, Rangoon Pol 7 Burma Burma-U.S., No. 014225.

132. Letter, P.W.M. Vereker to Miss P. Stanbridge, 16 November 1966, FO371/186159; Letter, W.I. Combs to R.H. Hanbury-Tenison, 17 November 1966, FO371/185974.

133. *Towhlanyei Kaungsi ei Hluthsaungchet Thamaing Akyinchut*, p. 218; FO 371/185948.

134. PREM 13/3071

135. The guns were almost certainly Israeli made Uzi submachine guns.

10

PREPARATION FOR TRANSITION
(March 1967 to February 1972)

In wars of rebellion, there is other knowledge required ... not only knowledge of the country, but the disposition of the people.

George Washington

Five years after seizing power, Ne Win had experienced many frustrations and disappointments. He readily admitted that the economy was dysfunctional, that the government had no adequate development plans, that its statistical base was woefully inadequate, that rice production was falling, and the men upon whom he was relying to build a socialist economy did not know what they were doing. But still he pressed on and did not change course. His underlying motive for the revolution that he had created could not be achieved by turning back. Burma had to be pulled up by its bootstraps and self-government restored. Moreover, Burma existed in the midst of a hostile world. The Americans were deep into their Southeast Asian quagmire, with the battle in Laos and Vietnam threatening Cambodia. Thailand, sanctuary to Ne Win's political and insurgent opponents, was locked into the American embrace. Myanmar apparently had amicable relations with its other neighbours, Pakistan, India and China, but the world was an uncertain place and no one could predict the future. As during the previous two years, so through the next few, Rangoon was occasionally a venue for quiet diplomacy to attempt to resolve the wars in Indochina. Ne Win stayed as far from such diplomacy as possible and claimed he was not in the habit of consulting with United Nations (UN) Secretary General U Thant, or anyone else, over the war in Vietnam or other matters.[1] Preserving his neutrality in the Cold War came above all else.

Nevertheless, this did not mean that he did not take his responsibility and opportunities as a statesman on the world stage seriously. When U Thant visited Yangon in February and March 1967, he arranged, via the Soviet Undersecretary at the United Nations, Alexi Nesterenko, to have a secret meeting with North Vietnamese representatives in Yangon. North Vietnam, of course, was not a member of the world body. As Thant recalled in his memoirs:

> I arrived in Rangoon on February 24 and called on Generals Ne Win and San Yu the next day. They told me a delegation from Hanoi would arrive in Rangoon in a few days, and described to me the arrangements that had secretly been made for my meeting with the North Vietnamese delegation, whose arrival in Rangoon would not be announced, as requested by Hanoi. At 9 P. M. on March 2, a senior Burmese military officer took us from the government guest house to the residence of the North Vietnamese consul general. Normally the drive would have taken about six or seven minutes, but since press cars were trailing us, we took a roundabout route to mislead the journalists. I arrived at the destination twenty minutes later, with no sign of any press cars in view (Thant 1977, p. 73).

Ne Win could look back on his and his government's diplomatic activities during the previous five years as a success. Myanmar was as isolated as it could be from the wars and potential wars surrounding it. Relations with China were cordial, the Communist giant's leaders frequent visitors with Ne Win, and China's £30 million loan for twelve development projects in key industrial sectors, given in 1961 after the settlement of the border agreement, was contributing to socialist construction (Steinberg and Fan 2012, p. 88). Relations with India were also cordial and Ne Win was on friendly, if not intimate, terms with the top Indian leadership.[2] Standing aloof from the dispute between Sukarno's Indonesia and the new state of Malaysia, *Konfrontasi,* Myanmar preserved its neutrality in Southeast Asia's most threatening rift. Even relations with the United States, after years of strain and suspicion, were on an even and mutually beneficial basis. Small amounts of American military equipment were made available at significantly reduced prices[3] and the pledge of assistance in extremis, made by President Kennedy, was implicitly underscored by the state visit Ne Win made to Washington the previous year.

However, past achievements do not necessarily ensure future success. If the situation in Southeast Asia was hostile, so was also now China, previously seen as a friend and supporter, now entering into the thralls of the Cultural Revolution which was about to spill over from being an internal crisis into international relations, engendering a fundamentally different attitude towards Burma and Ne Win. In Burma, while domestically the army had been able to contain the Communist and ethnically designated insurgents whom it faced, for nearly two decades now, none of them had been defeated or eliminated. The Myanmar army, the People's Army, with approximately 122,000 men and a few women (Aung Myoe 2009, p. 33, Table 2.1), faced possibly 14,000 ethnically designated rebels, mainly under the banner of groups speaking for the Kayin, Kachin, Shan, and Bengali Muslims, and another 1,000 hard-core White Flag Communists and perhaps 200 Red Flag supporters. The White Flags, operating primarily in the Bago Yoma, were isolated and posed little threat to the government and the other groups were scattered across large but separate swathes of the country and were incapable of combining their forces to take on the government in a serious attempt to overthrow the regime.[4]

Ne Win's opponents from the regime he had ousted and described by many of his colleagues as "rightists" were obviously angry at his treatment of them, but were either incarcerated or ineffective in their opposition to his rule. Their incarceration was one of the prices they had to pay not only for their previous incompetence, but also for the revolution he wanted to carry out. Reality, unpleasant as it was, had to be faced. He had a larger goal and that was to change the attitudes and skills of the indigenous population of Myanmar. As he remarked to the outgoing British ambassador in September 1967, it was unfair to blame the leader. After all, "what the leader could do was limited by the nature of his people."[5] Therefore, he had to change his people and get his domestic arrangements in order. In the fifth year of the revolution, Ne Win largely stayed at home and tended to the routines of managing the state and trying to get the socialist economic system to produce the goods and services which would fulfil its promise.

The people he wanted to change had, until then, been relatively moderate and tolerant in responding to the treatment Ne Win had given them during the previous half decade. Most who thought about politics shared his nationalist vision and his socialist rhetoric. The soldiers with whom he worked most closely believed in him as their leader, even if they felt the "rough side of his tongue". The loyalty of the army to Ne Win was in no doubt, but he wanted to build a party to rule as a socialist politician, not merely as a military dictator. Party and constitution building was proving to be slower and more difficult than he expected. The Worker's Councils and the Peasant's Councils, filled at the top with former Communists and strong socialists, as well as his military colleagues, talked the talk of the workers and peasants revolution, but somehow were not connecting closely with the people they were meant to lead. Both the Worker's Councils and the Peasant's Councils were tasked not only with increasing production for the achievement of socialism, but also to contribute to national defence (Steinberg 1970, pp. 136–37). Never lost sight of was the link between domestic and defence and foreign policy. People's militias began to be formed again to defend the revolution, but their loyalty might be in doubt if tested.

Thorough nationalization of the economy and the health and educational systems[6] inherited from the British, and modified by the civil governments of the 1950s, had been accepted, if grudgingly, even by the people most affected. "Kicking out the Indians", as many had seen the nationalization of the economy, had undoubtedly been popular with many ardent nationalists unaffected initially by the disorder in the economy. Those who were dislodged, but remained, had found positions in the trade corporations and state run schools and hospitals. In many ways, things continued as before, but with tighter rations and in a drabber and rather militarized manner. Ration-book socialism worked, but only if you did not work too hard, and the black market was available for what the state could not provide. Five years into the revolution, no solutions to these problems were in sight and new problems were about to emerge which would severely test the Ne Win regime and his resolve. The people whom Ne Win led, and sought to change, were having their patience tested. Perhaps Ne Win felt tested as well.

In 1967, the economy was facing an increasing balance of payments deficit and rice production was declining, as was per capita income. Although rice production was badly affected by a cyclone which hit the coast of Rakhine in May, Rakhine having been hit by another cyclone the previous year, the rice crisis and prices of commodities was largely a man-made, not a natural, disaster. When U Nu and the other politicians tried to capitalize on the cyclone tragedy by using a disaster fund-raising campaign as a ruse for what the government saw as political agitation, their activities were eventually banned,[7] but not before Nu was able to once more demonstrate his popularity (Law-Yone 2013, p. 171). Nu's public appearances, recorded in the government press, "drew admiring and respectful crowds" (Trager 1969, p. 108; see also Butwell 1969, p. 869). Paddy production had reached a peak of 8.37 million tons in 1964–65 but declined to 6.53 million tons in 1966–67, while rice exports had fallen by more than half during the same time from 1.47 million tons to 0.55 million tons.[8]

The rapid and nearly complete nationalization of the economy had resulted in severe shortages in goods, including rice, as farmers avoided the monopolistic state-purchasing system for the much more lucrative black market. Hoarding of rice by peasants was also a complaint often made by the government. The fact that farmers failed to repay agricultural loans extended to them in previous years meant that there was a shortfall in the ability of the government to incentivize production. The government's efforts to keep urban rice prices low was also working as a disincentive to production, and consequently there was a shortfall in rice available for export, thus hitting the ability of the government to import goods now in very short supply. Cooking oil and other basic commodities became very expensive and some have argued that Ne Win used anti-Chinese riots in mid-1967 as a diversion from the government's mismanagement of the economy (for a summary of these views, see Steinberg and Fan 2012, pp. 109–11).

Despite Ne Win's articulation of the economy as at the heart of his government's policy, he allowed economic management to remain the preserve of Tin Pe and Ba Nyein. Not until October 1967 was the Burma Socialist Programme Party's Socialist Economic Planning Committee established, with Ne Win as its Chairman. Not until January 1971 did the Party form a Long-Term Plan Formulation Committee. This eventually produced a report and plan directives for submission to the first party congress (Tin Maung Maung Than 2006, pp. 115–16). In the meantime, the economy floundered.

In this uncertain atmosphere, Ne Win looked for support and assistance where he could find it, particularly if it came from a non-threatening source. West Germany became one such source, with Japan another. Ne Win and U Thi Han, the Foreign Minister, met for more than an hour in late May 1967 to discuss cooperation between the government in Bonn and Burma.

The talks were prompted by a visit by Dr Rolf Lahr, the permanent secretary of the German foreign ministry, who was accompanied by Ambassador Keiser. Lahr outlined German foreign policy towards Asia as predicated on three principles: non-interference in domestic affairs, cooperation and assistance, and the promotion of peace. These were all highly satisfactory to Ne Win and the conversation, which covered both the question of divided Germany and economic cooperation, was described as "hearty". It was the continuation of a deepening relationship.[9] Though official state-to-state relations strengthened after 1967, the ongoing relationship between the Fritz-Werner Company, expanding from arms manufacturing to economic development projects, and the Myanmar army was the larger part of Ne Win's German connections. That relationship went back to 1956, eventually building three arms and ammunition factories in Yangon and on the west side of the Ayeyawady River near Pyay.[10]

While Ne Win was considering relations with Germany, more immediate problems arose in Yangon. On 19 June, the Ministry of Education banned the wearing of unauthorized badges by students while in school uniform. This was directed at the wearing of Mao badges which the Chinese embassy had been distributing as part of the effort to export the Cultural Revolution to the world.[11] Soon students of Chinese descent at the 259 now nationalized Chinese schools, in the presence of Chinese embassy and Xinhua news agency staff, began to protest against the ban and, on 26 June, thousands of Burmese began attacking Chinese-owned shops and the Chinese embassy in retaliation.[12] Martial law was soon declared but not before 50 to 80 persons were reported to have been killed, including a Chinese technician when the Chinese embassy was attacked and looted by a Burmese mob. Martial law in Yangon was to last throughout July as the situation remained very tense. On 29 June, the Chinese ambassador was withdrawn, the Chinese aid programme soon terminated, and Chinese journalists expelled. Radio Beijing then began a campaign of vilification of the Ne Win government, accusing it of being "counter-revolutionary, fascist and reactionary", and Ne Win of being "Burma's Chiang Kai-shek".[13] Fighting with the Burma Communist Party escalated in July, opening a new front along the Chinese border in the Kokang region, with the assistance of Chinese "volunteers". A new front had been opened in the civil war as China began directly aiding the BCP in its fight with the government, another consequence of the Chinese Cultural Revolution. The export of the Cultural Revolution had put *Pauk-phaw* (cousinly relations) in suspension and all of Ne Win's cultivation of the Chinese leadership had apparently come to nought (a good account of the riots and their consequences is Fan 2012, pp. 234–56).

That the two crises occurred at approximately the same time may have been fortuitous for Ne Win, as his firm stand against the Chinese showed him to be a sincere and devoted Myanmar nationalist. His critics need to ask what the public response would have been had the government not taken firm action against the students, backed by a foreign government which was believed to be intrinsically hostile to Myanmar and was supporting an armed insurgency in the country. The Chinese effort to export the Cultural Revolution to Myanmar impinged on Myanmar state sovereignty and the state's obligation to maintain order. Any government would have responded similarly. Nonetheless, it has been suggested that a contributing factor to the anti-Chinese mood in Yangon was the alleged "increasingly xenophobic atmosphere that had enveloped the country after Ne Win's seizure of power" (Smith 1999, p. 225).

Ne Win himself was often accused of being a xenophobe.[14] The standard definition of xenophobia, the noun of the adjectival form, is "an intense or irrational dislike or fear of people from other countries". If we examine Ne Win's personal life, it is difficult to see how he could be described as a xenophobe. He travelled the world, dealing with people from many nations and had house guests from Europe, Japan and the United States. His personal cook and valet was an Indian, Raju. He preferred to holiday in England and, increasingly, in Germany and elsewhere in Europe. His tastes were cosmopolitan. That he pursued nationalist economic policies which he believed were designed to force Myanmar to develop through the utilization of its own resources, including human resources, as yet undeveloped, there can be no doubt. However, on this, he and the people with whom he worked were no different from many other leaders in Asia and Africa in the 1960s and beyond. There was clearly no fear of people from other countries and, of course, rationality or irrationality is a contingent judgement. As Furnivall argued in *Colonial Policy and Practice*, since there was no single, unified society in colonial Burma, there could be no common will and therefore no common view of the country's interest. To attempt to create a common will was an aspect of Ne Win's goals. That is not the same as xenophobia. Framing domestic policies for the benefit of the indigenous population is, afterall, one of the key justifications for nationalism.[15] If socialism and nationalism equate to xenophobia, then probably half or more of the world's population was xenophobic in the 1950s, 1960s and 1970s.

Whilst Ne Win's government was coping with the anti-Chinese riots in Yangon, near the border where Thailand, Myanmar and Laos meet, there were reports of heavy fighting between the KMT forces and a drug caravan belonging to Khun Sa, an opium warlord who had formed a local unit of militia in 1963 known as the Ka Kwe Ye (KKY), nominally loyal to the Burmese government. The Laotian Air Force was reported to have intervened and made off with the opium for themselves. Fighting continued later in July in the same area between Khun Sa's KKY and Shan State Army and KMT troops. The Communist Chinese government also became involved in border affairs, protesting on 11 August that the Burma Air Force had intruded into Yunnan, claiming also that Burmese troops had fired into Yunnan and had crossed the border on at least twenty-seven occasions. As relations with China deteriorated and the instability of northern Myanmar grew, riots broke out in the west of the country at Sittwe over apparent rice shortages, and resulted in a number of deaths on 19 August. There were also reports of protests over inflation and food prices in other parts of the country (Smith 1999, p. 225).

However, Ne Win was in London then, having left Yangon on 6 August for further medical treatment from Dr Sir Clifford Naunton Morgan.[16] Learning of his presence in London, the Mahadevi of Mongmit, the doughty Mabel from East London, wife of Sao Hkun Hkio, U Nu's foreign minister, drove to Wimbledon and parked her car in the driveway of the residence at which Ne Win normally resided when in London. Mabel had been expelled from Burma the previous April, perhaps as a result of her conversations with Princess Alexandra in January. Her Wimbledon protest was to demand the release of her husband from the detention he was enduring, now in its fifth year. Having made her point and gained adequate publicity and embarrassment for both Ne Win and the British government, she departed after a second day's "park in", having been told that Ne Win was not in the house but at a nursing home receiving treatment.[17] Ne Win himself returned to Yangon on 31 August.

Three weeks later, the Japanese Prime Minister, Eisaku Sato, arrived in Yangon for a three-day visit.[18] According to a Japanese report to the United States embassy, on the first day of Sato's visit, he and Ne Win met twice, the second time at Ne Win's initiative, for a total of two hours and forty-five minutes. The conversation centred on China, Vietnam, the Soviet

Union, and economic cooperation. At the end of the visit, Sato, who had met with Ne Win in October the previous year, was apparently struck by the naivete of the Burmese but the intelligence and keen mind of Ne Win. As a result, he wanted to do something for Burma.[19] He was followed two months later by the West German Chancellor, Kurt Kiesinger.[20] Soon after Kiesinger's departure, Ne Win hosted a dinner for the delegates to the Colombo Plan Coordination Council dinner in Yangon on 27 November. In earlier years, Ne Win had intentionally avoided appearing overtly involved with the British Commonwealth oriented Colombo Plan, but the change in relations with China made looking in that direction, and others, including the Soviet Union and Eastern Europe, advantageous if for no other reason than to remind China that Myanmar had options (Badgley 1967, p. 756).

The growing problems along the Chinese border were exacerbated when a delegation of Kachin rebels visited China in August/September, led by Brang Seng, the leader of the Kachin Independence Organisation (KIO) until his death in 1994. A second Kachin delegation, led by Zau Tu, met with Chou En-lai and other Chinese leaders, as well as Thakin Ba Thein Tin and former Captain Naw Seng, now in exile in Beijing. Chinese support for Ne Win's enemies was accumulating.

On 25 December, Ne Win invited the American ambassador and Mrs Byroade to a Christmas dinner along with three Austrian doctors, house guests of the Ne Wins. Presumably one of them was Dr Hoff who had become a close friend of the family. Ne Win, in the ambassador's estimation, appeared to be preoccupied and concerned about his personal security, though insisting that he enjoyed his trips around the country where the security cordon around him was relaxed such that he could talk with the people. Uncharacteristically, Ne Win used this primarily social occasion to discuss politics, particularly his concern that the Chinese were attempting to subvert the "ethnic tribes" on the border, that is, the Kachins.

Ne Win did not seem particularly concerned about this, however, as there were "39 different tribes and dialects" among the Kachins and the Chinese would have to expend a huge effort to unite them against the government. He was of the belief that it would take at least two generations before the problem would be resolved, even if the Chinese did not intervene in the area. "He said that Burma would stand up to China in a proper and dignified stance, no matter what … just now it was a matter of trying to deal with lunatics. … " He then went off on a long discourse on Burma's problems with China historically.[21]

Two days after the dinner, Ne Win departed Yangon for an almost week-long tour of the Ayeyawady Delta, followed two weeks later with another week spent touring the Rakhine state. Ne Win's flurry of touring, which involved visits to development projects, government-owned factories and military bases, drew the attention of the West German ambassador. He noted that Ne Win, after being withdrawn and unavailable for most of the previous year, was now making himself available to the public.[22] Whether as part of a charm offensive, a display of confidence, or a desire to rally the country in the face of growing Chinese support for Shan, Kachin and Communist insurgents, the government released 127 political detainees on 27 January 1968. Among them were Dr Ba Maw, Edward Law-Yone, Sao Hkun Hkio,[23] U Kyaw Nyein, former Brigadier Aung Gyi, and former Chief Justice U Myint Thein.

After more than a year of not making a major public address, Ne Win spoke for more than two hours at another, and final, "Peasants Seminar" at the old Rangoon Turf Club grounds,[24] now renamed the Hsaya San Grounds, after the nominal leader of a peasant revolt in the early 1930s, the memory of whom the Revolutionary Council promoted as a national hero (Aung-Thwin 2011). In his speech, Ne Win regretted the delays in organizing the Peasant's Councils which were to protect and guide the peasants' political and economic affairs. The reasons for the delays were myriad, especially as they were not as physically concentrated as the urban workers. Of particular need amongst the farmers, Ne Win believed, was their education, including: (1) expanding their knowledge and intellectual horizons; (2) providing them with the capacity for clear and critical thinking; and (3) learning to be considerate and fair in their dealings with others. He extolled the peasants to abandon their alleged traditional apathy, which he attributed to their belief in *kan* or karma, and seize the opportunities placed before them.

Three days later, on 3 March, in a relaxed mood, Ne Win met the visiting American golf champion, Paul Harney, who was a guest of the United States Information Agency. With almost the entire Revolutionary Council present, except Brigadiers Tin Pe and San Yu, but saying little, Ne Win sat with Harney and his embassy aide, pressing food and drink upon them, before playing seventeen holes of golf at seven over par on the Defence Golf Course. Colonel Tin U followed behind, managing Ne Win's security. Irritating his opponents, he danced a little jig when he made a long putt. After a thirty-minute golf clinic, Ne Win left the links after nearly four hours. "The General, at this meeting, seemed like a thoroughly likeable man", even providing Harney with cold tablets from his pocket.[25]

On 15 March, Ne Win and Daw Khin May Than flew to India on what was to have been a week-long private visit.[26] On his arrival at the airport in Delhi, Ne Win "rushed down the gangway and shook hands down the line bef ore the chief of protocol caught up with him and led him back to be photographed by the president, vice-president and [the prime minister] Mrs. Gandhi." He left "his wife far behind" as he resumed shaking hands with the small delegation sent to receive him. Amongst the large diplomatic corps, only the Singapore High Commissioner, the Thai ambassador, Prince Prem Purachatra, and the acting head of the Myanmar embassy, in the absence of Ambassador Daw Khin Kyi, came to greet him. Looking "cheerful" buy "a little embarrassed", Ne Win was apparently in a hurry to get to his hotel.[27]

According to the British High Commissioner to India, Mr John Freeman, the co-signatory of the Let Ya–Freeman Agreement, which established the British Services Mission which Ne Win finally despatched in 1954, the Indian side insisted on a number of meetings as they were agitated about possible Chinese military incursions into Northeast India or Northwest Burma. Reports of Chinese-armed Nagas reaching the Indian border across Burma from China had been received during the previous months. Ne Win considered these reports exaggerated and felt that India was overstating the Chinese threat. In reviewing domestic affairs in Myanmar, Ne Win regretted having to arrest his opponents, but there were threats to assassinate him which could not be ignored. As for relations with the United Kingdom, he indicated that his government did not like being lectured by British bankers and officials over Burma's leaving the Sterling Area, in anticipation of the Wilson government's expected devaluation against the United States dollar in November 1967, a move which would have further undermined Myanmar's already slim international reserves.[28]

Approximately a month after returning from India, Ne Win left for a trip to Singapore, his first since the island state was expelled from Malaysia. The trip was in combination with a visit to Malaysia as well, three days in the first and five in the second.[29] In Singapore, Ne Win attended the standard state banquet and had several conversations with top leaders as well as touring the new Jurong industrial estate. Speaking on the cusp of the formation of the Association of Southeast Asian Nations (ASEAN) in August 1967, which other non-Communist Southeast Asian leaders were pushing Ne Win to join, he felt impelled to state a position on regionalism in a speech in Singapore:

> In South East Asia today, there are powerful forces at work — forces which have their origin in countries of the region and which have their origin outside the region. The interplay of these forces will influence the future of South East Asia. Though the conflict between the forces outside the region casts its shadows over the political scene, we in Burma believe that ultimately only the forces of the region will prevail and play a decisive role in determining the kind of South East Asia we shall have to live in.
>
> For our part, we look forward to the kind of South East Asia in which every nation will be free to live its own life in its own way. We believe that in such a community of nations it will be possible for each nation also to live in peace and friendship with its neighbours. But such a situation will not come about of itself: all the nations of the region will have to work for it steadfastly. It is to fit in with those objectives that we have fashioned our national policy (quoted in Aung Myoe 2006, p. 5).

He and Prime Minister Lee once more had a round of golf but Ne Win demonstrated no security concerns on that occasion as he had in Yangon three years earlier (Lee 2000, p. 361). In a similar manner, the Malaysian itinerary consisted of dinners, meetings, and golf sessions.[30] Nothing of substance was agreed, but certainly the talks concerned ongoing developments in global and regional politics. Myanmar remained aloof from ASEAN, then composed of the five anti-Communist states in the region, all having defence agreements or military pacts with Western states.

The routines of official foreign visits and managing day-to-day affairs of state were suddenly interrupted when Daw Khin May Than had a health crisis, reported as a cardiovascular illness. She and Ne Win arrived in London on 11 May 1968 and went directly to the London Clinic. Health and Education Minister Hla Han, who was at that time on a trip to West Germany, immediately cancelled all of his engagements and rushed to London to be with Ne Win.[31] While Daw Khin May Than recuperated in the London Clinic, Ne Win, amongst other things, had another lunch with Prime Minister Harold Wilson.

The conversation over lunch covered various topics, including the nuclear non-proliferation treaty which had just been opened to accession. Ne Win, whom Wilson thought was very well-informed on the subject, refused to sign on behalf of Burma, on the grounds that the treaty was unfair as long as those powers who had nuclear weapons refused to give them up.[32] As to the situation in Southeast Asia, the possible increase of Chinese influence in the region as a consequence of the

Vietnam War did not necessarily mean that the countries there would buckle to Chinese pressure. As he said, "Although a weaker creature, when cornered by a tiger, a stag would fight to the death." Ne Win tended to dismiss the idea of cooperation amongst the states of Southeast Asia as unlikely because of their conflicting interests and strong sense of nationalism.[33]

Remaining in London until 29 June, on the day before departure he had a meeting with Her Majesty, the Queen, in which they allegedly discussed the situation in China and the ongoing insurgency in Myanmar.[34] Even after her treatment in London, Daw Khin May Than was still not well. Ne Win was very solicitous of her health and expressed concern at a party the Myanmar representative of Pan American airlines hosted. He was considering purchasing a portable kidney dialysis machine for her.[35] One was eventually installed in the military hospital at Mingaladon but was apparently never used by her. A planned trip by the Ne Wins to Germany in October appeared also to have been cancelled because of her condition.[36]

Though Myanmar, under Ne Win's leadership, was attempting to maintain its neutralist and non-aligned credentials during the height of the ever more complex Cold War, its allegiance to one of the key principles of non-alignment, non-interference in the internal affairs of other states, sorely tested the principle of neutrality. In contrast to his position on most international crises of the period, including the war in Vietnam, Ne Win led his government to a firm stand in opposition to the Soviet invasion of the reformist Communist state of Czechoslovakia under the government of Alexander Dubcek. This, of course, pleased the countries in the Western bloc, particularly West Germany, which was increasingly worried about the development of relations between Myanmar and East Germany.[37]

In the midst of dealing with many matters that had been in abeyance during his unexpected period abroad, Ne Win still had time to entertain foreign guests. One was the "touchy", indeed "rather humourless and a bit pompous", Professor Alan Woodruff, at that time Professor of Clinical Tropical Medicine at the London School of Hygiene and Tropical Medicine. In Woodruff's honour, a dinner for fifty was arranged, which included Daw Khin May Than's father, Dr Ba Than, then Rector of Medical Institute Number 1, where Dr Willcocks C. Manson-Bahn was advising on tropical medicine for one year. Ne Win was almost the only Myanmar who spoke throughout the entire evening, though many members of the Revolutionary Council and their wives were also present.[38]

High on his agenda at that time was the work of preparing for the Annual Commanders' Conference which would take place within a month, followed immediately by the Third Party Seminar. The two meetings had been postponed until late September, having been originally scheduled for earlier in the year. Ne Win's concluding speech at the commander's conference commenced with a brief discussion about the planned organization, again by the army, of armed people's militias to assist in fighting the growing insurgency.[39] Insurgency had been growing amongst the ethnic minorities, especially in the north and east of the country as a consequence of a number of interrelated phenomena in the late 1960s.

One, of course, was the Chinese Communist support for Kachin and other insurgents. Another was the ready availability of small arms leaking from Thailand, Laos and Vietnam into Myanmar. A third was the growth of the black market with increasing quantities of jade, cattle, opium and other products being smuggled mainly to Thailand, in exchange for the commodities unavailable because of the deficiencies of the socialist economy. Ideologically, the perception that the government was Bamar-dominated, despite efforts to separate religion and ethnicity from politics, added to the justifications advanced for insurgency by a growing number of local elites in the name of putative "group rights" (Renard 1996, pp. 6–7; McCoy 1991, pp. 367–69, 424–25). Ne Win drew attention in a speech to the necessity of vetting those who volunteered to take up arms to defend the state unless they were proven to be loyal. This lead to the perception that it was mainly the Bamar that the government trusted because of the recruitment of Bamar during and after the civil war period.

Ne Win then launched into a lengthy historical discourse on the rise of states and the use of violence in state and class formation until the industrial revolution in England. He linked this to the rise of imperialism and the growth of the middle class as first traders, then exploiters. Diverting to a discussion on the rise of parliament, Cromwell, and the beheading of Charles I, he explained, "What I want to stress here is the dangerous nature of militarism", having drawn attention to the role of Colonel Thomas Pride and the fear of the army on the part of the parliament.

He next turned to the French Revolution and the rise of Napoleon. Napoleon may have started out with good intentions but he became enamoured with power and was the creator of nepotism. Ne Win wished

to stress that the lesson that could be learned from the French Revolution
and Napoleon was that "at a time of political unrest, there were few
organisations or men a country could rely on". However, he went on a
few paragraphs later,

> It is very important that we should not be like Napoleon. We
> should work for the welfare of the country. If we acted like
> Napoleon, not only we, but the country we love and people we love
> would also suffer. The country would suffer more than we do. Power
> is now in our hands. We must not use it to serve our selfish interests.
> It is our responsibility to re-invest this power in the hands of the
> people.

Calling on all of the army to work sincerely, for even if projects fail,
"If a body in power works sincerely in the interests of the country, the
people will trust them even if they have to live in poverty." Continuing,
he said,

> Whoever is working dishonestly, whether he be from the army or from
> outside, is sure to meet his downfall.
>   We will have to continue to work for the country. When we are
> gone, others will take our place. For me, I do not want to take the
> leadership for too long. If we do not take the leadership, others will
> do it. Those who take the political leadership of the country should
> see that there is no disorder.
>   An army is an organisation formed to defend a country. A
> country has a right to form an army but if the army goes beyond its
> responsibility of defence, it is transgressing its role.

He then reverted back to his discussion of history, drawing attention to
how the United States army, though growing out of unusual circumstances,
became the tool of imperialists when it fought the Spanish but refused
to give the Philippines the independence that the Filipinos had expected.
As for the Myanmar army, it came out of the Burma Independence
Army and its successors but it had to use former British soldiers out of
necessity. He then discussed at some length the problems with the British
Services Mission in the days after independence when the British had
insisted on raising Shan, Kachin, Chin and Kayin regiments. With no
explication of motive or purpose of the British, he noted that the army
needed ammunition and equipment but were faced by conditions posed
by the British.

However, faced with the intransigence of the British and the need to raise troops to defend Yangon, Ne Win recounted how he sent men, some just privates, to various towns in the districts in 1949 to raise more men to return to Yangon to defend the city. This was the origin of the initial levies, but some of them turned against the army and were used by politicians, while others became dacoit levies, so "they had to be disbanded at last" for they fought against the people. The politicians, however, without the interests of the country at heart, raised the Union Military Police (UMP) as an army composed of men who were once from the BIA or BDA, but had been rejected by the army on reorganization. The UMP, like the levies, "brought more turbulence than benefit to the country" because, rather than being one disciplined force, it was in reality a number of smaller forces following different political leaders. Even when the UMP had been brought under the army, some politicians tried to use it as a force to coerce people to vote in the 1960 elections. However, as Ne Win noted, "Arms, no matter how they are used, cannot influence the people's thoughts."

Having reviewed the history of the Myanmar army, Ne Win turned to the topic of a transition towards a new political order and constitution. On this, the army had to guard against corruption in all forms, including flattery and religiosity. They had to practise honesty and to also accept former politicians who had demonstrated their honesty and loyalty to the country back into politics. The army was now involved in politics and, "If politicians are no good, we are no good either." The officer corps had to learn to delegate and share responsibility with others. Referring again to the formation of the levies to assist the army, Ne Win also justified the role of the army in the administration of social and economic affairs but, just as in war times, civilians, including politicians, rally to defend the country, so soldiers were expected to do more than mere blind fighting. They have to be with the people. Perhaps unwittingly, through his stumbling oratory, he was laying out the rationale for the military's political dominance in Myanmar for the next half century and beyond.

This oration, a long version of the history of the use of force and an implicit discussion of a number of criticisms of the army, was a defence of its role, but also a warning of the dangers of remaining in power for too long or without the right motives. The theme of unity was the major point with which Ne Win started his address six days later at the conclusion of the Third BSPP seminar.[40] In the interim between his two speeches, a dramatic development had occurred in the country's politics. Recalling that the country was behind because it had been enslaved, and also because of the lack of unity and internecine conflicts, the fruits of independence had only been slightly tasted, especially by the workers and peasants. Turning to specifics, he drew attention to the release of political detainees the previous January. Some in the party had seen this as a sign of turning to the political right. That was not the case. Those who were detained were because they were angry and therefore "could not think objectively". They were seeking arms and attempting to assassinate the leaders of the state and party. Most of those detained were "our personal friends", but for reasons of state, regrettably, they had to be taken into custody. However, as the right-wing countries in world politics were facing many difficulties now, the danger of the release of the rightists injuring the country was remote. Also, those released were citizens and fellow Myanmar.

Turning to internal party unity, Ne Win argued that this could only be achieved through interparty dialogue and discussion. People should be broadminded, especially those at the top, and listen to the opinions of others, even when they disagreed with their own beliefs. People should not be afraid of retaliation if they expressed their opinions. Also, cliques and factionalism were to be avoided because, though such behaviour grew out of the human trait of selfishness and ambition, factionalism should be excluded from the party. He then went through a litany of factionalism in Myanmar politics, going back to the *Myanma Athin Chokkyi* (General Council of Burmese Associations, or GCBA) split in 1922, caused in part by the British offering the dyarchic constitutional order. Noting that his first teachers from the national high school in Pyay refused to take government employment for many years, one being his English teacher, the elder brother of General San Yu. He believed this was an example of true patriotism, but even they eventually had to seek government employment.

The failure of the GCBA to remain united in opposition to the British gave rise, he argued, to the *Dobama Asiayon*, but eventually it also split, for either principled or personal reasons. Ne Win was uncertain which caused the parties to factionalize. The faction leaders told their followers, however, "Only we really love the country and only we really work for the country." The other faction, they accused, was composed of "spies". And, "we believed what our hsayas (leaders/teachers) said". He only learned they were wrong when they got to Hainan and began training with members of the other faction. However, even back in Myanmar, and after they had chosen Dr Ba Maw as the leader of the government, the Thakin party was not truly united. Thakin Ba Sein and Thakin Tun Ok, through personal ambition which led to factionalism, fell for a Japanese ruse. Rather than consulting with their colleagues in the party, they accepted an offer to fly to Japan for political training, with the promise at the end that they would return to Yangon and oust Dr Ba Maw. Of course, they were arrested and put into exile when they reached Singapore. Ne Win claimed to have seen through the ruse but could not persuade the two to abandon their plans.

Ne Win then briefly reviewed the many splits which occurred following the union of the Communist Party and the army within the Anti-Fascist Organisation (AFO). After the British returned, the Burma Communist Party (BCP) splited into two. Then the People's Volunteer Organisation, formed out of the army, divided into pro- and anti-Communist factions. The Communists split from the Anti-Fascist People's Freedom League (AFPFL), as the AFO came to be known. Continuing on the theme of unity, Ne Win then said

> Speaking about communists, news we received the other day was most tragic. Some might say I should be overjoyed over the elimination of the enemy. But I know and I believe that certain personalities among communists are true patriots. The death of every true patriot is a loss to the country. Of course I have no comment about the other personalities amongst the Communists who are headstrong in their actions with no regard for the country. This is our attitude toward patriots even if they are our arch enemies.[41]

He was referring to the death of Thakin Than Tun on 24 September. Thakin Than Tun, the leader of the White Flag Communist Party, was assassinated by his own party members in an excess of revolutionary zeal as the Burma Communist Party emulated the behaviour of the Chinese Communists during the Cultural Revolution.

Rambling on, including a reference to the split in the AFPFL which lead to his 1958 Caretaker Government, Ne Win stated that when he referred to patriotism, he did not mean narrow and extreme nationalism. To paraphrase his colloquial expression, Myanmar needed to share in order to help others who did not have full bellies. By way of conclusion, he remarked,

> It is better to consult than to come to a decision on your own. This is the democracy we want. Before coming to decisions, study all facets of the issue. We must look not only at what is under our eyes but also at things beyond. Don't think that the sprinter who comes in first

in a 100 meter dash at 11 seconds under your eyes is the best man. Somewhere else some other sprinter might be doing the distance at 10 seconds. When we look at a thing, we must visualise how it will look from the other side. In fact we should look at it from all angles before we make our decision. This will help up to minimize the chance of error. Even then mistakes are sometimes made. After all, mortals are not infallible. That is all.

While that was all of Ne Win's speech-making that day, he was to make similar speeches for years to come. The ideals enunciated proved impossible to achieve, despite his intentions. Indeed, his personal behaviour often belied his intentions. Meanwhile, affairs of state and the joys of travel lay more immediately ahead.

With the increasing support for the Communists provided by China, insurgent activity was heavily reported in the government media. During the third quarter of 1968, firefights of over 30 minutes in duration more than doubled over the previous quarter and the government took the offensive, launching 141 raids against the insurgents' 83, reversing the ratio of the previous quarter. The insurgents were unable to mount large offensives, with the Communists raising raiding parties of up to 100 men.[42] The levies that Ne Win discussed in his speeches included the Ka Kwe Ye, Khun Sa's opium-smuggling band which eventually turned into a Shan separatist force. The use of these groups was a stopgap measure taken to deal with the growing threat from China. In exchange for turning a blind eye to their smuggling activities, Khun Sa and his men could carry on as long as they served to keep out the Communists. When they joined with the Shan separatists, as they eventually did, the army began to pursue them along with the other insurgent forces in the Shan State. According to a Burmese employee of the American consulate in Mandalay who observed KKY in Lashio, the troops were comprised of Shan and other ethnicities, but the officers, like Khun Sa, were of Chinese descent, some probably ex-KMT. Their relations with the regular army were bad and they were known to be used as smuggling bands by so-called "upper class" or rich Shan families, the former Sawbwa.[43]

Ne Win's state visit to West Germany, which was initially indicated as cancelled due to Daw Khin May Than's health condition, was back on again by 8 August. At that time, Ne Win indicated that he wanted a state visit of only three or four days, with a light schedule of events. After the formal visit, they would spend some additional time in Europe.[44] The West Germans went to great lengths to make Ne Win happy, noting how pleased he was that the in-flight menu was printed in Burmese and the state crest hung on the back of the door to the cockpit on his Pan Am flight to the United States two years earlier. He requested to fly into Germany with Lufthansa and internally with the German air force.[45] As for speech-making, Ne Win indicated that he wished to make only one speech, on the occasion of a breakfast with the President of the Federal Republic.[46]

As with Ambassador Byroade, Ne Win apparently got on easily with the West German Ambassador, Rolf von Keiser. They met for an hour on 14 October to discuss plans for Ne Win's German visit during which Ne Win made no special requests other than, in the interests of his wife's health, the schedule be as informal and relaxing as possible.[47] They discussed a number of familiar topics, including the location of a German-assisted glass factory, which Ne Win believed should be located between Chauk and Pyay. On larger developmental topics, he once more discussed the country's lack of technically trained people, including accountants, and the consequences of Burma having been dominated by the British, Indians and, most recently, the Chinese. He had to guard against this happening in the future as it appeared to be occurring in Indonesia. After once more relaying the story of the Thirty Comrades and how he had been comrade-in-arms with people like Kyaw Nyein at one point, they turned to the topic of the German reunification. Ne Win was convinced that the Soviet Union would not invade another country in Eastern Europe for fear of setting off a world war. Relaxed and calm throughout the conversation, Ne Win could not be stopped during a lengthy discourse on the Japanese occupation of the country during the Second World War.

Ne Win's state visit to West Germany took place from 17 to 19 October 1968, after which he planned to visit Austria and perhaps London.[48] The President of the Federal Republic, Heinrich Lubke, who was known for his interest in the developing world, greeted Ne Win on arrival and pledged Germany's continuing assistance to Myanmar. In talks with the German Chancellor, Kurt Kiesinger, they reviewed the situation in Eastern Europe and Myanmar's relations with China. Ne Win refused to take a position on the question of the two Germanys.[49] On China, Ne Win mentioned the presence of many Chinese troops on their common border and that symbolically, relations had improved since the previous year, as the Myanmar charge d'affaires had been invited to the May Day Celebrations in Beijing. Nonetheless, for relations to improve further, Beijing would have to abandon its support for insurgency in the country.[50] From Germany, the Ne Wins departed for Vienna, returning to Yangon on 2 November.[51]

Ne Win's speeches during the latter half of 1968 and his discussions with the West German ambassador about the struggles of the young men in the anti-fascist resistance and the civil war were once more reminiscences of the days of unity amongst the nationalists of the *Dobama Asiayon*, the Thirty Comrades and the Anti-Fascist Organisation. Thoughts of their united struggle against the British, the Japanese and then the British again, may have lain at the back of Ne Win's mind as he formed the Union of Burma Internal Unity Advisory Board on 29 November. The members of the Board included U Nu, U Kyaw Nyein, and other former leaders.[52] While memories of the past may have played a role, the crisis on the Chinese border and ongoing problems in the Myanmar economy doubtless were more immediately on his mind. The failure of the unity talks with the armed insurgents in 1963 were in some ways a precursor to the offer implicit in the formation of the Board. This offer of possible collaboration with the former political elite was seen by many in the BSPP as an offer to the rightists. If the revolution was moving to the right, however, there was no sign of it in the economic policy. All cinemas were nationalized on 9 December and on the 27th of the same month, all remaining factories were nationalized.[53]

Despite her ill health the previous year, Daw Khin May Than accompanied Ne Win on an inspection tour of the South East Command area for six days after Independence Day in January 1969. They made inspections of the paper and sugar mills and visited the salt and pearl-culture industries in the region. Ne Win then set out on 27 January for a four-day visit to Pakistan, which was believed for discussions with his counterparts on relations with China.[54] He and Ayub Khan met for two hours on 28 January but Ne Win spent most of his time touring development projects.[55] Secret meetings were also held with Chinese diplomats in an attempt to restore cordial relations (Steinberg and Fan 2012, p. 120).

Other than hosting Indian Prime Minister Indira Gandhi on a state visit to Yangon at the end of March, and addressing the first meeting of the Central People's Peasant's Council, Ne Win confined his activities to non-public activities during the first months of 1969. This led to much speculation about rivalries and policy rifts within the Revolutionary Council and struggles between rightists and leftists. Hard facts, however, were hard to find.

Ne Win and his family arrived in London again on 4 April 1969, partly so that Daw Khin May Than could receive treatment for her renal condition. In a clearly relaxed mood, Ne Win met with Harold Wilson, this time at the Prime Minister's country retreat, Chequers, where they played a round of golf and had lunch. The main topic of the lunch was the forlorn British hope of gaining compensation for expropriated assets following the waves of nationalization.[56] He also met with Her Majesty the Queen, who was briefed on recent British visitors to Myanmar, which had included General Bernard Ferguson of Chindit fame; Lord Mountbatten and Princess Alexandra (1967); and Arthur Bottomley, Dorothy Woodman and Alan Woodruff (1968).[57] Ne Win, his wife, daughters and son left England for Germany on 2 May.

In Germany, they were the guests of the Fritz-Werner Company. Ne Win stayed at the private home of Dr Meyer and originally intended to remain for approximately six days but later decided to linger an additional week, cancelling a planned trip to Vienna. Dr Hoff came to Germany to see him instead. He enjoyed his stay in Geisenheim, Hessen, where Fritz-Werner had its headquarters, playing golf and visiting various German officials and industrialists, as well as spending time in the vineyard of Countess Metternich.[58] Ne Win and his family returned to Yangon around 18 or 19 May.

On 1 June, the thirty-three-member Union of Burma Internal Unity Advisory Board submitted its report to the government.[59] A number of recommendations were made, with the majority, twenty-two members, proposing a return to a multi-party political system, while eleven favoured the one-party system. U Nu, who presented a separate report in February, before departing on a religious retreat to India in April, proposed that power be handed back to him so that he could return it constitutionally to Ne Win (Butwell 1969, pp. 870–71). In addition to Nu's proposals, the various members of the Board called for a greater degree of autonomy for the ethnically designated states, while Kyaw Nyein advocated a more centralized state. The day after the report was issued, Ne Win discussed it in a non-committal manner on Myanmar radio, indicating that it would have to be studied carefully. The government eventually rejected the recommendations but published them in their entirety in the state controlled press. As with the 1963 peace talks and despite all the problems faced, the failure of the rightist politicians to fall into line with the direction Ne Win wanted did not halt the march to the construction of a socialist one-party constitutional order.

The failure of the Unity Advisory Board gambit meant that the only remaining option, it seemed, was to press on with Ne Win's ill-defined plan for a new state structure which would replace the colonial and immediate post-colonial apparatus. A key part of that apparatus was much changed in spirit and in personnel, but still remained largely intact in the shape of the British-inspired civil service. The civil service had long been a bane of Myanmar nationalists and leftist politicians and dismantling it became one of the eventual aims of the constitutional order that Ne Win was to carry out in five more years. As a step in that direction, the first deputy ministers were appointed to take over the duties previously carried out by the permanent secretaries of the ministries. The fact that the first four were also regional commanders at the time of their appointment was not unnoticed[60] and became part of how the regime that Ne Win created proved to be so strong and stable long after he was gone. Creating safe career paths for the officer corps after retirement, either in the Party or the bureaucracy or both, became a pillar of an unusually stable political order.[61]

The appointment of deputy ministers at that time, however, may have been contingent on the resignation of U Thi Han the previous month, the only civilian member of the Revolutionary Council and a trusted source for Western diplomats. Thi Han's departure further closed off information to the outside as to what was going on in the Revolutionary Council. Known for his sympathy for the views of some of the members of the Unity Advisory Board and his disenchantment with the Burmese Way to Socialism, Thi Han's departure meant that another voice that would and could stand up to Ne Win was eliminated from his circle.[62]

On 11 July, Ne Win and Daw Khin May Than departed again for London where they remained for slightly less than a month. While she received treatment for her kidney disease, they also took an excursion to the Isle of Man.[63] Soon after their return, the Ne Wins had lunch with Princess Alexandra and her husband, Angus Olgilvy, who had stopped over for three hours in Yangon on 15 August.[64] Eleven days later, Daw Khin May Than departed for Vienna to attend the funeral of Dr Hans Hoff, her late psychiatrist.[65] While she was away, United States Senator Mike Mansfield made another visit to Yangon in search of a solution to the American wars in Southeast Asia. He met with Ne Win who apparently said nothing new or startling, and the new Foreign Minister, Maung Lwin, was "extremely reluctant to stray off of platitudes".[66] Byroade's successor as American ambassador, who had not seen Ne Win for nearly a year after presenting his credentials, was more than a little miffed at Ne Win's reception of Mansfield. Mansfield drove directly to Ne Win's house on arrival and was invited for an intimate family dinner, along with his staff, but excluding the Ambassador (Oberdorfer 2003, pp. 363–64).

At about the same time, U Nu had gone on a religious pilgrimage to India, where he met with Bo Let Ya and Edward Law-Yone (Butwell 1969, pp. 873–76). Law-Yone had received a passport after writing to Ne Win and requesting an interview. It was promptly granted and when they met, Law-Yone was "seized … in a long bear hug before leading him into his private office". During the interview, Ne Win, as Law-Yone often said he did, went from mournful and embarrassed, to petulant and self-regarding. Lamenting that "all people ever did was find fault" and he had to put up with "grumbles about whether he had the people's mandate". When Law-Yone popped the request that he wanted passports with which to take his family to Thailand and England, Ne Win immediately agreed to have them issued. He was also apologetic about the arrest not only of Law-Yone and other senior members of the political elite, but also the harsh interrogation that followed the arrest of Law-Yone's daughter, Wendy, who he had known as a child. When Law-Yone asked after Daw Khin May Than, Ne Win said that she was in poor health and that Law-Yone, who had previously been very close with her, could see her in a room down the hall. He demurred but requested that his son Byron, who had recently graduated from medical school, should also be allowed to leave. Ne Win granted that request and acknowledged with "a slight tinge" in his expression when Law-Yone indicated that he would smuggle his assets out of the country via foreign embassies (Law-Yone 2013, pp. 172–73).

From Indian, Nu and Law-Yone went to London where Nu announced at a press conference that he was going to form a new Parliamentary Democracy Party (PDP) and would begin to collect arms with which to overthrow the Ne Win regime within one year. He would eventually join with Bo Yan Naing and others who had been attempting the same thing since 1964. At the end of October, Nu had travelled from London to New York and had been allowed by his old confidant U Thant to use the United Nations as a venue to mount a verbal attack on Ne Win and his government. Nu was subsequently given asylum in Thailand and allowed to form a government-in-exile there (Law-Yone 2013, p. 187). Senior members of the Myanmar government were convinced that the U.S. Central Intelligence Agency (CIA) was either directly, or indirectly, funding Nu's movement.[67] Together with members of the Karen National Union, Dr Ba Maw's son, Zali, and Bo Yan Naing, apparently had conversations with SEATO representatives in October 1969 (Thet Tun 2011, p. 110) and American veterans, former residents in Myanmar, were assisting Nu's movement. Were Ne Win's problems getting out of control?

At the Annual Commanders' Conference, preceding the Fourth BSPP Seminar, Ne Win made two speeches, largely repeating what he had said on previous occasions. The danger to the army of remaining in power for too long was reiterated, as well as the need to involve the public in politics. His deputy, General San Yu, discussed again the People's Militia and the need for unity and renewal in the army.[68]

The Fourth Party Seminar, held from 6 to 11 November, was opened by Ne Win with a speech which focused on three topics: the conversion of the cadre party into a people's party, the writing of a new state constitution, and the general situation in the country. After a brief reference to papers placed before the meeting on the draft party constitution, Ne Win turned to the writing of a new state constitution. He began with a lengthy discussion of how the British attempted to sow discord between people of the former frontier areas and the rest of the country and how, because of the exigencies of negotiating independence, the socialist ideals that General Aung San had enunciated had been obviated. Other topics requiring attention in a new constitution were the banning of the use of religion for political purposes; the right of recall of legislators; limiting the president's powers, including the unrestrained right of granting pardons; the monopoly the legal profession had in the judiciary; and the right to penalize holders of office who abused their trust. These were all grievances against the old constitutional order which were frequently heard from leftist politicians in the 1950s.

In terms of the political system, Ne Win indicated that the question of a multi-party or a single-party system was still to be determined, but his preference for the latter was stated obviously. The key problems he saw in the multi-party system were not only that the politicians failed to deliver what they had promised, but that the system of funding elections allowed the rich to get their way after the elections, to the detriment of the workers and peasants. He even revealed how he and Bo Set Kya had borrowed money to help finance the AFPFL campaign in 1952. However, he conceded that this and other problems in the functioning of the multi-party system in the past was the result of both the ignorance and laziness of the Burmese in contrast to the foreigners who took advantage of them. Another problem he alluded to was the issue of how the ethnically designated state governments related to the central government. The 1947 Constitution had created a clash of interests in this regard which had to be resolved. All in all, he advocated a form of "direct democracy" in which, somehow, the people were involved in government.

In concluding his discussion of his ideas for a new constitution, Ne Win placed particular emphasis on the future of the ethnically designated states, apparently confusing, as many did and still do, the people with the territory, and imputing ideas of advanced and backward developmental traits.

> All I want is to get the Burmese and the people of the frontier areas more and more intimate with one another. It is a two-way traffic, and talks alone will not bring any results. Practical application of the ideas must be made. I said at the Union Day celebrations about the more developed section of the people pulling up those left behind, of course, making certain personal sacrifices for the delay caused in waiting for those lagging behind to come up. Although the Burmese may be ahead here, compared to world standards, they are much behind others. Efforts must be made to make those lagging behind to come up on level with us.
>
> There are persons who want to seize power. Some of them strike an attitude to the effect that they will do what they like, whatever may be said of them. Well, if they want to fight, let them. We will fight back, for we have been fighting all our lives. That is all about this.[69]

He then turned to current affairs, particularly the security situation in the country.

Referring to U Nu's recently launched movement to overthrow his government, Ne Win indicated that he preferred them, the "white", to the alternative, the "red". He, however, had taken power in order to benefit those who had sacrificed for independence but had yet to be rewarded, that is the workers and peasants. The leadership he had assumed was a burden and he had been up the previous few nights agonizing over his speech, hence he was then "indisposed". Though he eschewed class analysis as there were both good and bad people in every class, Ne Win felt that the majority of the proposals advanced by the Internal Unity Advisory Board, and also U Nu's proposal, favoured the rich over the poor and therefore had to be rejected. He agreed with the thrust of the minority report to the Board but had not met the eleven authors, since doing so would generate untrue rumours that the authors had met and discussed other matters with him.

Turning to the problem of insurgency, Ne Win revealed the wide diversity of the ethnically designated armed groups and how even small bands of 50 or 60 caused widespread chaos and trouble for the army which, for the most part, fought with loyalty and dedication. He then turned to the area of the Chinese border and gave details of the fighting in the area north of Kengtung in the eastern Shan State, noting that in the first eight months of that year, there had been eight major engagements with the Burmese Communists, with government casualties amounting to 133 deaths, of which 10 were officers. He believed, but was not certain, that 355 Communist insurgents had been killed. Deviating to discuss the 1963 peace talks with the insurgents, and comparing them to the 1969 Internal Unity Advisory Board, in both of which the participants believed the government was weak and had to come to terms with their position, which Ne Win indicated was a false belief, he returned to the border and the fact the Communist boasted of having foreign support.

This, however, was no cause for alarm. Ne Win also indicated that his government did not have the ability, or the desire, to retaliate against those who supported the insurgents from outside. With regards to all of Myanmar's neighbours, Myanmar wanted to have peace and would remain neutral in their affairs. Especially for China, and drawing no particular attention to Thailand despite U Nu's activities there, Ne Win said that he wished they could overcome the legacy of the anti-Chinese riots of 1967 and restore relations to how they had been before.

> Even though our relations with a neighbour are at this juncture embarrassed, we shall not resort to the short-sighted policy of looking elsewhere for aid in the solving of our problems. Restoration of friendship is our constant objective. Love does no bloom forever, nor can hatred persist that long. Not among the people only but among nations as well, that holds true. Just because we have fallen out once, it does not mean that we must be foes forever. As I have said, it is better for neighbours to live in amity than in anger and bitterness, and we shall on our part, always try to live together in peace and amity.[70]

Though state-to-state relations with China were soon restored, the Chinese continued to provide material assistance to the Communist-led insurgents in the north of the country for another decade.

Five days later, Ne Win gave the concluding speech at the Party Seminar, this time half the length of his opening oration. After making two minor statistical corrections to his remarks on the first day, he turned only to two topics: the making of socialist law and the current condition of the economy. On the former topic, he was eloquent on the basis of law in customs and traditions and subsequent changes. He pointed out that the current legal system was one which made the law the tool of the two professions which lived off of crime, the police and lawyers. Finding a way around the problem of money and power was a challenge they faced in drafting the new constitution.

On the subject of the economy, Ne Win touched briefly on the need to increase production of agricultural crops, particularly rice, and minerals. Developing peasant and other organizations to stimulate and guide production had yet to be completed. Foreign trade was a problem too, as contracts of sale could not be committed till products were in hand and competition was keen. However, Ne Win said, "Internal trade is our real problem. I say trade only by convention. Internal distribution may be more appropriate to socialism. Today distribution is defective although it has slightly improved over the past."[71] In the villages, the situations were not as bad as in the cities for the villagers were able to manage the situation themselves, but there were constant complaints of the people's stores in the towns though urbanites were favoured with government shops. People should bear more responsibilities and expanding the cooperatives would be the way forward. Ne Win went on to discuss the problems of indebtedness and the wasteful living habits of the people. They had to learn to be diligent and frugal if they were to develop the country.

He told the story of a soldier, who after being given permission to visit the village of his birth, on returning told an officer that the village where he had grown up was "destroyed". What he meant was that the village, which had long been poor and without adequate water supplies, was next to one of the newly constructed dams the government had built. Now the village was growing rice and had a much improved income basis, but the life of the people had deteriorated because now everyone sat around all day playing cards and drinking. The Burmese people needed to learn not to drop their oars but row on to the finish, as in a story that General Aung San used to tell.

> Victories cannot be won immediately as might be anticipated. Obstructions, disruptions and opposition are natural. But the more obstructions there are the more resolute we must be. The whole nation must cultivate such a dauntless spirit. Even after victories have been accomplished, we might fall back if we relented in our efforts. We must always be industrious and tenacious. In conclusion I must say that we ourselves must imbibe such a spirit.[72]

Soon after the Party seminar, Ne Win, as often the case, set out on another tour of the country, this time in the central zone, visiting

Mandalay, Kyunchaung, Sale, Malun and Sinde.[73] Unusually, he was accompanied by a foreigner, his close friend Dr Meyer, the Chairman of the Fritz-Werner Company. The towns he visited were all, in Ne Win's view, possible development sites. At Sinde, for example, Myanmar's first industrial training centre for engineering, under the auspices of the Ministry for Industry Two, and with assistance of the Federal Republic of Germany, opened in 1979. Another five such institutions were opened only after Ne Win's death, with the assistance of China and South Korea.

During their travels together, Ne Win explained to Meyer why he had let U Nu travel abroad, against the advice of many of his colleagues in the government. Nu was, in Ne Win's view, very popular amongst the people living in the country, and therefore he was more of a danger inside the country than outside. Though some advised Ne Win to find a way of eliminating Nu while he was in Thailand, Ne Win was of the view that his movement was hopeless, unable to raise large amounts of financial support and, in the end, just "an empty box".[74] When Nu released a statement calling on the people to rise up against Ne Win, it was reprinted in both Burmese and English in the government press. Just over a month after his conversations with Dr Meyer, Ne Win cheerfully hosted a dinner for U Nu's Thai hosts, Deputy Prime Minister General Prapas Charusathien and Communications Minister Air Marshall Dawee Chulasapya.[75] Ne Win often saw the latter when he visited Bangkok. Ne Win was certainly aware of the reports that Nu's activities in Thailand had been facilitated not only by the Thai government, but also by retired CIA agent William Young, who organized the anti-Communist guerrillas in Laos, and Dr Gordon Seagrave's son, Sterling (Elliott 1999, p. 376). Other collaborators from the United States included Baird V. Helfrich and Stanley Booker, both of whom had done business in Burma prior to 1964 after serving in Force 101 during the Second World War raising Kachin levies.[76] Edward Law-Yone, who had also worked with the forerunner of the CIA during the Second World War, and was Nu's chief fundraiser, received US$1 million in 1972 with the promise of another US$12 million in two instalments if Nu's forces reached Yangon. The money was said to come from an unknown Canadian oil company named Asmara.[77]

The two Thai ministers were in Yangon, along with the other dignitaries, to attend the fifth Southeast Asian Games, hosted by Myanmar. Students used the occasion to attempt to embarrass the government, leading to the closure of a number of schools and universities, but, despite delegating the opening of the Games to General San Yu, Ne Win and Daw Khin May Than hosted a number of formal dinners. Whether the general public was concerned with the student protests is uncertain, but they were probably pleased that Myanmar won the most number of gold medals, 57, the most silver medals, 46, and the second-most bronze medals, 43, being pipped by Thailand by three. Despite Myanmar's eschewing of pro-Western regional organizations, the Games had a distinctly rightist bias, with no Communist country in attendance but South Vietnam represented along with Laos, Malaysia, Singapore and Thailand.

After the usual Christmas and Gregorian New Year holidays, and the marking of Myanmar's 22nd year of Independence, Ne Win and Daw Khin May Than made another visit to India from the 15th to the 22nd.[78] The year 1970 was going to be another one with much international travel for Ne Win and his wife. He had to turn down an invitation to visit West Germany in May because of obligations to attend the Osaka EXPO 70, after which he would be going to the United Kingdom so that Daw Khin May Than could receive medical attention. He was already planning in January, however, to spend some time with Dr Meyer in Germany in June or July. In an hour long, informal interview with the West German ambassador in his private quarters, Ne Win seemed relaxed and at ease.[79] Apparently, however, he had a mild heart attack sometime not long after this interview.[80]

Ne Win's apparent sense of security with his multiple opponents, Communist and non-Communist, inside and outside the country, was at a time of increased fighting along many of the country's borders. Nu's party attempted several forays into Myanmar in Tanintharyi and elsewhere, in each case repulsed by government forces. They also linked up with various Mon and Karen rebel groups to form a Nationalities United Liberation Front, a point that was widely publicized inside the country. The remnants of the original Burma Communist Party, now much reduced by the attrition of more than two decades of conflict and more recent internal purges, had made their way to southern China, where they had been rearmed. They then returned to the border area and established bases from whence they attempted to capture government controlled towns, including Lashio (McCoy 1991, p. 425). Meanwhile, the economy did not particularly improve, and while there was no intention of abandoning socialism, there were moves to encourage at least a modest tourist industry with the issuing of visas longer than 24 hours, up to seven days from 28 May. Brigadier Tin Pe, the architect of the socialist economy under Ne Win, was moreover nearing the end of his power. Often ill and incapable of work, by April he was in Edinburgh receiving medical treatment and retired from government service in August. He resigned as a minister and left the Revolutionary Council on 14 November, the day after Thakin Soe's arrest. Radicalism was on the wane.

With Tin Pe's removal from the Revolutionary Council, economic policy began to drift in a more conservative direction, though the fundamentals of state ownership of the major economic assets of the country were not abandoned. However, typical of the slightly more liberal regime, both Aung Gyi and Tin Pe prospered in retirement, in part as a consequence of the decision in May 1970 to acknowledge the role of the private sector in the economy (Badgley 1971, p. 153). As Aung Gyi was able to buy raw materials from government shops for his private tea shop at subsidized prices, so also Ne Win apparently ordered the Ministry of Education to print textbooks at Brigadier Tin Pe's family printing works (Chit Hlaing n.d., p. 23). Many others, outside the Revolutionary Council, but former colleagues in the *Dobama Asiayon* and the resistance, even after being arrested for suspected dissident political activities, such as Thakin Ba Tin, were given jobs in government corporations after the nationalization of the firms for which they had worked.[81] The youngest of the Thirty Comrades, who had joined the Communists but returned to the legal fold, was given a house by Ne Win, and Thakin Soe was assured, via Thakin Tin Mya, that Ne Win promised he would not be executed after his treason trial in January 1973.[82]

Ne Win and Daw Khin May Than departed for Japan to attend Expo 70 and open the Myanmar pavilion on 14 April 1970. They travelled via Manila, and made a brief visit there to meet with the President and Mrs Marcos.[83] Prime Minister Sato again met with Ne Win and once more discussed the Japanese aid programme to Myanmar (Liang 1990, p. 152). At Expo 70, the Myanmar exhibition was hailed by many, including the Japanese press and BBC television, as a "must visit". The high quality handcrafts and carvings were extolled, as were Myanmar-made goods in the markets of Yangon at that time. At least one experienced visitor to Myanmar that year wrote enthusiastically about the cultural and educational programmes of the country, particularly the Illiteracy Eradication Campaign. He also noted the expansion of higher education, to which English had been reintroduced, but noted the declining standards as numbers increased (Badgley 1971, pp. 149–50). In 1971, Myanmar was awarded a UNESCO prize for its literacy programmes.[84]

Their visits to the Philippines and Japan, totalling over three weeks, ended on 8 May when they arrived in London for another visit of about seven weeks, before going on to Germany on 26 June 1970.[85] The visit was very low key, focusing on medical attention for both Ne Win and his wife, though his was minor, once more for his sinus troubles.[86] He also called upon the Queen. After about ten days in West Germany, visiting with Dr Meyer, the Ne Wins returned to London. Daw Khin May Than had treatment for her kidney problems, but he had no official calls or engagements, treating the second half of their visit, like the first, as a private holiday. They left the UK and arrived in New Delhi for a three-day visit on 8 July, returning to Yangon on 11 July. In total, they had been abroad for nearly three months. Within two months of his return, the family moved from the old British Governor's mansion, which suffered cracking following a mid-year earthquake, back to the family home on Inya Lake, the chief of staff's residence, 26 Ady Road.

During these travels, Ne Win apparently gave no interviews and saw few people other than on a personal and private basis. There were no records of conversations with foreign officials or dignitaries, as in the past. Similarly, on one of his few occasions in 1970s to entertain foreigners who provided a record of their conversations, he was remarkably reticent to talk other than about his concerns for his wife's health. Unlike the rambunctious discussion held in June 1964, when Ne Win met with Professor Frank Trager in 1970, who was treated as a semi-state guest, he avoided all political talk other than indicating that "countries should stand on their own feet". At two informal family dinners, Ne Win, who looked very healthy, was clearly concerned about the health condition of his wife.[87] This was increasingly the pattern of Ne Win's encounters with Western diplomats and others. Rare were the causal chats of the kind he had previously enjoyed with Ambassadors Byroade and Keiser, or even Paul Gore-Booth. At 60 years old, he had served near or at the pinnacle of political power for half his life.

November was a particularly busy month for Ne Win, again largely devoted to international travel. However, before then there appeared one rumour that was to dog his remaining life. On 30 October 1970, the *Bangkok Post* announced that Ne Win had suffered a massive heart attack and had died; the next day, the same newspaper reported him receiving the Cambodian ambassador. That his government began making decisions which mystified the public added to the pool of rumours and speculation into which anyone could dip or add. Following a year of preparations, an order was given at 6 a.m. on 6 December 1970 to switch from left-hand to right-hand drive. Justified by a mooted Asian highway which was to cross Myanmar, the rumour that circulated then was that Ne Win consulted a fortune teller who advised, cryptically, to switch from the left to right in order to avoid disaster. While most believe the prediction was an urge to abandon socialism and return to a market economy, Ne Win was said to have drawn the conclusion that switching driving sides was a better way to meet the prophecy. Despite such tales, there was no evidence of Ne Win being particularly superstitious, though many of his advisers and close colleagues were. However, knowing the depth of belief amongst large swathes of the Myanmar population in superstitious practices, he may well have used the appearance of superstition from time to time to confuse his opponents without actually believing it himself.

Ne Win made his third trip to India that year, for just two days from 8 to 9 November.[88] Whether the closer relationship between India and Burma was the cause, at least state-to-state relations with China improved significantly at about the same time, with the Burmese ambassador returning to Beijing in mid-month. The Chinese ambassador to Burma returned the following March. After his quick trip to India, Ne Win and Daw Khin May Than made a slightly longer visit to Manila again, from 18 to 21 November,[89] before returning to Yangon and then departing for London on the 28th. In between, he hosted a dinner to mark the Golden Jubilee celebrations of National Day in Yangon, and received the credentials of the new Philippine and British ambassadors on the eve of his departure.[90] Immediately upon arriving in London, Ne Win entered a private clinic for treatment of urinary problems. After a spell in hospital, he met with the new British Prime Minister, Edward Heath, on 22 December. Most of his European visit was in London, but the last week was spent in Germany at the private residence of his friend, Dr Meyer of Fritz-Werner. After six weeks, Ne Win returned to Yangon on 9 January 1971.[91]

Though there was cocktail party chit chat, picked up by an East German diplomat, that Ne Win's extensive absence from the country was prompting criticism of him not only among the general public but also among members of the Revolutionary Council, there was no evidence that this was the case.[92] Ne Win's health was clearly suffering at this time and he was back in London six weeks later. His plane was met at 9:15 in the morning of 21 February 1971 by an ambulance at Heathrow Airport and he was taken directly to King Edward VII Hospital for Officers, having previously cancelled a planned trip to Nepal.[93] He apparently had a bad case of stomach or intestinal ulcers and had arrived in London in order to undergo surgery.[94] He remained in the hospital for more than three weeks, leaving only on 16 March.[95] Amongst his visitors were the left-wing Labour member of parliament, Tam Dalyell. Dalyell thought Ne Win was so ill that he could probably die. Nonetheless, they had a discussion of China's changing policy towards Myanmar as well as problems involving drilling operations, presumably for oil or gas, in Myanmar.[96] Ne Win had visited an offshore oil exploration vessel of the Myanmar Oil Company, the M.V. *Jason*, just five days before he was taken ill.[97]

U Nu's attempt to oust Ne Win from power, after two years, was faltering. Former member of the Revolutionary Council, and former head of the Burma Air Force, Tommy Clift, on Nu's behalf, thus sought the help of the British government to convince Ne Win while he was in hospital to step down from power.[98] The British Foreign Secretary, Alec Douglas-Home, lost no time in scotching any such possibility.[99] Indeed, the British were rather impressed with some aspects of Ne Win's Burma. As the newly installed Ambassador in Yangon, E.G. Willan, wrote in his "First Impressions" letter:

> I have now met and talked to most of the members of the Revolutionary Council, to the extent they permit themselves to any serious discussion with a foreign diplomat. They do not for the most part strike me as sinister or ill-intentioned men. They are personally affable (some even jolly). In uniform they look like any group of middle-age, seniorish officers anywhere. Out of it they are strikingly unmilitary.
> ... they do not live particularly ostentatious or luxurious lives, nor do they as individuals flaunt that single-minded concentration on self-enrichment so familiar in many developing — and developed — countries.

With regards to Ne Win, Willan noted his many British friends, citing in particular Basil Clark, head of the BBC's Burmese language radio service, Dr G.E. Marrison of the British Museum, and Mr P.D. Trevor-Roper, an ophthamalic surgeon and long-time gay-rights campaigner.[100]

Ne Win remained in London until 5 April, convalescing from his medical treatment. After another brief private visit to Germany, he proceeded on to Yangon via Tehran and Delhi, and was expected back in Yangon in mid-April.[101] However, he was once more taken ill and returned to London where he was photographed, in his pyjamas, being carried off a plane at Heathrow on a stretcher. His ulcer was apparently bleeding and he was rushed back to hospital. However, additional surgery was not required and he was out of hospital within a week. He was fit enough to attend the dress rehearsal of a Myanmar ballet on 21 April, and though expected to leave London two days later,[102] he remained in the United Kingdom until 20 May and then Germany until 2 June, an absence of over three months. He was not idle during that time, of course, and met with the Malaysian Prime Minister, Tun Abdul Razak, among others.[103] Nonetheless, over a period of more than six months, Ne Win had been in Myanmar for a total of forty-four days.

On 28 June, the first Congress of the Burma Socialist Programme Party was held in a newly erected hall constructed of all natural, local materials — wood, bamboo, nipa palm, and jute canvas — at the site of the Central School of Political Science at Mingaladon. The Congress was opened by a speech by Chairman Ne Win.[104] In his speech, Ne Win once more called for unity within the party as it converted itself from a cadre into a mass party, and also for unity amongst the "national races", the various ethno-linguistic groups in the country.[105] He also mandated the drafting of a new state constitution, a necessary step to complete the socialist revolution and allow the army to return power to civilians.

Ne Win's speech was more focused than many he had given in the past. The problem of uniting the country politically under a new constitutional order was clearly uppermost in his mind. As usual, he reviewed a good deal of history, in particular on the alleged British policy of "divide and rule" and the efforts of the Bogyoke Aung San and others to overcome the political and economic divides between the so-called national races, which was the legacy of history which Myanmar nationalists inherited. Prior to that, however, he gave an insight into his view of pre-colonial Burmese history, a view which shared a great deal with the standard British-taught, but now Marxist-influenced, version of that history.

> During the first period [i.e., pre-colonial times] difficult communications resulted in isolation of the national races. The prevailing mentality of the ruling class reflected selfish and feudalistic thinking. There also prevailed the narrow interests of the family and the clan. In that context the Burmese kings and their courtiers, supposed to represent the Burmese people, the most advanced and cultured race, were selfish and narrow-minded. The relations with other national races were at best minimal and were not as between equals.
>
> Even in terminology, these peoples were referred to as primitive. I only point this out as a historical fact. The rulers of the day not only established such wrong relations with the remote areas but they ruled with the sword over the regions they could reach. Even with the Burmese who were their own kin, these feudal rulers practised the law

of the jungle exploiting and bullying one another. In short, this kind
of rule would not make for national unity. All they cared for was to
oppress and exploit other races.

The attitude of the rulers was then adopted by the Burmese people, who
considered themselves superior to the other races; therefore the problem
of national unity was caused by the Burman and they must correct their
attitudes.

As a step in the direction of ending army rule and returning power
to the people, four civilians were admitted to both the Revolutionary
Council and the Central Committee of the party after the Congress. The
transition from the Revolutionary Council to a more legitimate, popularly
based, civilian government, had begun. None, however, were appointed
ministers, and when a cabinet reshuffle took place after the Congress, only
military officers were confirmed in its eleven places, while General San Yu
was anointed as General Secretary of the BSPP.[106] San Yu was appointed
Deputy Prime Minister at the same time as new deputy ministers were
appointed two months later.[107] Ne Win's concluding speech at the end of
the two-week Congress reiterated many old themes, reverting to a discussion
of religious and other terminology.[108] In the following month, he took the
opportunity of correcting two errors which had been drawn to his attention
in his concluding speech relating to the interpretation of Buddhist texts.
Speaking at a meeting on drafting the constitution and national unity,
he also apologized to members of the Myanmar Language and Literature
Commission for calling them all "half-baked". He conceded he should have
said that only "some" of them were "half-baked".[109]

Ne Win was referring to the fact that he had assigned three men at
the Language Commission to prepare a spelling manual and dictionary,
a collection of scientific terms, and a grammar, specifying that Min
Thu Wun, U Thein Han, and U Aye Maung were responsible for each
respectively. However, they worked very slowly and, moreover, as elderly
gentlemen, reverted to Pali, and much of what they wrote was not relevant
to the contemporary style of writing. Hence, the three knew to whom
Ne Win referred when he said they were "half baked". The three elderly
men were very disappointed that Ne Win had rejected their work and
one felt suicidal. Ne Win then re-organized the Language Commission,
appointing new members, including U Thaw Kaung and U Tin Aye, to
rewrite the dictionary. He also ordered pulping of the orthography prepared
by Min Thu Wun. Later, Ne Win invited the three elders to his home and

personally apologized for calling them "half baked" in public. Ne Win then kept a close eye on the Language Commission and visited it frequently in the first half of the 1970s.[110]

While concentrating on Party affairs and the conversion of his military rule into a civilian state, Ne Win's mind would never have been far off the implications of international affairs. While U Nu's revolt from Thailand was fizzling out, even the Thai cabinet was getting upset with his antics, though he remained close to Ne Win's dinner guest of the previous year, Air Chief Marshall Dawee.[111] More importantly, on 15 July, the White House announced that U.S. President Nixon would visit China the following year. Ne Win discussed the implications of the proposed Nixon–Mao meeting, with his own imminent visit to China in mind, when he met with the brother of United States Senator John Tunney in late July. Jay Tunney was Vice-President of Orion Petroleum of Denver, Colorado, an oil and gas exploration and development company. He, along with former White House Chief of Protocol Lloyd Hand, whom Ne Win had met in 1966, avoided discussing oil, but with reference to Nixon's forthcoming visit to China, Ne Win suggested that it might lead "to the possibility of enhanced U.S. business opportunities in Burma's economic development which could follow in the wake of an improvement in U.S.–P.R.C. relations".[112]

Two weeks after proffering these remarks, Ne Win was in Beijing, where he had more than fifteen hours of talks with his old acquaintance, Chou En-lai. The "Chiang Kai-shek of Burma" also met with Mao Tse-tung during the visit. Apparently the meetings were friendly and, though China regretted the events of 1967, its government had to defend its citizens. However, Chou once more indicated that overseas Chinese should obey the law of the country of their residence, and Ne Win assured him that Chinese who applied for citizenship in Myanmar would receive it. He also inquired as to how those Chinese who were adversely affected by the 1967 riots should be compensated, to which Chou replied that this was an internal matter for Myanmar to resolve. China offered to resume its aid programme, but apparently the question of Chinese assistance to the Burma Communist Party was not raised. Ne Win returned to Yangon via Gaungzhou, but with a minimum of the elaborate sightseeing that the Chinese had provided in the past, other than a tour with Chou, a singular honour for Ne Win. There was only one museum visit.[113]

Not long after his return from China, Ne Win hosted an informal family dinner to mark the occasion of a visit by Sir Robert Bradlaw, a friend of Ne Win, who was a visiting World Health Organisation consultant on dental education. Also included in the party was the British Ambassador, Edward Willan. Ne Win freely discussed his meetings with Chou En-lai, describing him as charming, and the atmosphere as one of goodwill. His only regret was that he had been unable to sleep through a performance of "The Red Detachment of Women", as he usually did when attending an opera or ballet, because of all the "banging".[114]

Ne Win was once more plunged into Party work. The Central Committee met in September and approved the First Four-Year Plan for the economy, expected to run from 1971/72 until 1974/75. Party development as well as economic development were also on his mind if the Burma Socialist Programme Party was going to develop as a viable ruling party. On 7 August, the Party established the Lansin Youth Organising Committee as a new endeavour to bring the young into the party and, as noted above, on 21 August Ne Win addressed a meeting on national solidarity and the drafting of a new constitution.

Having been in Myanmar for most of the preceding four months, Ne Win and Daw Khin May Than returned to London on 8 October, accompanied by his now frequent companion, Dr Meyer. He was apparently visiting London primarily for medical, including minor heart surgery, and dental attention, and declined most invitations.[115] He met with Lord Mountbatten, dined with Dr Htin Aung, played golf and caught a cold which required him to check in again at the King Edward VII Hospital and, because of his hospitalization, he was unable to dine with Prime Minister Heath in the first week of December, though they did have a brief meeting.[116] At that time, Ne Win assured Heath that while racial tensions in Malaysia were delicate and Communist activity was increasing in Thailand, Chinese influence was not on the rise in Southeast Asia.[117]

Amongst those he invited to his "Spartan" Wimbledon residence, in the words of a Foreign Office memo, were Basil Clark and his wife and Mark Dodd, head of the BBC World Service, and his wife. Ne Win struck up a conversation several times with the New Scotland Yard officer attached to him for security purposes, one Sergeant Scrace. He described Ne Win as "a man's man". He even advanced the view to Scrace that, perhaps in a year or two, once the Myanmar economy was running smoothly, he might retire to England.[118]

While resting in London, the noted journalist of the London *Daily Telegraph*, Claire Hollingsworth, visited Myanmar and subsequently published an article "on how Gen. Ne Win regiments his country: Burma's rebellious road to socialism". Thinking that she was writing an article to commemorate the Fourteenth Army's retaking of Burma in 1944–45, Hollingsworth had been assisted by the British embassy in her week-long visit to Yangon. When the article appeared on 12 October 1971, the embassy was less than pleased as they saw the article as part of the propaganda campaign of U Nu's Parliamentary Democracy Party movement in Thailand. They catalogued a number of errors in her report which were typical of much reporting on the country at that time:

> It would be a waste of time to try and comment on all the inaccuracies but for the record there have, in recent years, been no attempts, formidable or otherwise, to overthrow the regime of General Ne Win, whose position needed no re-establishing (paragraph 1), there is no evidence that the student riots in Rangoon a year ago (a very minor affair — see our reports at the time) were in any way inspired by the clandestine radio, that there were any in Mandalay or that a large part of the townspeople sympathised with them. No units in the Burmese army defected and there was at no time any suggestion of a national uprising (paragraph 4). The account of the military situation in paragraphs 5–8 is, as you will realise, pure fantasy. There have been regular flights to Bhamo for many years (paragraph 9). As far as we know there is no truth at all in the story officers' wives visiting Bangkok for shopping (paragraph 13). Those of us who live here are unconscious of any atmosphere of "intense fear" (paragraph 18). Queues are not the most conspicuous feature of the city (paragraph 17). Bread and rice are freely available and unrationed. The frequently repeated reports of the small annual clothe ration ignores the fact that this is related only to one particular type of state produced state price controlled cloth: other types of cloth can be bought freely both in the People's Shops and markets.[119]

Ne Win had a lengthy chat over lunch on 14 November with Arthur Bottomley, the Labour member of Parliament who had been involved in the negotiations surrounding the drawing of the Shan States and the Frontier Areas into independent Burma before independence. At about that time, Daw Khin May Than was travelling to Myanmar via Frankfurt in order to attend the funeral of her father, Dr Ba Than. However, because of labour strike action at Heathrow Airport, she could not get back in time.[120] Bottomley reported the gist of their conversations back to the Foreign Office. Ne Win discussed at length U Nu's attempt to oust him from power, and he believed that the British were in touch with the people from Nu's time in power. As for Nu's threat to his power, Ne Win was dismissive, even though he suspected that former Brigadier Aung Gyi was conspiring with Nu. U Ba Swe was not intriguing against him, and Ne Win said his old friend U Kyaw Nyein, he had had to visit to convince him not to attempt suicide while in detention. As for his own politics, Ne Win was not very optimistic about the future of his party, but the single-party system had to be tested. In regard to his subordinates, he said "he was reasonable with those who played fair but gave no quarter to those who were unfair to him".

In regard to his sixth and most recent visit to China, Ne Win said little but indicated that, in his view, one of the reasons the Chinese supported the ethnically designated insurgents along their common border was because the Americans did the same with the Karens along the Thai border. As for British assistance, even of a technical kind, he refused to accept, because if he accepted aid from the UK, he would have to take it from the others too. In any event, he did not trust the Foreign Office people, as they favoured the minorities. Particularly, he did not like Sir Richard Allen, the British Ambassador from 1956 to 1962, nor his predecessor, Paul Gore-Booth. He particularly resented the apparent fact that Gore-Booth encouraged and facilitated the foreign education and residence of Aung San's surviving children, Aung San Oo, who was then studying in the United States, and Aung San Suu Kyi, then about to marry an Englishman met via the Gore-Booths.[121]

Ne Win intended to return to Yangon on 20 December, but the outbreak of war between India and Pakistan, resulting in the eventual creation of Bangladesh, caused him to change his plans, and he departed on 6 December instead, travelling via Tokyo. He was sent off by a large party, including Professor Aung Than, Daw Khin May Than's dentist brother then in the UK on a study mission, Professor Sir Robert Bradshaw and a Mrs Leech.[122] On his return to Yangon, Ne Win entertained Sir Ronald and Lady Bodley-Scott, he being the distinguished author of a number of critical medical treatises, especially in the field of cancer, at his house over the holiday period.[123]

Ne Win would have been preoccupied by many thoughts during that period. Relations with India were strained because of its war with Pakistan. Burma could no longer remain neutral between India and Pakistan. On 13 January, in breach of one of the government's firmest principles of non-interference in the domestic affairs of other states, Myanmar recognized the new, Indian-favoured, state of Bangladesh, what had been East Pakistan. China and the economy would also have been on Ne Win's mind, as was the continuing insurgencies. The CIA estimated that the army, still at about 122,000 men, was facing, not 14,000 insurgents, as it did five years earlier, but 20,000. Despite the self-inflicted wounds of the Cultural Revolution, the Burma Communist Party was now fielding a 4,000- to 5,000-man force, trained and armed by China, operating from the Chinese border down through the northeastern Shan State to just north and west of Mandalay.[124]

Ne Win had other concerns closer to home as well. Relations with Daw Khin May Than were strained during the latter part of 1971. While he was having medical treatment in London, she made a separate visit on her own to Germany. When Sergeant Scrace described Ne Win as a "man's man", he may well have been thinking of some pithy expressions from the General on men's relations with women. In January 1972, they finally had a big row,[125] and she moved out of the family home with the children and stayed in another residence not far from the Inya Lake Hotel.[126]

Lord Mountbatten arrived in Yangon on 9 February, having been expecting to tour the country with Ne Win and Daw Khin May Than. However, he was informed in advance that the Ne Wins had separated and therefore they would have to tour alone. Ne Win made excuses of having meetings with the Malaysian prime minister and so on, but Mountbatten was convinced the marital row was the real reason. Ne Win met him at the airport as, at the same time, he was seeing off the Hungarian Premier, Mr Jeno Fock, who was returning to Europe from a visit to Hanoi.[127] As Mountbatten recorded in his diary, despite his problems, Ne Win "was very cheery and cheerful and full of apologies at not being able to come round, and asked us to come back early to Rangoon so that we could come and see him for a gossip before the Union Day dinner".[128] On 11 February, Mountbatten and his family, visited Ne Win:

> He received us in his own house which he built after the war on Inya Lake, and very charming it was, much smaller and more compact than the real State House. We had a ten minute friendly talk about every sort of matter, and then suddenly he turned round and with charming candour told us the sad story that he and Katie were divorced. He said it happened about a month ago and was a great

shock to him, but matters had risen which he could not disregard. They remained good friends, but now lived apart. He had given her one of his houses and the children were divided between them (Ziegler 1989, p. 230).

They then drove in a motorcade to the old State House for dinner and entertainment for 4,000 people to mark Union Day. Mountbatten and his son-in-law and daughter were the only foreign guests.

A few months after Mountbatten's last visit to Burma, he gave an interview with Basil Clarke of the BBC Burmese Service. He remarked,

> Over the years I've been back to Burma on numerous occasions, '48, '56, I think another time in the '60s, again in '67 and certainly in '72, and it has always been as a guest of General Ne Win, who became a great friend. This last time I was fascinated by the people, well-fed, well-clothed and as happy and gay as the Burmese people always are. They seem to be a very happy and contented lot. I went up to Lake Inle, up to Taunggyi. We then went to Maymyo where I saw the Defence Services College. I was very impressed. They have got 400 young Burmese boys learning to be officers of the army, the navy and the air force. Every young man in Burma wants to join the armed forces, which is very good. They pick the most marvellous men.[129]

After the Mountbatten party had left, Ne Win did indeed entertain the Malaysian Prime Minister, Tun Abdul Razak, who visited Burma "informally" to try to get Ne Win to join ASEAN. After two days from 16 to 18 February, at Sandoway, the Rakhine beach resort where Ne Win often entertained foreign visitors, they returned to Yangon where Ne Win hosted a formal banquet for the Malaysian delegation. Razak apparently hoped that ASEAN's 1971 pledge of a Zone of Peace, Freedom and Neutrality (ZOPFAN), which he had sponsored, would entice Burma in joining the Association. Ne Win, appearing "cheerful, vigorous, and evidently fit", replied that Burma was already neutral and would join ASEAN when they were truly neutral.[130] The normalization of relations with China since 1967, though not restoring the warmth of earlier years, nonetheless would have convinced Ne Win that his strategy, at least for his country, was best for preserving independence (Holmes 1972, pp. 686–700).

Being temporarily without a hostess, Ne Win received the visiting Soviet Minister for Culture, Madame Ekaterine Alekseevna Furtseva, a reportedly attractive protégé of Khrushchev and one of the few women to reach the pinnacles of power in the Communist Republic, not once but twice, hosting dinners for her on her way to and from Hanoi on 24 February and 3 March. Nonetheless, perhaps exasperated with women, Ne Win and a party of nine, all male, set off for Zurich on 23 March, either for a medical check-up or perhaps to conduct business. He had previously visited Zurich in May 1971. He was eventually known to be staying at the Three Crowns Hotel in Vevey.[131] They remained there until 12 April when Ne Win returned to Yangon and reportedly had a dizzy spell. Daw Khin May Than then returned to their residence to look after him.[132]

After ten years in power and with recurring health and marital problems, and seemingly bored with routine, Ne Win's promises to hand power back to the people seemed not implausible. He had always kept his word in the past, and he had adequate reasons to orchestrate a change in his circumstances. Having paid relatively little attention to the details of government during the previous few years, as he was often travelling, his trustworthy colleagues could carry on without him. But would he allow them to do so or could his interest in government, and life more widely, be rekindled? Was ten years long enough for Ne Win to have changed Myanmar and its people?

Notes

1. Telegram, Byroade to Secretary of State (SOS), 4 March 1967, reporting UN Secretary General U Thant's press conference following a meeting with North Vietnamese officials that day in Yangon. Also, Airgram A-54, Byroade to SOS, illegible, October 1967, both in Correspondence, Box 235, LBJ Library.
2. In May 1967, India and Myanmar signed a Boundary Agreement providing for the formal demarcation and delimitation of the tradition, i.e., British, boundary between the two countries. Than Han, *Common Vision: Burma's Regional Outlook* (Washington, D.C.: Institute for the Study of Diplomacy, School of Foreign Service, Georgetown University, 1986), pp. 11–12.
3. In subsequent years, according to a retired senior army officer in Yangon interviewed in 2006, officers from the United States military attachés offices in Bangkok would arrive in Yangon and offer to sell surplus equipment to the Myanmar army. The Burmese would reply that they were poor and had

little money. The Americans would say, make an offer, and ridiculously low prices were immediately agreed.

4. Estimates of insurgent numbers vary. These come for a CIA assessment made in September 1966 but the same report gives maximum numbers equaling about 25,000. Central Intelligence Agency, "Current Intelligence Weekly Special Report: Burma Under Ne Win", 2 September 1966, pp. 3–4, Box 235, LBJ Library.

5. Notes on Farewell Interview with General Ne Win by L.J.D. Wakely, 14 September 1967, FCO15/95.

6. The centralization of university administration meant that academic staff came under civil service regulations and appointments were made by the Ministry with the university having no influence in the matter. When this was explained to a recent Oxford University graduate, she interpreted it as "warning her not to try to return to Burma — at least not yet". Note, P.H. Gore-Booth to Mr Bollard, 1 May 1967, FO15/65, explaining an exchange of letters between Miss Aung San Suu Kyi and the Director of the Economics Faculty at Yangon University.

7. Burma Socialist Programme Party Central Committee Headquarters, "Political Report of the Central Organising Committee of the Burma Socialist Programme Party Submitted to the First Party Congress", in *The First Party Congress 1971: Speeches of the Chairman of the Party Central Committee and Political Report of the Party Central Organising Committee* (Yangon: Burma Socialist Programme Party, March 1973), p. 154.

8. Table 66, Production of Selected Crops, p. 153 and Table 155, Domestic Exports of Principle Commodities, p. 285, in Central Statistical and Economics Department, Revolutionary Government of the Union of Burma, *Statistical Yearbook 1967* (Rangoon: New Secretariat).

9. Dr Lahr and Ambassador Keiser to AA, 27 May 1967, AA PA AV Nuuers Amt 2.160, 345–47.

10. See Roman Deckert, "Strong and Fast: German Arms in Burma", English translation from the *Small Arms Newsletter* of the German Campaign Against Small Arms, November 2007, available at <http://www.bits.de/public/articles/kleinwaffen-nl11-07eng.htm> (accessed 4 May 2013). See also S. Aung Lwin, "The Burma Connection", no date, available from The Burma Buro, Josephinestrasse 71, 4630 Bochum, Germany. A corrective to this source is provided by Andrew Selth, *Burma's Armed Forces: Power without Glory* (Norwalk, Conn.: EastBridge, 2002), p. 140.

11. The Communist government of North Vietnam, which was then allied with China in the war to reunify Vietnam in the face of American opposition, also banned the acceptance and wearing of Mao badges. Qiang Zhai, *China and the Vietnam Wars, 1950–1975* (Chapel Hill: University of North Carolina Press, 2000), p. 152. Many other governments in Africa and Asia took similar

stands. See David I. Steinberg and Fan Hongwei, *Modern China-Myanmar Relations: Dilemmas of Mutual Dependence* (Copenhagen: NIAS Press, 2012), p. 116, fn. 88.

12. A fictionalized account of the riots is given by Hla Oo in "Rice Riots to Race Riots", in The *Scourge of Burma and Four Short Stories* (N.p.: the author, 2010), pp. 81–88.

13. Also publishing statements in a similar vein by BCP leaders in exile such as Thakin Ba Thein Tin, an example being "The Military Government of Ne Win, the Chiang Kai-shek of Burma, Is Bound to Fail! The People Are Bound to Win!", *Peking Review*, no. 29, 14 July 1967.

14. For example, see his obituaries in *The New York Times* and the London *Telegraph*, 6 December 2002 or Stan Sesser, "A Rich Country Gone Wrong", *The New Yorker*, 9 October 1989, reprinted in Sesser, *The Lands of Charm and Cruelty: Travels in Southeast Asia* (New York: Alfred Knopf, 1993), pp. 177–238.

15. According to J.E. Hoare of the South and South East Asia Section of the Foreign Office Research Department, Daw Aung San Suu Kyi explained Burmese attitudes toward Indians, Chinese, the British and Japanese. Summing up a note on a talk she gave at St. Antony's College, Oxford, on 13 November 1979, he wrote, "Her views also seem to me to reflect accurately what we know of the views of Ne Win." Memo to Dr Roe, SEAD, 15 November 1979, FCO.

16. Papers in PREM 13/3071; FCO57/83 and FCO15/95.

17. Clippings from *The Times*, 10 and 12 August 1967, FCO15/88.

18. 20 to 22 September. See *Towhlanyei Kaungsi ei Hluthsaungchet Thamaing Akyinchut* [Concise History of the Actions of the Revolutionary Council] (Rangoon: Printing and Publishing Corporation, 2 March 1974), p. 220.

19. Airgram, R.W. Zimmerman to Department of State, 19 October 1967, Burma Correspondence, Box 53, LBJ Library; see also Chi-shad Liang, *Burma's Foreign Relations: Neutralism in Theory and Practice* (New York: Praeger, 1990), p. 152.

20. Ibid., p. 224.

21. Telegram, Byroade to SOS, 26 December 1967, Rangoon 1669 Pol 15-1 Burma xr Pol Burma-Chicom, No. 74.

22. Ger Emb YGN Amb Kaiser to AA, 19 January 1968, AA PA B 37 Bd. 376, 70–72.

23. Sao Hkin Hkio saw Dorothy Woodman when she visited Myanmar in April 1968. Though he had been released for three months by then, he had yet to write to his wife, Mabel. Letter, Mabel Hkun Hkio to David Lane, MP, 28 May 1968, FO15/70.

24. Myanmar Hsoshelit Lansin Pati Baho Kowmitti Danakyut, *Myanmar Hsoshelit Lansin Pati Okkatakyi ei Hkit Pyaung Towhlanyei Thamaing win Meinkhun Paungkyut* [Collected Speeches of the Era Changing Revolution

History of the Chairman of the Myanmar Socialist Programme Party], Vol. 2 (Yangon: Myanmar Socialist Way Party Central Committee Headquarters, Party Publications Unit, July 1985), pp. 185–94.

25. Airgram, Byroade to SOS, 9 March 1968, containing Clifford E. Southard's account of Paul Harney's golf match with General Ne Win, Pol 15-1 Burma, no. 166.

26. *Towhlanyei Kaungsi ei Hluthsaungchet Thamaing Akyinchut*, p. 219; paper in FO1041/6.

27. Edmund Baker, ed., *The Accidental Diplomat: The Autobiography of Maurice Baker* (Singapore: World Scientific, 2014), pp. 133–34.

28. Record of Conversation between the High Commissioner (New Delhi) and General Ne Win, 16 March 1968, FO1041/6.

29. *Towhlanyei Kaungsi ei Hluthsaungchet Thamaing Akyinchut*, p. 219.

30. *The Guardian*, vol. XV, no. 3 (May 1968).

31. AA Mr or Mrs Fischer to German embassy in Rangoon, 10 May 1968, AA PA AV Neuers Amt 2.160, 336; also Mr or Mrs Weil, Yg to AA, 11 May AA PA AV Neuers Amt 2.160, 337; also papers in FO15/83 and FO15/95.

32. Myanmar did not accede to the treaty until 2 December 1992, after China had done so earlier in that year.

33. Papers in PREM 13/2071; FCO15/826.

34. FCO15/826; FCO15/83: FCO15/95

35. Telegram, Rangoon to SOS, 22 July 1968, Pol 15-1 Burma, No. 03708.

36. Ger Emb Ygn Weil to AA, 25 July 1968, AA PA B 37 Bd. 377, 836.

37. Ger Emb Ygn Keiser to AA, 13 September 1968, AA PA B 37, Bd. 377, 843–46.

38. Letter, Trafford Smith to D.F. Murray, 11 September 1968; Letter, Trafford Smith to D.F.B. LeBreton, 30 August 1968; Letter, D.F.B. Le Breton to K. Hamilton Jones, Yangon, 9 August 1965, FCO15/90.

39. "Tatmadaw Nyilahkan Meinhkwun" [Army Conference Speech], 21 September 1968, *Myanmar Hsoshelit Lansin Pati Okkatakyi ei Hkit Pyaung Towhlanyei Thamaing win Meinkhun Paungkyut*, Volume 2, pp. 267–305; a translation is available in *Forward*, vol. VII, no. 5 (15 October 1968): 4–11.

40. *Myanmar Hsoshelit Lansin Pati Okkatakyi ei Hkit Pyaung Towhlanyei Thamaing win Meinkhun Paungkyut*, Volume 1, 27 September 1968, pp. 101–15. Translation can be found in *Forward*, vol. VII, no. 6 (1 November 1968): 6–9.

41. Senior General Saw Maung recalled these words in a speech on 5 July 1988. He was a Major in 1968 and reported to Ne Win about Thakin Than Tun's demise. Saw Maung said, according to the translation of his words in *The Working People's Daily* of 6 July 1989,

I was very happy. I'm saying this very frankly. That was how I thought at that time, but not now. There is no reason for me to feel happy about it

now. At that time our General, General Ne Win came. I reported the matter
to him. What he said was ... in fact the BCP is our enemy. You might
think that it was a thing to be happy on the death of a person whom you
regarded as an enemy. But you think carefully. Actually he had followed the
wrong path. He was one of those who played an important role during the
struggle for independence. He also said that he could have done greatly for
the country if he had done things correctly. No other citizen than ours has
been lost.

42. Tally provided in telegram, Rangoon to SOS, 23 November 1968, Box 235,
    Burma Cables, Volume I, LBJ Library.
43. Telegram, Rangoon to SOS, 13 November 1968, Box 235, Burma Cables,
    LBJ Library.
44. Germany embassy in Rangoon, Weil to AA, 8 August 1968, AA PAB 08
    Bd.1 603, 378 and 9 August 1968, AA PA B 37 Bd. 377, 837.
45. Weil to AA, 30 August 1968, AA PA B 08 Bd.1 603, 382–83; also, Ambassador
    (to the United Nations) Boeker to AA, 21 September 1969, AA PA B 08
    Bd.1 603, 388.
46. Keiser to AA, 18 September 1968, AA PA B 08 Bd.1.603, 385–87.
47. Ger Emb Ygn Amb Keiser to AA, 14 October 1968, AA PA B 37 Bd. 376,
    689–891.
48. *Towhlanyei Kaungsi ei Hluthsaungchet Thamaing Akyinchut*, p. 223; Papers in
    PREM 13/3071; FCO15/826.
49. Dr Munz, 23 October 1968, AA PA B 08 Bd. 1 603, 406–7.
50. Contents of General Ne Win's talks with the State Chancellor, 18 October
    1968, AA PA B 37, Bd. 377, 851–53. At that time, Myanmar was still willing
    to be provocative toward China as with Dr Maung Maung's unusual article
    in the *Bangkok Post*, "Burma — A Slap at the Reds", 24 November 1968,
    apparently designed to show the Thai government and others that Ne Win's
    government was not afraid of the Chinese.
51. *The Guardian*, vol. XV, no. 12 (19 December 1968).
52. *Towhlanyei Kaungsi ei Hluthsaungchet Thamaing Akyinchut*, p. 16; *The Guardian*,
    vol. XVI, no. 1 (January 1969).
53. *Towhlanyei Kaungsi ei Hluthsaungchet Thamaing Akyinchut*, p. 41.
54. Ibid., 219.
55. *The Guardian*, vol. XVI, no. (March 1969).
56. PREM 13/3071
57. Briefing note, 29 April 1969, FO15/826.
58. Ger Emb Ygn Mr Weil to AA, 29 April 1969, AA PA B 08 Bd. 1.110, 304;
    AA internal memo by Mrs Schoettle, 5 May, 12 May, 16 June 1969, AA PA
    B 08 Bd.1.110, 306–7, 310 and 314–15.
59. *Towhlanyei Kaungsi ei Hluthsaungchet Thamaing Akyinchut*, p, 116.
60. *The Guardian*, vol. XVI, no. 8 (August 1969); Ger Emb Amb Keiser to AA,
    9 July 1969, AA PA B 37 Bd. 445, 542–43; Silverstein, "Political Dialogue
    in Burma", p. 138.

61. See "Destroy the Bureuacracy! Transformation of the Civilian Bureaucracy in the Name of the Revolution", in *Strong Soldiers, Failed Revolution: The State and Military in Burma, 1962–88*, by Yoshihiro Nakanishi (Kyoto: Kyoto University Press, 2013), pp. 142–68.

62. Ger Emb Amb Keiser to AA, 24 June 1969, AA PA B 37 Bd.445, 538–41.

63. Papers in FCO5/826 and *The Guardian*, vol. XVI, no. 9 (September 1969).

64. *The Guardian*, vol. XVI, no. 9 (September 1969).

65. Telegram, Rangoon to FCO, 27 August 1969, FCO15/826.

66. Airgram, Rangoon to SOS, 30 August 1969, Leg 7 Mansfield xr Pol 15-1 Burma, no. A-227.

67. Letter, A.D.P. Smart to J. Watts, 4 June 1971, FCO15/1381, based on a conversation with Deputy Director of Intelligence Colonel Tin U. On the saga of Nu's efforts to raise funds, see Wendy Law-Yone, *Golden Parasol: A Daughter's Memoir of Burma* (London: Chatto and Windus, 2013), pp. 188 and 201–6.

68. Telegrams, Rangoon to SOS, 4 November and 6 November 1969, Pol 17: Burma-US, No. 186393 and Pol: Burma, No. 298.

69. *Address Delivered by General Ne Win, Chairman of the Burma Socialist Programme Party at the Opening Session of the Fourth Party Seminar on 6th November 1969* (Yangon: Burma Socialist Programme Party, November 1969), pp. 29–30.

70. Ibid., p. 37.

71. Ibid., p. 6

72. Ibid., p. 18.

73. *The Guardian*, vol. XVII, no. 1 (January 1970).

74. Ger Amb Keiser to AA, 4 December 1969, AA PA B 37 Bd. 445, 593–94.

75. *The Guardian*, vol. XVII, no. 1 (January 1970).

76. OSS-101 Association Newsletter, Spring/Summer 2008, p. 4.

77. Martin Smith, *Burma: Insurgency and the Politics of Ethnicity*, 2nd ed. (London: Zed Books, 1999), p. 277. Law-Yone wrote that the amount agreed was two million dollars initially and another two million when the government was able to execute the agreement. *Golden Parasol*, pp. 203–4.

78. *Towhlanyei Kaungsi ei Hluthsaungchet Thamaing Akyinchut*, p. 219.

79. Ambassador Rolf von Keiser to AA, 30 January 1970, AA PA AV Neuers Amt 2.160, 351–52.

80. PREM 11/4650

81. Carolyn Wakeman and San San Tin, *No Time for Dreams: Living in Burma Under Military Rule* (Lanham, Maryland: Rowman and Littlefield, 2009), pp. 20–21. Thakin Ba Tin who was one of the founders of the *Dobama Asiayon*, was commissioned in the BIA and was subsequently tortured by the Japanese *Kempetai*. After independence, he worked closely with Bo Let Ya and was imprisoned in 1958 and again in 1963. He received medical treatment

before his death in 1965 at the Defense Services Hospital. Chit Hlaing, "The Tatmadaw and My Political Career", unpublished paper, translated by Kyaw Yin Hlaing, p. 27. After his death, his widow sold state lottery tickets and his daughter worked for a government newspaper.

82. Interview with Major (rtd) Htway Han and Thakin Tin Mya, 11 March 2006.
83. *Towhlanyei Kaungsi ei Hluthsaungchet Thamaing Akyinchut*, p. 221.
84. John Badgley, "Burma: The Army Vows Legitimacy", *Asian Survey*, vol. XII, no. 2 (February 1972): 181. The literacy programme, which involved getting volunteer students to teach in the villages was initially received with enthusiasm. Wakeman and San San Tin, *No Time for Dreams*, pp. 40–41.
85. Papers in PREM 11/4650 and PREM 13/3071.
86. Telegram, Rangoon to SOS, 6 June 1970, Pol 15-4 Burma.
87. Airgram, Rangoon to SOS, 5 September 1970, Pol 2-1 Burma, No. A-192.
88. *Towhlanyei Kaungsi ei Hluthsaungchet Thamaing Akyinchut*, p. 219.
89. Ibid., p. 219.
90. *The Guardian*, vol. XXIX, no. 1 (January 1971).
91. Letter, A.B.P. Smart to W.J. Watt, 15 January 1971, FCO15/1387; Ger Emb Ygn Ramisch to AA, 11 January 1971, AA PA B 37 Bd. 584, 644. During this visit, Ne Win donated a pavilion in Geisenheim to display Burmese products and crafts as a gesture of gratitude to the assistance the Fritz Werner Company had provided Myanmar.
92. GDR GC YGN Thomas to MFAA, 20 January 1971, AA PA MFAA C 112 73, 1097–98.
93. Telegram, FCO to Rangoon, 22 February 1971, FCO15/1387.
94. Ger Emb Ygn Ramisch to AA, 22 February 1971, AA PA B 37 Bd. 584, 640–41, also 656–57.
95. Telegram, FCO to Rgn, 16 March 1971, FCO15/1387.
96. File Note, 8 March 1971, FCO15/1385.
97. *The Guardian*, March 1971.
98. Note on Meeting with Tommy Clift at the President Hotel, Bangkok, on 2 March 1971 by P.A. Knapton, Wing Commander, Air Attaché, 2 March 1971, FCO15/1381.
99. Telegram, Douglas-Home to Bangkok, 4 March 1971, FCO15/1381.
100. First Impressions of Burma by E.G. Willan, 25 February 1971, FCO15/1387. For information on Mr Trevor Roper, see his obituary in *The Guardian* (London), 6 May 2004.
101. Telegram, FCO to Rgn, 30 March 1971, FCO15/1387; Mr Ramisch of German embassy in Rangoon, report to AA, 1 April 1971, AA PA 152819, 354; AA Berendonck to Ger Emb Ygn, 7 April 1971, AA PA B 37, Bd. 584, 662.

102. Telegram, FCO to Rgn, 21 April 1971, FCO15/387.

103. Record of Conversation between FCO Minister Douglas Home and Tun Abdul Razak, 23 April 1971, FCO15/1387.

104. *Towhlanyei Kaungsi ei Hluthsaungchet Thamaing Akyinchut*, p. 27.

105. *Myanmar Hsoshelit Lansin Pati Okkatakyi ei Hkit Pyaung Towhlanyei Thamaing win Meinkhun Paungkyut*, Volume 1: 159–79, translated in *Forward*, vol. IX, no. 23 (15 July 1971): 4–7.

106. *Towhlanyei Kaungsi ei Hluthsaungchet Thamaing Akyinchut*, pp. 161, 254, 255.

107. Ibid., pp. 161, 256.

108. *Myanmar Hsoshelit Lansin Pati Okkatakyi ei Hkit Pyaung Towhlanyei Thamaing win Meinkhun Paungkyut*, Volume 2, pp. 180–92.

109. Ibid., vol. 2, pp. 32–38.

110. Discussions with U Thaw Kaung, March and July 2013, and email from Thant Thaw Kaung, 8 August 2013.

111. Letter, C.W. Squire, Bangkok to FO, 8 July 1971, FCO15/1386.

112. Airgram, Rangoon to SOS, 30 July 1971, Pol 2-1 Burma, No. A127.

113. Liang Chi-shad, "Burma's Relations with the People's Republic of China: From Delicate Friendship to Genuine Cooperation", in *Burma: The Challenge of Change in a Divided Society*, edited by Peter Cary (London: Macmillan, 1997), p. 73; Liang, *Burma's Foreign Relations*, p. 91; papers in FCO15/1876.

114. Letter, Wilan to D. McD. Gordon, 27 August 1971, FCO15/1385.

115. Letter, A. Carter to H.E. Rigney, Rgn, 8 October 1971, FCO15/1388.

116. Note by FCO to Rigney, Rgn, 22 October 1971, FCO15/1387; Letter, Col. Ko Ko To Douglas-Home, 29 October 1971, FCO15/1388.

117. Note on Meeting between the Prime Minister and General Ne Win, 21 December 1971, PREM 11/4650.

118. Notes in FCO15/1388.

119. Letter, Chancery, Rangoon to South East Asia Department, FCO, 21 October 1971, FCO15/1383.

120. Letter, Douglas Home to Ne Win, 11 November 1971, FCO15/1388.

121. Notes by Mr Smart of conversation with Arthur Bottomley, MP, 17 November 1971, FCO15/1388.

122. Notes in FCO1388. This could be a Mrs Leach, the wife of the British mining advisor to the Caretaker Government during 1958–59.

123. Letter, E.G. Willan to A.B.P. Smart, 18 April 1972, FCO15/1522.

124. Directorate of Intelligence, Central Intelligence Agency, Intelligence Report: "Peking and the Burmese Communists: The Perils and Profits of Insurgency", RSS No. 0052/71, July 1971, p. 98, LBJ Library.

125. Apparently over the marriage of one of her daughters from her first marriage to someone Ne Win considered unsuitable. Telegram, Willan to FCO,

24 March 1972; Letter, H.E. Rigney to A.B.P. Smart, 10 March 1972; Letter, E.G. Willan to A.B.P. Smart, 18 April 1972, FCO15/1522.

126. Now L'Opera Italian restaurant.

127. *Towhlanyei Kaungsi ei Hluthsaungchet Thamaing Akyinchut*, p. 224; FCO15/1513.

128. Philip Ziegler, ed., *From Shore to Shore, the Final Years: The Diaries of Earl Mountbatten of Burma, 1953–1979* (London: Collins, 1989), p. 229. See also Letter, Mountbatten to Dennis (probably Greenhill, permanent secretary of the Foreign Office), 2 March 1972, FCO15/1513.

129. Lord Mountbatten's interview with Basil Clarke, BBC Burmese Service, 20 July 1972, PC/C-1, Part II.

130. Letter, E.G. Willan, to D. McD. Gordon, 25 February 1972, FCO15/1519.

131. Telegram, Willan to FCO, 24 March 1972; Letter, E.G. Willan to A.B.P. Smart, 18 April 1972, FCO15/1522.

132. Letter, E.G. Willan to A.B.P. Smart, 18 April 1972, FCO15/1522.

11

TRANSITION AND SMALL CHANGE
(March 1972 to February 1978)

Behold, I sent you forth as sheep in the midst of wolves: be ye therefore
wise as serpents and harmless as doves.

Matthew 10:16

By 1972, opposition to Ne Win's revolution appeared enfeebled, but still
a nuisance and a potential threat. No one could predict the future but,
as ever, yesterday's enemies might be tomorrow's assets. As Ne Win had
by 1972 been fighting on all sides for thirty years — against imperialists,
fascists, communists, separatists, racists, religionists, capitalists, chauvinists,
and the merely misguided — he could cope with nuisances, though they
and other irritations apparently undermined his health and equilibrium. The
tensions of the previous five years appeared to have been weathered. Though
the Chinese were still providing support for the Burma Communist Party
(BCP), the party itself generated little enthusiasm amongst the majority of
the population, and the rebellion was kept going only with the assistance
of ethnic separatists and Chinese-dominated border minorities. Still, small
urban cells persisted amongst the students and intellectuals. The attempt
by U Nu and his Parliamentary Democracy Party (PDP), the old right of
Myanmar, had failed to rally the people to its banner and the Americans
and the British, while they may have considered the possibility of supporting
Nu's movement briefly, had realized the futility of that option. Better not

411

to stir the cauldron of Myanmar politics for fear of losing the country's neutrality in the Cold War.

Nu's link with Karen and other separatist forces had damaged his credibility with the majority of the population, and the Karen National Union (KNU) and its armed wing, the Karen National Liberation Army (KNLA), though still a potent insurgent force, was in no position to threaten Ne Win's regime. India was reassured of Burma's neutrality in its conflicts with Pakistan and China, and when pressed to decide, had proven that its neutrality was tempered by realism, as in the recognition of its new, and troublesome protégé, Bangladesh. Ne Win's radical brand of neutralism, though paying a heavy price in terms of delayed economic development, was ensuring peace for the overwhelming majority of the population. That peace and stability was welcomed by many then as a respite from the chaos of the previous decades. Most who were adults in the early 1970s had lived through the turmoil of the Second War World, the resistance, and the Civil War. Those memories were strong and Ne Win's kind of peace, and unwillingness to tamper with the fundamental institutions of Myanmar society, particularly Buddhism, was welcome. When the horrors inflicted on the faith by the Khmer Rouge became known later in the 1970s, many thanked Ne Win for keeping Communism out of Myanmar, even if at the cost of his brand of socialism.

Intermittent fighting persisted in parts of the country, but the delta and the Bago Yoma were both now largely free of insurgent forces, thanks to sweeping battles by the army during the previous few years. The army, despite its modest size and rudimentary equipment, was the People's Army, and had proven itself worthy of the tasks that were given to it. Stretched sometimes to cover all its responsibilities, military and administrative, the army and its officer corps, apparently loyal to Ne Win, had proven themselves to be adequate for the job.[1] His most loyal lieutenants, Brigadier San Yu, Colonel Hla Han, Colonel Lwin, Colonel Sein Win and others, could be trusted not only to manage affairs in his absence, but also to ensure that when he returned from his forays abroad, on government business, personal matters, or both, he would still be the most important person in Myanmar.

Despite the problems with the economy, projects of the kind mooted at various times by Ne Win, combining both industrialization and the revival of Myanmar traditions were under way. Hino trucks, Mazda cars, National light bulbs, radios, and electrical equipment were being assembled with the reparation funds provided by the Japanese. Nonetheless, the economy was increasingly demonstrating Myanmar's self-sufficiency and if foreign clothing and medicines were scarce, traditional medicines were being revived. Perhaps best at evoking the spirit of the Revolution in all of its aspects, and its most significant monument, was the Karaweik Palace. A project commenced by Colonel Sein Win in the 1960s, construction began in 1972, resulting in two elaborately carved mythical birds on stable bases in the Kandawgyi Lake opposite the Shwe Dagon Pagoda. Combining ten traditional crafts, including lacquerware, carving, metal work, and stucco work, the deck between the two birds provided restaurants and performance areas for traditional Myanmar music and dance (Moore 2009).

One element of the Karaweik that had to be imported, however, was the tinted glass that is found in many of the windows and decorations in the ornate building. Perhaps inevitably, given the scarcity of imported materials, and the open nature of the grounds of the Karaweik construction site, some of the glass slipped into the black market and was used to make spectacles. This led the wags of Rangoon to go about saying that under the Burmese Way to Socialism, they were all wearing rose coloured glasses.[2] While many doubted the government's claims of economic change, few were willing to challenge the prevailing doctrines. Better to go along than to become an object of attention.

In these circumstances, conditions seemed set fair to press on with the revolution which Ne Win had foreseen, but not explained, a decade earlier. On 20 April 1972, eight days after returning to Yangon from his Swiss holiday, Ne Win and twenty other senior officers resigned from the army. For the first time in three decades, Ne Win was officially no longer a soldier, though for most, he would always be the General. His desire to be a politician had, however, been achieved. According to Revolutionary Council Announcement Number 99, the cabinet was re-organized, with fifteen members now. Ne Win remained Prime Minister as well as Chairman of the Council, underlining that there was more continuity than change in the announcement.[3] Two civilians were added to the cabinet and Brigadier San Yu was promoted to full General rank, with the posts of Chief-of-Staff, Defence Minister, and Deputy Prime Minister. At the same time, Colonel Tin U was promoted to Brigadier and made Deputy Chief-of-Staff (Wiant 1973, p. 100). Ne Win spent much of May that year in Maymyo, sleeping late and playing golf, and going on a tour in the Northwest Command Area, before returning to Yangon.[4]

Ten days later, the first draft of what would become the new constitution of the Socialist Republic of the Union of Burma, prepared by a ninety-three member commission, chaired by General San Yu, was published. There would then commence an eighteen-month period of consultation, with members of the drafting commission hosting meetings throughout the country to explain the new constitution and the people's role in the new order. Out would go the old colonial legacy of legal and bureaucratic institutions, in would come Myanmar made new people's courts, people's administrations, and people's police. Steps were already in place to ensure the smooth transition to the new order, with the reform of Tanintharyi Division to create the Mon State, and an expansion of Yangon division and the unification of the northern and southern Shan States.[5] The Central Security and Administration Committee (SAC) was reformed on 1 July, state and divisions SACs were reformed on 20 July as were the various level economic-plan implementation committees.[6] On 7 August, both executive and judicial powers were given to reformed SACs as a step in the implementation of the people's judicial system, in keeping with Ne Win's idea as explained in 1969 to turn the administration of justice over to the people and out of the hands of lawyers and the police. At the same time, the bureaucracy was reformed, with the abolition of the old British districts and sub-districts.[7] In his role as chief exhorter of the country, Ne Win met with "intellectuals and working intelligentsia" in June to encourage them to use the country's natural resources effectively and efficiently.

While supervising and guiding these domestic issues, Ne Win was also, of course, shaping the country's foreign policy, just as he did when he was abroad. The Bangladesh Foreign Minister, Abdus Samad Azad, arrived for a four-day visit to thank the government of Myanmar for its prompt recognition of his country earlier in the year.[8] Despite Myanmar's neutrality in the Cold War, at least the British embassy felt that Western governments had more access, limited as it was, to the government than their Eastern European colleagues, in particular the East Germans.[9] This may well have been a reflection of the anti-Communist sentiments of the government, particularly as the Burma Communist Party was at that time carving out an enclave on the border which the army found impossible to dislodge, given the stiffening provided to the Communist forces by Chinese "volunteers". A long low-level siege was to take place on Myanmar's northern marches for the next two decades.

Nonetheless, Ne Win needed to maintain the perception of balance in Myanmar's foreign relations and, certainly with that aim in mind, he left Yangon for an official visit to Hungary from 13 to 19 July, having stopped off en route to have lunch with the Italian President, Guilio Andreotti, in Rome.[10] From Budapest, he flew to London again, and Daw Khin May Than, with their three children, arrived soon after.[11] According to the recently promoted Captain Scrace, his Special Branch minder, Ne Win indicated that his divorce from Daw Khin May Than was still under way and that, though living together, they led very separate lives. He mainly played golf and lunched twice with his doctor friends but otherwise never went out, while she was seeking medical treatment for her kidney disease. However, she refused to use the kidney machine at King Edward VII hospital.[12]

Ne Win remained in London for just over a month. Before his departure, he did meet with Prime Minister Heath for half an hour and also the Foreign Secretary, Sir Alec Douglas-Home, both on 8 August. Ne Win told Heath that relations with Thailand would remain un-reconciled as long as U Nu was allowed to harbour there. The other two topics of conversation were the divisions Ne Win perceived within the ageing Chinese leadership and the growing Japanese influence in Singapore.[13] His conversation with Douglas-Home also touched on China. Ne Win, noting that Chou En-lai liked straight talk, said that Chou would get on well with Home. He also said that he had not raised the issue of Chinese support for the BCP during his visit to China the previous year, but indicated that he would do so in future. As for Myanmar's prompt recognition of Bangladesh, Pakistani then President Zulfikar Ali Bhutto and he were friends, and he had told Bhutto that he would not have objected if Pakistan had broken off relations with Myanmar over the issue.[14]

While Ne Win was in London, the then Foreign Minister of Myanmar, U Kyaw Soe, flew in to consult with him on his way to an imminent Non-Aligned (NAM) Foreign Ministers Conference in Georgetown, Guyana. At that conference, where statues of four of the six founders of the Non-Aligned Movement were unveiled, U Nu and Sukarno were noticeably absent.[15] Myanmar took a more active role than normal. Doubtless thinking of the impact of its actions on the perceptions of Myanmar in the Cold War context, as well as its neutralist principles, the Myanmar delegation lodged five formal reservations, in particular objecting to the seating of a National Liberation Front (NLF) for South Vietnam delegation and a delegation of supporters of Cambodia's ousted Prince Sihanouk. Recognition of the NLF and Sihanouk, ousted in a coup by General Lon Nol in 1970, would be acts of interference in the domestic affairs of the states. Though

acting on the principle of non-interference, these reservations would not
have pleased the Chinese, who were supporters of both the NLF and
Sihanouk.[16]

After his month in London, on his return Ne Win chaired a meeting
of the Central Committee of the Burma Socialist Programme Party (BSPP)
from 25 to 27 September where, amongst other business, the process
of the transition to a civilian government and eventual party rule was
discussed.[17] He then addressed a Party Consultative Conference on
29 September. In his speech, Ne Win discussed at length problems
over supplies of rice and cooking oil, noting public concern about the
availability of supplies. In addition to exhortation and admonition, he
tried to reassure his audience that the government was acting in the best
interests of the public. He also discussed the replacement of 20 kyat
banknotes with 25 kyat notes of local provenance. Previously, Myanmar
banknotes had been printed in England or Australia but, with new
German presses, they were being produced in the country. The change
had led to speculation about another demonetization, as had occurred
in 1964, and he reassured the public on that point, though threatening
black market operators and smugglers at the same time that their illegal
wealth would be seized.[18]

That same day, Daw Khin May Than once more flew from Yangon to
London for medical treatment, accompanied by Dr Mya Oo. Ne Win was
initially expected to follow her, arriving on 2 October, but then postponed
his journey to arrive on the 6th.[19] In the event, he flew on 30 September,
but had been airborne for about an hour when Daw Khin May Than died
at Fulham hospital. Remaining in London for a few days, one day mainly
in bed, another playing golf and visiting friends in Walton-on-Thames, he
flew back with his children and her body on the 3rd, arriving in Yangon
on the 4th. Daw Khin May Than was buried on the 6th in a simple
religious ceremony for the family only at Kyandaw Cemetery. Her body
had been available for viewing the previous day by diplomats and others
and, on the final part of the journey to the cemetery, her coffin had been
drawn by nurses, marking her own nursing career and interests.[20] For the
final steps to her resting place, the coffin was carried by her son Pyo, three
sons-in-law, nephew Dr Lyn Aung Thet, and Maung Maung Chaing, the
son of Colonel Chaing.

Ne Win was badly shaken by the death of his wife, despite their
estrangement. Sixteen years his junior, but every bit his equal in terms of
pose and personality, they had raised six children together, three from her

previous marriage, and three of their own. Her unwillingness to submit to dialysis, that certainly contributed to her death at the relatively young age of forty-five, was difficult to understand, particularly because of the high quality health care she received and her own medical background. Though she was raised in a medical family and was aware of the advances in modern medicine, Ne Win could not persuade her to undertake the treatment which might have saved her life. For weeks after her death, one of his children would often sleep on the floor in his room in order to provide him with companionship. Having been together for two decades, he may have come to depend upon her more than he thought. Many felt that he had lost much of his humanity and sympathy for others after her departure. As the British ambassador wrote at the time:

> Ne Win cannot be the easiest man to live with, but she understood his moods, was one of the few people who could handle him, and to some extent humanise him.[21] She was vigilant over his physical well-being and gave him a normal, relaxed family life. She was devoted to their children, who she had at time to shelter from their father's wrath. She was an accomplished hostess, clever, witty, and charming, far more at ease than he in international company and fitting easily into the role of Head of State's wife. In recent years the Ne Wins felt obliged to keep themselves increasingly aloof when in Burma and she came to rely mainly on old friends, both Burmese and foreign, for an outlet for her inherent sociability. She had strong likes and dislikes but was fundamentally kind hearted. There are many people in Burma who felt that in really serious trouble they could always in the last resort seek her intervention. Above all, she had great personal courage, and knowing for some years that she had not long to live, never let it show.

Though criticized by staunch socialists and others for the advantages that she and Ne Win enjoyed as head of state and wife, including holidays abroad, he continued,

> In fact by any but Burmese standards their life style was modest. When an earthquake caused minor damage to the vast late-Victorian Government House they moved with relief into a villa he had acquired as Chief of Staff. This must be one of the least assuming residences of a Head of State, and apart from the unavoidable security which hemmed them in, they lived much like any British or anglicised army officer or official (golf clubs in the dining room and dogs underfoot). But it is true she was no convinced socialist and her influence

must usually have been on the side of moderation, pragmatism and humanity.

Turning to Ne Win himself, the ambassador, who was concerned his access to Ne Win would possibly deteriorate in Daw Khin May Than's absence, wrote:

> The crucial question however is the effect of his wife's death on Ne Win himself. He leant heavily on her, and when he landed at Mingladon Airport with her body he was visibly deeply distressed (and members of the Revolutionary Council were in tears). He is a hard man and will get over it. But it will not be surprising if his colleagues find him even more autocratic, irascible and hard to approach. They will certainly miss her ability to feel the temperature or put in a helpful word. I doubt if there will be much talk of his voluntary retirement, the temptations of which must now seem much reduced. In any case this is scarcely the moment to think of abandoning his responsibilities. The astrologers predicted that September would be inauspicious for Ne Win and they were not wrong. ... His sense of duty (and lack of confidence in his colleague's ability) will probably keep him on the job. After last year's alarm he seems to have kept pretty fit this year, but with no wife to support him, watch his health and diet and act as lightning conductor, his staying power may be affected. In the long run the chances of dying in harness are probably enhanced.[22]

However, funerals and bereavements aside, the conspiracies, and rumours of conspiracies, of politics still occurred. Some days before Daw Khin May Than's funeral, Military Intelligence arrested a number of persons, perhaps as many as 200 in Yangon, for allegedly plotting to overthrow the government. A month later Aung Gyi, Ba Swe and Kyaw Nyein were all arrested for allegedly plotting to assassinate the cabinet. The first arrests had taken place while Ne Win was abroad and included U Rashid, U Nu's former Mining Minister. Rashid and most of those detained were released on 9 October. There were reports prior to then that Nu's movement from Thailand was attempting to land armed militants in the delta around Pyapon but these were never confirmed.[23] President Soeharto of Indonesia, another general in power but pursuing very different policies from Ne Win, other than staunch anti-Communism, visited on 16 November. Closely aligned with the United States, Soeharto had ended his predecessors tryst with socialism and China, for the kind of policies Ne Win might have pursued if he had

had the atomic scissors he told Harrison Salisbury about in 1966 to allow him to drag Myanmar out to sea.[24]

With the departure of Ambassador Byroade, the gradually improving state-to-state relations with China, and the preoccupation of the new Nixon administration in ending its wars in Vietnam, Cambodia and Laos, Myanmar and Ne Win had limited relations with the United States by the early 1970s. As indicated by his remarks to Senate Mike Mansfield in 1969, Ne Win had nothing to contribute in assisting the United States to exit from the quagmire it had created. However, in 1971, one of the by-products of that quagmire, the growing market in the United States for illegal drugs, particularly heroin, which had followed American troops home from the Indochina War, caused the United States once more to take an interest in Myanmar. President Richard Nixon's special representative for international drugs control, New Jersey politician Nelson G. Gross, visited Myanmar a second time in mid-1972 in an attempt to interest the Revolutionary Council in accepting anti-drug equipment.

On his first visit in October 1971, Gross had been rebuffed, getting no support for a conference he wished to organize on the drug problem involving Burma with the United State's anti-Communist allies in mainland Southeast Asia.[25] Gross at that time attempted to induce the British ambassador to persuade Lord Mountbatten to convince Ne Win to meet with the President's special representative. The ambassador refused to do so,[26] possibly thinking, because such a conference would compromise Myanmar's neutrality, that Mountbatten's credibility with Ne Win would be undermined if he did. The Americans were getting desperate to gain access to Ne Win on the subject, and the American ambassador, then Edwin Martin, also approached the West German embassy, explaining a scheme to buy the entire opium crop of Burma in order to get it off the streets of American cities, and hoping to use Ne Win's German friend, Dr Meyer, as an intermediary. The ambassador was no more enthusiastic for the idea than his British counterpart.[27] Later schemes to buy up the opium crop avoiding the Myanmar government as an intermediary were eventually abandoned by the United States government.

However, Gross was to meet with Ne Win on 18 January 1972, the day before his divorce from Daw Khin May Than was announced. Gross had attempted to see Ne Win in England through several intermediaries and eventually Dr Meyer, to whom Gross appealed as an intermediary when in Germany, prevailed upon Ne Win to meet the American. However, prior to that, Ne Win insisted on a letter from President Nixon requesting him to meet with Gross. After much delay on Ne Win's part, including waiting for an official copy of the letter, the invitation to Gross was extended. In the words of Kenton Klymer, "Gross left the meeting very pleased, even euphoric", for Ne Win had expressed strong views on suppressing the opium trade.[28] Gross' subsequent enthusiasm for quick action to assist the government of Burma in controlling the opium production and smuggling operations, including the provision of sophisticated military equipment and training, were typical of the kind of American overenthusiasm which made Ne Win suspicious. Had he known of Gross's suggestion that the experience of the Central Intelligence Agency's airline, Air America, and the U.S. military in South Vietnam be drawn into any assistance scheme, he would have killed it at once.[29]

The bulk of Myanmar's poppy production was in areas near the Chinese, Laotian and Thai borders in the control of various insurgent armies. Some, while posing as ethnic champions, such as Khun Sa, were in the drug smuggling business primarily to make money. According to Nelson Gross, Ne Win's view of the Ka Kwe Ye (KKY), of which Khun Sa was a major factor, was that they "lie, cheat and steal". "Cracking down on them" was the only solution.[30] For the poor farmers of the area, poppy was one of the few cash crops they could grow to supplement their modest incomes. The American offer of assistance was rejected.[31]

The general Burmese attitude at this time was that the drug problem was not theirs but the creation of the imperialists, going back to the British and now the Americans, and it was their responsibility to deal with it. If there were no market, there would be no production. That view would change in time. The Revolutionary Council had asked the United Nations to authorize the legal and controlled growing of opium for medical purposes in 1962, as was done in India. Despite Ne Win's appointment of an Opium Enquiry Committee in 1964 to redraft Myanmar's legislation to comply with the United Nations Single Convention on Opium, the government did not ratify the convention until 1972. The bureaucracy worked slowly unless Ne Win intervened. In the meantime, the government had declared the cultivation of poppy as illegal and had attempted to close all of the opium dens in the country. However, failing to get UN cooperation in 1962, the problem was left to drift for another decade (Renard 1996, pp. 49–50).

However, the increasing attention given to the growing opium trade in the Shan and Kachin states, as well as the persistent insurgency in the area, in part funded by the drug trade, was impelling the government to respond. In January 1973, the government ordered the KKY to disband and surrender their weapons (Lintner 1999, p. 273). In the middle of January, a United Nations drug team was permitted for the first time to enter the so-called Golden Triangle, which included parts of the Kachin and Shan states, on an inspection tour.[32] The Americans were also putting pressure on Thailand at this time to control the drug trade, and, in March 1973, Thailand's Deputy Prime Minister, General Chatichai Choonhaven, whose father, Field Marshall Phin Choonhaven, the Thai coup-maker intimately involved in the activities of the CIA and KMT in the 1940s and 1950s and subsequent drug smuggling operations (Seagrave 1995, pp. 155–66), visited Rangoon to discuss the demarcation of the border between the two countries (McCoy 1991, p. 431). U Nu's self-proclaimed "government-in-exile", though now largely moribund as a military movement, was still extant in Thailand, and Burmese awareness of Thai support for Shan and other insurgents made cooperation difficult.

And still, the socialist revolution rolled forward. On 1 January 1973, the Blind Persons Cooperative Benefit Plan and the Disabled Persons Producers Cooperative Benefit Plan were introduced.[33] In March, the Revolutionary Council announced another reshuffle of deputy ministers,[34] and the Party Central Committee approved the second draft of the new state constitution. From 7 to 10 April, the BSPP held a special Extraordinary Conference to amend the tenure of the First Party Congress and also to amend the constitution of the party itself,[35] followed by another reorganization of the lower-level economic plan implementation committees.[36] The gradual shift to accepting more foreign assistance for Myanmar's economic development took a significant turn when the government joined the Asian Development Bank (ADB) at the same time as the Extraordinary Party Conference. Even some edging in the direction of a return to foreign investment was revealed in February 1972, when the Myanmar Oil Company accepted one million dollars worth of technical assistance from the Gulf Oil Corporation of the United States to undertake a survey of offshore oil reserves.[37] Further exploration and production-sharing agreements were reached in 1975, but when gas was found offshore, the well was capped (Martin 1975, p. 132), allegedly because of Ne Win's concern about the political implications of developing Myanmar's gas industry at that time. Having large American-owned oil companies establishing major installations with their own personnel in the country might not only antagonize China but also undermine Ne Win's desire to achieve autarky and self-reliance. The gas could remain in the earth until it was needed and Myanmar had the capacity to exploit it. Nonetheless, before long, the government abandoned the policy pursued since 1962 of financing development from internal savings and began increasingly to accept foreign aid and loans, up to 30 per cent of development spending (Sylvan 1979, pp. 117–19).

In the meantime, General Ne Win, within less than nine months of his wife's death, remarried. The new bride, Daw Ni Ni Myint, thirty years younger than Ne Win, and a distant relative of Daw Khin May Than, was a lecturer in history at Yangon Arts and Science University. She had assisted Daw Khin May Than in earlier years in managing her extended household, including during the time she moved out of the marital home from January to April 1972, and had been known to Ne Win for some time.

Though Khun Sa had been ordered to disband his Ka Kwe Ye units and after his capture was in detention in Mandalay, his troops had managed to kidnap two doctors from the Soviet Union working on an aid project near Taunggyi. Their release was dependent upon his release. Kidnapping became something of a problem for the government at this time, with a West German drilling expert captured by the Kachin Independence Army in 1975 near Namtu, in the northern Shan State, and reportedly released after the payment of a quarter of a million dollar ransom by the German government. In the case of the two Soviet doctors, they were released in exchange for the government giving Khun Sa his freedom.[38]

Ne Win went abroad for the first time since his return with Daw Khin May Than's body on 18 April, travelling first to Thailand and then to Japan.[39] It seems likely that in his talks in Bangkok, he made it clear that improved relations would be dependent upon Thailand resolving the issue of U Nu's "government-in-exile". Just a month after his visit, Nu was ordered by the Thai authorities to leave the country,[40] and he departed a month later to travel to New York where he had accepted an offer to teach at New York University, Professor Frank Trager's institution.[41] He later toured the United States, giving lectures on Buddhism.[42] He handed his movement over to Bo Let Ya,[43] Nu's former Minister of Defence, and Aung San's right-hand man, who led it for another five futile years. Bo Let Ya remained in exile in the hills east of Myanmar until his death in 1978 at the hands of his alleged allies, the Karen National Liberation Army (Khin Let Ya 2012, pp. 10–11). Bo Yan Naing then re-took command of the dwindling insurgent band. In Japan, Ne Win doubtless discussed continuing Japanese economic assistance.

Following Nu's departure from Thailand and the extradition of opium warlord Lo Hsing-Han to Myanmar, cooperation in the effort to control illicit drug production with the United States and Thailand increased. From 11 to 17 June, Ne Win paid return calls to Indonesia and Malaysia.[44] Both visits were remarkably causal and relaxed, with lots of time to play golf. Conversations centred on the Association of Southeast Asian Nations (ASEAN), which Myanmar was once more encouraged to join, now that the Vietnam War was nominally over. Ne Win insisted that Myanmar was more neutral than any ASEAN member and Myanmar would therefore remain aloof from the organization.[45] It would have been natural though for the leaders of the non-Communist states of Southeast Asia in the mid-1970s to seek Myanmar's membership of any regional organization if, for no other reason, that it was the American failure in Vietnam that led them to conclude that the best protection against domestic opponents was not Western alliances but Southeast Asian resilience and non-interference in other's affairs; in other words, the Ne Win way (Acharya 2012, p. 125). Also, China's relations with Southeast Asia would also have been on their lists of discussion points. To underline the point, though prodded by the host nation, Algeria, Ne Win refused to attend the Fourth Non-Aligned Summit in Algiers in September, even though he was just across the Mediterranean Sea in Europe at the time. There was much speculation in Yangon as to whether he would attend, but in the end he did not and Myanmar's delegation, while filing dissenting motions on five points including Cambodia and Vietnam, as before, on this occasion did not even bother to address the meeting.[46] The NAM was becoming irrelevant and part of what Ne Win saw as the futility of much Third World political posturing.

The construction of the new single-party socialist state continued throughout 1973, step-by-step and systematically, as the newspapers repeatedly said. Indeed, routine was becoming the norm of the late Revolutionary Council government. Ne Win played an increasingly smaller role, leaving major activities to his subordinates, led by San Yu, though he still occasionally toured development projects, spending three days in upper Myanmar in late July. According to Brigadier Thaung Dan, then Minister for Information, Culture and Social Welfare, and Vice Chief-of-Staff of the Armed Forces, all of his fellow ministers were bored at meetings and slept through San Yu's speech at the Annual Commanders' Conference in August. Thaung Dan, considered to be a genuine leftist, hoped to escape his ministerial duties to return to the military after the forthcoming constitutional referendum and then elections, and believed the government actually had the correct policies but the government itself was incompetent. He also reported that Ne Win was very angry at the "economic obstruction of members of the Peasants Council", referring to the collaboration of farmers with businessmen to hoard paddy and keep prices high. In an unreported speech to the Central Committee on 6 August, Ne Win had spoken harshly of the peasantry.[47] As Ne Win had discussed with the United States ambassador and the Chinese premier ten years earlier, the peasantry were very conservative but they had to be made to change their behaviour for their own good and for the good of the country.

At this time, the Revolutionary Council issued the 1973 Socialist Republic of the Union of Burma referendum law and formed a constitutional referendum committee, chaired by former Kachin Duwa, Dingra Tang, with twenty-six other members, unusually all civilians. Then followed the Sixth Meeting of the BSPP Central Committee. It formed a 310-member Burma Socialist Programme Party referendum commission.[48] Soon after the conclusion of the Central Committee meeting, Ne Win and Daw Ni Ni Myint departed for a month-long visit to Switzerland and England; however, not before meeting with a visiting Thai delegation, led again by General Chatichai Choonhaven, who was hoping for more cooperation from Myanmar now that Nu was no longer in Thailand. Little of consequence resulted from the visit. Though U Nu was no longer a point of contention, Thailand continued to harbour other opponents of the Myanmar government.[49]

Soon after Ne Win's return from holiday abroad, the Duke and Duchess of Kent visited Myanmar as his guests. He met them at the airport on 26 September and took them to the state guest house. They then toured Bagan and Mandalay with Ne Win and Daw Ni Ni Myint before flying to Thandwe to stay at Ne Win's beachside residence. While at Thandwe, as the roof was leaking where she sat at a meal, the Duchess used her umbrella to gather water into a drinking glass. In a playful mood, Ne Win topped it up by pouring his water on her umbrella. Ne Win did not attend a final lunch in the Kent's honour and a subsequent reception as it was the first anniversary of the death of Daw Khin May Than and he did not want to upset his children.[50] The visit was such a success that the British government were considering whether to accept an invitation extended by Ne Win to Princess Margaret, the Queen's sister.[51]

While Ne Win was larking about with rainy season high jinks with members of the British royal family, *The New York Times* was speculating about the direction that Myanmar was going under his unseen leadership.

The paper reported that he was increasingly aloof, not having seen the United States ambassador for more than a year, and cancelling his attendance at annual diplomatic banquets. Though he allowed his government to open itself to multilateral assistance, as indicated by its ADB membership, he allegedly did not trust foreigners. Apparently, it was believed he spent most of his time playing golf with his bodyguards.[52] While socialist construction carried on in Yangon, the government's insurgent opponents within the country, particularly the various Shan and Karen groups, were reaching out to attempt to form alliances with the Burma Communist Party and its Chinese backers in Yunnan (Lintner 1999, p. 454).

Following a Second Party Congress in October 1973, which Ne Win addressed, an eight-point programme for the party was laid out,[53] and a number of measures were then undertaken leading up to a national referendum on the new constitution.[54] Among them was the decision at the Congress to change the base year of a Twenty Year Plan for economic development to coincide with the coming term of a national legislature under the forthcoming constitutional order, from March 1974, at which time a second four-year plan would come into effect. This was intended to simplify accounting and accountability issues for the *Hluttaw* as the body legally responsible to supervise and guide the economy.

Ne Win himself toured the Chin hills and surrounding areas and Kawthoolei and Tanintharyi in the latter half of October and Kyaukpyu and Sittwe for a few days in early December, meeting local officials.[55] The formation of the Mon state from part of Tanintharyi, the renaming of Kawthoolei as Karen, and the creation of Rakhine state, were all promises that U Nu had made prior to the 1962 coup. Ne Win was now making them a reality, but unlike Nu, keeping religion and politics as far apart as possible. The national referendum on the new constitution was held from 15 to 31 December, in an atmosphere that many in central and lower Myanmar remember as having been festive. Unsurprisingly, given that the only option available was a continuation of Revolutionary Council rule, 90.1 per cent of the electorate voted for the new constitution, formally ending nearly twelve years of military government.[56]

However, in the midst of these reforms, the slow drift to the right was continuing. In October, for example, it was announced that private traders could purchase eighty-one different products directly from government factories for redistribution, thus weakening the monopoly of the people's stores and cooperatives. Some previously nationalized shops reopened in new premises, such as the famous Indian photography shop S.N. Ahuja, and private tea shops and restaurants reappeared in larger numbers. Ne Win's interest in Myanmar's industrialization, which remained under state domination, was emphasized by his four-day visit to the Sittaung Paper Mill, the local salt works and its surrounding regions in what would be the new Mon and Kayin states after the constitution was ratified.[57]

Ne Win, after twelve years in power, as Chairman of the Revolutionary Council metamorphosed into the President of the Socialist Republic of the Union of Burma on 2 March 1974. This followed single-party elections to choose the members of the new national legislature, the *Pyithu Hluttaw* (People's Assembly) and people's bodies at all levels of administration, a total of 252,446 positions, held on 26 January. The first session of the First *Pyithu Hluttaw*, with 451 members, convened on Peasants' Day, the anniversary of the coup. Before then, Ne Win had received the Australian Labour Prime Minister, Gough Whitlam, on a four-day visit, marking an increasingly close relationship between the two countries. Whitlam urged Ne Win to join ASEAN, but he replied categorically that Myanmar "could not join … until all of the organisation's members recognised China, and all US bases were removed from Thailand".[58] After the visit, Australia enhanced its small aid programme in Myanmar, centring on road construction, well-drilling in the dry zone, and veterinary health, as well as education and medical equipment.

As one of its final acts, the Revolutionary Council issued the Narcotics and Dangerous Drugs Law and Rules, part of an attempt to control the increasing threat of drugs within Myanmar as well as abroad. Also, the drug trade was growing in importance as a source of funding for the government's insurgent opponents. Opposition did not dissipate as a result of Ne Win's dream of unity under the new order. Separate from the low-level conflict in the north, Let Ya's PDP forces, together with Karen forces, briefly occupied Myawaddy on the Thai border on 18 March, and the next day students burned down the police box opposite Yangon Arts and Sciences University in Hledan (Lintner 1999, pp. 454–55).

The new government, with Ne Win as Chairman of the *Pyithu Hluttaw* and therefore President, had a new cabinet, with executive authority in the government devolved theoretically on the new Prime Minister, former Brigadier Sein Win. The creation of a parliament, civilian cabinet and constitutional presidency were not, however, the most significant changes on that day. With the new order in place, Ne Win sought to oversee both the party and the army. Therefore, when the constitution came into effect, he maintained San Yu as the General Secretary of the Party, and General Thura Tin U was given the post of Commander-in-Chief of the Armed Forces. Ne Win supervised both, as Party Chairman and President. As long as both remained loyal to Ne Win, stability was ensured, though inevitably rumours abounded about alleged rivalry between San Yu and Tin U to inherent the top job when Ne Win finally stepped down. One victim of the reorganized government was U Ba Nyein, one of three members of the Revolutionary Council not appointed to the new Council of State. He also lost the Cooperatives Ministry (Martin 1975, p. 130).

The British ambassador, Mr E.G. Willan, paid a departure call on Ne Win on 1 April 1974. Ne Win, who "looked fit, but tired", gave Willan a detailed lecture on the factionalism of the Chinese leadership of the past two decades culminating in the Cultural Revolution and the current anti-Confucius Campaign. In terms of Chinese leadership, Ne Win personally liked Chou En-lai but did not trust him. He felt that the increasing support from China for the BCP and its non-communist insurgent allies was not prompted by Chou but was the result of anti-Chou elements in the party and army. There was no point in complaining about this as it would only harm relations, though sometimes Yangon had to complain about things going on in Yunnan that were not known in Beijing. Turning to Myanmar's relations with its other troublesome neighbour, Thailand, Ne Win "was scathing about Air Marshall Dawee's recent claim that Chou En-lai had told him that China would stop supporting the Thai communists". It would not or could not, he was not sure which. Ne Win then told the story of one of his visits to China where he was shown a dog and a tiger living in the same cage. Ne Win said the tiger looked content but the dog "seemed very uneasy".[59]

Ambassador Willan, in his valedictory despatch at the end of his tenure in Yangon, reflected on conditions in the country in 1974. He wrote, "No one who has known a real police state would now describe present-day Burma in those terms." People freely criticized the government and while there was corruption, it was of a petty nature.[60] At that time, the Malaysian Prime Minister, Tun Abdul Razak was paying a private and low- key visit to Myanmar. April 1974 and the months that followed were a significant period for the region, as the consequences of the American defeat in Vietnam became apparent. Thailand was now under a weak civilian government for the first time in decades following the student uprising of October 1973. The new government's foreign minister, Charoonphan Israngkul Na Ayudhya, visited Yangon from 10 to 14 October. Three days after his departure, the Khmer Rouge occupied Phnom Penh. The next day, Ne Win commenced a nine-day visit to South Asia. As China and Thailand, his eastern neighbours, were troublesome, maintaining good relations with neighbours on the West became important.

Ne Win first visited Pakistan, where he apologized again to Prime Minister Bhutto for Myanmar's prompt recognition of the independence of Bangladesh. Much of the visit was devoted to visiting Buddhist sites in Muslim Pakistan.[61] After three days, Ne Win went on to Delhi where he met alone with Prime Minister Indira Gandhi for nearly two hours.[62] Three days later, he was back in the air to Dacca, the new capital of Bangladesh. Accompanied by Dr Maung Maung, U Hla Han and U Hla Phone, Ne Win was the first foreign head of state to visit the new state. However, there was no business conducted between the two sides on this visit.[63] The next day, South Vietnam was reunified with the north as People's Army tanks rolled on to the lawn of the presidential palace in Saigon.

On his return from South Asia, Ne Win chaired the fourth meeting of the BSPP Central Committee, reviewing and confirming government decisions and appointments.[64] It was very much business as usual, but underneath, resentment was growing, particularly among the workers for whom, along with the peasants, the revolution was said to have been launched. Whether out of economic grievances, or being encouraged by the anti-regime leftist underground, itself encouraged by the Communist victories in Vietnam and Cambodia, or by the BCP from Yunnan, workers struck in the oilfields at Chauk and unrest spread to Mandalay in May. The Worker's Councils, rebranded the Worker's *Asiayon*, were clearly not providing the leadership which was expected. The party leadership, primarily from the army, was not connecting with the workers or the peasants. Worker's real incomes had been severely reduced as a consequence of the state's previous attempts to finance development from domestic savings (Sylvan 1979, pp. 136–38). It was alleged that food shortages were the main grievance, and when the protests spread to Yangon, the army attempted to quell the disputes. Textile and dock workers were fired upon (Lintner 1999, p. 455). A number of them were arrested, tried and convicted of violating the Construction of Socialism legislation, but recognizing the workers' grievances, the government also established a Workers' Demonstrations Enquiry Committee on 9 July which invited testimony either in person or in writing.

Against the backdrop of unrest in Myanmar's cities, Ne Win and Daw Ni Ni Myint set off on 24 May on a trip to Malaysia, Australia and New

Zealand. While in Malaysia, there was little of substance discussed and a good deal of golf played.[65] From 27 May to 4 June, Ne Win toured Australia, visiting Sydney, Melbourne and Canberra and viewing prize cattle studs. A scheduled thirty-minute meeting with Prime Minister Whitlam turned into a two-hour session. Despite two untoward incidents, including the spraying of the interior of the aircraft in which he arrived with insecticide, which Ne Win had asked not be done presumably because of his repeated sinus problems, and an automobile accident in Melbourne in which Ne Win bumped his head, the visit was an apparent success.[66] Myanmar subsequently requested assistance in training officers at staff colleges and on technical courses, but after the removal of the Whitlam government the following year, none of the places offered were taken up by Myanmar (Selth 1990, pp. 9–10). Ne Win then set off for New Zealand which, like Australia, he had not visited previously.[67] By the time Ne Win and his party returned to Yangon, the strikes at 42 factories around the city were almost over, with 22 strikers killed and another 61 injured, including 13 police officers, according to the government.[68]

When asked whom he wanted to meet in Australia, Ne Win said Lord Casey, the anti-Communist former diplomat and governor-general who frequently visited Asia, Geoffrey Fairbairn, an Australian academic who wrote on Communism in Asia (his publications include Fairbairn 1968), and L.A. Crozier, the former manager of the Mawchi Mine whom Ne Win had met and assisted in 1958. Earlier in 1974, Crozier had visited Yangon on his way home from Liberia and was invited to lunch with Ne Win. Crozier subsequently wrote,

> We had an interesting conversation although I was somewhat impolite in pressing the General for information as to whom the Burma Army had been fighting in Northern Burma. I had been told by a friend of mine who had been with the army in the North that they had fought the Chinese Red Army, but the General would not give me any information. I later heard that they had been fighting tribal levies deployed against them by the Chinese.

As they parted after lunch, "the General put his arm around my shoulders and gave me a little hug" (Crozier 1994, pp. 112–13). Some xenophobe!

Three years after President Nixon's special drug envoy attempted to see General Ne Win in Yangon, by which time Nelson Gross may well have been in prison,[69] an agreement was reached with the United States government on drug suppression in northern Myanmar. On 29 June

1974, the United States agreed to provide Bell 205 helicopters to be used in a campaign against drugs, but not, somehow, against the insurgent forces that traded in them (Lintner 1999, p. 455). The deal had been negotiated by the United States embassy and the government of Myanmar. At that time, the embassy viewed the government for all of its shortcomings tolerantly. Its support for education was particularly appealing to American diplomats, such as John Lacey, then deputy chief of mission. Lacey, with the CIA station chief Clyde McAvoy, on one occasion flew up to the Shan state and viewed a heroin distillery at the end of trails from Myanmar on the Thai border. Lacey believed this evidence of the refining of the opium into heroin within Burma had convinced the government to launch its drug eradication programmes with United States assistance.[70]

Earlier, when Lacey and his CIA colleague began producing information, in conjunction with the U.S. Drug Enforcement Agency and Thai intelligence, that the Ka Kwe Ye was involved in the trade, was probably when Ne Win ordered their disbandment in January 1973. Ambassador Edwin Martin, who met with Ne Win only once during his time as ambassador, persisted in lobbying other members of the army about the growth of the opium problem for Myanmar, especially as the use of heroin was becoming a problem in the country. That was when the government started to act against the trade, in the Ambassador's view. The sight of the refinery of Lo Hsin-han was the clinching move.

> Once they found out it was true, plus the fact — and I think, there again, they began seeing they were themselves beginning to have a drug problem among their youths — they turned over a leaf and began to go after the problem. They bombed the refineries, and they went after Lo Hsin Han and assigned a special force of four or five battalions to go after the Ka Kwe Ye. They cornered them down by the Thai border, and just at the time the troops were surrendering, Lo went across the border, and the Thais arrested him, much to his surprise. He'd always been able to go across, because the Thais, as I said, didn't have any particular love for the Burmese, and vice versa, but that's another thing that we'd worked on to try to get some cooperation between the Thais and the Burmese.[71]

In total, the government accepted eighteen American helicopters to assist in suppressing the drug trade and, in 1976 and 1977, the army undertook four major campaigns against the Shan and Communist opium armies along the Thai border in cooperation with the Thai army. While large quantities of raw materials required for the distillation of heroin were seized, the border refineries remained largely untouched, so the army turned its attention to destroying the poppy fields further north that supplied the raw opium. As cheap weapons from Vietnam became scarce following the American defeat, Khun Sa, and eventually the Burma Communist Party, became the major actors in the opium smuggling business, squeezing out the many smaller Shan groups (McCoy 1991, pp. 425–26)

As a consequence of declining air traffic to and from Mingaladon Airport, international airlines no longer regularly stopped at Yangon. Ne Win had to fly to Singapore or Bangkok in order to take connecting flights. At some point during 1974, on one of Ne Win's several trips abroad, he called on Singapore's Lee Kuan Yew. Lee suggested that he and Ne Win should "coordinate" their policies in order to get the United States, China and the Soviet Union "to maintain a presence in the region, so as to have some power balance". Ne Win was not in the least interested (Lee 2000, p. 360). Trying to manipulate the big powers was not Ne Win's style.

On 12 July 1974, Ne Win and Daw Ni Ni Myint arrived in Europe, initially London, for a visit of approximately a month. While in London, he called on the Queen at Buckingham Palace but apparently made no other official calls. After eight days in London, he flew to Geneva, returning from there to Yangon on 7 July, arriving two weeks before another Extraordinary Party Congress to amend the tenure of party unit executive committees and amend the Party constitution.

Indonesian President Soeharto made a state visit to Yangon in early September 1974. While Myanmar had received many foreign dignitaries over the years, few were state visits. Zairian leader General Mubuto Sesu Seko Kuku Ngbenka WaZa Bangka had a brief state visit over two days in January 1973. On that occasion, he shocked his Burmese hosts by pouring the champagne given to him for a toast on the ground. Apparently such was a Congolese custom. Soeharto was more conventional and stayed longer. Ne Win and the Indonesian military leader spent much time together touring Mandalay, Bagan and Yangon. Much golf was played but apparently little business conducted.[72] Though seemingly remote and aloof from day-to-day state affairs, as well as avoiding foreigners, Ne Win's personal diplomacy was still at work, making friends and avoiding making enemies.

On 4 October, Ne Win and his party arrived in Rome for a private visit.[73] Three days later he flew to Belgrade to meet with President Tito. He visited a hydroelectric and copper complex at Bor, but resisted Yugoslav efforts to develop Myanmar's copper reserves. Tito pressed him on several other points, including Myanmar's relations with Israel and its cool relations with Communist Vietnam. Despite this, or perhaps because, Ne Win apparently largely ignored lesser officials than Tito at other meetings.[74] Expected to return directly to Yangon from Yugoslavia, Ne Win instead detoured to Switzerland, where he remained with his wife and entourage until 30 October.[75] His unexplained diversion to Switzerland was apparently for health reasons. When the British Airways representative in Yangon flew to Switzerland on 23 October to escort Ne Win on his return trip, he found him in a clinic in Montreux.[76]

Two days after his return from Switzerland, Ne Win hosted the Japanese Prime Minister, Kakuei Tanaka. Tanaka's visit apparently involved no substantive discussions but had been insisted upon by Ne Win when he heard that the Japanese leader was also visiting Australia and New Zealand.[77] In a speech in Yangon, Tanaka "described Burma-Japan friendship as 'one of the closest in the world'" (Liang 1990, p. 152). Also visiting Ne Win in November was Mark Dodd, head of the BBC World Service, who had last visited Ne Win in London in 1971. Dodd and British Ambassador O'Brien were invited to join Ne Win for an informal family dinner on the 20th. Two ministers were also present. Their conversation ran over the world food situation and problems of the current Myanmar crops caused by flooding. Ne Win, whose voice was thickened and had been treated for a throat related issue in Montreux, impressed O'Brien with his knowledge both of history and Buddhism, a subject most people thought he knew, or cared, little about.[78]

Agitation against the Ne Win regime, in its new guise, returned in December and soon became, because of the individuals involved, if only briefly, a subject of international media attention. This was the death, and subsequent controversy over the burial, of former United Nations Secretary General U Thant. U Nu's former secretary died on 25 November 1974 in the United States. The world around Ne Win was changing. Old colleagues and adversaries were passing away. Marshall Chen Yi, for example, had died two years earlier. The Americans were defeated in Vietnam, and a week after U Thant's demise, Vientiane, the capital of Laos, fell to Communist forces, effectively ending the civil war which had been the backdrop to Ne Win's coup of 1962.

Domestic political opponents of Ne Win and his military-led revolution, most of whom did not believe his was a "genuine" socialist revolution, and often sympathetic to the Burma Communist party, had organized themselves into loosely affiliated "reading" or "study" groups.[79] After the 1964 National Solidarity Act outlawed all political organizations not affiliated with the BSPP, these amorphous but potent organizations continued to persist underground in Myanmar's major cities (Kyaw Yin Hlaing 2013, pp. 234–35). Students were often a focus of their activities, and combined with the government's own propaganda about the role of students in the independence struggle, going back to the students' strikes of the 1920s and 1930s, they needed little encouragement when given a cause with which to rally opposition to the government.[80] Reminded daily as they walked on the campus of the destruction of the Students Union building in the previous decade, the funeral of U Thant, with the international attention it would receive, was too good an opportunity to embarrass the government to be refused. Coming after the workers' strikes earlier in the year, the image of a government in crisis would become embedded in many minds.

Initially, the government had not been requested to make any specific arrangements for U Thant's funeral, and it was presumed that the family and the United Nations would make the necessary arrangements.[81] When the coffin arrived in Yangon, it was taken in a United Nations van and eventually placed for the public to pay respects at the Kyaikkasan Grounds prior to burial at the Kyandaw Cemetery, where Daw Khin May Than was buried. Ne Win apparently had no role in the arrangements and while he may have been dissatisfied with U Thant for allowing U Nu to use the UN as a venue to announce his attempt to oust him, as Thant had done nothing further to assist Ne Win's enemies, and time had passed, Ne Win's ire at Nu's now dead former associate would have lessened. To Ne Win's most severe critics, however, this would seem unreasonably sanguine.

On the day of the funeral, 5 December, a crowd estimated to have been as large as 50,000 gathered at the Kyaikkasan Grounds. Led by students and some monks, they seized the coffin and marched for two hours carrying the body to the site of the former Students Union building on the campus of the Arts and Sciences University. From there, they took the body to the Convocation Hall and placed it on display. General Ne Win ordered the army not to become involved in the matter, though General Kyaw Htin was to monitor developments. Thakin Tin Mya, who, at Ne Win's request, wrote a paper on how to provide an appropriate burial for the former world statesman, was asked to talk with the students.[82]

Two days later, U Thant's brother, U Thaung, and his son-in-law, Dr Tin Myint Oo, invited the leaders of the students and monks for a meeting. Seven students and two monks came. At the meeting, a letter from the government was produced by the family which said that a suitable burial spot would be made available and a mausoleum constructed for U Thant next to that of Queen Supayalat, the last queen of Myanmar, at the foot of the Shwe Dagon Pagoda, and near that of Thakin Kodaw Hmaing.[83] In addition, no reprisals would be taken against those who had seized the body. However, the letter made no mention of a state funeral for the former Secretary General, which had become the primary demand of the protest leaders.

At that meeting, the majority present decided to accept the government's offer, but four — three students at the Yangon Institute of Technology and a medical student — dissented, insisting that he be buried at a so-called Peace Mausoleum which was being constructed on the site of the former students union. On 8 December, at 12 noon, the coffin was carried to a quickly assembled "Peace Mausoleum", from whence, after religious rites were conducted, it would be escorted, as U Thant's family wished, to the permanent site below the Shwe Dagon. When the announcement was made to remove the body, the students began to shout "do not remove the body" and others joined in. Soon the body was entombed in the makeshift mausoleum and the United Nations flag draped across it. That night, Myanmar Athan broadcast that the students had gone against the wishes of U Thant's family, had illegally seized government property, primarily construction materials for a new university library, had trespassed on the university campus, and consequantly legal action would be taken against them as a result.

For two days nothing much happened, though students and monks stood vigil at the site of the coffin in order to protect it. Then, on 11 December, martial law was declared and the army moved on to the campus. Previously, the army and military intelligence had surrounded the campus area quietly and systematically, and then, after the student numbers had dwindled down to approximately 3,000, with 200 monks also present, stormed the campus, arresting all they could capture and taking possession of the coffin. In what the British ambassador subsequently described as a "classic textbook operation", no one was killed and few injured.[84] However, in demonstrations over the next few days against the government action, officially 9 died and 74 were injured, with 1,800 arrested. The government closed all schools and universities, and a 9 p.m.–4 a.m. curfew was imposed in Yangon. One other casualty of the U Thant affair, as it became known, was a planned trip to meet with President Ne Win by Singapore's Prime Minister, Mr Lee Kuan Yew. Because of the demonstrations, the visit was postponed.

As usual after such an event, in the subsequent telling and retelling of it, the story gets more and more lurid. In some accounts, the soldiers, usually described as from the "uncivilized" ethnic minorities, bayoneted students and monks with abandon, while a giant machine ripped down the mausoleum as damsels clung on to the coffin and were crushed to death. Subsequently, Yangon became a war zone with persons being indiscriminately machine gunned while the public attacked party and government buildings.[85] I made my first trip as a tourist to Yangon for one week in early January 1975, three weeks after these events, and became subject to the curfew on my first night.[86] Knowing no one in the city at that time, one day I bought a ticket from Burma Travel and Tours, the government travel agency, for a tour of Yangon. I was the only passenger, and when the bus in which I was riding passed the university campus, I was called to the back by the young tour guide and told that hundreds had been shot on the spot we were now passing.

The next day, I took a *lei-bein* (very small Mazda truck used as a taxi) to the campus and walked around. The site of the temporary mausoleum was largely clear and the only evidence of the dramatic events of the previous month was a few strips of film which must have been removed from onlookers' cameras. The campus was completely open and I walked across accompanied mainly by some very unfriendly dogs which kind tea shop sellers soon shooed away. The mood at the time, however, was epitomized by the behaviour of soldiers patrolling Yangon in the first few days after the riots. Youths sporting long hair or wearing bell-bottom trousers, signs of Western decadence and dissidence, were summarily detained and given haircuts or their trousers shortened. They were soon ordered to halt such behaviour by their superior officers.[87] Displaying what I took to be the nationalist zeal of an army veteran, one man abused me for wearing a black-market army slouch hat that I had purchased to ward off the sun until he was, in turn, firmly encouraged by his wife, with the aid of her umbrella, to shut up.

After the event, people began to speculate about who had been behind the so-called U Thant affair. The daughter of Sao Shwe Thaik wrote to Lord Gore-Booth. Giving a livid account of what allegedly occurred, she wanted the British government to intervene. When Gore-Booth discussed the matter with Daw Aung San Suu Kyi, she, in his words, took "a characteristic Burmese anti-Shan line that these demonstrations were contrived by Shan influences and that there [sic] were inexcusable because they had no hope of succeeding and simply cost human lives". She was "not prepared to concede that there might have been something spontaneous about the whole thing".[88]

Student activists again attempted to embarrass the Ne Win regime the following year when, on 23 March 1976, several hundred demanded the right to mark the 100th anniversary of the birth of Thakin Kodaw Hmaing, a grand old man of nationalist literature and a winner of the Stalin Peace Prize for his efforts to reconcile the government and the Communists before his death in 1964. Seeing the planned march as an unauthorized political stunt, which would also remind the world of the previous year's U Thant affair, the authorities denied permission but the students marched anyway. When they reached the mausoleum of Thakin Kodaw Hmaing, on the other side of that of Queen Supayalat from U Thant's, the leaders were arrested and the students dispersed by the army. Again, universities were once more closed. However, this was the last major demonstration by students against the government for more than eleven years. Campuses remained outwardly quiet and apolitical from then until the end of the Ne Win era, perhaps because one of the key organizers of this event, and the demonstrations of 1974, disappeared, probably to Thailand, where he met with the remnants of Nu's PDP under Bo Let Ya.[89]

The quiet was hiding, however, an increasing passive resistance to the government's socialist road. Part of the problems of the economy certainly stemmed from the familiar litany of inadequate data, complex management structures, uncoordinated decision-making, and the international situation, but the underutilization of equipment and the spasmodic supply of raw materials for industrial processes contributed to a malaise amongst the employees of the subsidized public companies. Despite years of socialist construction, beginning before the Revolutionary Council came to power, the unchanged structure of the economy and the predominance of the private sector were still apparent. Were it not for that and the black market, many items required by the public would not have been available. In a year-end assessment by the new East German ambassador, he identified the root of the problem as the over-reliance of the government on economic measures to change the society. What was missing, he argued, was political leadership and engagement with the public to change conditions. The handover of power from the army to the party in March 1974 had, in fact, changed little and, moreover, expectations of change were soon thwarted. Until and unless the party, under Ne Win's leadership, could connect with the people, the future looked bleak. Few would disagree with his assessment, though it was probably more sympathetic to the regime than the calculations of the ambassador's capitalist colleagues.[90]

Ne Win, a member of the *Pyithu Hluttaw* from Mayangone Township, where his residence was located, briefly attended a first extraordinary session of the legislature from 13 to 16 January and then its third regular session from 10 to 18 March 1975. In between, he had removed the Minister for Mines, Dr Nyi Nyi. Nyi Nyi, one of the few civilians brought into the upper reaches of the government, was a geologist educated at Imperial College, London. Serving first as Deputy Minister for Education under Colonel Hla Han, who wore many hats, Nyi Nyi was responsible for the switch from teaching many subjects at university level into Burmese. As Minister for Mines, he had been responsible for the efforts of the government to develop its then largely unknown oil and gas resources, both on and off shore. His downfall came when he was identified in *Time* magazine as one of the upcoming young men of Asia. This drew the ire of other ministers who did not appreciate his education, his Chinese ancestry, or his affinity with Ne Win.[91] Much of Ne Win's time in the next few years seems to have been devoted to protecting his subordinates from one another. Nyi Nyi was an early casualty. Like others, however, who fell by the way, he was found a comfortable niche in which to move, first as ambassador and then a long career at UNICEF in New York (Hinton 2009, pp. 99–100). A cabinet reshuffle followed the third session of the *Pyithu Hluttaw*.

In the first week of May, Ne Win toured the northwest, western and central command areas, visiting industrial installations. Though he was now the civilian president of a republican government, when he travelled, it was still referred to in the press as visits to the military command regions, presumably because they were responsible for his security and housing during his visits to these areas. At that time there were rumours that he had a heart attack in April, though he was reported fit and well at the end of the month or the beginning of May by the West German ambassador.[92] Rumour of the heart attack was partially confirmed, however, in June when the departing British ambassador's wife paid a call on Daw Ni Ni Myint. She reported that Ne Win had been "very ill" in April.[93] Ne Win kept a very low profile throughout 1975, making no major public speeches and appearing little in public after his May tour. Amongst his appearances in the press during this period was a report in July of his meeting with a special representative of North Korea whom he received at his residence over a bowl of *ohno kaukswe* (coconut noodle soup) but left to San Yu and the other ministers to entertain for the remainder of his visit.[94]

Despite the introduction of the new political system the previous year, 1975 was typical in the problems that faced the party, the state and the economy during the entirety of Ne Win's twenty-six years in power. He only learned too late that, as J.S. Furnivall wrote, "Leviathan himself must fail unless he can adapt himself to human nature" (Furnivall 1939, p. 137). These problems were summarized nicely in a notification issued on 13 July by the Council of People's Justices, calling for greater punishments for this litany of ills:

> ... unscrupulous persons are endangering the State by committing major political, economic and social crimes: high treason and rebellion affecting State security; defamation of the State; robbery, arson; illegal departure for abroad; illegal entry from abroad; crimes which endanger the State's socialist economic system established under the Socialist Economic Construction Act; theft and destruction of public property; co-operative cases; smuggling of goods to and from abroad; slaughtering and smuggling abroad water buffaloes, cows, elephants used in agriculture, forestry and other sectors; gambling affecting socialist social conduct and morals; bribery; embezzlement of funds; various methods of undermining conduct and physical well-being; narcotics; prostitution; crime affecting the Lansin Party which leads the State; crimes under the law or the violation of Party Discipline. ... (quoted in Arumugam 1976, p. 167).

By attempting to control, if not monopolize, almost all of human life other than religion, the Revolutionary Council and its Party successor had created a world which drove citizens to violate the many laws which had been put in place. If the institutions of order could keep the most egregious violations in check, the government could maintain a tenuous grip on the society and the economy as long as international conditions remained favourable. That remained the case for only another decade or so.

Meanwhile, at some point around 1975, Ne Win may have secretly entered monkhood. According to Sao Htun Hmat Win, a Harvard-trained Director of Religious Affairs of the Ministry of Home and Religious Affairs. He is reported as saying:

> U Ne Win, during his 26 years, took an interest in sasana only in the last 16 years. In the beginning, religion and state must be separate. But afterwards he realised that it not was easy to change the spiritual directions of the people. He ordained for a few months around 1975 and studied the scriptures. I was his instructor. I can tell you that he was very sincere. He learned scriptures and built the pagoda. He became a king builder, and I was in charge of the central committee. Soldier, politician . . . now U Ne Win is a religious man. You cannot bluff yourself! A Myanmar must be like this ... only slowly can he change (Jordt 2007, p. 184).

On 11 November 1975, Ne Win made a largely unnoticed four-day visit to Beijing at the invitation of the Chinese government, the second visit in four years.[95] Relations were slowly being restored and this visit allowed the two governments to reiterate the principles of non-interference and pacific relations which had been promulgated before the anti-Chinese riots of 1967. With Mao clearly waning in health and power, Deng Xiao-ping was Ne Win's major interlocutor, though he did have an audience with Mao (Steinberg and Fan 2012, pp. 133 and 398). He was reported to have said, after leaving the presence of the Great Helmsman, "Useless mother fucker. That was a waste of time."[96]

The visit had been preceded by visits to Beijing by Myanmar's foreign minister and deputy trade minister, as well as various sporting teams. Despite China's continued support for the Burma Communist Party, the pauk-phaw relationship was being rebuilt. While in Beijing, on what was a relatively short visit, Ne Win also met with Prince Sihanouk, now resident there while the Khmer Rouge ruled in Phnom Penh.[97] It was believed in diplomatic circles in Yangon that, after the visit, Ne Win was upset that Deng Xiao-ping, despite their three friendly meetings, still refused to cut support for the BCP. Ne Win's old interlocutor, Chou En-lai, was then gravely ill with cancer and died two months after the visit.

If worries on the Chinese border occupied Ne Win and his government at the end of 1975, so also did the Bangladesh border, though not perhaps as immediately pressing. However, the continuous flow of illegal Bengali immigrants into north Rakhine was becoming an increasingly delicate political problem for the government of that area as well as for relations with the western neighbour. As the Bangladesh ambassador to Yangon told his British counterpart, there were "upwards of ½ million Bangalee trespassers in Arakan whom the Burmese had the right to eject". He was pleased, however, that the government had taken no such action, especially at a time when there was political disorder in his country, following the assassination of the prime minister and the establishment of a military dominated martial law administration. He believed that the flow had been stemmed, however.[98]

Whether it was frustration with Myanmar's neighbours, his government's handling of the economy, his personal life, or just life itself, Ne Win finally boiled over on Christmas Eve. Ne Win was having a quiet night at home, watching a movie on the open-air roof of his residence with some senior colleagues and old friends, including U San Yu, U Hla Han, and General Tin U. Their enjoyment of the movie, however, was apparently interrupted by loud, Western, "rock and roll" music by a local band known as ELF, with lots of drums, coming across the lake from the Inya Lake Hotel, 400 or so yards away. Gathered at the ballroom of the hotel were some of the cream of Yangon society youth, and a number of diplomats and their families, numbering 800 to 1,000, including the British ambassador's daughter,[99] and a Mr R. Wingfield-Hyde, an archivist. Ne Win, faced with the interruption of his evening, got in a car[100] and was driven around the lake, where he marched into the ballroom and smashed the drums.

The dance party was interrupted, in the midst of a rendition of 'Killing Me Softly' sung by one Sett Maw, not only by Ne Win but also the eight soldiers with bayonets and semi-automatic rifles who followed him in at about 11:20 at night. Yangon in those days was largely asleep by 9 p.m. Ne Win reportedly punched a middle-aged Burmese hotel security officer and grabbed a protesting Norwegian by his jacket. The Norwegian, a Mr Finn Teith, subsequently fell off the terrace of the ballroom while trying to retrieve his wife's handbag. In the meantime, former Colonel Hla

TABLE 11.1

**Chiefs of Staff or Commanders-in-Chief of the Armed Forces,
1948–2011**

From	To	Name
4–1–1948	31–1–1949	Lt. General Smith Dun
1–2–1949	20–4–1972	General Ne Win
20–4–1972	1–3–1974	General San Yu
1–3–1974	6–3–1976	General Thura Tin Oo
6–3–1976	3–11–1985	General Thura Kyaw Htin
4–11–1985	22–4–1992	General Saw Maung
22–4–1992	31–3–2011	Senior General Than Shwe

Han had arrived outside the hotel main entrance with four lorry loads of troops.[101] The next day, the American-originated Lions and Rotary Clubs were banned. Whether there was a connection between Ne Win's dramatic entrance at the party and that decision is unknown, but the two clubs had met at the Inya Lake Hotel.

Concerns other than matters of state may have contributed to Ne Win's rage. Relations with his young wife of less than two years were obviously strained and it was noted that she did not attend the annual pre–Independence Day dinner hosted by Ne Win on 3 January 1976.[102] She and Ne Win were subsequently divorced and it was suspected that Ne Win had taken a new paramour, one Dr Daw Sein Sein Khin.[103] Dr Sein Sein Khin was, indeed, a very close companion of Ne Win for two decades, but their relationship was, according to her, platonic. However, apparently because he enjoyed her company, he blocked her from taking up posts abroad on two occasions.[104]

Ne Win lost not only a wife but also a close colleague of many years in March. On 6 March 1976, General Tin U was forced to resign and was replaced by General Kyaw Htin. Kyaw Htin would occupy the top spot in the military until 1985 and the Minister of Defence portfolio until 1988. Tin U, who was believed to be popular with the troops, as Ne Win had been when in command, was accused of corruption and eventually dereliction of duty. It was believed that his wife was particularly avaricious and made use of military attachés abroad to provide her with items unavailable in Yangon, including hardware for a new home they were building and medicine and syringes for their ailing son. She was a very formidable woman and many soldiers were frightened of her, it was claimed.[105] Ne Win apparently, out of frustration, threatened to resign as Party Chairman and all of his other posts because of factionalism within the party and disaffection between the party and the army (Maung Maung 1999, pp. 42–43).

Ending three months of upheaval, Ne Win departed for the calm of Switzerland on 25 March. On arrival, he checked into a clinic for a medical check-up and remained in the country until 15 May. Believing that London was no longer safe to visit because of the threat posed by the Irish Republican Army's mainland bombing campaign, Ne Win decided to avoid England that year. While he was in Geneva, Ne Win was visited daily by a senior partner of the Swiss jewellery firm, Zalcman Samooria, and his apparently attractive blond wife.[106] Zalcman, along with British jeweller I.P. Roberts of Merrs. Benj. Warwick, was a major purchaser of Myanmar precious stones, for which he was honoured at the 25th Jade, Gems and Pearls Emporium held in November 1987.[107] On his return from Geneva, the British Airways representative in Yangon sat with Ne Win. He reported him to be in "excellent form, alert, lively, full of questions about British aviation".[108]

In early July, the government arrested fourteen soldiers, including three captains, for plotting to assassinate Ne Win and other top leaders. Led by Captain Ohn Kyaw Myint, Captain Win Thein, and Captain Tun Kyaw, they had apparently identified U San Yu and head of Military Intelligence Brigadier General Tin U as among their prospective victims.[109] The so-called "Captains Plot" trial ended on 11 January 1977. Former Chief-of-Staff General Thura Tin U, not to be confused with Military Intelligence Brigadier General Tin U, also known as "Spectacles Tin U", was implicated at the trial and subsequently convicted for not having revealed the plot or taken action to put a stop to it. Ne Win was said to have become angry at Tin U who, after his dismissal from office, continued to receive many powerful persons in the government at his home. Suspecting Tin U was plotting against him, he used the opportunity of the trial to put him out of circulation.[110] He was given a sentence of seven years but released three years later under a general amnesty. Ohn Kyaw Myint was sentenced to death, Captain Win Thein to life imprisonment, and the rest to lesser terms of imprisonment.[111]

Problems with the economy continued to dog Ne Win's regime, and reversing previous policy, Myanmar began to seek both bilateral and multilateral economic assistance in 1976. Under World Bank auspices, a Burma Consultative Meeting was held in Paris by Western and industrialized countries — Australia, Canada, France, West Germany, the United Kingdom, the United States, and Japan — to pledge economic aid under the vague rubric of "mutually beneficial economic assistance" by which Myanmar state-owned economic enterprises could interact with foreign aid providers. However, rather than develop a foreign investment law, which might have been seen as feasible under the new economic arrangements, such investments would be dealt with on a case-by-case, or ad hoc, basis (Than Han 1986, pp. 14–15). Given the lack of legal protection for foreign investments in Myanmar, unsurprisingly, none were forthcoming. No direct private foreign investment ever occurred, but the government and multilateral loans accepted became part of the reason the BSPP regime fell twelve years later.

On 13 August 1976, the new Malaysian Prime Minister, Hussein Onn, visited Yangon for more golf and discussions of regional affairs. On 18 August, Ne Win left again for Switzerland for another reported medical check-up.[112] On 16 October, Ne Win returned after a six-week absence, again sitting with the British Airways (BA) representative, a Mr Emery. Ne Win spent part of the journey telling Emery about his encounters with Mao Tse-tung, whom he described as the "Robin Hood of Asia", even though he had his sinister side. At the airport in Geneva, he was seen off by a new lady in his life, June Rose Bellamy, or Yadana Nat Mai.[113] Twenty-two years younger than Ne Win, born in the Shan State, the daughter of an Australian horse racing entrepreneur and a princess of the last royal family, she had married an Italian doctor with whom she had two sons. In 1976, now divorced, she was residing in Florence, Italy. She had contacted Ne Win the previous year in order to get a visa in an attempt to visit her dying mother. Ne Win then met with her in Europe on his next visit, and on a second meeting, asked her to marry him.

On 2 November, British Airways was requested to fly June Rose Bellamy to Yangon.[114] She and Ne Win were subsequently married in a simple ceremony on the first anniversary of his assault on the rock band at the same venue, the Inya Lake Hotel. Earlier in the month, Ne Win hosted a dinner for BA's Mr Emery and his wife, along with B.E. Paunceford and his wife, from the British embassy. Over a four-and-a-half hour dinner,

Ne Win was "genial and jovial". Introducing June Rose as his fiancée, and clearly "captivated by his lady", he peeled oranges and placed them in her mouth and that of Mrs Emery. The meal of European cuisine was marked only by modest drinking and social chit-chat, with politics and weightier matters being entirely excluded.[115]

An extraordinary BSPP Party Congress was held on 29 and 30 October, in the anodyne words of a government information booklet,

> To solve the political organisational and economic difficulties of the State being encountered, to convene the Third Party Congress as soon as possible; to amend the tenure of the Second Party Congress, and to decide on the proposed amendments to the Constitution.[116]

While it did these things, its purpose, in Ne Win's view, was to strengthen the party and increase its autonomy from the army in order to better cope with the economic and political problems the country was facing. Getting the new constitutional order to function as he intended was more difficult than perhaps it had been expected to be.

Between the extraordinary Party Congress and the Third Party Congress, held from 21 February to 1 March 1977, Ne Win entertained a number of guests from neighbouring countries as the consequences of the partial American withdrawal from Southeast Asia became apparent. The new President of Communist Laos, the "Red Prince", Prince Souphanouvong, visited Myanamar from 19 to 23 January 1977. Two days later, the new Thai Foreign Minister, Upadit Pachariyangkun, of the recently installed military government of General Kriengsak Chamanant, paid a three-day visit to Yangon. And then, from 11 to 15 February, the widow of the late Chou En-lai, Madame Deng Ying-chao, paid a courtesy visit in her capacity as Vice Chairman of the National People's Congress. Madame Deng's visit was treated as a state visit and was very emotional for Ne Win. He had wanted to fly to Beijing at the time of Chou's death but had been dissuaded by the Chinese government. At a banquet in her honour, as he spoke about his relationship with Chou, he broke down and wept. It took him ten minutes to compose himself and resume his remarks.[117] Soon after the Congress, Ieng Sary, the Deputy Prime Minister and Foreign Minister of the new Khmer Rouge government in Cambodia, arrived in Yangon, staying seven days, from 7 to 14 March. Whether Ne Win, now the senior head of state of the region, could be enticed to become more active in Southeast Asian affairs was being tested. He apparently was not.

Being sought after by those abroad did not, however, ensure political success at home. The Third Party Congress, having been moved forward as a result of decisions of the Extraordinary Party Congress the previous year, was to resolve the questions generated by the removal of Tin U and re-establish the Party firmly under Ne Win's control. Meeting in February, one of the main functions of the Congress was to elect a new Central Committee and Party Inspection Committee. Under the new rules, at least 55 per cent of the members of the next Central Committee were to be newly elected, presumably to bring new faces, ideas and energy into the upper reaches of the party. In fact, the party failed to achieve that aim and, in terms of representation of ethnic minority groups, the new Central Committee was even less representative of the nation's ethnic diversity than the old one. However, in elections from the Central Committee to the Central Executive Committee there was remarkable change, with seven senior military officers removed and replaced primarily by long-retired officers who worked in the party secretariat. They then moved into the ministerial posts previously held by former defence ministry directors-general or regional commanders.

This had come about because those who conducted the balloting had manipulated the process in order to attempt to remove Ne Win from the chairmanship. When the Central Committee vote was announced, Ne Win had come in third in the ballot, behind San Yu and Kyaw Soe. Ne Win, in a rage, left the Congress and went home, refusing to see anyone except Chief of Military Intelligence Brigadier General Tin U. Tin U, eventually with Chief of General Staff General Kyaw Htin and one other, convinced Ne Win not to resign, as he intended to do, but to purge the party of those who voted against him. Tin U then created a list of those he wanted out of the party and gave it to Ne Win. The purge took place, resulting in the expulsion of 113 congress members, four of whom, from the party secretariat, were also purged from the Central Executive Committee.[118] Members of the Party secretariat who were purged were prosecuted for misappropriating party funds and stealing party condensed milk and sugar. Ne Win was reported to have said about them subsequently, "these mother-fuckers wanted to get to the top through a shortcut".[119] A second Extraordinary Party Congress was then called for the following October to elect a new central committee as well as abandoning the rules Ne Win had introduced the previous year to ensure party autonomy. Ne Win, having been humiliated, in his view, by party members, had allied with his army colleagues to regain control of the party, thus defeating his own effort to create party autonomy. He was truly hoisted on his own petard (Nakanishi 2013, pp. 129–37).

Following the two party congresses, Ne Win was unusually busy, touring upcountry, viewing factories and meeting troops, again visiting the language commission, debating spelling reforms with linguists. He also called at the party headquarters at least twice a week, something he had not previously done, as well as going to army offices and demanding to see reports on various matters. San Yu, who had been much seen in the public eye following the removal of General Tin U, was now eclipsed and Ne Win became once more the centre of public attention.

From 6 to 8 April, Ne Win made a routine state visit to Nepal. The economy was never far from his mind, particularly between 10 and 12 April, when a special envoy from Japan visited him, presumably to discuss Japanese desires for economic reforms in Myanmar, as their aid was important in propping up the government's industrialization schemes, but with little result. The visit was also in preparation for the visit to Myanmar of new Japanese Prime Minister, Takeo Fukuda, from 10 to 12 August. Maintaining good relations with Japan and West Germany were amongst his priorities. Myanmar's international credit standing, despite the faltering economy, was high because of the prudent way in which the government, under Ne Win, conducted its financial activities. Unusually for a developing country, Myanmar paid off United States "PL480" Food for Peace loans in U.S. dollars, rather than Kyat and following a meeting of the Burma Aid Group in Tokyo in November 1976, negotiated its first private sector loan from an American and British banking consortium.[120]

From 27 April to 12 May 1977, Ne Win made his third visit to China in the decade to once more attempt to negotiate an end to Chinese support for the BCP. If he had been exasperated at the end of 1975, he must have been reaching the end of his tether with the Chinese. In diplomatic language, he made it clear in his speeches and toasts that common problems needed to be resolved, otherwise there was a risk to their friendship. In a speech at a banquet hosted by Vice-Premier Li Xiannian, Ne Win was very clear on the point. While the Chinese avoided the subject of disagreements in their remarks, they were fulsome in their expressions of goodwill, with Premier Hua Guofeng hosting two dinners in Ne Win's honour, as well as Ne Win again meeting the ailing Mao (Steinberg and Fan 2012, pp. 139 and 399). In order to make it clear to the Chinese of his cooperative attitude, despite his chagrin at the continued Chinese support for the BCP, Ne Win did not see the visiting Soviet deputy foreign minister who visited Yangon after his return from Beijing.

Ne Win's tribulations in 1977 concerned not only the party and the army, or foreign relations, however. Family matters were also of a cause of annoyance. During another visit by an old Japanese friend of Ne Win, he and his new bride, June Rose Bellamy, apparently had a major argument which led to physical violence in which both suffered injuries. She was seen the next day, 28 May, at the airport, flying back to Italy, with a black eye.[121] Also in May, Ne Win's younger brother, former Thakin Hla Htun, passed away.[122] In July, his son, Pyo Win, married Daw Yin Yin Nwe. At his meeting with the departing United States Ambassador David Osborn, the next day, Ne Win was not in an affable mood. He made clear to Osborn that he "expected to remain in sole command for a long time to come and had no intention of delegating any of his functions to anyone else". Furthermore, "he showed his contempt to the Burmese people whom he thought were indolent and in need of firm guidance." If running Myanmar was hard work, however, it was "much harder to run a family than a country".[123]

July brought visitors from two predominantly Muslim neighbours of Myanmar, Bangladesh and Indonesia, with the foreign minister of the latter visiting in late July. Prior to that, the recently installed President of Bangladesh, Ziaur Rahman, arrived on 20 July for a three-day get-to-know-you visit. The relatively young president, then 41 to Ne Win's 67, former Major General Rahman had risen to power through the chaos of Bangladesh politics and, after finally seizing absolute power in April 1977, banned party politics and ruled through martial law until his assassination in 1981. The content of their talks was unknown but the recent involvement of a Bangladesh military attaché in a separatist plot in Rakhine State would have been discussed.[124] The military attaché, according to Burmese Military Intelligence, was planning to assassinate Rahman and Ne Win when they visited Sittwe (Morshed 2001, p. 59).

Also, certainly the border between northern Rakhine State and Bangladesh would have been an issue for before long the government responded to public pressure to act against the many illegal immigrants in the area. Nine months later, the immigration department, in conjunction with the army, launched "Operation Naga Min". The operation was designed to check on the identity cards of all residents in the area as locals had been complaining for some time over pressure on land and other resources as a consequence of the thousands of Bangladeshis who had fled from the civil war in their country. As a consequence of "Operation Naga Min", thousands fled back across the border into Bangladesh where they were no more welcome than in Myanmar. Typical of how the government dealt with foreign governments at that time, when Western embassies requested a briefing on relations with Bangladesh from the Ministry of Foreign Affairs, they were told that all they needed to know was in the newspaper.[125]

On 25 July 1977, Ne Win addressed the successor organization to the Peasant's Councils the Revolutionary Council had established, the first Peasants Asiayon Conference at Kaba Aye Hill in Yangon. In a typical speech, he reviewed the history of the exploitation of the peasantry since colonial days and how "comprador and foreigner scions" had taken the land from the peasants, as well as how they continued to be exploited under the Anti-Fascist People's Freedom League's All Burma Peasants' Organisation. Now, however, though there was still much work to be done, and just holding meetings and passing legislation would not change things, the situation of the peasantry had improved. Because of the formation of the Peasants Asiayon to guide the farmers in their work, the government was going to simplify the issuing of crop loans and give them in one instalment, rather than in two. In the past, it was believed that many farmers would squander their loan money but with the Asiayon to guide them, that danger had passed.[126] The eighth session of the First *Pyithu Hluttaw* met for six days at the end of August, passing the Enterprise Protection Law, which offered the security of protection from nationalization for private businesses.

The mid-1970s were marked by other efforts to enhance opportunities for those in remote areas. The illiteracy programme was extended from the original seventy-seven townships covered from its commencement in 1965 to other, more remote regions. In 1975, a programme of four- or five-year university degrees by correspondence under the supervision initially of Yangon Arts and Sciences University faculty was launched. From an initial enrolment of nearly 19,000 students, by the 1978–79 academic year nearly 48,000 were involved. Also, in June 1975, seventeen regional colleges were opened, with an additional three over the next two years. With a focus on technical education, the most successful recipients of two-year diplomas would be eligible for enrolment in the final two years for full degree courses at university. Three years after launching the colleges, more than 30,000 students were enrolled. Both the correspondence courses and the regional colleges were said by the regime's critics to be efforts to distribute the students for political reasons, but the government said it was to extend educational opportunities more equally for the benefit of students in rural and remote centres. Though the three largest regional colleges were in Yangon, enrolling more than 5,000 students each, the other seventeen were in towns such as Myitkyina, Pa-an, Shwebo, Yeinangyaung, Taunggyi, and Lashio, which previously had not had tertiary educational institutions.[127]

On his way to visit North Korea, which he did from 20 to 23 September 1977, Ne Win stopped again in Beijing, staying four days, from the 16th to the 20th, for further talks with the Chinese leadership. It was originally believed that he would be in China for just one day. Amongst speculation that he was considering reorienting Myanmar's foreign policy toward a more pro-Western position, Ne Win had talks with both Premier Hua Guofeng and the recently restored Vice-Premier Deng Xiao-ping. Following Mao's death, Deng had briefly been eclipsed by the so-called Gang of Four. Ne Win's conversations centred on recent developments within China, following the turmoil that persisted after Mao's death the previous year, and relations with the United States, Japan and Yugoslavia (Steinberg and Fan 2012, pp. 139 and 399). Diplomats in Yangon after the visit were led to believe that Ne Win was frustrated by the unwillingness of the Chinese to raise the issue of their support for the BCP, despite their desire to hold up relations with Myanmar as a model for the countries of Asia and Africa.[128] His efforts since his last visit to China, where he had made it clear, though diplomatically, his frustration with the different ways the Chinese Communist Party dealt with Myanmar had yet to take effect.

Subsequent to Ne Win's visit to North Korea, he departed for a private holiday in England, arriving on 28 September and departing on 23 October. While he was in London, he approached the West German government in regard to a possible visit to Berlin where he sought a meeting with the President of the Federal Republic, Walter Scheel. Scheel had been West Germany's aid minister and foreign minister before assuming the presidency, and in those regards was known by Ne Win. As he was unwell in early October and unable to meet with Ne Win, the visit was cancelled. Later in October, however, Myanmar Foreign Minister U Hla Hpone made a visit to East Germany.

Ne Win addressed the opening session of an extraordinary party congress on 14 November 1977. In his speech, he noted that a clique within the party had put their own interests over those of the state or the party. He emphasized that the state's interests were paramount and the party would have to give way if there was a contradiction, but in this case it was obvious that selfishness and power seeking were a danger to the party and the state. In one of his shorter orations, he urged party members to live within their means and set an example in order to earn the respect and support of the people.[129] In his concluding remarks three days later, Ne Win drew attention to two aspects that had existed since the formation of the party fifteen years earlier. One was the need to draw together those organizations which "had been divided and had been fighting and killing one another" previously, and the other was the warning issued to him by his anti-Communist army colleagues of bringing outdated ideologues into the party. Ne Win underscored his belief in the need for unity to overcome past divisions and hence the necessity of allowing those who wished to try to work together. If they betrayed the trust placed in them, however, they had to be dropped. However, what they had faced in 1977 were politicians who had joined the party "with ulterior motive and the work of opportunists". They had to be purged from the party. Regrettably, all of the party upheaval had got in the way of production, so all should return to work and strive to their utmost for the country.[130]

In a move which would have pleased the government of China, Ne Win became the first and only foreign head of state to visit Cambodia, then known as Democratic Kampuchea, under the Khmer Rouge. China was the major ally of the Khmer Rouge, a government which practised autarky on a scale that made Myanmar look positively internationalist. The visit commenced on 26 November 1977, and included meetings with senior government officials and a visit to Angkor Wat.[131] To demonstrate that relations with China were definitely on the mend, China's new reformist leader, Deng Xiao-ping, now firmly in control of the government in Beijing, arrived in Yangon for a five-day visit commencing 26 January 1978, two months after Ne Win's visit to Phnom Penh. He appeared to be attempting to coax Ne Win into an anti-Soviet/anti-Vietnamese nominal alliance. The day after Deng left Yangon, the BCP launched a campaign along the Chinese border (Liang 1997, p. 75). Ne Win was rumoured on the diplomatic cocktail circuit to have been angry again that Deng did not raise the topic of Chinese support for the BCP and that Myanmar might now look to the West for support.[132] According to Ezra Vogel, "Ne Win expressed concern about China's continuing ties with

Communist insurgents in Burma and other parts of Southeast Asia, which China was not ready to break." This had a limiting effect on their cooperation, though cultural and economic ties were strengthened after Deng's visit (Vogel 2011, p. 277).

Before Deng's visit, however, Ne Win made a tour of Northeast Command at Lashio to review the fighting in the north against the Communists. At that time, the BCP had troops operating in three command areas, the Northern and Eastern, as well as the Northeastern. Ne Win's guide on the tour was General Htun Ye, who had joined the Burma Defence Army and attended the Mingaladon officer training course during the Second World War. Htun Ye, who at that time had no particular command post, impressed Ne Win with his knowledge of the enemies' activities not only in the Northeast, which he had previously commanded, but in all three regions. From those conversations, the idea of Bureaus of Special Operations was born to coordinate from the General Staff Office operations against the enemy (Aung Myoe 2009, pp. 73–74). Ne Win, though out of the army for six years by then, was still giving the army strategic guidance in collaboration with his old colleagues from the anti-imperialist campaigns of the 1940s.

After a tumultuous year, in which Ne Win appeared to be losing his grip on power, but then firmly regrasped it, the Second *Pyithu Hluttaw* met on 2 March 1978. He may have expected that, having installed the new constitutional order in 1974, life would get easier after the trauma of the death of Daw Khin May Than and continuing problems of the economy and insurgency. However, as the years 1975, 1976, and 1977 demonstrated, change is fraught with uncertainty and uncertainly leads to danger. Having seized the tiger's tail, Ne Win still could not relax his grip.

However, for many of his countrymen, the dramas that filled his life, to the extent that they were known, rather than merely conjectured, were just part of the political spectacle which they had been led to expect. Though Myanmar was still fraught by insurgency, life for most went on much as it had always been. The economy, though not flourishing, was stronger than it had been for years, and while most luxuries, and some necessities, were scarce, food was plentiful and inexpensive, jobs not too demanding, and while life was poor, there was a shared penury which somehow made it easier to bear. The army remained a popular career choice for the young and the party provided means of assuagement. Socialism in the Burmese way could not be made in a day. In the meantime, the army was doing its best to defend the nation from the forces of colonialism and neo-colonialism, Communism and separatism. As for the insurgency, to paraphrase another author writing about another country that faced prolonged civil war years earlier,

> In a larger sense, too, the world went on its way despite the immediate disturbance of the wars. The fact of conflict of course weakened the body politic, and loosened the ties between the realm and the government, but there is no evidence of general desolation or dislocation. Few towns or cities were affected by disturbances, and only those in the immediate vicinity of battles would have suffered from the factional struggle. The vast resources of the Buddhist monkhood were not touched, and in general the monks remained as distant observers of the conflict. The law courts were still in session, but now presided over by the lowest in the land. The calamities and misfortunes of the war fell only upon the soldiers, especially the officers (adapted with thanks from Ackroyd 2012, p. 392).

Notes

1. For a fictionalized, and sometimes overly dramatic, account of how the under-resourced army conducted operations in the civil war at that time, see Hla Oo, *Song for Irrawaddy* (N.p.: The author, 2007).
2. As told to the author by Dr Tin Maung Maung Than, December 2012.
3. *Towhlanyei Kaungsi ei Hluthsaungchet Thamaing Akyinchut* [Concise History of the Actions of the Revolutionary Council], (Rangoon: Printing and Publishing Corporation, 2 March 1974), pp. 161, 254 and 255.
4. Interview, Dr Kyaw Win, 21 March 2007.
5. *Towhlanyei Kaungsi ei Hluthsaungchet Thamaing Akyinchut*, pp. 181 and 182.
6. Ibid., p. 182.
7. Ibid., pp. 9, 10, 182 and 192.
8. FCO15/1518
9. Letter, C. Thompson to A.R. Michae, 1 June 1972, FCO15/1520.
10. *Towhlanyei Kaungsi ei Hluthsaungchet Thamaing Akyinchut*, p. 223; press clipping, 4 August 1972, FCO15/1516.
11. Note, C.W. Squire to Sir E. Norris, Private Secretary of the Secretary of State, 31 July 1972, FCO15/1522.
12. Letter, A.R. Michae to H.E. Rigney, 31 July 1972, FCO15/1522.
13. PREM 11/4650; note by A.R. Michael, 5 September 1972, FCO15/1523.
14. Record of Conversation with Sir Alec Douglas-Home and General Ne Win, 8 August 1972, FCO15/1523.

15. While the unveiling of a statue of U Nu at that time would have been embarrassing, Ne Win insisted that Nu's role in the founding of the movement be adequately acknowledged in an article on the movement published in Yangon by U Pe Kin, a distinguished member of the Myanmar foreign service and former ambassador to China. Interview with Major (rtd) Htway Han, 11 March 2006.

16. Letter, E.G. Willan to A.B.P. Smart, 18 September 1972, FCO15/1516. While Ne Win was in London, United State Senator Mike Mansfield made one of his periodic visits to the region, including Myanmar. He met with some Myanmar officials and concluded, as before, that it was best the United States do not become too deeply involved in the affairs of Myanmar. *Winds of Change: Evolving Relations and Interests in Southeast Asia: A Report by Senator Mike Mansfield to the Committee on Foreign Relations, United States Senate* (Washington, D.C.: U.S. Government Printing Office, 1975), pp. 3–6.

17. *Towhlanyei Kaungsi ei Hluthsaungchet Thamaing Akyinchut*, p. 52.

18. Myanmar Hsoshelit Lansin Pati Baho Kowmitti Danakyut, *Myanmar Hsoshelit Lansin Pati Okkatakyi ei Hkit Pyaung Towhlanyei Thamaing win Meinkhun Paungkyut* [Collected Speeches of the Era Changing Revolution History of the Chairman of the Myanmar Socialist Programme Party], Volume 1 (Yangon: Myanmar Socialist Way Party Central Committee Headquarters, Party Publications Unit, July 1985), pp. 237–54.

19. PREM 11/4650

20. Prem 11/4650; Letter, A.R. Michael to W.L. Ward, 9 October 1972, FCO15/1523; Despatch, E.G. Willan to Douglas Home, 10 October 1972, Letter, A.R. Michael to W.L. Ward, 9 October 1972, FCO15/1513; PREM 15/760.

21. A perception shared by Dr Maung Maung following her death in an article in the *Working People's Daily*, 4 October 1972.

22. Letter, E.G. Willan to Sir Alec Douglas-Home, 10 October 1972, PCO15/1513.

23. FCO15/1513

24. R.E. Elson, *Suharto: A Political Biography* (Cambridge: Cambridge University Press, 2001).

25. Telegram, Willan to FCO, 27 October 1971, FO15/1392.

26. Letter, Willan to D. McD. Gordon, 5 November 1971, FCO15/1392.

27. Germ Emb Ramisch to AA, 25 October 1971, AA PA B 37 Bd.584, 637–39.

28. Forthcoming book on United States-Burma/Myanmar relations, by Dr Klymer. I am indebted to Dr Klymer for the information on Gross's meetings with Ne Win and the activities surrounding it.

29. Bunker (in Vietnam, for Gross) to Rogers, 21 January 1972, Tel. 957, RG 59, SNF 1970–73, Box 169, folder DEF BUL 1/1/70, NAII. I am indebted to Dr Klymer for this reference.

30. I am indebted to Dr Kenton Klymer for the quotation.

31. Letter, H.E. Rigney to A.B.P. Smart, 27 June 1972, FCO15/1534.

32. *New York Times*, 15 January 1973.

33. *Towhlanyei Kaungsi ei Hluthsaungchet Thamaing Akyinchut*, p. 99.

34. Ibid., p. 146

35. Ibid., p. 29.

36. Ibid., p. 57.

37. *Forward*, 1 March 1972, pp. 23–25.

38. The release of Khun Sa was negotiated by his associate, Thai General Kriangsak Chamanan. See Bertil Lintner, *Burma in Revolt: Opium and Insurgency since 1948*, 2nd ed. (Chiang Mai: Silkworm Books, 1999), pp. 319 and 455.

39. *Towhlanyei Kaungsi ei Hlutsaungchet Thamaing Akyinchut*, p. 219; Chi-shad Liang, *Burma's Foreign Relations: Neutralism in Theory and Practice* (New York: Praeger, 1990), p. 152.

40. *Washington Post*, 24 June 1973.

41. Ne Win was said to have once referred to Trager as "the little CIA", presumable because of his affiliation with the National Security Agency. Trager's book, *Why Vietnam?* (London: Pall Mall, 1966) was seen as an apology for United States anti-Communist policies in Asia. See his obituary in *The New York Times*, 31 August 1984.

42. Nu and his son came to Cornell University in the winter of 1973–74 and lectured to an enraptured group of hippy students about the various layers of reality, mental sparks and how Buddhists understand physics better than nuclear scientists. The audience was left rather bemused. Though avowedly a non-political visit, as a condition of his visa to the United States, on the evening of his lecture he could not resist discussing politics privately at a dinner held in his honour. His son, Maung Aung, spoke more vehemently against Ne Win than did his father. The author chaired Nu's lecture and chauffeured him to and from the dinner.

43. *New York Times*, 25 July 1973.

44. *Towhlanyei Kaungsi ei Hluthsaungchet Thamaing Akyinchut*, p. 219.

45. Airgram, Kuala Lumpur to Secretary of State (SoS), 26 June 1973, Pol 7 Burma xr Pol Burma-Malaysia; Letter, P.J. Dunn, Kuala Lumpur, to S.J. Bill, 26 June 1973, FCO/1736.

46. GDR Emb Ygn Dr Esche to Deputy M.F. AA. Dr Willerding, 22 August 1973, MFAA AA PA MGAA C 1.115 77 GDR MOFA, 1082–88; Letter, E.G. Willan to C.W. Squire, 20 September 1973, FCO15/1736.

47. Airgram, Rangoon to SoS, 15 August 1973, reporting on an evening spent by a local member of the United States embassy with Thaung Dan, Pol 12 Burma.

48. *Towhlanyei Kaungsi ei Hluthsaungchet Thamaing Akyinchut*, pp. 33, 146, 240, and 238. For details of the constitution drafting procedures and the public consultation process, see Albert D. Moscotti, *Burma's Constitution and the Elections of 1974*, ISEAS Research Notes and Discussions No. 5 (Singapore: Institute of Southeast Asian Studies, September 1977).

49. GDR Emb YGN, Dr Esche to deputy MFA, Dr Willerding, 22 August 1973, MFAA, AA PA MGAA C 1.115 77 GDR MOFA, 1082–88.

50. Letter, E.G. Willan to Douglas-Home, 4 October 1973, FCO15/1741.

51. Note to Mr Youde, 9 November 1973, FCO 15/1741; Letter, J.S. Chick, Rangoon, to Miss L.M. Bullock, 30 November 1973, FCO15/1736.

52. *New York Times*, 29 September 1973.

53. *Towhlanyei Kaungsi ei Hluthsaungchet Thamaing Akyinchut*, pp. 29 and 33.

54. Ibid., pp. 1, 47, and 148.

55. The *Guardian*, vol. 21, no. 1 (January 1974): 7.

56. *Towhlanyei Kaungsi ei Hluthsaungchet Thamaing Akyinchut*, pp. ya, 34.

57. The *Guardian*, vol. 21, no. 2 (February 1974): 7.

58. T.D. Allman, "A New Look for the Old Brigade", *Far Eastern Economic Review*, vol. 83 (11 March 1974): 24.

59. Letter, E.G. Willan to C.W. Squires, 1 April 1973, FCO15/1876.

60. E.G. Willan to James Callaghan, 8 April 1974, FCO15/1871.

61. Letter, J.R. Paterson, Islamabad to P. Draw, 25 April 1974, FCO15/1873.

62. Letter, J.C.S. Stitt to L.M. Deas, 1 May 1974, FCO15/1873.

63. Letter, N.J. Thorpe, Dacca, to A.R. Murray, 30 April 1974, FCO15/1873.

64. Letter, P. Sullivan to M. Chapman, 21 May 1974, FCO15/1869.

65. Letter, L.J. Middleton, Kuala Lumpur, to P.R. Spendlove, 3 June 1974, FCO15/1873.

66. Letter, G.W. Hewitt, Canberra, to L.M. Bullock, 11 June 1974, FCO15/1873.

67. R.D. Lavers, Wellington, to K.W. Kelly, 9 June 1974, FCO13/1873.

68. Telegram, Rangoon to FCO, 10 June 1974, FCO13/1869.

69. Gross resigned in early 1973 and returned to New Jersey where he was arrested and convicted on five counts of perjury and tax fraud connected to an earlier Senate election. Paroled in 1976, he died in 1997 at the hands of teenage kidnappers. Obituary, *New York Times*, 27 September 1997.

70. Interview, John A. Lacey, Deputy Chief of Mission, Rangoon, 1972–75, Association for Diplomatic Studies and Training, 2012, Burma, pp. 114–16.

71. Interview, Edwin Webb Martin, Ambassador, Burma (1971–73), Association for Diplomatic Studies and Training, 2012, Burma, pp. 100–5, quotation from p. 105. Once convinced of the problem, the government became very cooperative with the American embassy on the drug suppression matter. Interview with Richard M. Gibson, Vice Consul, Rangoon (1974–75), Association for Diplomatic Studies and Training, 2012/09, Burma, p. 134.

72. Letter, O'Brien to Callaghan, 9 September 1974, FCO15/1877.

73. Letter, J.S. Chick, Rangoon, to M. Chapman, 20 August 1974, FCO15/1873.

74. Letter, P.L. Thomas, Belgrade, to A. F. Green, 20 August 1974, FCO15/1873;
    Letter, P.L. Thomas, Belgrade, to A. F. Green, 14 October 1974, FCO15/1873;
    Letter, C.L. Booth, Belgrade, to Andrew Green, 16 October 1974,
    FCO15/1873.

75. Letters, F.J. O'Brien to C.W. Squire, 24 October and 30 October 1974,
    FCO15/1873.

76. Letter, F.J. O'Brien to C.W. Squire, 4 November 1974, FCO15/1873.

77. Letter, T.J. O'Brien to C.W. Squire, 15 November 1974, FCO15/1878.

78. Letter, T.J. O'Brien to C.W. Squire, 22 November 1974, FCO15/1870.

79. In 1978 and 1982, I had occasional discussions with lecturers at the Yangon
    Arts and Sciences University. This impressed upon me the view that Ne Win's
    Burmese Way to Socialism was not "genuine".

80. Thakin Lay Maung, one of the first member of the *Dobama Asiayon*, "whom
    student leaders say for years had been running secret training classes in
    organization and agitation". Martin Smith, *Burma: Insurgency and the Politics
    of Ethnicity*, 2nd ed. (London: Zed Books, 1999), p. 270.

81. According to a third hand account passed on years after the event, the possibility
    of a state funeral was raised at a cabinet meeting. Ne Win is reported to have
    grunted at the suggestion and left the room. His colleagues therefore assumed
    that he did not favour the idea. I am grateful for an anonymous reviewer
    of the manuscript for this story. However, very few, if any, ministers would
    have had the temerity to propose anything in cabinet not already known to
    be favoured by Ne Win. This story lacks verisimilitude.

82. Interview, Thakin Tin Mya, 6 January 2006.

83. Lieutenant Colonel (retired) Ba Yi and Thakin Tin Mya, in an interview on
    30 January 2006, stated that the government had indicated to U Thant's
    family earlier that the plot of land at the Shwe Dagon would be available
    for his entombment and that government facilities would be made available.
    However, Ne Win insisted the army not be involved and that the Party should
    handle the matter. He sent Thakin Tin Mya to talk with the students but to
    no avail. Ex-Communist Tin Mya was convinced that his former colleagues
    instigated the student action. For an account of how students at the Yangon
    Institute of Technology were drawn into the demonstrations, see Hla Oo,
    "U Thant Uprising", in *Scourge of Burma and Four Short Stories* (N.p.: The
    author, 2010), pp. 73–79.

84. Despatch by T.J. O'Brien, 12 December 1974, FCO15/1071; Letter, T.J.
    O'Brien to C.W. Squires, 30 December 1974, FCO15/1070. For a fuller
    account, see Andrew Selth, "Death of a Hero: The U Thant Disturbances in
    Burma, December 1974", Centre for the Study of Australian-Asian Relations,
    Paper No. 49 (Brisbane: Griffith University, April 1989).

85. See, for example, Hla Oo, "1974 U Thant uprising — a first hand account", New Mandala blog site, 23 July 2008, available at <http://asiapacific.anu. edu.au/newmandala/2008/07/23/1974-u-thant-uprising-a-first-hand-account/> (accessed 21 May 2013). The commentary which follows is also instructive. See also Henry Soe Win, "Peace Eludes U Thant", *Asian Tribune*, 25 January 2006, available at <http://www.asiantribune.com/?q=node/11810> (accessed 21 May 2013).

86. I describe my arrival in Hkin Nint U, Myint Kyaung, and Maung Zeya, eds., *U Thaw Kaung 75th Hnitpyi Ahtein ahmat Mudita Sasu* [Collected Papers in Honour of the 75th Birthday of U Thaw Kaung] (Yangon: Myanmar Book Centre, 2013), pp. 259–63.

87. Ne Win's son Pyo was one of those caught up in the army's attack on Western decadence. He was at a golf links with his father one day and mentioned to him that young men were being given haircuts against their will. Ne Win asked General Tin U whether that was the case and Tin U said it had happened previously but had been stopped. The next day Pyo drove into town and was stopped by a private of the 1st Chin regiment at a makeshift check point and taken to a 2nd lieutenant. The officer said he had orders to cut his hair regardless of who he was but Pyo was eventually released. Ne Win and Pyo's sisters had been informed of the incident via a friend of one of the sisters and were worried about whether Pyo had had a haircut until he got home unscathed. Ne Win, though initially concerned, reprimanded him for going into town. Later that day General Tin U was called in to see Ne Win and then the haircuts ceased. Email from Pyo Win, 28 January 2015.

88. Letter, Lord Gore-Booth to Thomas Brimelow, FCO, 11 March 1975, FCO15/2038.

89. Despite the claim that the student was hung upon returning to Yangon within two weeks of meeting with Bo Let Ya, there is no evidence to support the accusation. Smith, *Burma: Insurgency and the Politics of Ethnicity*, pp. 270–71.

90. GED Emb Ygn Amg Kuhnel to MFAA, 16 December 1974, AA PA MGAA C1.115 77 GDR MOFA 1065–81.

91. Two members of the Council of State, retired colonel Kyaw Zaw and U Than Sein (Rakhine) in particular, were said to have insisted on his removal. Both were dropped from the Council of State in 1978.

92. Letter, T.J. O'Brien to C.W. Squires, 8 May 1965, FCO15/2038.

93. Letter, T.J. O'Brien to C.W. Squires, 17 June 1975, FCO15/2038.

94. *The Guardian* and *Working People's Daily*, 25 July 1975.

95. The visit was arranged as part of the internal conflicts within the Chinese leadership at that time. See Frederick C. Teiwes and Warren Sun, *The End of the Maoist Era: Chinese Politics During the Twilight of the Cultural Revolution, 1972–1976* (Armonk, New York: M.E. Sharp, 2007), p. 404 and fn.7, p. 385.

96. Interview with a retired senior army officer present at the time, March 2007.

97. Chi-shad Liang, "Burma's Relations with the People's Republic of China: From Delicate Friendship to Genuine Cooperation", in *Burma: The Challenge of Change in a Divided Society*, edited by Peter Cary (London: Macmillan, 1997), p. 73; Australian Department of Foreign Affairs Backgrounder, 21 November 1975, FCO15/2042; Letter, T.J. O'Brien to P.J.E. Male, 18 November 1975, FCO15/2042; Letter, N.M. Fenn to D.M. March, 19 November 1975, FCO15/2042.

98. Talk with Mr K.M. Kaiser, Bangladesh Ambassador in Rangoon by T.J. O'Brien, 23 December 1975, FCO15/2041.

99. She provides an account of the evening in Harriet O'Brien, *Forgotten Land: A Rediscovery of Burma* (London: Michael Joseph, 1991), pp. 104–6.

100. Interview, retired Major Htwe Han, 11 March 1911. He was said to dislike modern Western music and Western classical music. Interview, Prof. Dr Hc Mult. Franz Gerstenbrand, 14 September 2008.

101. Letter, T.J. O'Brien to A.M. Simons, 29 December 1975, FCO15/2039.

102. Letter, J. Chick to A.K Goldsmith, 15 January 1976, FCO15/2146.

103. Letter, T.J. O'Brien to Simons, 26 February 1976, FCO15/2146. According to the British Ambassador, Daw Sein Sein Khin was a 45-year-old Consultant Anaesthetist at the Central Woman's Hospital and apparently, a friend of Ne Win's children.

104. Private communication with a long-time friend of Dr Sein Sein Khin, 3 August 2013.

105. Interview with Lieutenant Colonel Ba Yi and Thakin Tin Mya, 30 January 2006. *Far Eastern Economic Review*, 9 April 1976, p. 9.

106. Letter, O'Brien to Simons, 5 May 1976, FCO15/2146.

107. *Forward*, December 1987, pp. 21–22.

108. Letter, O'Brien to Simons, 17 May 1976, FCO15/2146.

109. AAP-Reuters in *The Melbourne Age*, 21 July 1976.

110. Interview with Major (rtd) Htway Han, 11 March 2006.

111. Frank N. Trager and William L. Scully, "Burma in 1977: Cautious Changes and A Careful Watch", *Asian Survey*, vol. XVIII, no. 2 (February 1977): 149. Also convicted were the commanders of the Northern and Southern Regional Commands and a General Staff Officer, whom Tin U had appointed.

112. Whether it is for security reasons, particularly the Irish Republican Army bombing campaign in mainland Britain, or disaffection with his British cardiologist, Ne Win increasing travelled to Switzerland for health care. Letter, T.J. O'Brien to A.M. Simons, 26 February 1976, FCO15/2146.

113. Letter, T.J. O'Brien to A.M. Simons, 18 October 1976, FCO15/2146.

114. Letter, R.J. O'Brien to A.M. Simons, 2 November 1976, FCO15/2146.

115. Letter, B.E. Paunceford to A.K. Goldsmith, 17 December 1976, FCO15/2146.
116. *Facts about Burma* (Yangon: Printing and Publishing Corporation, December 1983), p. 110.
117. Tang Shuyi, "Former Chinese Ambassador to Myanmar Cheng Ruisheng's Interview", *International Herald Leader* (Beijing), 26 December 2003.
118. A list of fifty from the Central Committee and six from the Alternate Central Committee is given in Researcher, *A Concise History of Myanmar and the Tatmadaw's Role 1948–1988, Vol. I* (Yangon: News and Periodicals Enterprise, January 1991), p. 144.
119. Interview, Lieutenant Colonel Ba Yi, 30 January 2006.
120. Trager and Scully, "Burma in 1977", pp. 143–44. However, it was believed by many diplomats in Yangon that the Myanmar government paid off the loan in kyat as the United States diplomats could access local currency at favourable rates, according to one who lived there at the time. Embassy expenses were also believed to be paid in kyat.
121. FRG Emb Amb Linser to AA, 9 August 1977, AA 1782–1787. However, the ambassador may have got his date wrong as she was reported to have stayed one or two nights at U Lay Maung's residence near Ne Win's home. She subsequently explained that she had made a common mistake of married women; she believed she could change him and his policies.
122. Letter, O'Brien to Simons, 2 December 1977, FCO15/2146. The ambassador's report may have been incorrect as Ne Win's family record U Hla Htun's death as being on 3 June 1976.
123. Letter, O'Brien to Simons, 15 July 1977, FCO15/2146.
124. Burma: Annual Review for 1977, 30 December 1977, FCO15/2317.
125. I was living in Yangon at that time and had infrequent contacts with the Australian embassy from which I learned of this. For details of "Operation Naga Min" and its consequences, see Moshe Yegar, *Between Integration and Secession: The Muslim Communities of the Southern Philippines, Southern Thailand, and Western Burma/Myanmar* (Lanham, Maryland: Lexington Books, 2002), pp. 53–55.
126. *Myanmar Hsoshelit Lansin Pati Okkatakyi ei Hkit Pyaung Towhlanyei Thamaing win Meikhkun Paungkyut*, Volume 2, pp. 19–200; translated in *Forward*, vol. XV, no. 11 (1 August 1977): 2–3.
127. See the Socialist Republic of the Union of Burma, Ministry of Education, "Development of Education in Burma, 1976/77–1977/78", Report to the 37th Session of the International Conference on Education, Geneva, 5–14 July 1979.
128. Ger Emb Ygn Amb Linsser report to AA, 3 October 1977, 1885–89.
129. *Myanmar Hsoshlet Lansin Pati Okkatakyi ei Hkit Pyaung Towhlanyei Thamaing Win Meinhkun Paungkyut*, Volume I, pp. 367–69, translated as "Be Humble and of Unassailable Integrity", *Forward*, vol. XVI, no. 3 (1 December 1977): 2–3.

130. Ibid., pp. 369–71, translated as "Always Have Revolutionary Vigilance", *Forward*, vol. XVI, no. 3 (1 December 1977): 4.

131. Bertil Lintner, "China: Burma and Khmer Rouge Regime", *Searching for the Truth: Magazine of Documentation Centre of Cambodia*, no. 7 (July 2000): 2–4. Ezra F. Vogel, in his well regarded biography, *Deng Xiaoping and the Transformation of China* (Cambridge, M.A.: Belknap Press of Harvard University Press, 2011), p. 277, states that this visit took place ten days after Ne Win's last meeting with Deng. This is an error. Ne Win last met Deng nearly two months before the Cambodia trip.

132. Letter, J.W. Richards to R.E. Allen, 17 April 1978, FCO16/2321.

12

PURIFYING THE SANGHA, UNIFYING THE NATION, AND MAINTAINING GENUINE NEUTRALITY
(March 1978 to February 1988)

The only way to erect such a Common Power, as may be able to defend them from the invasion of Forraigners, and injuries of one another, and thereby to secure them in such sort, as that by their owne industrie, and by the fruites of the Earth, they may nourish themselves and live contentedly; is to confere all their power and strength upon one Man, or upon Assembly of men, that may reduce all their Wills, by plurality of voices, unto one Will: which is as much as to say, to appoint one man, or Assembly of men, to beare their Person; and every one to owne, and acknowledge himself to be the Author of whatsoever he that so beareth that Person, shall Act, or cause to be Acted, in those thing which concerne the Common Peace and Safetie; and therein to submit their Wills, every one to his Will, and their Judgements to his Judgement.

Hobbes, "The Generation of a Commonwealth", *The Leviathan*

Ne Win commenced his sixteenth year in power, and his fourth as President, in a calmer mood than was apparent during the previous years. He spent ten days around the Burmese New Year, *thingyan*, in Maymyo in 1978 with some of his children, playing golf, rather than going abroad as often in the past. However, he had a mishap of some nature and had to be flown by helicopter to Mandalay on 24 April. Nonetheless, three days later he was receiving departing ambassadors as usual.[1] One of the achievements of the socialist revolution, the People's Health Plan, had commenced on 1 April. For all the problems of the economy, some of the social reforms that were dreamt of at the time of the 1962 coup were at least being realized, if only on paper. However, the cost was significant in other terms and it was believed by the British ambassador that Myanmar was then holding 1,500 political prisoners, many having been arrested in the workers and students demonstrations in 1974.[2] Others would have been insurgents and other rebels caught in military campaigns against the Communist and ethnically designated separatists. However, as the economy improved, the international situation evolved in ways posing no immediate threat to the country, Ne Win's confidence grew and, within two years, there would be a significant liberalization within the boundaries of the one-party state.

Myanmar's relations with its neighbours continued much as before, neither particularly cooperative nor actively hostile. General Kyaw Htin was invited to China in June 1978, where he was given a grand tour of Beijing, Shanghai, and Kunming. Kyaw Htin was reportedly told in his talks with leading Chinese officials, which included Prime Minister Hua Guofeng, that if Ne Win came to Beijing once more, Chinese aid to the Burma Communist Party (BCP) would be reduced.[3] Relations with Bangladesh also remained an irritant. The country's foreign minister, Tabarak Husain, visited Ne Win in early June as the number of Bangladeshis fleeing back across the border as a result of the check on their immigration status under "Operation Naga Min" was said to have reached nearly 200,000. By July, an agreement was reached by which many of those who had fled would be repatriated if they could demonstrate their longevity of residence. However, international politics took up less and less of Ne Win's time. In his final decade in power, he travelled abroad much less frequently and devoted himself to detailed attention of economic development projects within the country. As Cold War tensions, and American power and attention, waned in Asia, Myanmar began to be seen as less important, and Ne Win became less sought after than in earlier years.

In what was becoming increasingly a quiet posting, diplomats spent a good deal of time considering the nature of Ne Win's regime and contemplating why he had made the decisions he had over the years. In one such rumination by the British Ambassador, Charles Booth, who was on his third posting to Burma, reflected that Ne Win was "a fascinating enigma". "An undoubted patriot, he scarcely disguises his contempt for what he regards as the laziness and pusillanimity of the average Burman." "Capable of charming a bird out of a tree and an intelligent and fascinating conversationalist, he is foul tempered, vindictive and cruel. ..." He was also described as uxorious and an invisible dictator.[4] In another rumination on Ne Win, Booth recalled Ne Win's comments to Maurice Collis in 1966 that he wanted to "give the Burmese people back their country".[5] Despite his repeated spells of ill health and hospitalizations, he was "in good health" and "extremely fit for a man his age", then sixty-eight.[6]

Booth, who deplored the arrest of political prisoners and their detention without trial, as well as how the investigations of suspected Bangladeshis were conducted in Rakhine, nonetheless concluded some months later that:

> Burma is no Ethiopia or Cambodia. Its rulers are basically decent men.
> Ne Win is personally squeamish about shedding blood. ... This kind
> of regime will continue as long as one can foresee. One either comes
> to terms with it and tries to influence it, or one abdicates.[7]

While Ne Win ran his dictatorship through the Burma Socialist Programme Party (BSPP) which he chaired, and the government of which he was president, his real power base was in the army, then under the control of his trusted colleague for forty-five years, General *Thura* Kyaw Htin. Having joined the Burma Defence Army in 1943 and, after attending the Japanese-organized Officer Training School at Mingaladon, Kyaw Htin, ten years Ne Win's junior, was attached to his commander's Fourth Burma Rifles. The army he headed was instructed to follow the discipline towards the local population that Ne Win had developed in "Operation Flush" in 1947. In the words of the British military attaché in Yangon in 1978:

> Battalions in action have the strictest instructions to cooperate with
> the local population, to buy their supplies from them, and to protect
> them from retaliation. The Burma army does not have a reputation
> of a marauder within its own country. Discipline is strict and on the
> whole behaviour toward the ethnic groups is very good.[8]

While the desertion rate from the army was relatively high and constant, at 300 to 500 per month, the troops, who signed up for ten years, were largely peasants and replacements were not difficult to recruit. However, efforts were made to keep up morale, which was especially high among the students at the Defence Services Academy, by rotating operational troops back to their bases where their families were well provided with the essentials of life. The Burma army was also remarkable at that time for having only six generals.[9]

Deng Xiao-ping continued to court Ne Win towards the end of 1978, as he had in January. On 14 November, he stopped in Yangon, as Chou En-lai had often done, for a four-hour meeting and lunch with Ne Win and Daw Ni Ni Myint, the Chairman's former wife with whom he has now reconciled. Deng was certainly thinking at that time of the twenty-five year Treaty of Friendship and Alliance which the Soviet Union and Vietnam had signed eleven days earlier in Moscow.[10] Six weeks later, Vietnam invaded Kampuchea (Liang 1997, p. 74), and the Khmer Rouge regime fell in Phnom Penh on 7 January. China attacked Vietnam on 17 February. If the American war had brought complications and dangers to Ne Win's world, fighting amongst the Communist powers brought other threats. If there was a silver lining in this situation, Thailand was now preoccupied with its eastern borders and the feeble remnants of U Nu's anti-Ne Win forces collapsed after the death of Bo Let Ya.

However, the Thai and Chinese arming of the Khmer Rouge for the next decade made weapons easily available and the Karen, Kachin and other insurgent groups in Myanmar now had a ready supply of weapons and ammunition from which to buy, even if, as eventually happened, the Chinese government cut off supplies from Yunnan. The necessity of the black market, given the failure of the Burmese Way to Socialism to provide many goods in demand, ensured that smuggling became a financial lifeline to the insurgents in search of revenue to top up the "taxes" they imposed on villagers in areas under their control. Despite the Thai government's complicity with the black marketeers, state security came first, and on 4 March 1979, Ne Win flew to Bangkok for two days of talks with Thai officials on the emerging situation in Southeast Asia.[11]

While Ne Win prized his close relations with West Germany, Japan and other sources of support for his government, he increasingly remained a stickler for protocol and the protection of his time and activities. When Hildegard Hamm-Brucher, the Minister of State in the West German Foreign Office, visited Myanmar in early 1979, she requested to meet with

Ne Win, and though the embassy in Yangon so requested, the meeting was denied. This apparently caused the minister some angst and the ambassador was at pains to explain that the head of state only received other heads of state or government. Unless there was a problem with which to deal, he would not normally meet with a foreign minister. In the event, however, relations between West Germany and Myanmar were in good form, she was reassured by the ambassador, and Ne Win was a great admirer of the German resurrection after the devastation of the Second World War.[12]

To assist Myanmar's development, and to further restore state-to-state relations to what they had been prior to 1967, China offered a new economic and technological cooperation agreement following Deng Xiao-ping's first visit to Yangon in 1978. Amounting to RMB1 billion, or approximately US$63 million, the offer was for a loan, with the first seven years interest free, for a number of projects including the Yangon-Thanlyin bridge, textile machinery and three rice mills. Less liberal than the terms offered in 1961, it provided much needed support to shore up Myanmar's weak economy and slow development. Prime Minister Maung Maung Kha signed the agreement on a three-day visit to China in July 1979 (Steinberg and Fan 2012, p. 399).

Ne Win was considering a trip to England in early July 1979, but because of an unspecified ailment, postponed the visit.[13] He then intended to visit in August but turned around and returned home, getting only as far as Singapore. On 27 August 1979, Earl Mountbatten of Burma was assassinated off the Irish coast by an Irish Republican Army bomb. The man whom Ne Win first met in Kandy in September 1945, but refused to see in 1956, was the first foreigner invited to visit Myanmar after the 1962 coup and had become a firm friend. Ne Win had in later years seen the Queen's cousin frequently on his visits to London or during Mountbatten's three visits to Myanmar after 1962. Two days after Mountbatten's death, after initially indicating that Ne Win would not attend the funeral, first class tickets were booked for him, Dr Maung Maung, U Lay Maung, and others, including Ne Win's personal doctor and the head of Military Intelligence, to fly to London via Singapore.[14] However, on arrival in Singapore, the British Airways flight was delayed because of mechanical difficulties; after Ne Win and his party rested in a hotel, they returned to the airport but as the plane was taxiing, it burst a tyre. Ne Win then cancelled the journey and returned to Yangon,[15] sending Rear Admiral Chit Hlaing, who served as a pall bearer, and six other Myanmar naval and air force officers as a guard of honour at the funeral on 5 September.[16]

Though Ne Win became increasingly less involved personally in international diplomacy, he was still capable of pulling off surprises, even if via remote control. Long unimpressed by the effectiveness of so-called Third World efforts to change the international order or establish peace and security for developing nations, Myanmar withdrew from the Non-Aligned Movement (NAM) at the Havana Summit of the heads of government on 7 September 1979. The venue at the capital of pro-Soviet Union Cuba, and a number of outstanding issues which impinged on the NAM as a result of the trilateral relations of China, the United States, and the Soviet Union, inspired the withdrawal. Particularly important was the support that was given to Vietnam after its invasion of Cambodia (Ang 2013, pp. 24–26). Of course, Ne Win did not attend the event, having attended no such conference for the previous decade and a half. In his brief speech at the Summit, the head of the Myanmar delegation, Foreign Minister Myint Maung, said,

> The principles of the movement are not recognizable anymore. They are not merely dim, they are dying. Differences of views and outlooks are only to be expected, but deliberate deviations from the basic principles can only be fatal to the movement. And it is not enough for the movement to just exist in name. There are among us those who wish to uphold the principles and preserve their own and the movement's integrity. But obviously there are also those who do not, and deliberately exploit the movement to gain their own grand designs. We cannot allow ourselves to be so exploited.[17]

Not only had the division in the organization over the Soviet invasion of Afghanistan that year tarnished the credentials of the movement, but also the Vietnamese invasion of Cambodia had done the same (Misra 1981, pp. 49–56).

After the announcement was made in Havana, Ne Win called in the ambassadors of Sri Lanka, Pakistan, India, Nepal and Bangladesh, to reinforce the message that Myanmar would not rejoin the Non-Aligned Movement until it sorted itself out. He said, repeating the words spoken by U Myint Maung, "we are not prepared to be made fools of or to be exploited." The NAM meetings were disgracefully mismanaged and the organization had become the tool of certain interests, implying the Soviet Union.[18]

Beijing was doubtless pleased by Myanmar's action at Havana but did not embarrass the Burmese by saying so. Nonetheless, China's Foreign Minister Huang Hua subsequently visited Myanmar twice in November 1980.

Between his visits, the Myanmar army launched its largest campaign to date, known as "Min Yan Aung", against the BCP in the northeast. Twenty-five battalions were engaged in an attempt to capture the BCP headquarters at Panghsang. Chinese support had lessened. Fighting continued into early January but the ultimate prize, the headquarters, was not achieved, though a forward base was established within 25 km of it. Unusually, but denoting the importance of China in Myanmar's foreign policy considerations, Ne Win received Huang Hua at his residence on 25 November 1980.[19]

Ne Win made his first, and apparently only, visit to Laos from 22 to 24 October 1979. Relations between Myanmar and its war-torn neighbour had been minimal since the then king visited a year after the Revolutionary Council came to power. Now under the control of the Lao People's Revolutionary Party, backed by the governments of the Soviet Union and Vietnam, Ne Win had an interest in ensuring that Vietnam and Laos did not start to supply arms to the Burma Communist Party just as it seemed that Chinese support was wavering. Ne Win had to tread warily in Laos. While the achievement of the neutrality of Laos was a lost cause from 1975, if not years before, convincing the government of President Souphanouvong that good neighbourly relations were in both their interests was a priority. In both Ne Win's remarks in Vientiane and in the joint communiqué issued at the end of the visit, the importance of cooperation on their mutual border and the principles of non-interference in the internal affairs of other states were emphasized (Aung Kin 1980, p. 110). Coming not long after Myanmar's withdrawal from the Non-Aligned Movement, underlining these points to Soviet-aligned Vietnam and Laos once more demonstrated Ne Win's determination to remain non-aligned and neutral in the Cold War, now a Cold War of the great Communist powers. China made no comment on Ne Win's visit, possibly viewing it as benign, but essential.

Domestically, Ne Win took a keen interest in various projects which his government had commenced, including the Myanmar Gems Corporation, which he visited on 27 November 1979. He also toured the Northwest Command for three days in early December, inspecting the Sagyin Marble Factory at Madaya, the Paleik Textile Mill, the Mandalay Institute of Indigenous Medicine, and the Mandalay National Museum, as well as four pagodas, including the Maha Myatmuni. At this time, he often invited along the Professor of Zoology at Yangon Arts and Sciences University as a travelling companion and raconteur (Tin Aung n.p., pp. 1–4). On 10 and 11 December 1979, Ne Win chaired the Tenth Meeting of the

BSPP Central Committee. The matters which particularly concerned him included the adequacy of rice for domestic consumption, improvements in the education system, getting the members of the cooperative societies to take their responsibilities seriously, and the forthcoming referendum on the national citizenship law.

On 13 December 1979 and in keeping with his interest in cooperatives as a pillar of the socialist economy, Ne Win inspected Cooperative Societies in Kamayut and Mayangon townships, and a primary goods retail shop, as well as the Kaba Aye Central Cooperative Training School. There he discussed the work of the research department and the Cottage Industries Department. His inspections were quite detailed, down to the godowns, canteen, ice and candle production, finished goods and other manufacturing processes.[20] He returned for a second inspection on 20 August 1980.[21] Nothing seemed too petty to arouse the Chairman's interest. The 17th Gem, Jade and Pearl Emporium at the Inya Lake Hotel was also inspected on 14 February 1980.[22] He spent six hours at the hotel, along with Council of State Secretary San Yu and eight other senior members of the government examining the displays and making recommendations for improvements.[23] He apparently also visited the Emporium twice more, before its conclusion, on 26 and 29 February.[24]

Miss Patricia Byrne, the new United States ambassador, presented her credentials to Ne Win in January 1980. She reportedly found Ne Win looking older than she had expected and suffering, throughout their meeting, from sinus trouble. In a friendly exchange, Ne Win made it clear that Myanmar would remain remote from conflicts in former French Indochina, where she had served previously. While he opposed the recent Soviet invasion of Afghanistan, small countries like his could do nothing about it and the United States would have to oppose Soviet expansionism.[25] On that theme, Ne Win noted in a meeting with the outgoing West German ambassador the following month that the Soviet Union had intervened in Angola, Ethiopia, South Yemen, Iran and Cambodia, as well as Afghanistan, and the Western response to all these efforts had been ineffectual. Ne Win discounted the notion that in the Kremlin there were liberals who were arguing for a less aggressive foreign policy and deserving of encouragement from the West. As for relations with China, aid to the BCP had been reduced "to some extent", but officials in the provinces, meaning Yunnan, often operated outside the control of Beijing.[26]

Unreported, Ne Win had a narrow escape on the return trip to Yangon from Minbu via Mandalay on 24 January 1980. He had gone to Minbu to study religious texts and visit various Buddhist relics, but did not visit the Mann oilfields nearby as he often did in the past. When he travelled upcountry, he normally flew in a Union of Burma Airways Fokker F-28, which was preceded by an Air Force plane, a stretched version of the F-27 manufactured by the American Fairchild company, carrying his security contingent for the next destination. On that day, the first plane took off from the old Mandalay Airport but crashed shortly after due to engine failure. All but one of the forty-five passengers, all of whom were well-known and trusted by Ne Win, were lost. On arrival back in Yangon, the passengers on the second flight were obviously saddened at the loss of so many of their compatriots, many of whom had been colleagues since the 1940s. Afterward, Ne Win, together with members of his family, attended the funerals of all who died as well as visiting the bereaved at their homes and ensuring they were looked after.

Ne Win's acquaintance with royalty received a boost when the King and Queen of Nepal visited Yangon for three days, from 2 to 4 March 1980. Ne Win and Daw Ni Ni Myint hosted a dinner for King Birenda Bir Bikram Shah Dev and the Queen on 3 March, after receiving them at his residence.[27] The visit presumably was of greater religious than political significance, as the Buddha had been born in what is now the Lumbini region of Nepal and most of the population of Nepal, like the Lao, Cambodians, Thai, Sri Lankans and Burmese, are followers of Theravada Buddhism. The King's visit was connected with the most important domestic religious event in Myanmar in 1980, the unification and purification of monkhood. The day after the King's departure, Ne Win was meeting and dining with graduating students from the Academy for the Development of the National Races Course 11 at Ywathitgyi, another project started under his government in which he took a special interest.[28] On 15 March, he presided over the annual meeting of the BSPP Central Committee, prior to the *Pyithu Hluttaw* meeting on the 17th, and on the 25th he pursued another of his interests when he attended a seminar of indigenous medicine practitioners at the Saya San Hall at Kyaikkasan Ground, as well as a display of indigenous medicine plants at the Kandawgyi Lake.[29] Two days later, he hosted a dinner in honour of Armed Forces Day.[30]

Soon after, another of his interests, the revival of Burmese literature was briefly the focus of Ne Win's attention. The BSPP had organized, as mass and class bodies in support of the socialist revolution, the Workers and Peasants Asiayon, followed by Party youth groups, the Luyehkyun (outstanding student) scheme, various labour volunteer projects, including the literacy campaign, and the Model Workers and Model Peasants campaigns, with holiday camps and special study tours. However, despite his early indication of concerns about preserving and strengthening Burmese culture, nothing had yet been done to organize the literati in support of the revolution. That was amended on 4 April 1980, when the First Conference of the Literary Workers Organisation was held, in keeping with Ne Win's speech at the First Party Congress in 1971.[31]

While establishing new, state-sponsored bodies, Ne Win also saw to the closure of colonial-era institutions when he discovered their continued existence. In 1980, after being invited to the 70th anniversary meeting of the Burma Research Society, he ordered that the publication of its journal be taken over by the Ministry of Industry 2. With that, the publication of *The Journal of the Burma Research Society* ceased, and the society with it. Ne Win saw the society as the instrument of colonialism, and therefore of no value for the new socialist Burma (Tin Aung n.p., pp. 27–29).

The long sought unification and purification of the Buddhist monkhood in Myanmar was also accomplished under Ne Win's auspices but in his absence, as he restricted his public activities to secular affairs. Whether his study of Buddhist principles and close affiliation with influential senior monks lay behind this achievement is difficult to ascertain.[32] Whatever the level of Ne Win's involvement in the matter, the First Congregation of the Sangha of All Orders met with 1,226 members from 24 to 27 May 1980 and formed the 33-member state Sangha Nayaka Committee. The formation of the committee was intended to moderate sectarianism in the monkhood, provide a means to differentiate bogus from genuine monks by having a system of monastic identity cards and registration, and to ensure that non-Buddhist cults, such as nat worship, did not sully the purity of the faith (Tin Maung Maung Than 1988, pp. 26–61; 1993, pp. 6–100). Two years earlier, the Ministry of Home and Religious Affairs had seen to the reinstatement of two honorary monastic titles which had not been awarded since 1962. The title of Agga Maha Pandita, created in 1915, and Abhidaja Maha Ratha Guru, established in 1953, were again awarded in 1979 (Rozenberg 2010, p. 126). At the conclusion of the Congregation, Ne Win advised the Sangha Nayaka Committee to build a pagoda to mark its success. Such a pagoda would house an image of the Buddha and a hairstand relic which had been donated by the King of Nepal during his visit in March (Aung Kin 1981, p. 104).

As he had managed to reconcile the various factions of the Sangha, on the final day of the Congregation, Ne Win called a meeting of the BSPP Central Executive Committee, the central organs of state power, and the council of state to hear his proposal for the establishment of a system of state honours for the nation which would serve as a means of overcoming the political divisions of the past. The next day, Order No. 2/80 was issued offering a 90-day amnesty for all insurgents to mark the Sangha congregation. Bo Thet Tun, the BCP commander in the northwest and U Nu, then in Bhopal in India, among many other opponents of Ne Win at home and abroad, both accepted the amnesty. In total, 2,189 persons accepted the amnesty, including Bohmu Aung, Bo Yan Aung, and Saw Kya Doe who returned from Thailand. Less well-known politicians, such as U Thu Wei, a follower of Kyaw Nyein and for many years a journalist in Bangkok, also returned to Myanmar.[33] Lo Hsin Han and Thakin Soe were also released from prison and Thakin Soe's death sentence was lifted. After the amnesty period ended, Burma Communist Party leader Thakin Ba Thein Tin wrote to Ne Win seeking peace talks. Kachin Independence Organisation (KIO) leader Brang Seng came to Yangon to discuss having peace talks and the talks were held in Myitkyina from 17 to 19 November with a second round between 18 and 21 December. In addition, 3,944 prisoners were released and all death penalties were commuted. Ne Win's long sought national unity might once more be within reach.

The amnesty announcement and the plans for the award of honours and pensions to those whom, in the past, had served the nation and the state were part of a process of national reconciliation orchestrated by Ne Win in his now more confident mood. The intention was to achieve what had been sought through the idea of leftist unity in 1948–49, the parleying with the insurgents in 1963, and the Unity Advisory Board in 1969. All those had failed, but Ne Win and his colleagues thought they could yet create national harmony through their own demonstration of goodwill and honest intentions. The plan Ne Win outlined was not only to award honours to those who had worked for the independence of the country but also financial rewards so that they could live in dignity. Such a scheme had been considered soon after the coup in 1962, but then pertained only to the Thirty Comrades, and eventually fell by the side as the government became overwhelmed with the tasks of governing.

In presenting the scheme in a typical speech, Ne Win reviewed the history of the country since the kings attributing the defeat of the Konbaung dynasty by the British to infighting among the numerous descendants of the polygamous monarchy. He explained the reason he was discussing the past was to draw lessons for contemporary politics.

> In our country, even up to the present day, there are those who are creating disturbances. They are not familiar with history. I myself found out these facts only when I studied them now. It is not right if all want to be king, if all want to be ministers. One must serve in one's own suitable place and if any threat from a foreign country should arise we must all be united. In this age there is no reason to face threats from other countries. Even if such threats do not seem to exist in succeeding generations it is best to be united among ourselves. Best for our present age as well as future ages. This is why unity is being emphasised. ... . If people taking up politics are to place the honour of the country first, the interests of the country first, and their own interest second or third ... not only other persons but all of us ... they would serve the country in whatever capacity they are capable no matter who became leader. That is what I wish to say.

He then turned to those who had resisted the British and given service to the state and nation at the time of independence and subsequently. Starting with the Shan Wuntho Sawbwa (for an account of his resistance campaign, see Ni Ni Myint 1983, pp. 212–14) through the nationalist movement in all its guises to General Aung San's cabinet, the Caretaker Government, and the efforts of his own government, all had sought to create an independent state and nation. He again discussed at some length the three nationalists whom he knew from Pyay and how they had to compromise their nationalist attitudes in order to make a living. He also mentioned by name Brigadiers Tin Pe, Aung Gyi, Aung Shwe, and Maung Maung, all of whom he had dismissed because of personal or political differences.

> I will tell you about the endeavours of these individuals. Leave aside their defect and there may also be certain things one may not like. However, during the Japanese time when we were preparing to fight back the Japanese, in '42 and '43 ... at that time I told these four what I wanted and asked them to attend to the details ... and they carried out the work. In fighting against the Japanese the struggle was carried out according to eight command areas. All these plans were carried out by them.

In awarding honours, Ne Win emphasized that even Communists and members of the National United Front, those who had worked together in the resistance at one time, and then later "went different ways due to differences in political ideas", should be included.

He briefly concluded his remarks, noting that the amnesty had also been announced to mark the purification of the Sangha being carried out by the Sayadaws.

> This is not something which can be done every day nor every year. This is something which has to be done due to appropriate time and causes. It is an extremely unique and sacred activity. Hence in recognition of, in consideration of, and in reverence for this unique and sacred activity, there is the matter of giving amnesty to those guilty of political and criminal offenses.[34]

Not long after, the government allowed Ashin Vicittasarabhivanmsa, a noted monk who had worked closely with U Nu, to established two Sangha universities in Yangon and Mandalay with financial support coming not from state funds but from wealthy private donors. Buddhist missionary work became the focus of the two institutions which were apparently more successful than the previous government-funded Buddhist university that Ne Win had closed in the early 1960s. Since the fall of Ne Win's government in 1988, two more privately funded Buddhist universities have been founded (Khammai Dhammasami 2007, p. 22).

Myanmar was not only reviving past traditions in religion and culture, including handicrafts and the arts, but also pressing ahead and catching up in terms of modern technology. Skipping the black-and-white phase of television experienced by many other countries at that time, Myanmar commenced colour television broadcasting on 1 October, first on an experimental basis, and then becoming regular from 1 November 1980 onward. Initially for only a few hours in the evening and on Sundays, television sets, placed in the streets of Yangon, became community hubs and before long translations of *Columbo* scripts were being sold on the streets and children would come running at the sound of the theme to the *Woody Woodpecker* show. Those with televisions could watch old black-and-white Burmese movies on Sunday afternoons, including those of A-1 Tin Maung and Collegian Ne Win.

Indications of Ne Win's relative optimism and relaxed attitude at this time, as well as concerns about his health and mortality, were revealed at a dinner for Professor Frank Trager and his wife, on another visit to Myanmar. Dr Maung Maung was the only other guest on that occasion. Ne Win only drank tea and a little wine at the dinner. He discoursed for twenty minutes on an undiagnosed stomach complaint and his continuing problems with his sinuses. The food was bland and apparently designed for someone with stomach trouble. The only politics discussed over the table were some thoughts Ne Win had about enhancing the political powers of the seven states and the need to conciliate with his old political opponents in his remaining years. He was then seventy years of age. He also noted that he was in frequent contact with U.S. Senator Mike Mansfield and was on friendly terms with former Senator Edmund Muskie, then President Jimmy Carter's secretary of state.[35]

Ne Win presided over the first day of the twelfth meeting of the BSPP Central Committee but did not attend the second day's proceedings, leaving them in the hands of his trusted deputy, U San Yu. However, again unusually, as with the earlier reception of the Chinese Foreign Minister in November 1979, Ne Win met with the visiting Thai Foreign Minister, Air Chief Marshall Siddhi Savetsila, on 18 June,[36] prior to a visit by Thai Prime Minister Prem Tinsulanonda just over a month later. Ne Win hosted a dinner for the Prime Minister, who was the guest of Prime Minister Maung Maung Kha, on 24 July, the first day of his three-day stay.[37] Following the Vietnamese invasion of Cambodia, Ne Win was willing to enhance relations with non-Communist Southeast Asian governments and he also received Singapore's Minister for Trade and Industry, Goh Chok Tong and the First Permanent Secretary of the Singapore Foreign Ministry, S.R. Nathan, on 10 July.[38] Less than a month later, on 5 August 1980, he met with the Deputy Prime Minister of Singapore, Mr S. Rajaratnam.[39]

During this flurry of visits from foreign dignitaries, at the invitation of Ne Win, U Nu returned to Myanmar from his exile in India after eleven years. On arrival at the airport, he was received by the President's military assistant, and driven off directly to meet with Ne Win. He was housed in the official state guest house and assured of the right to remain in the country either permanently or temporarily, as he wished. Nu indicated that he wished to devote himself to the promotion of Buddhism, both at home and abroad.[40] He was encouraged by Ne Win when he began a project to translate the Tipitaka, the Buddhist canon, into English. U Nu was made President of the Pitaka Translation Society soon after; this was announced in his presence at the Ministry of Religious Affairs at Kaba Aye Hill the following month.[41]

Soon after the departure of the Thai Prime Minister and the arrival of U Nu, a ceremony to mark the beginning of the construction of the pagoda that Ne Win advised the State Sangha Nayaka to erect commenced.

On 27 July 1980, the Full Moon of Waso, with the entombment of the sacred relics of the Buddha donated by the King of Nepal, in a ceremony overseen by senior monks and conducted by the Yangon People's Council Chairman and the Ministers for Home and Religious Affairs and Construction, the Maha Wizaya Pagoda was consecrated on a hillock on the south side of the Shwe Dagon Pagoda, where previously the army records office stood.[42] Unusual in design, with a hollow stupa and an interior circular outer hall noting all of the regions of Myanmar, it was built using private donations, mainly from the Yangon city bus line operators committee, but overseen by the Yangon government and the Ministry of Home and Religious Affairs.

On 11 August 1980, according to the monthly magazine, *Forward,* "Burma Socialist Programme Party Chairman and President U Ne Win had an intimate and friendly meeting and gave a luncheon to his colleagues of the Freedom and Revolutionary Struggles at the President House, on Ahlone Road".[43] The lunch was for the recipients of the Naingngan Gonyi Award. Photos of the event showed a smiling Ne Win in a higher chair than his guests, surrounded by former colleagues and one-time enemies from the country's political left and political right. In one photo, Thakin Soe sat on his left and U Nu on his right.[44] In others, Ne Win was seated next to or seen greeting Saw Kya Doe, Mahn Ba Saing, Saya Tha Hto, all Kayin leaders, U Kyaw Nyein, U Ba Swe, and others.[45] A film of the event was shown in all cinemas.

Whether it was seen by the participants as Ne Win saw it, a sign of political reconciliation and his dominance of the state, remains a moot point. Subsequently, Brigadier Maung Maung, an attendee, who tended to see the drab side of life at the best of times, claimed the bonhomie of the affair was forced and the entire event was "a wholly uncomfortable and artificial occasion". Thakin Soe was the butt of many remarks, according to Maung Maung, at one point it being said that had he taken power, most of those at the table would now be dead. He did not deny this, but claimed that if he had taken power, the country would not be in any worse mess than it was. This retort was well received.[46] The next day, Ne Win met with a Special Envoy of President Kim Il-sung of North Korea, Mr Hwang Jang Yob, on a week-long visit to Yangon.[47] The BSPP and the Workers' Party of Korea had fraternal relations.

Ne Win was off on another inspection tour on 21 August 1980, driving from Yangon to Pyay, making a stop in Thayawady. The next day, he and his party, which included General Kyaw Htin, Agriculture Minister

Ye Gaung, and various party and government officials, inspected the North
Nawin Dam project. Ne Win had last visited the project in August the
previous year. He went over the plans for the dam and the development
of agriculture in this region, including discussions with local farmers. On
23 August, he toured another project of interest to him, the Industrial
Training Centre at Sinde, along with Industry (2) Minister Col. Maung
Cho. He also met one Lieutenant Colonel Than Shwe, the Director of the
Heavy Industries Corporation, at Sinde. The party returned to Yangon by
car on 24 August.[48] Perhaps the plane crash in 1979 encouraged him to
use more land transportation.

Having hosted the King and Queen of Nepal in March, Ne Win
was hobnobbing with Princess Alexandra and her husband, Angus
Ogilvy, from 16 to 19 September. The Princess was entertained by Ne Win
on several occasions.[49] He also gave her a broach, among other things,
which he designed himself, the first time he had crafted a piece of
jewellery.[50] New dimensions were being added to his life as golf and alcohol
waned.

Ne Win had a busy year at home in 1980 and made only two overseas
trips. He also attended the usual round of ambassadorial meetings. On one
such occasion, he informed the departing Malaysian ambassador that while
Myanmar wished to have good relations with all Southeast Asian countries,
it still would not join the Association of Southeast Asian Nations. Indeed,
he chided them for opposing Vietnam for its invasion of Cambodia, despite
the Foreign Ministry condemning Vietnam's invasion and close ties with the
Soviet Union. He also indicated that he could not accept an invitation to
visit Malaysia that year because of his health. He was "outspokenly hostile
to the Soviet Union, critical of [U.S.] President Carter, and as friendly as
ever to the Chinese leadership in spite of mounting evidence that Chinese
support for the BCP is as substantial and as effective as before", wrote the
British ambassador.[51]

Ne Win visited China for the eleventh time from 20 to 23 October
1980 in order to hold talks again with Deng Xiao-ping, Hua Guofeng,
Li Xiannian, and the new Chinese premier, Zhao Ziyang.[52] During
that visit, Deng arranged a meeting between Ne Win and the chairman
of the Burma Communist Party, Thakin Ba Thein Tin, without telling
Ne Win. According to Ba Thein Tin, they met for 90 minutes and arranged
subsequent meetings, the first of which Ne Win attended, but reached no
agreement (Silverstein 1982, p. 183). Needless to say, Ne Win was not
pleased. Relations between the two countries, through increasingly frequent

meetings between the two states' top leaders, remained less than cordial. With the army still fighting the Burmese Communists, and that party's key leaders residing in China, relations could not yet become fully normal. In order to maintain a balance between his rival neighbours, Ne Win departed less than a month later for an official to India. The brief visit, from 20 to 22 November, included most importantly meetings with Prime Minister Indira Gandhi. Among other things, he wanted to thank her for encouraging U Nu to return to Myanmar, as he had asked her to do. The trip concluded with a stopover in Dacca for brief talks with Bangladesh President Ziaur Rahman.[53]

Back home, Ne Win hosted a three-day meeting from 11 November at his office for senior educationalists and top state officials on educational matters.[54] The meeting broached the subject of re-introducing English as a medium of instruction at the universities as well as strengthening the teaching of English in pre-university education. In his concluding remarks, Ne Win indicated that education was the most important investment the country could make and great efforts at improvement were necessary.[55] Investment in the economy was beginning to see results. In 1980–81, the economic growth rate was reported to have been 8.3 per cent with an average growth rate of 6.7 per cent in the first three years of the four-year plan period. Prices were reasonably stable and production in many sectors had met or exceeded the targets set, though problems were lurking ahead (Silverstein 1982, pp. 185–87). Perhaps because of Myanmar's withdrawal from the Non-Aligned Movement in 1979, and to demonstrate nonetheless its willingness to play a role in world affairs, the government sought to become a member of the governing body of the International Labour Organisation in November 1981.[56]

In November, Ne Win hosted a dinner for six doctors from the Royal College of Surgeons in Edinburgh, led by Professor John Gillingham, a leading neurosurgeon. Gillingham had come to Myanmar earlier to operate on Ne Win's step-daughter, Lei Lei, who was suffering from the after effects of meningitis. They were in Yangon to interview potential candidates for further medical study in the United Kingdom. Though well, Ne Win was beginning to show his age and had cut down on golf and whiskey, according to the British ambassador, who was also present at the dinner. Ne Win's then wife, Ni Ni Myint, was not present, indicating that they had had another rift, possibly over whether her mother could be admitted to the military hospital. Ne Win's daughter Sanda, herself a doctor in the army medical corps, had objected to taking a civilian into the hospital and

Ne Win supported her position. Besides discussing his own health condition, Ne Win also inquired as to whether there were texts in London on Myanmar indigenous medicine removed by the British in 1886. It was clearly a topic of interest to him.[57] Politics was avoided throughout the evening.

To mark Independence Day in 1981, Ne Win presented the Aung San Tagun, an honorary state award, to seven veterans of the Minami Kikan, the Japanese organization which had trained the Thirty Comrades four decades earlier. Also granted the award was the widow of the founder of the Minami Kikan, Colonel Suzuki (Seekins 2007, p. 38). At the end of the evening, led by Bohmu Aung, the old comrades lined up, and at the command from Aung to salute Ne Win, bowed to him in the Japanese manner, an honour which he then returned with misty eyes (Maung Maung 1999, p. 169).

As Ne Win was remembering his Japanese mentors, his former British foes were thinking kindly of him. The British Foreign and Commonwealth Office issued a "Background Brief", entitled "Developments in Burma", in July. Generally optimistic, it noted that "President Ne Win, who has ruled Burma since 1962, has recently made determined moves to reconcile the warring groups within the country and to set the economy on a more productive path." It drew attention to the recent amnesty and the release of 4,000 political and other prisoners, the return from exile of U Nu, and the purification and organization of the Sangha. Also on the author's mind would have been the recently failed peace talks with both the Communist Party and the Kachin Independence Organisation.[58]

Ne Win did not forget his old British friends either, awarding the Aung San Tagun title to the British Labour politician Arthur Bottomley on 16 February. Since the agreement the previous year to his proposal for honours and pensions for Burmese nationalist heroes, he had held several other award granting ceremonies. One such ceremony was held on 6 February. In the early part of the year, as was now customary, Ne Win hosted Independence and Union Day dinners and visited the Gems, Jade and Pearl Emporium.[59]

Ne Win's visit to China the previous October was followed by a twenty-three-member delegation from Beijing which arrived in Yangon on 26 January. After visiting a number of industrial projects and holding talks with ministers, Ne Win received Premier Zhao Ziyang on the evening of 29 January and hosted a dinner in his honour.[60] While China still recognized the Burma Communist Party as a fraternal party, support for it was dwindling, and state-to-state bilateral relations were on the mend. This was certainly a consequence of the careful diplomacy that Myanmar had practised towards China through difficult years, but was also a by-product of the intra-Communist Cold War.

It was claimed that in April 1981, Ne Win came up with the idea for the 300 river water pumping stations of the kind one now sees along the banks of the Ayeyawady and Chindwin rivers in central Myanmar, providing irrigation water to the parched land of the dry zone. On a visit to Minbu, he was said to have inquired what the farmers grew in that area. When told that they grew merely beans and pulses because there was inadequate water for rice cultivation, Ne Win exploded and pointed to the river. Ne Win shouted at General Kyaw Htin, "Why can't you guys do something about it? Those lazy motherfuckers from the Agri-Forest Ministry should do something, fucking anything." Mechanical engineers were soon assigned by Colonel Ye Gaung, the Minister responsible, and allegedly US$80 million was spent developing a pump which, after one year, was irrigating a thousand acres of cotton, with another thousand the following year. The soil was too sandy for paddy. When shown the results in 1983, Ne Win was said to have remarked:

> You know, with that sort of money, I know exactly what sort of crop they should be growing here! Do you know which one? Shwe-Bins (gold trees). Fucking Shwe-Bins, fucking idiots. Eighty million bucks for 2000 fucking acres of bloody cotton! Motherfucking thieves.

The Shwe-Bin pumps project was then abandoned only to be revived under the post–Ne Win military government which, abandoning fiscal prudence for development, had created conditions for growing rice in the same areas as a result of the silt which the pumps have brought out of the river to enrich the soil along with the water.[61]

On 8 August 1981, Ne Win addressed the sixth and final day of the Fourth Party Congress. In his speech, he explained that he was stepping down as President of the Socialist Republic. He gave two reasons. One was to establish a tradition of handing over power "in a spirit of unity at the right time" and under the appropriate conditions. Another was that no man could escape old age, illness and death. He, at the age of 71, had already experienced old age and illness, with death inevitable. He handed the presidency over to San Yu, eight years his junior. Ne Win also indicated that he wished to give up the party chairmanship but, as he said, "my comrades have asked me to continue to watch their work, to give

advice and guidance". This revealed, in his estimation, that "our people
are not fully confident of themselves", and he urged them to develop their
independence.[62]

He then turned to the economy, laying down a number of principles
or axioms as to what the economy should be like. In sum, it was a call
for prudence and self-reliance. Income had to exceed expenditure and
loans, and loans had to be repaid. Borrowing should not be excessive and
industrialization should not be for its own sake, but for the utilization of
Myanmar's own products and resources. Perhaps glimpsing the future, he
said, "I say these things because I do not want our country to go bankrupt,
as we would, if we carry on without being careful about the points
I have mentioned and if we are not able to repay the loans when due."
Though Myanmar had to borrow to develop, it still had the economic
resilience not to be dictated by its creditors and that was a position which
should be maintained in order to secure both political and economic
independence.

The world economy was the third section of his discourse. Mentioning
a number of economic problems historically and in different countries
in relation to the values of currencies and the costs of raw materials for
industry, and perhaps, unknowingly foreseeing the Plaza Accord four years
later, Ne Win averred that the capitalist economies of the West and Japan
were in an economic war. This economic war "had been going among the
countries said to be friends ... for a long time covertly". As a consequence,
for the foreseeable future, aid and soft, low interest rate, loans would be
scarce as the world looked to Ne Win to be on the verge of an economic
crisis similar to that in the early 1930s. Therefore, economic prudence was
not only necessary for maintaining Myanmar's independence, but also a
condition of the real world.

Referring to party matters, in terms of membership recruitment,
Ne Win wished to reverse the party's usual practice of seeking "able and
good" persons and to change it to seeking "good and able" persons. Good
people, even if not competent, could be trained, whereas able people who
were not good would use the party for their own purposes and do the
party much harm. Earlier in the year, a number of party members at the
township level had been arrested for corruption. He also chastised party
members who tried to exclude capable people from the party so as to
protect their own positions. They were not acting in the interests of the
state or of the people.[63]

By then, both the Party and the bureaucracy were becoming increasingly
dysfunctional. The expression *ma lok, ma shok, ma pyot* (don't do any work,

don't get implicated, don't get fired) had become the slogan for the civil service and Party apparatchiks. Hiding behind the expression *ana-de* (to be restrained for fear of offending), even minor decisions were avoided, with the excuse that the matter had been put up to a higher level and no response had yet been received. This was compounded by the practice of many officials of so-called "double grazing", whereby individuals got themselves appointed to more than one post in order to increase their income. The Party itself became dependent upon gifts from wealthy individuals in order to host the ceremonies and events that the leadership expected to be observed (Kyaw Yin Hlaing 2003, pp. 5–58).

For over a week at the turn of the year, Ne Win was on an inspection tour by air of the Central, Southwestern, Western and Northwestern Command Areas, returning to Yangon on 3 January 1982. Oilfields and heavy industries, both for defence and civilian purposes, were visited as well as a lengthy visit to Party and local government institutions and offices in Pyay Township which had been the central point of his tour, and of course his birthplace.[64] Less than a month later, Ne Win made a second inspection tour, this time by train, to industrial projects in the Central and Northwest Command Areas. He visited sugar mills, a paper mill, a metallurgy research project, textile mills and dam projects, particularly at Yezin, now part of Naypyitaw. Travelling the area by car, he visited Pyinmana and Meiktila and went to the Tetma Test Well, an oil exploration project, by helicopter. Ne Win also had time to study *parabeiks* (palm leaf manuscripts) at the U Ponnya Pitakai Taik, before visiting the Sedawgyi Dam project and returning to Yangon from Mandalay. It was a whirlwind trip.[65] Freed from the presidency, he could indulge his interests in Myanmar's history and culture as well as its economic development.

From the late 1970s until the early 1980s, the fruits of the Revolutionary Council were beginning to ripen, and thanks to the acceptance of foreign aid and loans, a significant injection of capital, by Burmese standards, had given the economy a fillip. When Ne Win visited the Gems Emporium and Union Day exhibitions and dinner in 1982 with President San Yu as his guide and host, he had reason to believe that the revolution might succeed after all. He could now relax and let others get on with managing what he had wrought. He trusted the ministers, now in place for several years, to get on with their tasks though he still kept a close eye on them. Nonetheless, it was time to relax, as he did with students at the Academy for the Development of National Groups dinner hosted on 5 March 1982 by the new General Secretary of the BSPP, U Aye Ko, who had taken over U San Yu's place on his elevation as president.

Five days later, U Aye Ko was presenting his report on behalf of the Central Executive Committee of the BSPP to the Sixth Meeting of the Party Central Committee with Ne Win was presiding. The nearly five-and-a-half hour long meeting also received reports from the party Discipline and Inspection Committees and the Ideology Study Group. Joint General Secretary Tin U then presented a number of proposals and announced the results of ballots of persons elected to fill vacancies on various party bodies. The second day's proceedings were devoted to amending various party rules and regulations.[66]

By travelling abroad less frequently and giving up the minutiae of day-to-day management of the President's office, including receiving foreign guests and ambassador's credentials, to the trustworthy, if lacklustre, San Yu, Ne Win could indulge in his own interests more deeply, if spasmodically. He continued his practice of micro-managing aspects of the state and its development projects. He would assign tasks to his subordinates or colleagues and then study how well they had succeeded in what he wanted to get done.[67]

Many of his activities during his final six years as Party Chairman remain, for now, unknown, but on 5 June 1982, Ne Win called a seminar of leading council of state members and ministers to hear reports from the members of the Indigenous Medicine Board and the Institute of Indigenous Medicine in Mandalay.[68] Based on Ayurvedic concepts and influenced by Buddhism, traditional Burmese medical practices were revived during the Second World War when other varieties of treatment became unavailable. Indigenous medicine is now practised in most parts of Myanmar, with 5 hospitals, 194 clinics, and 8,000 practitioners. After independence, it came under state supervision and the Indigenous Medicine Board became the regulatory body under the head of state. In 1976, the Institute of Indigenous Medicine was founded and the Board's authority amended several times between 1966 and 1987.[69] Indigenous medicinal plants were cultivated in the gardens of army guest houses where Ne Win often stayed when on tour. The codification of Myanmar indigenous medicines was significantly advanced under Ne Win's auspices.[70]

Ne Win's journeys abroad, though few, became increasingly open to speculation. On 2 July 1982, he and Daw Ni Ni Myint departed for West Germany. Seen off and received on his return on 21 July by no ambassadors, Ne Win was accompanied by General Kyaw Htin, the Chief-of-Staff, and Minister for Industry 2, U Maung Cho, as well as Attorney General U Lay Maung.[71] Most likely, given Maung Cho's responsibilities for heavy industry, in which the Germans were deeply involved, they went on the trip as guests of the Fritz Werner Company and Giescke and Devrient of Munich, the suppliers of security printing presses.

A week later, Ne Win addressed the Third Central Body Meeting of the reorganized War Veterans Organisation held in the Saya San Hall at the Kyaikkasan Ground on 29 July 1982. He began his remarks with an indication of his semi-retired status as Party Chairman: "I have decided to talk less, work as much as necessary, and rest when I should and can." He undertook a lengthy discussion of the political origins and institutional history of the army, noting that an official history was being compiled. His account revealed nothing particularly new. The importance of his remarks lay in his emphasis, both early in his discourse and at the end, that the Myanmar army was different from other armies where soldiers "must be foolhardy and rash" and "rough, reckless and obeyed orders thoughtlessly". The Myanmar army had to be educated for it had many tasks, economic, administrative and military, and had to see its responsibilities in the round. The army was "based on the working class and the peasantry of the masses, and ... founded by and with real and genuine politicians who really served the interests of the country". They had to ensure that that "mental make-up" did not disappear so that the army could "perpetually serve the country with this spirit".[72]

Ne Win felt moved to speak again in 1982, addressing the Seventh Meeting of the BSPP Central Committee on 8 October at the President's House on Ahlone Road. His topic was the Citizenship Law which was being passed at that time. He again began with a review of history, though he insisted he did "not wish to hurt anyone" and he would "try not to do so". "However", he said, "the truth might perhaps hurt somebody sometimes." Of course, Ne Win was referring to the unfettered immigration of foreigners, mainly South Asians, and to a lesser extent, Chinese, into Myanmar during the colonial period. This had given rise to a mixed population of indigenous persons, guests, mixed race persons, and the offspring of immigrants. After explaining the content of the two nationality acts passed at the time of independence to give "guests", i.e., immigrants, and their offspring, Myanmar citizenship, Ne Win noted two problems with the legislation. One was that the Minister for Immigration had sole discretion on the granting of citizenship and the other was that there were many persons who had not taken action under the existing legislation to regularize their status. Also, there were now a third group, those who had arrived in Myanmar subsequent to independence. Something had to be done to regularize the status of those persons who had arrived, or were descended from persons who had arrived, between 1824 and 1948 in order to distinguish them from the post-1948 entrants who came under different auspices, often illegally.

As for those to whom the 1948 laws applied, Ne Win said,

> If we could do something definite to define their rights, they will be happy. We on our part must be magnanimous. In reality too we cannot be but magnanimous. ... We are, in reality, not in a position to drive away those people who had come at different times for different reasons from different lands [before 1948]. We must have sympathy on those who had been here for such a long time and give them peace of mind. We have therefore designated them *eh-naingngan-tha* (Associate Citizens) in this law.

Associate citizens would not be allowed to be involved

> in matters involving the affairs of the country and the destiny of the State. This is not because we hate them. If we were to allow them to get into positions where they can decide the destiny of the State and if they were to betray us we would be in trouble.

He then explained, by way of example, the problem posed for the government by associate citizens who had siblings abroad. Through their networks of overseas relatives, they often became involved in smuggling to the detriment of the state. This could not be allowed. Those who had arrived and applied for citizenship under the 1948 legislation would be made *eh-naingngan-tha*. These persons will gradually disappear as they become assimilated into the Myanmar society with the passage of generations.

> This is the first time we are taking action to enable those who have been in our country since before independence to escape from a life of uncertainty about their nationality. If necessary qualifications are met, they can live in our county; if they live correctly and properly, their grandchildren will become full citizens. ... I would also like to tell our true citizens, the Burmese, that they should not treat such persons arrogantly, saying that they came from abroad or they are guests, but should realise that one day they will become one of us and all will be travelling in the same boat.[73]

What Ne Win was addressing was a problem left over from colonialism, the plural society that J.S. Furnivall described in 1948 and in which

Ne Win and his generation had grown up. In political terms, that society could "be distinguished by three characteristic features: the society as a whole comprise[d] separate racial sections; each section [was] an aggregate of individuals rather than a corporate or organic whole; and as individuals their social life [was] incomplete" (Furnivall 1956, p. 306). What Furnivall was highlighting was that the legacy of free immigration had created a polity without "the unitary society that western people take for granted" (Furnivall 1956, p. 307). Such a unitary society creates a national will, and makes shared sacrifice possible in times of crisis and shared wealth in times of plenty. This was the basis of a modern integrated society, a prerequisite for a democracy, which Myanmar lacked. Overcoming that condition was essential for national unity, and through the racially loaded language of the colonial period in which people discussed the question of national integration, Ne Win was proposing an end to the residues of the plural society as well as ensuring that post-1948 immigration was regulated.

The third session of the *Pyithu Hluttaw* convened for a four-day meeting and passed the Burma Citizenship Law, Law No. 4 of 1982 three days later. The legislation established three types of citizenship: citizen, associate citizen, and naturalized citizen. The first applies to all persons whose ancestors were residing in the country before 1824, that is national races, and the second, those who fit the category of persons who acquired citizenship under the 1948 legislation, whose families had arrived before 1948. All others would require naturalization. The legislation stated nothing about differential rights between categories of citizenship.[74] By the 1980s, many of the remaining persons of Indian descent had essentially integrated into Burmese society and their grip on the economy ended, especially in Yangon, which had been transformed from an Indian to a Burmese city (Tin Maung Maung Than 1993, pp. 585–623 and Khin Maung Kyi 1993, pp. 624–65). Despite its emotiveness, the new legislation concerned a very small proportion of the population, perhaps about 4 per cent, and proved to be very popular with the majority (Taylor 1993, pp. 666–82).

On 30 October, Ne Win was off once more to Pyay, where he met with officials from Pyay, Shwedaung and Paukkaung Townships, as well as Bago Divisional Party and government officials, and the officers of the 66th Light Infantry where he spent the night before returning to Yangon by plane the next morning. He spent over one-and-a-half hours discussing applications for

Party membership; cultivation and weather conditions; work to be carried out according to the supply of irrigation water; control and suppression of crop pests of all kinds; the production of bio-gas for widespread use as a fuel substitute in rural areas and about augmenting rural water supply through collective sinking of tube wells and their long term maintenance.[75]

A week later, he inspected once more the Sittang Pulp and Paper Mill, and then the Thaton Tyre and Rubber Factory, the Salt Industry at Htanbinchaung, and the Mupun No. 1 Pottery Plant before discussing Party membership matters with Mon State officials. He travelled for just three days, with a packed itinerary.[76] In December, he made an inspection tour of Kayah State and Taunggyi, where agricultural, road construction, and animal breeding and agriculture were the topics of investigation.[77]

In 1983, Ne Win varied the usual routine of Independence Day, Union Day, Gems, Jade and Pearl, and Armed Forces Day dinners and exhibitions, and visits to the graduating students of the Academy for the Development of National Groups with a two-day nostalgic trip to Dedaya at the Ayeyawady Delta. It was at Dedaya that he had served in the resistance and he went back to meet old resistance fighters still living in the area. At Kunpalaung village, Ne Win greeted resistance veterans and was received by the Southwest Command commander and local Party officials. From Kunpalaung, he went to Thegon and met the village council and former resistance members and then motored to Dedaye town. After Dedaye, he proceeded to Chaunggyi village. The next morning, joined by Industry (2) Minister Maung Cho, Ne Win went to the Ahmar Base Camp of the oil exploration activities in Bogale township of the Myanmar Oil Company. There he discussed the offshore operations of the corporation before returning to Yangon.[78]

These routines, tedious as they were, were what kept the top of the leadership of the Party and the state on their jobs and, in some ways, became the essence of governing. Ne Win presided over the BSPP Eighth Central Committee meeting at the President's Office on 10 and 11 March. Nine days later, he was off with a large entourage including ministers for a tour of the Northwest and Central commands. He visited the Paleik textile mill and mining projects at Kawlin and Kyaysintaung. Returning to Mandalay, he visited the Metallurgical Research and Development Centre at Ela and then the No. 2 Paper Mill at Yeni.[79] Ne Win's visits were not merely junkets. He left, as the newspapers repeatedly said, "necessary instructions and guidance", and expected to receive further information on the follow-up of his visits. Such a report-back meeting was held on 18 March when the Ministers for Agriculture and Forests and for Construction, as well as the Joint General Secretary of the Party, presented reports consequent to Ne Win's visits to Dedeya in February and Kayah State and Taunggyi in December the previous year.[80] Ne Win's great interest in many topics took him to an exhibition of cover designs for books, periodicals and calendars by the Ministry of Information at the Tatmadaw Hall in May.[81] He had other matters on his mind in May, however.

No matter what important matters of state concerned him, Ne Win still had time for other pursuits and interests. He eventually abandoned the zoology professor as a travelling companion and instead sometimes brought along professors of physics, mathematics and chemistry after some of his ministers gave him books on these subjects. With the professor of physics he often discussed the search for quarks, an elementary particle of matter. During one of his excursions to Mandalay, Ne Win was reminded of the legend that the Natmauk Ruby, part of the royal regalia which disappeared in 1885, might have been dropped in the Boke-ta-loke lake in the royal compound. He then ordered the draining of the lake in a vain search for the stone. On another occasion, he had a Buddha image tested because of rumours that it was made of a special alloy (Tin Aung n.p., pp. 7–10).

The penultimate major personnel crisis in Ne Win's long career occurred on 17 May 1983 when he forced Brigadier General Tin U, known as "Spectacles Tin U", to resign from the government. He was subsequently prosecuted for corruption. Also dismissed at the same time was the then Home Minister, Colonel Bo Ni, a protégé of Tin U. Since the purge of the BSPP in 1977, Tin U had been placing his own personnel in key posts in the government and his power was significant, sometimes referred to as Number One-and-a-Half, indicating that he was on the cusp of succeeding Ne Win as the most powerful man in the country.[82] Tin U was noted for a number of publicly lauded development projects, including the honey industry and the proliferation of quail's eggs in the market. In 1982, about the only thing for sale in the Inya Lake Hotel gift shop were jars of honey. Rumour had it that Ne Win suspected Tin U of attempting to engineer his removal as early as 1981 when Tin U was said to have proposed that General Kyaw Htin leave the army to assume the joint secretary post in the party, vacated when U Thaung Kyi died of a heart attack,[83] thus allowing his own man to take over the army. Instead, Ne Win made Tin U joint secretary.

Ne Win had apparently ordered Tin U to take action against Bo Ni who was believed to be protecting "Goldfish" Myint Thein, a gold dealer suspected of smuggling the metal out of the country, from prosecution. Bo Ni's wife was known to have travelled abroad with "Goldfish" and his wife. People eventually came to Ne Win and not only told him that Tin U was protecting Bo Ni and his misdeeds, but also about the victims of Tin U's own activities. This included attempting to remove the head of the national police force.[84] Several persons Tin U had had purged from the BSPP in 1977 were re-admitted after investigation following his removal.

According to one who overheard Ne Win's encounter with Tin U when he was dismissed, they met in a room on the upper floor of his Ady Road residence. Ne Win, shouting very loudly, was obviously furious. He demanded to know why Tin U allowed his son to accept expensive wedding gifts from businessmen. To paraphrase, he said something to the effect, "you put other people in jail very easily but you did not take action against your own people. You must also be involved in their corrupt activities as well. You are very partial. You did what you should not have done." When asked where the money came from for the wedding of Tin U's son, which Ne Win had refused to attend, his claim that it came from relatives was unacceptable. Tin U, who entered the house as the second most powerful man in the country, left facing arrest and prosecution for corruption.[85] In the style of those days, the departure of Tin U and Bo Ni was announced in small notices on the back page of the newspaper the next day.

Purged along with Tin U and Bo Ni were Major General Tin Sein, the Minister for Fisheries and Livestock, U Soe Thin, a member of the Council of People's Attorneys, his protégés in military intelligence, Brigadier Myo Aung, Colonel Kan Nyunt, and Colonel Thein Aung. In total, nine were imprisoned, Tin U for exceeding his authority and misusing public funds. The others were imprisoned for various derelictions of duty and corrupt activities. Subsequent to these arrests, there was a major reshuffle of party and government positions and a thorough reorganization of intelligence services in both the army and the civilian sides of the government (Tin Maung Maung Than 1984, pp. 118–19).

The Party Central Committee was obviously involved in the removal as such a key official as its Joint General Secretary. The ninth meeting of the Central Committee was held on 21 July, with Ne Win presiding, to confirm Tin U's resignation and that of six other members. In addition,

Bo Ni had been found to have violated party rules and was expelled from the Party on 29 June by the Party Discipline Committee. The Central Committee then voted in former General Tint Swe as a member of the Central Executive Committee and former General Sein Lwin as Tin U's successor as Joint General Secretary.[86] In keeping with procedure, the *Pyithu Hluttaw* was called into Special Session to receive a report from the Council of State on the group's removal and the appointment of Major General Min Gaung as Bo Ni's replacement as Minister for Home and Religious Affairs and U Sein Tun as Minister for Livestock and Fisheries.[87] Colonel Aung Koe was appointed head of military intelligence. The Tenth Meeting of the Central Committee convened on 29–30 September and deliberated, under Ne Win's auspices, on various reports, prior to the regular session of the Third *Pyithu Hluttaw* from 3 to 6 October. The *Hluttaw* was still meeting in temporary facilities in the Central Meeting Hall of the President's compound as a new *Hluttaw* building, under construction for some time, was not yet completed.[88]

The 1980s saw a marked increase in the ability of the army to push the various insurgent forces back to the borders with China, Laos and Thailand. This was reflected in the attempts in 1980 and 1981 by the Kachin Independence Army and the BCP to seek peace terms with the government, but the failure of those overtures demonstrated the confidence of the army that it could eventually defeat the insurgents. Every attempt by the insurgents in these years to penetrate army lines failed and, by 1983, the army was able to continue campaigning in the rainy season, demonstrating a capacity not previously developed. In particular, the Karen National Union (KNU) was feeling extreme military pressure, with the army capturing a strategic mountain peak overlooking key KNU bases on the border. The KNU would soon switch tactics and become involved in an international propaganda campaign against the government as their military capacity, relative to that of the army, waned.

Ne Win, now confident of his position with Tin U removed from office and the insurgencies confined mainly to the relatively remote border areas, continued his minute investigations of development projects. At the end of August 1983, he made a three-day inspection visit again to the North Nawin Dam project. Travelling by car to Pyay and then on to Shwedaung, he oversaw the construction of the textile mill there. The next day, his party proceeded on to Nyaungchedauk where the Heavy Industries Ministry had constructed a factory making engine parts. From there they went to Sinde once again to visit factories and technical schools under Lieutenant Colonel

Than Shwe. The next day it was visits to the North Nawin Dam and then the ceramic factory at Tharrawaddy before returning to Yangon by car.[89]

In early October, the South Korean President, Chun Doo-hwan, was on an official visit to Yangon for talks with President San Yu. As was routine on such occasions, Chun was to lay a wreath on 9 October 1983 at the tombs of Aung San and others assassinated on the cusp of Independence. However, North Korean agents had managed to slip past Myanmar intelligence and plant a bomb in the roof at the site. Fortunately for Chun, but not for 21 other persons, including 17 South Koreans, the bomb was set off prematurely, with horrifying consequences. Ne Win was at home at the time of the incident, but as soon as he learned of it, he was driven to the guest house where the South Korean President was staying. After a tense standoff between Ne Win and Chun's security teams, the two men met and Ne Win apologized profusely that the outrage had happened in his country.

Two days later, thanks to tips from local villagers in the delta, one of the North Korean terrorists was captured and killed but not before killing three Burmese soldiers. Two others were arrested the next day. One admitted his complicity in the crime and was given a life term of imprisonment while the other was convicted and hung.[90] The head of military intelligence, Colonel Aung Ko, in his new post for only a few months, was apparently on the golf course at the time of the bombing. Whatever the case, he and his organization had to accept responsibility for allowing the North Korean agents the opportunity of planting and detonating the bombs and as a result, were dismissed. After Aung Koe's dismissal, Ne Win sought a replacement and, on the recommendation of U Tint Swe, appointed Colonel Khin Nyunt to the post.

Before the round of dinners and exhibitions rolled around once more in the new year, Ne Win's interest in nostalgia led him to host a dinner for former university football players at the President's House on Ahlone Road. He was pictured chatting and joking with ten old time footballers, including U Saw Belly and U Hundley.[91] At the end of February 1984, he was back touring the Central Command region once more. Visits to Pyay, the site of his youth, were becoming routine. His touring programme was particularly light, compared to earlier ones, visiting only the rustic jaggery boiling works at Byugon village in Pyay township on the first day. The next day he was shown around the new No. 3 Chemical Fertilizer plant of the Petro-Chemical Industries Corporation at Kyawswa village and he returned to Yangon by plane early the next morning from Pyay Khittaya airfield.[92] He did not preside at the Eleventh Meeting of the BSPP Central Committee on 8–9 March, leaving it to General Secretary Aye Ko.[93]

Ne Win's apparently lax attention to detail in the first few months of 1984 was ended on 11 April with a visit to inspect the Universities' Computer Centre, which housed Myanmar's only computer at that time, a large machine manufactured in the United Kingdom by International Computers Limited (ICL).[94] The belief in Yangon then was that the only information that the computer processed was army pay and it was believed to be the last such computer in operation. His penchant for inspections continued on 24 April with a visit to a tin smelting and refining plant at Thanlyin, opposite Yangon. He arrived on the launch *Bandoola*, named after the allegedly irascible chief of the Burmese forces who occupied Manipur and Assam, and died at the hands of the British at the end of the First Anglo-Burmese War.[95] In between these two visits, Ne Win once more inspected the Kinda Dam project in Mandalay Division and the Defence Services Academy at Maymyo. He also visited the Maymyo Iron and Steel Mill and a special metal exploration camp in Patheingyi township. The Kinda hydro-electric project was also inspected as was the textile mill at Palaik.[96]

The June issue of *Forward* magazine, the official English language record of the Ne Win years, gave the flavour of the times in an editorial entitled, "Party Chairman's Inspection Tours". It said,

> During the last month, Chairman of the Burma Socialist Programme Party U Ne Win inspected several work places and gave the management and workers his views and instructions. ...
>
> During these inspection tours the Chairman met local Party and administration officials to hear their respective reports and to give his views and instructions. There instructions are being taken by the local leaders and officials as directives for improvement of their work.
>
> The working people of the country have been giving their best to the implementation of plans for socialist construction under the guidance of the Party and with the strength of national solidarity. It is ten years since the base year of 1973–74 when the Party laid down the 20 year long-term economic plan, and now after ten years the volume of productivity and service had more than doubled. That improvement is obviously due to the cooperative endeavour of the working people under the correct leadership of the Party.
>
> The Chairman's occasional tours of inspection contribute much to the socialist construction of the country, and the working people are gratified by such vision: they feel encouraged in their arduous work of nation-building.[97]

As one member of the Party used to say when reading the various achievements of the socialist economy in the 1980s, "could be, could not be, could be, could not be ... ."

Despite the scepticism of others, Ne Win continued his rounds of inspections, visiting the brass and copper works in Tampawaddy Ward of Mandalay on 11 May and the No. 1 Copper Project at Salingyi the next day.[98] With General Kyaw Htin and the Minister for Heavy Industry Maung Cho, Ne Win was off to West Germany again in mid-June. His frequent and very lengthy stays abroad were over and he returned on 9 August,[99] possibly having had a brief visit to London during the seven weeks he was abroad. A joint venture was established with Fritz-Werner to manufacture goods for export. It apparently never materialized before the end of the socialist era (Zollner 1994, p. 199). Ne Win also visited the Giesecke and Devrient Company which provided the presses and other equipment for the secure printing facility at Wazi that had been established in 1972 for the printing of Myanmar currency.[100] San Yu had returned from London just two weeks before Ne Win's departure for a medical check-up, almost certainly for his heart problem. Ne Win met him at the airport on his return,[101] and together the two inspected the new Yangon General hospital, constructed with Japanese aid, located at the corner of Bogyoke Aung San and Pyay Roads.[102] This historic site, where the old British-built Rangoon Prison had once stood, had become, after the socialist revolution, "St. John's *zei*" (market), next to St. John's Catholic convent. This unofficial market, opened only in the evening, was a site for the sale of smuggled electrical and other goods from Thailand, before the construction of the hospital.

Although receiving few foreign guests in the mid-1980s, Ne Win did receive former British Prime Minister Edward Heath, together with Foreign Minister Chit Hlaing, on 3 September 1984.[103] Ne Win, of course, had lunched with Heath several times in London previously. The following month, Ne Win was back inspecting the heavy industrial installations at Sinde and the copper works of the Defence Service Industries in the Central and Western Command areas, before returning to Yangon by plane.[104] On 11 October, he resumed chairing meetings of the Party central committee and on 28 October saw off President San Yu on an official goodwill visit to China with a party which included Deputy Minister of Defence and Vice Chief-of-Staff (Army), Lieutenant General Saw Maung.[105] Ne Win was off to the Western Command from 3 to 7 November where he made a detailed inspection of pearl cultivation works and other marine activities along the Rakhine coast in the vicinity of Thandwe.[106] On 20 November 1984, Ne Win, together with Dr Maung Maung and General Kyaw Htin, flew to New Delhi as the official guests of the Indian government. He was received at the airport by Prime Minister Rajiv Gandhi and, after paying respects at the site of the cremation of Indira Gandhi, assassinated three weeks earlier, called on the President of India, Shri Zail Singh. The visit was just an overnight stop, and he returned to Yangon in the early afternoon of 21 November. Having been hosted at a dinner by the President on the first day of the visit, the morning of the second was occupied by a meeting with the Prime Minister.[107]

From 6 to 9 October, Ne Win, accompanied by Dr Maung Maung, U Maung Cho and Kyaw Htin, toured the Western and Central Command areas.[108] The same party toured the Western Command area for four days in early November. The usual round of Party and *Hluttaw* meetings took place in between, with little to note and Ne Win rarely attending. In December, Ne Win, together with Kyaw Htin and other ministers, visited the Central and Northwest Command areas for four days. Once more, the Yeni paper mill, the Ela metallurgical research station, the Thayetkhon special metals project, the Maymyo iron and steel plant, and the Yinmabin copper project received the Chairman's attention.[109]

In addition to his usual round of dinners and inspections in the first three months of the year, Ne Win added a visit to the Myanmar Language Commission on 11 January 1985. There seemed to be no subject in which he was not interested in the most minute detail.[110] Nearly a quarter of a century after 1962, the same themes that Ne Win mentioned in his first orations continued to recur as government policy. For example, at about the same time as his visit to the Language Commission, his government was attacking so-called decadent culture which was to be combatted by promoting "traditional" or "national culture".[111]

On 21 January, Ne Win travelled to the most remote towns in northern Myanmar, Putao and Machanbaw, where Aung Gyi went on his internal exile in 1962 and 1963, meeting with Kachin army commanders and party officials as well as viewing local dances.[112] He returned to Kachin State again, spending two days at Myitkyina, at the end of March.[113] He left, with Kyaw Htin and Maung Cho, for another quick trip to West Germany on 23 January,[114] returning on 4 February 1985.[115] Soon after, he was off to inspect pearl cultivation again in Tanintharyi.[116] The Sedawgyi and Kinda multi-purpose dam projects got another inspection from Ne Win in mid-April.[117]

Though development projects, cultural preservation, and domestic affairs appeared to dominate Ne Win's mind and time during the mid-1980s, foreign relations was never far out of his ken. He renewed his relations with China when the President of China came to Yangon on an official visit as a guest of President San Yu. Ne Win and Li Xiannian met on two occasions on 5 and 10 March. The Myanmar media underscored that President Li was meeting Ne Win in his capacity as Chairman of the Burma Socialist Programme Party, leaving the impression that the Chinese state, at least, recognized the legitimacy of the ruling Party and its Chairman by inviting him for an official visit.[118] Soon after Li's departure, Ne Win presided over the Thirteenth Meeting of the BSPP Central Committee.[119]

Ne Win took up the invitation which was accepted by President San Yu on 4 May 1985 when he flew to China as the guest of Deng Xiaoping in his capacity as Chairman of the Central Advisory Commission of the Communist Party of China and Chairman of the Military Commission of the State Council of the People's Republic of China. This, his twelfth and last, visit to China, lasted five days. Included in his party were Daw Ni Ni Myint, his daughter Daw Sanda Win, and son-in-law, U Aye Zaw Win. He met a number of other senior Chinese figures, in addition to Deng, including State Councillor Ji Pengfei, Premier Zhao Ziyang, the Chairman of the National People's Congress Standing Committee, Peng Zhen, and Communist Party of China General Secretary, Hu Yaobang.[120] The meeting with Hu would have confirmed to Ne Win and his colleagues that China had now accepted the Burma Socialist Programme Party as the sole legitimate party in Myanmar and any residual support for the Burma Communist Party had now ended, despite allowing aged BCP leaders to live in China.

This was confirmed in Ne Win's talks with Deng. When Ne Win noted that there were significant battles being fought between the Burma Communist Party and the Myanmar army at that time and inquired on the extent of the Chinese assistance, Deng indicated that there was none. He did, however, state that some BCP leaders were receiving medical treatment in China and others had settled down there with their families. Assistance, as appropriate, would continue to be given to them. Subsequently, relations with China improved even more markedly.[121] CCP General Secretary Hu stated that in terms of relations with Communist parties in other countries, China would not impose its will. As summed up by a senior Myanmar diplomat, the Chinese position was that while China could not disavow parties friendly to it, it would not be actively involved with them either. "How governments deal with their internal Communist parties is their own concern and problem" (Than Han 1986, p. 17).

If relations with one of Myanmar's potentially troublesome neighbours were then in an obviously tranquil phase, relations with another remained fraught. In November 1985, the Foreign Minister, Admiral Chit Hlaing, took up the responsibility of negotiating the marine borders of Myanmar with India and Bangladesh with his counterparts. According to him, negotiations with India were quite easy and the two sides agreed after advancing reasonable proposals. However, negotiations with Bangladesh were quite difficult because both Chit Hlaing and his Bangladeshi counterpart put forward palpably unreasonable claims. When Chit Hlaing was asked by Ne Win to explain the failure of the negotiations with Bangladesh, he replied that the unreasonable demands were instructions from Prime Minister U Maung Maung Kha. Ne Win then passed him a file which showed that the Prime Minister had instructed him in error. Maung Maung Kha was then summoned and given a vigorous scolding by Ne Win. According to the Admiral, Ne Win was "very short tempered. He threw things at people."[122]

Despite claims by the Planning and Finance Minister and others that the economy was growing at 6.6 per cent a year and that the planned targets had nearly been achieved in the 1984–85 economic plan, problems clearly existed in terms of foreign exchange, as both imports and exports were down on the previous year.[123] Five days after his return from his successful China trip, Ne Win was inspecting the operation of the Union Bank of Burma, the central bank for Myanmar.[124] The desire to examine the minutiae of government services never seemed to tire. He was at the General Post Office in the middle of August for a report on postal activities.[125] His visit to the bank may have once more stimulated his ulcers. Whatever the case, with his usual overseas travelling companions Kyaw Htin and Maung Cho, he and Daw Ni Ni Myint departed on 7 June. They apparently visited West Germany, France, and Switzerland for a health check-up.[126] In Switzerland, he visited the Pilatus Company from which the Myanmar air force bought PC-6 and other short take-off and landing airplanes designed for search and rescue missions in remote areas.[127] The Burma air force also used them for pilot training and, when armed, used them in combat (Selth 2002, pp. 206–7). They returned on 15 July,[128] two weeks before the convening of the Fifth BSPP Party Congress which re-elected Ne Win for another term as Party chairman.

The Party Congress, held at the Central Institute of Political Science, commenced on 2 August with an address by Ne Win. In his speech, he first discussed the construction of the temporary facilities for the Congress, noting the necessity to build in harmony with Myanmar's environment and traditions, as well as to prevent waste and overconsumption. The other main point of his remarks was that the election of the new Central Committee should give due consideration to keeping some experienced members while bringing on some new persons so that the party had both the advantages of experience as well as new ideas. In perhaps a prescient comment, Ne Win reiterated that if there was ever a time when the interests of the party and the state differed, the interests of the state must come first.[129] Nothing was said or done at the Congress that presaged the change which was coming in the Party's direction. Ne Win's remarks were remarkably sanguine and without much significance. There was no offer to step down as chairman, unlike four years earlier. Nonetheless, there was a small innovation with the election of U San Yu as Vice-Chairman of the Party.

Memories of Thailand, a country he had visited frequently and of which he knew many of the key leaders, would have been stirred when Ne Win met with the visiting Commander of the Royal Thai Army, General Arthit Kamlangek.[130] Nostalgia would also have been on the menu when Ne Win met the visiting former President of the United States, Richard Nixon, who arrived in Yangon on 15 September and was hosted at a dinner by Ne Win.[131] Health concerns were never far away for Ne Win and he must have been considering options if President San Yu were to pass away. His silent partner for many years departed for both Japan and the United Kingdom on 9 November for medical treatment,[132] and did not return until 21 January 1986.[133]

In October 1985, elections for the Fourth *Pyithu Hluttaw* commenced and Ne Win voted on the first day of the balloting on 6 October. The electoral process for the *Pyithu Hluttaw* and lesser bodies continued until 20 October because of security problems in some areas. Fifty-five per cent of the electorate voted for the 489 members of the *Pyithu Hluttaw*, 976 members of the 14 state and divisional people's councils, 22,850 members of the township councils, and 166,763 ward and village tract people's councils. This elaborate process of one-party democracy was overseen and guided by the 2.3 million members of the BSPP which took its guidance in turn from the Central Committee and its Chairman, Ne Win. When the new *Pyithu Hluttaw* was seated in November, it looked much like the old. Whether the relatively low voter turn-out for a one-party state election concerned

Ne Win or his colleagues is unknown, but it might have suggested to them that after four elections and a lacklustre economic performance, the Party was failing to connect with the voters.

In the meantime, Ne Win once more visited various institutions, including the computer centre at the university in Yangon and that of the Myanma Oil Company. Toward the middle of the month, from the Eastern and Northeast Command areas, he toured the Shan State, holding talks with senior military personnel at Lashio and Kentung on the campaign against the ongoing Communist and Shan insurgencies, as well as visiting development projects and discussing Party affairs.[134] Ne Win showed no sign of diminishing interest in managing Myanmar in all aspects. At the end of the month, he was inspecting factories in the Northwest Command area.[135] Three days later, he was chairing a meeting of the Party Central Committee and for the next three days, he observed, apparently for the first time since he stood down as President, the proceedings of the first session of the Fourth *Pyithu Hluttaw*, now meeting in the new *Pyithu Hluttaw* building on Pyay Road opposite the Shwe Dagon and the old British army parade ground, presently the People's Park.[136] From that meeting, a new Council of State and the other central organs of state power were formed, along with a nineteen-member cabinet with twenty-eight deputy ministers. There were few new names in the top positions. No one could claim that Ne Win did not know what was going on half-way through his 75th year.

Ne Win had launched the revolution in 1962 in the hope that economic development and equality across the country would undermine, and eventually end, the insurgencies which had plagued the country since independence. However, by 1985, the level of insurgency remained high, though in the following three years it began to taper off as the army launched enhanced campaigns, particularly against the smuggling gangs along the Thai border, and China's support for the Communists in the north was terminated. However, as late as the 1984–85 fiscal year, the army fought 13 major battles and 1,879 minor battles in the Eastern and Southeastern Command areas along the Thai border. In the Northern and Northeast Command areas, the army fought 9 major and 1,910 minor skirmishes against largely Kachin Independence Army and BCP forces.[137]

Problems in the economy, after what had appeared to be a halcyon period in the late 1970s and early 1980s, were now taxing the government's capabilities. Inflation had returned as a consequence of shortages in the market and food prices were threatening political stability, especially in the cities. Though the Asian Development Bank (ADB) estimated inflation that year at less than 10 per cent, in key commodities such as rice and cooking oil, the increases were greater.[138] In a dramatic move on 10 November 1985, the government demonetized the kyat for a second time since the coming to power of the Revolutionary Council. Kyat notes valued at 25, 50 and 100 were withdrawn in an effort to undermine smugglers' profits and reduce the money supply available since this was the only way possible for an economy with no effective banking system. New notes were issued, in some cases, in exchange for a small amount of old notes, in the denominations of 15, 35 and 75 kyat.[139] The move had little effect on inflation, which the government reported to be 15 per cent the following year, while the Asian Development Bank claimed it was 22 per cent.[140] An emergency session of the *Pyithu Hluttaw* was called on 23 December 1985 to ratify the decision and the Party General Secretary, U Aye Ko, addressed a meeting of leading officials to impress upon them the need to increase production in the state and cooperative sectors of the economy.[141] Again, no new ideas were advanced and any idea of reform was left unsaid. The socialist economy was to be continued despite the unfavourable international climate. The Party also responded to the growing economic problems by calling a meeting of senior members at the Party Central Committee headquarters to discuss reducing the prices of necessities. Ne Win did not attend and, again, no new ideas were advanced, just exhortations to try harder to increase production through the cooperatives and the state-owned enterprises.[142]

Having been in power for a quarter of a century by 1986, Ne Win was seen as a senior figure, despite Myanmar's relative isolation and lack of integration into world trade networks. Though holding no formal government post, when other heads of government came to Myanmar, they wanted to meet with him. For example, Singapore's Prime Minister, Lee Kuan Yew, together with a delegation of senior Singapore ministers and officials, called on Ne Win at his home on Ady Road for nearly two hours on 16 January 1986.[143] Lee found Ne Win, "despite Burma's 20 years of economic stagnation, ... as distrustful of foreign powers as ever. He spoke of being locked in a 'battle of wits' against elements outside Burma who wanted to make as much as they could at the expense of his country." Lee found the lack of development deplorable and when he subsequently tried to convince Prime Minister Maung Maung Kha to develop the tourism industry, he got no response (Lee 2000, pp. 361–62). Later in the year, Ne Win also received the First Deputy Prime Minister of Singapore, Goh Chok Tong.[144] On 24 February, he met with the Deputy Prime Minister and Minister for Foreign Affairs of Thailand, Air Chief Marshall Siddhi Savetsila. The same applied to the few Europeans who visited, the most prominent being the President of the Federal Republic of Germany who, while on a state visit as the guest of President San Yu, met with Ne Win for more than an hour at the state guest house.[145]

In addition to the usual official dinners and exhibitions, Ne Win attended a dinner as Party Chairman on 21 February 1986. Hosted by U Aye Ko as Vice-President while San Yu was abroad, the dinner was for musicians, dancers and singers of both traditional and modern Myanmar music. It was a gala event to which members, and their wives, of all the leading organizations of the Party, including youth, motion picture, theatrical, and literary organizing committees, and the Army, as well as the government, were invited. The dinner was preceded by a dance performance by the Pyidaungsu Padetha (Plentiful Union) dance troupe.[146]

On 5 March 1986, Ne Win, accompanied by San Yu, visited the Maha Wizaya Zedi, the pagoda he had proposed in 1980 to mark the purification and unification of the Sangha after the First Congregation of All Orders or sects. While at the pagoda, the architect, U Ngwe Hlaing, explained its construction and Ne Win and his party went round examining the result, paying particular attention to the Gandakuti Cave inside the stupa.[147] The dome of the cave has the image of the stars as they were seen on the day the pagoda was consecrated in 1980. The next day, Ne Win was back presiding over a two-day meeting of the fourth meeting of the BSPP Central Committee, the ritual which preceded the second session of the Fourth *Pyithu Hluttaw* later in the month.[148]

In addition to pagoda construction, irrigation was also on Ne Win's mind in March. He visited the Sedawgyi and Kinda multi-purpose dam projects once more as well as the Kobinchaung dam project and the Mahananda lake renovation project in Shwebo township. At each stop a leading irrigation department official, such as U Saw Vawter Loo, made a presentation and Ne Win gave advice and guidance. The trip, by plane, car and helicopter, lasted for three days from 16 to 19 March.[149] Two days later, Ne Win was welcoming to his home Princess Sirindhorn of Thailand who was visiting Myanmar for ten days. On the first day of her visit, Ne Win hosted a reception and dinner in her honour. After her return from touring the country, he hosted a second dinner for her on the 29th and saw her off at the airport on the 31st.[150] Ne Win took particular care over the itinerary of her visit. On the day she visited the Shwe Dagon Pagoda and the National Museum, then in a colonial era building on lower Pansodan, she requested to visit the Pagan Bookshop on 37th Street. Ne Win forbade the visit on the grounds that the 37th Street was too dirty and decrepit for the Royal Princess to see.[151]

After a particularly busy month of March for the 76-year-old Ne Win, he was off again for a medical check-up in London on 2 April 1986, this time, apparently, at the Cromwell Hospital. He was accompanied only by Deputy Prime Minister and Minister for Defence Kyaw Htin and a member of the Council of People's Attorneys, U Lay Maung, as well as his wife, Daw Ni Ni Myint.[152] He returned two months later on 29 May.[153] His personal frugality and regard for public expenditure was legendary, though at times, particularly in terms of his foreign travel, he could be extravagant. In the mid-1980s, Thura U Tun Tin, the Deputy Prime Minister and Minister for Finance and Planning, insisted that he travel to Europe in a specially chartered plane, rather than in a normal commercial flight as previously. When learning that delegates to a party congress were eating butterfish, Ne Win said, "those mother fuckers are wasting the public money."[154] He was known for often eating only vegetables, which he was said to be able to cook well.

Ne Win knew that time was passing and his old comrades were dying around him. When U Kyaw Nyein died of cancer on 26 June 1986,[155] he went to his home to pay his respects. Also present were U Nu and U Ba Swe, amongst others. Before Ne Win entered the room which contained the coffin, Military Intelligence officers asked everyone to leave. Nu then left for his residence and Ba Swe and others went to a separate room, while Ne Win gave his condolences to the family.[156]

Despite, or perhaps because of, Ne Win's attention to detail, and his reliance on a relatively small circle of intimates with whom he had worked for years, moving projects forward, political, economic, or infrastructural, took a long time in socialist Burma. Four years after the third meeting of the War Veterans Central Organising Body in 1982, the organization's first conference was held in the Saya San Hall at the Kyaikkasan Grounds. Ne Win, as Patron, spoke on the first day of the two-day meeting on 30 July 1986. In his relatively brief remarks, he made three main points. The first point was the fine traditions of the army and the need to maintain those traditions and pass them on to future generations. The second point was that the organization should first have regard to *cettana* (positive volition), second, proficiency, and third, goodwill.

His third point was with reference to an article in the most recent July issue of *Sitpyan* (literally, War Returnee, or Veteran) magazine. That article had described Ne Win as the father of the army. He wished to correct that article by insisting that Bogyoke Aung San was the true father of the army and that in the early days of the BIA and BDA, Ne Win was, along with others, looking after the young in the army. Aung San was the leader. After Aung San's death, Ne Win became the leader, so he should be considered the second, or foster, father of the army. He also mentioned that when he took over the leadership of the army during the troubled years of 1947–49, he integrated the soldiers and military police who had previously served the British into the army. He stressed that it was important to remember that those who had served the British also served the independent army of Myanmar as loyal soldiers.[157]

The Party Central Committee held its fifth meeting from 9 to 10 October prior to the meeting of the *Pyithu Hluttaw* on 13 October. On the first day of the *Hluttaw*, Ne Win inspected a display of gold and silver artefacts found in Shwedaung township earlier in the year.[158] The Council of Ministers report once more made note of the twin problems of rising consumer prices and declining export earnings which were putting a severe strain on the ability to import necessary consumer goods as well as spare parts and industrial raw materials. However, no new plans were advanced on how to tackle these problems and the people were merely exhorted once more to consume frugally and work harder.[159] No parallels or lessons were drawn from other socialist economies, such as that of China, which since Deng Xiao-ping's resurrection, had abandoned autarky and austerity for experiments in economic reform and opening up to foreign investment, as well as agricultural reform, or Vietnam which in the same year announced its new policy of *Doi Moi* or Renovation to a more market-oriented economy.

Meanwhile, Ne Win was addressing the Myanmar Language Commission for the second time in two years, where he received reports on the compilation of books on Myanmar orthography, grammar, dictionaries, including of mathematical terms, and a Myanmar-English dictionary. He then provided detailed instructions to the effect:

> ... that just as it was required to have rules of pronunciation and grammar to ensure a correct understanding of what one meant in speaking to one another, so also it was necessary to precisely follow grammar rules in writing; if errors slipped into the texts of books,

they could cause controversy for coming generations; in prescribing the spellings of words, it must be decided through deliberation with reason; in writing words relating to a specific field of study, it was necessary to be conversant in that field of study; in writing an account of work done on the dictionary, it was necessary to mention not only those who carried it out at present, but also those who had done so earlier; and as members of the Language Commission present at the meeting were ones close to the literary world and writers, [they should] convey to them an exhortation for themselves to know well the rules of written language and to adhere to them in their literary works.[160]

This was micro-management to a degree. The following month he took members of the Language Commission, along with a number of senior ministers and academics, to read the Maha Ledi stone inscriptions at a repository of writings by the Maha Ledi Sayadaw in Monywa. After discovering that the inscriptions were unsuitable to be used as a guide to contemporary spelling (Tin Aung n.p., p. 16), Ne Win then carried out the usual round of touring the mining and metallurgy projects in the Northwest Command from 14 to 18 November. The next day, he inspected the 24th Gems, Jade and Pearl Emporium, brought forward from its usual February date.[161] From 20 to 25 December, in his last full year as Party chairman and leader of Myanmar, Ne Win undertook an intense level of activity of touring the Northeast and Northwest commands. He met with, seriatim, Party and People's Council functionaries from 22 townships around Lashio, and Shan State Party officials. He then visited the army hospital at Lashio, army fish-breeding ponds and hot springs recreation grounds, private silver and brass works in Sagaing, the Seinban Cooperative society foundry manufacturing spare parts, the Tampawaddy brass Buddha moulders at Sutaungpyi Pagoda at the Mandalay Palace grounds, and supervised the cleaning of the palace moat.[162] The visit to Lashio and the military units in the area may have been due to some very severe fighting which took place in early January when the army retook Pangsai (Kyuhkok) from the Communists, with the loss of 175 government troops and 591 enemy in 18 separate engagements.[163]

At some point, also in 1986, Ne Win and an entourage, including academics, toured industrial development projects on the west bank of the Ayeyawady River, as he often did. Many of these developments were placed in uneconomic locations because the priority in their development was either national security or the economic development of the regions. On this tour, amongst the facilities examined, was the glass factory built at

Pathein. Pathein had no market for the factory's production, having lost its utility as a teak crate export centre. As a consequence, glass manufactured at the plant was crushed to be used as raw materials in order to keep the operation functioning.[164] Most state-owned economic enterprises, as such institutions were known, unsurprisingly, were loss-making.

President San Yu travelled abroad once more for medical attention in January. Seen off by Ne Win, he had heart surgery in Texas on 18 January 1987,[165] and returned to Yangon on 7 February.[166] Since Deng Xiaoping's visit to the United States in early 1979, and especially after Ne Win's triumphant visit to Beijing in 1985, relations with both the United States and China had been unusually warm. China had received a number of high-level ministerial visitors and entertained them lavishly. The United States government was quite pleased with the government of Myanmar's anti-drug efforts, known as "Operation Moe Hein", which had grown from year to year. High level United States officials, such as the Attorney General, exchanged views with Myanmar officials[167] and, from 1980 onwards, middle level officers from the army were sent for training in the United States (Riley and Balaram 2012). Especially in regard to anti-narcotics efforts, "Washington wished some of our other partners like Mexico, Thailand and Colombia would" would have been as cooperative.[168]

However, amongst many less-well-informed foreign observers, many fantasies existed in the late 1980s. Perhaps Ne Win's micro-management style encouraged these fantasies, with the problems of the economy becoming more apparent. He was even believed to have changed time and made the sun to stand still! As the chief consular officer of the American embassy in Yangon from 1986 to 1988 explained: "People used to ask 'What's the time difference between Bangkok and Rangoon'? The joke was 50 years. In fact, it was 30 minutes, because the Ne Win regime had decreed that time difference as one more way to separate Burma from its neighbours."[169] The Indian Empire and its railways no longer existed, even in memory. To those who saw Ne Win as the all powerful, he ruled his nation as if it had no history!

One of the accusations, or excuses, which was sometimes made of Ne Win's behaviour in regard to the economy was that he was ill informed and mislead. While it may be true that his ministers and their reports to him were intentionally misleading, he was said to have his own sources of information on market conditions and prices. He talked to his relatives and other persons in the party and the army at lower ranks to find out what was going on. As he thought many of his ministers were incompetent, he took a close look at matters which came his way. At the same time, he gave his ministers great latitude to get on with their responsibilities and often complained that they would not leave him alone. They kept pestering him for decisions so much "that his pubic hair had turned grey"![170]

Though foreign dignitaries no longer called on Yangon as frequently as they did during the height of the Cold War, they still came in small numbers, such as Romanian President Nicolae Ceausescu and his wife, Elena. Ne Win first met them when he visited Bucharest in June 1966. The couple were executed by firing squad with the downfall of the Communist regime in Romania on 25 December 1989, less than two years after meeting Ne Win at the state guest house in Yangon.[171] Also in April, Ne Win once more chaired a meeting of the Party Central Committee prior to a meeting of the *Pyithu Hluttaw*. Then he, together with Daw Ni Ni Myint, General Kyaw Htin, Industry Minister (2) Maung Cho, and some of his family members, departed for Texas and Oklahoma in the United States.[172] They also visited France and West Germany on this trip, in particular visiting the Pavilion of Myanmar arts and handicrafts near the Fritz-Werner headquarters in Wiesbaden. There were also displays of items Myanmar had for export. The visit to Paris was cut short, however, apparently as a result of confusion over the Ne Win party's reception by the French hosts from the Schlumberger company, and they spent only one night there.[173]

As with many of his trips, this trip also combined business with pleasure. United States President Ronald Regan phoned Ne Win to welcome him on his arrival in the United States. Ne Win brought along Maung Cho in order to discuss the purchase of second-hand drilling and other technology with American oil companies to boost oil and gas production in Myanmar.[174] Ne Win was also said to have attempted to patch up a marital dispute of an American couple who were old friends of his, but the husband refused to allow him into the house.[175] In all, he was in the United States for over six weeks, from 3 April until his return on 20 May.[176] Soon after, Ne Win saw off and welcomed back President San Yu who made a state visit to South Korea, the highest level exchange between the two countries since the bombing of Korean ministers in 1983.

The failure of the government to respond to the growing economic malaise of the country finally drove Ne Win to act. Increasing domestic prices, growing unemployment in urban areas, and a serious balance of payments crisis had all to be addressed. Business as usual and exhortations to the masses alone could not be tolerated. However, neither a way forward nor a new path was laid down by the Party Chairman. Rather, Ne Win called for a unique meeting of the BSPP Central Executive Committee, the Council of State, and the Central Organs of State Power party fractions (units) on 10 August.

In his opening speech, Ne Win indicated that the meeting had been called to receive preliminary reports on the conditions of the country and the success of the socialist revolution. Reviewing the work of the Revolutionary Council briefly and then the BSPP government, he noted that there were successes as well as failures but he felt that "innovative intellectual inputs designed to improve and further develop contemporary achievements" were required and should be submitted by the time of the next meeting of the Central Committee. Drawing on his interest in medicine, he said that they could "begin looking for the right medicine and the right kind of treatment only when we are able to pin-point the disease". Noting that things had changed since 1962 or even 1974, Ne Win called on the members of the various bodies to think of ways to "catch up". However, catch up with what was unclear; indeed, the nature of the reports and proposals he sought was unclear, although he did suggest that changes in the constitution might be in order.[177] Brief comments from the party fractions, the Council of State, the Council of Ministers, the Council of People's Justices, the Council of People's Attorneys, and the Council of People's Inspectors were then made on a report from the Party General Secretary, U Aye Ko.[178]

Twelve days later on 22 August, a second smaller meeting of members of the Party Central Executive Committee, and Council of State and central organs was called in which Ne Win gave more specific and extensive instructions. The reports he wanted should differentiate between current work and long-term proposals for work and reforms in social, economic as well as political affairs.[179]

Ne Win then set off four days later for another three-day inspection tour of the Central Command area. Wearing garments and a hat which appeared to have been bought on his Texas trip, he visited various cooperative shops in Pyay, looking not only at the foodstuffs on sale but also checking the accounts. On the second day, he inspected the township of his birth, Paukkaung, and examined a site where antiques had been recovered near Ye-U village in Chaungkaung village tract. He returned to Yangon the next day.[180]

The government, having assured the public that there would be no further demonetization following Ne Win's two meetings on the economic situation, suddenly ordered a third demonetization on 5 September 1987. This time no compensation was given to those holding 25, 35 and 75 kyat notes. When the new currency was issued in 45 and 90 kyat denomination, this was said to have been a sign of Ne Win's superstitious attachment to the number 9. Why he chose 9 in 1987 and not in 1985, tea shop gossip did not suggest. Whatever the case, it was a severe blow to the government, an act of folly that a leader with a surer grip on the realities around him would not have made. University students were the first to organize protests. This led to the closure of higher education institutions and the sending of the students back to their homes, thus ensuring their anger would be spread more widely across the country. Inflation, control of the money supply (monetarism in Thatcherite terms), and a rumour that the KNU was going to flood the country with counterfeit notes were all advanced to justify an act which, in the public mind, could have no justification in reality.

While Ne Win was touring the Kyunchaung Fertilizer plant and the Kinda multi-purpose dam once more in late September and the Gems Emporium on 28 October,[181] worries about the economy must have weighted heavily on his mind. He was aware of the changes going on around Myanmar in the world economy but could not make up his mind as to what should be done in Myanmar. Economic nationalism, or socialism, together with political independence, were the goals of the revolution Aung San had led and this ideal was never far from Ne Win's thoughts. He returned to that theme in a speech given on the concluding day of the BSPP Seventh Central Committee meeting on 9 October 1987:

> Burma regained political independence on 4 January 1948. Although Burma became politically independent, the economy of the country was not in the hands of the Burmese. The wholesale business and financial business were all in hands of foreigners. The Burmese had only a little share in retail business. An independent nation may be politically independent but its independence is not complete if we cannot decide for ourselves economic matters and if we cannot control it ourselves. If its economy is not strong, there is the danger of being controlled and manipulated by others as freely as they like. When did we remove this danger? It was at the advent of the Revolutionary Council in 1962.

Ne Win then recounted the problems the post-colonial government and the Revolutionary Council faced in taking advice from foreigners. In particular, he related how the government had lost foreign exchange when a foreign dealer was told to sell British pounds when sterling was about to decline in value, but instead, bought more, thus losing money for the country when the pound was devalued in 1967 (Bo Thanmani 1991). He also told of bogus foreign companies that shipped bricks into the country, rather than the goods ordered. During the 1950s, though the government controlled the foreigners and gave free rein to the Burmese, "... our people were rather lazy, and they also had no experience and so they only did what others told them to do."

From Ne Win's perspective, the problem of the economy was still closely related to integration. He discussed how citizens, including guest citizens, whose children and grandchildren would become in time full citizens, were now given free rein in the economy. He said, with regards to the immigrants and their descendants:

> What I would like to say to such persons with emphasis is that they have come to our country, live here, and earn their living here and so, they should make up their minds once and for all to live together with us in weal and woe and through thick and thin. They are the ones who do business most. Take what they should get and enjoy the rights they should enjoy, but if they do business only serving their selfish ends too much, there will be "problems".

He then urged business people to ensure that they paid fair prices for the goods and services they bought from the peasants and workers, and not exploit them or be excessively greedy. The same applied to Burmese as well, and he extolled them to improve their business skills. "However, if anybody — be he a bonafide citizen or be a guest citizen — does business with undue greed to make oneself rich, that person is bound to meet with danger some day."

So in the short term, while the socialist planned projects would proceed, there would be some liberalization of the economy but Ne Win was not specific as to how much, but the threat to those who exploited the opportunities provided was there, though the consequences were ambiguous. As to the long term, he briefly examined the condition of the world's capitalist economies and leftist or socialist economies. Both were facing problems, so some middle way must be found.

> What it is like is that the disease has been discovered, but the medicine has not yet been found and nobody knows what medicine to give. We are included in this category. Since we are included, how shall we

change? Is it necessary for us to change the principles? Last month
we decontrolled rice because it is the most important for us. This is
the beginning of the change. We shall have to take into consideration
to what extent we should change and how, on the basis of our own
experiences as well as the experiences from the world. We must lay
down new principles after taking all these considerations. With this
I conclude.[182]

Ne Win's reference to the decontrol of rice was a reference to the fact
that the government had abandoned its monopoly on the rice trade and
trade in other basic commodities. The result was a sudden upsurge in
prices, leading the government to re-impose controls soon after. This not
only inhibited incentives for production but was also another blow to
government credibility.

While the economy was threatening to collapse and no solution to
its ills were yet discovered, another long-standing problem faced by the
government was being dealt with firmly by the army. From May onward
through 1987, the army had been mounting major campaigns against the
troops of the Burma Communist Party, the Kachin Independence Army
and the Karen National Union, undermining the economies of these anti-
government forces but also squeezing the black market. As the army got
a firmer and firmer grip, especially along the border with Thailand, the
ability of the smugglers to supply consumer goods in the black market,
particularly in Yangon, was being squeezed, thus contributing to price
inflation.[183] Public humiliation added to the actual economic distress when
Burma, along with Chad, Afghanistan, Ethiopia, Bangladesh, and Haiti, was
declared a least developed nation (LDC) by the United Nations. Achieving
LDC status was supposed to be a means of achieving debt relief, but in
Myanmar's case, it merely brought debt default in the next few years when
Ne Win's successors stopped payment on Myanmar's sovereign debt after
foreign assistance was terminated.

On 20 November, the Princess Royal, daughter of Queen Elizabeth
II, arrived in Yangon and Ne Win received her at the state guest house.
However, it was left to San Yu, Maung Maung Kha and other ministers
to show her around the country on her four-day visit, though Ne Win
did personally bid her farewell at the Yangon airport VIP lounge on
23 November.[184] Though the Myanmar press did not report the news,
Princess Anne was visiting the country in her capacity as President of the
Save the Children Fund (UK), which provided support for poor children
in developing countries. Sometime earlier in 1986 or 1987, unannounced,

perhaps for fear of the impression it gave of weakening Myanmar's self-reliant health and educational systems, permission was given for a Chin doctor in Kalemyo to open a health clinic supported by a German Christian charitable group. Other cracks in the decisions made after 1962 were emerging.

Ne Win went to Bangkok in early December to present a gift to King Bhumipol Adulyadej on his sixtieth birthday. On 26 November, in the presence of Ne Win and other senior state officials, the chairman of the State Sangha Nayaka Committee and fifteen other senior monks, consecrated a jade Buddha which Ne Win took to Bangkok the next day to present to the King. He was received and sent off at the airport in Bangkok by Princess Sirindhorn on the same day.[185] Many believed that "U Ne Win just followed advice of his astrologers, as some predicted that 1988 would be a bad year and prospect of political conflicts loomed large. The presentation of the Jade Buddha was to ward off the imminent downfall of the regime" (Aye 2009, p. 154). This groundless rumour perhaps reflected the cynicism that surrounded Ne Win as he ended his 25th year of rule. However, it ignored his increasingly close identity with the Sangha and Buddhist practices more generally, as well as Ne Win's acquaintance with the Thai royal family going back over four decades. On 15 December, Ne Win and San Yu met with visiting Indian Prime Minister Rajiv Gandhi who presented the text of a work by the famous Konbaung dynasty general, Maha Bandoola, which had been placed in a museum in India by the British.[186]

As Myanmar entered its last year of BSPP rule, despite the economic chaos and the humiliation of being declared a Least Developed Country, life for Ne Win was as per normal, with public dinners for Independence Day and a tour from Mandalay to the Northwest Command region from 23 to 27 January 1988 to inspect industrial, indigenous medical, agricultural and other projects and industries, including the metallurgical facilities at Ela.[187] Then, it was Union Day dinner and an inspection once more of indigenous medicine research in Yangon on 22 February. The Prime Minister of Malaysia, Dr Mahathir bin Mohamad, was received by Ne Win three days later and Ne Win bid farewell to him on the 28th.[188] On 29 February, Ne Win met the visiting Crown Prince of Thailand. Then it was dinner with the graduates of the Academy for the Development of National Groups on 1 March and another dinner for the Thai Crown Prince on 3 March before bidding him farewell on the 5th. Armed Forces Day exhibition and dinner were duly attended on 25 and 27 March respectively. In between dinners and visitors, Ne Win had time for another quick, less than a day, tour of the Central Command region, visiting a pagoda and the South Nawin dam project.[189] These routines were about to end.

Notes

1. Letter, C.L. Booth to A.M. Simons, 4 May 1978, FCO15/2324.
2. "First and Third Impressions of Burma", by C.L. Booth, 31 May 1978, FCO15/2320.
3. Letter, C.L. Booth to A.M. Simons, 29 June 1978, FCO15/2321.
4. "Is there anything to be said for Ne Win's Burma?", 13 July 1978, FCO15/2318.
5. "First and Third Impressions of Burma", by C.L. Booth, 31 May 1978, FCO15/2320.
6. Letter, C.L. Booth to B. Smith, 22 September 1978, FCO15/2318.
7. "Has Britain a Stake in Burma?", by C.L. Booth, 29 November 1978, FCO15/2322.
8. Letter, R.G. Farrer to B. Smith, 20 October 1978, FCO15/2325.
9. Ibid.
10. Letter, C.L. Booth to B. Smith, 30 November 1978, FCO15/2321.
11. *Far Eastern Economic Review*, vol. 103, no. 11 (16 March 1979): 7.
12. Ne Win vitae, pictures 50 and 51; Letter, FRG Emb Ygn Amb Linsser to GA, pictures 60 and 61, 23 March 1979.
13. Telegram, Farrar to FCO, 8 June 1979; Telegram, Booth to FCO, 2 July 1979, FCO15/2465.
14. Telegrams, Rangoon to FCO and MOD, 29 August 1979, and two telegrams on 31 August 1979, DEFE 49/22.
15. As told to the author by a retired Singapore foreign ministry official, 4 February 2013.
16. Ceremonial Programme of Mountbatten Funeral, 5 September 1979, DEFE 68/350.
17. Quoted in Than Han, *Common Vision: Burma's Regional Outlook* (Washington, D.C.: Institute for the Study of Diplomacy, School of Foreign Service, Georgetown University, 1986), p. 13. In the printing of this quotation, an error is made in the footnote but the text makes it clear that this is from the Havana Summit, not the Belgrade Summit of a decade earlier when similar fears were raised. Ne Win was encouraged to attend that summit but he chose to stay away.
18. Telegram, Rangoon to FCO, 8 January 1980, FCO15/2628.
19. *Forward*, vol. XVIII, no. 7 (1 April 1980): 23.
20. *Forward*, vol. XVIII, no. 5 (1 February 1980): 2.
21. *Forward*, vol. XIX, no. 1 (1 October 1980): 24.

22. *Forward*, vol. XVIII, no. 5 (1 February 1980): 2 and 24.

23. *Forward*, vol. XVIII, no. 7 (1 April 1980): 2.

24. *Forward*, vol. XVIII, no. 8 (1 May 1980): 2.

25. Letter, Charles Booth to Head of Chancellery, 22 January 1980, FCO 15/2628.

26. Letter, Charles Booth to Head of Chancellery, 31 January 1980, FCO 15/2623.

27. *Forward*, vol. XVIII, no. 8 (1 May 1980): 2.

28. Ibid., p. 23.

29. Ibid., p. 24.

30. *Forward*, vol. XVIII, no. 9 (1 June 1980): 23.

31. *Forward*, vol. XVIII, no. 8 (1 May 1980): 3–9.

32. Dr Ingrid Jordt attributes Ne Win's encouragement of the purification as an apparent response to the political unrest of 1974, but provides no evidence of a link between the two events. Ingrid Jordt, *Burma's Mass Lay Meditation Movement: Buddhism and the Cultural Construction of Power* (Athens: Ohio University Press, 2007), p. 180.

33. U Thu Wei organized the Democracy Party under which a number of descendants of the old AFPFL contested the 2010 elections in the face of condemnation by the National League for Democracy. He was encouraged to return by his parents, who came to Thailand to get him with the assistance of General Tin U and U Kyaw Nyein. Kyaw Nyein apparently believed that the amnesty was a sign that Ne Win was going to re-establish multi-party politics. Interview, U Thu Yei, 25 March 2009.

34. Myanmar Hsoshelit Lansin Pati Baho Kowmitti Danakyut, *Myanmar Hsoshelit Lansin Pati Okkatakyi ei Hkit Pyaung Towhlanyei Thamaing win Meinkhun Paungkyut* [Collected Speeches of the Era Changing Revolution History of the Chairman of the Myanmar Socialist Programme Party], Vol. I (Yangon: Myanmar Socialist Way Party Central Committee Headquarters, Party Publications Unit, July 1985), pp. 386–99; translated as "President Ne Win's Speech on Naing-Ngant Gonyi Award", *Forward*, vol. XVIII, no. 10 (July 1980): 3–7.

35. Letter, Charles Booth to Head of Chancellery, 15 September 1980, FCO15/2623.

36. *Forward*, vol. XVIII, no. 11 (1 August 1980): 2–3.

37. *Forward*, vol. XVIII, no. 12 (1 September 1980): 3–7.

38. *Forward*, vol. XVIII, no. 11 (1 August 1980): 23–24.

39. *Forward*, vol. XIX, no. 1 (1 October 1980): 23.

40. Telegram, Farrer to FCO, 30 July 1980, FCO15/2623.

41. *Forward*, vol. XIX, no. 3 (1 December 1980): 23.

42. Theikpan Myint Oo, "Religious Treasures from Nepal", *Forward*, vol. XIX, no. 1 (1 October 1980): 3–7.

43. *Forward*, vol. XIX, no. 1 (1 October 1980): 24.
44. Also present were U Ba Swe, U Kyaw Nyein, Thakin Tin, Thirty Comrades Bo Phone Myint, Bo Bala, Bo Min Gaung, Bohmu Aung, and Bo Zinyaw, Hanson Saw Kya Doe, San Po Thin, Ma Hnin Si, Daw Saw Mya, U Htain Lin, retired Brigadiers Maung Maung, Aung Gyi, Aung Shwe and Tin Pe, Vidura Thakin Chit Maung, and former Fourth Burma Rifles and Communist Bo Thet Tun. See Maung Maung, *The 1988 Uprising in Burma*, Yale University Southeast Asia Studies Monograph no. 49 (New Haven: Yale University Southeast Asia Studies, 1999), *passim*, pp. 140–58.
45. *The Guardian*, 12 August 1980.
46. Letter, R.G. Farrar to P.A.A. Brooks, 15 August 1980, FCO15/2624.
47. *Forward*, vol. XIX, no. 1(1 October 1980): 2.
48. Ibid.
49. Ibid., pp. 12–13. Also *Forward*, vol. XIX, no. 2 (1 November 1980): 2 and 24.
50. Comment by U Lay Maung, Myanmar foreign minister, Confidential Record of Conversation between the Lord Privy Seal and the Burmese Foreign Minister, 23 September 1980, at 10:15 a.m., in the Foreign and Commonwealth Office, FCO15/2629.
51. Letter, C.L. Booth to R.P. Flower, 30 May 1980, FCO15/2628.
52. *Forward*, vol. XIX, no. 3 (1 December 1980): 2.
53. *Forward*, vol. XIX, no. 4 (1 January 1981): 2.
54. *Forward*, vol. XIX, no. 3 (1 December 1980): 13–14.
55. *Forward*, vol. XIX, no. 4 (1 January 1981): 2.
56. Letter, Ministry of Foreign Affairs, Myanmar, to Embassy of Her Britannic Majesty, Rangoon, 4 November 1980, FCO15/2626.
57. Letter, Charles Booth to K.F.X. Burns, 21 November 1980, FCO15/2627.
58. FCO973/181
59. *Forward*, vol. XIX, no. 7 (1 April 1981): 2.
60. Ibid.
61. Hla Oo, "Irrawaddy Waters and Ne Win's Gold Trees", in *The Scourge of Burma and Four Short Stories* (N.p.: The author, 2010), pp. 58–65.
62. Following nationwide elections, the Third *Pyithu Hluttaw* met for its first session on 9 November and elected San Yu as president.
63. *Myanmar Hsoshelit Lansin Pati Okkatakyi ei Hkit Pyaung Towhlanyei Thamaing win Meinkhun Paungkyut*, Vol. 1, pp. 430–42; translated in Burma Socialist Programme Party Central Committee Headquarters, *The Fourth Party Congress 1981: Party Chairman's Speech and Political Report of the Central Committee* (Yangon: Burma Socialist Programme Party, June 1985), pp. 183–93.
64. *Forward*, vol. XX, no. 5 (1 February 1982): 2–3.

65. *Forward*, vol. XX, no. 6 (1 March 1982): 2–4.
66. *Forward*, vol. XX, no. 7 (1 April 1982): 3–5.
67. Interview with retired General Khin Nyunt, 18 July 2013.
68. *Forward*, vol. XX, no. 10 (1 July 1982): 2–3 and 31.
69. *Legal Status of Traditional Medicine and Complementary/Alternative Medicine: A Worldwide Review* (Geneva: World Health Organisation, 2001), pp. 135–37.
70. See *Myanmar Taingyin Hsei Pyinna Akhyeikhan Tabawtaya:mya* [Basic Principles of Myanmar Indigenous Medicine] (N.p.: Indigenous Medicine Department, Department of Health, Government of the Union of Myanmar, 2007).
71. *Forward*, vol. XX, no. 11 (1 August 1982): 2–3.
72. *Myanmar Hsoshelit Lansin Pati Okkatakyi ei Hkit Pyaung Towhlanyei Thamaing win Meinkhun Paungkyut*, Vol. 2, pp. 348–70, translated in *Forward*, vol. XX, no. 12 (1 September 1982): 2–12.
73. Ibid., pp. 49–63, translated in *Forward*, vol. XXI, no. 2 (1 November 1982): 2–5 and 10.
74. An English translation of the law is found in *Forward*, vol. XXX, no. 2 (1 November 1982): 24–31.
75. *Forward*, vol. XXI, no. 3 (1 December 1982): 2.
76. *Forward*, vol. XXI, no. 3 (1 December 1982): 3–4 and 6.
77. *Forward*, vol. XXI, no. 7 (1 April 1983): 11.
78. *Forward*, vol. XXI, no. 6 (1 March 1983): 2–6.
79. *Forward*, vol. XXI, no. 7 (1 April 1983): 2–7.
80. *Forward*, vol. XXI, no. 7 (1 April 1983): 11.
81. *Forward*, vol. XXI, no. 9 (1 June 1983): 3.
82. Amongst those that Tin U eliminated, or gave trouble, before his own dismissal were U Lay Maung, U Thaung Dan, U Hla Han and U Aye Kyaw. "He made a lot of enemies", according to U Htway Han, BSPP Secretary One. Interview with Major (rtd) Htway Han, 11 March 2006. One of his targets was the head of the Myanmar police, Sandhurst-educated Brigadier Shwe Than. To protect him, Ne Win removed him from the police and put him in charge of the government shipping company, Myanmar Five Star Line.
83. Thaung Kyi had been in London for medical treatment for three weeks in October 1979. Telegram, Booth to FCO, 4 October 1980, FCO15/2465.
84. Interview, Lieutenant Colonel Ba Yi, 30 January 2006; Ba Yi was Director of BSPP Headquarters.
85. Interview, Lieutenant Colonel Ba Yi, 30 January 2006.
86. *Forward*, vol. XXI, no. 11 (1 August 1983): 2–3.
87. Ibid., pp. 4–7.
88. *Forward*, vol. XXII, no. 2 (1 November 1983): 2–10.

89. *Forward*, vol. XXII, no. 1 (1 October 1983): 2–3.
90. Ibid., p. 119; also, *A Lingering Nightmare: The Rangoon Bombing* (Seoul: Korean Overseas Information Service, October 1984); *International Renegades: North Korean Diplomacy Through Terror* (Seoul: Korean Overseas Information Service, December 1983).
91. *Forward*, vol. XXII, no. 3 (1 December 1983): 2.
92. *Forward*, vol. XXII, no. 6 (1 March 1984): 4–5.
93. *Forward*, vol. XXII, no. 7 (1 April 1984): 10–12.
94. *Forward*, vol. XXII, no. 8 (1 May 1984): 13.
95. By this time, Ne Win had apparently discovered that Bandoola was a Muslim. See Tin Aung, "Travels with Numero Uno", unpublished paper, circa 2000, p. 7.
96. *Forward*, vol. XXII, no. 8 (1 May 1984): 4–5.
97. *Forward*, vol. XXII, no. 9 (1 June 1984): 1.
98. Ibid., pp. 2–3.
99. *Forward*, vol. XXII, no. 1 (1 July 1984): 2 and vol. XXII, no. 12 (1 September 1984): 2.
100. Interview with former General Khin Nyunt, 18 July 2013.
101. *Forward*, vol. XXII, no. 8 (1 May 1984): 14 and vol. XXII, no. 10 (1 July 1984): 3.
102. *Forward*, vol. XXIII, no. 1 (1 October 1984): 2–3.
103. Ibid., *p.* 4; *Working Peoples' Daily*, 4 September 1984.
104. *Forward*, vol. XXIII, no. 2 (1 November 1984): 2.
105. Ibid., pp. 3–5.
106. *Forward*, vol. XXIII, no. 3 (1 December 1984): 2.
107. Ibid., pp. 3–4.
108. *Working People's Daily*, 10 October 1984.
109. *Working People's Daily*, 8 December 1984; *Forward*, vol. XXIII, no. 4 (1 January 1985): 2–3.
110. *Forward*, vol. XXIII, no. 5 (1 February 1985): 3–4.
111. Economist Intelligence Unit, *Quarterly Review of Thailand, Burma*, no. 1 (1986): 33.
112. *Forward*, vol. XXIII, no. 4 (1 February 1985): 5.
113. *Forward*, vol. XXIII, no. 8 (1 May 1985): 2.
114. *Forward*, vol. XXIII, no. 4 (1 February 1985): 6.
115. *Forward*, vol. XXIII, no. 6 (1 March 1985): 3.
116. Ibid., pp. 4–5.
117. *Forward*, vol. XXIII, no. 8 (1 May 1985): 4–5.
118. *Forward*, vol. XXIII, no. 7 (1 April 1985): 4–5.
119. Ibid., pp. 6–8.
120. *Forward*, vol. XXIII, no. 8 (1 June 1985): 4–13.
121. Interview with retired General Khin Nyunt, 18 July 2013.
122. Interview, Admiral Chit Hlaing, 12 March 2006. See also Kaiser Morshed,

"Bangladesh-Burma Relations", in *Challenges to Democratization in Burma: Perspectives on Multilateral and Bilateral Responses*, by International Institute for Democracy and Electoral Assistance (Stockholm: International Institute for Democracy and Electoral Assistance, 2001), p. 60.

123. "Explanation of 1985-86 Plan", *Forward*, vol. XXIII, no. 7 (1 April 1985): 41–43 and 50.
124. *Forward*, vol. XXIII, no. 9 (1 June 1985): 15.
125. *Forward*, vol. XXIII, no. 12 (1 September 1985): 2–3.
126. *Forward*, vol. XXIII, no. 10 (1 July 1985): 2.
127. Interview with retired General Khin Nyunt, 18 July 2013.
128. *Forward*, vol. XXIII, no. 11 (1 August 1985): 2.
129. The proceedings of this Party Congress were never, to my knowledge, published before the Party was abolished in 1988. This information is based on *Forward*, vol. XXIII, no. 12 (1 September 1985): 4.
130. *Forward*, vol. XXIV, no. 1 (1 October 1985): 3.
131. Ibid., p. 2.
132. *Forward*, vol. XXIV, no. 3 (1 December 1985): 2.
133. *Forward*, vol. XXIV, no. 5 (1 February 1985): 3.
134. *Forward*, vol. XXIV, no. 2 (1 November 1985): 2–7.
135. *Forward*, vol. XXIV, no. 3 (1 December 1985): 3.
136. Ibid., pp. 4–17.
137. Economist Intelligence Unit, *Quarterly Economic Review of Thailand, Burma*, no. 2 (1985): 27.
138. *Asian Development Outlook* (Manila: Asian Development Bank, 1990), Table A9, Changes in Consumer Prices, p. 230.
139. Some speculated that the move was made to mark Ne Win's 75th birthday, giving another permutation of his birth date.
140. Ministry of Finance and Planning, Central Statistical Organisation, *Selected Monthly Economic Indicators*, no. 3 (May–June 1990): 15; *Asian Development Outlook*, p. 230.
141. *Forward*, vol. XXIV, no. 4 (1 January 1986): 2–3.
142. Ibid., pp. 4–6.
143. *Forward*, vol. XXIV, no. 6 (1 March 1986): n.p.
144. *Forward*, vol. XXV, no. 4 (1 January 1987): 4–5.
145. *Forward*, vol. XXIV, no. 6 (1 March 1986): n.p.
146. Ibid., p. 3.
147. *Forward*, vol. XXIV, no. 7 (1 April 1986): 4.
148. Ibid., pp. 6–9.
149. Ibid., pp. 5 and 46.
150. Ibid., pp. 14–22.
151. Information provided by the late U Ba Kyi, owner of the Pagan Bookshop.
152. *Forward*, vol. XXIV, no. 8 (1 May 1986): 2.

153. *Forward*, vol. XXIV, no. 9 (1 June 1986): 2.

154. Interview with Lieutenant Colonel Ba Yi (retired), 30 January 2006.

155. Personal communication with Bo Bo Kyaw Nyein, 1 August 2013.

156. Interview, U Thu Yei, 25 March 2009.

157. "Bogyoke Aung San, The First Father of the Tatmadaw, U Ne Win, the Second Father of the Tatmadaw", *Forward*, vol. XXIV, no. 12 (1 September 1986): 2–3.

158. *Forward*, vol. XXV, no. 2 (1 November 1986): 5.

159. Ibid., pp. 2–3 and 6–14.

160. Ibid., p. 4.

161. *Forward*, vol. XXV, no. 3 (1 December 1986): 2–4.

162. *Forward*, vol. XXV, no. 4 (1 January 1987): 2–3.

163. *Forward*, vol. XXV, no. 5 (1 February 1987): 8–9.

164. Myat Thein, *Economic Development of Myanmar* (Singapore: Institute of Southeast Asian Studies, 2004), p. 105 and p. 120, fn. 6. On an earlier trip to this factory, Ne Win discovered that all the glassware manufactured was being sold to Singapore and shipped in good teak cases. This was a scam to export expensive teak as packing materials. Tin Aung, "Travels with Numero Uno", pp. 4–5.

165. *Forward*, vol. XXV, no. 5 (1 February 1987): 3–4.

166. *Forward*, vol. XXV, no. 6 (1 March 1987): 3.

167. *Forward*, vol. XXIV, no. 7 (1 April 1986): 47.

168. Interview, Victor L. Tomseth, Association for Diplomatic Studies and Training 1012/09, Burma, p. 158.

169. Interview with Aloysius M. O'Neill, Chief Consular Officer, Rangoon (1986–88), p. 166, Association for Diplomatic Studies and Training 2012/09, Burma, p. 166.

170. Interview with Lieutenant Colonel Ba Yi, 30 January 2006.

171. *Forward*, vol. XXV, no. 7 (1 April 1987): 7.

172. *Forward*, vol. XXV, no. 8 (1 May 1987): 2.

173. Interview with retired General Khin Nyunt, 18 July 2013.

174. Ibid.

175. Confidential email exchange, June 2013.

176. *Forward*, vol. XXV, no. 9 (1 June 1987): 2.

177. *Forward*, vol. XXV, no. 12 (1 September 1987): 2–3.

178. Ibid., pp. 3–4.

179. Ibid., p. 5.

180. *Forward*, vol. XXVI, no. 1 (1 October 1987): 2.

181. *Forward*, vol. XXVI, no. 2 (1 November 1987): 2–3.

182. *Forward*, vol. XXVI, no. 2 (1 November 1987): 6–7 and 13.

183. *Forward*, vol. XXVI, no. 1 (1 October 1987): n.p. and vol. XXVI, no. 2 (1 November 1987): 32–33.

184. *Forward*, vol. XXXVI, no. 3 (1 December 1987): 5–7.
185. Ibid., pp. 2–4 and 22.
186. Chi-shad Liang, *Burma's Foreign Relations: Neutralism in Theory and Practice* (New York: Praeger, 1990), p. 136. *Forward*, vol. XXXVI, no. 3 (1 December 1987): 2.
187. *Forward*, vol. XXVI, no. 5 (1 February 1988): 2–4.
188. Ibid., pp. 2–5.
189. *Forward*, vol. XXVI, no. 7 (1 April 1988): 2–7 and 10–12.

13

FAILURE AND FAREWELL
(March 1988 to December 2002)

You are the community now. Be a lamp for yourselves. Be your own
refuge. Seek for no other. All things must pass. Strive on diligently.
Don't give up.

Attributed to the Buddha

The final fourteen years of Ne Win's life were marked by initial crisis,
eventual withdrawal into meditative peace, and final farce. The crisis
had been ignited the previous year when Ne Win had admitted that the
regime he had led for twenty-five years had reached a dead end and that
reforms of a significant, but still ill-defined nature, were essential. He
was perhaps hesitant to introduce radical economic and political reforms
because of uncertainty about the consequences and regret at the loss of the
socialist ideal which his leader, Aung San, had established. The decision
to demonetize the kyat for the second time in two years, after pledging
not to do so, had removed the last vestiges of faith in the government's
promises, at least among those who were directly affected, a large swathe
of the population.

For the politically aware public, the humiliation their nation received
by being officially declared a "Least Developed Country" by the United
Nations, together with other international mendicants, removed the final
shred of faith in the Burmese Way to Socialism. In the resulting mood
of despondency and despair, with factories closed or on short time due to

shortages of spare parts and raw materials, and the shelves in shops bare, it took little to set off public outrage. Moreover, there were those who saw opportunities in the crisis to remove Ne Win and his regime, both on his political left and right. Even many of the Burma Socialist Programme Party (BSPP) faithful were disillusioned, as were some of the security forces, despite their continued loyalty to the government and the chain of command. This was made clear to Ne Win in a report submitted to him by U Tin Aung Hein, a highly respected figure in the government and the party. In the report, he detailed how the party had, over time, become ossified and ineffectual, despite the revolutionary intentions of its inspiration. For the younger generation, those born after 1962, who knew little of the history that Ne Win often recounted, past battles counted for little; it was present difficulties which mattered.

As devastating firestorms commence from an unseen spark, so events in Myanmar between March and September 1988 progressed from urgings by a former colleague to full-scale public protests of a kind never before seen in the country. Perhaps the least important of the many events that marked this dramatic period was the circulation of a letter, the first of three, by former Brigadier Aung Gyi to his Bogyoke pointing out the ways in which Indonesia had modernized its economy and the problems that UN agencies and others were facing in Myanmar, ending with a note on the impending economic crisis and an alleged threat of famine.[1] It is highly unlikely that Ne Win learned anything from the letters he did not already know, as he himself had identified the impending crisis the previous year. One letter from Aung Gyi, on 9 May, was addressed to Bo San Yu, and others in the government, as well as former members of the Revolutionary Council, and another, on 8 June 1988, addressed to Ne Win, once more discussed the destruction of the students' union building twenty-six years earlier and the handling of student demonstrations more recently. The letters were distributed to diplomats and others interested in the future of the country, who regarded them as a sign of growing dissent.

Another event, however, was much more important for the final unravelling of the socialist revolution. It began as a completely apolitical brawl in a tea shop between students from Rangoon Institute of Technology (RIT) and local youths on 12 March over what type of music to play. Drunken locals began to beat the students and other students then came to their assistance. The police arrested some local men, including one Zaw Zaw, but he was released the next day after the intervention of an associate of his, rumoured to be a high-level local Party official. Learning of Zaw Zaw's release, students in significant numbers proceed to stone the tea shop and the offices of the local People's Council from whence the order to release Zaw Zaw had come. The conflict then spread, as local residents turned their wrath on the students while attempting to defend their property. Fires were set and eventually the police arrived. Three or four hundred students, and about the same number of locals, were said to be involved. The police separated the two groups and drove the students back to the RIT campus by dousing them with water hoses from fire engines but, after fifteen minutes, they ran out of water. The police then used tear gas and shotguns to control the crowd. In the end, five students were wounded and one, Phone Maw, died on the evening of 13 March. A second student, Soe Naing, passed away in Rangoon General Hospital on 13 April.

Anger at the police's handling of the event, now spread to include the local People's Council, and then the larger government, the *Pyithu Hluttaw* being in session at the time just down Insein and Pyay Roads from RIT. Prior to then, Ne Win had been presiding at the regular meeting of the BSPP Central Committee on the morning of the tea shop brawl. That meeting proposed nothing significant to address the country's economic ills. The next four evenings, students protested and arrests were made, 625 according to the police, of whom 484 were released by 1 April. However, by then the tea shop brawl was forgotten and the death of the students at the hands of the police, and the alleged disappearance of other students, became the focus of students' anger. Their anger soon spread and became part of the "proof" that the government was not only incompetent but also callous.[2] On 17 March, in an attempt to calm the situation, the government appointed a three-person commission to investigate the events and issue a report and recommendations. That report was not issued until 13 May, and then only in summary form. What it did not say was more important than what it did.

In the meantime, on 11 April 1988, Ne Win, accompanied by Daw Ni Ni Myint, Dr Maung Maung, U Thaung Tin and U Ohn Kyi from the Council of State, Deputy Prime Minister and Defence Minister General Kyaw Tin, U Lay Maung of the Council of People's Attorneys, and U Maung Cho, Minister of Industry 2, and others from the Chairman's office and the Ministry of Defence, left for a six-week visit to Germany and Switzerland, mainly to Munich and Zurich. The composition of his entourage indicated that they had legal and industrial business to conduct, as well as a typical hot-season holiday around Buddhist New Year. They returned on 26 May.[3] This was Ne Win's last trip to Europe and the West.

On returning to Myanmar, Ne Win still bore down on the details of the short-term issues he had discussed in his speech to the Central Committee in September. He and a large party drove to Pyay and spent the night of 16 June 1988 at the 66th Light Infantry Division headquarters, as he had often done in the past, before driving the next day to Kyangin Township via the recently completed Pathein–Monywa highway which opened up north–south land transportation on the West bank of the Ayeyawaddy River where he had marched with his troops in the Burma Independence Army (BIA) in 1942. At Kyangyin, they inspected the methanol plant constructed there. From Kyangyin, they drove for about an hour to the Heavy Industries Factory No. 2 at Htonbo and in the evening visited Heavy Industries Factory No. 4 at Padaung Township. Having crossed the Ayeyawady, they spent the night again at Pyay and returned to Yangon the next morning.[4] This was Ne Win's final tour. He was on the road from 16 to 19 June.

During that time, students began renewed protests over their economic and educational situation, commencing on 15 June and not brought under control until the 21st, when the universities were once more closed, after reopening only on 20 May, and the students rusticated. A curfew was imposed in Yangon also on the 21st, and rioting began about this time in Pyay and Taunggyi between Muslims and Buddhists, with clashes occurring in lesser towns as well. Once more, as Ne Win once said, it was necessary for the army to keep the "bearded fellows", meaning Muslims, separate from the "bald headed fellows", meaning Buddhist monks.[5] At about this time, students, claiming to speak for the Yangon University Students Union, issued a demand for the re-establishment of a legal and independent students union addressed to the "Fascist government of Ne Win".[6] The choice of the adjective "Fascist" would have alerted anyone in the army that the demand had originated from Communists.

However, others took a less confrontational posture *vis-à-vis* the government and Ne Win. U Nay Min, a lawyer for one of the Muslim men swept off the streets during the communal clashes, and subsequently a political prisoner, filed a lawsuit against the Burma Socialist Programme Party on 4 July for the wrongful arrest of his client. He also wrote unsuccessfully to Ne Win through a friend on that day but later learned that Ne Win had ordered a postbox be kept open for him at the Yangon General Post Office, with instructions that letters be delivered to him twice a day. U Nay Min then wrote via that channel and believed that his argument that the judicial system was being brought into disrepute by the events following the March tea shop incident and subsequently was taken up by Ne Win. In any event, his client and others were released on 7 July.[7]

In the face of the growing crisis, now not just of the economy but also of public disorder, on 7 July, an Extraordinary Party Congress was called for 23 July. The day before, Ne Win summoned a meeting of four senior counsellors: San Yu, U Myint Maung, chairman of the Council of People's Attorneys, U Tin Aung Hein, chairman of the Council of People's Justices, and Dr Maung Maung. Ne Win began the meeting by showing them a copy of the summary of the report on the deaths resulting from the tea shop incident of March as printed in the newspapers in May. The publication of a summary was unusual, for normally in such circumstances, the entire report would be published. Ne Win asked the group, "doesn't it look like a cover up?" (Maung Maung 1999, p. 46). Ne Win ordered that expelled students from Rangoon Institute of Technology have their cases reviewed for re-admission immediately and they were invited the next day to re-apply. After being told incomplete accounts by Myint Maung and Tin Aung Hein, as well as San Yu, of what had transpired, "The chairman closed the meeting with these remarks: 'I have decided what should be done and I made the decision before I met you, and you are not responsible for it. Yes, and I have the guts to go through with it!'" According to Dr Maung Maung, "he didn't tell us then what [the decision] was. Nor did I think he told anyone until the very eve of the Extraordinary Party Congress and even then only the inner circle. ..." (Maung Maung 1999, p. 49). Ne Win then ordered the release of the full report, which revealed that forty-one persons had suffocated on the night of 18 March when they were locked in a police *kyut-ka* (custody truck), though none were said to have been students (Maung Maung 1999, pp. 62–63).

At the Extraordinary Party Congress, Ne Win once more launched a surprise: his resignation as Party Chairman. He began his speech, which was broadcast live on radio and television, and reported verbatim in the newspapers the next day, by saying:

> Party Congress delegates, I speak on matters for calling this Extraordinary Party Congress and the matters to be presented, discussed and approved by this Congress and carried out. I believe that the 1988 March and June bloodshed and disturbances were meant by those who took part in them and those behind them to show lack of confidence in the Government and the Party leading the Government.

Unlike in 1962 when students occupied the Rangoon University Students Union, Ne Win did not claim that the events of the preceding months were part of a Communist or other conspiracy to overthrow the government, though the military government which succeeded the BSPP following the September 1988 coup subsequently stated this to be the case,[8] just as Party Joint Secretary General Aye Ko implied, without being specific in his speech immediately following Ne Win's resignation.

Therefore, Ne Win went on to say,

> It is necessary to assess whether among the people of the entire country, a majority is behind those lacking confidence or a minority. As I believe that holding a national referendum on what they wish — a one party system or a multi-party system — would answer the question, I am asking the Party Congress to hold a referendum.
>
> If the majority want a multi-party system, the present Constitution's provisions under Chapter II, Paragraph II for the sole political party leading the State will have to be substituted with wording in consonance with a multi-party system. A suitable lapse of time would of course be needed for convenient movement of people, production of ballot cards and other requirements.
>
> Roughly said, it should be set up no later than end of September. It should be held earlier than that if possible. If, after the referendum more votes are for a multi-party system, elections must be held at the earliest for a new parliament. Parties formed by bona fide citizens, organisations and individual citizens will have to register themselves with the election supervisory body.

He then went through some details of how an election could promptly be held to elect a new parliament which would have the power "to write the Constitution and other necessary laws according to its own wishes". In the meantime, he wanted the existing government and its institutions "to assert control as much as possible to keep the country from disarray till the organisations formed by the *Hluttaw* can take over". After briefly discussing the implications for the party if the referendum outcome was to keep the one-party system, Ne Win then unexpectedly said, "While the Party may carry on with its present role, I should like to make special mention of my own role", and sat down.

U Htway Han came to the podium. It was clearly a very emotional moment for Ne Win. Then Central Committee Headquarters Secretary and a retired air force officer, Htway Han subsequently explained,

On that day [i.e., 23 July], I was asked to come to him. When I saw him, he said, "I have decided to resign. I have written it out. When I call you, you come and read it." I asked him to reconsider. He said he had already decided. I couldn't say anything more. When I asked General San Yu to do something about it, he just said he knew nothing about it. So I returned to my seat. After a while, I was asked to go to the podium. I read out what he asked me to read. He said U San Yu, U Aye Ko, U Sein Lwin, Gen. Kyaw Htin and U Tun Tin also wanted to retire. What happened was that he asked them to leave before the meeting. He just said, "I am resigning. You should all quit as well."[9]

The words that the 78-year-old Ne Win had written and Htway Han read out were:

As I consider that I am not totally free from responsibility even if indirectly for the sad events that took place in March and June and because I am advancing in age, I would like to request Party members to allow me to relinquish the duty of Party Chairman and as a Party member. In order to do so, Paragraph 14 subpara (c) of the Party rules will have to be amended.[10] I request you to do so. If you do not want to amend the rule, I request this Party Congress to treat it as a special exemption.

Formerly, whenever I talked of relinquishing the Party chairmanship, my confidants and colleagues prevented me and, unhappily, I have had to stay on in this political *samsara*.[11] This time my confidants have not only consented to allow me but have also asked that they too be allowed to leave along with me and have entrusted their resignations to me.

They are (1) U San Yu, (2) U Aye Ko, (3), U Sein Lwin, (4) U Tun Tin, (5) U Kyaw Htin. There are others, quite a number, who have as seniors been shouldering high responsibility, who want to retire, leave the party. I would like this Party Congress to accede to their wishes to do so after transferring responsibility with the emergence of the new Hluttaw. I want to tell those wanting to retire, wanting to leave the Party, to tender their resignation in time while this Congress is in session.

Ne Win then resumed speaking, summarizing what he had just said and written and then stating, "multi-party system, or one-party system, which of the two the people support, may I conclude, declaring that I shall leave the political arena and turn away from politics".

He then turned to more recent developments, noting that perhaps the disorder in Taunggyi, Pyay and Yangon in June was a consequence of the government's attempts to maintain order using minimum force. He noted that he had restrained the army from being used to suppress the disorder in Pyay which broke out again on 16 July and lasted until 22 July. At this point Ne Win made remarks which were often quoted as constituting a threat to the populace. However, what he actually said was fairly commonplace in a situation where the government was facing severe disorder. What was more significant was the way in which he seemed to qualify his resignation:

> There is what I said earlier that I would retire from politics. Although I said I would retire from politics, we will have to maintain control to prevent the country from falling apart, from disarray, till the future organisations can take full control. In continuing to maintain control, I want the entire nation, the people, to know that if in future there are mob disturbances, if the army shoots, it hits — there is no firing into the air to scare. So, if in future there are such disturbances and if the army is used, let it be known that those creating disturbance will not get off lightly.

Then, sensing his audience was getting restless and agitated by the unexpected development implicit in his resignation, he told them to "be patient and listen to what I have to say".

Ne Win then recounted, perhaps angered by Aung Gyi's third letter, his role in the events of 7–8 July 1962 and the destruction of the Rangoon University Students Union building. On learning at about 5 p.m. on 7 July that eight or nine policemen had been injured on the campus and that students were holding out in the Union building, Ne Win ordered that they be warned that if they did not submit to arrest, large caliber arms would be used against them. If they did not come out, a recoilless gun would be fired to drive them out, preferably before dark that day. On the morning of 8 July when he heard the explosion at the Union building, Ne Win telephoned the Myanmar Athan station near the campus, the headquarters for the group concerned with the campus, and inquired. Colonel Kyaw Soe told him that it had been dynamited. The Revolutionary Council at that point, in the spirit of the army's collective responsibility doctrine, admitted to dynamiting the building and Ne Win made his "sword with sword and spear with spear" broadcast. Kyaw Soe told him that the decision to blow up the building was reached after discussions among members of the Revolutionary Council at the Myanmar Athan crisis headquarters.

Then, some months later, when Ne Win was accused by foreign journalists of having ordered the destruction of the Union building while drunk, he inquired of Kyaw Soe what had actually happened on the night of 7–8 July. Using evidence from Aung Gyi's public letter of 9 May 1988 and a report written by Colonel Hla Han in 1963, Ne Win said that Aung Gyi had told the group at the broadcasting station, who were in a feverish mood, that he and others felt that the Union was a Communist nest, and that Aung Gyi would get Bogyoke's permission to blow it up. He visited Ne Win at his home, but did not mention the matter of blowing up the Union building, yet he returned and said that "Bogyoke" had approved it. Ne Win concluded:

> So, these two points are, as I said earlier, what was told to others without my knowledge but as if I knew; as if I had asked them to, and others destroyed it as they had been told that I agreed. So, taking the above mentioned points into consideration, I conclude by asking the entire people to judge for themselves who the real culprit was in the destruction of the union building.[12]

Ne Win apparently did not attend the remaining three days of the Congress. After he spoke, he called Dr Maung Maung and U Tin Aung Hein for a brief chat. As Maung Maung recalled, he said, "'What do you think of what I said? ... Are you surprised?' He looked brighter and lighter having had it out." (Maung Maung 1999, p. 50).

After Ne Win left the hall, Party General Secretary U Aye Ko presented a report on the state of the party and the nation. Noting the poor economic performance in recent years, the growing trade deficit, the dependency of the economy on the black market, and the inadequacies of the health and education systems, he also reported on the near bankruptcy of the state, including the fact that the debt service ratio (annual repayments to export earnings) had risen from 15.11 per cent in 1977–78 to 59.14 per cent in 1986–87. Given Myanmar's precarious balance of payments situation and meager foreign exchange reserves, the situation was unsustainable and default on the loans loomed. In the last decade of Ne Win's chairmanship, the country had gone from mini-boom to mega-bust. Aye Ko then proposed a number of steps, some already agreed, cautiously to liberalize the economy in important sectors.[13]

The second day of the Congress was devoted to debating the proposals placed before the Party the previous day. The fifteen delegates chosen to speak on behalf of each state and division and the army unanimously supported Ne Win remaining as chairman. As reported the next day in the *Working People's Daily*,

> Citing instances of practical achievements, [delegates] also described how the Party Chairman and other Party leaders are personalities with great historic traditions and rich experiences fully able to provide leadership to overcome difficult and stringent conditions being faced in the country. Moreover they emphatically expressed great concern that the country would be left in disorder and disarray if the leaders of such great traditions resigned.
>
> It is clear that their discussions in this matter of resignation of the Party Chairman and the other Party leaders at this Extraordinary Party Congress reflect not just their individual sentiments but those of the delegates of the regions to this Congress and those of the entire mass of Party members.
>
> The Party Congress delegates are totally unconsenting about these matters of permitting the resignation of the Party Chairman, other leaders from the Party membership, and similar resignations of other persons in leading positions. ... Some who are shouldering duties in leadership are still able in respect of age and health to go on undertaking responsibilities of the Party and the State. That there is need for continuity in leadership and continuity in endeavours for realisation of the objectives of the Party has also been stressed in the discussions of the Party Congress delegates.[14]

Twelve delegates, who spoke on Aye Ko's economic reforms, and a further three on the idea of revising the party philosophy, supported the proposals. When the Congress met for the final day, it decided to reject Ne Win's and his colleagues' resignations, as well as the idea of a referendum on whether a multi-party system should be adopted or the one-party system prevail. The economic reforms, however, were accepted. Aye Ko, on behalf of the leadership, replied to the effect that the rejection of the resignations could be circumvented through the clause that allowed members to resign for reasons of ill health or old age. The official press report of the final day of the Party Congress made no reference to Ne Win's suggestion of a referendum on the party system, but Maung Maung reported that while the army delegation remained neutral on the matter, there was a rumour that Ne Win would not object to the rejection of his proposal and therefore it was voted down (Maung Maung 1999, p. 52). According to the Constitution, only the *Pyithu Hluttaw* could authorize such an event, but, of course, the *Hluttaw* merely agreed with whatever the Party proposed and the Party Congress, perhaps fearful for the delegates' futures, chose to reject change.

The next afternoon, the Central Committee of the Party met at the *Pyithu Hluttaw* building. The Central Committee members ignored the Party's decision to reject Ne Win's resignation, and with U Sein Lwin, in his capacity as Joint General Secretary presiding, elected him as the second Party Chairman and therefore the third President of the Socialist Republic of the Union of Burma. General Kyaw Htin was elected to succeed Sein Lwin as Joint General Secretary and U Khin Maung Gyi, Dr Maung Maung, and Lieutenant General Than Shwe were elected to fill the vacancies on the Party Central Executive Committee. The choice of the latter three had significant implications for what lay ahead. In a brief speech accepting his election, Sein Lwin did not mention the past or Ne Win.[15] While these events were transpiring, Prime Minister U Maung Maung Kha, Home Minister U Min Gaung, the head of police, and the attorney general were all dismissed from office.

The choice of Sein Lwin as Ne Win's successor, in as much as he was one of those, along with new Joint General Secretary Kyaw Htin, who was slated to resign with Ne Win, surprised many. Though many believed the choice of Sein Lwin was made by Ne Win, seeking a tough man to put down the protests and defend the regime, those close to the party inner circle believed that Ne Win would have preferred Kyaw Htin and was concerned that the ballot had been rigged to ensure Sein Lwin's success. That evening, Sanda Win telephoned Ne Win's personal physician and the head of army medicine, Brigadier General Kyaw Win, MBBS, saying that her father was unwell. The doctor immediately left to attend to Ne Win but found him in good health. He advised he drink a little brandy and honey.

Ne Win asked Kyaw Win what he was doing when Sanda called him and, when told he was having a drink with Colonel Khin Nyunt, Head of Military Intelligence, and U Set Tun,[16] and despite it being nearly mid-night, Ne Win asked Kyaw Win to invite them to his house. When they arrived, Ne Win said that as he was no longer Party Chairman and President, he wished to move to his daughter's home nearby. When Set Tun protested, Ne Win said words to the effect,

> Hey, Set Tun, you should not be using the things you are not entitled
> to. I am neither the President, nor the Party Chairman. I should not be
> enjoying all those privileges. You return the house to the government
> and reassign all the people working in this compound to government
> departments. You do it tomorrow.

He also advised Kyaw Win to move to the Medical Research Department,
which he had indicated he wished to do several months earlier to pursue his
research on malaria. Ne Win did not move out of his house immediately,
however, as Sein Lwin, when learning of the request, talked him into
staying during Vassa or Wadwin, the three months of the Buddhist lent,
and convinced him that it was inauspicious for both of them to move
during the rainy season.

After Sein Lwin's appointment, the unrest in the streets grew. Despite
using repressive tactics, arresting many, including Aung Gyi, and firing into
crowds, the government appeared to be losing control. A general strike
was called on 8 August, now known as 8–8–88, and many civil servants
and others poured into the streets in defiance of the government. Ne Win,
however, feeling that his advice had been ignored, withdrew to his home
and refused to meet with senior officials. When Sein Lwin requested to
see Ne Win, he gave instructions that he was sleeping and did not wish
to be disturbed. It was impossible for him to be asleep, as the noise of
the demonstrators was quite loud and could easily be heard on Ady Road.
Once, when shots were heard, Ne Win indicated that they were probably
fired by monks.

Quite quickly, pressure for Sein Lwin to resign grew and eventually
General Kyaw Htin, the senior officer closest to Ne Win, was urged
to go see him. Kyaw Htin, not wanting to be seen as the man who forced
Sein Lwin from office, sent two other men, U Ohn Kyee and U Tha
Kyaw,[17] to see him instead. This displeased Ne Win but he heard them
out. They said that Sein Lwin should resign and Dr Maung Maung
should succeed him instead. Ne Win agreed and told them to get on
with it. Claiming that they did not know how to arrange it, Ne Win
asked them to tell Sein Lwin that he wanted him to resign from all his
official posts, while he would arrange to convince Maung Maung to
accept the chairmanship and presidency, thus creating a hiatus of several
days when the country had no president. Afterwards, Sein Lwin said that
if Ne Win ordered him to dig a grave and bury himself alive, he would
do so.[18]

Sein Lwin had remained Party Chairman and President for just seventeen days. Dr Maung Maung succeeded him on 19 August as the third and final Party Chairman and fourth and final Socialist Programme Party President of Burma, holding office for just a month. Four days later, the martial law that Sein Lwin had imposed was lifted and all persons arrested in the previous demonstrations were released. This was apparently the consequence of an exchange between U Tin Aung Hein and Daw Aung San Suu Kyi.

Aung San Suu Kyi expressed to Tin Aung Hein her wish to address a public meeting on 26 August which, under then prevailing rules, would not have been allowed. She also wanted the government to stop arresting protestors. Tin Aung Hein asked her to control the demonstrators and convince them not to abuse the army and government servants, and cease castigating Ne Win in particular. She apparently agreed to do so. Tin Aung Hein then went to Ne Win's house on the evening of 23 August and informed him of his meeting with Suu Kyi. Also present were Dr Maung Maung and two other state councillors. They considered the proposition and Ne Win ordered that martial law be lifted not only in the area where Suu Kyi wished to hold her meeting, but also throughout Yangon and Pyay. Moreover, all persons recently arrested, including senior people like Aung Gyi, should be released. When one of the councillors objected to the release of Aung Gyi, Ne Win said, "release them all. Don't keep him." Two days later, Aung Gyi addressed a rally on the Padoma Ground denouncing Ne Win.[19]

Despite Maung Maung's efforts to mollify the demonstrators while adhering to constitutional principles, which the government's opponents saw as obfuscation, the demonstrations continued to grow and the government lost control over large parts of the city. Moreover, insurgent groups along the border were taking advantage of the chaos to attempt to enhance their own positions. According to Htway Han, Ne Win then orchestrated Maung Maung's removal and the replacement by an army government known as the State Law and Order Restoration Council.[20] It was not difficult to orchestrate because Maung Maung handed power willingly to General Saw Maung and the army (Maung Maung 1999, pp. 221–30 and passim). However, as Ne Win had drawn away from involvement in ongoing affairs, a way had to be found for him to re-enter the governing process in order to bring a resolution to the crisis.

During the time of his presidency, Dr Maung Maung met regularly with General Kyaw Htin as Minister of Defence, U Aye Ko as Party Joint Secretary, and General Saw Maung as Commander-in-Chief of the Armed Forces at the Party headquarters and the War Office. Saw Maung was quite indecisive and deferential to his superiors, particularly Aye Ko whom he looked to as his mentor. However, when the protestors attacked and looted Medical School Number One on Myoma Kyaung Road, and surrounded soldiers at the Ministry of Trade Building who were under orders not to fire and had subsequently to be rescued by monks, Saw Maung and Khin Nyunt went on the evening of 17 September to see Ne Win at his home. Ne Win listened to what they had said and then sent them away, saying he would think about it.

The next day, Saw Maung and Khin Nyunt told Kyaw Htin and Aye Ko that they had gone on their own to see Ne Win. Aye Ko became very angry and demanded to know why they went to see Ne Win without telling him and Kyaw Htin. Not long after, on the same morning, Ne Win asked Maung Maung, Khin Nyunt, Aye Ko, Kyaw Htin, and Saw Maung to come to his residence. He explained that he understood the situation was getting very bad from the government's perspective and he had called Khin Nyunt and Saw Maung to see him the previous evening, thus relieving the pressure on them from Aye Ko. He said that he did not want to interfere but would do so if the country or the army faced disintegration. Now he believed that disintegration appeared to be immanent.

Aye Ko and Kyaw Htin proposed imposing military rule on Yangon and Mandalay. Ne Win asked them why only these two cities. The government was defunct. If the military were to rule, they should rule the whole country. In effect, Ne Win recommended what was known in Latin America as an *autogolpe*, a self-coup (Fukuyama 2012, p. 140). Dr Maung Maung immediately agreed with him and from then on, a military coup was a *fait accompli*. Aye Ko and Kyaw Htin turned to Saw Maung and asked to be arrested. He told them to just return home and avoid anyone dressed as a soldier for protesters were masquerading as soldiers. Maung Maung, however, was not relieved of work and Saw Maung relied on him to draft the various statements and documents issued by the military government in its early days, with Khin Nyunt liaising between the former president's office and the war office.[21] It was doubtless Maung Maung who translated the name of the new military government in language thought to fit with English language usage at a time of political crisis, the State Law and Order

Restoration Council, which journalists and diplomats quickly turned into a mnemonic, SLORC. The name in Burmese, *Naingngantaw Nyein Wut Pi Phya Hmu Te Hsaug Yei Konsi*, translates literally as the "Council to Build a Composed and Tranquil State".

For the next nearly four and a half years, the government, led by General Saw Maung, and composed entirely of senior military officers, governed in a manner unlike that pursued by the BSPP under Ne Win. The economic reforms tentatively discussed in 1987 and 1988 were embraced with alacrity, despite certain restrictions mainly related to national security. The offer of a referendum on the political system had, by late into Dr Maung Maung's month in office, transmogrified into a promise that multi-party elections would be held, and the army government maintained that pledge. Elections were held in May 1990 with a significant caveat added in advance that before the army could hand over power to a civilian government, a constitution would have to be drafted and ratified in a referendum. The overwhelming winner in that election was the National League for Democracy (NLD), led, though under house arrest, by Daw Aung San Suu Kyi, the daughter of Ne Win's leader from the Thirty Comrades. Until she was placed under house arrest in July 1989, she had led a civil disobedience campaign accusing the army of being Ne Win's "pocket army" and not the national or people's army. This drew the retort from senior SLORC leaders that she was trying to split the army and was the unwitting tool of enemies of the state.

Clearly, as demonstrated by the May 1990 election results, the NLD was then the most popular political party in the country, gaining slightly less than 60 per cent of the votes and, thanks to Myanmar's "first past the post" electoral system, more than 80 per cent of the seats. The remnant of the BSPP, the National Unity Party (NUP), its General Secretary being U Khin Maung Gyi, demonstrated some residual support for the old order, winning just over 25 per cent of the votes, but gaining only ten seats (Taylor 1991, p. 204). The NLD had two wings, one identified as the students and intellectuals, who had dominated the movement on the streets in 1988–90, and the other, identified as the uncles, was composed mainly of former senior military officers who had parted company with Ne Win between 1961 and 1976.

Chief among them was former General Aung Gyi, though he left the party after only two months, accusing Aung San Suu Kyi of being surrounded by Communists, particularly Thakin Tin Mya, and formed his own party in late 1988. With Aung Gyi's departure, the chairmanship was assumed by former General Tin U, who had been removed and jailed by Ne Win in 1976. When Tin U was placed under house arrest, at the same time as Suu Kyi, the chairmanship was assumed by former General Aung Shwe, whom Ne Win had sacked in 1961 and sent abroad as an ambassador until 1975. The party spokesperson for years was former Colonel Lwin, General Maung Cho's brother who served as Finance Minister in the 1970s. The uncles, who included other senior ex-military and government figures from the Ne Win years, dominated the party Central Committee. Their opposition to Ne Win may have driven them into politics as much as an affinity with the ideology of democracy.

Ne Win, after ensuring that Saw Maung and the army had taken control of the government, disappeared from the public scene, but diplomats, journalists, tea shop pundits and, most importantly, Aung San Suu Kyi, persisted in believing that he was still in charge of the government. No amount of gainsaying, or even government actions contrary to Ne Win's style, could undermine such views. Ne Win himself may have been frustrated by the lack of activity he had been thrust into after fifty years in the public eye. He briefly interrupted his political oblivion when he showed up, in uniform and uninvited, at the annual Army Day dinner on 27 March 1989 in his capacity as patron to the War Veterans Organisation.[22] Then, on 2 April, he paid a visit to the annual Army Day exhibition in Tatmadaw Hall on U Wisara Boulevard. These appearances were politically embarrassing for Saw Maung, who had not mentioned Ne Win in his Army Day address, and the other members of the military government who were trying to keep a distance between themselves and the old order. Saw Maung must have struggled with great inner turmoil caused by the need to maintain his authority as the head of state and the army, and his loyalty and respect for his former leader, the stepfather of the Myanmar army. The following year he gave himself the title of Senior General, a rank higher than Ne Win ever assumed, in order to boost his authority over his military colleagues.

Saw Maung remained in charge of the government until he had a nervous breakdown around November or December 1991. Ne Win's involvement in his removal as Chairman of the SLORC and Commander-in-Chief of the armed forces and the replacement with General Than Shwe was his last known political involvement. Saw Maung, who was under great pressure following the arrest of Daw Aung San Suu Kyi in July 1989, the 1990 elections, and the brief renewal of Karen National

Union insurgency in the delta, as well as the ongoing military campaigns, particularly along the Thai border, to end the insurgency through force if ceasefire agreements could not be reached, had become increasingly incoherent and behaved strangely. On one occasion, he claimed he was Kyansittha, the third king of the Bagan era after Anniruddha, whose name, literally translated, means "the remaining soldier". His ability to continue governing was brought into question by those with whom he worked most closely.

The process of Saw Maung's removal was prolonged and had to be carefully and properly managed for fear of causing a fissure in the army. To remove a head of state, minister of defence and commander-in-chief was not something to be taken lightly, whatever the cause. Before he was removed, he was assessed by members of the army medical corps. Both Ne Win and Maung Maung took a personal interest in the process. Should dissent break out in the government or the army over Saw Maung's dismissal on medical grounds, or in the belief that his subordinates, particularly his successor, General Than Shwe, or the Secretary One of the SLORC, Colonel Khin Nyunt, had done so contrary to the chain of command and for their own personal advantage, an unfortunate precedent of insubordination would have been established. Than Shwe and Khin Nyunt were involved at all stages in Saw Maung's removal, with Ne Win and Dr Maung Maung advising them on the process.[23] However, that was the limit of Ne Win's involvement in army affairs. Formally, Saw Maung was finally removed on 23 April, having passed the post of Minister of Defence to General Than Shwe on 20 March 1992. When his wife received news of his dismissal, she rushed to Ne Win's house, only to be assured by him that she and the family would be properly looked after and that he supported the change both for the good of the country and for Saw Maung himself.[24]

Perhaps to ease General Than Shwe into the role as the new head of state, a handwritten letter from Ne Win requesting that his photograph be removed from government offices and other public places was published in the Myanmar language edition of the *Working People's Daily* on 24 May 1992. Since 1962, Ne Win's photograph had been hung for more than twenty-five years, usually next to a photograph of Aung San. Ne Win was beginning to fade from public memory, just as he had faded from the public stage. The old soldier was now 82 years of age and in the early 1990s, spent much of his time at his wife's residence playing chess with members of his security detachment.

Five years after stepping down from the Party Chairmanship, Ne Win's involvement in the management of the upper reaches of the military leadership and the government had finally waned to little more than shadows and rumours. The larger problem he referred to in the 1970s on how to manage a family remained, however. There were indeed problems in his private life, as he drew ever closer to his daughter, Daw Khin Sanda Win, a medical doctor by training and a retired army major, and her husband, U Aye Zaw Win. They became involved in various business projects, including a hotel and communications systems, sometimes with German firms. His children's attempts to use his name and, therefore the residual influence of Ne Win, to their advantage leaked out to the international press. On 25 August 1993, *Asiaweek* published a brief article about Sanda Win's influence-peddling on behalf of her husband, of which several senior military men were said to have complained to Ne Win.[25] After an unpleasant altercation between her and the wife of a senior officer at a social function, Ne Win felt driven to go to the officer's home to apologize to him and his wife, lamenting that he could not control his daughter.[26]

From then on, Ne Win's life became entirely private and personal, despite much speculation to the contrary. In January 1994, he journeyed to Singapore for medical treatment, probably vascular irritation, as well as for dental and optical attention. Lee Kuan Yew, then Senior Minister of Singapore, called on him at his hospital and found a man looking much healthier than the "sickly person" he had met in 1986. Ne Win told Lee that he had been tormented for two years after he stepped down from office in 1988 about what was happening in the country, but in 1990 he started reading about and practising meditation seriously. When they met again, three years later, on another medical-related trip to Singapore, Ne Win, then 86, looked much healthier and hardier. He said he refused to discuss affairs of state with the generals' government and while he was worried about his family and their activities, he found relief in meditation (Lee 2000, p. 363). According to Ne Win's youngest brother, after retirement, he took up Vipassana (insight) meditation, and when not meditating or playing chess, read a great deal about Buddhism.[27]

Ne Win, accompanied by his daughter Sanda, his son-in-law and one grandson, visited Indonesia's President Soeharto in late September 1997. Soeharto hosted a dinner for the party and Ne Win visited the grave of Soeharto's late wife, Tien. While there was much speculation that somehow

Soeharto would become involved in a democratization scheme in Yangon, predicated on the assumption that Ne Win was still running Myanmar's government; it all, of course, came to nothing. Ne Win left Jakarta on 24 September for a short flight to Singapore where he again had a medical check-up.[28]

A year later, in late September 1998, and now at 88 years of age, Ne Win flew back to Singapore for further medical attention. There were rumours that he had died, but it was more likely that he had suffered from a stroke or heart attack.[29] The previous March, a party had been hosted by his daughter for a number of friends at the Sedona Hotel in Yangon. No one from the government or army attended.

The loss of power and influence did not come easily to some of Ne Win's family, particularly his grandsons. As the late 1990s wore on, his grandsons, whom he was said to dote upon, became virtual laws to themselves, leading a gang of over twenty young men around Yangon. Known as the Scorpions, the gang was broken up and many members were arrested in 2001.[30] There were rumours that they were involved in criminal activities, but it was more likely that they were just behaving as young men above the law.

The final farce of Ne Win's long life occurred on 7 March 2002 when the government arrested his son-in-law, Aye Zaw Win, and his three grandsons, Aye Ne Win, Kyaw Ne Win, and Zwe Ne Win, at the Oriental House Restaurant on Myoma Kyaung Road. Sanda was not arrested, but placed under house arrest so that she could continue to look after her father who was now getting very weak. Two days later, at a special press conference, Major General Kyaw Win, deputy head of military intelligence, explained the reasons for their arrest and the placing under house arrest of Ne Win's daughter. They were said to be plotting a coup to detain the three senior persons in the government, Senior General Than Shwe, General Maung Aye, and Lieutenant General Khin Nyunt, and put in place a government which recognized the authority of Ne Win.

On 18 March, a second press conference supplied further details of the alleged plot, including that those arrested had suborned the company commander assigned to provide Ne Win's security in order to carry out the plot, and that two regional commanders, some distance from Yangon, were allegedly involved. Their dubious business practices, which the government had ignored in the past, were noted, as were paraphernalia designed by one of the grandsons implying the existence of a Ne Win royal family. The whole incident smacked of fantasy and black magic as well as farce. The four arrested were placed on trial, found guilty and sentenced to death on 27 September 2002. Some of those convicted accused their lawyers of being tools of the government and declared they would not exercise their right of appeal. Aye Ne Win was quoted as shouting at his lawyer, "I have not been able to see my mother since we were arrested. What are you doing about that? Since you have been hired by the authorities you may as well do their bidding."[31] They appealed and lost. Aye Zaw Win and the youngest son, Zwe Ne Win, were released following the coming to power of President Thein Sein in 2010. Daw Khin Sanda Win was released earlier from house arrest, in December 2008. The other two grandsons were released from prison in November 2013.

It is unlikely that Ne Win knew of, let alone was involved in, the coup plot as it was so poorly planned and unlikely to have been successful. Moreover, it undermined one of his firmest principles, the necessity of maintaining the unity of the army and the sanctity of the chain of command. If he was aware of the coup, it is unlikely that he understood what was proposed. One of his doctors suspected that he had a minor stroke or brain lesions in his latter years and his mental faculties had become muddled.[32] Half-way through his 93rd year, he became increasingly weak and his death on 5 December 2002, while not expected, was not a surprise.[33]

Ne Win died at about 7:30 in the morning and was cremated in a simple Buddhist ceremony six hours later. He left instructions in the form of a handwritten note on 20 June 1989, the day he learned of the death of Dan Rose,[34] that his cremation should take place within thirty hours of his passing. Military Intelligence officers took control of the arrangements and, as he had also requested, his ashes were thrown into the nearby Hlaing River.[35] Only his daughter, Daw Khin Sanda Win, stepdaughter Thida Win, son U Ngwe Soe, a close cousin, a few other relatives and friends, just over a dozen, were present at the cremation. Others came to attend and pay their condolences to the family but were turned away by the authorities.

A simple notice of his death appeared in the Myanmar press the next day, noting that his wife Daw Khin May Than, son U Kyaw Thein, son U Aye Aung Win, and daughter Dr Daw Lei Lei Win pre-deceased him, and his familial survivors were U Ngwe Soe, Daw Thida Win, Dr Daw Thawda Win, Dr Daw Khin Sanda Win, U Pyo Wei Win, and Dr Daw

Kyai Hmon Win. Thanking those who had assisted and apologizing for the way the news was being announced to the people he knew, the notice from the family ended. In the starkness of the notification, the only trace of his long and eventful life was the echo of Ne Win's concluding one of his addresses to his comrades in the army or the party, "that is all".

Notes

1. The letters can be accessed at <http://asiapacific.anu.edu.au/newmandala/2011/06/17/aung-gyis-letters-to-ne-win>.
2. A good example of how rumour generates misinformation and half-truths is a *New York Times* account of the events of March. Published on 29 May, it stated that one student was killed in the tea shop in a brawl over debt, and the number arrested was 3,000.
3. *Forward*, vol. XXVI, no. 8 (1 May 1988): 2 and vol. XXVI, no. 9 (1 June 1988): 2.
4. *Forward*, vol. XXVI, no. 10 (1 July 1988): 2–3.
5. Earlier in May, Muslims of Bengali descent had attempted to take over the local administration in Maungdaw township and clashed with the security forces.
6. These and other events between March and September 1988 are catalogued in Khain Hkant, *8888 Dimokayeisei Ayeitowpun Hmattan* [Record of the 8888 Democracy Revolution] (Yangon: Kyee Hla Maung Sapei Taik, January 2013). A useful summary in English is found in Hans-Bernd Zollner, *The Beast and the Beauty: The History of the Conflict between the Military and Aung San Suu Kyi in Myanmar, 1988–2011, Set in a Global Context* (Berlin: Regiospectra, 2012), pp. 19–50.
7. Email communication with former political prisoner and confident of U Nay Min, June 2013.
8. *Naingngan Anka Theinpaik ywuyei: atwe Bama Pyi Kommyunit Pati Politbyuyo ci. Kyasinhmumya: hnit. LutHsaunghkyekmya* [Schemes and Activities of the Burma Communist Party Politburo to Seize State Power] (Yangon: News and Periodicals Corporation, January 1990) and Khin Nyunt, *Web of Conspiracy, Complicated Stories of Treacherous Machinations and Intrigues of the BCP UG, DAB, and Some NLD Leaders to Seize State Power* (Yangon: News and Periodicals Corporation, January 1991).
9. Interview with Major (rtd) Htway Han, 11 March 2006, former secretary of the BSPP.
10. This rule barred resignation from the party for reasons other than health.
11. Buddhist cycle of rebirth.

12. *Working People's Daily*, 24 July 1988. The speech is also translated in Maung Maung, *The 1988 Uprising*, pp. 39–41.
13. *Working People's Daily*, 24 July 1988.
14. *Working People's Daily*, 26 July 1988.
15. *Working People's Daily*, 27 July 1988.
16. Set Tun had been an artillery captain in the late 1950s and early 1960s. He was erroneously implicated in the incident on the Yangon University campus in the latter half of 1962 when two army officers drove onto the campus and were forced to abandon a car (a Volkswagen) by students, who subsequently set fire to the car. In a decision made by then Brigadier Aung Gyi, Set Tun was dismissed. He eventually returned to the infantry and was connected with both the 99th and the 66th Light Infantry Divisions, the latter at Pyay. Once, in the mid-1970s, Ne Win met Set Tun at Pyay and then brought him back to Yangon to serve as an assistant to his ADC, Captain Aye Kyaw. He continued to serve Ne Win until 1996 or 1997 when he was finally able to retire. Private communication, 13 August 2013.
17. Both were members of the Council of State. Ohn Kyee, born in 1924 in Einme, had joined the army during the BIA period and had risen through the ranks of the army and the party. Tha Kyaw had a similar career. Born in Sittwe in 1921, he was involved in making contacts with the British in the early days of the resistance.
18. Interview with Dr Kyaw Win, 21 March 2007.
19. Interview with Thakin Tin Mya, 13 March 2006.
20. Interview with Major (rtd) Htway Han, 11 March 2006.
21. Interview, Dr Kyaw Win, 21 March 2007.
22. Interview with a retired senior member of the army.
23. Interview with Dr Kyaw Win, 21 March 2007.
24. He eventually died of a heart attack in July 1997 at age 68.
25. *Asiaweek*, 25 August 1993, p. 58.
26. Confidential interview
27. Interview, U Thein Nyunt, 10 July 2012.
28. *The Nation*, 25 September 1997.
29. Reuters, 28 September 1998.
30. "Last members of the notorious Scorpion gang given amnesty", Mizzima news agency, 12 October 2011.
31. Seth Mydans, "Four Relatives of Myanmar's Ex-Strongman Sentenced to Death", *The New Work Times*, 27 September 2002. The American embassy report on the trial is contained in a telegram to the State Department dated 27 September 2002 and released via Wikileaks.
32. Interview with Univ. Prof. Dr Hc Mult. Franz Gerstenbrand, Vienna, 14 September 2008.

33. The United States charge d'affaires, Ms Carmen Martinez, reported his passing in a telegram entitled "Ding Dong Ne Win is Dead ... Finally", in a lame attempt to make light of the event by borrowing a phrase from the "Wizard of Oz". Telegram, 6 December 2002, issued by Wikileaks.
34. Daniel Rose was the American who facilitated Ne Win's first trip to the United States and sold arms to the Myanmar army during the civil war. Ne Win wrote, on learning of his death, that Dan Rose was a "true friend and whom I love like a brother". I am indebted to Dr Aung Myoe for drawing my attention to the note which was posted on the popularmyanmar.com website (accessed 4 December 2013).
35. Interview with U Thein Nyunt, 10 July 2012.

EPILOGUE
What to Make of Ne Win?

History not Theory.
Patriotism not Internationalism.
Evolution not Revolution.
Direction not Destruction.
Unity not Disruption.

Razumov's Credo in Joseph Conrad's Under Western Eyes

Despite what is known of his life, in many ways, Ne Win remains an enigma. There is too much unknown to form a rounded and satisfactory understanding of the man. He was a man of his time, and that time is now gone. The issues which inflamed nationalist politicians in Myanmar and other colonies in the 1920s and 1930s are all but forgotten, except by historians. The changing alliances and the violence of war and revolution in the 1940s throughout Europe and Asia are now the romance of movies and historical documentaries. The global Cold War and the anti-colonialist, anti-capitalist rhetoric of Third World leaders of the 1950s and 1960s are now marketed as Che Guevara and Ho Chi Minh T-shirts. The collapse of socialism and Communism is now taught as inevitable by the sons and daughters of the neoclassical economists who developed monetarism and privatization in the 1970s and 1980s. Men and women born in this century will find it hard to understand how once white skin was a necessary badge for admission to the centres of global power and wealth, or that men brought the world to the cusp of nuclear war over ideological shibboleths of Communism and Democratic Capitalism. Even if we knew more about Ne Win, it is doubtful we would know how to understand the world as he and his generation of Myanmar nationalists did.

However, some aspects of his character, purposes and intent do show through his words and actions. Of course, over a lifetime of more than nine decades, his opinions changed as he learned new things, experienced new sensations, and observed the world around him alter, seemingly imperceptively, but cumulatively, significantly. However, like most people, Ne Win was probably not as adaptable to change as he thought he was or perhaps he should have been, particularly towards the end of his political career. He was born in a township in the middle of a province of British India and died in a nation whose government was considered a pariah by the Western governments which had seen him for twenty-six years as a champion of anti-Communism and the nation he governed, the quiet hub around which the international politics of South, Southeast and East Asia's conflicts were waged. While those conflicts often ruffled the porous borders of Myanmar, Ne Win held the centre in check, at huge cost in terms of material wealth, but in the process saved many lives from the wars and revolutions that dominated those regions between the 1940s and the 1980s. Either during his years in power, or in the previous nearly a decade and a half from Myanmar's regaining independence, had he chosen to take a different path than he did, the history of the cold and hot wars of Asia in the second half of the twentieth century would almost certainly have been different.

The dominant interpretation of the meaning of Ne Win's life, at least in the English speaking world of journalism and academia, is that he was a tyrant who ultimately failed. As Ferdinand Mount wrote about another politician, "History to the defeated does not just say alas or pardon; history in the shape of obituaries ... sneers and patronises."[1] The first scholarly work to assess the politics of his attempt at revolution through the Revolutionary Council and the Burma Socialist Programme Party (BSPP) describes it as a failed revolution which created an anachronistic regime.[2] That regime was remarkably stable, something very unusual for military governments (Nakanishi 2013, p. 4). The secret to Ne Win's, and his military successors', long survival was control over the personnel of the armed forces and regular reassignment of members of the officer corps before retiring them into positions in the civil administration or economic institutions (Nakanishi 2013, p. 216). For better or worse, his successors continued this process and ensured the stability of the government which succeeded the BSPP's reign for another twenty-two years, despite the united efforts of Western governments and domestic and exiled political opponents to shift it from its self-appointed task. Despite Ne Win's desire to be seen as a politician, and not only as a soldier, and to create a party through which to govern, it was ultimately the army which was the basis of his power and the power of the state that he led. He failed to create a durable political system not largely dependent on the military for its existence.

Institutionally, the policies of the Revolutionary Council and the BSPP were also failures. The Party, and its mass and class organizations, did not resonate with genuine enthusiasm after a few years. Rather, they became bureaucratic routines in which their members had to participate as part of their employment to gain access to subsidized goods. As Ne Win and his revolution avoided not only the rhetoric of class conflict, but the mass mobilization campaigns of the Chinese and Vietnamese Communist parties, Myanmar avoided the chaos of the Communist revolutions which did, at least for a time, engage with the mass of the peasantry. The denouncing of landlords, capitalists, bureaucrats, intellectuals, and priests, as the evil human residue of feudalism, colonialism and capitalism, was not for Ne Win. Ne Win's revolution was largely one of live and let live, allowing time to liquidate the alleged inequities of the past. Given the economic disaster of 1987–88, and the draconic measures taken in 1988–89 to restore order and to reform the economy, it was remarkable that the successor to the BSPP still managed to gain 25 per cent of the votes in the 1990 elections. Though few would believe it today, there were still those who believed in socialism and had fond memories of the Lansin Youth organization, the literacy campaigns, the model peasants and workers, and the Luyehkyun scheme for outstanding students. In some unseen ways, they live on in new guises, denying their origins.

However, longevity and fond memories are not measures of success. Most certainly, no economist would point to Myanmar under Ne Win's guidance as a success story. Often one has heard economists and economist manqué claim that Myanmar under the British was the richest colony in Southeast Asia and the most promising economy in the region in the early 1950s. Presumably never having read Furnivall's *Colonial Policy and Practice* (Furnivall 1956), or examined the destruction of the Myanmar

TABLE 1

(a) Per capita GDP in Myanmar and Four Other Asian Countries in 1950–54, 1960–64, and 1985–89
(1985$: annual averages for the five years shown).

Country	1950–54	1960–64	1985–89
Myanmar	245	361	556
India	617	800	1,142
Philippines	896	1,204	1,627
Thailand	804	1,027	2,790
Taiwan	967	1,387	6,708

(b) Per capita GDP in Myanmar and Four Other Asian Countries in 1960–64 and 1985–89
(1985$: annual averages for five years shown)

Country	1960–64	1985–89
Myanmar	361	556
China	487	1,283
Indonesia	583	1,688
Malaysia	1,544	4,082
Singapore	1,899	9,578

Adapted from Anne Booth, "The Burma Development Disaster in Comparative Historical Perspective", *South East Asian Research*, Vol. 11, No. 2, Table 3, p. 145.

economy as a consequence of the Second World War, a credulous world put the blame for this economic disaster at the feet of Ne Win. Indeed, as demonstrated in Table 1 above, on a per capita GDP basis, Myanmar was an economic disaster, but the disaster did not start in 1962, its origins were earlier. Myanmar has been amongst the poorest countries in Asia since the end of the Second World War. In economic terms, the tragedy is, of course, that it has not only never caught up with other Asian economies but, relatively speaking, has fallen further behind. However, by persisting in failed policies long after outside observers, and some inside, described them as failures, Ne Win and his government did less than they might have been able to do to reverse Myanmar's economic decline. Of course, this assumes that economic growth, rather than domestic economic and social restructuring or international independence was, or should have been, the number one priority of the government.

The economic disaster which was created during the Ne Win years can be demonstrated from the many ways in which the Revolutionary Council and its successor Party government pursued their policies. Those policies were fundamentally the same as that pursued by the Anti-Fascists People's Freedom League governments in the 1950s, although, as Ian Brown argues (Brown 2013), pushed to extreme and beyond the point where they had any chance of succeeding, either comparatively or in their own terms. The unwillingness of Ne Win and his government to come up with viable alternative policies was the root of the economic failure. Most people would lay the blame on Ne Win himself, and surely he carries the largest responsibility. By the time he had come to recognize the necessity for change, he had surrounded himself with old colleagues with neither the technical competence nor the economic or political imagination to break free from the socialist dogma they had all been taught at the knee of Aung San as ventriloquized by the Revolutionary Council and the Burma Socialist Programme Party, both of which Ne Win chaired. Neither Aung San nor Ne Win had any economic training, but like most anti-colonial politicians, the rhetoric of socialism and anti-capitalism was mesmerizing and the logic of capitalism and international finance simultaneously enervating and enchaining. Independence came first.

No Myanmar nationalist politician during Ne Win's lifetime apparently ever aspired to the rhetorical level of many third world leaders such as Sukarno or Nkrumah, but they would have thoroughly understood and sympathized with these words:

> They talk to me about progress, about "achievements", diseases cured, improved standards of living.
>
> I am talking about societies drained of their essence, cultures trampled underfoot, institutions undermined, lands confiscated, religions smashed, magnificent artistic creations destroyed, extraordinary *possibilities* wiped out.
>
> They throw facts at my head, statistics, mileages of roads, canals, and railroad tracks. ...
>
> I am talking about millions of men torn from their gods, their land, their habits, their life — from life, from the dance, from wisdom ...
> I am talking about millions of men in whom fear has been cunningly instilled, who have been taught to have an inferiority complex, to tremble, kneel, despair, and behave like flunkeys. ...

I am talking about natural *economies* that have been disrupted — harmonious and viable *economies* adapted to the indigenous population — about food crops destroyed, malnutrition permanently introduced, agricultural development oriented solely toward the benefit of the metropolitan countries; about the looting of product, the looting of raw materials.

They pride themselves on abuses eliminated.

I too talk about abuses, but what I say is that on the old ones — very real — they have superimposed others — very detestable. They talk to me of local tyrants brought to reason; but I note that in general the old tyrants get on very well with the new ones, and that there has been established between them, to the detriment of the people, a circuit of mutual services and complicity (Cesaire 2000, pp. 42–43).

Perhaps too polite to point these arguments out to the British and later other Westerners who proffered capitalist nostrums to them, and feeling little need to whip up the nationalist sentiments of their fellow countrymen, such rhetoric did not need to be enunciated. Ne Win positively eschewed it, for in his view, rhetoric changed nothing.

Given the overriding nationalist goal of undermining the plural economy and the plural society which it generated, a goal of every nationalist politician from the 1930s onwards, the policies that the Revolutionary Council pursued were a success. By the 1970s, the overwhelming bulk of the economy was in government or indigenous entrepreneurial, including peasant, ownership. While a large proportion of landless labourers still existed, and the land reform scheme a muddle, foreign landlords and foreign owners of the limited means of industrial production were eliminated. The country might have been an economic disaster in many eyes, but it was a Myanmar economic disaster (Taylor 1995, pp. 45–63). As Dr Ba Maw said in 1962, as long as it was a *Burmese* way to socialism, it would be acceptable while any other way would not. Distributive justice was also a goal of economic policy and, for all its faults, Myanmar under Ne Win had an economy where the extremes of wealth and poverty observed in other, more economically developed societies, did not exist. Yangon and other cities came down to the level of the village, as soldiers and their families raised chickens and pigs within a few blocks of downtown. Moreover, there were no large rubbish dumps with scavengers living off the detritus of the rich, as found in other Asian capitals deemed as more successful.

It is not difficult to argue, within the terms of conventional economics, that the Myanmar economy was a disaster twenty-six years after Ne Win seized power. Myanmar's GDP growth during the period of his rule averaged less than 4 per cent a year (Myat Thein 2004, p. 55, Table 3.1), and with population growth at about 2 per cent per annum, little real increase in the standard of living of the population could be realized. Though inflation, until the final two years of BSPP rule, was normally kept in check, the collapse in foreign trade, and the emphasis on large-scale industrial projects, left little for increasing private consumption. Workers' wages were squeezed to pay for development which should have, but did not, reward future generations, and peasant producers denied any incentive to produce more for the state. Where there was growth in private consumption, the main beneficiaries were the black marketeers. The heavy emphasis on investment in the development of processing and manufacturing, to the neglect of agriculture, had not paid dividends (Myat Thein 2004, p. 61, Table 3.2). The mistake of the inherited fixation on industrialization from the days of civilian rule of the New Burma in the New World, with smoke pouring from chimneys above a sawtooth line of factory roofs, was never realized even after forty years of trying. Myanmar was not the only country in Southeast Asia to make that mistake.[3] While Myanmar's capitalist neighbours, such as Thailand, economically developed with their open economies and the receipt of significant foreign investment from Japan, the United States and Western Europe, Myanmar remained on a drip feed of limited foreign assistance and loans. The loans were sufficient, however, to cause the bankruptcy of the state in 1988, because the dividends they needed to generate did not materialize.

In the light of other criteria, criteria which stemmed not from the industrial revolution and the notion of the power of nations, but of coping with human needs, perhaps Ne Win's time might be judged more tolerantly, though far from glowingly. During his period of rule, the population of the country grew by an estimated 73 per cent, from 22.8 million to 39.4 million. During that time, paddy production roughly kept pace with population growth, despite some periods of decline, and in as much as exports declined, an increase in per capita consumption was indicated. This was despite the inhibitions placed in the way of production, but a consequence of irrigation schemes and the introduction of high yield rice varieties in the early 1970s. People probably ate more protein during the Ne Win era than earlier periods, if the increase in livestock production were to be a guide: sheep and goats by 184 per cent (510,000 to 1,458,000), pigs by 376 per cent (643,000 to 3,019,000), chickens by 332 per cent (7,756,000 to 33,483,000), and ducks by 150 per cent (2,416,000 to 6,032,000).

In the education sector, leaving aside quality, schools were starved for funds for teaching materials and supplies, and foreign exchange for the purchase of educational aids from abroad became nearly non-existent in the end. The number of primary schools grew by 118 per cent (14,464 to 31,499) while the number of primary teachers by 337 per cent (43,091 to 188,417). Non-discriminatory basic education was available to a larger proportion of the population than at any time in the past. The increase in the numbers of teaching personnel at all levels is striking. Middle schools, of which there were 770 in 1962, had increased to 1,702 in 1988, but the number of teachers had grown by 537 per cent, up to 44,958 (from 7,059). Officially, at least, the staff/student ratio was 27 to one at the primary and the middle levels. At the high school level, though relatively few pupils continued to that level because of an inability to pay the ancillary costs of an allegedly free system, there were just 250,000 students in 1988. That, however, was still an increase of 207 per cent over 1962 (when the number was a mere 81,503), with an increase of teachers of 482 per cent.

Agricultural, teacher training, and other vocational schools saw similar increases, with particularly strong growth in technical high schools, from 1 to 12 for the entire country. No doubt, the quality of the teaching was poor, and finally, towards the end of Ne Win's rule, the legalization of so-called "tuition classes or schools" took place, making a virtue of a necessity. A similar story of growth in numbers, if not in quality, could be observed at the university level. The number of university teachers grew 418 per cent, from 1,206 to 6,250. Student numbers grew more than 1,000 per cent, from 20,000 to 256,000. However, higher education was often disrupted by political unrest, with all universities closed in the mid-1970s for three consecutive years, and many students studied under a poorly resourced distance-learning scheme. Also, the cost of education precluded many who could have benefitted and this held back development. In the education sphere, despite the expansion of personnel and provision during the Ne Win period, Myanmar still ranked among the less-developed countries in Asia, such as Sri Lanka.

In terms of health care, the number of hospitals and hospital beds increased slightly faster than the growth of the population, but the production of doctors, nurses and midwives was prodigious, with Myanmar becoming an exporter of doctors at one time. The number of doctors working in the country increased by 744 per cent, from 1,907 to 16,087 between 1962 and 1988. Nurses and midwives increased 563 per cent from 2,476 to 16,425. Moreover, the quality of health education did not deteriorate as badly as in other spheres of education. Medical degrees in Myanmar were recognized in England long after those of many former colonies were denied British certification. The number of dispensaries and health centres increased more rapidly and much work was done to increase rural public health, sometimes at the cost of urban development.[4] Station hospitals and people's hospitals, while not providing all kinds of services, were available in most townships, and while patients' families had to bring their own food and often purchase medicine on the black market, there was a strong effort to provide basic health care to the public.

In terms of human development indicators, Myanmar's literacy rate increased from 57 per cent in 1960 to 80 per cent by 1986. Life expectancy at birth had increased from 43.8 years to 59.2 years, an increase of 35 per cent. Income, on the other hand, on a per capita basis, had grown by 44 per cent, from 1,047 kyat to 1,510 kyat, according to Myat Thein (Myat Thein 2004, p. 114, Table 4.16). Myanmar was still a poor country and few jobs were available for those with university degrees outside of government service.

Despite the failure of the socialist governments to change the overall structure of the economy and the labour force from that inherited from the British, significant spending as a proportion to total public spending, averaging 20 per cent a year of total state investment, was devoted to infrastructure development. However, the inefficiency of the socialist management system and the inadequacies of communications and power production, destroyed what little gains were made. By 1980, Myanmar still had only two telephones per 1,000 persons, a provision worse than the average for other least developed nations (Myat Thein 2004, pp. 109–11). Nonetheless, to Ne Win's and the BSPP's credit, and an indication of their intentions, social sector development during the socialist era outshone other development indicators. The road to hell was at least paved with good intentions.

What other aspects of Ne Win's rule need to be examined? Certainly one that his critics would hold up for condemnation was his treatment of the political opposition to his regime, both from the left

TABLE 2

Social Sector Indicators in Myanmar and Other Countries, 1960–80

	Myanmar 1960	Myanmar 1980	Average of 33 Low Income Countries 1980
GNP per capita US$		170	260
Adult literacy rate %	60	70	50
No. enrolled in primary school (% of age group)	56	84	94
Life expectancy at birth	44	54	28.5
Infant mortality rate (per 1,000)	129	101	94
% population with access to safe water		35 urban, 20 rural	31
Population per physicians (persons)	15,560	5,260	5,810
Daily calorie supply as % of amount required		103	47

Adapted from Myat Thein, *Economic Development of Myanmar* (Singapore: Institute of Southeast Asian Studies, 2004), Table 4.15, p. 113.

and from the right. Indeed, many persons were arrested and interrogated using harsh and cruel methods. The exact numbers will never be known. While there was no exculpation for such practices, had his opponents from the Anti-Fascist People's Freedom League (AFPFL) period remained in power, it is unlikely that they would have been more regarding of civil liberties than they had been in the 1950s, particularly in regard to the ethnically designated insurgent leaders or suspected or actual members of the Burma Communist Party (BCP). It is equally unlikely that the leaders of the BCP, had they succeeded in forcing Ne Win from power, would have been any more regarding of civil rights, and perhaps a good deal less. In the Cold War era, the high regard which is now paid for civil rights, real and declared, did not exist. As diplomats wrote at the time, Burma did not seem as oppressive then as it came later to be described (for a less charitable view, see Donnison 1970, pp. 173 and 181–82). Ne Win was capable of being ruthless, but all of his political opponents died either in combat, at the hands of others, or in their beds. Myanmar has not experienced the mass bloodshed that occurred in other Southeast Asian societies, such as the widespread massacre of alleged political opponents overseen by the Indonesian army in 1965, or the Khmer Rouge in the 1970s, despite years of civil strife.

The nationalization of the press, and the imposition of censorship on all forms of publishing, did lead to a great diminution of the availability of ideas and opinions contrary to that of the officially approved state dogma. Much of the censorship was petty and frustrating in its stupidity. Much was self-defeating for the absence of real news meant that the tales concocted in tea shops became accepted versions of events, however implausible. It was, however, much easier to isolate the country in those days before the invention of satellite television and the Internet. Given the absence of local news, the newspapers were full of international news and many ordinary people were much better informed on world affairs than their counterparts abroad. Ne Win was not opposed to allowing international media to be made available, and when the Thatcher government threatened to close the BBC Burmese Service broadcasts in the late 1980s, he wrote personally to ask that they be maintained. Ironically, in 1988 the BBC Burmese Service became a key source of information inside the country on the anti-BSPP campaign to bring down his government (Kyaw Yin Hlaing 2004, pp. 402–4).

Perhaps the greatest victim of the closure of alternative news and information to that of the government was the government itself. Cut off from new ideas and new developments in economic theory and the sciences, Myanmar's academics and intellectuals, technicians and entrepreneurs, became out of touch with the latest developments in their respective fields. The universities were eventually starved for scientific journals, in part because of the shortage of hard currencies in their budgets with which to buy the materials they required. Physics teachers often got the latest news on developments in their field not from scholarly articles, but popularized versions in publications like *Time* magazine. However, still some small bits of innovation and change were undertaken. The teaching of international relations was begun at both Mandalay and Yangon universities in 1982, under the auspices of Ne Win's wife, Daw Ni Ni Myint, as a way of getting away from the stifling ideological teaching of politics by the Party.

If, by any contemporary standard, the socialist revolution Ne Win led was an economic, political and intellectual mistake, other questions arise about why he introduced the policies he did, and why he persisted with them beyond the point of obvious failure. The expression he used in the 1960s that once he had "grabbed the tiger's tail, it was difficult to let go", was no excuse. Letting go was difficult, but not impossible. Other socialist systems changed and adapted. The argument sometimes heard was that he did not know how bad the situation was persuades only on the margins. He may have been isolated, mislead and bamboozled from time to time, but he had his own sources of information. Moreover, Ne Win was aware that he could be and would be misled by subordinates trying to excuse or explain away failures of policy or execution. If he saw their elucidations as evasive, he may have concluded that the policy was correct, but the implementation was fallacious. However, the weight of evidence of the failure of the system was so great that to believe this one must assume he refused to face reality. Nothing in his behaviour suggests that was a trait of his.

The answer, it would appear, was not that he did not know the revolution was a failure, but he feared the alternative. In the relatively benign international atmosphere of the 1980s, it would have been acceptable to China under Deng and his successors for Myanmar to have re-engaged with the world economy and abandoned socialist autarky. The Japanese government had been pushing Myanmar in that direction for over a decade. He could see the development of Thailand and

Singapore for himself. However, change brings uncertainty and he had surrounded himself with party leaders, ministers, and the party itself, as demonstrated at the final Party Congress, that loathed change. Change threatened their livelihoods and status. Evolution, rather than revolution, would have to be attempted, but the ultimate crisis of 1987–88 was too deep and sudden to allow for an evolutionary approach. Well before the 1962 coup, Myanmar, for reasons of national security, had opted out of the American hegemony that provided the prosperity for much of East and Southeast Asia (Berger 2004). Opting back in would be both difficult and potentially raised the threats to domestic stability that the overeager Americans, and their rogue agencies, brought in the past.

Moreover, Ne Win did not believe that the men with whom he had to work with were sufficiently competent to undertake change of such a large measure. In addition, he still despaired of the Myanmar people who, despite being shoved and pushed, beaten and bullied, were still, in his eyes, the same rather lazy, gullible people who had lost the country's economic and political independence in the nineteenth century. He had only twenty-five years towards the end of the twentieth century to remake a nation with more than a thousand years of history behind it. Would reopening not bring back the same economic and political interests that undermined Myanmar's independence in the 1950s and threatened to kill any chance of achieving the goals of the nationalist movement of the 1930s and the anti-imperialist struggles of the 1940s?

Ne Win could not be sure, and therefore it was better to be cautious than to rush forward without a plan. What that plan should be, however, was no longer as obvious as it had seemed in the 1960s when he turned the economy over to Tin Pe and Ba Nyein. The modification of the radical autarky of the Revolutionary Council, as carried out through the planning mechanism of the 1970s and 1980s, had already demonstrated how easily Myanmar could become entangled with international financial interests. To go further down that road meant the end of the dream for which he and his army had fought in the 1940s and 1950s. If he opened the floodgates of reform, would the British, the Americans, the South Asians and the Chinese not be back once more sucking the economic and cultural essence out of the marrow of Myanmar's bones? It was doubtful, furthermore, whether the state had the capacity to impose change, particularly on the peasantry. The existing system benefitted some, to the cost of many and, at the local level, those who had power also had wealth.

When Ne Win told Lee Kuan Yew of the torment he felt at the direction the country was taking in the first few years after 1988, and only eventually found peace through meditation and resignation, he was revealing perhaps more than he realized. One heard little of his views after 1988, just rumours that he was still controlling the government. However, the military government he put in place behaved very differently from any government he ever led, from nomenclature and propaganda, to major policy issues (for details of that period, see Taylor 2009, pp. 375–506). Ceasefire agreements, rather than political and military integration, with former Communist and ethnically designated insurgent groups were sought and, in many cases, achieved. Areas along the border became no-go zones for the government and its army, an abnegation of sovereignty Ne Win would never have countenanced. The economy, except for a few strategic sectors, was thrown open to foreign investment. Indigenous entrepreneurs were identified and provided with state assets and access to land and raw materials. Tourists were welcomed and plans for large-scale tourism, including foreign-owned hotels and resorts, were developed. Though spurned for its human rights record by Western governments and the international multilateral financial agencies which they control, neighbouring countries were encouraged to and did invest and trade with Myanmar.

In terms of other aspects of domestic policy, there was also a dramatic shift. Throughout Ne Win's period, the government was never able to raise adequate revenue to maintain itself and develop the country. Infrastructure projects were postponed and the country's highway and railway systems were little changed between 1948 and 1988. Now, despite the curtailment of almost all forms of external economic assistance, road and railway, bridge and airport, construction went ahead at seemingly breakneck pace. Military expenditure, in U.S. dollar terms, more than doubled from the niggardly amounts of government budgets under Ne Win, in the first year he was out of office and more than doubled again in the next seven years (Selth 2002, pp. 132 and 134, Figures 10 and 13). These, and post–Ne Win development projects, were consequently paid for through the sacrifices of the poor, through their labour and endurance of years of high inflation of the kind that Ne Win would not have tolerated. The security printing presses at Wazi, built to protect the kyat from the costs of printing Myanmar's currency abroad, now printed money with abandon to pay for the development of the infrastructure of the country. Many standards of service provided by the socialist state also suffered, including the educational and health systems, as the underfunding that they had endured in the socialist era was compounded. Even the name of the country in English and other Western languages was changed from the colonial Burma, which Ne Win had used, to Myanmar.

Moreover, the cult of Aung San was diminished in prominence, in part because his daughter, Daw Aung San Suu Kyi, was the most obvious symbol of opposition to continued army rule. Whereas Ne Win always referred to Aung San Suu Kyi as "my leader's daughter", and would not listen to criticism of her,[5] the state-controlled media occasionally described her contumeliously. Aung San's advocacy of socialism was forgotten and his position as the founding father of the army was diminished as the military traditions of the country would said to stem from Anawratha, Bayinnaung, and Alaungpaya, the kind of warrior kings Ne Win denounced as the feudalists who first created ethnic strife in the country. When conflicts occurred with neighbouring states, they were no longer referred to as merely "the other country", but named, and in some cases, denigrated. Ne Win would not have thought this sensible.

The rapid adoption of Western modes of dress, and the tolerance for rap and rock music the new military government provided, Ne Win would not have tolerated, seeing this as a decadent attack on traditional Burmese culture. The ostentatious displays of religiosity on the part of senior government ministers who were shown paying elaborate homage to senior Buddhist monks almost daily in the media would have looked impious and inappropriate to Ne Win. His strong advocacy of the separation of state and religion had lessened in the final years of his rule, but only marginally, and nothing like the displays led by his successors. Their ostentation included even taking upon themselves grand titles of the kind he would have rejected. The rank of Senior General was invented and promotions in the army were handed out with a liberality which would have shocked him.

The army was clearly happy to be outside of the control of the Party and its chairman after 1988. It began a policy of aggrandisement which the country could ill afford in its current state of finances. Therefore, it turned to China and other governments willing to provide loans and give military assistance in order to rapidly expand the army from less than 200,000 to more than 400,000. Defence training and educational facilities were also enlarged and annual intakes were doubled in many cases. By turning to China and other friendly Asian governments for assistance, the government developed a degree of dependency on its neighbours which Ne Win would have abhorred. Neutrality was being compromised. The Western orientation to arms purchases quickly gave way to Eastern European and predominantly Chinese equipment (Selth 2002, pp. 133 and 137, Figures 11 and 14). Many of the things he may have feared might happen if change came, did. Even his own family could not resist. As he once remarked, "My chaps can stand any amount of adversity, but prosperity is something some of them cannot withstand." (Maung Maung 1999, p. 118). Corruption and conspicuous consumption on the part of the new military rulers soon became widespread and much grander than the petty corruption of the socialist period.

Though Myanmar's neutrality was being compromised, it was not completely undermined despite the application of Western economic sanctions because of another legacy of Ne Win. The government of Myanmar was not particularly concerned about the sanctions. Myanmar's ratio of GDP to trade was among the lowest amongst developing countries, at less than 4 per cent, comparable to Albania or North Korea. Trade was not a significant factor in the official economy. Prior to the imposition of American investment sanctions and the 1997 Asian financial crisis, the termination of bilateral and multilateral economic assistance was quickly overcome as a result of foreign investment, particularly in offshore gas production and mining. Not only had Ne Win left the gas and minerals in the ground until they were needed, he created a state which could survive on a modest income until and unless the economy improved. Of course, the limited health and educational provision which was inherited from the socialist era suffered from under-investment, as state and regime security took priority.

Ne Win's socialist revolution was a failure, he held on to power for too long, and was unwilling to change sufficiently to save his reputation. However, any assessment of a person's life should not only consider the latter half. Ne Win had had a political and military career at the centre of Myanmar's politics since the late 1930s. If he governed alone for twenty-six years, he governed with others for nearly as long. His role in the formation and leadership of the Burma Independence Army, the Burma Defence Army, the Burma National Army, the Patriot Burmese Forces, and the British Burma Army, in the decade leading up to independence was significant and cannot be ignored in any assessment of his life. His leadership following the assassination of Aung San and then the civil war that engulfed Myanmar helped, perhaps ensured, the survival of the British plans for Burma's independence and the continuity of the government under U Nu and the AFPFL for ten years.

Consider what would have been the consequences if Ne Win had been induced, as he was urged, to switch his allegiance from Nu's government to the Communists at the height of the civil war. Almost certainly, the government would have either fallen quickly to the Communists or, in order to maintain a grip on power, turned to the British and Indian governments for support. One of the prices for that support would have been to come to terms with the demands of the Kayin and Mon insurgent groups to turn the mutinying ethnic armies against the predominantly Bamar army. Quite likely, as demonstrated by the behaviour of Naw Seng, the Kachin and other ethnic troops would have defected to fight for the autonomy of their areas. Would China or the United States have stood back and allowed Myanmar's civil war to lead to the complete breakup of the country into Communist and ethnically controlled armed enclaves? What happened subsequently in Korea and Vietnam suggests not. Ne Win and the army he led forestalled major international armed conflict in Asia for two years and in Southeast Asia for more than a decade. Maybe it would not have happened like this, but it might have.

To speculate again, what would Ne Win's reputation have been had he chosen to retire in 1974 or 1981? Either of these dates would have been possible and appropriate. In 1974, he could have departed as the man who had finally made the socialist revolution work. Twice he would have been seen as the saviour of the nation who had handed power back to the people in the form of a constitutional government after resolving political and social issues. Though he had taken the country through difficult economic adjustments, the economy was now under the control of the indigenous population and relations with neighbours were once more restored to levels of threat that could be managed. The festive atmosphere of the constitutional referendum would have been his departure party. Had he stepped down in 1981, when he threatened to do so, he would have left at a time when it seemed as if the socialist economic system might actually succeed. The economic development of neighbouring countries was just gaining momentum, so invidious comparisons were not yet common place. When the economy collapsed six or seven years later, the blame would have been put on the shoulders of his successors, not Ne Win.

However, he did not step down when he might have, and when he did go, he left nothing in his wake but a vacuum that he was soon drawn back into at least to the extent of engineering or supervising his successors through to 1992. Had his words at the 1988 Extraordinary Party Congress not been so ambivalent on the question of a referendum on changing the party system, he might have been able to manage the transition to a multi-party system. Many people still looked to him for solutions to the country's problems. Had he been more forceful and insistent on economic reforms and brought in economic advisers, including foreign advisers as he had done in the 1950s, he might have been able to steer Myanmar from a socialist economy to a more mixed system as happened in China and Vietnam. However, he did not. He had apparently grown too tired to think anew or too fearful of change to risk forcing through policies whose outcomes were difficult to predict.

This book is a political biography. Speculation on the part of the author about motives and intents has been avoided as much as possible. This book is not about Ne Win's personality or private life except as it was seen to impinge on his public activities. Nor is it an attempt to confirm or, more likely, deny the many exaggerated claims that have been made over the years about his alleged irrational or implausible behaviour. However, some efforts have been made to try to understand the kind of man Ne Win was, and how he changed, if he did, over the years. Robert Caro, in his multi-volume biography of Lyndon Johnson, suggests that while Lord Acton may have been correct when he said that "power tends to corrupt and absolute power corrupts absolutely", it is not necessarily the case. Caro goes on, however, to argue that power is greater at revealing a man. In Johnson's case, his achievement of the presidency of the United States revealed his hidden commitment to civil rights and the creation of a more equitable society.

What did power reveal about Ne Win? The answer to that depends a great deal on the period of his life that is being examined. His control of the army in the 1950s revealed a man who did not seek power, but rather stability and, often, pleasure. The puritanical streak which was revealed after 1962 was well-hidden. As Lord Gore-Booth wrote, Ne Win then "... played a somewhat elusive part in Burmese public life, alternating between bursts of energy and an enjoyment of golf, racing and family life". Gore-Booth further noted that Ne Win "had an instinct for power and political manoeuvre unusual among Burmese in public life and much of the history of Burma over the period is a history of how he used those skills" (Gore-Booth 1974, p. 213). He alternated between periods of intense and often detailed administrative and planning activities, and of holiday, relaxation, and concerns for his health which sometimes seemed to verge on hypochondria.

His behaviour during the civil war, when he could have seized power in his own name, or that of the Communist Party, suggests a man who strongly believed in orderly government and the need for loyalty to whatever organization to which he was responsible. Despite his misgivings about how the AFPFL government functioned until 1958, he served it loyally. When he handed power back to Nu in 1960, he revealed a man who kept his word. However, as he got drawn more and more deeply into the politics of Myanmar as the threats of the Cold War developed further, and the possibility that internal fissiparous tendencies became stronger, a greater loyalty was revealed and that was loyalty to the unity and independence of Myanmar. That loyalty and his belief that the policies that he had advocated in the past would more quickly and effectively establish the socialist republic that independence sought to achieve caused him to order the coup of 1962.

Having grasped "the tiger's tail", Ne Win appears to have quickly realized that he had taken on a task more complex and difficult than he had expected. In 1958, when Maung Maung and Julian Licht were discussing economic policy, he walked out of the room and left it to them to discuss. In 1962, that option was not available, unless he turned the economy over to Aung Gyi. However, Aung Gyi was soon perceived to be inadequately loyal to the socialist ideal and perhaps insufficiently loyal to Ne Win, to be allowed his own way and was discarded within a year of the coup. Because Ne Win saw all politics and policies as interrelated, and that foreign policy and national security took priority over domestic policy, the nostrums of Tin Pe and Ba Nyein were more appealing than the more outward looking economic strategies proposed as alternatives. Only when Tin Pe's health failed, and his economic policies had demonstrated convincingly their failure, did Myanmar switch to a more orthodox system of national planning. While in the 1970s, Ne Win revealed a willingness to compromise his desire for autarky, he would not give up the nationalist ideal of Myanmar socialism. While he was dedicated to socialism as an ideological abstract, his ideas on the subject were obscure and vague. Unlike his discussions of Buddhism which were grounded in wide reading and study, his socialism was ethereal and largely ethical in content, not programmatic.[6]

He displayed ideas about economics, widespread in Myanmar and other developing countries, that markets are inherently skewed in favour of the rich and profits are by their nature immoral. The price of an item should be what it cost to produce, not what it would fetch in the market.[7]

Power also revealed another characteristic in Ne Win which he shared with the majority of his fellow Myanmar and that is a belief that Myanmar is a multi-ethnic nation. However, unlike many other political leaders, Bamar and those claiming rights on behalf of ethnic minorities, he did not see ethnicity, "national races", as justifying differential political treatment. Tracing ethnic conflict back to Myanmar's history, as did the British, Ne Win saw unequal treatment growing out of feudalism and monarchical political practices. The solution to that was to divorce politics from ethnicity and treat everyone equally as citizens of a modern Myanmar state. Cultural differences existed and should be celebrated as part of the inherited culture of the country, but cultural differences did not justify political privileges on the part of either minorities or the majority. As with other problems, Ne Win saw the solution to ethnic conflict in Myanmar as a long-term proposition which only time and understanding would resolve. His establishment of the Institute for the Development of National Races, an experiment in multicultural living and learning, designed to create teachers from all groups with a Myanmar vision, was one consequence of his idealism. Though he sometimes spoke in the stereotypical terms of his generation, his dealing with individuals often belied his words. For example, as long as his Anglo-Burmese colleagues in the army accepted his political programme, they remained in place. Only when they dissented politically, did they remove themselves or he dismiss them. Ne Win was an egalitarian but not a romantic.[8]

Power also revealed in Ne Win a devotion to the borders of Myanmar as inherited from the British. He held as the primary obligation of the army to defend the country's borders and ensure that the country did not fall apart. Indeed, it may have been fear of that possibility that ensured he remained loyal to U Nu's government in 1949. The sanctity of borders, however, had to be preserved with the means that were available. His recognition of Myanmar's relative military and economic weakness required him to pursue joint strategies of military suppression of those seeking to dismantle the inherited borders of Myanmar and political co-optation and compromise on all but first principles. Also, he took a long view of the conflicts that his army faced. A quick military solution to the separatist problem did not exist. The demands, in the name of politicized ethnicity, to break up Myanmar would not end until all political leaders understood that they had more to lose breaking away than remaining in the country. The development of that perception was only partially in the hands of the government of Myanmar. Neighbouring countries also played a role, and his government had no capacity to change their behaviour other than by dealing with them on a principled basis. He was a realist, not a romantic.

Perhaps the most important thing that Ne Win in power ever revealed was his innate ability to understand the domestic and international political problems of other political leaders both in Myanmar and abroad. He could see problems from the position of the other side, and therefore was able to craft responses which protected Myanmar's and his interests while not worsening relations. He took a long-term view of problems and analysed options coolly and rationally. Despite his well-known temper[9] and tendency to enter into a rage, he controlled himself whenever an important and fundamental policy problem appeared. Despite his petulance, he was remarkably cool and composed when it came to the big questions of Myanmar and international relations, appreciating the importance of power, or its absence, in determining affairs. He also considered the long-term implications of issues long after short-term ones were resolved. His extended periods abroad offered him opportunities to study how the rest of the world operated and to understand their political issues. He used that knowledge to Myanmar's advantage in the Cold War.

Finally, power revealed in Ne Win what it does in almost all men and woman who achieve it: power, once acquired, is hard to give up. It is not so much the perks and privileges of power as the exhilaration of making history. He was aware of this danger, at least in his early years in power but as he felt he had found no worthy successor, or perhaps having made it impossible for anyone of comparable competence to succeed him, giving up power was nearly impossible until time and circumstances forced it upon him.

What power did not reveal in Ne Win was how he had changed over the years. The scoffer at religions in the 1950s became the serious student of Buddhism by the 1970s. Nonetheless, he largely kept his religious interests restricted to his private life. In his final decade, if not sooner, he read and studied Vipassana meditation. Earlier, he had taken a deep interest in the history of Buddhism in Myanmar. However, unlike many Myanmar politicians and military leaders both before and after him, Ne Win did not attempt to claim great religious insights or ostentatiously display his Buddhist faith. Many people claimed that he was very superstitious. His alleged attachment to the number nine was often cited as proof, particularly the issuance of 45 and 90 kyat notes in 1987. The contrary issuance of 75 kyat notes in 1985 was said to mark his 75th birthday, though most people would have believed him to be 74 in 1985. The choice of different denominations, of course, could be explained as ensuring that the old currency did not remain in circulation, thus fleecing the illiterate.

It is doubtless the case that many people in Myanmar, as elsewhere, do participate in activities that would appear to derive from non-rational beliefs. Ne Win may well have been surrounded by such persons. However, no evidence was discovered which would convince a sceptic that he was indeed superstitious.[10] Even if he was, there was no evidence to suggest that this shaped his decisions on fundamental matters of policy. Most claims of the superstitious basis of his actions were, of course, proposed by persons with no knowledge of what Ne Win was thinking or intending at the time of taking the actions. Many times, no superstitious explanation was offered, especially if the decision was one which received approval. To those who wish to believe in astrological or other superstitious beliefs and practices, there is no dislodging their faith despite repeated failures of prediction. In Myanmar, one finds as much scepticism about superstition as one does in the rest of the world. The credulous are always with us. In fact, nothing revealed about Ne Win, as opposed to fantasy, suggests credulity.

Though there is no monument of Ne Win in Myanmar, many still abominate him and his memory. However, he was a major figure not only in Myanmar's history, but also in Cold War history. His lack of vanity, his disregard for what the world thought of him and his actions, his willingness to drive his people to retake control of Myanmar against what he saw as their languorous and unsophisticated nature, shaped many aspects of the Myanmar that exists today. What he wanted to build, an autonomous socialist state was not, perhaps could not be, achieved. His larger goal of creating a unified society which was in the hands of its own population remains a work in progress. All of what he attempted may yet disappear, rather as he has returned to the stardust from which we all may have come. But if the country for which he fought does become a united, self-governing, and culturally distinctive nation, proud of its history, appreciative and conserving of its traditions, and does not become just another country seduced by the power and glitz of globalization and inane mass culture, then his monument will be Myanmar itself. Like the socialist dreams of his generation, that is probably impossible and his place in Myanmar and Cold War history thus will remain unmarked.

Notes

1. "Selwyn and the Real World", *The Spectator*, 26 May 1978, p. 4. Also, Ferdinand Mount, *Cold Cream: My Early Life and Other Mistakes* (London: Bloomsbury, 2008), p. 262. Mount added that the obituaries of the defeated can also be used to add to the mythology and fantasy that their enemies love to retail. See, for example, the obituary of General Ne Win in *The Telegraph* (London), 6 December 2002.
2. Yoshihiro Nakanishi, *Strong Soldiers, Failed Revolution: The State and Military in Burma, 1962–88* (Kyoto: Kyoto University Press, 2013), p. xix. Dr Nakanishi also describes the Ne Win era as producing a "crooked" (his quotation marks) government, but he does not explain what he meant by "crooked" other than implying it was anachronistic, an adjective he also uses to describe the military and party governments in Myanmar between 1962 and 2011.
3. It was not until the end of 1986 that Vietnam's economic leaders recognized that it was a mistake to rush into industrialization before they were ready. Sophie Quinn-Judge, "Victory on the Battlefield: Isolation in Asia: Vietnam's Cambodia Decade, 1979–1989", in *The Third Indochina War: Conflict between China, Vietnam and Cambodia, 1972–1979*, edited by Odd Arne Westad and Sophie Quinn-Judge (London: Routledge, 1966), p. 222.
4. These statistics, and those above, are drawn from comparisons between *Report to the People by the Union of Burma Revolutionary Council on the Revolutionary Government's Budget Estimates for 1970–71* (Rangoon: Central Press, 1971) and the *Review of the Financial, Economic and Social Conditions for 1989/90* (Rangoon: Ministry of Planning and Finance, 1989).
5. Interviews with Singapore diplomats, May 2013.
6. Interview with Prof. Dr Hc Mult. Franz Gerstenbrand, Vienna, 14 September 2008.
7. See Furnivall, *Colonial Policy and Practice: A Comparative Study of Burma and Netherlands India* (New York: New York University Press, 1956, reprint of Cambridge University Press edition, 1948), pp. 290–303, for a discussion of the contingent basis of economic rationality and accepted practices.
8. Rather like another often misunderstood man of an earlier generation in another country, the German-American H.L. Mencken. See Charles Scruggs, *The Sage in Harlem: H.L. Mencken and the Black Writers of the 1920s* (Baltimore: Johns Hopkins University Press, 1984).

9. His temper certainly led many of his colleagues to fear him and they consequently made erroneous, often stupid, decisions on the basis of misinterpreting causal remarks. Often these had unfortunate consequences for army and government personnel who were mistakenly arrested or dismissed, some even being called back if the error were discovered. Tin Aung, "Travels with Numero Uno", unpublished paper, circa 2000, pp. 17–19 and *passim.*

10. In February 2014, I received a manuscript which claimed that Ne Win was a strong believer in astrology. However, the author made no claim to have actually witnessed Ne Win's alleged astrological interests. The only instance was the author wrote that he "immediately assumed he [i.e., Ne Win] was doing it [not handing him travel money until last because he was Saturday born] at the bidding of the astrologer." The author who has a PhD in physics from an American university, as a consequence of this event, and at his mother's behest, made a donation to a pagoda to earn merit. Ibid., pp. 20–21.

APPENDIX
Radio Address by Colonel Naywin
(7–5–45), to the People of Burma

Comrades and Countrymen,

You have known by now with what aims the Burmese Army has come into existence and of what stuff it is made. Its one and only aim is to fight for Burmese freedom and it is to that aim that practically the whole of Burmese Youth have dedicated their lives. You have also seen that it is a united front put up by all the indigenous races that call themselves Burmese. Thus it is that the Burmese Army which is composed of the Burmese, Shans, Kachins and Karens has been looked upon by all as not only the hope of the country but also as its very life and soul. For it is this Burmese Army which has, in the name of the People's Freedom Army, declared war on the Fascist Japanese and is actively engaged in fighting them on the Burmese front. Bitterly have they fought for the liberation of their soil from Fascist clutches and as bitterly with they continue the fight till that menace is completely eradicated. And it is our purpose here no less our duty to tell the people in as clear and simple words as possible the reason for the step we have taken. We wish every single Burmese to understand that in taking this historic step, the Burmese army is neither guided by sheer irresponsibility of youth, as their enemy has been inclined to attribute, nor is it a meaningless, opportunist movement some of the people have tried to make out. Members of the Burmese Army will certainly not let their blood and sweat flow so freely nor let their wives and children suffer mortal agonies at the hands of the Japanese Military Police nor let the Burmese villages go up in flames without having a firm conviction in the righteousness of their action.

We were not unawares of what terror and ravages Japanese Fascism has wrought in China. At the same time, we as realists believed that without the help of a foreign power, in those days, we could not successfully struggle against the British and achieve our independence. It happened that in view of the international situation prevailing then, Japan was and could be only foreign ally we could look up to. Secret negotiations went on and the Burmese Revolutionary Group demanded from accredited representatives of the Japanese Government solemn pledges of independence for Burma. That pledge was given by the Japan and this fact, briefly and simply, accounted for the cooperation which the Burmese young men extended to the Japanese Forces during the first phase of the war. Later, on January 21, 1942, just after the fall of Hongkong, the Japanese Premier General Tojo confirmed this pledge in his statement made in the Imperial Diet.

> As regards the Philippines, if the peoples of those islands will hereafter understand the real intentions of Nippon and offer to co-operate with us as one of the partners for the establishment of the Greater East Asia Co-prosperity Sphere, Nippon will gladly enable them to enjoy the honour of independence. As for Burma what Nippon contemplates is not different from that relating to the Philippines.

To those who are as freedom-loving as the Burmese are, such an expression of definite promise could not but receive their wishful credence especially when it was found, to all appearances, to be more satisfactory that the British statement that the Atlantic Charter shall not be applicable to India and Burma. We reasoned to ourselves also that since Japan would never be able to occupy India without being able to rally the active support of the Indians, by granting Independence to Burma and thus prove that she has no territorial ambitions, political expediency and circumstances would compel her to redeem her Independence pledge to Burma as well as to the Philippines and other East Asiatic countries. Hence our decision to making our alliance with Japan and fighting side by side with her against the British in 1942.

Out first regrets came with the fall of Moulmein. Doubts began to awaken in Burmese minds when the Japanese for the first time broke their promise of declaring Burmese independence and handing over the administration of the town to the Burmese themselves as soon as Moulmein fell into their hands. Since that time began discussions among the Burmese regarding the questionable character of Japan's promises. Their regret and resentment was certainly not improved as time went on and greater contact with the Japanese more and more unmasked their aggressive nature in all manner of dealings. It was fortunately in good time that we found out our mistake and we had been able to send a section of our youth leaders to foreign countries to seek foreign aid.

Disillusionment came a second time when, the occupation of the whole of Burma having been completed, the Burmese Independence Army (As it was then called) gathered together at Mandalay. What was the disappointment and fury in the hearts of these young patriots when "Burmese Independence Army" was converted into the Burma Defence Army"! It was no consolation to know that the Burmese Army had then reached a considerable strength. They forthwith planned to turn the B. I. A., not into B. D. A. as the Japanese desired but into a Burma Revolutionary Army as their whole souls desired, but three big factors prevented their plans from ripening into action. The first is that Premier Tojo of the Japanese Government happened to have just declared his government's intention to recognise Burmese Independence in his Diet Speech, the second is that the Burmese troops were then yet lacking in training and experience, and the third is that the Japanese Fascists were then at the height of their military power. Leading members of the Burmese Army had therefore decided to bide their time and allow discretion to form the better part of their valour.

Then came the declaration of Burmese Independence which we all found out presently, was just a declaration. As soon as the Burmese found that the independence which they proclaimed to the world was poles apart from the independence which they have aspired for and looked forward to and that instead of enjoying the rights of real sovereignty their territory was mutilated, their economy ruthlessly exploited and their civil liberties completely cast aside, their plans and decisions to overthrow Japanese Fascism began to take concrete shape. They made up their minds neither to rest nor pause till they have redressed the wrong they have, with the best of intentions, made to the country, and then felt equal to the many dangers that would await them, their families and their associates, should the Japanese Military Police but get an inkling of their extremely hazardous plan. Nothing but their inherent love of freedom gave them the courage to brave the inhuman tortures of the Japanese military police as they crossed the borders between Burma and foreign countries, organised revolutionary parties in all parts of the country, secretly circulated guerrilla pamphlets, giving practical training wherever possible and doing the while all they can to impeded the progress of the Japanese war effort. This huge subversive movement having completed, they attempted four times to effect a general rising and all the times their plans aborted.

This time, which is the fifth time in the history of the Burmese Army, we have successfully carried out our plans. I will not give you a rough outline of the Burmese Army's activities, to give you an idea of the loyalty and death-defying spirit of our comrades as well as to give due recognition to the admirable co-operation that we have received from our own people, the gallant villagers and towns-people alike.

(a) We have been able to successfully negotiate with the Japanese Military Authorities to send our troops to various districts, to which they have been assigned, despite the fact that the entire Burmese Army has all along been stationed in Rangoon.

(b) We have been able to procure sufficient arms and ammunitions from the Japanese Army within the space of a few days from the date on which the revolution is to break out.

(c) We have been able to combine our troops with revolutionary parties in Prome, Allanmyo, Pyinmana, Toungoo, Pegu, Mandalay and other Delta towns and thereby obtain perfect coordination.

(d) We have been able to send our men to India to seek outside military assistance and supply of arms.

(e) We have been able to contact the Allies successfully.

(f) We have been able to combat the Japanese in Upper Burma and Arakan and defeat them thoroughly.

(g) We have been able to give training to villagers of various districts in guerrilla forms of warfare, and by the time the revolution is started have already organised straight-shooting guerrilla fighters all over the country.

All these, you will agree with me, are not such as can be achieved overnight, especially when there was a horde of Japanese Military Police and their secret agents and unscrupulous informants. All this certainly an uncommon feat which any nation in the world would feel proud of, for the Burmese have demonstrated to the world that Japan who is a rival power among the World Powers and is the most ruthless of all Fascist Powers has at last reaped bitter defeat at the hands of the Burmese.

Even the Allied Nations have admitted that for sheer grit and guerrilla fighting technique, it is difficult for any other nations to surpass Japan.

And Burmese today have beaten the Japanese in their own game, as is much evident in the operations in the delta districts of Pyapon, Maubin, Bassein, Insein, etc., and in Mandalay, Toungoo, Pyinmana and other places where the Burmese successfully drove them out and redeemed the Burmese towns from their bands. It was against the Burmese Army that has to forestall the Japanese plans of subjecting the city of Rangoon to a scorched-earth demolition and occupy the city before they can carry out their plans. The most effective part of the Burmese Army's activities is the complete breakdown of transportation and communications of the Japanese Army in Burma. The typically Burmese techniques of guerrilla fighting is sure to find a place in the pages of the world's military science.

I think I have made it clear enough that the Burmese Army is not only the hope of the country but its very life soul that is neither irresponsibility of youth that lay behind their historic step nor a meaningless opportunist movement as I have earlier pointed out. Hence to the people of Burma who have for four hapless years been exposed to the most gruelling form of hardship, danger and disease, I wish to give this solemn pledge. That for the freedom of every small state that even like ourselves are in mortal dread of the Fascist menace, we are firmly resolved to drive back the Japanese Fascism to its native home and to give our lives to achieve our objective of Burmese freedom. With this pledge on my lips I urge you, comrades and countrymen to give us yet more of our willing co-operation and help, for before you all, ever loyal and true, we stand in readiness to fight for our cherished freedom, our one objective and our very life.

In *From Fascist Bondate to New Democracy: The New Burma in the New World*. Appendix 2 B., pp. 28-38.

BIBLIOGRAPHY

Archives

Chinese Ministry of Foreign Ministry Archives. The references refer to file/ document numbers.

Das Bundesarchiv or Archive of the Federal Republic of Germany are organized as AA, meaning Auswartiges Amt or German Foreign Ministry; PA refers to Political Archive; B 12 refers to the respective department; and Bd refers to the band or volume where the document is found.

India Office Archives and Records, now in the British Library: BOF refers to Burma Office files, the system in effect when I accessed the Burma papers.

National Archives (U.K.), i. e., the Public Record Office, Kew: FO and FCO refer to files in the Foreign and Foreign and Commonwealth series; DOM refers to the Dominions Office files; WO refers to War Office files; and PREM refers to the Prime Minister's Department files.

National Archives and Records Administration (U.S.): most files are found in RG59. The United States State Department Archives.

The Walinsky Papers are at the Cornell University Library. I am indebted to Professor Ian Brown for this information.

Interviews

Association for Diplomatic Studies and Training, Burma, Country Reader, available at <http://adst.org/wp-content/uploads/2012/09/Burma.pdf> (accessed 11 February 2013).

U Aung Gyi, Yangon

U Ba Yi, Yangon

U Chan Aye, Yangon

Ambassador Cheng Ruisheng, Beijing

U Chit Hlaing, Yangon

U Chit Hlaing (retired admiral), Yangon

U Chit Myaing, Washington, D.C.
U Edward Law-Yone, Camp Hill, Pennsylvania
Prof. Dr Franz Gerstenbrand, Vienna
U Htwe Han, Yangon
U Khin Nyunt, Yangon
Dr Kyaw Win, London and Yangon
U Min Nyi, Yangon
U Ngwe Thein, London
U Pyo Wei Win, London
Dr Soe Lwin, London
U Than Nyunt, Yangon
U Thaw Kaung, Yangon
U Thein Nyunt, Yangon
U Thu Yei, Yangon
Thakin Tin Mya, Yangon

WORKS CITED

Publications in Burmese

Baho Komiti Winlaung:mya: ei Koyei: Hmattan: Akyinchok [Biodata of Candidate
  Members of the Central Committee]. Yangon: Myanmar Hsoshelit Lansin
  Pati, 1971.

Bo Thanmani. *Ba Kyaunt Sterling Ngwekyei Neipei Hma Myanmar Naingngan
  Hnote Htwet Khe Thalei Bah Dway Gayet Yite Khe Tahlei* [Why Did Myanmar
  Withdraw from the Sterling Area and What was the Impact?]. Yangon: News
  and Periodicals Corporation, 1991.

Hkin Nint U, Myint Kyaung, and Maung Zeya, eds. *U Thaw Kaung 75th Hnitpyi
  Ahtein ahmat Mudita Sasu* [Collected Papers in Honour of the 75th Birthday
  of U Thaw Kaung]. Yangon: Myanmar Book Centre, 2013.

Hpa Has Pa La Ahpweikyok. *Tawhlanyei Sakhaung* [Revolution Memorial]. N.p.:
  N.p., N.d.

Khain Hkant. *8888 Dimokayeisei Ayeitowpun Hmattan* [Record of the 8888
  Democracy Revolution]. Yangon: Kyee Hla Maung Sapei Taik, January
  2013.

Khin Let Ya. *Hpei Hpei Bo Let Ya* [Daddy Bo Let Ya]. Yangon: Zwun Pwint Sa Ok,
  2012.

Ko Ko Maung Kyi (pen name for U Chit Hlaing). *Pyamashonnaing thaw Nainganyei
  Akyaung* [Political Affairs Which I am Unable to Leave without Saying].
  Yangon: Thiyi Myanma Sapei, 2012.

Lei: Maung. *Myanmar Nainganyei: Thamaing* [History of Myanmar Politics].
  Yangon: Sapei Beikman Press, 1974.

Min Maung Maung. *Tatmadaw hnin Amyotha Naingngan Uhsaunghmu Ahkankagna*
  [Collected Articles on the Army and National Politics]. Yangon: News and
  Periodicals Corporation, July 1995.

Myanmar Hsoshelit Lansin Pati Baho Kowmitti Danakyut. *Myanmar Hsoshelit Lansin Pati Okkatakyi ei Hkit Pyaung Towhlanyei Thamaing win Meinkhun Paungkyut* [Collected Speeches of the Era Changing Revolution History of the Chairman of the Myanmar Socialist Programme Party]. Two volumes. Yangon: Myanmar Socialist Way Party Central Committee Headquarters, Party Publications Unit, July 1985.

Myanmar Hsoshelit Lansin Pati Ukkatakyi ei Hkit Pyaung Towhlanyei Thamaing Mein Kwan Paung Hkyut [Collected Era Changing Historical Speeches by the Chairman of the Myanmar Socialist Programme Party]. Vol. 2. Yangon: Myanmar Hsoshelit Lansin Pati Central Committee Headquarters, 1985.

Myanmar Taingyin Hsei Pyinna Akhyeikhan Tabawtaya:mya [Basic Principles of Myanmar Indigenous Medicine]. N.p.: Indigenous Medicine Department, Department of Health, Government of the Union of Myanmar, 2007.

Naingngan Anka Theinpaik ywuyei: atwe Bama Pyi Kommyunit Pati Politbyuyo ci. Kyasinhmumya: hnit. LutHsaunghkyekmya [Schemes and Activities of the Burma Communist Party Politburo to Seize State Power]. Yangon: News and Periodicals Corporation, January 1990.

Nu. *Nga Hnit Yathi — Bama Pyi 1941–1945* [Five Seasons in Burma 1941–1945]. Yangon: Myanmar Pyi Saok Taik, 1946, 2nd printing, 1961.

Pyihtaungsu Myanmar Naingngan Towhlanyei Kaungsi [Union of Myanmar Revolutionary Council]. *Myanmar Hsoshelit Lansin Pati ei Witheitha Latkangmya* [Specific Characteristics of the Myanmar Socialist Programme Party]. Yangon: Myanmar Socialist Programme Party, Party Affairs Central Committee, 4 September 1964.

Saw. *Gyapan Lan Nyunt* [Japan Points the Way]. Yangon: Thuriya, 1936.

Sein Tin, Takkathu. *Yebaw Thon-gyaik Mawkun* [Record of the Thirty Comrades]. A:manthit Sapei, 1st printing, 1968; 5th printing, 2010.

Sit Thamaing: Pyutaik hnit Tamataw Mawkuntaik Hmuyoun [Military Museum and Defence Services Archive Department]. *Tatmadaw Thamaing: 1824–1945, First Part (Defence Services History, 1824–1945)*. Yangon: News and Periodicals Corporation, 1994.

Thein Pe Myint. *Kyaw Nyein*. Yangon: Pyithu Sapei Taik, 1962.

Tin Mya. *Fascist Tawlonyei Danakyuk hnit Tain (10) Tain* [The Fascist Revolution Headquarters and the Ten Divisions]. Yangon: Pyi Loung Kywat Hpyan Hkyi Yei Hla Maw Sapei Taik, 1968.

Towhlanyei Kaungsi ei Hluthsaungchet Thamaing Akyinchut [Concise History of the Actions of the Revolutionary Council]. Rangoon: Printing and Publishing Corporation, 2 March 1974.

Unpublished papers in Burmese

San San Myint. "Hpa Hsa Pa La Khit Myanma Naingnanyei Thamaing 1948–1958" [Myanmar Political History of the Hpa Hsa Pa Lat Era 1948–1958]. Unpublished Masters thesis, Rangoon Arts and Sciences University, 1979.

Thein Nyunt. "U Ne Win Akyaung Thi Kaung Saya Akyetalet Akyou" [Some Information About U Ne Win]. Photocopied typescript. Unpublished paper. N.p.: N.d.

Thihmat Hpweya Koyei: AchetAlatmya [Biographical Information for Recalling]. N.p.: N.p., N.d. (Available outside the Ministry of Information, News and Periodicals Department, Thein Byu Street, Yangon, for free in 2008.)

Publications in English

Articles

Adeke, Ademola. "The Strings of Neutralism: Burma and the Colombo Plan". *Pacific Affairs*, vol. 76, no. 4 (Winter 2003–04): 593–610.

Aldrich, Richard J. "Legacies of Secret Service: Renegade SOE and the Karen Struggle in Burma, 1948–50". *Intelligence and National Security* 14, no. 4 (Winter 1999): 130–48.

———. "American Intelligence and the British Raj: The OSS, the SSU and India, 1942–1947". *Intelligence and National Security (Great Britain)* 13, no. 1 (Spring 1998): 132–64. Also in Richard J. Aldrich, Gary D. Rawnsley, and Ming-Yeh T. Rawnsley, eds. *The Clandestine Cold War in Asia, 1945–1965: Western Intelligence, Propaganda and Special Operations*. London: Frank Cass, 2000.

Arumugam, Raja Segaran. "Burma: Political Unrest and Economic Stagnation". In *Southeast Asian Affairs 1976*. Singapore: Institute of Southeast Asian Affairs, 1976.

Aung Kin. "Burma in 1979: Socialism with Foreign Aid and Strict Neutrality". In *Southeast Asian Affairs 1980*, edited by Leo Suryadinata and Ng Shui Meng. Singapore: Heinemann Asia, 1980.

———. "Burma in 1980: Pouring Balm on Sore Spots". In *Southeast Asian Affairs 1981*. Singapore: Heinemann Asia, 1981.

Aung San. "The Resistance Movement". In *Burma's Challenge (1945)*. Rangoon: Tathetta Sapei, March 1974.

Badgley, John. "Burma's Military Government: A Political Analysis". *Asian Survey*, vol. 11, no. 6 (August 1962): 24–31.

———. "Burma: The Nexus of Socialism and Two Political Traditions". *Asian Survey*, vol. III, no. 2 (February 1963): 89–95.

———. "Burma's Zealot Wungyis: Maoists or St. Simonists?" *Asian Survey*, vol. V, no. 1 (January 1965): 55–62.

———. "Burma's China Crisis: The Choices Ahead". *Asian Survey*, vol. VII, no. 11 (November 1967): 753–61.

———. "The Union of Burma: Age Twenty-Two". *Asian Survey*, vol. XI, no. 2 (February 1971): 149–57.

———. "Burma: The Army Vows Legitimacy". *Asian Survey*, vol. XII, no. 2 (February 1972): 177–81.

Bigelow, Lee S. "The 1960 Election in Burma". *Far Eastern Survey*, vol. 29, no. 5 (May 1960): 70–74.

Booth, Anne. "The Burma Development Disaster in Comparative Historical Perspective". *South East Asia Research*, vol. 11, no. 2 (2003): 141–71.

Butwell, Richard. "Civilians and Soldiers in Burma". In *Studies on Asia 1961*, edited by Robert K. Sakai. Lincoln: University of Nebraska Press, 1961.

———. "Burma Doesn't Want Aid". *New Republic*, 3 September 1966.

———. "U Nu's Second Comeback Try". *Asian Survey*, vol. IX, no. 11 (November 1969): 868–76.

Butwell, Richard and Fred von der Mehden. "The 1960 Election in Burma". *Pacific Affairs*, vol. 33, no. 2 (Summer 1960): 144–57.

Callahan, Mary P. "Building an Army: The Early Years of the Tatmadaw". *Burma Debate*, vol. IV, no. 3 (July/August 1997): 7–11.

———. "Sinking the Schooner". In *Gangsters, Democracy, and the State in Southeast Asia*, edited by Carl A. Trocki. Southeast Asia Program Series no. 17. Ithaca: Cornell University, 1998.

Cheesman, Nicholas. "How an Authoritarian Regime in Burma used Special Courts to Defeat Judicial Independence". *Law and Society Review*, vol. 45, no. 4 (2011): 801–26.

Chit Myaing. "In His Own Words". *Burma Debate*, vol. IV, no. 3 (July/August 1997): 11–24.

Clymer, Kenton. "The Trial for High Treason of the 'Burma Surgeon', Gordon S. Seagrave". *Pacific Historical Review*, vol. 81, no. 2 (2012): 245–91.

Everton, John. "The Ne Win Regime in Burma". *Asia* (Autumn 1964): 1–17.

Fan Hongwei. "The 1967 Anti-Chinese Riots in Burma and Sino-Burmese Relations". *Journal of Southeast Asian Studies*, vol. 43, no. 2 (June 2012): 234–56.

Furnivall, J.S. "The Fashioning of the Leviathan". *Journal of the Burma Research Society*, vol. XXIX, no. 3 (1939): 1–37.

Guyot, Dorothy Hess. "Communal Conflict in the Burma Delta". In *Southeast Asian Transitions: Approaches through Social History*, edited by Ruth T. McVey. New Haven and London: Yale University Press, 1978.

Holmes, Robert A. "China-Burma Relations Since the Rift". *Asian Survey*, vol. XII, no. 8 (August 1972): 686–700.

Ikeda, Kazuto. "The Myaungmya Incident during the Japanese Occupation of Burma: Karens and Shwe Tun Kya". In *Reconsidering the Japanese Military Occupation of Burma (1942–45)*, edited by Kei Nemoto. Tokyo: Research Institute for Languages and Cultures of Asia and Africa, Tokyo University of Foreign Studies, 2007.

Khammai Dhammasami. "Idealism and Pragmatism: A Dilemma in the Current Monastic Education Systems of Burma and Thailand". In *Buddhism, Power and Political Order*, edited by Ian Harris. London: Routledge, 2007.

Khin Maung Kyi. "Indians in Burma: Problems of an Alien Subculture in a Highly Integrated Society". In *Indian Communities in Southeast Asia*, edited by K.S. Sandhu and A. Mani. Singapore: Institute of Southeast Asian Studies, 1993, reprinted 2006.

Kyaw Yin Hlaing. "Reconsidering the Failure of the Burma Socialist Programme Party Government to Eradicate Internal Economic Impediments". *South East Asia Research*, vol. II, no. 1 (March 2003): 5–58.

―――. "Burma: Civil Society Skirting Regime Rules". In *Civil Society and Political Change in Asia*, edited by Muthiar Alagappa. Stanford: Stanford University Press, 2004.

―――. "The Politics of Language Policy in Myanmar: Imagining Togetherness, Practising Difference?" In *Language, Nation and Development in Southeast Asia*, edited by Lee Hock Guan and Leo Suryadinata. Singapore: Institute of Southeast Asian Studies, 2007.

―――. "The Four-Eights Democratic Movement". In *State Violence in East Asia*, edited by N. Ganesan and Sung Chull Kim. Lexington: The University Press of Kentucky, 2013.

Laidlaw, Richard B. "The OSS and the Burma Road, 1942–1945". In *North American Spies*, edited by Rhodri Jeffrey-Jones and Andrew Lownie. Lawrence: University of Kansas Press, 1991.

Law-Yone, Edward M. "Dr. Ba Maw of Burma". In *Contributions to Asian Studies 16: Essays on Burma*, edited by John P. Ferguson. Leiden: E.J. Brill, 1981.

Liang Chi-shad. "Burma's Relations with the People's Republic of China: From Delicate Friendship to Genuine Cooperation". In *Burma: The Challenge of Change in a Divided Society*, edited by Peter Cary. London: Macmillan, 1997.

Lintner, Bertil. "China: Burma and Khmer Rouge Regime". *Searching for the Truth: Magazine of the Documentation Centre of Cambodia*, no. 7 (July 2000): 2–4.

Martin, Edwin W. "The Socialist Republic of the Union of Burma: How Much Change?" *Asian Survey*, vol. 15, no. 2 (February 1975): 129–35.

―――. "Burma in 1975: New Dimensions to Non-Alignment". *Asian Survey*, vol. 16, no. 2 (February 1976): 173–77.

Maung Maung. "Burma — A Slap for the Reds". *Bangkok Post Sunday Magazine*, vol. XXII, no. 327 (24 November 1968).

―――. "Daw Khin Mae Than". *The Working People's Daily*, 4 October 1972.

Min Shin. "Back from the Wars". *Forward*, vol. 1, no. 11 (7 January 1963): 25–27.

Misra, K.P. "Burma's Farewell to the Nonaligned Movement". *Asian Affairs*, vol. XII, part 1 (February 1981): 49–56.

Morshed, Kaiser. "Bangladesh-Burma Relations". In *Challenges to Democratization in Burma: Perspectives on Multilateral and Bilateral Responses*, by International Institute for Democracy and Electoral Assistance. Stockholm: International Institute for Democracy and Electoral Assistance, 2001.

Mya Maung. "Socialism and Economic Development in Burma". *Asian Survey*, vol. IV, no. 12 (December 1964): 1182–90.

Nemoto, Kei. "Between Collaboration and Resistance: Reconsidering the Roles of Ba Maw and Aung San in Their Context of Asserting Burmese Nationalism". In *Reconsidering the Japanese Military Occupation of Burma (1942–1945)*, edited by Kei Nemoto. Tokyo: Research Institute for Languages and Cultures of Asia and Africa, Tokyo University of Foreign Studies, 2007.

Pelz, Stephen E. "Documents: 'When Do I Have Time to Think?' John F. Kennedy, Roger Hilsman, and the Laotian Crisis of 1962". *Diplomatic History*, vol. 3, no. 2 (Spring 1979): 215–29.

Quinn-Judge, Sophie. "Victory on the Battlefield: Isolation in Asia: Vietnam's Cambodia Decade, 1979–1989". In *The Third Indochina War: Conflict between China, Vietnam and Cambodia, 1972–1979*, edited by Odd Arne Westad and Sophie Quinn-Judge. London: Routledge, 2006.

Sadan, Mandy. "The Kachin Photographs in the J.H. Green Collection: A Contemporary Context". In *Burma: Frontier Photographs 1918–1935*, edited by Elizabeth Dell. London: Merrell, 2000.

———. "The Kachin Photographs: A Documentary Record of Contact". In *Burma: Frontier Photographs 1918–1935*, edited by Elizabeth Dell. London: Merrell, 2000.

Selth, Andrew. "Burma's Mythical Isles". *AQ-Australia Quarterly*, vol. 80, no. 6 (November–December 2008): 24–28 and 40.

Silverstein, Josef. "Politics in the Shan State: The Question of Secession from the Union of Burma". *Journal of Asian Studies*, vol. 18, no. 1 (November 1958): 43–57.

———. "The Federal Dilemma in Burma". *Far Eastern Survey*, vol. XXVIII, no. 7 (July 1959): 97–105.

———. "First Steps on the Burmese Road to Socialism". *Asian Survey*, vol. IV, no. 2 (February 1964): 716–22.

——— and Julian Wohl. "University Students and Politics in Burma". *Pacific Affairs*, vol. 37, no. 1 (1964): 50–61.

———. "Burma: Ne Win's Revolution Considered". *Asian Survey*, vol. VI, no. 2 (February 1966): 95–102.

———. "Problems in Burma: Economic, Political and Diplomatic". *Asian Survey*, vol. VII, no. 2 (February 1967): 117–25.

———. "Political Dialogue in Burma: A New Turn on the Road to Socialism?" *Asian Survey*, vol. X, no. 2 (February 1970): 133–41.

———. "Burma in 1981: The Changing of the Guardians Begins". *Asian Survey*, vol XXII, no. 2 (February 1982): 180–89.

Taylor, Robert H. "Politics in Late Colonial Burma: The Case of U Saw". *Modern Asian Studies*, vol. 10, no. 2 (April 1976): 161–94.

———. "Burma in the Anti-Fascist War". In *Southeast Asia under Japanese Occupation*, edited by Alfred W. McCoy. New Haven: Yale University Southeast Asia Studies, 1980.

———. "Perceptions of Ethnicity in the Politics of Burma". *South East Asia Journal of Social Science*, vol. 10, no. 1 (1982): 7–23.

————. "The Burmese Concept of Revolution". In *Context, Meaning and Power in Southeast Asia*, edited by Mark Hobart and Robert H. Taylor. Ithaca, New York: Cornell University, Southeast Asia Program, 1986.

————. "Burma: Defence Expenditure and Threat Perceptions". In *Defence Spending in Southeast Asia*, edited by Chin Kin Wah. Singapore: Institute of Southeast Asian Studies, 1987.

————. "Myanmar in 1990: New Era or Old?" In *Southeast Asian Affairs 1991*, edited by Sharon Siddique and Ng Chee Yuen. Singapore: Institute of Southeast Asian Studies, 1991.

————. "The Legal Status of Indians in Contemporary Burma". In *Indian Communities in Southeast Asia*, edited by K.S. Sandhu and A. Mani. Singapore: Institute of Southeast Asian Studies, 1993, reprinted 2000.

————. "Disaster or Release? J.S. Furnivall and the Bankruptcy of Burma". *Modern Asian Studies*, vol. 29, no. 1 (February 1995): 45–63.

————. "Colonial Forces in British Burma: A National Army Postponed". In *Colonial Armies in Southeast Asia*, edited by Karl Hack and Tobias Rettig. London: Routledge, 2006.

Thaw Kaung. "Mirrored in Short Stories: Some Glimpses of Myanmar Life and Society in the 20th Century". In *From the Librarian's Window*. Yangon: Myanmar Book Centre, 2008.

Thet Tun. "A Critique of Louis J. Walinsky's *Economic Development in Burma, 1951–1960*". *Journal of the Burma Research Society*, vol. XLVII, part 1 (June 1964): 173–82.

Tin Maung Maung Than. "Burma in 1983: From Recovery to Growth?" In *Southeast Asian Affairs 1984*, edited by Pushpa Thambipillai. Singapore: Institute of Southeast Asian Studies, 1984.

————. "The *Sangha* and the *Sasana* in Socialist Burma". *Sojourn*, vol. 3, no. 1 (February 1988): 26–61.

————. "Burma's National Security and Defence Posture". *Contemporary Southeast Asia*, vol. 11, no. 1 (June 1989): 40–60.

————. "*Sangha* Reforms and Renewal of *Sasana* in Myanmar: Historical Trends and Contemporary Practice". In *Buddhist Trends in Southeast Asia*, edited by Trevor Ling. Singapore: Institute of Southeast Asian Studies, 1993.

————. "Some Aspects of Indians in Rangoon". In *Indian Communities in Southeast Asia*, edited by K.S. Sandhu and A. Mani. Singapore: Institute of Southeast Asian Studies, 1993, reprinted 2006.

Trager, Frank N. "Burma: 1967 — A Better Ending than Beginning". *Asian Survey*, vol. VIII, no. 2 (February 1968): 110–19.

————. "Burma: 1968 — A New Beginning?" *Asian Survery*, vol. IX, no. 2 (February 1969): 104–14.

———— and William L. Scully. "Burma in 1977: Cautious Changes and A Careful Watch". *Asian Survey*, vol. XVIII, no. 2 (February 1977): 142–52.

Tun Aung Chain. "Managing the Politics of the Family: Bayinnaung". *Myanmar Studies Journal*, no. 1 (December 2013): 25–59.

Whittam, Daphne E. "The Sino-Burmese Boundary Treaty". *Pacific Affairs*, vol. 34, no. 2 (Summer 1961): 174–83.

Wiant, Jon A. "Burma: Loosening Up on the Tiger's Tail". *Asian Survey*, vol. 13, no. 2 (February 1973): 179–86.

———. "Burma 1973: New Turns in the Burmese Road to Socialism". *Asian Survey*, vol. 14, no. 2 (February 1974): 175–82.

Zollner, Hans-Bernd. "Fritz Werner in Burma: A Study on the German-Burmese Relations after World War II". In *Tradition and Modernity in Myanmar*, edited by Uta Gartner and Jens Lorenz. Berlin: Berliner Asien-Afrika-Studien Bd. 3/1, 1994.

Books

A Lingering Nightmare: The Rangoon Bombing. Seoul: Korean Overseas Information Service, October 1984.

Acharya, Amitav. *The Making of Southeast Asia: International Relations of a Region*. Ithaca: Cornell University Press and Singapore: Institute of Southeast Asian Studies, 2012.

Ackroyd, Peter. *The History of England, Volume I: Foundation*. London: Pan, 2012.

Address Delivered by General Ne Win, Chairman of the Burma Socialist Programme Party at the Opening Session of the Fourth Party Seminar on 6th November 1969. Yangon: Burma Socialist Programme Party, November 1969.

Address Delivered by General Ne Win, Chairman of the Burma Socialist Programme Party at the Closing Session of the Fourth Party Seminar on 11th November 1969. Yangon: Burma Socialist Programme Party, November 1969.

Alexander, Garth. *Silent Invasion: The Chinese in South-East Asia*. London: MacDonald, 1973.

Allen, Louis. *Burma: The Longest War 1941–45*. London and Melbourne: J.M. Dent, 1984.

An International Terrorist Clique North Korea. Seoul, Korea: Korean Overseas Information Service, n.d.

Andrus, J. Russell. *Burmese Economic Life*. Stanford, California: Stanford University Press, 1948.

Ang Cheng Guan. *Singapore, ASEAN and the Cambodian Conflict 1978–1991*. Singapore: NUS Press, 2013.

Anti-Fascist People's Freedom League. *From Fascist Bondage to New Democracy: The New Burma in the New World*. Rangoon: 1945.

Asian Development Outlook. Manila: Asian Development Bank, 1990.

Attlee, Clement. *As It Happened*. London: Heinemann, 1954.

Aung Myoe. *Building the Tatmadaw: The Organisational Development of the Armed Forces in Myanmar, 1948–1958*. Strategic and Defence Studies

Centre, Working Paper no. 327. Canberra: Australian National University, November 1998.

———. *Military Doctrine and Strategy in Myanmar: A Historical Perspective*. Strategic and Defence Studies Centre, Working Paper no. 339. Canberra: Australian National University, September 1999.

———. *Officer Education and Leadership Training in the Tatmadaw: A Survey*. Strategic and Defence Studies Centre, Working Paper no. 346. Canberra: Australian National University, May 2000.

———. "Regionalism in Myanmar's Foreign Policy: Past, Present and Future". ARI Working Paper Series no. 73. Singapore: Asia Research Institute, September 2006.

———. *Building the Tatmadaw: Myanmar Armed Forces Since 1948*. Singapore: Institute of Southeast Asian Studies, 2009.

———. *In the Name of Pauk-Phaw: Myanmar's China Policy Since 1948*. Singapore: Institute of Southeast Asian Studies, 2011.

Aung-Thwin, Maitrii. *The Return of the Galon King: History, Law and Rebellion in Colonial Burma*. Athens: Ohio University Press, 2011.

Aye, Henri-Andre. *The Shan Conundrum in Burma*. N.p.: N.p., private printed, 2009.

Ba Than. *The Roots of the Revolution: A Brief History of the Defence Services of the Union of Burma and the Ideals for which They Stand*. Rangoon: Director of Information, 1962.

Badgley, John H. and Aye Kyaw, eds. *Red Peacocks: Commentaries on Burmese Socialist Nationalism*. New Delhi: Readworthy, 2009.

Baker, Edmund, ed. *The Accidental Diplomat: The Autobiography of Maurice Baker*. Singapore: World Scientific, 2014.

Bates, H.E. *The Purple Plain*. London: Michael Joseph, 1947.

Bayly, Christopher and Tim Harper. *Forgotten Wars: Freedom and Revolution in Southeast Asia*. Cambridge, Mass.: The Belknap Press of Harvard University Press, 2007.

Becka, Jan. *Military Rule in Burma*. Brussels: Free University of Brussels, 1969.

———. *The National Liberation Movement in Burma during the Japanese Occupation Period (1941–1945)*. Prague: Oriental Institute in Academia, Czechoslovak Academy of Sciences, 1983.

Beisner, Robert L. *Dean Acheson: A Life in the Cold War*. Oxford: Oxford University Press, 2006.

Berger, Mark T. *The Battle for Asia: From Decolonisation to Globalisation*. London: RoutledgeCurzon, 2004.

Brown, Ian. *A Colonial Economy in Crisis: Burma's Rice Cultivators and the World Depression of the 1930s*. London: RoutledgeCurzon, 2005.

———. *Burma's Economy in the Twentieth Century*. Cambridge: Cambridge University Press, 2013.

Burma and the Insurrections. Rangoon: Government of Burma, 1949.

Burma Gazetteer, Prome District, Volume B. Rangoon: Office of the Superintendent, Government Printing, Burma, 1913.

Burma Provincial Banking Enquiry. *Report of the Burma Provincial Banking Enquiry Committee, 1929–1930, Volume I: Banking and Credit in Burma*. Rangoon: Superintendent, Government Printing and Stationery, 1930.

Burma Socialist Programme Party Central Committee Headquarters. *The First Party Congress 1971: Speeches of the Chairman of the Party Central Committee and Political Report of the Party Central Organising Committee*. Yangon: Burma Socialist Programme Party, March 1973.

———. *The Fourth Party Congress 1981: Party Chairman's Speech and Political Report of the Central Committee*. Yangon: Burma Socialist Programme Party, June 1985.

Burma Socialist Programme Party Central Organising Committee. *Party Seminar 1965: Speeches of Chairman Ne Win and Political Report of the General Secretary*. Yangon: Burma Socialist Programme Party, February 1966.

———. *Foreign Policy of the Revolutionary Government of the Union of Burma*. Yangon: Burma Socialist Programme Party, 1968.

Butwell, Richard. *U Nu of Burma*. Stanford, California: Stanford University Press, 1963.

Cable, James. *The Geneva Conference of 1954 on Indochina*. London: Macmillan, 1986.

Cady, John F. *A History of Modern Burma*. Ithaca: Cornell University Press, 1958.

Callahan, Mary P. *Making Enemies: War and State Building in Burma*. Ithaca: Cornell University Press; Singapore University Press, 2004.

Campagnac, Charles H. *The Autobiography of a Wanderer in England and Burma*. Raleigh, North Carolina: Sandra L. Carney, 2010.

Caro, Robert A. *The Years of Lyndon Johnson: The Passage of Power*. New York: Alfred A. Knopf, 2012.

Castle, Timothy N. *At War in the Shadow of Vietnam: U.S. Military Aid to the Royal Lao Government 1955–1975*. New York: Columbia University Press, 1993.

Cavoski, Jovan. *Arming Nonalignment: Yugoslavia's Relations with Burma and the Cold War in Asia (1950–1955)*. Cold War International History Project Working Paper no. 61. Washington, D.C.: Woodrow Wilson International Center for Scholars, April 2010.

Central Statistical and Economics Department, Revolutionary Government of the Union of Burma. *Statistical Yearbook 1967*. Rangoon: New Secretariat.

Cesaire, Aime. *Discourse on Colonialism*, translated by Joan Pinkham. New York: Monthly Review Press, 2000, first published in French in 1955.

Chao Tzang Yawnghwe. *The Shan of Burma: Memoirs of a Shan Exile*. Singapore: Institute of Southeast Asian Studies, 1987.

Cheng Siok-Hwa. *The Rice Industry of Burma, 1852–1940*. Singapore: Institute of Southeast Asian Studies, 2012. Reprint of Kuala Lumpur: University of Malaya Press, 1968.

Collis, Maurice. *She was a Queen*. London: Faber and Faber, 1937.

————. *The Journey Up: Reminiscences 1934–1968*. London: Faber and Faber, 1970.

————. *Diaries: 1949–1969*, edited and introduced by Louise Collis. London: Heinemann, 1977.

Conboy, Kenneth and James Morrison. *The CIA's Secret War in Tibet*. Lawrence: University of Kansas Press, 2002.

Corley, T.A.B. *A History of the Burmah Oil Company, Volume II: 1924–1966*. London: Heinemann, 1988.

Crozier, Brian. *The Morning After: A Study of Independence*. London: Methuen, 1963.

Crozier, L.A. *Mawchi: Mining, War and Insurgency in Burma*. Australians in Asia no. 11. Brisbane: Centre for the Study of Australia-Asia Relations, Griffith University, March 1994.

Darby, Philip. *British Defence Policy East of Suez 1947–1968*. London: Oxford University Press, 1973.

Defence Services Museum and Army Archives Office. *Tatmadaw Thamaing: 1824–1945, Part One (Army History 1824–1945)*. Yangon: News and Periodicals Corporation, 1994.

Dommen, Arthur J. *Conflict in Laos: The Politics of Neutralization*. Revised ed. New York: Praeger, 1971.

Donnison, F.S.V. *Public Administration in Burma*. London and New York: Oxford University Press for the Royal Institute of International Affairs, 1953.

————. *Burma*. New York and Washington: Praeger; London: Ernest Benn, 1970.

Elliott, Patricia W. *The White Umbrella: A Woman's Struggle for Freedom in Burma*. Bangkok: Friends Books, 1999.

Elson, R.E. *Suharto: A Political Biography*. Cambridge: Cambridge University Press, 2001.

Enriquez, Colin Metcalf Dallas. *The Races of Burma, Compiled under the Orders of the Government of India*. New York: AMS Press, 1981, reprint of 2nd ed., published Delhi: Manager of Publications, 1933.

Evans, Julian. *The Semi-Visible Man: The Life of Norman Lewis*. London: Cape, 2008.

Facts about Burma. Yangon: Printing and Publishing Corporation, December 1983.

Fairbairn, Geoffrey. *Revolutionary Warfare and Communist Strategy: The Threat to South-East Asia*. London: Faber and Faber, 1968.

Fan Hongwei. "China-Burma Ties in 1954: The Beginning of the 'Pauk Phaw' Era". ICS Working Paper no. 2009–21. Kuala Lumpur: Institute of China Studies, University of Malaya, 2009.

Fellowes-Gordon, Ian. *The Battle for Naw Seng's Kingdom: General Stillwell's North Burma Campaign and Its Aftermath*. London: Leo Cooper, 1971.

Foley, Matthew. *The Cold War and National Assertion in Southeast Asia: Britain, the United States and Burma, 1948–1962*. London: Routledge, 2010.

Foreign Relations of the United States 1946, Volume VIII: The Far East. Washington, D.C.: United States Government Printing Office, 1971.

Fraser, George MacDonald. *Quartered Safe Out Here: A Recollection of the War in Burma*. London: Harper Collins, 2000.

Fredholm, Michael. *Burma: Ethnicity and Insurgency*. Westport, Conn.: Praeger, 1993.

Freedman, Lawrence. *Kennedy's Wars: Berlin, Cuba, Laos and Vietnam*. New York and Oxford: Oxford University Press, 2000.

Fukuyama, Francis. *The Origins of Political Order from Prehuman Times to the French Revolution*. London: Profile Books, 2012.

Furnivall, J.S. *Colonial Policy and Practice: A Comparative Study of Burma and Netherlands India*. New York: New York University Press, 1956, reprint of Cambridge University Press edition, 1948.

———. *The Governance of Modern Burma*. New York: International Secretariat, Institute of Pacific Relations, 1960.

Garver, John W. *The Sino-American Alliance: Nationalist China and American Cold War Strategy in Asia*. Armonk, New York and London: M.E. Sharpe, 1997.

Geographer, The, Office of the Geographer, Bureau of Intelligence and Research, United States Department of State. "International Boundary Study No. 42, Burma-China Boundary". Washington, D.C., 30 November 1964.

Gibson, Richard M., with Chen Wenhua. *The Secret Army: Chiang Kai-shek and the Drug Warlords of the Golden Triangle*. Singapore: Wiley (Asia), 2011.

Gore-Booth, Paul. *With Great Truth and Respect*. London: Constable, 1974.

Gray, William Glenn. *Germany's Cold War: The Global Campaign to isolate East Germany, 1949–1969*. Chapel Hill and London: University of North Carolina Press, 2003.

Halle, Louis J. *The Cold War as History*. London: Chatto and Windus, 1967.

Hanna, Willard A. *Eight Nation Makers: Southeast Asia's Charismatic Statesmen*. New York: St. Martin's Press, 1964.

Hilsman, Roger. *To Move A Nation: The Politics of Foreign Policy in the Administration of John F. Kennedy*. New York: Delta, 1964, 1967.

———. *American Guerrilla: My War Behind Japanese Lines*. Washington, D.C.: Brassey's, 1990.

Hinton, K.T. Ch'iu. *The Ellipses of Katherine Ch'iu Hinton*. New York: Tower Books, 2009.

Hla Oo. *Song for Irrawaddy*. N.p.: The author, 2007.

———. *The Scourge of Burma and Four Short Stories*. N.p.: The author, 2010.

Holroyd, Michael. *Works on Paper: The Craft of Biography and Autobiography*. London: Little Brown, 2002.

Hopkins, Harry. *New World Arising: A Journey of Discovery through the New Nations of South-East Asia.* London: Hamish Hamilton, 1952.

International Renegades: North Korean Diplomacy Through Terror. Seoul: Korean Overseas Information Service, December 1983.

Is Trust Vindicated? The Chronicle of Trust, Striving and Triumph: Being an Account of the Accomplishments of the Government of the Union of Burma: November 1, 1958–February 4, 1960. Rangoon: Director of Information, Government of the Union of Burma, 1960.

Jacobs, Seth. *Cold War Mandarin: Ngo Dinh Diem and the Origins of America's War in Vietnam, 1950–1963.* Lanham, Maryland: Rowman and Littlefield, 2006.

———. *The Universe Unraveling: American Foreign Policy in Cold War Laos.* Ithaca and London: Cornell University Press, 2012.

Johnson, Haynes. *The Bay of Pigs: The Invasion of Cuba by Brigade 2506.* London: Hutchinson, 1965.

Johnson, J.J., ed. *The Role of the Military in Developing Countries.* Princeton: Princeton University Press, 1962.

Jones, Thomas. *Lloyd George.* London: Geoffrey Cumberlege, Oxford University Press, 1951.

Jordt, Ingrid. *Burma's Mass Lay Meditation Movement: Buddhism and the Cultural Construction of Power.* Athens: Ohio University Press, 2007.

Kaznacheev, Aleksandr. *Inside a Soviet Embassy: Experiences of a Russian Diplomat in Burma,* edited by Simon Wolin. London: Robert Hale, 1962.

Keenan, Paul. *Saw Ba U Gyi.* N.p.: Karen History and Culture Preservation Society, March 2008.

Khin Let Ya. *Paintings of Bo Let Ya.* Yangon: Zunn Pwint Publishing House, May 2012.

Khin Maung Saw. *Myanmar Literature Project Working Paper No. 10:13, Material on Two Political Dictionaries.* Passau: University of Passau, 2008.

Khin Nyunt. *Web of Conspiracy, Complicated Stories of Treacherous Machinations and Intrigues of the BCP UG, DAB, and Some NLD Leaders to Seize State Power.* Yangon: News and Periodicals Corporation, January 1991.

Khin Yi. *The Dobama Movement in Burma (1930–1938).* Ithaca: Southeast Asia Program Monograph, 1988.

Kin Oung. *Who Killed Aung San?,* 2nd ed. Bangkok: White Lotus, 1996.

Kirby, S. Woodburn, R. Roberts, G.T. Wards, and N.L. Desoer. *The War Against Japan, Volume IV: The Reconquest of Burma.* London: Her Majesty's Stationery Office, 1965.

———. *The War Against Japan, Volume V: The Surrender of Japan.* London: Her Majesty's Stationery Office, 1969.

Kyaw Win, Mya Han, and Thein Hlaing. *Myanmar Politics 1958–1962, Volume III,* translated by Hla Shein. Yangon: Win Aung, April 2011.

Law-Yone, Wendy. *Golden Parasol: A Daughter's Memoir of Burma*. London: Chatto and Windus, 2013.

Leach, Edmund R. *The Political Systems of Highland Burma: A Study of Kachin Social Structure*. Boston: Beacon Press, 1965.

Leary, William M. *Perilous Missions: Civil Air Transport and CIA Covert Operations in Asia*. Washington and London: Smithsonian Institution Press, 2002.

Lee Kuan Yew. *From Third World to First: The Singapore Story, 1965–2000*. Singapore: Times Media, 2000.

Legal Status of Traditional Medicine and Complementary/Alternative Medicine: A Worldwide Review. Geneva: World Health Organisation, 2001.

Leigh, Michael D. *Conflict, Politics and Proselytism: Methodist Missionaries in Colonial and Postcolonial Upper Burma, 1887–1966*. Manchester: Manchester University Press, 2011.

Lewis, Norman. *Golden Earth*. London: Cape, 1953.

——. *The Single Pilgrim*. London: Cape, 1953.

Liang, Chi-shad. *Burma's Foreign Relations: Neutralism in Theory and Practice*. New York: Praeger, 1990.

Lintner, Bertil. *Burma in Revolt: Opium and Insurgency since 1948*, 2nd ed. Chiang Mai: Silkworm Books, 1999.

Longmire, R.A. *Soviet Relations with South-East Asia: An Historical Survey*. London: Kegan Paul, 1989.

Ma Ma Lay. *A Man Like Him: Portrait of a Burmese Journalist, Journal Kyaw U Chit Maung*, translated by Ma Thanegi. Ithaca, New York: Cornell University Southeast Asian Program, 2008.

Mannin, Ethel. *Land of the Crested Lion: A Journey Through Modern Burma*. London: Jarrolds, 1955.

Maung Maung [Dr]. *Grim War Against the KMT*. Rangoon: U Nu Yin Press, 1953.

——, ed. *Aung San of Burma*. The Hague: Martinus Nijhoff, 1962.

——. *Burma and General Ne Win*. London: Asia Publishing House, 1969.

——. *To a Soldier Son*. Rangoon: Sarpay Beikman, 1974.

——. *The 1988 Uprising in Burma*. Southeast Asia Studies Monograph no. 49. New Haven: Yale University Southeast Asia Studies, 1999.

Maung Maung [U; Brigadier retired]. *From Sangha to Laity: Nationalist Movements in Burma, 1920–1940*. New Delhi: Manohar, 1980.

——. *Burmese Nationalist Movements, 1940–1948*. Edinburgh: Kiscadale, 1989.

McCoy, Alfred W. *The Politics of Heroin: CIA Complicity in the Global Drug Trade*. Brooklyn, New York: Lawrence Hill Books, 1991.

McEnery, John H. *Epilogue in Burma 1945–1948: The Military Dimensions of the British Withdrawal*. Bangkok: White Lotus, 2000; originally published Tunbridge Wells: Spellmount, 1990.

Mencken, H.L. *Prejudices: A Selection*. New York: Vintage Books, 1955.

Mendelson, E. Michael. *Sangha and State in Burma: A Study of Monastic Sectarianism and Leadership*, edited by John P. Ferguson. Ithaca: Cornell University Press, 1975.

Ministry of Finance and Planning, Central Statistical Organisation. *Selected Monthly Economic Indicators*, no. 3 (May–June 1990).

Mole, Robert. *The Temple Bells Are Calling: Memories of Burma*. Bishop Auckland, County Durham: Pentland Books, 2001.

Moore, Elizabeth. *Karaweik Palace*. Yangon: Phoe Pyae Press, 2009.

Morrison, Ian. *Grandfather Longlegs: The Life and Gallant Death of Major H.P. Seagrim, GC*. London: Faber and Faber, 1947.

Moscotti, Albert D. *Burma's Constitution and the Elections of 1974*. ISEAS Research Notes and Discussions no. 5. Singapore: Institute of Southeast Asian Studies, September 1977.

Mount, Ferdinand. *Cold Cream: My Early Life and Other Mistakes*. London: Bloomsbury, 2008.

Muggeridge, Malcolm. *Like It Was*. London: Collins, 1981.

Mya Han and Thein Hlaing. *Myanmar Politics 1958–1962, Volume IV*, translated by Sai Aung Tun. Yangon: U Win Aung, April 2001.

Mya Oo. *History of Medical Education in Myanmar During Colonial Administration*. Yangon: Institute of Medicine 1, 9 May 1995.

Myanmar Department of Health. *Myanmar Health Care System, Health in Myanmar*. Naypyitaw: Myanmar Department of Health, 2011.

Myat Thein. *Economic Development of Myanmar*. Singapore: Institute of Southeast Asian Studies, 2004.

Myint Kyi and Naw Angelene. *Myanmar Politics 1958–1962, Volume II*, translated by Hla Thein. Yangon: Historical Research Centre, Ministry of Culture, 2007.

Myo Myint. *Confronting Colonialism: King Mindon's Strategy for Defending Independence (1853–1878)*. Yangon: Ministry of Religious Affairs, 2012.

Myoma-Lwin. *Dha-Byet-See: The Gun that Saved Rangoon*. Woodstock, U.K.: Writersworld, 2011.

Nakanishi, Yoshihiro. *Strong Soldiers, Failed Revolution: The State and Military in Burma, 1962–88*. Kyoto: Kyoto University Press, 2013.

Nash, Manning. *The Golden Road to Modernity: Village Life in Contemporary Burma*. New York: John Wiley, 1965.

Naw, Angelene. *Aung San and the Burmese Struggle for Independence*. Copenhagen: Nordic Institute of Asian Studies, 2001.

Nemoto, Kei, ed. *Reconsidering the Japanese Military Occupation of Burma (1942–45)*. Tokyo: Research Institute for Languages and Cultures of Asia and Africa, Tokyo University of Foreign Studies, 2007.

Newhall, Sue Mayes. *The Devil in God's Old Man: Life and Work of the Burma Surgeon*. New York: W.W. Norton, 1969.

Ni Ni Myint. *Burma's Struggle Against British Imperialism, 1885–1895*. Rangoon: Universities Press, 1983.

Nu, Thakin. *Toward Peace and Democracy*. Rangoon: Ministry of Information, 1949.

———. *From Peace to Stability*. Rangoon: Ministry of Information, 1951.

———. *Burma under the Japanese: Pictures and Portraits*, translated by J.S. Furnivall. London: Macmillan, 1954.

———. *U Nu — Saturday's Son*, translated by Law Yone and edited by Kyaw Win. New Haven and London: Yale University Press, 1975.

O'Brien, Harriet. *Forgotten Land: A Rediscovery of Burma*. London: Michael Joseph, 1999.

Oberdorfer, Don. *Senator Mansfield*. Washington and London: Smithsonian Books, 2003.

On Kin. *Burma under the Japanese*. Lucknow: Lucknow Publishing House, 1947.

Pearn, B.R. *A History of Rangoon*. Rangoon: American Baptist Mission Press, 1939.

Peres, Shimon. *Battling for Peace: A Memoir*, edited by David Landau. London: Orion Books, 1996.

Porter, Gareth. *Perils of Dominance: Imbalance of Power and the Road to War in Vietnam*. Berkeley: University of California Press, 2005.

Pye, Lucien W. *Politics, Personality and Nation-Building: Burma's Search for Identity*. New Haven: Yale University Press, 1962.

Renard, Ronald D. *The Burmese Connection: Illegal Drugs and the Making of the Golden Triangle*. Boulder and London: Lynne Rienner, 1996.

Report on Public Instruction in Burma, 1927 and *1940*. Rangoon: Superintendent, Government Printing and Stationery, 1927 and 1940.

Report to the People by the Union of Burma Revolutionary Council on the Revolutionary Government's Budget Estimates for 1970–71. Rangoon: Central Press, 1971.

Researcher. *A Concise History of Myanmar and the Tatmadaw's Role 1948–1988*. Two volumes. Yangon: News and Periodicals Enterprise, January 1991.

Review of the Financial, Economic and Social Conditions for 1989/90. Rangoon: Ministry of Planning and Finance, 1989.

Rice, Edward E. *Mao's Way*. Berkeley and Los Angeles: University of California Press, 1972.

Richards, C.J. *Burma Retrospect and Other Essays*. Winchester, England: Herbert Curnow, The Cathedral Press, 1951.

Rozenberg, Guillaume. *Renunciation and Power: The Quest for Sainthood in Contemporary Myanmar*, translated by Jessica L. Hackett et alia. Monograph no. 59. New Haven: Yale University Southeast Asia Studies, 2010.

Russell, Francis. *President Harding: His Life and Times, 1865–1923*. London: Eyre and Spottiswoode, 1969.

Rust, William J. *Before the Quagmire: American Intervention in Laos, 1954–1961*. Lexington: University Press of Kentucky, 2012.

Saha, Jonathan. *Law, Disorder and the Colonial State: Corruption in Burma c. 1900*. London: Palgrave Macmillan, 2013.

Saito, Teroko and Lee Kin Kiong. *Statistics on the Burmese Economy: The 19th and 20th Centuries*. Singapore: Institute of Southeast Asian Studies, 1999.

Salisbury, Harrison E. *Orbit of China*. London: Secker and Warburg, 1967.

Sanda. *The Moon Princess: Memories of the Shan States*. Bangkok: River Books, 2008.

Sandu, K.S. and A. Mani, eds. *Indian Communities in Southeast Asia*. Singapore: Institute of Southeast Asian Studies, 1993, 2006.

Sanger, Clyde. *Malcolm MacDonald: Bringing an End to Empire*. Liverpool: Liverpool University Press, 1995.

Scruggs, Charles. *The Sage in Harlem: H.L. Mencken and the Black Writers of the 1920s*. Baltimore: Johns Hopkins University Press, 1984.

Seagrave, Gordon S. *Burma Surgeon*. New York: Norton, 1943.

———. *Burma Surgeon Returns*. New York: Norton, 1946.

———. *My Hospital in the Hills*. New York: W.W. Norton, 1955; London: R. Hale, 1957.

Seagrave, Sterling. *Lords of the Rim: The Invisible Empire of the Overseas Chinese*. London and New York: Bantam Press, 1995.

Secretary of State for Burma. *White Paper on Burma Policy, Statement of Policy by H.M. Government*. London: His Majesty's Stationery Office, 1945.

Seekins, Donald M. *The Disorder in Order: The Army-State in Burma since 1962*. Bangkok: White Lotus Press, 2002.

———. *Historical Dictionary of Burma (Myanmar)*. Lanham, Maryland and Toronto: Scarecrow Press, 2006.

———. *Burma and Japan Since 1940: From 'Co-prosperity' to 'Quiet Dialogue'*. Copenhagen: NIAS Press, 2007.

Sein Tin, Tekkatho (co-translator Kan Nyunt Sein). *Thakin Ba Sein and Burma's Struggle for Independence*. Saarbrucken: VDN Verlag Dr. Muller Gumbh and Co., 2011.

Sein Win. *The Split Story: An Account of Recent Political Upheaval in Burma: With Emphasis on AFPFL*. Rangoon: The Guardian, 1959.

Selth, Andrew. "Death of a Hero: The U Thant Disturbances in Burma, December 1974". Centre for the Study of Australian-Asian Relations, Paper no. 49. Brisbane: Griffith University, April 1989.

———. *Assisting the Defence of Australia: Australian Defence Contacts with Burma, 1945–1987*. Canberra: Strategic and Defence Studies Centre, Australian National University, October 1990.

————. *Burma's Armed Forces: Power Without Glory*. Norwalk, Conn.: EastBridge, 2002.

Sesser, Stan. *The Lands of Charm and Cruelty: Travels in Southeast Asia*. New York: Alfred Knopf, 1993.

Shah, Sudha. *The King in Exile: The Fall of the Royal Family of Burma*. New Delhi: HarperCollins India, 2012.

Shizno, Maruyama. *The NAKANO School: Memoirs of a Member of the Takuma Kikan*. Tokyo: Heiwa Shoba, 3 April 1948.

Shute, Nevil. *The Chequer Board*. London: Pan Books, 1962; first published London: Heinemann, 1947.

Silverstein, Josef, ed. *The Political Legacy of Aung San*. Southeast Asia Program Series no. 86. Ithaca, New York: Cornell University Press, June 1972.

————. *Burma: Military Rule and the Politics of Stagnation*. Ithaca: Cornell University Press, 1977.

Singh, Balwant. *Independence and Democracy in Burma, 1945–1952*. Ann Arbor, Michigan: Centre for South and Southeast Asian Studies, University of Michigan, 1993.

Singh, Uma Shankar. *Burma and India, 1948–1962*. New Delhi: Oxford and IBH Publishing, 1979.

Slim, William. *Defeat into Victory*. London: Cassell, 1956.

Smith, Donald Eugene. *Religion and Politics in Burma*. Princeton: Princeton University Press, 1965.

Smith, Dun. *Memoirs of the Four-Foot Colonel*. Southeast Asia Program Data Paper no. 113. Ithaca, New York: Cornell University, May 1980.

Smith, Martin. *Burma: Insurgency and the Politics of Ethnicity*, 2nd ed. London: Zed Books, 1999.

Steinberg, David I. *Burma's Road to Development: Growth and Ideology Under Military Rule*. Boulder, Colorado: Westview Press, 1981.

————. *Burma: A Socialist Nation of Southeast Asia*. Boulder, Colorado: Westview Press, 1982.

Steinberg, David I and Fan Hongwei. *Modern China-Myanmar Relations: Dilemmas of Mutual Dependence*. Copenhagen: NIAS Press, 2012.

Strachan, Hew. *The Politics of the British Army*. Oxford: Clarendon Press, 1997.

Tarling, Nicholas. *Britain, Southeast Asia and the Onset of the Cold War 1945–1950*. Cambridge: Cambridge University Press, 1998.

————. *Britain, Southeast Asia and the Impact of the Korean War*. Singapore: Singapore University Press, 2005.

Tatsuro, Izumiya. *The Minami Organ*, translated from Japanese by Tun Aung Chain. Rangoon: Translation and Publications Department, Department of Higher Education, March 1981.

Taylor, Robert H. *The Foreign and Domestic Consequences of the KMT Intervention in Burma*. Southeast Asia Program Series no. 93. Ithaca, New York: Cornell University, 1973.

————. *Marxism and Resistance in Burma, 1942–1945: Thein Pe Myint's 'Wartime Traveler'*. Athens, Ohio: Ohio University Press, 1984.

————, ed. *Dr Maung Maung: Gentleman, Scholar, Patriot*. Singapore: Institute of Southeast Asian Studies, 2008.

————. *The State in Myanmar*. London: Hurst; Honolulu: University of Hawaii Press; Singapore: NUS Press, 2009.

Teiwes, Frederick C. and Warren Sun. *The End of the Maoist Era: Chinese Politics During the Twilight of the Cultural Revolution, 1972–1976*. Armonk, New York: M.E. Sharpe, 2007.

Than Han. *Common Vision: Burma's Regional Outlook*. Washington, D.C.: Institute for the Study of Diplomacy, School of Foreign Service, Georgetown University, 1986.

Thant. *View from the UN*. Newton Abbot and London: David and Charles, 1977.

The Nine Months after the Ten Years. N.p.: N.d. [1959].

The Pentagon Papers: The Defense Department History of United States Decisionmaking on Vietnam (The Senator Gravel Edition). Volume II. Boston: Beacon Press, n.d.

Thein Pe Myint. *Selected Short Stories of Thein Pe Myint*, translated by Patricia M. Milne. Southeast Asia Program Series no. 91. Ithaca, New York: Cornell University, June 1973.

————. *Sweet and Sour: Burmese Short Stories*, translated by Usha Narayanan. New Delhi: Sterling, 1999.

Thet Tun. *Waves of Influence*. Yangon: Thin Sapay, 2011.

Tin Maung Maung Than. *State Dominance in Myanmar: The Political Economy of Industrialization*. Singapore: Institute of Southeast Asian Studies, 2006.

Tinker, Hugh. *The Union of Burma: A Study of the First Years of Independence*, 4th ed. London: Oxford University Press, 1967.

————, ed. *Burma: The Struggle for Independence, Documents from Official and Private Sources, Volume I: From Military Occupation to Civil Government, 1 January 1944 to 31 August 1946*. London: Her Majesty's Stationery Office, 1983.

————, ed. *Burma: The Struggle for Independence, Documents from Official and Private Sources, Volume II: From General Strike to Independence, 31 August 1946 to 4 January 1948*. London: Her Majesty's Stationery Office, 1984.

Tocqueville, Alexis de. *The Old Regime and the French Revolution*. New York: Anchor Books, 1955.

Tolstoy, Leo. *War and Peace*. London: Penguin, 1997.

Trager, Frank N. *Burma: From Kingdom to Republic, A Historical and Political Analysis*. London: Pall Mall Press, 1966.

————. *Why Vietnam?* London: Pall Mall Press, 1966.

Trumbull, Robert. *The Scrutable East: A Correspondent's Report on Southeast Asia*. New York: David McKay, 1964.

Tucker, Shelby. *Burma: The Curse of Independence.* London: Pluto Press, 2001.

Tun Pe. *Sun Over Burma.* Rangoon: Rasika Ranjani Press, 1949.

Turnell, Sean. *Fiery Dragons: Banks, Moneylenders and Microfinance in Burma.* Copenhagen: NIAS Press, 2009.

Two Reports on Vietnam and Southeast Asia to the President of the United States by Senator Mike Mansfield. Washington, D.C.: United States Government Printing Office, 1973. Reprinted report of 18 December 1962.

Ulanovsky, Rostilav. *National Liberation: Essays on Theory and Practice.* Moscow: Progress Publishers, 1978.

Vespa, Amleto. *Secret Agent of Japan: A Handbook of Japanese Imperialism.* London: Victor Gollancz, 1938.

Viet Nam and Southeast Asia: Report of Senators Mike Mansfield, J. Caleb Boggs, Claiborne Pell, and Benjamin A. Smith to the Committee on Foreign Relations, United States Senate. Washington, D.C.: United States Government Printing Office, 1963.

Vogel, Ezra F. *Deng Xiaoping and the Transformation of China.* Cambridge, MA.: Belknap Press of Harvard University Press, 2011.

Wakeman, Carolyn and San San Tin. *No Time for Dreams: Living in Burma Under Military Rule.* Lanham, Maryland: Rowman and Littlefield, 2009.

Walinsky, Louis J. *Economic Development in Burma, 1951–1960.* New York: Twentieth Century Fund, 1962.

Warren, Alan. *Burma 1942: The Road from Rangoon to Mandalay.* London and New York: Continuum Books, 2011.

Wessendorf, Larah. *The Era of General Ne Win: A Biographical Approach of His Military and Political Career Considering Burmese Traditions of Political Succession.* Berlin: Regiospectra, 2012.

Westad, Odd Arne. *The Global Cold War: Third World Interventions and the Making of Our Times.* Cambridge: Cambridge University Press, 2007.

Who's Who in Burma 1961. Rangoon: People's Literature Committee and House, 1961.

Williams, Francis. *Twilight of Empire: Memoirs of Prime Minister Clement Attlee.* New York: A.S. Barnes, 1962.

Winds of Change: Evolving Relations and Interests in Southeast Asia, A Report by Senator Mike Mansfield to the Committee on Foreign Relations, United States Senate. Washington, D.C.: United States Government Printing Office, 1975.

Woodman, Dorothy. *The Making of Burma.* London: The Cresset Press, 1962.

Wyatt, Woodrow. *Southwards from China: A Survey of South East Asia since 1945.* London: Hodder and Stoughton, 1952.

Yegar, Moshe. *Between Integration and Secession: The Muslim Communities of the Southern Philippines, Southern Thailand, and Western Burma/Myanmar.* Lanham, Maryland: Lexington Books, 2002.

Yoon, Won Z. *Japan's Scheme for the Liberation of Burma: The Role of the Minami Kikan and the "Thirty Comrades"*. Athens, Ohio: Ohio University Southeast Asia Program, 1973.

Zan, Spencer. *Life's Journey in Faith: Burma, from Riches to Rags*. Bloomington, Indiana: Author House, 2007.

Zhai, Qiang. *China and the Vietnam Wars, 1950–1975*. Chapel Hill: University of North Carolina Press, 2000.

Ziegler, Philip, ed. *From Shore to Shore, the Final Years: The Diaries of Earl Mountbatten of Burma, 1953–1979*. London: Collins, 1989.

Zollner, Hans-Bernd, ed. *Soe, Socialism and Chit Hlaing, Memories*. Myanmar Literature Project Working Paper no. 10:10. Passau: Passau University, n.d.

———. *The Beast and the Beauty: The History of the Conflict between the Military and Aung San Suu Kyi in Myanmar, 1988–2011, Set in a Global Context*. Berlin: Regiospectra, 2012.

Unpublished papers in English

Asia Research Institute. "Thakin Than Tun's Speech of Greetings to the 2nd Congress of the Communist Party of India". Asia Research Institute, National University of Singapore, Documentary Database, The Cold War in Asia (1945–1980). Available at <http://www.ari.nus.edu.sg/docs/SEA-China-interactions-Cluster/TheColdWarInAsia/1948%20Thakin%20Than%20Tuns%20Speech%20of%20Greetings%20to%20the%202nd%20Congress%20of%20the%20Communist%20Party%20of%20India.pdf>.

Chit Hlaing. "The Tatmadaw and My Political Career", translated by Kyaw Yin Hlaing. N.d.

Clymer, Kenton. "The United States and the Guomindang (KMT) Forces in Burma, 1949–1954: A Diplomatic Disaster", 2012.

Guyot, Dorothy. "The Political Impact of the Japanese Occupation of Burma". Unpublished PhD dissertation, Yale University, 1970.

Kyaw Zaw Win. "A History of the Burma Socialist Party (1930–1964)". Unpublished PhD dissertation, Wollongong University, July 2008.

Maung Maung. "Some Aspects of the 'Caretaker Government' 1958–1960: An Experiment in Democratic Process". N.p.: N.d., possibly 1999 or later.

Ministry of Education, Socialist Republic of the Union of Burma. "Development of Education in Burma, 1976–77/1977–78". Report to the 37th Session of the International Conference on Education, Geneva, 5–14 July 1979.

Myo Myint. "China Factors in Myanmar Foreign Policy", 21 March 2009.

Nyun-Han, N. "Burma's Experiment with Socialism". Unpublished PhD dissertation, University of Colorado, 1970.

Riley, Mark S. and Ravi A. Balaram. "The United States International Military Education and Training (IMET) Program with Burma: A Case Study of 1980–1988 Programming and Prospects for the Future", October 2012.

Sylvan, David Jonathan. "The Illusion of Autonomy: State 'Socialism' and Economic Dependence". Unpublished PhD dissertation, Yale University, 1979.

Taylor, Robert H. "The Relationship between Burmese Social Classes and British-Indian Policy on the Behavior of the Burmese Political Elite, 1937–1942". Unpublished PhD dissertation, Cornell University, 1974.

Thein Pe Myint. *Critique of the Communist Movement in Burma*. Mimeographed, circa 1967.

Tin Aung. "Travels with Numero Onu". Unpublished paper, circa 2000.

Yoon, Won Z. "Japan's Occupation of Burma, 1941–1945". Unpublished PhD dissertation, New York University, 1971.

INDEX

About the Author

Robert H. Taylor was formerly Professor of Politics and Pro-Director of the School of Oriental and African Studies (London) and subsequently Vice-Chancellor of the University of Buckingham. Earlier he taught at Wilberforce and Sydney universities. More recently, he was a Visiting Professor at City University of Hong Kong and Visiting Professorial Fellow at the Institute of Southeast Asian Studies where this volume was drafted. Educated at Ohio University, Antioch College, and Cornell University, he is the author of a number of scholarly publications on Myanmar and Southeast Asia, including *The State in Myanmar* (2009; in Burmese, 2014), *The State in Burma* (1987; in Thai, 2006), *Marxism and Resistance in Burma, 1942-1945* (1984), and *The Foreign and Domestic Consequences of the KMT Intervention in Burma* (1973). A contributor to *In Search of Southeast Asia: A Modern History* (1987) and *The Emergence of Southeast Asia: A New History* (2005), he edited, among other works, *Dr. Maung Maung: Gentlemen, Scholar, Patriot* (2008) and *The Politics of Elections in Southeast Asia* (1996). In addition to his academic career, Professor Taylor has worked as a consultant to the oil and gas industry and served as a lay member of the United Kingdom Immigration and Asylum Tribunal. A frequent traveller to Myanmar since 1975, he lived there for extended periods in the 1970s, 1980s and since 2000.

CPSIA information can be obtained
at www.ICGtesting.com
Printed in the USA
LVHW080156140123
737122LV00003B/87

9 789814 620130